THE IVP NEW TESTAMENT COMMENTARY SERIES

Acts

William J. Larkin Jr.

Grant R. Osborne
series editor

D. Stuart Briscoe
Haddon Robinson
consulting editors

INTERVARSITY PRESS
DOWNERS GROVE, ILLINOIS, USA
LEICESTER, ENGLAND

To the memory of
David Robert Sanderson

InterVarsity Press
P.O. Box 1400, Downers Grove, Illinois 60515, U.S.A.
38 De Montfort Street, Leicester LE1 7GP, England

© *1995 by William J. Larkin Jr.*

InterVarsity Press®, U.S.A., is the book-publishing division of InterVarsity Christian Fellowship®, a student movement active on campus at hundreds of universities, colleges and schools of nursing in the United States of America, and a member movement of the International Fellowship of Evangelical Students. For information about local and regional activities, write Public Relations Dept., InterVarsity Christian Fellowship, 6400 Schroeder Rd., P.O. Box 7895, Madison, WI 53707-7895.

Inter-Varsity Press, England, is the book-publishing division of the Universities and Colleges Christian Fellowship (formerly the Inter-Varsity Fellowship), a student movement linking Christian Unions in universities and colleges throughout the United Kingdom and the Republic of Ireland, and a member movement of the International Fellowship of Evangelical Students. For information about local and national activities write to UCCF, 38 De Montfort Street, Leicester LE1 7GP.

USA ISBN 0-8308-1805-7
UK ISBN 0-85111-680-9

Printed in the United States of America ⊗

Library of Congress Cataloging-in-Publication Data

Larkin, William J.
   Acts/William J. Larkin, Jr.
      p.   cm.—(The IVP New Testament commentary series; 5)
   Includes bibliographical references (p.).
   ISBN 0-8308-1805-7 (hardcover: alk. paper)
      1. Bible. N.T. Acts—Commentaries.   I. Title.   II. Series.
   BS2625.3.L374   1995
   226.6'077—dc20   95-12621
   *   CIP*

British Library Cataloguing in Publication Data

A catalogue record for this book is available from the British Library.

17	16	15	14	13	12	11	10	9	8	7	6	5
09	08	07	06	05								

General Preface

In an age of proliferating commentary series, one might easily ask why add yet another to the seeming glut. The simplest answer is that no other series has yet achieved what we had in mind—a series to and from the church, that seeks to move from the text to its contemporary relevance and application.

No other series offers the unique combination of solid, biblical exposition and helpful explanatory notes in the same user-friendly format. No other series has tapped the unique blend of scholars and pastors who share both a passion for faithful exegesis and a deep concern for the church. Based on the New International Version of the Bible, one of the most widely used modern translations, the IVP New Testament Commentary Series builds on the NIV's reputation for clarity and accuracy. Individual commentators indicate clearly whenever they depart from the standard translation as required by their understanding of the original Greek text.

The series contributors represent a wide range of theological traditions, united by a common commitment to the authority of Scripture for

Christian faith and practice. Their efforts here are directed toward applying the unchanging message of the New Testament to the ever-changing world in which we live.

Readers will find in each volume not only traditional discussions of authorship and backgrounds, but useful summaries of principal themes and approaches to contemporary application. To bridge the gap between commentaries that stress the flow of an author's argument but skip over exegetical nettles and those that simply jump from one difficulty to another, we have developed our unique format that expounds the text in uninterrupted form on the upper portion of each page while dealing with other issues underneath in verse-keyed notes. To avoid clutter we have also adopted a social studies note system that keys references to the bibliography.

We offer the series in hope that pastors, students, Bible teachers and small group leaders of all sorts will find it a valuable aid—one that stretches the mind and moves the heart to ever-growing faithfulness and obedience to our Lord Jesus Christ.

Author's Preface

The longer I have studied Acts according to the guidelines for this series, the more I am convinced that Acts has a vital message for today. Aside from the differences in technology and place in history, our increasingly post-Christian world is looking more and more like the pre-Christian world in which the missionary witnesses of Acts operated. How the gospel witness advanced boldly, intelligently and persuasively in the various thought worlds of that day has much to teach us. How the church lived out its multicultural unity gives us a much-needed model in our various strife-torn, ethnically pluralistic settings. Above all, Acts evangelizes us and turns us into evangelists. It reminds us again and again, with clarity and power, that what God has promised he has fulfilled in sending his Messiah to suffer and rise from the dead so that repentance for the forgiveness of sins might be proclaimed in his name among all the nations (Lk 24:46-47).

Luke's writings have been an object of my study and reflection for twenty-five years. First in seminary, where Bertil Gärtner, Graham Stanton and Bruce Metzger mentored me, then in Ph.D. studies under C. K.

Barrett, Luke's thought has been my "set text."

In my seminary teaching, "Acts in Historical, Theological and Missiological Perspective" has been an annual offering. I am indebted to generations of students, whether prefield Christian workers, national church leaders or veteran missionaries, for the enriching interaction they have provided me on Luke's message in Acts and its application to today.

More directly related to this project, thanks must go to the administration of Columbia Biblical Seminary and Graduate School of Missions for providing the 1991-1992 study leave in which the bulk of the research and writing was completed. Peggi Simmons, seminary faculty secretary, was a great help in final preparation of the manuscript. I appreciate very much the opportunity the John Mark Class of Eau Claire Presbyterian Church, Columbia, South Carolina, gave me to teach Acts, episode by episode, over a two-year period. The input of colleagues who "test-drove" commentary portions as they prepared to preach is also greatly appreciated.

It is always appropriate to thank immediate family members for their patience and encouragement as they live with the project day in and day out. I thank Edna, Thomas and Priscilla for their sacrifice of love.

I dedicate this commentary to the memory of David Robert Sanderson, 1944-1969, budding New Testament scholar, seminary classmate and friend. May this begin to be a worthy substitute for the commentary he did not live to write.

Introduction

☐ Preaching Acts Today

When we study and preach or teach Acts today, we are struck by how distinctly unfamiliar yet strangely familiar it is. We are not first-century persons, hampered by all the physical and cultural limitations of a pre-scientific society. At the same time we have our own limitations: we do not live in the age of the apostles and do not have direct contact with those who experienced the ministry of Jesus immediately. It takes some work to "walk in the sandals" of those first Christians.

Yet in some ways our post-Christian, postmodern world has come full circle. The worldview of many outside the church is not unlike the approach to spiritual things of pre-Christian first-century pagans. And the church faces similar challenges in communicating the changeless gospel message and in nurturing the faith of converts within an increasingly hostile environment.

Luke would not be surprised that Acts can communicate the good news to the late-twentieth-century person who is asking, though in different words, "What must I do to be saved?" (Acts 16:30). After all, that's

why he wrote it. And for the Christian, Luke's work provides an encouraging and challenging model of what God can do with a Spirit-filled people who are completely devoted to him.

The Contemporary Relevance of Acts

With its pattern of early church message, life and mission, Acts can serve as a sheet anchor in the choppy seas of contemporary life. It models a way of communicating the gospel message which constructively engages other worldviews while maintaining integrity. It bristles with confidence that the Christian message can withstand the close scrutiny of public inquiry. This gives us courage in a secularized culture, where religious faith is not welcome in the "public square."

Acts clearly sets out the church's mission: world evangelization. Whether lulled into complacency by universalism or into indifference by viewing missions as the specialty of certain persons, the church will be awakened by Acts, which declares that being on the move with the gospel witness across cultural thresholds is the church's number-one job.

Today church life tends to be fragmented or distorted by the constraints of modern culture. Acts gives us a welcome pattern of balance and wholeness, showing how spiritual characteristics such as love, joy and unity were lived out in mutual ministry to the whole person. That wholeness extended to racial and ethnic relations, with the challenge to visibly express oneness in Christ. And when the church must live in a hostile environment amid resurgent religious fanaticism, Acts shows us how to do so with courage and wisdom.

The twentieth century's crimes against humanity and the future prospect of doom—whether by limited or not-so-limited nuclear war or by environmental pollution—has turned many postmodern persons into cynical pessimists. The postmodern does not think it's possible to make sense out of history. But Acts has good news. God is at work in history. He brought his salvation near in Jesus Christ. Now in preparation for his return, he continues to do his work through the church, bringing the saving message to people to the ends of the earth.

Today there is hunger for the Spirit but "confusion about who He is and how we become riverbeds for the flow of His unlimited power" (Ogilvie 1983:15). While Acts has often been the battleground for de-

bates about how the Spirit is present today, it is an indispensable testing ground for both discerning God's will for the church and evaluating current experience.

Faithfulness and Relevance in Interpretation

The historical and cultural gap between the first century and today can create difficulties both for understanding Acts and for seeing its relevance. But study of the text's grammatical and literary features and historically based word meanings, as well as the historical context that the text points to or reflects, can help us uncover what the author intended to say to his first readers. This intended message is the foundation for any discovery of relevance and building of authoritative application.

If Luke's challenging and refreshing picture of the church, history and the Holy Spirit were not enough to assure his writing's relevance for today, his purpose and view of history certainly would be. The writer pens Acts so that his readers will positively respond to God's saving message, intended for all time and for all nations (Lk 24:47; Acts 1:6-8). Luke sees history with Jesus at the center point. All before his arrival is the age of promise. All after his first coming, which inaugurates the age of fulfillment, is one period—the last days. Since we, the early church and Luke's audience live within the same period of redemptive history, Acts' account of God's dealings with the early believers has immediate relevance for us.

Still, the reality of the difference between the early church's historical generation and ours makes us raise questions—legitimate questions—about how to convert the text's immediate relevance into appropriate authoritative application.

Authoritative Application

From the outset, two extremes in application must be avoided. We must not make Acts give us too much normative content: we must read it with a proper historical sense of the true *pastness* of much of its content. On the other hand, we must not go to the other extreme and conclude that Acts can offer us nothing authoritative in terms of either principles or practice. God may indeed have inspired the biblical writer to present early church practice as historical precedent with normative value, to

declare detailed normative mandates in teaching or preaching, and to teach and model divinely approved principles of thought and action throughout the narrative.

What guidelines should we follow as we seek material for application? Scripture contains commands and promises that we can apply directly or indirectly (Larkin 1993:354-60). *Direct* application involves taking the text's commands and promises and obeying them or claiming them in the same form as they were given. We apply these directly because the biblical writer does not restrict the recipient. He does not present cultural conditions for fulfillment; indeed, he may supply a universal rationale. This type of mandate or promise is to be directly applied if it is not limited by teaching elsewhere in Scripture. Acts 2:38-39 is a case in point.

When the command or promise is directed to a restricted audience or has certain first-century cultural conditions for its implementation, we should apply it to ourselves *indirectly*. The writer intends us to take the principle behind the command or promise and obey or embrace it in culturally appropriate ways. Such an approach should also be followed for statements of truth and narrative examples that yield principles.

Readers in the late twentieth century have a fairly sophisticated literary and historical consciousness. It is not hard for us to distinguish between material intended for direct application and that which should be applied indirectly. We have no difficulty seeing the apostles' command to choose seven, for example, as calling for indirect appropriation today (6:3). The number of servers or administrators will vary with human resources and the need.

Some materials for application seem to stand in a middle ground. They have a specified recipient or cultural conditions for fulfillment. Yet if we find ourselves in similar circumstances today, the application to us must be direct. If not, then we must apply indirectly by finding a culturally appropriate form for expressing the underlying principle. The Jerusalem Council's decree would still have force for Gentile Christians fellowshipping with Jewish Christians who keep a kosher table (15:28-29).

Which actions of Luke's narrative were intended to be directly applied

Notes: Introduction Werner G. Marx (1980) gives valuable background on the status,

as normative historical precedents? Which have illustrative value, intended only for indirect application? Which decisions and actions were simply reported as historical detail, necessary to the progress of the narrative but without normative value?

The interpreter should consider at least three factors in deciding whether Luke intends a historical action to have normative value. (1) Do positive statements in the presentation and the event's immediate context show that Luke wants his readers to imitate the action? (2) Does Luke present the principle behind the action in a teaching portion elsewhere in his two-volume work, especially in Jesus' teaching in the third Gospel? (3) Does Luke create an unambiguous pattern of practice, showing that the historical precedent became a sustained practice?

Consider the summary description of early church life (2:42-47), which comes at the denouement of the Pentecost account. It concludes with Luke's approving comment "And the Lord added to their number daily those who were being saved" (v. 47). We may rightly expect to uncover some normative essentials of church life in this passage, though each detail must be sifted through the sieve of the original cultural and historical conditions to see whether it was intended to be applied directly or indirectly. In the matter of prayer (2:42) we may find help in Jesus' teaching (Lk 18:1-8). If we look for a sustained pattern, we see that throughout Acts prayer is the church's very life-breath (Acts 4:24; 6:4, 6; 12:5, 12; 13:3; 20:36; 21:5).

□ Historical Setting: Author, Date, Audience

Although the author of Acts does not identify himself, the first-person "we passages" (16:10-17; 20:5-15; 21:1-8; 27:1—28:16) probably indicate that he was a traveling companion of Paul. That he was the author of the third Gospel may be concluded from the addressee, Theophilus, and from similarities of interest, language and style. Church tradition consistently testifies from the second century onward that the author is Luke the beloved physician (Col 4:14), a Gentile Christian often associated with Syrian Antioch. This identification best explains all the New Testament evidence.

training and practice of physicians in ancient times, especially their activities as litterateurs.

Date

To determine when Luke wrote Acts, we must begin with a time frame bounded by the last events recorded in the book (A.D. 62) and the terminus of the expected life span of a traveling companion of Paul (A.D. 85). The two choices within this time frame are the early sixties and sometime in the seventies to mid-eighties, the former being more likely.

Acts uses Roman authorities to support an apologetic for Christianity's innocence. One of the book's main concerns is the reception of Gentile Christians into a predominantly Jewish Christian church. Paul plays a prominent role in the narrative. All these features point to a time before Nero's persecution (A.D. 64), Paul's martyrdom (c. A.D. 64-66) and the fall of Jerusalem (A.D. 70).

When we look at Acts alongside the challenges facing Christianity in Rome in the late fifties and early sixties, as reflected in Romans and Philippians (for example, Phil 1:12-20), we can find many parallels. Each responds to the Jewish polemic against Christianity as a threat to civilized life. Each deals with the Judaizers' challenge to the legitimacy of Paul's Gentile mission (compare Rom 13:1-8 with Acts 18:12-17; 24:5; 26:30-32; 28:22; compare Rom 2:11-29; 10:9-21 and Phil 1:15-18 with Acts 1:8; 10:34-43; 15:1-29; 21:20-26).

Acts devotes so much space to events of A.D. 58-60 (chapters 20—28) that it is likely the events had just occurred. We best explain the accuracy of geographical, political and sociocultural details, humanly speaking, if the work was produced close to the events it describes.

Finally, an early sixties date makes the apparently abrupt ending of Acts understandable. Luke reports the course of early church history only as far as he knows it. This does not include Paul's death, even though Luke has prepared his readers for it (20:24-27). But the early sixties also brings the narrative to a point where Paul is able to fulfill the book's purpose. Though a prisoner, Paul in Rome—the empire's center, to which and from which "all roads lead"—boldly and without hindrance

---

As for dates, Donald Guthrie (1990:363-65) effectively answers arguments for a second-century origin, a theory that by and large has been abandoned. I. Howard Marshall (1971:219-20) properly critiques reasons given for a nineties date. F. F. Bruce (1988:11-13) puts forward a case for an origin between A.D. 70 and 85, a view that seems to be growing in popularity among conservatives. D. A. Carson, Douglas J. Moo and Leon Morris (1992:192-94) make the strongest recent case for a date in the early sixties.

preaches the kingdom of God and teaches about the Lord Jesus Christ (28:31). In that way he confirms the truth of a gospel that claims that God's plan is for the good news to be proclaimed to all nations (Lk 1:4; 24:46-47; Acts 1:8).

Audience and Occasion

Luke wrote Acts to Theophilus, a Gentile, who is representative of the intelligent Roman middle-class reading public among whom Paul's case had sparked interest (Acts 28:30; Phil 1:13; see Bruce 1954:31). Theophilus is a real person, a patron of the work and a high Roman official; the dedication and the use of the title "most excellent" (Lk 1:3) indicate this. He has been informed about the gospel but is confused about its certainty, since he hears it amid strongly dissenting voices. Unbelieving Jews attack its innocence before the state (see Acts 17:5-9; 18:13; 24:5-9). Judaizers are attacking the legitimacy of a salvation by grace for Gentiles (15:1-2; 21:20-21). Theophilus's Roman contemporaries despise this eastern cult (16:20-21; 25:18-20; Tacitus *Annals* 15.44). Based on the discussion of purpose, below, I conclude that he is not yet a Christian.

Purpose

There is no unanimity among scholars concerning Luke's exact purpose in writing Acts (see Gasque 1988a:119). The complexity of Acts allows scholars to posit many different purposes. Further, many scholars are unable to identify a precise historical setting and occasion for the work (Marshall 1989:54). Yet there does seem to be agreement in regard to certain factors that must be considered in any answer to the question of purpose: preface (Lk 1:1-4), details, central themes and literary genre (Gasque 1988a:119).

Evangelism, Not Edification Luke expresses his purpose in his pref-

Mary Moscato (1976) summarizes the main positions concerning Luke's audience.

Schuyler Brown (1978:100) and Richard Longenecker (1981:217) give good summaries of the various proposals for Luke's purpose in Acts.

W. Ward Gasque (1988a and 1988b), I. Howard Marshall (1989), David L Allen (1990), Mark A. Powell (1991) and Carson, Moo and Morris (1992:202-13) are helpful for their characterizations of the current debate in scholarly studies in Acts and for their bibliographies.

ace this way: "so that you may know the certainty of the things you have been taught" (Lk 1:4). The kind of knowledge *(epiginōskō)* Luke desires for his readers includes both recognition of the truth about facts and Spirit-aided insight (Lk 24:16, 31; Acts 4:13; 12:14; 22:24, 29; 23:28; 24:8, 11; 25:10).

Luke says he wants his readers "to know the certainty *[asphaleia]*" of the things they have been taught. Not only is this certainty the exact truth based on a clear understanding of the evidence (Acts 21:34; 22:30), but it also involves the firm assurance that such truth has personal significance for the reader (2:36). In Peter's Pentecost sermon, Old Testament promises and the New Testament fulfillment events converge to interpret and validate the witness that Jesus is indeed the Messiah and Lord. And in so doing they provide firm assurance that Jesus is the Lord on whose name we must call if we are to be saved (2:21, 37-38). Luke wants his readers to have that assurance (Dillon 1981:226).

The NIV translation "so that you may know the certainty *of the things you have been taught [peri hōn katēchēthēs]*" (Lk 1:4) might lead us to conclude that Luke's purpose is not evangelistic but edificatory. Although *katēcheō* became a technical term in the church for the instruction of new believers, in biblical usage it can also refer to simply informing someone about something. Luke uses it both ways in Acts (instructing, Acts 18:25; informing, 21:21, 24). The phrasing of Luke 1:4 parallels that of Acts 21:21, 24, where *katēcheō* means "to inform." From the content of Luke-Acts we see that the "things" of Luke 1:4 are historical accounts and not doctrinal discourses. These two factors combine to suggest that Theophilus is the object of evangelism, not catechesis.

Acts frequently highlights Romans as the recipients of, and often positive responders to, the gospel witness (Cornelius, Acts 10:1-11:18; the Philippian jailer, 16:25-34; Felix and Festus, 24:10-26; 26:1-29). The theological themes of Acts may be drawn out of the framework of the gospel message (see below, "Theology"). The book's literary genre is general history (Aune 1987:139-40). All these factors support an evangelistic purpose.

Historical Reliability Since Luke's purpose is to evangelize Theophilus and his compatriots through a thoroughly and accurately investigated, orderly account of events that demonstrate the truth of the gospel, Acts'

historical reliability is foundational to the author's aims (Lk 1:1-4). Luke is not alone in this. A number of ancient historians introduced their works with claims of accurate investigation and goals of presenting "the truth as it actually happened" (Lucian *How to Write History* 49-50; also see Diodorus Siculus *Library of History* 1.4.4; Josephus *Against Apion* 5.1-5; Hemer 1989a:90-91).

Unless we redefine historical writing so that a mixture of fabrication and fact is acceptable (L. T. Johnson 1992:7), we must continue to judge Luke's claims to historical reliability by an uncompromising standard of truthfulness. This we do by answering two questions: (1) Did Luke have access to the events reported, so that he had the capacity to write reliable history? (2) Did Luke write an account that is in any way self-contradictory or that conflicts with other biblical witnesses to the events (Paul's letters) or other ancient literary or archaeological evidence?

Luke did have access to the events. First, he participated in many of them. Although some scholars have attempted to explain the "we passages" as based on a travel journal that came into Luke's hands or as a literary device he employed (Praeder 1987), the various features of this phenomenon in Acts are best explained by authorial participation (Longenecker 1981:224).

Luke tells us that he depended on sources as well as his own experience. "Those who from the first were eyewitnesses and servants of the word" handed to him "the things that have been fulfilled among us" (Lk 1:1-2). It is not possible to isolate literary sources in Acts, given the uniformity of Luke's style and the lack of extant potential source documents (Dupont 1964). For every section of Acts, however, there are identifiable personal acquaintances of Luke who were eyewitnesses to the events recounted:

☐ Acts 1—5, Mark and Barnabas

☐ 6:1—8:40, Philip [see 21:8] and Paul

☐ 9:1-31, Paul

☐ 10:1—11:18, Peter through Mark

☐ 11:19-30; 13:1-4; 14:26-28, the Antioch church

☐ 12:1—13:13, Mark

☐ 12:25—28:31, Paul

☐ 16:10-17; 20:5-15; 21:1-8; 27:1-28:16 ("we passages"), Luke himself

The term *servant (hypēretēs)*, which emphasizes helping by strictly following orders, in this context points to accurate witness to what happened (see 13:5; 26:16).

As to internal consistency, many scholars claim that the differences among the three reports of Paul's conversion (Acts 9; 22; 26) show that Luke was not interested in writing a historically accurate account (Haenchen 1971:323; Lake 1979b:195; Lohfink 1976; Hedrick 1981). These differences are not historical contradictions, however, but features well suited to each historical setting: original telling, defense before a Jewish mob, defense before a Gentile governor (Bruce 1988:188, 419).

There is no final contradiction between the picture we get of Paul in Acts and the picture given by his letters. Concerns about discrepancies in theology and behavior (Vielhauer 1966; Haenchen 1971:112-16), as well as the progress of major events (Acts 15 compared to Galatians 2; the collection for Jerusalem and Acts 21) have been satisfactorily addressed by Gasque (1978) and Bruce (1976). The differences are no more than what one would expect between a self-portrait by Paul and Luke's appreciative picture, painted for a different audience and purpose. Yet in some circles the negative assessment of Acts in this matter continues (see Krodel 1986:14; Tyson 1985; L. T. Johnson 1992:7).

Even skeptical critics give Luke high marks for his "factual fastidiousness" when it comes to geographical, social and political minutiae (Koester 1982:2:50). But those who see this accuracy simply as the result of the kind of research a good historical novelist would do (L. T. Johnson 1992:5) are guilty of anachronistic thinking. Reference works that would make such research possible did not exist in the first century. Eyewitness participation in the events remains, according to Colin J. Hemer, the "easiest [and] most satisfying hypothesis." "It is the only basis," he continues, "on which I feel able to account for certain features which need a sufficient explanation" (Hemer 1977b:39; also see Hemer 1989a; Baugh 1990).

The speeches of Acts have often been understood as Luke's own compositions and hence historical fabrications (Tyson 1985). Some stake out a middle ground, in which Luke, not in free composition, but with historical realism, writes the speeches, depending on traditional material (Pillai 1979:111). But given the content, vocabulary and style of each,

there is still no impediment to taking the speeches as containing in verbatim, precis or summary form the substance of what was said on the occasions cited (Bruce 1974). In sum, Luke not only intended to write a historically reliable work but succeeded in doing so.

□ The Text of Acts

The text-form of one third-or fourth-century manuscript, the uncial Bezae Cantabrigiensis (Codex D), commonly called the Western text, is ten percent longer than the Alexandrian text-type, the usually accepted text. The additional material includes interesting historical detail that may be authentic, though the text-form itself is probably secondary. A copyist smoothed out grammatical difficulties and clarified ambiguous theological points (Carson, Moo and Morris 1992:201; also see Parker 1992; Strange 1992). Where important, I will note Western readings.

□ Theology

Luke's summary of the gospel message provides a helpful framework for expounding his theology. "This is what is written: The Christ will suffer and rise from the dead on the third day, and repentance and forgiveness of sins will be preached in his name to all nations, beginning at Jerusalem. You are witnesses of these things" (Lk 24:46-48).

God Fulfills His Promise

"This is what is written" asserts that the gospel message's origin is not human religious tradition but divine revelation. It was promised through the prophets and is now fulfilled in the death and resurrection of Christ and the church's worldwide evangelistic mission. Although the impact of such an argument is greatest for Jews whose ancestors received the prophetic promises (Acts 2:17, 21, 39; 10:36; 13:32; 15:16), its effect is not lost on Gentiles. They too will be impressed with a message about saving events promised long ago but now fulfilled. From this initial theme flows Luke's theology of God the Father, the Scriptures, history and the end times.

God the Father In the proclamations to Gentile audiences, Luke presents God as transcendent and immanent (17:28-29), as Creator (14:15; 17:24; also see 4:24) and as sustainer and controller of history,

particularly salvation history (14:17; 17:26; compare 1:7). In the preaching to the Jews he highlights God's active intervention in history to accomplish his saving purposes (7:2-47; 13:17). The climax of God's saving acts is bringing Jesus the Messiah to Israel in fulfillment of the promises God made through the prophets (13:23, 33). He legitimized Jesus' person and work through signs and wonders (2:22; 10:38). By his "set purpose and foreknowledge" Jesus was handed over to suffering and death (2:23; 4:28), and by his power God raised Jesus from the dead (2:32; 3:26; 13:34; 17:31). He gave to the Son the promise of the Spirit, who, poured out on Pentecost, both validates the claim that Jesus is truly Lord and Christ and empowers the church in its worldwide witness (1:4, 8; 2:33, 36). The Father has appointed Jesus as judge of all at the end of time and has given his resurrection as proof (17:31).

The Scriptures The Spirit-inspired Word of God (4:25; 28:25) contains prophetic promises now fulfilled (2:25-32) and prophetic typology now applied (13:47). Its content may serve as proof for the truth of an argument (7:42; 28:25-28) or prophetic legitimation of a conclusion concerning God's working in current circumstances (15:16-17). It provides ethical mandates (23:5). It is the objective reference point for the reader who seeks to understand the truth and significance of the gospel message.

History and the End Times God's intervention in history to accomplish his salvation necessarily molds Luke's view of history. The present is "the last days." It is the time of the continuance of Jesus' ministry (1:1), though in a different form: by the Spirit through the church. It is the time of the Spirit's outpouring "on all flesh" and the universal proclamation of the gospel (Acts 2:17, 21).

Luke also has the end in view, especially in terms of final resurrection and judgment at Christ's second coming (1:11; 3:21; 17:31; 23:6; 24:15, 25; 26:6-8). But what is in the forefront and distinctive is the current period of salvation history, "the last days." The gospel message itself binds together under the rubric of scriptural fulfillment the two main features of "the last days": Jesus' ministry and the church's mission (Lk 24:46-48).

The Messiah Who Suffers and Rises

The gospel message focuses on a Messiah who suffers and rises from the

dead on the third day. Luke develops his christology in terms of titles by emphasizing that the Scriptures prophesy both the death of the Messiah, Son of David, as well as his resurrection (17:3; 2:31).

Christology: His Titles Jesus' identity as the Messiah is argued forcefully (9:22; 18:5). Other messianic titles—"prophet," "righteous and holy one" and "servant"—are used to highlight the culpability of the Jews and to link Jesus' suffering and his present glory as manifest in his resurrection and miraculous activity through the church (3:13-14, 22, 26; 4:30). While the term "Son of God" is used sparingly (9:20; 13:33), the term "Lord" predominates. It refers to Jesus in his resurrected, exalted position as Lord of all (10:36; compare 2:36). "The Lord" is the source of salvation for all those who will believe in him (2:21; 9:42; 16:31). It is the word of the Lord that is preached and spreads (8:25; 12:24; 13:49). The Lord himself guides the church's mission and enables it to advance (2:47; 9:10).

Luke uses many titles for Jesus that combine in a unified portrait of "the 'Messiah-Servant' who is seen, as the story progresses, to be a 'more than Messiah' figure in that he is the Lord" (Marshall 1989:54).

Christology: His Work Luke focuses on Jesus' earthly ministry, death, resurrection, exaltation, current reign and return. He emphasizes that God according to his messianic promise brought to Israel a Savior, Jesus (13:23). This man, announced by John the Baptist and divinely anointed with the Spirit's power, conducted a public healing ministry, including the conquest of demons (2:22; 10:38-39; 13:24-25). Such miraculous doing of good demonstrated God's approval.

Though Jesus was the holy and righteous one, innocent of any wrongdoing, the Jewish people, and especially their leaders, rejected him and had him put to death by crucifixion (2:23; 3:13-15; 4:10; 5:30; 7:52; 8:32-35; 10:39; 13:28). Yet all this was according to God's saving plan as announced by the prophets (2:23; 3:18; 4:11; 7:52; 10:39, 43; 13:28-29; 26:22-23). This salvation is recognized as a key theme in Luke's writing (Marshall 1971: chap. 4).

Luke emphasizes Christ's resurrection as the central event in God's saving purposes. Of all of Christ's work, it is the immediate source of salvation blessings (2:33-39; 3:26; 4:10-12; 5:31; 13:37-39). Not only was Messiah's resurrection prophesied in Scripture (2:24-32; 13:32-37; 17:3;

26:23), but it was an objective historical event for which there are undeniable proofs and eyewitnesses (1:3, 22; 10:40-41; 13:31). In fact, the main task of the apostles is to bear witness to this resurrection and its saving significance, especially as a prototype of the coming resurrection (1:22; 3:15; 5:32; 10:40-41; 13:31; 22:14-15; 23:6; 24:15, 21). This witness also serves as a warning that the resurrected Lord will come as final judge (10:42; 17:31).

Christ's ascension-exaltation places him in the position of "Lord of all." From the right hand of the Father he pours out salvation blessings and actively empowers and guides the church in its witness (2:33-36; 9:10). His name becomes "hypostatic" as Luke seeks to describe the spiritual effects of his unseen presence when the church acts in his authority (2:38; 3:16; 4:10, 12, 30; 8:12, 16; 10:43, 48; 16:18). Christ's soon return will involve final resurrection and judgment (1:11; 3:20-21; 17:31; 23:6; 24:14-15; 26:6-8).

The Salvation to Be Preached

The second half of the gospel message introduces the conditions for and results of receiving salvation, as well as the human method and scope of its dissemination: "and repentance and forgiveness of sins will be preached in his name to all nations" (Lk 24:47). As the Third Gospel substantiates the first half of the gospel message, so Acts validates the truthfulness of the second half. It shows Theophilus that the gospel message he has heard is the same one that the Lord Jesus charged to his disciples.

Responding to the Gospel Though the word *faith* is not used in this summary, Luke does use it as the general term for the whole process of responding to the gospel. So central is faith that *believer* is a very common term to denote a Christian (as in 2:44; 4:32; 15:5; 18:27; 21:25; 22:19). God's grace and election are at work producing saving faith (15:11; 13:48). Several times faith is mandated as the proper condition for salvation (10:43; 13:39; 16:31).

It is the word of God, the gospel message, to which persons must

Because of slightly superior manuscript attestation and the probabilities of copyists' practice, the UBS text prefers the reading "repentance unto the forgiveness of sins" for Lk 24:47 (Metzger 1971:188).

respond in faith (4:4; 8:12; 11:21; 15:7; 17:34; 18:8). When they come to saving faith in response to signs and miracles, Luke usually notes that preaching of the word was also present (8:12-13; 13:12; 19:10-11, 19-20; exceptions are Acts 5:14; 9:42). Luke makes explicit that the way of faith must be followed by Gentiles as well as Jews (15:11).

Faith involves a commitment characterized by repentance and conversion. This also is a gift of God (5:31; 11:18, 21). It is a universal condition that all must meet if they are to avoid final judgment (17:30-31). *Repentance* and the related term *conversion* refer to a complete turnaround from sin, darkness, Satan's authority and idols, to God, light, God's kingdom and the Lord (8:22; 9:35; 14:15; 20:21; 26:18). In his final articulation of the gospel message, Luke notes that true repentance will issue in deeds worthy of repentance (26:20).

Open confession of faith and baptism are other aspects of receiving salvation. Though these are not mentioned every time a conversion is described in Acts, they are commanded at the beginning (2:38). Further, they are mentioned at significant junctures in the church's advance in mission to different ethnic groups and as a practice in all of Paul's missionary journeys (8:12, 13, 36, 38; 10:47; 13:43, 48; 16:15, 33; 18:8; 19:5).

Acts presents a mixed pattern concerning the sequence of factors in conversion—personal response of faith and repentance, outward manifestation of the Spirit, water baptism (8:12, 15; 10:44-48; 19:2-6). Further, the coming of the Spirit is not consistently presented as a second experience separated in time from conversion. The mixed pattern may well be due to God's initiative in mercifully persuading Jewish Christians, through the outward sign of the Holy Spirit's coming on various ethnic groups, that he had indeed regenerated them (10:47; 11:15; 15:8-9). This limited purpose for the manifestation led to the mixed pattern and probably indicates that it is not normative for all Christians.

Salvation Blessings With the phrase "forgiveness of sins" Luke captures the results of salvation. When combined with his use of "salvation" words as well as *grace* and *joy,* this gives a comprehensive picture of salvation blessings.

The parallel passages throughout the commentary have been gleaned from a study of the Greek vocabulary of Acts. Readers familiar with Greek are encouraged to refer to a Greek New Testament.

From the very beginning the concept of salvation expressed in words such as *Savior, save* and *salvation* serves as an overarching theme. Explaining the Spirit's coming at Pentecost, Peter concludes his quotation from the prophet Joel with the promise, "And everyone who calls on the name of the Lord will be saved" (2:21). Luke consistently presents spiritual rescue as "being saved" (2:47; 11:14; 16:31). He stresses the divine initiative in the process through the passive voice, and he points to faith as the condition for salvation (2:47; 15:11; 16:31). Jesus is the only source of salvation (4:12; 5:31; 13:23). In accounts of healings, *salvation* and related terms are sometimes used for restoration of physical wholeness. In each context such restoration is a sign of the spiritual wholeness available in the name of Jesus (4:9, 12; 14:9, 15).

Grace portrays salvation benefits in two ways. It is the divine enabling for a person to believe and receive salvation (15:11; 18:27). It is the divine power and quality of life that becomes manifest in the lives of believers, so that it can be said that great grace rests on them or that they are full of grace (4:33; 6:8; 11:23).

Joy is the portion of those who believe the gospel message, especially Gentiles (8:8, 39; 13:48, 52; 16:34). Luke says their joy is in response not only to the liberation they find in Christ but also and particularly to the knowledge that this salvation is intended for them too (13:46-48).

Though forgiveness of sins is mentioned only four times in Acts, the context is such that this benefit becomes Luke's standard description of salvation. In Peter's Pentecost sermon and in Paul's final exposition of his gospel, those who are converted are said to receive forgiveness of sins (2:38; 26:18). This is a blessing from heaven itself (5:31; 13:38).

It is in the church that these salvation blessings come to fullest expression. Spiritual qualities find expression in patterns of living. The church's unity and grace are seen in the fellowship it practiced, especially the breaking of bread. The believers took meals together regularly, even daily, which probably included the celebration of the Lord's Supper (2:42, 46; 20:7, 11). Their fellowship overflowed in the practical compassion of Dorcas (9:39), the hospitality of the newly converted Lydia (16:15; compare 10:48; 16:33-34) and the Jerusalem church's sharing of goods with those in need (2:42-47; 4:32-37; 6:1-6).

The churches showed the spiritual quality of trust, total dependence

on the Lord (16:5; see 6:5 and 11:24 for descriptions of individuals). This they did by the consistent practice of prayer, both individually and corporately (1:14; 2:42; 6:4; 10:9; 13:2; 16:25; 20:36; 21:5). In fact, in two important summary statements Luke highlights prayer as an essential of church life and one of the main duties of church leaders (2:42; 6:4). Specific occasions for prayer included the advance of the church's mission, whether in preparation, confirmation, commissioning, empowerment or deliverance (1:14; 6:6; 8:15; 9:40; 12:5, 12; 13:3; 14:23; 28:8).

With faithfulness the church adhered to the apostles' teaching (2:42). Luke stresses the teaching activity of the church, which had both an evangelistic and an edificatory dimension (evangelism, 4:2, 18; 5:21, 28, 42; 15:35; 20:20; 28:31; edification, 11:26; 16:4-5; 18:11). He consistently notes how teaching and words of encouragement brought strength to the church (14:22; 15:32, 41; 18:23). The watchword is "Always remain in the grace you have received" (see 11:23; 14:22).

Because Luke focuses almost exclusively on the church's outwardly directed mission, he pays scant attention to details of its internal life and organization. No particular polity emerges as normative, although some spiritual characteristics of its organization emerge. The church manifests an organic unity, so that its multiple expressions in a region can be described in the singular: "the church throughout Judea, Galilee and Samaria" (9:31). A local expression is termed "the church at _____" (8:1; 13:1).

Such unity is grounded in a spiritual equality. All Christians view other members as their brothers and sisters (11:29; 15:1, 23, 36; 17:10, 14). This includes the leaders, who exercise their authority collegially, following the humble servant-leader role commanded by Christ (Lk 22:24-30). The decision-making process preserves all these traits. Each party, leader and congregation fulfills its role submitting its action to the others, and neither moving ahead without the approving consensus of the others (Acts 6:1-6; 15:22-29). The premier manifestation of God's salvation in the individual and the church is the presence of the Holy Spirit to empower and guide (2:4; 4:8, 31; 8:29; 10:19; 16:6-7).

The Preaching of Salvation

For Luke the church is a missionary church. Christ commands that this

salvation message "be preached in his name to all nations" (Lk 24:47). Three key concepts summarize Luke's teaching on the church's mission: proclamation/witness, the word as the gospel message, and the Spirit.

Proclamation/Witness Luke makes clear from the very climax of his Gospel and the opening of Acts that the church's main mission is proclamation/witness (Lk 24:44-48; Acts 1:8). He reiterates this theme at key points in the church's advance: Philip's mission to Samaria (8:5); Paul's first public act as a Christian (9:20); Paul's description to the Ephesian elders of his activities among them (20:21, 24-25); the climax of Acts, when Paul at Rome "preached the kingdom of God" (28:31). He even reports a witness which cites Jesus' commission (10:42).

The content of this proclamation/witness encompasses the resurrection, the person of Christ, salvation blessings and the kingdom of God (2:32; 3:15; 5:32; 8:25; 9:20; 10:41-42; 18:5; 19:13; 20:21, 24-25; 22:15; 28:23, 31). Luke stresses that eyewitnesses attested the facts of the salvation story (1:22; 5:32; 10:40-42; 13:31; 26:16; also see 26:26).

The Word The word of God is a key theological concept that Luke uses to encourage Theophilus toward salvation (Minear 1973:142). God takes the initiative in sending this word of salvation to Israel (10:36; 13:26). It is "the word" that Christian witnesses speak, evangelize, announce (4:31; 8:4, 25; 11:19; 13:5, 46; 14:25; 15:7, 35-36; 16:6, 32; 17:13). Converts are saved by hearing and believing, receiving and glorifying that word (2:41; 4:4; 8:14; 10:44; 11:1; 13:7, 44, 48; 17:11; 19:10). So central is "the word" to the church's mission that the apostles make their priority the "ministry of the word" and prayer (6:2, 4). And Luke can describe the church's growth as the word of the Lord's spreading and growing (6:7; 12:24; 13:49; 19:20).

God's empowerment of "the word" to saving effect is sometimes accompanied by signs and wonders that bear witness to it (4:33; 14:3). The word of God proclaimed is truly the bridge between salvation accomplished and applied.

The Spirit There is no explicit mention of the Holy Spirit in Luke's gospel summary, but his work is clearly implied by two aspects of its wording. The passive "will be preached" has no expressed agent. This leaves room for inferring that not only human beings but also God will be involved in the proclamation. Luke makes this explicit in Acts 5:32.

The phrase "in his name" points to the divine power and authority with which the proclamation goes forth. This too Luke brings out as the Holy Spirit's power when Jesus commissions the apostles in Acts 1:8.

What roles does the Holy Spirit fill in the purposes of God? The Holy Spirit inspired the prophets to predict salvation events, especially those that would involve hostility against God's Messiah and rejection of his message (Acts 1:16/Ps 69:25; 109:8; Acts 4:25/Ps 2:1-2; Acts 28:25-27/Is 6:9-10). This demonstrates that such events are not outside God's control and in no way invalidate Jesus' messiahship or the gospel message.

The Holy Spirit is the promised gift from the Father and from the exalted, reigning Son. He is first poured out at Pentecost on all who repent and believe in the Lord Jesus for salvation. The Holy Spirit's presence is a key salvation blessing. Speaking in tongues is an outward manifestation of his presence, a sign of regeneration. As I have pointed out, the lack of a consistent pattern of conversion and outward manifestation makes it unlikely that Luke sees such an outward manifestation as normative for all Christians.

In the church's life the Spirit provides power in witness. When Christians full of the Spirit testify, there is enabling, boldness and conviction (2:4, 17-18; 4:8, 13, 31; 5:32; 6:5, 10; 18:24-25). There may also be a power encounter in which Satanic opposition to the gospel is routed (13:9-12). The Spirit further supplies guidance, especially for the advance of the church's mission (8:29, 39). He may give specific instruction in combination with supernatural communication in order to overcome ethnic hesitation and move a Philip or a Peter to preach the gospel to Gentiles (10:19; 11:12). He guides Paul into his Gentile mission, both in its inauguration through the Antioch church and in its further thrust into Macedonia.

The Spirit can indicate God's purposes both positively and negatively (13:2, 4; 16:6-7). He can warn of negative circumstances surrounding an action. When Paul purposes in the Spirit to minister at Jerusalem and Rome, the Holy Spirit warns him of the persecution and suffering that await him. This works perseverance in Paul, and willingness to sacrifice (20:22-24; 21:4, 11, 13-14).

Finally, the Spirit's guidance promotes church unity. The Jerusalem Council decision that promoted spiritual equality and harmony between

believing Jews and Gentiles is prefaced with the words "It seemed good to the Holy Spirit and to us . . ." (15:28).

In church life, the Holy Spirit also facilitates edification. He fills leaders for serving, shepherding and prophesying (6:3, 5; 11:24, 28; 20:28). Accountability to the Spirit is central in church discipline (5:3, 9). No better picture of the Spirit's role in the church's growth and maturity can be found than in Luke's summary statement about the church in Judea, Galilee and Samaria: it "enjoyed a time of peace. It was strengthened; and encouraged by the Holy Spirit, it grew in numbers, living in the fear of the Lord" (9:31).

Scope of the Witness

That this gospel message would be preached "to all nations" raises several important issues in Luke's theology: the legitimacy of the Gentile mission, the relationship of Israel and the church, the relationship of the Christian to the law.

Luke establishes the Gentile mission's legitimacy by showing how God's hand of blessing was upon the witness to the Gentiles (10:45; 11:17; 13:48; 14:27; 15:3, 8, 12; 21:19). At a critical juncture, Peter's witness to Cornelius, there is an outward manifestation of the Spirit as there had been at Pentecost. This enables the apostles to understand and effectively argue for a gospel of grace that has come in the same way to Jew and Gentile alike. Luke points out that the Gentile mission is a fulfillment of God's purposes articulated in the Old Testament (13:47; 15:15-16). He repeatedly refers to Paul's commission to take the gospel to the Gentiles and his obedience to that call (9:15; 13:46; 18:6; 22:21; 26:17). In his last summary of the gospel message he includes the Gentile mission as part of its content (26:23).

If the Gentile mission is legitimate, what is the relationship of Israel and the church? Luke acknowledges the Jews' special place in God's salvation plan. When preaching to Jewish audiences, the apostles stress that according to the promise made to their ancestors God has brought a Savior to Israel, and that the gospel message must be preached to the Jews (3:26; 10:36; 13:23, 46):

It is Luke's custom to use *people (laos)* as a designation of the Jews in their special relationship to God (for example, 2:47; 3:12; 13:24). Two

times, however, he uses the same word to designate Gentiles who will respond to the gospel (15:14; 18:10). Gentiles have been under the sovereign control of God. God has allowed them to wander away from true worship; he holds them accountable for their guilt, but they are not viewed prejudicially. Only those who respond to the gospel message may rightly claim to be part of God's people.

Luke shows a continuity and discontinuity between Israel and the church. He views the church as the true Israel, responsive to God's fulfillment of his salvation promises in Messiah Jesus. Historically, the church begins as a predominantly Jewish Christian body that must integrate into itself the fruit of the Gentile mission. With that integration complete, the church becomes the new Israel, the new people of God, composed of both Jew and Gentile.

The church and individual Christians relate to the law within a context of the freedom of grace. Nevertheless, freedom must be used in love, to promote fellowship across ethnic lines (15:19). Ethnic diversity is respected, though within the limits of the written law of God, while unity encompassing that diversity is pursued (see 21:25).

With this stance the scope of the gospel message's audience, "all nations," Jew and Gentile alike, is affirmed, and the dynamic of the mission—"witnesses . . . to the ends of the earth" (Acts 1:8)—continues until the King returns. By the time Theophilus reached Acts 28:31, he must surely have known that the gospel message is true and that it was indeed for him and his compatriots (Lk 1:1-4). That same sure knowledge should be ours as well.

Outline of Acts

COMMENTARY

THE JERUSALEM CHURCH: ITS BEGINNING (Acts 1:1—2:47)

"Let the church be the church!" This rallying cry from John MacKay, missionary statesman and ecumenical leader of an earlier generation, needs to be heard and heeded again in our day. Pressures from without (secularization or resurgent religious fundamentalism) and from within (marketing or accommodation to the spirit of the age) work to keep the church from being the church.

As Luke seeks to convince Theophilus and other interested Romans that the implementation aspect of the gospel message is true (Lk 1:4; 24:47), he places before us what the church is to be and do: its missions mandate. As Luke begins, he gives the mandate's source, emphasizes the divine power needed to implement it, and portrays its divinely worked results in individual lives and in the dynamic fellowship that is the church.

☐ Preparation for Pentecost (1:1-26)

Luke skillfully begins Acts with a backward look that lays the groundwork for his second volume of historical narrative. In this "beginning of the beginning" he focuses on preparation for the coming of the empowering Holy Spirit. We need to hear his claim that by the Spirit's power the church will fulfill its mandate of preaching the gospel to the ends of the earth. What a difference that will make in how we offer or receive the message!

Jesus' Postresurrection Appearances and Ascension (1:1-11)

What in the world should the church be doing as we face a new millennium? Jesus' missionary mandate, which is a preview of the content of Acts, gives us the answer: *You will be my witnesses . . . to the ends of the earth* (1:8). The entire preface so undergirds and clarifies this command that we are led not only to the conviction that Acts must be viewed from a missionary perspective but to realize that we too must find our places in fulfilling that mandate, which is also a promise.

Review of the Gospel of Luke (1:1-5) Luke's review of his gospel stresses comprehensiveness: *all that Jesus began to do and to teach* (v. 1). It also provides forward-looking continuity with the second volume: presumably Acts will report what Jesus continued to do and teach (as in 2:47; 9:34; 14:3; 16:14; 18:10).

The review focuses on Jesus' postresurrection preparation of the apostles to be authoritative guarantors of the truth of his resurrection and the gospel's content. Luke notes that the risen Lord instructed the apostles whom he had personally chosen through the Holy Spirit (Lk 6:13), thereby emphasizing the authoritative link between the words and work of Jesus and the message and mission of the church.

Jesus qualified the apostles as guarantors of the truth of the resurrection by appearing to them repeatedly over a period of forty days (Acts

---

Notes: 1:1-11 Though the forms of appearance, farewell scene, commission and assumption story may have influenced the framing of this account (Palmer 1987; Mullins 1976; B. J. Hubbard 1977), the structure of Acts 1:1-11 is best understood as that of a preface to the second volume of a multivolume work (compare Josephus *Jewish Antiquities* 8.1; Diodorus Siculus *Library of History* 2.1; Herodian *History* 3.1; 41). The review (vv. 1-5) is followed by a preview that introduces the book's content through a recapitulation of the last events of the previous volume (Lk 24:44-53; Acts 1:6-11; compare Josephus *Jewish Antiquities* 7.380-82; 8.1).

The historicity of the ascension has been questioned (vv. 9-11). Some believe the early church originally understood Jesus' resurrection as a resurrection-exaltation to heaven and take the account of a separate ascension as a later development. In fact, some view it as Luke's historicizing the truth of Jesus' exaltation (Baird 1980:5). Yet the ascension is attested elsewhere in the New Testament (1 Tim 3:16; 1 Pet 3:22; also see Jn 6:62; Eph 4:8-10; Heb 4:14). Luke himself shows an awareness of the resurrection-exaltation as one continuous event that resulted in an outpouring of salvation blessings (Acts 2:32-33; 5:30-31). The ascension is the last resurrection "disappearance" in the form of visible ascension (3:21; O'Toole 1979b:106; Moule 1982:60).

1:1 *Began* binds Jesus' earthly ministry and the church's early mission into one history.

1:2 In Greek thought *apostles* were agents sent on a mission with the authority of the

1:22; 10:41-42). The many pieces of empirical evidence could lead to no other conclusion than that he was alive.

During his postresurrection appearances, Jesus spoke to the apostles "things pertaining to the kingdom of God." "Kingdom of God" became for Luke a shorthand phrase for the content of the early church's preaching (see 8:12; 19:8; 28:31). And rightly so, for the final reign of God has arrived "in the events of the life, death, and resurrection of Jesus, and to proclaim these facts, in their proper setting, is to preach the Gospel of the Kingdom of God" (Dodd 1964:24; Is 33:22; Zech 14:9; Lk 11:20).

The importance of such continuity for Luke's evangelistic purpose and the church's fulfillment of its missionary mandate cannot be overestimated. Here is the proof that a gospel message that claims to go back to the apostles can be trusted: the apostles received it from Jesus. Here too is the clearly articulated basis for belief that the gospel's key salvation event has actually happened. The empirical evidence of the empty tomb and the resurrection appearances point steadily in only one direction: Jesus is alive! We can boldly and unashamedly invite unbelievers to hear our witness and consider the evidence.

Luke's review climaxes with Jesus' command to wait for the Holy Spirit's coming (1:4-5; see also Lk 24:49). Jesus gave this instruction on

one who sent them (see Barrett 1978). In Jewish writings the term "apostle of God" was applied to the priesthood and to Moses, Elijah, Elisha and Ezekiel, "because there took place through them things normally reserved for God" (Rengstorf 1964:419).

To place the phrase *through the Holy Spirit* with *giving instructions* (as the NIV does) does not appear to further the passage's thought, while connecting it with *chosen* would (Jervell 1972b:88).

1:3 The ascension after forty days may be harmonized with the apparent departure on Easter Sunday evening in Luke 24:50-53, if Acts 1:9-11 is read as providing detail by which the account in Luke's Gospel may be fleshed out, and if the transitional connective at Luke 24:44 is allowed to indicate a break in sequence (E. F. Harrison 1986:43; Neil 1973:63).

1:5 Pentecostal and neo-Pentecostal or charismatic interpreters see this Spirit-baptism as a repeatable event in the life of the church. It is a distinct, subsequent-to-conversion experience, with speaking in tongues as its necessary sign (Holdcroft 1962:120-127; Bennett and Bennett 1971:27-35). The "Third Wave" of charismatic renewal does not insist on this separate experience but does claim the presence of "signs and wonders" today (Wagner 1988). Whether from the Reformed, dispensational or evangelical Anglican perspective, other interpreters see the promise of Spirit-baptism as fulfilled in the outpouring at Pentecost. All post-Pentecost converts receive it at conversion (1 Cor 12:13; Hoekema 1972:17-21; Unger 1974:60-63; Packer 1984:91).

a number of occasions (not only one, as in the NIV).

Luke understands the Spirit's baptism as occurring at Pentecost. It is a foreshadowing of the end-time deluge of the Spirit and fire (Is 66:15; Ezek 36:25-27; 39:29; Joel 2:28; Acts 2:1-13). "The future encounter with God's Holy Spirit-and-fire will be like an angry sea engulfing and sinking a boat, or like a massive surge of flood water suddenly sweeping down on a man as he attempts to cross the river and overwhelming him. It will be immense, majestic and devastating" (Turner 1981:51). This coming baptism, then, is to be an overwhelming eschatological experience of God's Spirit. It is unique, unrepeatable in church history.

Jesus promises that in a little while God will supply the church with all the resources it needs for fulfilling its missionary mandate. Lloyd Ogilvie observes, "We have been instructed in the things Jesus did, but know too little of what He continues to do today as indwelling Spirit and engendering power" (1983:26). Christians who have not done so need to appropriate the power that is already theirs, all because Jesus' promise was fulfilled at Pentecost.

Preview of Acts (1:6-11) The disciples' question *Lord, are you at this time going to restore the kingdom to Israel?*—which they asked repeatedly (NIV indicates only one asking)—was most natural for Jews to address to the resurrected Messiah.

Central to Old Testament faith was the conviction that God would in the end time fully restore his people to their inheritance in the land, where they would live securely without foreign domination (Jer 16:15; 23:8; 50:19; Hos 11:11; Joel 3:17). In response to Jesus' resurrection or to his teaching about the kingdom (Acts 1:3; also see Lk 22:28-30), the disciples want to know a date. Such a question is selfishly nationalistic and betrays an eagerness for the end of history and an ushering in of God's perfect reign. The disciples had consistently asked such questions throughout Jesus' ministry (Lk 19:11; 21:7).

Jesus' mild rebuke affirms that God alone is qualified to know such things, since by means of his own authority he has established the *times or dates,* the stages and critical events through which humankind must

---

1:6 The indefinite designation of the audience indicates that it is probably broader than the apostles (Haenchen 1971:142; see also Acts 1:22).

pass until the kingdom comes (compare Acts 17:26).

Acts 1:8 sets out clearly what the church is to be doing until Jesus returns. Through a command-promise, Jesus tells his disciples of the resources, content and scope of their primary task. The essential resource is God the Holy Spirit, who will come on them at Pentecost as he did on Mary at the incarnation (Lk 1:35). By this Spirit-baptism they will receive the supernatural ability to work miracles and preach effectively (Acts 4:7-10, 31, 33; 6:5, 8; 8:13). Their witness will be bold and will produce conviction leading to positive or negative decisions (2:37, 41; 4:8, 13, 31; 6:5, 10; 7:54-58).

The whole church, and each member of it, must take up this task. All who receive the apostles' teaching become witnesses (14:2-3; 22:15-18, 20). Richard Longenecker rightly concludes, "This commission lays an obligation on all Christians. . . . The Christian church, according to Acts, is a missionary church that responds obediently to Jesus' commission" (1981:256).

The mandate, expressed with a future-tense verb *(will be),* can be taken as both a command and a prophetic promise. Luke may well have intended that it be understood in both ways. Not only does he show the church obediently carrying out this mandate (2:47; 4:31, 33; 6:4, 7; 8:4; 11:19-20), but he also shows how God intervenes at strategic points to give impetus and direction for taking the mission across another cultural threshold or into a another geographical region (8:16-17, 26, 29; 10:9-16, 19-20; 11:20-21; 13:2; 16:9-10; 18:9-10; 23:11). God in his grace makes sure the mandate is completely fulfilled.

And so today the call for the church to be a missionary church is still in force. In 1974, at the first Lausanne Congress on World Evangelization, a gracious God refocused the churches' attention on the world's hidden people groups who have yet to hear the witness.

Jesus says to be his *witnesses.* To be a witness *(martys)* is to speak from personal knowledge of facts and their significance. The apostles, as eyewitnesses of the saving events, were witnesses in a unique sense. But all those who will believe and appropriate the truth of their testi-

---

1:8 As the portrayal of supernatural effectiveness in preaching elsewhere in Acts indicates (4:8, 13; 14:27; 16:14), this power is not limited to the performance of miracles that accredit

mony also qualify as witnesses.

The scope of the task is given in geographical terms. Acts presents the evangelization of the first two geographical regions (Jerusalem, 2:42—8:3; Judea and Samaria, 8:4—12:25). Luke probably has no particular place in mind when he uses the phrase *to the ends of the earth*. He is thinking of a mission that will reach throughout the whole earth in fulfillment of Isaiah 49:6 (Acts 13:47). Since the narrative concludes geographically in Rome—the empire's center, from which roads reach to the limits of the then-known world—the mission is potentially complete but actually remains unfinished.

When the scope of the task is viewed ethnically, however, we realize that by the time of the Jerusalem Council (15:1-35) "the gospel has already reached all possible manner of men" (Menoud 1978b:123). The gospel has been extended to Palestinian and Hellenistic Jews (2:5-13), Samaritans (8:4-13), a proselyte (8:26-40), a Gentile God-fearer (10:1-48) and pagan Gentiles (11:20-21; 13:46-48; 14:8-20).

Today the unfinished task remains a formidable challenge. But it is possible to complete the task—to take the witness to the ends of the earth and plant a church in each unreached ethnic group. For the 1989 Lausanne II Congress on World Evangelization in Manila, David Barrett calculated that there remain twelve thousand distinct cultural groups (1.8 billion persons) that have no church in their language and culture (Lausanne Committee 1989:13-14).

Among the 1.7 billion professing Christians in the world, we should be able to find 180 million true believers. They could serve as a more than adequate support base (fifteen thousand believers per unreached people group) to field a missionary force to penetrate each of the unreached groups. With such mobilization, each unreached people group could be evangelized in the foreseeable future.

There is a way. Where is the will? Current recruitment and deployment of missionaries falls far short. Currently only thirty thousand full-time Christian workers are at work among the 1.8 billion members of the twelve thousand unreached groups. Will the vision be caught, the mo-

---

the witnesses (contra Lake and Cadbury 1979:8).

Thornton's (1977) contention that the mandate is fulfilled to "the ends of the earth" in

mentum generated, so that in obedience to Christ the last great push to the ends of the earth will take place?

Immediately after Jesus gives this command, as the disciples are watching, he is taken up from the earth, and a cloud so envelopes him that the disciples can no longer see him. The cloud probably refers to the Shekinah glory, which at once manifests and hides the divine presence (Ex 19:16; 40:34). It may also point to Christ's return (Dan 7:13; Lk 21:27; Acts 1:11).

The disciples stand in awe, *looking intently up into the sky* for an extended period. Luke will use the verb "to look intently" often in Acts in connection with the miraculous (3:4, 12; 6:15; 10:4; 11:6; 13:9; 14:9).

Suddenly two angels appear—two witnesses (Deut 19:15)—to interpret God's mighty act in Jesus' ascension. Their gentle rebuke to the sky-gazing disciples implies that in the interim there is a task to be done: fulfillment of the missionary mandate.

The angels describe in simple terms what has just happened: Jesus has been taken up *into heaven.* The implications are unmistakable. Jesus will no longer be with the disciples in the way he was with them during his earthly ministry or in postresurrection appearances. In heaven Jesus is in a position of authority, at the Father's right hand, whence he can pour out salvation blessings as by his Spirit he directs and empowers the church's mission (Acts 2:33; 4:10-12; 5:30-31). The angels conclude with an affirmation of the certainty of Christ's return. He will come *in the same way* that he has gone.

The fact that the Great Commission is the last instruction of the risen, now ascended and imminently returning Lord gives it great weight. He is not mentioning an optional ministry activity for individuals with cross-cultural interests and churches with surplus funds. The Great Commission is the primary task the Lord left his church. The church must always be a missionary church; the Christian must always be a world Christian.

Waiting for the Spirit: The Election of Matthias (1:12-26)

Luke's report of the disciples' activities as they waited for the Spirit's

---

the evangelization of the Ethiopian or Schwartz's (1986) understanding of the phrase as meaning "to the boundary of the land, i.e. Israel," are not established from Acts.

· promised coming at Pentecost gives a pattern we would do well to emulate if we would prepare for an outpouring of the Spirit in revival. Though Pentecost was a unique inaugural event in the church's life, the steps that preceded it are essential for any fresh work of the Spirit.

United, Persistent Prayer (1:12-14) Obedient to their Lord's command to await the Spirit's coming in Jerusalem, the disciples return to the city (compare 1:4). They gather in a spacious room above the tumult and prying eyes of street traffic.

The assembly included three elements: the eleven apostles, women and Jesus' relatives. Luke explicitly names the eleven and in that way establishes the continuity between Jesus' ministry and the apostolic foundation of the church (compare Lk 6:14-16). Luke also draws attention to the faithful women who accompanied and physically supported Jesus in his ministry. They had witnessed his death and received the first news of his resurrection (Lk 8:1-3; 23:49; 24:1-11). Luke's discussions of women serve to indicate that barriers of gender are abolished among those who will participate in the church's witness in power. In referring to Jesus' family, Luke not only foreshadows the leadership that some of those relatives would exercise (Acts 12:7; 15:13; 21:18) but also highlights Jesus' messiahship and the link between the church and Israel.

This core of disciples, along with others, engaged in united, persistent prayer. They had not been commanded to pray, only to wait. But Jesus' own example at his baptism and his teachings, especially regarding how the Spirit would come in response to prayer, probably provided enough guidance (Lk 3:21; 11:13; 18:1, 8). The disciples' prayer was united, a quality that would characterize their common life under the Spirit's blessing (Acts 2:46; 4:24; 5:12). Their prayer was persistent. They devoted themselves to set times of daily corporate prayer until God answered from heaven.

1:12 The rabbis ingeniously calculated *a Sabbath day's walk* as two thousand cubits, or three-quarters of a mile (about eleven hundred meters), by interpreting Exodus 16:29 in the light of Numbers 35:5 (*m. Soṭa* 5:3).

1:13 It is hard to establish definite links between this *upstairs* room and the site of the Last Supper (Lk 22:11-13) or of the resurrection appearances (24:36). It is also not clear whether this is the house of John Mark's mother, Mary (Acts 12:12).

Simon the Zealot was probably a member of the nationalistic Jewish faction who were spiritual heirs of the Hasmonean insurgents (Josephus *Jewish Wars* 2.651; 4.160; 1 Maccabees 2:27).

The Fulton Street prayer meeting that sparked a revival in America in 1858 began with six people. Within six months there were ten thousand businessmen gathering daily for prayer in New York City, and within two years one million converts were added to the American church (Orr 1953:13). A. T. Pierson said, "There has never been a revival in any country that has not begun in united prayer, and no revival has ever continued beyond the duration of those prayer meetings" (quoted in Orr 1937:47). We must prepare for any fresh outpouring of the Spirit by united, persistent prayer.

Restored Integrity: The Election of Matthias (1:15-26) Luke singles out one event to record from those days of waiting. The legitimacy of the continuing witness to the twelve tribes of Israel (Lk 22:30) is affirmed by the apostles' filling the vacancy in their ranks. By detailing the apostolic requirement of being an eyewitness to the whole course of Jesus' ministry, including the resurrection and ascension, Luke emphasizes the continuity of eyewitness testimony which would be the church's foundation. And through it all he presents a prepared church with a restored integrity in its leadership.

Peter's speech to the 120 believers, introduced with much sense of occasion, declares the divine necessity of Judas' apostasy since what the Holy Spirit spoke through David long ago about him has now been fulfilled. Peter further emphasizes that Judas had received a place as one of the twelve, a position of service (see Lk 22:26, 28-30). He proceeds to quote the Old Testament Scriptures that predicted Judas's end and show the appropriateness of finding a replacement (Acts 1:20). Since the use of these texts, especially the first one, assumes the reader's acquaintance with the circumstances surrounding Judas's death, Luke provides a parenthetical statement about them. Judas's bloody suicide—a fall from

1:14 *Women* could refer to wives of the apostles (Lake and Cadbury 1979:11), but F. F. Bruce says they are the women who accompanied Jesus in his ministry and were present at the cross (1951:74).

1:18 Luke's and Matthew's accounts (Acts 1:18-19; Mt 27:3-10) may be harmonized if we understand that the Jewish leaders bought the land in Judas's name. Further, Judas may have attempted suicide by hanging himself but was actually killed when the rope broke and he fell headlong (A. B. Gordon 1971:98). According to another variant reading ("to swell" rather than *fall headlong*), after Judas died by hanging, his body swelled up during decomposition and burst (Metzger 1971:286).

a ledge on the southern slope of the valley of Hinnom—turned his property into cursed ground, twice defiled (Num 35:33; Deut 21:23; Mt 27:7-8; Acts 1:18-19). It became a cemetery for the ceremonially unclean and literally fulfilled the psalmist's imprecation: *May his place be deserted; let there be no one to dwell in it* (see Ps 69:25). Another imprecation establishes the legitimacy of the election to follow: *May another take his place of leadership* (Ps 109:8).

Peter now states the qualifications for an apostolic replacement. The apostle must be one who had accompanied Jesus' disciples from the time of John the Baptist's ministry until Christ's ascension, one who had been a witness to the resurrection and had seen the risen Lord. In other words, he must have witnessed the events that would be covered in the early church's gospel preaching (as in Acts 10:37-43; 13:23-41) and the Gospel of Mark. Peter stresses that the candidate must have been with Jesus' entourage *the whole time*—a most necessary qualification if he is to be an apostolic guarantor of the words and works of Jesus (compare 2:42; 5:32).

Public access to Jesus, as well as his authoritative relationship to his disciples, is captured in Peter's characterization of the time period: *the whole time the Lord Jesus went in and out among us*. Such a strong eyewitness requirement should further confirm to Luke's inquiring audience—and to us—that the early church's message can be trusted: it is grounded not in human opinion but in divinely wrought and humanly witnessed salvation-history events.

The believers—or possibly the apostles—set forth two candidates: Joseph Barsabbas (son of Sabba or Seba), who also had a Roman name, Justus; and Matthias. Neither is mentioned again in Scripture, though Judas called Barsabbas (see Acts 15:22) may have been Joseph's brother. Later tradition identifies Matthias as a missionary to the Ethiopians.

Now the believers—or again, possibly only the apostles—address a

---

1:20 The validity of Peter's interpreting the maledictions against the oppressors of the righteous as referring prophetically to Judas has often been questioned or excused (for example, Longenecker 1981:264; Bruce 1990:110). Support for his interpretation may be found in a messianic understanding of these psalms based on Davidic authorship, a literal reading of them (for example, the use of Judas's homestead as a "field of blood," a cemetery, means no living person dwells there; Ps 69:25) and Jesus' use of one of these psalms to describe his passion (Ps 69:4/Jn 15:25; also compare Ps 69:9/Jn 2:17; Ps 69:21/Jn 19:29; Ps 69:9/Rom 15:3).

prayer to the Lord Jesus. They ask him to indicate which of the two candidates he has chosen to fill the position vacated by Judas. With this prayer, in wording that echoes Jesus' initial calling of the twelve (Lk 6:13; compare Acts 1:2), they show they intend that this new apostle be chosen by Christ just as the other eleven were. An internal qualification of the apostle, possibly regenerate growth, may be hinted at when the Lord is addressed as the one who knows all hearts (compare Acts 15:8).

It is clear, though, that a replacement is being sought in the wake of apostasy; the believers are not intending to create a line of succession. Note how the prayer refers to Judas's defection and consequent end (compare 1:16-17, 20). One of the two apostolic candidates must receive, literally, "the place of this service and apostleship" (v. 25; NIV *this apostolic ministry*). Sin has reached even to the apostolic ranks. This is not outside the sovereign plan of God, for *the Scripture had to be fulfilled* (v. 16). Still, human responsibility and personal judgment are involved, and the ranks of leadership must be restored to full strength and spiritual integrity.

Lots are now cast. Each candidate's name is written on a stone, which is then placed in a container. The container is shaken and turned upside down until one of the stones springs or falls out. This method for discerning divine choice had a long history in Israel (Josh 18:6; 1 Chron 24:5; Prov 16:33).

Luke concludes by noting that the full complement of the twelve apostles has been restored. By principle, Matthias's election teaches us that restoration of integrity within the body of Christ is essential to preparation for revival. Wherever sin has created a breach and compromised the church's integrity, discipline, repentance and restoration must be pursued. J. Edwin Orr, that prodigious student of revivals, declared, "Revival is impossible apart from confession of sin among believers. It

---

1:21 The NIV inserts the verb *choose*. What Luke emphasizes is the necessity that one meeting the qualifications become a witness to the resurrection with the other apostles.

1:26 It was not a mistake to elect Matthias instead of letting Paul fill the vacancy. Paul did not meet the requirements, was not called to the Jewish mission, and recognized the abnormality of his apostolic calling (1 Cor 15:8; Longenecker 1981:267).

Given Old Testament background and practice, it was also not a mistake to cast lots. Casting lots does not seem, however, to have became normative practice in the early church after Pentecost (Marshall 1980:67).

must be confession to God, and it may be confession to one another. Every hindrance must go. Sin must be confessed in order that it may be cleansed. . . . Judgment must begin at the house of the Lord" (Orr 1937:50). Only a holy people, a repentant and restored people, are vessels fit to be revived.

□ Pentecost (2:1-41)

In the twentieth century Pentecost has become a source of confusion, embarrassment or division for Christians, even as it has become a curiosity, if not an object of ridicule, for non-Christians. What is repeatable— and what is unrepeatable—of that miraculous outpouring of the Spirit and speaking in tongues? Luke helps us sort through our various reactions so Pentecost can become the comfort and the challenge it was meant to be. Peter's speech speaks to the cause and significance of the event.

The Coming of the Spirit (2:1-13)

The story of the origin of a nation, a movement or an institution captures the imagination of later generations. Whether in the yearly remembrance of America's founding, the Fourth of July, or the twentieth anniversary of a key event in a movement, the civil rights march from Montgomery to Selma, Alabama, or the celebration of the New Testament church's birthday, Pentecost, each generation desires to recall in vivid detail what happened in those early days. A people reinvigorates itself by drawing

---

2:1 The theological background of Pentecost has been taken variously as the renewal of the covenant, the anniversary of the giving of the law on Sinai (Longenecker 1981:269), the reversal of Babel (Williams 1985:27), the fulfillment of Old Testament and New Testament prophecy concerning the Spirit's coming (Is 32:15; Joel 2:28-32; Marshall 1980:68) and the firstfruits of the wheat harvest (Russell 1986:58). Jewish tradition on the giving of the law in many languages (*b. Šabbat* 88b) makes very attractive a link between Acts 2 and Pentecost as the anniversary of the giving of the law (see Dupont 1979c:42). But the speech later in Acts 2 lacks allusions to Sinai and the law. Pentecost's initial significance as a feast of firstfruits, together with the biblical prophecies of the Spirit's coming, is the more probable background. The reversal of Babel may be a subordinate theme having to do with the church's universal mission. The theme of covenant renewal is not consistently developed throughout the account.

2:3 The tongues should be understood as divided in appearance, like flames of fire (Bauer, Gingrich and Danker 1979: s.v. διαμερίζω), not as a fireball of tongues that divided itself and come to rest on each (NIV).

comfort and challenge from the way it was in the beginning.

The Miracle (2:1-4) By the way Luke notes the arrival of the day of Pentecost, he marks it as a key event in salvation history *(symplērousthai, "was fulfilled" [NIV came];* see Lk 9:51). Pentecost, the Feast of the Firstfruits, was a most appropriate time for the Spirit to come. It was closely connected with Passover, just as the Spirit's coming would be associated with the saving events of the Lord's crucifixion and exaltation. The feast celebrated the first produce of the Promised Land, Israel's inheritance, just as the Spirit is the "firstfruits" of the salvation blessings to the believer (see Deut 26:1-11, especially vv. 9-11).

All together in one place, probably the upper room, the disciples in prayerful unity await the Spirit (Acts 1:14). Suddenly God gives signs of sound and sight. Their divine origin and supernatural character is clear. The sound is from heaven and is *like the blowing of a violent wind. The tongues that appear seemed* to be flames of fire. In the Old Testament such a loud sound often accompanied a theophany (Ex 19:16, 19; 20:18; compare Heb 12:19). A violent, rushing wind symbolizes the Holy Spirit (Ezek 37:9-14; compare Lk 16:16). The sound fills the whole house. What has arrived is an all-encompassing divine presence. The divided tongues like flames of fire, resting on each, also symbolize the Spirit of God, especially his power (Lk 3:16; compare Acts 1:8).

Those on whom the outward sign rests experience an inner filling with the Holy Spirit. This leads to a further external manifestation of his presence. Luke uses the verb *filled* in order to emphasize that although

---

2:4 Some take the disciples' experience to be a vocational empowerment to witness that is repeated in Acts and is described as filling (Stronstad 1984:53; Turner 1981:57). But others see the baptism and gift of the Spirit at Pentecost as both an initial, permanent endowment for the church (see the way it is referred to as a benchmark experience in 10:47; 11:17; 15:8) and a particular instance of vocational empowerment for inspired speech (Marshall 1977:355-56).

Jesus' giving of the Spirit during a postresurrection appearance (Jn 20:22) is best understood as an acted parable. It foreshadows Pentecost and reinforces the truth that the Spirit is Christ's gift to his church.

Interpreters have understood the nature of the tongues spoken as (1) ecstatic unintelligible speech, (2) intelligible foreign language, with several speakers speaking one language, (3) intelligible foreign language with one speaker communicating in several languages, (4) ecstatic unintelligible language that was heard in one's own tongue (Dupont 1979c:45). Luke presents it as intelligible foreign language. This phenomenon is different from the gift of tongues and interpretation in 1 Corinthians (Bruce 1990:115).

this is the initial endowment of the Spirit on the church, it is also an equipping with inspired speech for ministry. It is the first of many fillings the believers will know (4:8, 31; 9:17; 13:9).

As the Spirit inspires their speech, the believers are speaking in human languages other than their own native tongues. Here is a further sign that something extraordinary has happened. Acts 1:8 is being fulfilled all at once.

What of Pentecost does God want the church to expect in its life today? What is repeatable? What is unrepeatable? Those aspects of Pentecost that marked the inauguration of the Spirit's presence indiscriminately among the people of God appear to have fulfilled their purpose in the first Pentecost. We should not necessarily expect to see them again. The external signs of sound and sight and the foreign languages fall into this category. But in any age we should expect to find a church filled with the Holy Spirit, powerfully enabled to bear witness to Christ and his gospel.

If we are not so experiencing the Spirit's filling, why? Have we met the conditions of expectant prayer and cleansed lives? That is Pentecost's challenge. But what is its comfort? God has not abandoned his church. If he sent his Spirit before, he can do it again.

The Miracle's Effect (2:5-13) The *sound like the blowing of a violent wind* is evidently not isolated to the house. It attracts a crowd upon its occurrence, or possibly as the believers move out into the street and toward the temple. The curious throng, composed of devout Hellenistic Jews *from every nation under heaven* (compare Deut 2:25), is confused and then astonished *(existanto)* that each person hears in his or her native language the declaration of God's great deeds. Luke uses *existēmi* very selectively to describe the effect of the miraculous (Lk 2:47; 8:56; 24:22; Acts 8:13; 10:45; 12:16). We find it two times in this account, together with other "amazement" or "confusion" terms (*thaumazō, synchynō, diaporeō*—vv. 6-7, 12). Clearly, Luke wants us to sense what a

---

2:5 The vast majority of the crowd were residents (Haenchen 1971:168), not festal pilgrims, though some pilgrims were also present (compare v. 10).

2:9-11 Many different origins of the list of nations have been proposed: hellenistic history, geography or astrology; a Roman list of provinces; a Jewish list of diaspora regions; a pre-Luke tradition of the regions of Christian mission (Linton 1974:44). None of the alternatives

strong impact the Pentecost event had on the onlookers. They marvel that by a miracle of speaking or hearing, or both, they can understand Galileans, who were disdained for their indistinct pronunciation with its confused or lost laryngeals and aspirates (Bruce 1990:116).

The crowd's initial reaction shows us that God's powerful saving presence will always astonish us and challenge our current understandings of him and his ways. Turned toward God, our curiosity and surprise will become marveling, an important preparatory step to the believing reception of salvation blessings (Dupont 1979c:54).

People in the crowd enumerate their nationalities and places of origin. They begin with the far eastern border of the Roman Empire *(Parthians, Medes and Elamites)*, move westward through *Mesopotamia and Judea* (Israel, understood according to its God-given boundaries—Josh 1:4), and then encompass regions of Asia Minor in a circular counterclockwise fashion, commencing with the east: *Cappadocia, Pontus and Asia, Phrygia and Pamphylia.* The list then notes southern regions of the empire— *Egypt* and, west of it, *the parts of Libya near Cyrene.* Rounding out the list is *Rome,* the Empire's center, and two geographical extremities: the islands of the sea, represented by *Cretans,* and the desert places, represented by *Arabs* (compare Ezek. 30:5).

Each in his or her own language hears of *the wonders*—the great deeds—*of God.* Were these *wonders* the gifts of the Messiah and the outpoured Spirit (see 2:17, 33)?

This multilingual witness coheres with the universal offer of salvation in the church's message and its consequent worldwide mission. It also highlights the church's multicultural character. God affirms people as cultural beings. As many a Bible translator knows, our native language and culture is natural, necessary and welcome to us as the air we breathe. No wonder that when persons receive a Scripture portion in their own language, they rejoice: "God speaks my language!"

The crowd's astonishment progresses from marveling to perplexity.

---

explains all the names. A historical report of the Pentecost event itself is the best explanation.

2:13 The word translated *wine (gleukos),* with the marginal variant "sweet wine," normally refers to new wine, just vinted. Since the yearly vintage would not have taken place until after Pentecost, it probably refers to wine that had been kept sweet throughout the year (see Bruce 1988:59 for ancient methods for preserving sweetness).

They are trying to figure out the "why" of this miracle, both its cause and its significance. Some admit their inability to come up with an answer but show they are open for one as they wonder aloud, "What does this mean?" Others, for whom much of the speech is gibberish, mock, accusing the believers of being drunk with sweet wine (compare Lk 7:34).

How should we respond to the work of the Spirit in our midst? We must avoid the mockery of the scoffer who explains everything in empirical terms. We must be open to a divinely given explanation. The mixed reaction of the Pentecost crowd also teaches us that the "miraculous is not self-authenticating, nor does it inevitably and uniformly convince. There must also be the preparation of the heart and the proclamation of the message if miracles are to accomplish their full purpose" (Longenecker 1981:273).

Peter's Speech (2:14-41)

Humans were born to ask "Why?" From the chattering toddler tugging at his mother's skirts to the seasoned astrophysicist puzzling over her computer-enhanced images from outer space, the response to the novel is the same: Why? In fact, we ask this question in two directions. We want to know the cause, and we want to know the significance, especially for us.

To find an answer that satisfies both "whys," especially in regard to

---

2:14 The address, *Andres Ioudaioi kai hoi katoikountes Ierousalēm pantes,* should be compared with verse 5 and taken as a parallelism (Haenchen 1971:178), not indicating two distinct groups as Schneider (1980-1982:1:267), Longenecker (1981:275) and the NIV suggest.

2:17 There is variation in wording between Joel 2:28-32 and its quotation in Acts 2:17-21. Acts 2:17 has *in the last days, God says,* for "afterward"; it reverses two lines of Joel 2:28. Acts 2:18 adds *and they will prophesy* to Joel 2:29. Acts 2:19 adds *above . . . signs . . . below* to Joel 2:30. While the addition in Acts 2:18 is also a textual-critical matter, it may not have been part of Acts originally (Rodgers 1987). The other changes are explainable as appropriate inferences from the immediate context or as expansions for greater clarity and impact (Archer and Chirichigno 1983:149).

Some in Israel saw the outpouring of the Spirit as an event of the era preceding the end (1QH 4:31-34; 7:6; 1QS 4:2-6). Since Joel 2:28-32 is introduced by "afterward," an indefinite time marker pointing potentially to the distant future, Peter's appropriation of it as a prophecy of Pentecost using the pesher form, "This is _____," is a legitimate interpretation and does not violate the Old Testament context. Indeed, the Jews already treated the passage as prophetic of the age to come (Strack and Billerbeck 1978:2:615-17; see, for example, *Deuteronomy Rabbah* 6:14).

Because of Peter's Jewish mindset and his subsequent failure to embrace the Gentile

one's personal destiny, is to discover the best good news.

Apologia for Pentecost: Ultimate Cause and Saving Significance (2:14-21) Seizing the moment in the midst of the crowd's bewilderment and confusion, Peter addresses the people in Spirit-filled utterance (see 2:4). He begins with a formal address, *Fellow Jews,* which will soften as he proceeds (*men of Israel,* 2:22; *brothers,* 2:29). His message will explain the Pentecost event as God's saving acts (see also 4:12; 13:38: 28:28) and show its crucial importance for his hearers and for us.

Though those drunk and those filled with the Spirit are "carried out of themselves into an abnormal sense of freedom and expressiveness," the cause and the end results are entirely different (E. F. Harrison 1986:64). Peter with good humor dismisses this empirical explanation with further empirical evidence: in a culture where the first meal is not taken until ten o'clock, nine o'clock in the morning is too early in the day to find people drunk (see Josephus *Life* 279).

The ultimate cause and significance of the Spirit's empowerment is found in God and his saving purposes, as the prophet Joel foretold. *In the last days*—the final days of this age, the time when the "age to come" is inaugurated—God promises to pour out his Spirit on all people. Joel used the imagery of the vivifying impact of a Near Eastern torrential downpour on parched earth to picture the generosity, finality and uni-

mission immediately, some commentators argue that Peter's and his audience's understanding of *all people* here and *all who are afar off* in Acts 2:39 must be limited to Jews in Palestine and the diaspora (Haenchen 1971:179, 184; Longenecker 1981:286). Longenecker suggests that Luke, with his interest in the Gentile mission, reads into Peter's words more than was there. Instead of pitting Luke against Peter, it is better to understand Peter as speaking under the inspiration of the Spirit of an ethnically indiscriminate outpouring, which he and the Jewish Christians only gradually realized was the foundation for the Gentile mission (10:28, 34-36). In his commission Jesus had laid the groundwork for the mission to the Gentiles (Lk 24:47, "to all nations").

Are the *signs on the earth below* the miraculous darkness of Good Friday (Lk 23:44-45; so Bruce 1988:62) or the Pentecost event and the signs that followed (Acts 2:43; 4:16, 30-33; 5:12; so Marshall 1980:74)? The chiastic (reverse parallelism) structure of verses 19 and 20 makes *signs on the earth below* parallel to *blood and fire and billows of smoke.* Bruce's identification seems more accurate, although the crucifixion should be taken as only a foretaste of the *signs on earth* that announce the coming of the day of the Lord.

2:20 The "dreadful day of the Lord" (Hebrew) may be truly termed the *glorious,* or more properly "manifest" (LXX), *day of the Lord,* for it is the decisive revelation of the Lord as the Judge that makes the time fearsome.

versality of the Spirit's coming. And Peter declares that this is now happening before the very eyes and in the very hearing of his audience. In contrast to the selective and occasional outpouring of the Spirit on king and prophet in the Old Testament time of promise (1 Sam 10:10; 16:14; Ezek 11:5), here the Spirit comes without regard to age, sex, social status or, as Acts 2:39 indicates, ethnic origin.

What the Spirit empowers people to do is *prophesy.* Prophecy for Luke encompasses Spirit-filled speaking in other languages (2:12, 16), predictive discourse (11:27; 21:10; compare 9:10; 10:10; 16:9; 18:9, where dreams and visions guide the post-Pentecost church) and proclamatory witness (15:32). As the Old Testament prophets made God's will known by witnessing to his Word, so now, as Luther says, all Christians are Spirit-enabled to bear witness to "knowledge of God through Christ which the Holy Spirit kindles and makes to burn through the word of the gospel" (Stott 1990:74; compare Acts 1:8).

Joel and Peter remind us of the decisiveness of these last days by pointing to cosmic signs on earth and in heaven. The universe will reveal what a shambles sinful humankind makes of things by its constant assault on God's moral order. From this the human race should know that judgment must come at the day of the Lord (Is 13:6, 9; Ezek 30:3; Zeph 1:14-15). The hope held out by Joel is thus vitally significant. *And everyone who calls on the name of the Lord will be saved* (Acts 2:21/Joel 2:32).

Today, living in a time of rapid social change, moral decay, environmental crisis and seemingly unmanageable economic and political problems, we can identify with the apostle's and prophet's sense of the end. We are comforted that history is not out of control, for God is constantly at work. We live in the time of the Spirit's life-giving presence—and there is the challenge: will we call on the name of the Lord and be saved?

Apostolic Gospel at Pentecost: The Immediate Cause (2:22-36)
Who is this Lord? How can we know he can save? What does Pentecost have to do with this salvation? Peter directs the crowd's attention to Jesus

2:22-36 Peter's hermeneutic may seem strange to us, but when we start with his assumptions, his interpretation of Psalms 16 and 110 becomes logical and coherent (Stott 1990:76). The same may be said for the allusions to Psalm 132:11 and 2 Samuel 7:12-13. Our warrant for granting such assumptions is the christocentric interpretive practice of Jesus himself (Lk 20:41-44/Ps 110:1; Lk 24:25-27, 44-48).

Some rabbis, reading *lābeṭaḥ* in Psalm 16:9 as "securely" and *šaḥaṭ* in Psalm 16:10 as "pit,"

of Nazareth. He characterizes Jesus' earthly ministry as the arena of publicly witnessed divine power. Through him God did *miracles,* the power of God at work; *wonders,* astonishing, significant portents that point to God's presence; and *signs,* miraculous embodiments of spiritual truth. God accredited Jesus' mission by these marks of the messianic age and showed that it was the very beginning of the last days.

Peter next boldly implicates the crowd in Jesus' death. He was handed over into their power. With the help of lawless men—that is, Gentile Romans (NIV *wicked men)*—they did away with him through crucifixion. Peter sets their responsibility in tension with God's determined purpose and foreknowledge (compare Lk 22:22). Far from discrediting Jesus as God's Messiah, this shameful death was very much a part of God's set purpose and foreknowledge (see Acts 3:18; 13:29). Though Peter does not explicitly refer to Jesus' death as a vicarious atonement, he gives us the objective fact, which is the basis for such an understanding: an innocent man suffered and died.

But there's more. Human beings may have killed Jesus, but God brought him back to life. It was not a resuscitation but an eternal resurrection. In a remarkable mixed metaphor, death's agony became its birth pangs: death was in labor and unable to hold back the "delivery" of Jesus.

As Peter will go on to prove, with respect to Pentecost, Jesus' resurrection is the answer to the question "Why?" from both angles. It is Pentecost's immediate cause (vv. 32-33), and it is the ground for the saving significance of the Pentecost event.

Peter now argues, based on Scripture, that Jesus' resurrection is part of God's saving plan. In verses 25-28 he introduces a quote from Psalm 16:8-11 to explain Jesus' resurrection as the fulfillment of prophecy about the Messiah (NIV does not translate the Greek *gar,* causal connector between vv. 24 and 25). The psalmist declares that because of his ongoing relationship with the Lord God, he will not be shaken. This

came to the conclusion that some type of rescue in death was spoken of, if only the incorruptibility of David's corpse (*Midraš Ps* 16:10-11).

2:29 Whether the medieval building near Siloam, to the south of the city, is the ancient site of David's tomb is uncertain (Marshall 1980:76; see Josephus *Jewish Antiquities* 7.392-94; 13.249; 16.179-83; *Jewish Wars* 1.61).

accords well with Luke's portrayal of Jesus in his last hours (Lk 23:46/ Ps 31:5; the cry of dereliction is absent—Mk 15:34/Ps 22:1). The psalmist expresses joyful confidence that his flesh (*sarx*, NIV *body;* v. 26) will live in hope. He openly declares that there is no abandonment to Sheol or experience of decay, but rather the path of life and the joy of God's presence forever.

How is it possible to understand a first-person psalm attributed to David, in which he appears to speak of his protection from death, as a prophecy of the Messiah's hope in a resurrection out of death? Peter comes to such an understanding by using two hermeneutical principles: literal interpretation and a messianic reading of first-person Davidic psalms. Thus David, "not . . . as a mere person but David as the recipient and conveyor of God's ancient but ever-renewed promise," can predict the Messiah's experience (Kaiser 1980:225). Pointing to the well-known (and still extant) tomb of David, Peter contends that David could not be talking about himself. By a process of elimination, then, someone else must qualify to experience the literal fulfillment of this promise. That someone is the Messiah. For David was a prophet. He had received the divinely sworn promise of an eternal reign for one of his descendants, who would be the Messiah (2 Sam 7:12-13; Ps 132:12).

But how can a Messiah who suffers and dies also reign forever (Ps 22:15-16)? It is possible only if that Messiah rises from the dead. David was permitted to see ahead of time this vital stage in God's process of redemption. So he could speak confidently of Messiah's resurrection when he said that Messiah *was not abandoned to the grave, nor did his body see decay* (Acts 2:31). What a wise God to plan a path the Messiah would follow to effect salvation! What a merciful God to reveal a portion of that path to prophets, so that now, as we look back after the fulfillment, it all makes sense (see 1 Pet 1:10-12).

Now Peter moves from argumentation to proclamation (Acts 2:32). The great good news is that God has now raised to life the same Jesus who was crucified (v. 23). Peter adds his voice and those of the other apostles to the witness of the Scriptures. So confident is he of the apos-

_____

2:36 In Luke's and Peter's view, this Christology does not present Jesus as the adopted Son of God. Rather, by his resurrection and exaltation Jesus is able to function as Lord and Christ in a way he had not before. Now from heaven he dispenses salvation blessings and

tolic witnesses' compelling testimony that he can divide his presentation into two steps: (1) the Old Testament bears witness to a risen Messiah and (2) we bear witness to Jesus as the risen Messiah.

Peter unveils an even greater truth about Jesus which turns his audience into witnesses of God's saving grace. Jesus is the exalted Lord raised to the Father's right hand in heaven (see also v. 30). From that position of authority Jesus mediates the gift of the Spirit (Jn 14:16, 26; 16:7).

Peter now completes the second half of a chiastic (or reverse parallelism) construction that extends all the way back to verse 25. He has (a) preached Scripture proof of Jesus as the Messiah risen from the dead (vv. 25-28), (b) given an interpretation (vv. 29-31) and (c) made a kerygmatic proclamation (v. 32). Now he (c') proclaims Jesus as the exalted Lord and giver of the Spirit (v. 33), (b') gives an interpretation (v. 34) and (a') presents Scripture proof (vv. 34-35/Ps 110:1). This construction binds together Jesus' resurrection, his exaltation and his giving of the Spirit.

Again by a process of elimination and literal interpretation, Peter applies the Old Testament text to the Messiah. David is dead; we cannot claim that he has ascended to heaven. Then, following the lead of Jesus, Peter claims that David is addressing the Messiah when he says, "The Lord [God] said to my Lord [the Messiah]" (Lk 20:41-44/Ps 110:1). When Jesus asked how David could call his descendant "Lord," he was not simply making *Messiah* and *Lord* synonymous titles. When the One who is literally exalted to the right hand of the Father is called "Lord," he is addressed as more than an honored human descendant of David. The way Jesus formulated the question implied as much. Peter, unveiling what Jesus' question hinted at, declares him to be Lord in the sense of Yahweh. Jesus is God! (See also Acts 2:21, 36, 38.)

Peter calls his listeners to know for certain that God has openly avowed Jesus to be Lord and Messiah (compare Lk 1:4). Jesus may now rightfully be declared Messiah, since he has done Messiah's saving work and has been vindicated by God, who raised him from the dead. He may

directs the church's mission. There is no change in his nature. He had always been divine Lord and promised Christ, as Luke declares in the account of his birth (Lk 2:11).

properly be proclaimed Lord in the highest sense of the word, as the respectful designation of the unpronounceable name of God (YHWH). For by his resurrection-exaltation he has demonstrated that he is the ever-living and life-giving God, whom death cannot hold and who pours out the Spirit (Acts 2:24, 33).

Peter immediately reminds his listeners that it is this risen and exalted Messiah and Lord whom they have crucified. "They were not trifling with a Galilean carpenter, but God!" (Ogilvie 1983:71).

Application of Pentecost: A Call to Repentance and Promise (2:37-41) By the Spirit (Jn 16:8-11) the crowd feels the sharp pain of guilt (the NIV renders the verb literally, *were cut to the heart*). For Luke, this is as it should be: the heart, the inner life, is the source of all the thoughts, motivations, intentions and plans of sinful human beings (Lk 6:45; 12:34: 21:34; Acts 5:3-4; 7:39; 8:21-22; 28:27). Realizing they have killed the Messiah, their only hope of salvation, they desperately want to know, "Is there anything we can do about this? Or are we doomed to suffer God's certain wrath on the day of the Lord?" (see 2:20). They address Peter and the rest of the apostles, for it is the apostolic gospel, not a gospel of Peter, that they must receive and cling to (2:32, 42).

What will it take today to bring people to their knees—beyond admitting their anxiety (the awareness that something is wrong) to facing their guilt (the recognition that someone is wrong)? The sin of people today put Jesus to death just as surely as the sinful hatred of first-century people. This fact leaves no room for anti-Semitism. With Peter's first audience, we must return to the scene of the crime, the cross. We must face up to our guilt before almighty God, the Judge. We must throw ourselves on his mercy, asking, *What shall we do?* (v. 37).

Peter's invitation is to *repent*, "do an about face in your life's orientation and attach yourself to Jesus" (Talbert 1984:16). This turning from sin and turning to Christ is the necessary condition for receiving salvation blessings (Lk 13:3, 5; 15:7; 16:30; 24:47; Acts 3:19; 17:30; 20:21; 26:20). What about faith? It is mentioned in verse 44. John Stott observes, "Repentance and faith involve each other, the turn from sin being impos-

_____

2:38 Baptism in the name of Jesus only does not contradict the trinitarian formula in Jesus' commission (Mt 28:18-20) or the church's practice. What is being emphasized here is that the church is called to be Christ's; therefore Jesus' name will be prominent in reports of

sible without the turn to God, and vice versa" (1990:78).

Peter calls for each one of them individually *(hekastos,* but NIV *every one)* to *be baptized . . . in* (on the basis of) *the name of Jesus Christ*—that is, as Joseph Addison Alexander puts it, "by his authority, acknowledging his claims, subscribing to his doctrine, engaging in his service, and relying on his merits" (quoted in Stott 1990:78). By repentance and baptism we show that we have met the conditions for receiving forgiveness of sins and the gift of the Spirit. By making repentance and baptism conditions for the reception of salvation blessings, Luke does not imply that salvation comes by merit or ritual. He is not promoting some necessary second experience. He consistently presents both forgiveness and the Spirit as gifts of grace (3:19; 5:31; 13:38; 11:17; 15:8). The gift of the Spirit is the Spirit himself, who regenerates, indwells, unites, and transforms lives. All the fruit and gifts of the Spirit flow from this one great gift.

Peter now declares the universal extent of the salvation offer. He reaches out across time and space, generations and cultures *(your children and . . . all who are afar off*—that is, Jews of the diaspora and Gentiles; see Is 57:19; Eph 2:13). And he does not let his audience forget, even as he tells them their responsibility, that salvation is God's work from beginning to end. For the promise is *for all whom the Lord our God will call.* Those who respond are answering the *Lord our God's* effective call on their lives (compare Acts 13:48; 16:14). "He set me free to want what He wanted to give!" (Ogilvie 1983:72).

Now we have come full circle. The salvation promised by Joel (*and everyone who calls on the name of the Lord will be saved*—Acts 2:21/Joel 2:32) is accomplished by Jesus (*God has made this Jesus . . . Lord*—Acts 2:36). And it is humanly appropriated when one is *baptized in the name of Jesus Christ* (v. 38) with the assurance that the gift of salvation is *for all whom the Lord our God will call* (v. 39).

There were many other things Peter said to the crowd as *he warned them.* He kept on exhorting them to allow themselves to be saved, rescued from a *corrupt* (literally, "crooked") *generation.* The Old Tes-

---

rites of initiation into the church. See my commentary on this section for a discussion of the Spirit, conversion and baptism.

tament labeled the Israelites who wandered in the wilderness a "crooked generation" (Deut 32:5; Ps 78:8). Peter's use of this phrase intensifies the call to repentance. The "wilderness generation" experienced the judgment of God when it did not repent. So will those of the present generation if they do not answer God's call and turn to him in repentance.

The gospel call comes clearly and urgently today. "The question is not, shall I repent? For that is beyond a doubt. But the question is, shall I repent now, when it may save me; or shall I put it off to the eternal world when my repentance will be my punishment?" (Samuel Davies in Wirt and Beckstrom 1974:203).

Three thousand souls welcomed the word (compare 28:30), met its conditions and were baptized. They joined the ranks of the apostles and disciples in the nucleus of the New Testament church. "The *kerygma*, indeed, has the power to evoke that which it celebrates" (Willimon 1988:36).

We must not be negligent either in giving or heeding invitations. Lloyd Ogilvie strongly encourages pastors to make invitation a standard part of regular worship services. In whatever form—whether printing an invitation in the bulletin, designating a room for inquirers or calling people forward during a closing hymn—the Lord's call for those to be saved should be consistently present. "People are more ready than we dare to assume. And why not? The Holy Spirit is at work!" (Ogilvie 1983:73).

New Testament Church Life (2:42-47)

J. A. Bengel, the great Pietist commentator on the Bible, concluded his

---

2:41 A. T. Lincoln (1985:208; compare Haenchen 1971:188) wonders whether Luke did not overdo his numbers when he says *about three thousand* were baptized at Pentecost. There are practical questions of Jerusalem's population, space for a large crowd to meet without Roman interference, ability for a speaker to be heard and facilities to accommodate three thousand baptisms in one day. Longenecker (1981:287) ably answers Haenchen. Jeremias's later, more conservative estimate of Jerusalem's population—upper limit twenty-five to thirty thousand—is still enough to provide a pool for conversions (Jeremias 1969:83-84). The temple courts could accommodate 200,000. The gathering was not riotous; it was festival time, when the city was crowded with up to 125,000 pilgrims. The Pentecost crowd would not have attracted undue Roman attention in this milieu. Individuals have spoken without amplification to crowds as large as fifty thousand. The size of the crowd could have been accommodated by any of the common modes of baptism.

2:42-47 Luke uses summaries to conclude the six panels of Acts (6:7; 9:31; 12:24; 16:5; 19:20; 28:31) and to describe early church life in his first panel (2:42-47; 4:32-35; 5:12-16).

comments on Acts this way: "Thou hast, O church, thy form [pattern].
It is thine to preserve it, and guard thy trust" (Bengel 1860:1:925). We
must do this by examining Luke's portrait of a Spirit-filled community.

Four Commitments (2:42) The outpouring of the Spirit produced
not just momentary enthusiasm but four continuing commitments: to
learn, to care, to fellowship and to worship. *The apostles' teaching* probably included an account of Jesus' life and ministry, his ethical and
practical teachings, warnings about persecution and false teaching, and
the christocentric Old Testament hermeneutic. But at its center was the
gospel message. And so today, to devote oneself to the apostles' teaching
means evangelism as well as edification (4:2; 5:42; 15:35).

The apostles' *fellowship* and *breaking of bread* was a sharing of possessions to meet needs and of lives in common meals (2:44-46). What
an inviting way of life for our day, when "loneliness drives people into
one place, but that does not mean that they are *together,* really" (Ogilvie
1983:74).

Finally, Luke portrays *prayer* as integral to the church's life (compare
4:24; 6:4; 12:5; 13:3; 20:36). It is the essential link between Jesus and
his people as they carry out his kingdom work under his guidance and
by his strength (4:29-30; 6:6; 8:15; 14:23; 28:8). The reputation of the
vital, growing Korean church as a praying church shows that the maxim
is indeed true: "the vitality of the church was a measure of the reality
of their prayers" (Williams 1985:39).

Impact: Fear (2:43) The conviction of sin that followed Peter's Spir-

---

Throughout the passage Luke employs present and imperfect tenses, even periphrastics,
to emphasize the continuous nature of the occurrence or practice.

2:42 Some commentators give primacy to the spiritual nature of *fellowship (koinōnia;*
E. F. Harrison 1986:74) or see the *breaking of bread* and *prayer* as explaining it (Bruce
1988:73). Because of the wordplay with *koinos* (2:44) and the further descriptions in 4:32-
36, however, it seems best to take it as referring primarily to the sharing in material things
that flows from the believers' spiritual communion (compare Williams 1985:39).

Does *breaking of bread* refer to an ordinary meal, an agape feast of joy, a Jewish *ḥᵃbûrâh*
fellowship meal, the Lord's Supper, or the Lord's Supper in combination with one of the
others (Lake and Cadbury 1979:28; Bruce 1951:100; E. F. Harrison 1986:74; Longenecker
1981:290)? Since breaking of bread could be a signal to begin an ordinary meal, it served
as a metonymy for any meal (see 27:35). The phrase can also refer to the words of institution
and thus to the Lord's Supper. This double significance and the specification "after the
supper" in the words of institution (Lk 22:19-20) may point to an early Christian practice
of taking an ordinary meal bracketed by the Lord's Supper.

it-filled preaching (2:37) was not momentary panic but a continuing uneasiness among those who had not yet received the word. The *many wonders and miraculous signs* done by God through the apostles served only to intensify this conviction. Whether the "signs and wonders" element be taken as normative for today (Wimber 1986:21) or as simply the authentication of a fresh stage of revelation (Stott 1974:13), clearly Luke is certain that the church's presence will have an impact on society.

A Caring, Joyful, Transparent Fellowship (2:44-47) In expression of their Spirit-inspired togetherness, the believers pooled their resources. Individuals voluntarily sold property and goods, contributed the proceeds to a fund from which any Christian (and possibly non-Christians as well) could receive help, as he or she might have need. What a standard for today's church! Indeed, "what we do or do not do with our material possessions is an indicator of the Spirit's presence or absence" (Krodel 1986:95).

The community lived out its commitment to *the apostles' teaching* by gathering each day *in the temple courts* to hear instruction. They probably met in Solomon's colonnade, at the eastern end of the court of the Gentiles (5:12; compare 5:20-21, 42, and Jesus' practice—Lk 20:1; 21:37). In the temple they also fulfilled their commitment to prayer as they engaged in corporate worship.

Daily the community broke bread together in homes—sharing a meal, beginning it with the bread and ending it with the cup of the Lord's Supper (Lk 22:19-20; 24:35; Acts 20:7, 11). With constant intimacy, exultant joy and transparency of relationship they enjoyed the graces of Messiah's salvation in a true anticipation of his banquet in the kingdom (Lk 22:30; compare Acts 16:34). It was a gracious witness to *the people (laos),* "Israel as the elect nation to whom the message of salvation is initially directed" (Longenecker 1981:291).

Today growing churches manifest the same "metachurch" pattern: celebration, joining in large gatherings for worship and instruction, and

---

2:44 The Qumran community's practice differed in mandating the surrender of personal property when one joined the community (1QS 6). Jewish charitable practices—the weekly "poor basket" *(quppah)* for resident poor and the daily "poor bowl" *(tamhuy)* for transient poor—had some similarity to the church's practice, though the latter was not as standardized (Jeremias 1969:132-34).

cell group, meeting in home groups for fellowship and nurture.

Impact: Church Growth (2:47) Every day the Lord Jesus by his Spirit saved some, incorporating them into *their number.* God's plan is for churches to grow. The challenge for us is, "Will we meet the Scriptural conditions for growth: a dedication to be a learning, caring, fellowshipping, worshipping church?" Will we meet the one essential condition? "As empowering follows petition, so evangelism and Christian unity or community follow Pentecost. The empowering, moreover, is repeatable. So pray!" (Talbert 1984:17).

THE JERUSALEM CHURCH: ITS GROWTH (3:1—9:31)

Communal experiments and religious movements fueled by enthusiasm are often short-lived. Will the faith of Pentecost sustain itself? Will the church's mission mandate be fulfilled? Luke sets out to answer these questions, which lie at the heart of his reason for writing Acts. He hopes to persuade Theophilus and others that the gospel message is true by showing that it was indeed carried "to all nations."

Thus Luke unfolds before us the church's unstoppable advance even in the face of official opposition (3:1—4:31). After a look at the church's internal life (4:32—5:11), he highlights its mission's growing momentum in outreach into "all Judea," even as opposition grows (5:12-42).

Just when prejudice within and death-dealing hostility from without are about to hamper the church's witness, God raises up fearless messengers, Hellenistic Jewish Christians (6:1—8:40). They will complete Jesus' mandate (1:8) in microcosm. And to crown the triumph of the gospel, their chief persecutor, Saul, is converted and begins his ministry (9:1-31).

☐ A Healing Miracle and Its Consequences (3:1—4:31)

Crammed into first-story rooms of an undistinguished building in a suburb of Seoul are pews, a pulpit and other sanctuary furniture suitable for

---

2:46 *Every day* refers to both the temple activities and those *in their homes* (Bruce 1951:101), not just going to the temple (Schneider 1980:1:288).

2:47 *Epi to auto* (*together*, 2:44; *to their number*, 2:47) is not simply a local term. It is a quasi-technical term signifying union within the body of Christ (compare LXX Ps 122(121):3; 1QS 1:12, *yaḥad 'ēl*, or community of God; Delebecque 1980:82).

an auditorium seating five hundred to a thousand people, not the fifty to seventy-five who meet there for an organizing service. The overabundant furniture is a sign of their hope of what God will do through the preaching of the gospel in that place.

How is he going to do it? What is the divinely ordained pattern for the church's advance? Luke tells us in four episodes clustered around Peter and John's healing of a lame beggar. The church ministers via apostolic sign (3:1-10) and proclaims its saving significance (3:11-26). Religious leaders' opposition surfaces but is finally frustrated (4:1-22) as the church, in answer to prayer, continues in bold, Spirit-filled witness (4:23-31).

The Healing of a Crippled Beggar (3:1-10)

Modern medical care uses sophisticated equipment to monitor people with serious illnesses. Their "vital signs" give us hope. In spiritual matters, too, we live by signs. Luke's account of the healing of a crippled beggar serves as such a sign.

The Beggar's Need (3:1-3) According to Jewish custom, Peter and John live out Acts 2:42, 46, *going up to the temple* (both literally and spiritually) to pray and worship at the time of the evening sacrifice (Ex 29:39-40; Ps 24:3; 122:4). As they arrive, a man with no use of his legs because of a congenital condition is being carried to his accustomed begging place. The depth of his need is apparent to all. In these ordinary circumstances—apostles practicing their devotion to God, a lame man plying the only trade he knows, appealing to the generosity and piety of his peers—an extraordinary encounter occurs.

The Apostles' Offer (3:4-7) Peter fixes his eyes on the man, as later Paul will do when a miracle is about to occur (13:9; 14:9), and asks for the same attention in return. At first Peter disappoints the beggar by declaring his lack of money. This serves only to heighten the value of the great gift he does offer: complete health. But it is *in the name of*

3:1 NIV inserts *one day* so the transition from 2:47 will be smoother (compare the Western reading, *en de tais hēmerais tautais*—"and in those days").

3:2. Because no ancient Jewish source names a temple gate "Beautiful," the gate's identity is a matter of conjecture. Luke uses *hieron* ("temple") flexibly to indicate the entire temple mount area, including the court of the Gentiles (Lk 19:45) as well as the sanctuary precincts, beginning with the court of women (Lk 2:37). Both the Shushan, the east gate entrance to

Jesus Christ of Nazareth that it must be given. A name is an expression of a person's very essence. The power of the person is present and available in the name (Haenchen 1971:200). In the case of Jesus, the invocation of his name is a direct link between earth and heaven. It is not a magic formula but a simple recognition that if any salvation blessings are to come, they must arrive in and through the person of Jesus Christ. Jesus so commissioned his disciples (Lk 24:47) and the disciples so preached and ministered (Acts 2:38; 3:16; 4:10, 12, 30; compare the direct declaration "Jesus Christ heals you," 9:34).

Peter commands the man to walk (literally, continuous action—"be walking") and grabs him by the right hand to raise him up. "The power was Christ's but the hand was Peter's" (Stott 1990:91). So must the church ever act.

The Gift of Wholeness (3:7-8) *Instantly* (compare Lk 4:39; 8:44, 55) *the man's feet* (the term can also mean "tread" or "step") and ankle bones receive strength. Jumping up, he stands for the first time in his life. He tries out his new freedom by walking around; then, in a response natural to one who in faith realizes that he has been touched by God's power, he moves into the court of women and then the court of Israel, *walking and jumping, and praising God* (compare 2:47). He has become the living embodiment of the messianic age as predicted in Isaiah 35:6, "Then will the lame leap like a deer" (also see Lk 7:22).

Should we expect such miracles today? True, the apostles are no longer with us, and miracles seemed to cluster around them; even in the first century, miraculous signs were not everyday occurrences. But Jesus still is present by his Spirit in the church. So we should not be surprised if we hear reports of miracles, especially where an atmosphere of pervasive unbelief or false religion calls for a power encounter. But a healing miracle in the New Testament sense must have the following marks: It must be an instantaneous and complete deliverance from a grave organic condition. It must occur in response to a direct command in the

the court of Gentiles, and the Nicanor gate leading to the court of women are candidates for Luke's reference here (Lake and Cadbury 1979:32). Because of the renowned beauty of the Nicanor gate's Corinthian bronze decoration (Josephus *Jewish Wars* 5.201), the greater access that gate afforded to the city crowds, and how readily the apostles' movements can be explained in reference to it, it is probably the gate at which the beggar sat (Bruce 1988:80).

name of Jesus, and it must be publicly acknowledged as indisputable (Stott 1990:103).

Impact on the People (3:9-10) All the people (*laos;* see comment at 2:47), who had known the man in his previous condition, become witnesses to the miracle's authenticity. More than that, they *were filled with wonder* (awe felt in the presence of divine activity; compare Lk 4:36) *and amazement* (the state of being lifted out of one's habitual life and thought by encountering the power of God; compare Lk 5:26; Haenchen 1971:200). But this is not saving faith. Only two times do Luke's summary statements imply that witnessing a miracle leads directly to faith (Acts 9:35, 42). Witnessing miracles may contribute to a person's embrace of faith, but it cannot produce faith (see Lk 16:31).

That is why God's Word must now be preached. It will interpret the extraordinary and call for a decision. By the Spirit's power this proclamation will work repentance and saving faith in its hearers.

Peter's Speech in Solomon's Porch (3:11-26)

We moderns have relegated the word *repent* to a message on a sandwich board worn by some bearded cartoon figure. We chuckle at him in his lonely crusade to convince people that the end is near. We are about as ready to listen to such a message as was the temple crowd that gathered in amazement after the healing of the crippled beggar. Yet Peter does not hesitate to tell them—and us—that they should repent, and why.

The Setting (3:11) After the prayer service in the court of Israel, the apostles, with the beggar clinging to them, return through the Nicanor gate into the court of the Gentiles. All the people rush to see them, gathering at Solomon's colonnade, a many-pillared, three-aisled portico that ran the length of the eastern boundary of the court of Gentiles. The people are astonished, and their amazement is mingled with fear (com-

---

3:13 Luke's picture of Pilate's role in Jesus' trial and execution is not based on a later tradition that blamed only the Jews (contra Haenchen 1971:206). Rather, Pilate's actions make good sense in the light of Roman jurisprudence and the circumstances of first-century Palestine (Sherwin-White 1986; compare Jn 19:12).

3:14 Given Luke's use of *ho dikaios* as a messianic title elsewhere (Acts 7:52; 22:14) and the Old Testament and Jewish evidence (Is 53:11; Jer 23:5; 33:15; Zech 9:9; *1 Enoch* 38:2; 53:6), *Righteous One* here should be taken as a messianic title. Such a conclusion is less certain for *Holy [One]*. The Old Testament provides uncertain support (Ps 16:10; Is 41:14).

pare 3:10, 12; 13:41; Is 52:13; 1 Km 4:13 Sym).

The Miracle's Source (3:12-16) Peter seizes the moment and asks the people about their amazement (NIV has *surprise,* which may be too weak) and their staring (see comment at 3:4). If they think the miracle was produced by *power* resident in the apostles or by *godliness*—the superior practice of the duty one owes to God (compare 10:2)—they are mistaken.

Peter prepares the way for his Deuteronomy and Genesis quotes by declaring that *the God of Abraham, Isaac and Jacob* (compare Ex 3:6, 15) has in this healing *glorified his servant Jesus.* The title *servant* is an allusion to Messiah as the servant of the Lord featured in the servant songs of Isaiah. In particular it points to Messiah's suffering servant role in Isaiah 53. Boldly Peter alleges that the people *handed [Jesus] over* (compare Lk 9:44; 18:32; 22:21-22; 23:25; NIV adds *to be killed*) and *disowned him* by rejecting Pilate's judgment that he was innocent (Lk 23:13-25). Disowning *the Holy and Righteous One,* they asked that a *murderer be released* to them.

With a striking phrase, Peter asserts that "the crown prince" (NIV says *author*) *of life* has been deprived of life. *Life* in Luke can be a synonym for salvation (Acts 5:20; 11:18; 13:46, 48).

Today we are so jaded by constant exposure to violence through the news media that in our entertainment we demand ever more grisly acts of violence. Can we still be shocked by this "greatest crime in human history" (Barclay 1976:33) which Peter lays before his listeners? We must be, for only then will we be able to receive that great good news that Peter immediately declares: *God raised him from the dead. We are witnesses of this* (compare 1:22; 2:32; 4:10; 10:40-41; 13:30-31).

By faith (both the apostles' and the beggar's—compare 14:8-10) *in the name of Jesus* (that is, Jesus himself present in his resurrection power;

Luke does not use this title elsewhere as a messianic title in the absolute, unless Luke 4:34 be counted. It is best to take *holy* as a qualifier here, emphasizing that Jesus the Righteous One belonged to God in a special way (Marshall 1980:91).

3:15 *Archēgos* (NIV *author*) can mean "leader, ruler, prince; instigator; originator, founder" (Bauer, Gingrich and Danker 1979: s.v. ἀρχηγός). Johnston (1981)makes a solid case for the meaning "leader" in both of Luke's uses (Acts 3:15; 5:31) and for the Old Testament uses of it to refer to Messiah as Davidic crown prince (Hebrew *nāśî'* ["leader"]: Num 13:2 [compare LXX *archēgos*]; Ezek 34:24; 37:25).

---

compare 1 Kings 8:27-30), *this man . . . was made strong*. Literally, the Greek says, "Based on faith in his name this one . . . his name strengthened." "Faith is the manner and Jesus' name is the cause of the man's restoration" (Kistemaker 1990:130). In the end all is from Jesus, for faith is present not only as a human activity *(faith in the name of Jesus)* but also as a divine gift *(faith . . . through him)*. And today the economy is the same. There is no room for relying on manipulative, magical technique. All Jesus asks us to bring is humble dependence lived out in prayer and faith (Jas 5:14).

The Call to Repentance (3:17-26) Peter's transition from indictment to call to repentance is the empathic yet searching assertion that his compatriots *(brothers)* killed the Messiah in ignorance. They failed to recognize Jesus' true identity, though it should have been evident from his words and actions. This does not mitigate their guilt; rather, it makes their predicament all the worse (see Lk 23:34; Acts 13:27; see God's provision for sins of ignorance, Num 15:22-31).

Yet not even this ghastly mistake was outside God's plan, foretold through all the prophets (Lk 24:25-27, 46-47; Acts 2:23; 8:35; 13:27-29; 17:2-3; 26:22-23). The theme of Messiah's suffering can be traced through four of the five major prophets and one minor prophet (Is 53; Jer 11:19; Dan 9:26; Zech 13:7).

3:19 Luke uses *metanoeō* (NIV *repent*) for conversion, the decision of the whole person to turn around (Lk 3:8; 5:32), focusing at one time or other on turning from sin (Acts 8:22; 17:30) and to God (20:21). When the word is used in combination with *epistrephō* (NIV *turn*, here and 26:20), it points to the negative aspect (Laubach 1975:1:353-55). Marshall (1980:93) claims that here it points to the whole process and that *epistrephō* explains it. In the LXX, *epistrephō* consistently is used to translate the Old Testament word for conversion (*šûb*, Hos 5:4; 6:1; Amos 4:6). According to Luke it refers to the whole process of turning from sin to God (Acts 14:15; 26:18), as well as focusing on the positive aspect of the process (9:35; 11:21; 15:19; 26:20).

The *times of refreshing* have been identified as the restoration of the rule of God to Israel (Dillon 1981:548) and the final era of salvation (Marshall 1980:93). Yet because of some Jewish background (4 Ezra 11:46; Is 32:15 Sym; see Hamm 1984:207-8) and the parallelism with the preceding purpose clause, it seems best to take the phrase as referring to the positive counterpoint to the wiping away of sin. It is the refreshment of spirit, those "periodic seasons in which the forgiven and restored believer experiences the refreshing nearness of the Lord" (Kistemaker 1990:135; Stott 1990:93). These seasons come now, in the "last days," before the final era of salvation.

3:21 Some scholars equate the *times of refreshing*, the sending of the Messiah and the time when God will *restore everything*, and locate them in the current mission of Jesus through the church (Grässer 1979:118; Hamm 1984:211). Some understand *apokatastasis*

Peter commands the crowd to *repent,* renounce the sinful lives that led to Jesus' death, *and turn* (NIV adds *to God)* so that . . . sins may be wiped out (compare Ps 51:1, 9; Is 43:25) and *times of refreshing may come from* the presence of *the Lord*—that is, God the Father. Here is the immediate relief that the people can expect, since salvation is now accomplished and they are living in the last days (Lk 4:18-21; Acts 2:17-21, 38). But there is more. God will *send* to them *the Christ, who has been appointed* for them, at the end, when he restores all things (compare 2 Pet 3:13).

What positive motivations for repentance! Our slate has been wiped clean. Our parched lives are refreshed in the present by seasons of the Spirit's outpouring. Our future perfection is beyond imagination.

Peter now places his call to repentance in "promise-and-fulfillment" as well as eschatological perspective. Moses prophesied that God would raise up a prophet like himself, whom the people would be responsible to hear and obey (Lev 23:29; Deut 18:15-16, 19). If they didn't, they would forfeit their right to be part of the people of God. All the prophets from Samuel onward "proclaimed" *these days,* the days of fulfillment and of decision. Will Peter's hearers heed Jesus, the prophet like Moses, as he speaks his message through his apostles—"Repent . . . and turn to God" (Lk 24:47; Acts 2:38; 3:19)?

as "establishment" and the phrase *apokatastaseōs pantōn hōn* (NIV *to restore everything)* as indicating the perfect realization of the prophetic promises without specific reference to the restoration of all things (Marshall 1980:94). In light of the temporal progress indicated by the context and the Jewish background, it is best to take the sending of the Messiah as happening at the parousia and the times of restoration occurring then as well. In view of Old Testament and secular understandings of *katastasis* (note the cyclic views cited in Oepke 1964:1:390), it seems best to take the term as restoration in a universalized sense: "this final perfection awaits the return of Christ" (Stott 1990:94).

3:22-23 The text form of the Old Testament quotation (Deut 18:15-16, 19) follows neither the LXX nor the MT but a Palestinian text tradition found in the Dead Sea Scrolls and the Targum (de Waard 1971).

The promise in Deuteronomy 18:15-19, when interpreted literally, as in Judaism and early Christianity, is not that God from time to time would raise up prophets for the people but that there would be one prophet like Moses par excellence at the end of time—that is, the Messiah (1QS 9:11; 4Qtest 5-7; Jn 1:21; 4:25; 6:14).

Although Luke uses *anistēmi* (NIV *raise up)* and cognates quite frequently in reference to Christ's resurrection, we should understand the verb in verses 22 and 26 as pointing to his incarnation. That was when God fulfilled his promise by bringing the Messiah onto the stage of human history. A play on the two uses of the word may be present, especially in verse 26 (Hamm 1984:214), but it is not required for the passage to make sense.

Today this message is vital to the eternal destiny of not only ethnic children of Abraham, the Jews, but also that largest of hidden people groups, nominal Christians. If 75-80 percent of the world's Christians are Christian in name only, then one billion people need to be awakened out of their "smug assurance of salvation by biological birthright" (Kingsmore 1990:446; Willimon 1988:48).

Peter concludes with an encouraging appeal to the Jewish audience's place in salvation history. As "sons" *of the prophets and of the covenant* (NIV translates *hyioi* as *heirs*), they stand in line with those who received covenant promises of salvation blessings (compare Lk 1:72). In a text form closer to the Hebrew original than to the LXX, Luke gives us the foundational covenant promise: *Through your offspring* (literally "your seed") *all peoples on earth* (literally "families of the land") *will be blessed* (Acts 3:25/Gen 22:18). Understood literally and concretely, the "seed" is one person, the Messiah (compare Gal 3:16).

Peter's audience already received the promised salvation blessings in anticipation, when God sent his servant Jesus (compare Acts 3:13) for his earthly ministry. Now, in the preaching of the gospel and its reception through repentance, Jesus blesses his people by *turning each away from [his] wicked ways* (compare 26:23).

Too often today these salvation blessings are treated as cheap grace. Many claim to be Christians, yet their lives are not markedly different from the lives of others. Divorce rates do not vary greatly between professing Christians and the general population. Peter lets us know in clear terms that salvation is not simply a matter of wiping away sin (3:19) but also a matter of righteousness (3:26; 26:20).

Temple Arrest, Sanhedrin Hearing and Release (4:1-22)

The uninterrupted progress of the church in Acts 1—3 is quite unlike the situation in our world, but with the story of the apostles' arrest, incarceration and trial Luke brings us "down to earth." The progress of

---

4:4 The size of the church, five thousand males plus women and children—more than ten thousand in all—is a great work of God (2:47), but not impossible given a Jerusalem resident population of seventy thousand (low estimate thirty-five thousand) and the likelihood that this total included residents of surrounding villages (Jeremias 1969:83-84; Williams 1985:70).

the Jerusalem church did not occur without opposition. But advance it did, and therein lies the challenge to us: to accept the truth of its message and to be faithful in following its courageous example.

Official Opposition (4:1-7) The apostles were interrupted in their preaching by the sudden, dramatic appearance of hostile officials (*ephistēmi* is stronger than the NIV *came up to;* compare Lk 20:1; Acts 6:12; 17:5). *The priests* (Sadducean in conviction), *the captain of the temple guard* (a highly placed member of the high priest's family charged with temple security) and *Sadducees* (probably aristocratic laymen) *were greatly disturbed* (compare 16:18). *In Jesus* the *people* were being offered a particular instance of and foundational argument for the resurrection "from the dead" (NIV somewhat follows the Western text, *anastasei tōn nekrōn—the resurrection of the dead*).

The Sadducees, the priestly and lay aristocracy who had ruled the Jews in religious and political matters at the behest of foreign overlords since Hasmonean times, did not believe that anyone but the priests should be instructing the people in spiritual matters. They believed that the messianic age dawned with the Hasmoneans in the second century B.C. Anyone making messianic claims was at best mistaken and at worst a political revolutionary posing a threat to their comfortable position. In matters of doctrine they considered themselves traditional, holding only to the written Torah and rejecting the oral Torah, the sayings of the fathers, which the Pharisees accepted. One doctrine they did not find in the written Torah was resurrection from the dead (Josephus *Jewish Antiquities* 18.16-17).

Seizing *Peter and John, . . . they put them in jail until the next day* (compare Jesus' prediction, Lk 21:12). It was already evening, and the Sanhedrin normally commenced its judicial business only during daylight hours (*m. Sanhedrin* 4:1). Luke lets us know through the Sadducees' negative example that those with vested interests in power and comfort and with unbiblical preconceived notions will view the gospel

---

4:6 Annas served as high priest A.D. 6-15 (Lk 3:2). His son-in-law Caiaphas was presiding high priest A.D. 17-36. Both figured prominently in Jesus' trial (Jn 18:13-14, 24, 28). John is unidentifiable unless the Western reading *Iōnathas* is correct. Jonathan, son of Annas, served as high priest A.D. 36-37. Bruce (1990:150) proposes Annas's grandson John, son of Theophilus, as a possibility.

as a threat.

Luke will not allow us to think for a moment, though, that human beings had thwarted the advance of God's saving work. He immediately gives a summary statement on church growth: *many who heard the message* (literally, the word) *believed* (compare Lk 8:11-15; Acts 2:44; 3:22; 4:29, 31-32). The total church membership grew to about five thousand males, not to mention women and children. In our own day Muslim rulers' imprisonment of Christians also works to advance the gospel. Persecuted believers get to know one another in their confinement, forming a network for communication and support once they are released.

The next day the Sanhedrin convened. This highest legislative and judicial body in Israel consisted of seventy-one members from three groups: *rulers,* or temple officials, many from the high-priestly families; *elders* from the chief families, the landed gentry; and *teachers of the law,* professional Torah scholars who taught, expounded and applied the law, as well as arguing it in court. Identifying by name key members from the high-priestly component, Luke emphasizes the Sadducean viewpoint, which predominated in the council because of these members' prominence.

They placed Peter and John in their midst (the Sanhedrin sat in a semicircle—*m. Sanhedrin* 4:3). Just as they had challenged Jesus after he rid the temple court of the high-priest families' concession booths (Lk 20:2), so now they want to know *by what* kind of *power* (Acts 4:7; compare 1:8; 3:12; 4:33) or in *what* kind of *name* (3:6, 16; 4:10, 12, 17-18, 30) Peter and John had healed the beggar. Thus the council charged with distinguishing between truth and error in Jewish religion exercised its prerogative to test the basis for this healing. Their interrogation, however, was not unprejudiced. The emphatic placement of *you* in the question lets us know the contempt with which they hold these *unschooled, ordinary men* (4:13).

Whenever members of an establishment confuse their desire to maintain their own power with their duty to guard the public trust, sound

---

4:8 Luke's use of the aorist participle *(plēstheis)* helps us distinguish between the two types of filling in the Christian's experience: the Spirit's abiding presence, which is a sal-

judgment will invariably become impossible for them. Their blind ambition will keep them from seeing and comprehending the very truth they are to guard (see Jn 9:40-41).

Bold Declaration of the Word of Salvation (4:8-14) Peter, *filled with the Holy Spirit* (experiencing his "intense presence" and "abnormally strong" working), addresses the leaders (compare 9:17; 13:9). Their amazed reaction to the apostles' boldness and their inability to reply to Peter's scripturally and experientially based defense shows us the effect of the Spirit's filling (4:13-14). Jesus is here fulfilling his promise (Lk 12:11-12; 21:15). Peter's example is our challenge and encouragement. "What are we attempting which could not be accomplished without the Holy Spirit? What is there about our lives which demands an explanation? We will be 'filled with the Holy Spirit' when we dare to do what could never be accomplished on our own strength and insight" (Ogilvie 1983:98).

Peter begins his defense by reframing the council's question. The miracle—what they called simply *this*—becomes *an act of kindness.* Peter further defines it as *he was healed* (literally "saved," *sesōstai*). By introducing the word *sōzō,* which can refer to rescue from both physical dangers and afflictions (Lk 7:50; 17:19; 23:35-37; Acts 14:9) and the spiritual danger of eternal death (Lk 19:10: Acts 2:21, 40, 47; 4:12; 11:14; 15:11; 16:31), Luke initiates a wordplay that he will complete in verse 12. Finally Peter places John and himself in the background and concentrates on *the name of Jesus Christ,* the person of Jesus and his saving power (compare the same tactic before the crowd in 3:12, 16; see comment at 3:4).

Peter transforms his formal defense into evangelistic proclamation as he answers the council's question with an open invitation for them, along with all the people of Israel, to know that in *the name of Jesus Christ of Nazareth* the *man stands before* them completely *healed.* In his brief reference to Jesus' saving work—*whom you crucified but whom God raised from the dead*—Peter provides the authentic basis for the claim that Jesus' name can indeed have the power to heal. If Jesus had

---

vation blessing for every Christian (compare 6:5, *plērēs*), and the special moment of enabling, in this case inspiration, for ministry (Bruce 1988:92).

not been raised from the dead, the beggar could not have been healed (compare 2:32-33; 3:16).

Now Peter alludes to Psalm 118:22 to help the leaders understand that their rejection of Jesus and the Father's resurrection of him were the fulfillment of God's saving plan. A number of Jewish leaders had last heard this verse applied messianically by Jesus himself, as he interpreted their opposition to him (Lk 20:9-19). That opposition had manifested itself with the same question: "Tell us by what authority you are doing these things. . . . Who gave you this authority?" (Lk 20:2; compare Acts 4:7). Not heeding Jesus' interpretation, they had rushed on in blind rage to fulfill the prophecy. Would they in hindsight repent now?

Peter declares that Jesus has become *the capstone*. The NIV marginal reading *cornerstone* is more literal, picturing a stone at the base of a corner where two walls meet and take their line from it (Williams 1985:67).

Peter now declares the significance for every human being of Jesus' position: *Salvation is found in no one else, for there is no other name under heaven*—throughout the whole world—in which (NIV takes the instrumental understanding only, *by which) we must be saved.* These leaders know from the Old Testament that the God of Israel is the only Savior (Is 43:11; 45:21; Hos 13:4). Now Peter claims this role for Jesus Christ (compare 4QFlor 1:13; 1QH 7:18-19; *Jubilees* 31:19). And this name has been *given to men*.

In an age of religious pluralism, this radical claim is rejected outright by some (Hick and Knitter 1987). Others will admit the uniqueness of Christ in the objective accomplishment of salvation, but they say this text does not teach that it is essential to hear the good news about Jesus' saving work and consciously "name the name" (Sanders 1988). Such a bifurcation of the accomplishment and application of salvation runs counter to the explicit thrust of this verse. Peter makes his universal

---

4:11 The text form does not follow the LXX as Luke 20:17 does. It probably reflects an old tradition, possibly a testimony book (Barrett 1982:69). The differences in wording—*hymōn* applied to builders and *exoutheneō* instead of *apodokimazō*—drives home the application and heightens the reference to persecution (Williams 1985:67). The psalm itself provides no definitive information on the identity of the stone or the builders. Is it Israel being rejected by the nations? Is it the king being despised by the heathen or by skeptics in Israel? Among the Jews, interpretations ranged from Abraham to Jacob to David (Strack

claim by explicitly asserting that this name has been given to humankind as a means by which we must be saved (compare Lk 24:46; Acts 11:14). Appropriation of the name is an essential part of God's salvation transaction. To be true to Peter and Luke, we must never water down the fact that apart from Jesus there is no salvation for anyone—neither its accomplishment nor its appropriation.

Peter's Spirit-filled speech elicits amazement not unlike what the crowd experienced when they saw the crippled beggar walking (3:11). Peter's Spirit-endowed *courage* empowers him to tell the whole truth even though it will turn his judges into defendants and call into question their conviction that resurrections don't happen (4:10).

He tells an intelligent truth, skillfully handling the Scriptures to prove that all this happened according to God's plan (v. 11). Yet he and John have not had the rabbinic training required, humanly speaking, to sustain such theological argumentation. They are *unschooled*. They are *ordinary men,* more precisely "laymen." They lack the recognized credentials of a professional teacher of the law, which alone would command respect in the council. Nevertheless, amid their astonishment the council grasps the fact that these men *had been with Jesus.* Their Lord also lacked credentials yet handled the Scriptures in the same effective way. With a completely healed man (note the perfect-tense *tetherapeumenon)* standing before them as living proof of a truly risen Lord, the council has nothing to say in reply (compare Lk 21:15).

Today, as well, the Spirit's witness to the truth through Christ's messengers will be unanswerable, though still unacceptable, for many people. Here is the challenge not to hear the gospel message in vain. To be astonished at it, even to admit we cannot refute it, is not enough: we must allow it to do its saving work in our lives.

The Word of Salvation Frustrates the Opposition (4:15-22) The Sanhedrin confers in closed session over their dilemma. Jesus' followers

and Billerbeck 1978:1:876; e.g., *Midraš Ps* 118:20). In Jewish thought, religious leaders in Israel, both true and false, were seen as "builders" (Cairo *Damascus Document* 4:12, 19). Jesus, however, is the source and validator of the interpretation: stone = Messiah; builders = Jewish leaders (Lk 20:17, 19).

4:13 *Ordinary (idiōtes)* might refer to a lack of urbanity (E. F. Harrison 1986:93). It should be taken as explaining *agrammatoi* (NIV *unschooled*): Peter and John are laymen in matters of the law (compare Bruce 1990:152-53).

and their message are unacceptable, yet they have performed an *outstanding miracle* (literally, manifest sign). It is outstanding in that everyone knows about it, and a sign in that it points beyond itself to make claims for the dawn of the age of salvation in Jesus (compare 4:22; 8:6; Lk 11:16, 29-30). There is no denying the reality of this miracle.

Note that the council does not even consider seeking to discredit the apostles' message by marshaling evidence against Jesus' resurrection. Their pragmatic solution is to stop the spread of the message, either temporally or in degree, by warning the apostles *to speak no longer to anyone in* (on the basis of) *this name* (pointing to the divine power and authority of Jesus; Foulkes 1978:123).

Calling the apostles back in, they command them in the strongest terms possible to stop speaking (literally, proclaiming) and teaching on the basis of *the name of Jesus*. Thus the Sanhedrin not only seeks to cope with truth by the only effective means known—silencing it—but also creates a basis for further judicial proceedings against the apostles. And the method is still the same today. Tentmaking missionaries seeking to penetrate "creative access" countries should not be surprised to find people who are kept ignorant of the gospel's truth by those who control the media and make laws against "proselytizing."

Again taking the offensive, Peter and John command the council to make a judgment: is it right in God's presence to obey (literally, hear; compare 3:22) a human council, even one that views itself as ordained by and speaking for God, rather than God? They show their basic submission to the council's authority by calling on them to make that judgment (see 1 Pet 2:13-17). Yet at the same time, as our Lord did, they show the council members both the limits to their authority (compare Lk 20:25) and how they abuse it when they prohibit divinely commanded actions.

The council will need to make that judgment now, or in the very near future, for the apostles serve notice that they cannot help speaking what they have seen and heard. In obedience to the risen Lord's mandate they must continue to be eyewitnesses of these salvation truths (Lk 24:48; Acts 1:8; 3:15; 2 Pet 1:16-18).

4:15 Christian sympathizers in the Sanhedrin, such as Nicodemus, or Paul (Gamaliel's

Such a declaration of loyalty to God in the face of human opposition has been echoed often in church history, not least during the Reformation. Think of Martin Luther before the Diet of Worms, or the Scots Reformer John Knox, of whom it was said "He feared God so much that he never feared the face of any man" (Barclay 1976:41). And today the church faces the same challenge when confronted with human authorities that demand that it stop advancing in its mission. The church's willingness to keep spreading the Word despite threats of peril is clear evidence that its message is truly from God.

That Peter and John spoke and acted as they did should challenge Theophilus and others to consider the gospel's claims all the more closely. If these Jews were willing to put their highest tribunal on notice that they were going to continue to obey God, then their message must be true!

The council released them unpunished for two reasons. Judicially, they could not find a punishable offense on which to base a verdict (NIV's smoothing of the syntax obscures this point by referring to the *means* of punishment). This had not stopped them in Jesus' case (Lk 23:14-15, 22-25). Now *the people* make the difference. They are *praising God* (literally, glorifying God) for this *miraculously healed* man who *was over forty years old* (compare Lk 5:26; 7:16). To punish the human instruments of the miracle would not be a good move politically.

Luke ends his account of this episode in triumph. In reminding us of the man's helplessness, a congenital defect of long standing (see 3:2), he stresses the greatness of the miracle. But he also calls the miracle "this sign of healing." God's *act of kindness* has a significance beyond the beggar's physical restoration or even the amazement and praise of the crowd. It points to a salvation now offered to all in a gospel message whose proclamation, by the Spirit's power and the messengers' obedience, is unstoppable.

The Church's Prayer for Boldness (4:23-31)

When ordered to be silent, the apostles make clear that they "cannot

pupil) could have later supplied Luke with the information on the Sanhedrin's "closed-door" session (Kistemaker 1990:159; Stott 1990:98).

help speaking about what [they] have seen and heard" (4:20). How will they sustain such determination? The church looks in prayer to its sovereign Lord and finds the strength to continue its advances with boldness. In this way Luke gives further evidence for the truth of a gospel that is more than a sectarian Jewish message.

The Apostles' Report (4:23) The apostles are released, showing for the first time what Luke will contend consistently: Christianity is both innocent before the state and triumphant when its enemies seek to use state authority to hinder its advance (5:40; 16:35-40; 18:14-16; 23:28-29; 25:25-27; 26:32). They report to their own people—probably not simply the other ten apostles nor the whole assembly of more than five thousand, but their close friends and supporters, perhaps the original 120 of the pre-Pentecost upper room days (1:13-15; Kistemaker 1990:165). They report *all that the chief priests and elders had said,* particularly the threats (4:17-18, 21). (By referring to the Sanhedrin as *the chief priests and elders* Luke highlights the Sadducean loyalists among them.)

The first Christians were realists, and so must we be. These threats, coming as they did from the highest civil authority, had the force of law. Obedience to Christ in the midst of a hostile environment will be costly. Will we realistically face that cost?

The Prayer's Ascription (4:24-28) The news drives the believers immediately to their knees. In united (compare 1:14; 2:46; 5:12), urgent prayer they raise their voices to God the Father (either praying in unison, repeating the words of one apostle, or greeting his prayer with a hearty amen). They address God the Father as *Sovereign Lord (Despotēs).* Not common in Scripture, this divine title emphasizes the complete ownership God exercises over his servants (Lk 2:29; compare Jude 4; Rev 6:10). It was a common ascription in Jewish prayers (see Josephus *Jewish War* 7:323) and among the Greeks (see Aelius Aristides *Works* 37:1; Xenophon *Anabasis* 3:2, 13).

With such liturgical language, grounded in the Old Testament (such as Ex 20:11; Ps 146:6), the believers declare the scope of God's omnipotence. So they encourage themselves through praise that even the

---

4:25 The NIV has supplied *through* in order to overcome rough syntax, which is best explained as coming from Luke's source or as a very early copyist's error (Longenecker 1981:309; Metzger 1971:323).

threatening Sanhedrin is not outside God's sovereign control. Confessing the truth about God's relationship to our circumstances always brings encouragement, especially when we are aware of danger and feel out of control.

The prayer turns to an Old Testament text, Psalm 2:1, understood as foretelling the Messiah's suffering and making reference to a united (note the reverse parallelism: *nations . . . peoples . . . kings . . . rulers),* rebellious, conspiring, yet futile hostility against the Lord's *Anointed One.* Via the pesher method, the believers proceed to make immediate application to Jesus' suffering at the hands of a king, Herod (Lk 13:31; 23:6-12; see Bruce 1990:158); a ruler, Pilate; the Gentiles *(the nations);* and the people of Israel (*laoi—*literally, peoples—probably to maintain correspondence with the quote's wording).

This immediately raises a number of issues. Historically there is no inaccuracy in the believers' interpretation, for even though both Herod and Pilate declared Jesus innocent, they did cooperate with those who conspired against Jesus (Lk 23:6-25; Acts 3:13). The psalm is properly understood as messianic, for it speaks of a universal reign (Ps 2:8, 10-11; contra Marshall 1980:105; compare the pre-Christian Jewish messianic interpretation of the psalm, 4QFlor 1:18-19/Ps 2:1-2; also compare *Psalms of Solomon* 17:22-23/Ps 2:2, 9). Theologically, Jesus' anointing at a particular time—his baptism (see Acts 10:38)—does not contradict the fact that he was always Messiah, conceived by the Holy Spirit (Lk 1:35); his baptism may be viewed as the time when he "received the endorsement of the Father and the enduement with the Spirit" (E. F. Harrison 1986:97). The identification of Israel with the "peoples," in parallel with a pagan king represented by Herod, points out graphically that by rejecting Jesus, Israel was forfeiting its position as God's special people; if the Jews did not repent, God would view them no differently from Gentiles (see Acts 3:23).

The church's confessional ascription climaxes by celebrating God's sovereignty in the active accomplishment of his plan, as even his enemies do what his *power* (literally, hand) has predetermined (see 2:23;

4:26 The marginal explanation gives us the transliteration of the Greek *Christos* and Hebrew *māšîaḥ,* which is literally translated by the phrase *Anointed One.*

Lk 22:22). What a great encouragement! The very same group that is threatening these believers opposed their Lord. The persecutors' earlier success brought Christ's death but was really according to God's plan and by his hand. Surely any suffering these believers—or we—endure, then, is not outside God's control and will serve only to advance the purposes of the risen and reigning Messiah.

Prayer for Boldness (4:29-30) The church asks God to pay attention to the Sanhedrin's threats (4:17, 21) without further defining what they expect him to do about them. The easy transition from opposition to Jesus to threats against the apostles is possible because theologically there is a close identification of the people of God with their suffering and risen Lord, not only in continuing his work (1:1) but also in the pattern of his life (Lk 24:25-27; Acts 14:22; compare 1 Pet 2:20-25; 4:13). The *great* (literally, complete) *boldness* or candor the believers ask for is not only the freedom of speech of a Greek citizen versus a slave (Demosthenes *Orations* 9.3) but also the courage that stands up to all those who would limit the right to reveal the truth (Dio Chrysostom *Discourses* 32.26-27; Schlier 1967:872-73). Peter has already demonstrated such Spirit-filled boldness in declaring the whole truth to the Sanhedrin (4:8, 13; compare 28:31; the verb form, 9:27-28; 13:46; 14:3; 18:26; 19:8; 26:26). With this request we learn the believers' great concern is not for their own safety but for the mission's advance.

In the Greek, verse 30 is not a request (contra NIV; E. F. Harrison 1986:97) but a confident assumption of what will accompany the enablement to speak the word boldly ("while you stretch out your hand"). The believers understand the corroborative weight that the healings, signs and wonders have for their preaching of the gospel. The recent experience with the crippled beggar has taught them both the impact and the limits of a miraculous sign *through the name of your holy servant Jesus* (3:6-7, 16; 4:10, 14; see comments at 3:7-8).

When we realize that this statement is not a request but an assumption

---

4:31 *The place . . . was shaken* is not a vivid literary device to indicate a divine answer to prayer, borrowed from pagan religion (contra Haenchen 1971:228). The Pentecost narrative (2:2-4) and the prayer's request for God's presence are the proper background. In so saying I am not claiming that this event is a repetition of Pentecost (Bruce 1988:100). Old Testament theophany accounts may have an influence (as in Ex 19:18; Is 6:4).

of what God can do, we are freed from both the presumption and subsequent anxiety which come with demanding the miraculous from God.

The Answer: Spirit-Filled Witness (4:31) In answer to their prayer and in fulfillment of his promise (Lk 11:13), the place is shaken, and all—not just the apostles—are filled with the Holy Spirit (2:4; 4:8, see comment). They speak (literally, were speaking—continuous action at intervals) *the word of God* (God's great good news of salvation; 11:19; 13:46; 14:25) with boldness. The messengers are unstoppable. The mission continues with divine momentum. As Chrysostom observed about the place being shaken: "and that made them the more unshaken" (*Homily on the Acts of the Apostles* 11).

□ The Church's Common Life (4:32—5:11)

We would like to know so much more about church life in those early days. Luke lets us catch our breath from the action of the Jerusalem church's advance by giving us some tantalizing glimpses: a summary statement and a few vignettes about its inner life, which further develop 2:44-45.

General Description and Positive Example: Barnabas (4:32-37)

"Admirable but impractical"—that's what human beings through the ages have said about the communal ideal. Still, we wonder, Is there a way we can live together in harmony which at the same time liberates us from selfishness and assures us of support when we need it? Luke says a resounding "Yes!" and points us to a corporate salvation blessing: the church's common life.

Unity: Motive for Caring (4:32) Luke shows that the answer to the church's prayer (vv. 29-30) includes *much grace . . . upon them all* (v. 33), which results in a Spirit-given unity with practical outworking. *All the believers* (literally, "the congregation of those who believed," or the

---

4:32 The common life portrayed in Acts does not contradict the radical discipleship of the Gospel of Luke (Lk 14:33; 18:22; contra Kraybill and Sweetland 1983). Luke is aware of a change of economic arrangements after Jesus' departure (22:35-38), yet "having all things common" could also be seen as the way that Christians lived out their radical discipleship in community.

church in its corporate totality; compare 6:2, 5; 15:12, 30; see also 2:44) are *one in heart and mind (kardia kai psychē mia)*. This phrase masterfully brings together both the Greek ideal of friendship—"a single soul *[mia psychē]* dwelling in two bodies" (Aristotle in Diogenes Laertius *Lives of the Philosophers* 5.20)—and the Old Testament ideal of total loyalty (1 Chron 12:39, note Hebrew and LXX; compare Deut 6:5; 10:12). From this unity comes a mindset. Each member chooses not to look at his possessions as first and foremost his own. Rather, he chooses to see them as first of all available for common use.

Justin Martyr, the early Christian apologist, observed, "We who valued above all things the acquisition of wealth and possessions, now bring what we have to a common stock, and communicate to every one in need" *(Apology* 1.14:2-3). This is where the common life begins, with the heart and soul and a mindset (see Lk 9:24; 12:19, 22; 14:26; 12:34; Acts 2:46).

Mission: Context of Caring (4:33) The caring fellowship continues to be a witnessing fellowship. The apostles bear witness to the resurrection of the Lord Jesus (1:8, 22; 3:15; 5:32). They do so *with great power,* not miracles (as Bruce 1990:160) or the new life of the believing community (as Longenecker 1981:311), but effectiveness: their "utterances cannot be ignored by the hearers but force them to decision either for or against the gospel" (Marshall 1980:108). On *all* (the whole congregation, not just the apostles; this comment prepares for v. 34) there is *much grace,* God's sustaining favor (Haenchen 1971:231; compare Lk 2:40; not the favor of the people, as Kistemaker 1990:174, nor a spirit of generosity, see Stott 1990:106). Then and now it is God's power that makes the church effective in witness and in depth of fellowship.

Voluntary, Equitable Sharing: Method of Caring (4:34-35) Luke begins with the end result: *There were no needy persons among them*—an allusion to Deuteronomy 15:4. God's fulfillment of this covenant promise in the church demonstrates not only his faithfulness but also the fact that the church is the true Israel. In a voluntary, periodic fashion those with means sell real estate or houses, bring the proceeds and lay them at the apostles' feet.

Does this point to a customary practice in property transfer (Lake and Cadbury 1979:49), to an educational context (compare 22:3; Williams

1985:79) or to a political context (compare 2:35)? Whatever the background, it is clear that the apostles have full authority over the fund. As a development of the ad hoc arrangements of Acts 2:45 (see comment there), a common fund for the poor has been created, and the rich in the congregation keep it continuously supplied.

Jerusalem's tenuous local economy and Palestine's famines and political unrest placed some members in economic need. The displacement of the Galilean apostles and other members of the church's central core away from their normal means of livelihood, together with social and economic persecution, necessitated a ministry to meet economic needs (Longenecker 1981:310).

Should we see this process as normative for God's people in all times and all places? Whether because of Luke's supposedly unhistorical, idealized picture (L. T. Johnson 1981:129) or its supposed failure and lack of precedent in other churches (compare 11:27-30; 24:17; Rom 15:26) or the presence of examples that are really exceptions to the rule (Longenecker 1981:311), many have said this passage gives no normative teaching about structuring the church's common life. We must understand, however, that the structure Luke points to is not a coercive communism that dispenses with private property through once-for-all expropriation to a common fund. Luke never presents the system as a failure but rather sees all churches as living out not only their responsibility for the poor (Acts 20:35) but also their interdependence through caring for one another. The Jerusalem church just happened to be on the receiving end most of the time. Seen in this light, what Luke calls for is fully normative.

With a mindset of unity we will view our economic resources as available to meet others' needs. We will voluntarily, periodically supply our local assembly's common fund for the poor. Such a structure should not bind the Spirit's prompting to be generous as we encounter various needs, nor should it become a matter of obligation. If grace is on us, we will be gracious to others.

Barnabas: A Man Who Cared (4:36-37) Joseph, nicknamed Barnabas by the apostles, is a positive example. Luke translates the nickname for us: *Son of Encouragement,* that is, one who habitually manifests this quality (Bruce 1990:160). Barnabas is a "bridge person,"

bringing diverse parties together so that the cause of Christ advances and both older and newer believers are encouraged (9:27; 11:22-23, 25; 15:3, 12, 25; 30-35). For Luke he embodies the fully integrated life of external witness and care for the church's internal needs of "a good man, full of the Holy Spirit and faith" (11:24). We learn he is a Levite, from the tribe of priests and temple staff. He is from Cyprus, which had a large Jewish population in the first century A.D. (Philo *Legatio ad Gaium* 282). He has a *field* suitable for growing crops; he sells it and brings the proceeds to the apostles.

Admirable but impractical? No, admirable and doable when we keep in step with the Spirit. Where are the Barnabases for today's church?

Negative Example: Ananias and Sapphira (5:1-11)

This chilling account of the sudden deaths of Ananias (Hebrew, "the Lord is gracious") and Sapphira (Aramaic, "beautiful") makes us face the fact that God deals with sin, especially church members' deceit and lack of integrity. If God acts to preserve the integrity of the community that the gospel produced, we can have increased confidence in the truthfulness of the message itself (Lk 1:4). That's the good news for the inquirer. This narrative is bad news, though, for any who would take a casual approach to entering the kingdom of God.

A Man Who Was Good to His Family (5:1-6) Living out their unity with the believers, Ananias and his wife Sapphira sold real estate (see 5:3), brought and placed money at the apostles' feet. This action paralleled Barnabas's (4:37), with one significant difference. In collusion with his wife, Ananias *kept back part of the money for himself.* Literally, he embezzled from the sale price. This is paralleled in the LXX report of Achan's sin (Josh 7:1), in secular sources describing the pilfering of gold dedicated to the god Apollos (Athenaeus *Deiporosophists* 6.234) and in the keeping back of crops that had been declared common property in the Celtic tribe Vaccaei (Diodorus Siculus *Library of History* 5.34.3).

4:36 To find a Hebrew or Aramaic word meaning "encouragement" that will easily transliterate into *-nabas* has been a challenge for scholars. That Luke confused Manaen (= Menahem, "the comforter") with Barnabas (Acts 13:1; Haenchen 1971:232) strains credulity, given Luke's care in writing and his contacts with the Jerusalem church. There has been an attempt to link *paraklēsis,* whose range of meaning includes both "encouragement" and

Peter exposes the fraud. He knows the truth, whether by hearsay, reading Ananias's face or Spirit-empowered insight. By asking Ananias why Satan has filled his heart for the purpose of lying to the Holy Spirit and embezzlement, Peter exposes the spiritual battle that is raging (compare Lk 4:1-13). Satan now attacks Christ's mission from within as he had done through Judas and Peter (Lk 22:3, 31). The "father of lies" (Jn 8:44) starts in the heart, the source of all decisions concerning possessions and their relation to God (Lk 12:34; 16:14-15; Acts 8:21-22; contrast 2:46; 4:32). Ananias shows not simply a lack of honesty in bringing only a part of the sale price but also a lack of integrity—bringing only a part while pretending to bring the whole (Stott 1990:109).

Peter now exposes Ananias's full responsibility: he had full control over the property before it was sold, and over the sale price before he contributed any portion to the common fund (5:4). This statement can help us understand the arrangements of having all things in common (2:44; 4:32) and the practice of selling property and bringing the proceeds to the apostles as a contribution to a fund for the poor (4:34-37; compare 2:45), for it shows the voluntary, even periodic nature of the process. Peter again asks the piercing question "Why?" This sin, like all sin, is finally not against human beings but against God.

But sin blinds us to the true nature of the offense: that our sin is against God. Sin also blinds us so that we choose short-term gains in this life, heedless of the long-term loss in the next (Lk 9:24-25). For Ananias it was the possibility of being praised for his generosity while keeping a secure nest egg for his wife (Hebrew $k^e\underline{t}\hat{u}b\hat{a}b$, or dowry paid to a wife in the case of a unilateral divorce or at his death—see *m. Ketubot;* Derrett 1977:196).

As Ananias listens to this exposé (NIV's *when Ananias heard this* does not do justice to the simultaneous action indicated by the present participle), suddenly he falls down and dies (*exepsyxen,* used primarily in accounts of death as a result of divine judgment—Acts 5:10; 12:23; Judg

"exhortation," with prophecy (Hebrew $n^e\underline{b}\hat{u}'\hat{a}b$) through exhortation as the link. While this is satisfactory in terms of transliteration, the semantic link is too tenuous (Haenchen 1971:232; but see Jacobs 1979). Sebastian Brock's suggestion that following the Syriac Peshitta we find the link in the first-person imperfect *(nby')* of an Aramaic verb *(by')* meaning "to comfort" is the most promising path to a solution (Brock 1974).

4:21). God, the knower of all hearts, has assessed Ananias's unrepentant heart and immediately judged him for his sin (contrast Acts 15:8).

Such a punishment, "death at the hands of heaven," was a recognized penalty in Old Testament and Jewish law. The punishments for partaking of the priestly tithe while ritually unclean and the strange fire of Nadab and Abihu are the closest parallels (Lev 10:1-7; 22:9; *m. Keritot;* Derrett 1977:197). No wonder great fear comes upon the Jewish Christian bystanders (compare Acts 5:11; 19:17).

Such discipline certainly has its deterrent value. The hasty, unceremonious burial of Ananias shows the believers recognize that God's judgment has fallen on one who by his embezzlement had violated the transparent unity of the Spirit-filled assembly (see Lev 10:6; *Šĕmaḥot* 2:8). The young men (young in age, not office) cover his eyes and wrap his body in a shroud (*synesteilan;* the word *systellontos,* referring to a functionary related to burials, has been discovered on an inscription in a synagogue in Beth Shearim—see Safrai 1976:776). Without the traditional rituals of mourning, Ananias is taken outside the city and buried.

Beautiful Conspirator (5:7-11) Three hours later Sapphira arrives. Luke, given his mention of her ignorance, probably intends us to understand Peter's question to be about the agreed-upon false price, not the true price. Either way, his inquiry gives her an opportunity to confess or persist in her sin (compare Lk 22:48).

In response, Peter again uses the penetrating "why" question. The NIV emphasizes Peter's disbelief by phrasing it *How could you . . . .* He reveals his knowledge of the crime and points out its implications for their covenant relationship with God. In the wilderness the Israelites through their unbelief and murmuring against God were actually putting him to the test to see if he would indeed punish sin. At Kadesh Barnea they discovered that he does (Num 14:20-23; Ps 95:7-11; compare Deut 6:16). So Ananias and Sapphira learn that in this life God can, and when he chooses will, punish sinners either by immediate death or by some

---

5:5 That Ananias and Sapphira were Christians, truly regenerate, may be concluded with some degree of certainty when one compares and contrasts Acts 5:3, *Satan has so filled your heart,* with Luke's description of the regenerate and unregenerate heart elsewhere. He speaks of having a certain kind of heart turned in a certain direction (Lk 6:45; 8:15; Acts 8:21). The contrast between Peter's interaction with the couple and his conversation with Simon Magus, explicitly identified as unregenerate, is most clear (8:20-24). We have a basis

other means. This can happen to those who claim to be, and may truly be, a part of his covenant people, enjoy his salvation blessings and yet deliberately sin and remain unrepentant (1 Cor 5:5; 1 Jn 5:16-17).

For Christians today this is still a temptation: to so luxuriate in the love and grace of God that we do not take seriously the consequences of our deliberate sinning. But God will not be mocked (Gal 6:7-8).

In a prophecy and an effective judgment, but not a curse, Peter declares that the young men who buried Sapphira's husband (*the feet of* points to their function as transporters of the dead) are at the door and will soon carry out another corpse—hers. Luke heightens the impact with the phrase *at that moment* (5:10).

Thus Sapphira too experiences divine judgment by immediate death, and the believers again respond with dishonorable burial. The lack of reference to wrapping the body may reflect the Jewish custom that women could wrap both men and women, but men could wrap only men (*Šěmaḥot* 12:10).

Great fear comes on *the whole church*. This is the first reference in Acts to the body of Christians as the "church" *(ekklēsia)*. This term, though used in secular Greek to describe citizen assemblies (compare Acts 19:32, 39), derives its special theological meaning from its use by the LXX to consistently translate the Hebrew *qāhāl*, the assembly or congregation of God's people. For Christians to use this word to describe their corporate identity was to claim to be the true people of God, the rightful heirs of God's promised salvation blessings. To find it at the climax of this passage only heightens the seriousness of Ananias and Sapphira's sin and gives explicit justification for the severity of their punishment. And Luke lets us know that the dread extended to non-Christians as well.

The message of this for Christian and non-Christian alike is self-evident. Christians must realize that the selfless, transparent fellowship of the church must never be violated by selfish hypocrisy. Further, it is

for seeing the couple as regenerate when we take into account other teaching in Scripture concerning Christians' lying (Col 3:9), sinning against the Holy Spirit (Eph 4:30; 1 Thess 5:19) and experiencing punishment for postconversion sin, even to death (1 Cor 5:5; see Williams 1985:84). Further, we should remember that Ananias and Sapphira appear in an immediate context of Spirit-filled believers who are sharing their goods (Acts 4:32-37).

proper to employ discipline to guard the church's integrity, unity and purity. For the non-Christian, this account is a warning: Think twice before joining this holy fellowship. Are you willing to pay the price—fully renouncing wicked ways and full-heartedly embracing Christ and other believers in his body, the church?

□ The Apostles' Healing Ministry and Its Consequences (5:12-42)

Through skillful scheduling, a college basketball coach gradually exposes his team to stronger opposition over a long season so that it is brought to peak performance by national tournament time. In a similar way, God in his providence stretches the church by placing various challenges before it in this second cycle of the pattern of advance (contrast 3:1—4:31).

The Healing Ministry (5:12-16)

This last of three summary statements about Jerusalem church life (the first two were 2:42-47 and 4:32-35) holds up this mirror to all churches: What are you attempting that could not be done without the power of the Holy Spirit? We discover here how the church's confident expectation (4:29-30) was divinely realized.

Outreach: Supernatural Power (5:12) In fulfillment of the congregation's prayerful expectation, the church's mission continues to advance through the apostles' performance of *signs and wonders* (literally, "through the hands of the apostles"; compare 4:30). These miracles not only validate the apostles' message (see 2:22) and are tokens of the fullness of salvation blessings to be had in the kingdom at the end (2:19; 3:16-21; 4:9, 12, 22), but they also become a means of liberation from official Judaism, just as Moses' signs and wonders worked liberation from Egypt (7:36; see Deut 29:3; Ps 135:9; Jer 32:21). In both cases they are undeniable witnesses to God's power, and those in power react with frustration.

The special role signs and wonders play in salvation history, their clustering around key salvation events and new epochs of revelation, their extraordinary nature at those times and the fact they are performed mainly by the leaders should circumscribe our expectations concerning

the occurrence of signs and wonders today. Still, we are living in the same last days, and God is still at work mightily through his church (see comment at 3:7-8).

Just as miraculous is the church's unity in the wake of the Ananias and Sapphira incident. All together with one mind, purpose and impulse (as in 1:14; 2:46; 4:24) in Solomon's colonnade—see comment at 3:11; this was a place large enough for a good portion of their growing numbers—the congregation of believers worships, learns from the apostles and evangelizes (compare 2:42; 4:33; 5:25).

Is your congregation held together by anything beyond the homogeneity of ethnic background, socioeconomic circumstances and the goals and values that stem from them? It is the bond of the Spirit that makes outsiders marvel.

Impact on Unbelievers: Respect and Praise (5:13) Luke juxtaposes two contrasting statements about the church's continuing impact (NIV softens this by introducing the second with *even though*). In the light of the judgment on Ananias and Sapphira, *no one else* probably refers to non-Christians (Haenchen 1971:242) not believers (as E. F. Harrison 1986:105) or Jewish sympathizers (as Schwartz 1983). They *dared* not *join* ("come into the Christian community"—Krodel 1986:123; see Acts 17:34; less likely, "associate with, come near physically"—Longenecker 1981:317) *them* (the congregation, not the apostles). At the same time these unbelievers, termed *the people,* praised the congregation of Christians (see also 2:47; 19:17).

Does your church have this kind of impact? As John Stott notes, "This paradoxical situation has often recurred since then. The presence of the living God, whether manifest through preaching or miracles or both, is alarming to some and appealing to others" (1990:113).

The Church's Vitality (5:14-16) Luke now looks at the Christian community and the apostles from the angle of the results of God's work in supernatural power. In the midst of people's natural fear of joining, God continues to work in an ever greater way through the preaching of the gospel, so that a steady stream of men and women who believed (4:4) are being *added.*

A church alive with the power of God will be a growing church, with individuals regularly coming to the Lord for salvation and incorporation

into his body. Taking note of the circumstances, but even more taking hold of God's power, would you say that your own church is thriving in this way?

The effect of the apostles' *signs and wonders* ministry is heightened attraction: the sick are brought to them, even laid in the streets to intercept them, as in Jesus' early Galilean ministry (Lk 4:40-41; 6:17-19). There is heightened expectation—the hope that at least Peter's shadow with its healing power may fall on someone as he passes by.

The effect is a broadening scope for the church's mission. It very naturally enters its second phase, "witnesses . . . in all Judea," as crowds from the towns around Jerusalem, again in a constant stream, bring their sick and demon-possessed. (NIV margin *unclean* gives the literal translation, which points to the ritual impurity of those so possessed; they are unfit for worship in Israel [Williams 1985:88].)

Finally, the effect is total: *all of them were healed.* Whether during Jesus' ministry or when the church is on mission in Jerusalem, in Judea, in Samaria or on the island of Crete, "to the ends of the earth," God's power will effect a comprehensive healing when faced with human misery (Lk 4:40; 5:15; 6:17-19; Acts 5:16; 8:7; 28:9).

What difference is your church making? What evidences are there of the saving, healing power of God?

Consequences of the Healing Ministry (5:17-42)

A popular American TV news anchor of the 1960s and 1970s regularly signed off his broadcasts with "That's the way it is." Since his reports dealt only in human factors, they would have resonated with the Sadducean nobility, who believed all history was the result of human decisions (Josephus *Jewish Antiquities* 13.173). But the Sadducees were in for a surprise when they arrested the apostles. Certain things happened which forced them—and force us—to ask who was really in charge of the course of events.

The Apostles' Incarceration and Divine Release (5:17-26) The

5:15 *Peter's shadow* should not be understood against the background of first-century animistic thought about the beneficial and harmful effects of shadows. (The evidence marshaled by P. W. Van der Horst [1977] presents no exact parallel; the closest is the beneficial medicinal effects of trees' shadows mentioned by Pliny the Elder [*Natural History* 17.18]).

success of the apostles' witness and healing ministry (4:33; 5:12-16) fills the Sadducean high priest and his Sanhedrin associates (see comment at 4:1) with jealousy. This may originally have been "a passionate, consuming zeal focused on God, or rather on the doing of His will and the maintaining of His honour in the face of ungodly acts of men and nations" (Stumpff 1964:878; see Num 25:11; Ps 69:9). Yet because it is "not according to knowledge" (Rom 10:2), this zeal has devolved into jealousy. This is to be the reaction of the majority of Jews as the Christian mission proceeds (Acts 13:45; 17:5; compare Rom 10:19; 11:11).

The Sadducee nobility's jealousy further degenerates into "party spirit," focusing on the resurrection and the apostles' flouting of the high court's authority (4:2, 20, 31). They arrest (literally, "lay hands on") the apostles and incarcerate them for a trial the next day.

When zeal for God is not grounded in the whole truth of God or is mixed with human pride or opinion, it can easily become personal jealousy masquerading as piety. Such misguided zeal can do great harm to those who are the real messengers of God's truth.

Previously God allowed his messengers to remain in jail overnight (see 4:3); now, however, he sends his angel to liberate them. Luke presents angels as overcoming external opposition to and internal hesitation about the full accomplishment of the church's mission (8:26; 10:3; 12:7, 11, 23). The angel commissions the apostles to continue their witness. Taking a steadfast stand in the temple courts, the high priest's own turf and their accustomed place for evangelism and instruction (2:46; 5:12), they are to *tell the people the full message of this new life* (literally, "all the words of this life"). *Life* in the absolute, or with the adjective *eternal,* is one way Luke refers to salvation blessings (3:15; 11:18; 13:46; Lk 10:25; 18:18, 30; compare Acts 2:28/Ps 16:11). This phrase captures the truths that by God's Word the blessed life in covenant relationship is appropriated now, and that beyond death there is life in which God's salvation will be fully known forever (Deut 8:3; 32:47; Job 19:25-26).

Rather, the proper background is the Old Testament and Jesus' life and ministry. There the presence of God, often life-giving, comes as an "overshadowing" (Ex 40:35; Ps 91:1, 4; Lk 1:35; 9:34).

At daybreak the temple crier called, "Priests to worship, Levites to the platform, and Israelites to deputations" (*y. Šeqalim* 5:48d). And so at their earliest opportunity the apostles obey and resume teaching the people (Acts 5:21; Kistemaker [1990:199] takes the imperfect as simple continuous action, not as ingressive as does the NIV). What boldness the apostles show by the time and place of their witness! They are living out their prayer of Acts 4:29-30. God has taken note of the Sanhedrin's threats and actions and has delivered them from prison—yet it is not for their personal comfort but for the furtherance of their mission. This they obediently pursue, and so should all Christians.

In a fast-paced change of scene and collision of characters reminiscent of a Keystone Cops comedy, Luke portrays the powerlessness of the authorities to silence the church's message. Ignorant of the angelic liberation, the full Sanhedrin convenes and routinely summons the defendants. But *the officers* (Levites of the temple watch) find guarded, locked but empty cells, mute evidence that there has been supernatural intervention. *The captain of the temple guard* (see comment at 4:1) *and the chief priests* are more than just *puzzled (diēporoun)* at this. They are perplexed, at a complete loss to explain it. (*Diaporeō* is often used by Luke for the human response to an encounter with the supernatural—Lk 9:7; Acts 2:12; 5:24; 10:17.) Further, they are searching not just for the cause (as Longenecker 1981:320) or the significance (as Kistemaker 1990:202), but for the outcome (NIV; Haenchen 1971:250).

The leaders' negative example reminds us not to let our presuppositions blind us to what God might be doing. Those who do not believe in God's direct intervention in the affairs of humankind (Josephus *Jewish Antiquities* 13.173) could only be at a loss to understand how the apostles were liberated. Immediately they receive an answer to their perplexity. Someone breaks in and reports the apostles' open-air temple evangelism. Luke uses *look (idou)* selectively to point to unusual, supernaturally grounded occurrences (1:10; 2:7; 5:9, 25).

Springing into action, the captain and officers rearrest the apostles. They offer no resistance; the officers use no violent force. The church

---

5:28 Haenchen (1971:251) notes that the word *epagō*, which the NIV translates *make us*

still experiences the people's favor (5:26; compare 4:21; 5:13); the Sadducees hold sway in position only, "having the confidence of the wealthy alone but no following among the populace" (Josephus *Jewish Antiquities* 13.298).

The apostles' submission to the authorities models an important component of Christian civil disobedience: recognition of the legitimacy of political authority through one's willingness to accept the consequences for one's disobedience (compare Rom 13:1-7; 1 Pet 3:15-16). The underlying question posed by this extended arrest account is "Who's in charge?" Luke responds, "God!" God directly intervenes to promote his unstoppable mission through his people's obedient, bold witness. Will the Sadducee and the modern secularist have eyes to see?

Trial and Defense (5:27-32) The presiding officer's interrogation takes the form of two charges, bolstered by an opening reminder of the command given not to speak in Jesus' name (4:18). Disdainfully refusing to refer directly to Jesus *(this name . . . this man),* the high priest manifests a foreshortened perspective. He charges that by human effort the apostles *have filled Jerusalem with* their *teaching* and that they are carrying out a malicious verbal vendetta against the leaders, seeking to bring divine retribution down on them for Jesus' death.

The believers' teaching, however, had been received from their Lord and had spread by God's power (1:3; 4:33). True, they had consistently proclaimed the leaders' guilt for Jesus' death (2:23; 3:17; 4:10). Yet that was always accompanied by the good news of the offer of salvation (2:38-39; 3:19, 26; 4:12). In prayer the apostles had left those hostile to them in God's hands (4:29).

With Peter as the spokesperson and the other apostles indicating their assent (the Greek has *apokritheis* in the singular, followed by a plural finite verb), the defendants admit the charge of civil disobedience by reiterating the principle that obedience to God takes priority over the commands of human beings, whenever the two are in conflict (compare 4:19-20; Lk 20:25). John Stott well articulates the principle for us today: "If the authority concerned misuses its God-given power to command

---

guilty, is used in the LXX to describe divine retribution for sin (for example, Jer 6:19; Judg 9:24).

what he forbids or forbid what he commands, then the Christian's duty is to disobey the human authority in order to obey God's" (1990:116).

Peter answers the vendetta charge by immediately preaching the good news of salvation. He begins with common ground, *the God of our fathers* (compare another instance where a hostile Jewish audience is appealed to—22:14). He announces that God has *raised* up *Jesus,* not *from the dead* (as in NIV) but onto the stage of human history to fulfill his saving purposes (compare Judg 2:18; 3:9). The one God raised up the Jewish leaders *killed by hanging him on a tree* (see Lk 23:21). With this language Peter refers to Deuteronomy 21:23 ("anyone who is hung on a tree is under God's curse") and shows the depth of contempt with which the leaders had held Jesus—they had asked for a death that would place Jesus under God's curse (compare Acts 10:39; 13:29; Gal 3:13; Wilcox 1977). But through the resurrection-ascension, captured in the phrase *God exalted him to God's to his own right hand,* God has vindicated Jesus (Acts 2:34/Ps 110:1). He manifests Jesus as *Prince (archēgos;* see comment at 3:15) *and Savior.* It is the messianic Davidic prince (not Mosaic Messiah, as Marshall 1980:120) who is Israel's final Savior (Lk 2:11; Acts 2:36; 4:12).

Savior, like "Lord," is a bridge word that opens the way for viewing Jesus as God. The Old Testament is marked by the parallel themes that God will bring the final salvation and that the Messiah will bring it (Ps 106:47; 118:25-26; Is 63:8; Jer 17:14; Joel 2:32). The apostles reveal that God and the Messiah are one and the same, namely the Savior Jesus (Acts 2:21, 36, 38-40). The salvation blessings he gives *to Israel* are *repentance* (see comment at 3:19) *and forgiveness of sins* (2:38; 3:19-20, 26; 10:43; 13:38; 26:18; also Lk 24:47). Though the salvation blessings are not exclusively for Israel, it is appropriate to proclaim the fulfillment of salvation blessings to the ones whose ancestors had received the promises (Acts 3:26; 13:46). With this good news, it is almost as if the apostles are saying, "We have no vendetta against you. If you would listen to the good news, you would find the answer for your guilt." And that is ever the message of the Christian witness.

5:30 It is possible to interpret *egeirō* (NIV *raised*) as a reference to the resurrection (so the NIV, which adds *from the dead,* and some commentators, notably Marshall 1980:119; Schneider 1980-1982:1:395). However, the verb's placement at the beginning of a descrip-

The defense climaxes with two claims for the veracity of the gospel message. The apostles declare themselves witnesses, persons with first-hand experience of their testimony's content (compare 1:8, 22; 2:32; 3:15). And they say *the Holy Spirit* also bears witness. This is probably neither the gift of the Spirit in salvation (as Marshall 1980:120) nor the outward miraculous manifestations that salvation has come (8:15-17; 10:44-47; 15:8; as Krodel 1986:128). Rather, it is the Spirit's indwelling those who obey God, so that their witness is characterized by boldness and convincing conviction. Those who hear the truth either freely embrace or emphatically reject it (4:8, 31, 33-34; 6:5, 10; 7:55; compare Jn 16:8-11).

Who's in charge? In no uncertain terms Luke lets us know it is God who desires to save. What does he want of us? An obedience that embraces the good news and knows the presence of the Spirit.

Fury and a Call for Moderation (5:33-39) The apostles' defense, which actually manifests another instance of the charges against them, is more than the Sanhedrin could handle with sober judgment. Their jealousy and frustration (5:17, 24, 26) explode in a fury (literally, "sawn through"; compare 1 Chron 20:3; Acts 7:54) and a determination to do away with these men, as previously they had done with their Lord (Lk 22:2). Unless Peter's statement about Christ sitting at God's right hand as Prince and Savior is taken as a blasphemous attribution of deity to Jesus (compare Lk 22:69-71), there is no basis for a death-penalty verdict here.

In the midst of the furor a Pharisee, *Gamaliel, a teacher of the law* esteemed by the populace (*m. Sota* 9:15; Neusner 1971:373), takes the floor and has the apostles removed so that the Sanhedrin can go into executive session. Appealing for caution, he counsels a hands-off, wait-and-see policy (5:35, 38-39). Gamaliel makes his case by referring to two contemporary examples of failed revolutionary movements: Theudas (B.C. 4—see notes) and Judas the Galilean (A.D. 6/7). The former had either claimed to be a prophet or was a messianic pretender (Marshall 1980:122). The latter upbraided his fellow countrymen for paying taxes

---

tion of Jesus' saving work and the fact that all other uses pointing to the resurrection either are explicitly qualified (3:15; 4:10; 13:30; 26:8) or involve context pointers (10:40; 13:37) suggest this other sense (13:22; compare 3:26).

to the Romans (Josephus *Jewish War* 2.118). He founded the Zealot movement, whose credo was reminiscent of Peter's words (5:29). "They have a passion for liberty that is almost unconquerable, since they are convinced that God alone is their leader and master" (Josephus *Jewish Antiquities* 18.23). Gamaliel's logic presumably is that just as these movements died with the death of the leader (he is not precisely correct with respect to the Zealots—see Josephus *Jewish Antiquities* 18.25), Christianity too will soon die out, for its leader is now dead.

Gamaliel caps his argument with the principle that works of purely human origin come to nothing but those from God cannot be stopped; indeed, to oppose the latter is to fight against God (compare *m. 'Abot* 4:11). Though Luke presents the two options of verses 38 and 39 as conditional clauses, reflecting Gamaliel's uncertainty concerning the human origin and certainty concerning the divine origin of Christianity (NIV obscures this), it is not clear whether this suggests an incipient embracing of the truth of Christianity or a scoring of points against the Sadducees. The Sadducees believed only in human causation in history, while the Pharisees affirmed the hand of both human beings and God (Josephus *Jewish Antiquities* 13.171-73; 18.12-15; Robertson 1934:1018; compare Longenecker 1981:324).

This appeal persuades the council. The Pharisees (a transliteration of Heb *pᵉrûšîm,* "separated ones"), a small lay movement promoting strict adherence to the written and oral Torah, were a minority in the council. Their voice, however, carried great weight, often overruling the Sadducees, because of the favor they had with the people (Josephus *Jewish Antiquities* 13.298; 18.17).

Gamaliel's intervention again answers the question "Who's in charge?" by pointing to a God who providentially will use unbelievers within the ranks of official opposition to further his saving purposes. No human

---

5:36 Gamaliel refers to a revolutionary Theudas who was active before Judas the Galilean (active A.D. 6; Josephus *Jewish Wars* 2.117-18). If we identify this Theudas with the revolutionary referred to by Josephus (active under Cuspus Fadus A.D. 44-46; *Jewish Antiquities* 20.97-99), then Luke commits a historical error of order and creates an anachronism, for Gamaliel presumably gives the speech in the early 30s. Further, Gamaliel's claim that Judas's movement came to nothing is not true: the Zealots sustained Judas's vision and sparked the A.D. 66 war.

Though many would view the following suggestion as special pleading, there are good

situation is beyond his control and ordering.

And what of Gamaliel's counsel? It was good advice for the short run, since it encouraged unbelievers not to summarily dismiss Christianity's claims. Indeed, Luke gives his readers the same counsel of patience if they are to benefit from his writings and allow them to achieve their purpose (Lk 1:4). On the other hand, Gamaliel's words are also bad counsel, for good plans may fail and evil movements may succeed in the short term. The pragmatic test can fail us. In the long term, before God's judgment seat at the last day, we will know the truth that has triumphed, but then it will be too late. A wait-and-see approach to the gospel must be transformed into a decision-making stance. We must in repentance reach out and accept the forgiveness of sins that Jesus offers (5:31).

Verdict and Outcome (5:40-42) Persuaded by Gamaliel's appeal, the Sanhedrin backs away from having the apostles executed. Instead they are flogged (*derō*, a general term for punishment by beating or thrashing). This may have involved scourging with a whip thirty-nine times (*m. Makkot* 3:10-15; Haenchen 1971:254) or a lesser punishment (see Bruce 1988:117; compare Lk 22:63; Acts 16:37; 22:19). Again told not to speak in the name of Jesus, they are released.

In no masochistic fashion, but with spiritual eyes to see what suffering for the name of Jesus signifies about their eternal salvation, the apostles live out the dynamic of Jesus' beatitude (Lk 6:22-23) and respond to their physical suffering with joy. As far as Luke is concerned, two things bring Christians joy: contemplating salvation and the honor of being dishonored for Jesus' sake (Lk 10:20; Acts 8:39; 11:23; 13:48). Whether in singing hymns over the crackle of flames at the stake in centuries past or praising God while cleaning Chinese prison-camp cesspools in our own day, the hallmark of the Christian has been, and must continue to be, joy in suffering persecution (1 Pet 1:6; 4:13).

---

grounds for proposing that Luke is referring to another Theudas, a revolutionary active at Herod the Great's death (4 B.C.). Josephus reports many uprisings at Herod's death (*Jewish Antiquities* 17.269). Theudas, a contracted form of names such as Theodorus, Theodotus and Theodosius, was a common name in antiquity, as inscription and papyri show (Bruce 1990:176). Luke is as creditable a historian as Josephus; thus we should not too readily conclude that Luke clumsily misread Josephus. Further, Josephus published his work in A.D. 93, too late for Luke's use. Gamaliel's assessment of Judas's influence may have indeed been wrong.

In a brief summary statement Luke concludes his account of the first stage of the Jerusalem church's growth, the mission among Hebrew-speaking Jews. Daily in the temple courts and in homes (2:42-47), the believers continued teaching the good news, which is at the same time testifying that the Messiah is indeed Jesus (a confession, as in NIV and Bruce 1990:179; not a double name, as Lake and Cadbury [1979:63] suggest as an equal possibility).

Who's in charge? A God who empowers and leads his church in carrying out his mission in spite of opposition.

□ The Hellenistic Jewish Christian Witness (6:1—8:40)

MKs—missionary kids—are culturally "green." They are a mixture, having spent their formative years in two cultures: their parents' home culture and their parents' place of service. This makes them very fit to take the gospel crossculturally. Evangelist Luis Palau, born of British and Argentinean parents, is a good example.

It has ever been God's plan that the culturally marginal should be effective bearers of his message crossculturally. He began by raising up Hellenistic Jewish Christians (see notes). Though discriminated against (6:1-7), they bore a powerful witness to unsaved Jews, Hellenistic and Hebrew-speaking alike (6:8—7:53). Their persecution, in the wake of Stephen's martyrdom (7:54—8:3), actually advanced the church's mission across the cultural thresholds of Samaria (8:4-25) and "to the ends of the earth" (representatively, 8:26-40).

Appointment of the Seven (6:1-7)

Why is it that surveys of pastors' schedules often reveal that when it comes to preaching, their professed priorities greatly differ from their

---

6:1—8:40 Hellenistic Jewish Christians were Greek-speakers from birth, hailing from the Diaspora but now, out of "Zionist" fervor, residing in Jerusalem. Formerly they congregated in their own native-language synagogues, but since coming to faith in Christ they have met with the church, though probably with their own ethnic subgroup within the church.

6:1-7 Luke has skillfully placed this episode at a key transition point. He preserves the continuity of the Hellenistic Jewish Christian mission with the Jerusalem church's life and witness and at the same time accelerates the momentum of the mission's advance into new ethnic and geographical territory (Longenecker 1981:327). The episode's structure reflects Luke's literary pattern for narratives of threatening situations (peace, 6:1; threat, 6:1; reso-

actual practice? The Word is central to the church's growth—so central that Satan will use a congregation's expectations and traditions (often innocent in themselves) to distract ministers from what is required for effective proclamation of the Word. In the midst of great advance, the Jerusalem church faced the same problem.

The Church at Peace Faces a Threat (6:1-2) Luke notes the church's continued numerical growth as the apostles faithfully teach and evangelize (5:42). This success leads to an overload for the apostles in their administration of the common fund for the poor (4:35, 37; 5:1; compare Deut 1:9-10). As a result, the Grecian Jewish widows are being overlooked in the daily food distribution. The resulting complaints (compare Num 17:5) threaten to destroy the church's unity.

The fact that it is *Grecian Jews* (*Hellēnistoi;* Longenecker 1981:327-29 for a cogent discussion of the options for understanding this term) who complain against *Hebraic* believers (*Hebraioi;* see Longenecker 1981:332) shows that cultural tensions probably lie behind the oversight. Pious *widows,* having been removed from the temple dole—the weekly *quppâh,* or poor basket of foodstuffs (*m. Pe'a* 8:7)—are now dependent on the church's daily distribution (NIV specifies it more precisely than the Greek by adding *of food;* see Kistemaker 1990:221). But the apostles, Hebraic Jews, are not making sure the Grecian widows receive their share.

Hebraic Jews had a prejudicial sense of superiority over Grecian Jews, because of their own birthplace and language. Lack of communication between the groups also fostered suspicion. In fact, human diversity will always bring with it opportunities for prejudicial division and injustice.

Facing the problem immediately and openly, *the Twelve* gather the congregation (*plēthos;* see 4:32 for comment) and point out another

---

lution, 6:2-6; restoration, 6:7; see Tyson 1983:149). At the same time one can detect features of the "choice of supplementary leadership" form present in the Pentateuch (Talbert 1984:29: problem, 6:1-2; proposed solution, 6:3-4; qualifications of the new leaders, 6:3; setting apart of the new leaders, 6:5-6; see Ex 18:13-26; Num 11:16-25; 27:12-23; Deut 1:9-18; Daube 1976).

6:2 *To wait on tables* can refer to financial transactions or foodstuffs (Lake and Cadbury 1979:64) or foodstuffs closely associated with the common meal (Jeremias 1969:131) or the common meal itself (Tyson 1983:153).

threat: distraction from their calling, *the ministry of the word of God*. This activity is essential for church vitality and growth (see 6:7). The apostles are facing the decisions that come to leaders of a movement that is growing in numbers and complexity.

The Church Resolves the Problem (6:3-6) The Twelve instruct the congregation to *choose seven men* to take over this responsibility. That the diaconate is a function and not an office is clear from Luke's wording. He never uses the noun "deacon" (compare Phil 1:1; 1 Tim 3:8-13), though a noun and verb to describe the function are present *(diakonia,* Acts 6:1; *diakoneō,* 6:2; contrast 1:25). This passage probably did contribute, however, to the origin of the office (Coppens 1979:421). Luke stresses that this physical/social ministry has equal validity with the apostles' evangelism/edification ministry, for he uses *diakonia* to describe both (6:1, 4). The church must exercise both, and neither to the exclusion of the other (see Lk 10:38-42).

This division of labor is accompanied by a reiteration of the apostles' commitment to their calling: prayer and ministry of the Word of God. The apostles determine to be "busily engaged in, devoted to" these things, so that realistically they will take up all their time (Bruce 1990:183; compare 1:14; 2:42, 46). *Prayer* (literally, "the prayer") may have to do with leading the community's prayer services (Bruce 1990:183), or the apostles' intercession for the welfare of the community or effectiveness in preaching, whether individually or as a group (10:9; 13:3; Haenchen 1971:263; Stott 1990:121), or both. Prayer is central to the church's vitality and advance, as it was in Jesus' ministry (Lk 5:16; 6:12; 9:18, 28; 11:1; 22:41; see 18:1). The ministry of the Word "[sees] to it that the Word of God is communicated in power and in continuity with the apostles' teaching as its norm" (Krodel 1986:134). In the summary statement on growth, the necessity of this ministry is articulated for a third time (6:7; compare 6:2).

The proposed solution reveals the values that guided the decision: commitment to unity, to a holistic ministry and to growth by means of preaching and teaching. The decision-making process reflects equally

---

6:3 Whether the number seven is derived from the seven wards of Jerusalem (Lake 1979a:149) or Jewish representative boards or town councils, "Seven of the Town" (Williams 1985:106; Haenchen 1971:263) is unclear.

important values for church order. It is participatory, because of the church's spiritual equality (1:16; 2:17; 4:33; 6:3; 15:23). It involves distinct roles for leaders and congregation. The leaders (note it is collegial leadership) propose a solution and the criteria for implementing it. They also confirm the congregation's implementation (6:6). The congregation must "own" the proposed solution and do their assigned part (6:5).

If unity and growth are to be promoted, then, structures in the church must be flexible. Decision-making must be participatory, with distinctive roles for leaders and congregation.

The Twelve instruct the congregation to find seven men with a good reputation. The word order in the Greek makes it unlikely that the reputation is limited to being Spirit-filled, as the NIV suggests. The spiritual qualification *full of the Spirit* applies to those who have so fully given themselves to following Christ that God's saving, sanctifying and edifying grace is clearly and continuously manifest in their lives (6:5; 7:55; 11:24). The final qualification is wisdom—that skill in administration and business which will bring efficient and effective accomplishment of a task. Moral, spiritual, practical— these should be the hallmarks of all who sit on church boards. Only with such leadership will the real work of the church be done.

The whole congregation took ownership of the proposal, and unity was restored (6:5; compare 4:32). They brought forward names of seven men who may well have already been exercising leadership in the Grecian Jewish segment of the church. Except for Stephen and Philip (see 6:9—7:60; 8:4-40; 21:8), Scripture tells us no more of these men. Stephen's spiritual quality is particularly noted. Being *full of faith and of the Holy Spirit* probably points not to his working of miracles (as Haenchen 1971:263; see v. 9) but to his extraordinary depth of faith, as well as his singular life in the Spirit.

The leaders confirm the congregation's work by praying over and laying hands on these men. Though grammatically one could understand the people as doing this, Luke probably intends us to understand the apostles as the commissioners (compare 6:3). "The laying on of hands"

Full of the Spirit does not point to empowerment for a specific occasion (as in 4:8, "filled with the Holy Spirit"), nor to an endowment with a specific gifting, here wisdom: "practical wisdom . . . to manage the fund" (contra Williams 1985:104).

is used in Old Testament passages with the "choice of supplementary leadership" form. Hebrew *sāmak*, used in Numbers 27:18, means "to lean the hand on, exercise some force at the base of the hand at the joint" and has the significance of to "pour your personality—or a quality of yours relevant at this moment—into him" (Daube 1976:162; compare Num 27:20). What the apostles pass on to the Seven through the laying on of hands is not the Spirit, for the Seven already have the Spirit (Acts 6:3). Rather, they receive authority to work as the apostles' representatives in a specific task (Parratt 1969:213).

The Church, Restored, Continues to Grow (6:7) Having weathered the threat, the church returns to its normal condition: growth. So integral to growth is the Word of God, the message of salvation, that Luke uses personification, saying literally, "The word of God grew" (see 12:24; 19:20). As the seed possesses the power of growth, so "the word has in itself the power of life. . . . This independent force of the word of God makes it the preeminent instrument of salvation" (Kodell 1974:506; Acts 10:36; 13:26; 14:3; 16:32; compare 4:4; 11:1; 13:49; Lk 8:11). Luke's combination of *spread* (grew) and *increased* (multiplied) echoes the Old Testament command "Be fruitful and multiply," which was incorporated into covenant promises about the people of God (Lev 26:9; Jer 3:16; 23:3; compare Gen 1:28).

From among the priests, the core of the church's opposition (Acts 4:1; 5:17), a large number become obedient to the faith. The social gulf between the ordinary priests and the upper-class chief priests, who oppressed them economically, may explain the regular priests' openness to the gospel (Longenecker 1981:333). Still, the response of the priesthood reflects the total triumph of the church's mission. No segment of Jewish society was beyond the reach of the gospel. And today our churches should be marked by the same conviction—that the ministry of the Word is essential for growth and that growth is the normal condition of the church.

6:7 The multiplication was great in quantity *(sphodra)*, not in rate (as NIV).

The imperfect *hypēkouon* should probably be taken as continuous ("were being obedient"), not ingressive action (as in NIV, *became obedient*). It points to the priests' perseverance in the faith (Williams 1985:105).

6:9 The "Synagogue of the Freedmen" was probably not one center for weekly study and

Stephen's Witness and Arrest (6:8-15)

How attractive is the father or mother of a newborn, glowing with joy over God's good gift. Just as attractive is Stephen, a man full of the Holy Spirit. We are drawn to him.

What does a person "full of the Spirit" look like? By God's grace, can I be such a person?

Effective Witness in Deed and in Word (6:8-10) Stephen engages in an effective witness by deed and word, not unlike the apostles (5:12, 42). The Spirit-fullness he knows includes *grace* and *power,* so that he is able to do *great wonders* and miraculous signs. *Grace* further defined by *power* is not simply a miracle-working ability (compare 3:12). It is a more comprehensive "gracing" that includes effective preaching (6:9-10; compare 14:26; 15:40; 20:32). As part of a larger "apostolic" circle that included Philip and Barnabas, Stephen does miracles as a token of salvation's advance first to Hellenistic Jews and then to other peoples (8:6; 14:3; 15:12).

Should we expect more "Stephens" today? Though normally signs and wonders are the work of apostles and prophets at particular junctures of God's salvation history, Stephen's activity is witness to the fact that even "this restriction is not absolute" (Stott 1990:126). Let us pray to be full of the Spirit and let God's "gracing" do what it will.

Stephen's witness in the Hellenistic Jewish synagogues draws opposition. In theological debate, however, Stephen bests all comers; no one has an answer for him (compare Lk 12:12; 21:15; Jn 16:8-11). Stephen has conquered their minds. But God has not chosen through this witness to also conquer his opponents' wills and lead them to repentance and conversion.

Plot and Trial (6:11-14) Stephen's opponents resort to subterfuge. In private they prompt some to make the claim that they have heard Stephen speaking blasphemous things against Moses and God (also see vv. 13-14). In New Testament times blasphemy encompassed more than

---

exposition of the law, frequented by Jews from the four geographical areas noted (contra Metzger 1971:340). Rather, *Freedmen* probably denoted descendants of Jews taken to Rome as slaves by Pompey (B.C. 63) and later liberated (Strathman 1967a:265-66; Tacitus *Annals* 2.85; Josephus *Jewish Antiquities* 17.300; Suetonius *Tiberius* 36; Philo *Legatio ad Gaium* 155). They formed their own synagogue, as did all the other groups listed.

simply uttering the divine name (as in *m. Sanhedrin* 7:5); it was any slanderous or scurrilous word spoken against humankind or God or anything associated with his majesty and power (Lk 22:65; 23:39; compare 5:21; Num 15:30). The Hellenistic Jewish instigators and their agents arouse *the elders and the teachers of the law* and, for the first time, *the people* against the Christian witness (contrast Acts 2:47; 4:21; 5:13, 26). The opposition gathers such momentum that all rush on Stephen in a violent arrest (4:1; 19:29; compare Lk 8:29; Acts 27:15).

A Sanhedrin trial for blasphemy required witnesses, and the Hellenistic Jews make sure they are present here—though, as Luke is careful to point out, these are *false witnesses*. They are not false simply because they are opposing God's spokesperson. Rather, their testimony is a "subtle and deadly misrepresentation of what was intended" (Longenecker 1981:336). Comparing their words with Jesus' teaching reveals an identifiable mixture of truth and falsehood (v. 14; for v. 13 compare 21:28). Jesus did predict the temple's destruction, but he did not say he was its destroyer (Lk 21:6). When challenged for a sign to validate his right to drive the moneychangers from the temple area, Jesus responded, "Destroy this temple, and I will raise it again in three days" (Jn 2:19; compare Mk 14:58). Did Jesus of Nazareth predict that he would *change the customs Moses handed down?* No, Jesus was not an opponent of the law (Mt 5:17-18; Lk 16:16-17). Yes, Jesus did alter the customs of Moses, the oral tradition, when he found that allegiance to them meant nullifying the written law of God (Mt 15:1-9; Lk 6:1-5, 6-11).

Opposition tactics like these are still found today. When serious theological or religious debate is not successful, a personal campaign of lies may follow. And if the witnesses' or the message's integrity cannot be undercut this way, legal action may be pursued. Sadly, this path is followed by opponents of the truth within as well as outside the church.

Stephen's Godly Appearance (Acts 6:15) The defendant stands before the court in session, tier upon tier of dignified jurists of Israel's

---

6:13-14 The Jews had two sources for the content of their law: (1) the written Torah received by Moses on Sinai and (2) the oral Torah or the traditions of the fathers, the scribal interpretation of the written law, also believed to have come originally from Moses (*m. 'Abot* 1:1). Both had equal authority; both could be referred to as "law"; both could be said to be from Moses. In fact, *law* and *Moses* could be used to refer to an undifferentiated body of Mosaic legislation both oral and written. This may well be what the opponents desired

highest court. Stephen transfixes those who would be his judge. It's as though they cannot take their eyes off him (compare 1:10; 3:4, 12; 7:55). And no wonder: *his face was like the face of an angel!* Though this certainly reflects divine approval of his witness (Stott 1990:129) and parallels the effects of Moses' standing in God's presence (Ex 34:29, 35; Marshall 1980:131), Jesus' transfiguration is a better immediate model for what is happening here (Lk 9:29). So full of the Spirit, so full of wisdom, faith, grace, and power is Stephen that the glory of God shines from his face. To a greater or lesser extent, that's the way it is with all those who are full of the Spirit of God (2 Cor 3:18).

Stephen's Speech (7:1-53)

Human religious effort is a fact of life in almost every culture. Yet Stephen declares it is such effort that has kept Israel from knowing the righteous Savior and true worship.

Stephen's opponents see in his preaching a challenge to first-century Judaism's twin pillars of piety: the law and the temple (6:11, 13-14). Stephen now proceeds to answer these charges, not as one defending himself but as a witness to the gospel (Lk 21:13). He exposes the falseness of the charges as he affirms his loyalty to God's law and true worship. But more important, he reveals how religious effort, in this case first-century Judaism, is an obstacle to the true knowledge of God's saving provision, the Messiah. The words of historian John MacMurray about Jesus may be appropriately applied to Stephen: "The great contribution of the Hebrew to religion was that he did away with it."

Promise to Abraham and Preservation Through Joseph (7:1-16) The high priest, probably Caiaphas (he served in this capacity until A.D. 36; see 4:6), the Sanhedrin's presiding officer, asks Stephen whether the charges of blasphemy are true.

Stephen begins with respect *(brothers and fathers;* compare 22:1), yet commandingly: *listen to me!* (2:22; 3:22-23/Deut 18:15-16, 19). He de-

---

to point to when they used *Moses* and *law (nomos)* in verses 11 and 13. But Luke's use of *ethos* in verse 15 probably points us to a more specific focus of their opposition: the traditional temple service rules, an aspect of oral Torah (Schneider 1980-1982:1:439; see also Marshall 1980:130; compare Luke's other uses of *ethos* in Lk 1:9; 2:42; Acts 15:1; 21:21; 26:3; 28:17).

scribes the call of Abraham, how *the God of glory* appeared to him in Mesopotamia (the land of the Chaldeans [Acts 7:4], the southern region of modern Iraq). God's glory, pointing to his transcendence, begins and ends this episode (7:55; compare Lk 2:14; 19:38). God's appearance outside Palestine and apart from a tabernacle (contrast Ex 40:34-38) and temple (contrast Ezek 43:5) makes it clear that God's presence is not tied exclusively to a particular land or building. God called Abraham to participate in the same independence. He was to leave land and family and come to a land God would show him. Free of all human roots, he became totally dependent on God to provide his future, his inheritance.

Abraham obeyed in steps, proceeding with his immediate family to Haran, a flourishing city in the upper Euphrates valley at the intersection of important trade routes. After his father Terah's death, God "resettled" (NIV *sent*) him in Canaan, a location that Stephen relates directly to his audience (Acts 7:4). He may be indicating that their very presence in the land shows the fulfillment of the promise (Marshall 1980:135), or he may be relating Abraham's pilgrimage to the experience of the Hellenistic Jews, some of whom came from Mesopotamia (2:9).

There are both comparison and contrast here, for Stephen holds up Abraham as a model of faith in God's promise alone over against religious effort that finds security in the tangible. And today we too must be willing to say no to our dependence on religious effort and say yes to the God who calls us to follow him alone.

7:2-3 The reference to a call in Mesopotamia and not Haran, using the wording of Genesis 12:1, is not, in the final analysis, a discrepancy with the Genesis account (11:31). We need not conclude that Old Testament evidence is conflated here, as Williams (1985:118) proposes, or that Stephen relies on a variant Jewish tradition, as contended by Krodel (1986:140) and Kistemaker (1990:239; compare Josephus *Jewish Antiquities* 1.154; Philo *De Abrahamo* 70-72). If we keep in mind the Old Testament testimony to a divine call in Ur of the Chaldees (Gen 15:7; Neh 9:7) and the fact that the *waw* consecutive imperfect verb that introduces the quote at Genesis 12:1 can be translated as a perfect with the pluperfect meaning, "had said," as indeed the NIV does, there is no difficulty with Stephen's statement.

7:4 If Terah was seventy years old when Abraham was born (Gen 11:26) and Abraham was seventy-five when he left Haran for Canaan (12:4), and this occurred after Terah's death (Acts 7:4), Terah must have been 145 when he died. But Genesis 11:32 says he was 205. How do we account for the sixty years? It is not necessary to see the discrepancy as due to Luke's dependence on a variant textual tradition (as Marshall 1980:135; compare Samaritan Pentateuch Gen 11:32) or as an example of the natural reading of the text by an ordinary reader (Lake and Cadbury 1979:70), what Longenecker labels the conflation practice and inexactitude of popular Judaism (1981:340). Gleason Archer's (1982:378) solution over-

Abraham experienced fulfillment deferred. God did not give him the land, not even so much as could be paced off in one stride (see Deut 2:5). And he did not give him a child during the natural childbearing years. This was not so much to show that the covenantal relationship with God was to be cherished more than the promised inheritance (contra Longenecker 1981:340), though that may have been a part of it. Rather, God wanted to demonstrate to his covenant people that the tangible fulfillment of the promise is all God's doing, whether in the miraculous birth of an heir or in the miraculous deliverance from Egypt, which led to entry into the Promised Land.

Stephen now recounts how God in his mercy bolstered Abraham's faith in three ways. First, God frequently repeated his covenant promise (Gen 12:7; 13:15; 15:2, 18; 17:8; 24:7). Stephen alludes to the covenant renewal in the giving of the covenant of circumcision (Acts 7:5/Gen 17:8). In it God again promised to give the land to Abraham and to his seed for a possession. The NIV's *he and his descendants . . . would possess the land* is not accurate here; it also obscures the emphasis on God's active role in giving the land as a possession to Abraham and his seed.

Second, God gave a prophecy concerning what would happen to Abraham's family before they fully occupied the land. Quoting Genesis 15:13-14 (Acts 7:6-7), Stephen reports God's foretelling of sojourn, slavery and suffering during four hundred years in another country. But God also foretold deliverance: he would "judge" (NIV *punish*) that nation, and the

comes the difficulty. If we take Abraham not as Terah's eldest but as his youngest son, though he is mentioned first because of his prominence in the narrative, it is possible to propose that he was born some time after Terah was seventy, even sixty years later—that is, when he was 130. This would account for the missing sixty years and harmonize the passages.

7:6 Was Israel in Egypt 400 or 430 years (Gen 15:13; Ex 12:41)? Probably either the same time period was reported both as a round and as a more precise number (Kistemaker 1990:242) or the period was calculated in one case from the time of Isaac's birth and in the other from the giving of the promise (so the rabbis; see Strack and Billerbeck 1978:2:668-71).

7:7 The language of the last phrase, *they will . . . worship me in this place,* has affinities with Exodus 3:12. If it is identified as a quote of that verse, there is the problem of a switch of referents from Mt. Horeb to Canaan. We do not need to resort to a conflation or telescoping explanation (as Bruce 1988:134). The immediate context of Genesis 15 (especially v. 16) contains evidence that worship in Canaan is a valid implication of the passage (Marshall 1980:136). Stephen is thus not quoting or alluding to Exodus 3:12, though that verse and his words are "related in sense" (Archer and Chirichigno 1983:7).

nation would come out and worship God *in this place,* the land. This promise does not shift the focus from inheriting a land to being delivered out of Egypt and gaining the opportunity to worship (as Lake and Cadbury 1979:72). It continues the theme that God will provide the inheritance through a deliverance and highlights the purpose of the inheritance: to have a place where one may worship God. True worship becomes inextricably bound up with living in a covenant relationship with God and knowing the fulfillment of his promises (compare Lk 1:73-75).

Finally, there was an outward covenant sign: circumcision (Acts 7:8; Gen 17:1-16, especially vv. 9-12). Though circumcision was practiced at puberty, if not infancy, by most of the nations that had dealings with Israel in patriarchal times, only for Israel did it have covenantal significance (Bruce 1988:135). It was to be administered to one's sons, the next generation. Interestingly enough, this covenant sign was given before the birth of Isaac. Again, it was all God's doing. God took the initiative. Abraham simply had to receive the gift of the covenant sign and obediently apply it when the son of promise was born.

Stephen does not let us miss the covenant dynamic at work here. After mentioning the gift of *the covenant of circumcision,* he continues with what necessarily followed, introduced by "and so" *(kai houtōs;* NIV does not render *houtōs): And Abraham became the father of Isaac and circumcised him eight days after his birth.* This was not just a matter of covenant obedience (as Kistemaker 1990:243). It was a matter of God's covenant faithfulness. Stephen is no blasphemer. He approves of God's covenant ways.

And today we have the Scriptures, in which we may read God's covenant promises over and over again (Rom 15:4). We have biblical prophecy, which tells us enough of coming events to support our faith (Lk 21; Acts 1:6-7; Rev). We have a covenant sign, baptism, which we may take to ourselves (and as some believe, to our children) as a mark of God's covenant of grace (Col 2:9-12).

Stephen now lays the groundwork for the fulfillment of the prophecy

---

7:12 The NIV translation *grain* may reflect dependence on the Textus Receptus reading

concerning the nation's sojourn in another country (Acts 7:6). In the process he continues to unfold the dynamics of God's covenant relationship with his people. Further, there may be some typological parallels drawn to Stephen as the representative Christian of Jewish heritage opposed by his countrymen (see Richard 1979 on the polemical character of the Joseph episode). In jealousy the patriarchs sold their brother Joseph as a slave into Egypt (v. 9; Gen 37:11, 28). *God was with him* (see Gen 39:2-3, 21, 23) *and rescued him from all his troubles* (see Reuben's failed rescue plans, Gen 37:21-22 LXX, and the brothers' articulation of guilt, 42:21 LXX). Christians too face trouble (Acts 11:19; 14:22; 20:23).

God gave Joseph "grace and wisdom before Pharaoh" so that he was given responsibility over Egypt and all Pharaoh's palace. Contrary to the NIV rendering of 7:10—which must change the Greek word order in order to clearly present its chosen meaning for *charis* (NIV *goodwill*)—the words "grace" and "wisdom" should be taken together as indicating "divinely inspired skill in the reading of dreams" (Haenchen 1971:279; Gen 41:37-40).

Similarly, Stephen himself, full of wisdom and grace, has been made responsible for food distribution for God's people (Acts 6:3, 5, 8). Though Joseph's brothers and Stephen's opponents meant their attacks for evil, God is not thwarted, for he can turn it to good. In Joseph's case, God protected his chosen preserver of the covenant people, preparing the way for the survival of generations.

Famine struck Canaan as well as Egypt. Jacob and his family were on the point of starvation (*heuriskō* [NIV *could not find,* 7:11] in the negative imperfect points to "lasting inability"—Kistemaker 1990:249), and the covenant promises were on the verge of dying out in the fourth and fifth generations. Then they gained relief by sending to Egypt for food (see Gen 41:54, 57; 42:2, 5). Not only did Joseph preserve them alive, but on the second visit he revealed himself to them and effected a reconciliation (Acts 7:13; Gen 45:1-16).

Stephen concludes this portion of Israel's history with the note that

---

sita. The better attested reading externally is *sitia,* "food made from grain" (Metzger 1971:343).

Joseph sent for Jacob and the whole family, seventy-five souls, and so they settled in Egypt (Acts 7:14). He tells us of the patriarchs' deaths and their burial in Shechem in Canaan. So God's purposes—both his eternal covenant with Abraham to build a great nation and his prophecy that there would be a sojourn in another country—were being accomplished. Though trouble and exile from the land of promise seem to put the fulfillment of the promise even further away, the patriarchs had faith. Their final instructions were to have their bones buried in the land. And this their sons did in hope.

The constants of a covenant relationship, now as then, are God's word of promise and his powerful working to fulfill it, his presence in every place, and the necessity of obedient faith to lay hold of the promise.

Moses: Israel's Redemption and Rebellion (7:17-43) The history of the patriarchs focused on the dynamics of covenant relationship—living under God's blessing without customary code or tangible shrine. This next section looks at Moses and in its own kerygmatic way sets aside the charges leveled against Stephen. Stephen does this by laying the groundwork for two analogies that he will apply to his audience in the indictment (vv. 51-53). His recounting of the exodus and the experiences of the wilderness generation is marked by a strong theme of rebellion. Since Stephen explicitly states that Messiah is a prophet like Moses (v. 37; compare 3:22-23), it should not be surprising to find typological features in the history of Moses which match up with Luke's presentation of the life of Christ or even the body of Christ, the church. Though Stephen's audience may not have caught all the typological references, Luke's readership—and we—can benefit from them.

7:14 Did seventy (Hebrew text tradition Gen 46:27; Ex 1:5) or seventy-five (LXX text tradition Gen 46:27; Ex 1:5) go down to Egypt with Jacob (compare Philo *De Migratione Abrahami* 199-201, which mentions both)? As Archer explains it, both numbers can be taken as correct, depending on whether we count the descendants born to Joseph in Egypt as part of the family entourage (Archer 1982:378-79).

7:16 Genesis 23:3-20 describes Abraham's purchase of the cave of Machpelah for a burial site. Genesis 33:19 tells of Jacob's purchase at Shechem, where Joseph was later buried (Josh 24:32). Acts 7:16 says Abraham bought the property at Shechem. We need not conclude that Luke was confused or mistaken (as Krodel 1986:144; contrast Stott [1990:134], who says it is unlikely Stephen would have made such a mistake) or that he has again telescoped two accounts (as Bruce 1988:137). Rather, a case can be made that Abraham purchased the site at Shechem originally (compare Gen 12:6-7) and then forfeited his claim through his

Stephen recounts Moses' early years—his rescue as an infant, and the rejection that led to his flight from Egypt (7:17-22, 23-29). He places Moses' birth within the framework of the fulfillment of God's promises; in words that the NIV has somewhat obscured, he says emphatically, "Now when the time of the promise, which God confessed to Abraham drew near" (compare vv. 6-7). The Hebrew nation, he notes, was experiencing numerical increase, one of the blessings of the covenant (Gen 12:2; 17:2, 6; 35:11; 46:3; 47:27; Ex 1:7). Israel's population growth posed a problem for a pharaoh *who knew nothing about Joseph*. While this ruler is often identified as Ramses II (nineteenth dynasty, c. 1290-1224 B.C.; Bruce 1990:196), Archer understands the oppression as occurring over a number of dynasties starting with the later Hyksos and extending to Thutmose I (c. 1600-1514 B.C.; Archer 1964:215-21). Stephen's compressed statement does not let us know explicitly the motivation for the oppression or the nature of Pharaoh's ignorance—was it real or a conscious choice to forget in light of perceived menace (as Marshall 1980:139)? But the action he took is spelled out. He *dealt treacherously* (Acts 7:19; see Ex 1:10), exercising a crafty wisdom that *oppressed* the Jews (compare Acts 7:6; Ex 1:11). He practiced population control through infanticide (Ex 1:16, 22).

Into this situation Moses, a beautiful child, *fair in the sight of God* (NIV mg), was born. From the very start Moses was specially related to God and his purposes. Though hidden for three months, Moses too finally had to be exposed (Acts 7:21; *ektithēmi*, a technical term for infanticide by exposure; compare Philo *De Vita Mosis* 1.12; Diodorus Siculus *Library of History* 2.4.3). But *Pharaoh's daughter took him* (*aneilato*, literally "took

nomadic movements. Jacob then repurchased it in Genesis 33, just as Isaac had to do with wells (21:27-30; 26:26-32). Thus Archer concludes that though this detail is not recorded in Genesis, Stephen undoubtedly was aware of a reliable oral tradition that says Abraham bought a tract of land at Shechem near the oak of Moreh, where he had built an altar when first entering the land (Archer 1982:380).

7:20 The reading in the NIV text, *no ordinary child,* reflects a translation that treats *tō theō* as an idiomatic indicator of a superlative (Haenchen 1971:280), whereas the marginal reading treats the phrase literally. Though *asteios* may also be taken as "acceptable, well-pleasing" (Num 22:32 LXX), in light of other uses of "in the sight of God" in Luke, especially to describe Jesus (Lk 2:52; 24:19), it is probably best to follow the NIV marginal reading here.

up"). This is the verb used in the LXX to explain the derivation of Moses' name: "I drew him out of the water" (Ex 2:10). It is also a technical term for adopting a foundling (*Oxyrhynchus Papyri* 37:6; 38:6).

Pharaoh's daughter reared Moses as her own son. His education produced a man *powerful* in word and deed (compare descriptions of Jesus [Lk 24:19] and Apollos of Alexandria [Acts 18:24]). Moses' training is described in Jewish tradition but not in the Old Testament (Philo *De Vita Mosis* 1.21-24; Josephus *Jewish Antiquities* 2.236; compare Heb 11:25-26). Moses' protestations in Exodus 4:10 do not finally contradict this picture, for they either are Moses' self-interested self-deprecations with little basis in fact (Marshall 1980:140) or point to an early lack of eloquence that he overcame later (Bruce 1990:198).

The lessons for us from Moses' early life echo the lessons from Joseph's: God was, step by step, fulfilling prophecy concerning Israel's sojourn in Egypt. In the time of Moses the Jews experienced the mistreatment God predicted. Yet God was again faithful to his eternal covenant and displayed his power. He used Pharaoh's own daughter to rescue the Hebrew baby boy who would grow up to lead God's people out from under Pharaoh's oppression.

In an abortive bid for liberation, Moses encountered his people's rejection for the first time. Stephen maintains the momentum of a course of events moving to fulfillment. He uses fulfillment terms to speak of Moses' attaining manhood, "completing" *forty years (plēroō,* v. 23; compare 1:16; 3:18; 7:30). The number accords with rabbinic tradition, though the Old Testament is not specific (Strack and Billerbeck 1978:2:679; for example, *Genesis Rabbah* 100:10). At that time it "arose in Moses' heart" (the literal rendering; compare Jer 3:16) *to visit* "his brothers the sons of Israel." He probably intended to show concern and even to help (compare Ex 3:16; 4:31; Lk 1:68; 7:16). Indeed, when he encountered injustice he defended an oppressed Jew and avenged him by slaying the Egyptian oppressor (Ex 2:11/Acts 7:24). He supposed this brave act would be a rallying point for mounting a liberation movement (compare Philo *De Vita Mosis* 1.40-44). Surely his countrymen would understand that by this man, on whom God's hand had rested from birth (Acts 7:20), God would bring them salvation (Lk 1:71; compare terms about Jesus in Lk 19:10; Acts 4:12). But they did not understand, just as

their first-century descendants would not understand the mission of Jesus, the prophet like Moses (Lk 2:50; 18:34—compare Mk 10:34; see Lk 8:10 and Acts 28:26-27/Is 6:9-10; Lk 24:25).

This lack of understanding led to rejection (Ex 2:13-15/Acts 7:26-29). *The next day Moses* attempted to mediate between two Hebrews, and they shoved him aside. Rhetorically, they questioned the source of his authority and his motive—was it to murder, as he had the Egyptian?

At this word Moses banished himself to Midian, a region east of Aqaba in northwest Arabia. He became a *foreigner,* married and had *two sons.* The name of one, Gershom, commemorated Moses' alien status (Ex 2:21-22 LXX). In many ways Acts 7:29 is the climax of the subplot that began at verse 6: with Moses self-exiled as a common criminal, Israel was as far away from salvation as it could get.

As Stephen relates Moses' wilderness and ministry years, he details his call at the burning bush, his work as redeemer of Israel and finally how Israel rebelled against him (vv. 30-34, 35-38, 39-43). When the forty years of Moses' exile were "completed" (*plēroō,* again hinting that the events were a fulfillment of God's sovereign plan; compare vv. 17, 23), *an angel appeared* to him in a flaming bush at Mt. Sinai (compare v. 2; Ex 3:2; Judg 13:20-21). Because of the way in which *angel, the Lord's voice, the Lord* and *God* are used interchangeably in the Exodus account and here (Acts 7:31-33), we should probably understand this as a reverent way of describing a theophany of the transcendent God (Bruce 1988:140; Marshall 1980:141). It is not a reference to an angel "who bears the presence and authority of God himself" (as Kistemaker 1990:258). This vision (a supernatural sight experienced while one is awake or asleep; compare 10:3, 19) of a fiery bush that did not burn up (Ex 3:3) so attracted Moses' attention that he marveled (compare Acts 2:7; 3:12; 4:13) and moved toward it to make careful observation, "to master the mystery" (Bruce 1990:200; compare 11:6).

The Lord's voice came (NIV makes the voice an object of *he heard*), confessing the identity of this supernatural presence (Ex 3:6). By declaring, *I am the God of your fathers, the God of Abraham, Isaac and Jacob,* God told Moses that this revelation was in continuity with prior utterances of covenant promises. Moses' reaction to the spoken revelation, which had begun to interpret the vision, was to tremble and *not dare*

to look. This was indeed the right response to the news that he was standing in the palpable presence of the transcendent God (compare Is 66:1-2, 5).

God gave Moses some immediate instructions and a commission (Acts 7:33-34). "Because" he stood on *holy ground* (NIV does not translate *gar*), out of respect he must remove his sandals (v. 33/Ex 3:5). God prefaced his commission of Moses by revealing his covenant compassion for his people, which he would express in redemptive activity (Ex 3:7-8/Acts 7:34; compare 7:6, 19). Moses could take heart: he was not alone in this enterprise. God had declared his personal stake and role in liberating his suffering people.

This encounter in the desert at Sinai should remind Stephen's audience, Luke's readers and us that wherever God chooses to make himself known, there is holy ground. For a second time outside the Holy Land, God had appeared to a person of his choosing and made known a portion of his covenant promises and saving will. This presents a challenge to first-century Jews, so jealous for "this holy place," the temple, and to all others who cling to certain sacred spaces of their religious heritage.

Here Stephen changes style and begins a "passionate, rhetorically heightened indictment" (Haenchen 1971:282). Four instances of the demonstrative pointing to the redemptive work of "this Moses" occur in as many verses (vv. 35-38). God sent him as *ruler and deliverer* (compare vv. 23-29; 3:15; 5:31; Lk 24:21). The NIV has simple past, but the verb is *apestalken,* "has sent," a perfect tense pointing to the "abiding results of Moses' mission . . . a thought never absent from a Jew's mind" (Bruce 1990:201). Moses *led* the people *out of Egypt* (a key theme in the commission passage—Ex 3:8, 10-12). He did this with signs and wonders, not only in Egypt but also at the Red Sea and in the wilderness during the forty years of wandering (Ex 7—11; 14:21; Num 14:22).

7:35 The NIV introduces the phrase *by God himself,* which is not in the Greek but properly interprets the reference to the angel. Stephen is displaying his customary reserve in describing the intervention of the transcendent God in history. Exodus contains promises of both God's presence with Moses (Ex 3:12) and the angel of God's presence going before him (32:34; 33:2).

7:36 The NIV marginal reading, *that is, Sea of Reeds,* though it reflects a widely accepted literal rendering of the Heb *yam-sûp,* is misleading for two reasons. The Greek is clearly

Stephen now makes a direct connection between Moses and the Messiah by quoting the "prophet like Moses" prophecy (Acts 7:37/Deut 18:15; compare Acts 3:22-23 and the Jewish eschatological hope, 4QTestim; *Targum of Exodus* 12:42; *Ruth Rabbah* 5:6; *Pesiqta Rabbati* 15:10). The main parallel Stephen draws between Jesus and Moses, however, is their mistreatment and rejection by Israel (7:23-29, 39, 51-52). This becomes a powerful argument for the legitimacy of Jesus' messianic claims.

Just as rejection of Moses led to false worship and constant breaking of the law, so continued rejection of Jesus, the "prophet like Moses," will mean that the Jews will never be freed of their false worship (the idolizing of the temple) and false piety (the keeping of man-made customs; vv. 39-41, 53).

But Stephen is not finished with his own honoring of Moses. He was *in the assembly* (*ekklēsia,* pointing to the "day of assembly" when the people gathered to receive the law, Deut 4:10; 9:10; 18:16—though a Christian will hardly miss a possible allusion to the church). He served as a mediator between the angel and the people (NIV obscures this with a rearrangement of phrases) when on Mt. Sinai he received the living oracles to give to the Jews. The New Testament and Jewish tradition speak of the law as given through or in the presence of angels (Acts 7:53; Gal 3:19; Heb 2:2; Deut 33:2 LXX; *Pesiqta Rabbati* 21:7; Strack and Billerbeck 1978:3:554-56). The angel here, however, is probably another respectful circumlocution for the transcendent God present with human beings (compare Acts 7:30, 35). The law is "living oracles" not in the sense of giving life (as Krodel 1986:147) but in the sense of being Israel's very life (Deut 30:19-20; 32:46-47). By following the law, they would be able to live their earthly life to its fullest extent (Kistemaker 1990:262). With these words Stephen shows that the charge of blasphemer against Moses, the law and the customs handed down by Moses (Acts 6:11, 13-14) is baseless.

"Red Sea" *(Erythra Thalassē).* When all the occurrences of the phrase in the Old Testament are taken into account, the literal meaning of the Hebrew is unclear. The phrase is used to refer to the Gulf of Aqaba and the Gulf of Suez, two arms of the Red Sea (Num 14:25; Ex 10:19). In the account of the exodus crossing (Ex 13:18; 15:4) it also probably refers to a body of water directly linked to the Red Sea. "In sum, it is likely that the Israelites crossed not the 'Reed Sea' but the 'Red Sea,' specifically the southern end of the Bitter Lakes or the northern end of the Gulf of Suez" (R. L. Hubbard 1988:60).

Now Stephen comes to the people's rebellion against Moses and God's response (7:39-41, 42-43). The people rejected Moses' leadership (compare v. 27), and their heart's disposition was to live as though they were still in pagan Egypt (Ex 13:17; compare later Num 14:3-4). They adopted an empirical approach to their circumstances. Since they did not "see" Moses anymore, they demanded that an idol be their tangible spiritual leader.

Almost automatically, rejection of divinely sent leadership and of God's message issues in idol making. And so today, whenever the guidance of Scripture is set aside, humans will idolize the "wisdom" from some human source. Gurus, imams, priests and shamans guide us in our world of religious effort. Articulate professors, feisty talk-show hosts and charismatic movie stars become our moral and spiritual compasses in a secular world.

Idol making necessarily leads to idol worship. This Israel entered into with gusto, rejoicing in *what their hands had made* (Acts 7:41/Ex 32:4-6; compare Acts 17:24-25, 29). This last phrase will be central to Stephen's indictment of his audience (7:48-51). The first-century Jew's veneration of the temple was the same to God as worship of the golden calf.

God's punishment of the Israelites was to turn away from them and hand them over to the consequences of their sin (compare Rom 1:24, 26). He handed them over to the worship of (contrast Acts 7:7) the powers behind the idols, the host of heaven, those evil spiritual forces ever in mortal combat with God (1 Cor 10:20; Eph 6:10-13). That Israel practiced idolatry in the wilderness, even star worship of the type Stephen goes on to describe, is documented by the Pentateuch and the

---

7:42-43 The LXX and the New Testament correctly understand that the question expects a negative answer. The question about sacrifice to God in the wilderness does not assume either that there was exemplary worship without sacrifice in the wilderness (as Krodel 1986:148) or that there was sacrifice that included both the act and heart obedience (as Marshall 1980:145). Rather, in an indictment against unacceptable worship Amos points out the wilderness practice, which on the whole neglected sacrifice to God and replaced it with idolatry.

As the marginal readings of the NIV at Amos 5:26 show, there is some disagreement over how to best translate the reference to the foreign gods, given the Hebrew text and its LXX rendering. *Shrine of Molech* is an allowable rendering of *sikût malkᵉkem*, especially since Rylke Borger has shown that the cuneiform literature provides no support for "Sakkut" as the name of a deity (1988:81). Archer's explanation of the LXX rendering *Hraiphan* for

prophets (Lev 18:21; 20:2-5; Deut 4:19; Ezek 20:10-26; Hos 9:10). Stephen characterizes the sin by quoting Amos 5:25-27. *Molech* of the Ammonites was known as Venus' star. *Rephan* follows the LXX rendering of "Kaiwan," the Babylonian name for Saturn (E. F. Harrison 1986:132; Longenecker 1981:316-317). Amos details the further judgment God metes out: exile, the ultimate curse for covenant disobedience, removal from the enjoyment of the Promised Land.

Provision for Worship; God's Transcendence (7:44-50) Stephen abruptly, yet most appropriately, turns his audience's attention to *the tabernacle of the Testimony.* In the book of Exodus the golden calf incident intervenes between the giving of instructions about the tabernacle and its construction (Ex 25—27; 32—33; 36—38). In fact, Stephen develops a strong contrast between the idolatry condemned by Amos— *the shrine [skēnē] of Molech* and *the idols (typous)*—and *the tabernacle [skēnē] of the Testimony* constructed according to the *pattern (typon)* God gave Moses (Acts 7:43, 44). *The tabernacle of the Testimony* was God's provision of a structure for true worship. It contained the ark of testimony, a box holding the ten commandments written on stone (see Ex 25:10, 16, 21-22).

Again God took the initiative in revealing how he was to be approached. He enabled the Israelites to take the tent into the land under Joshua's leadership. God created a safe environment for his worship by expelling the nations already in Canaan (see Josh 23:9; 24:18). The promise made to Abraham so many generations before thus came true, and was maintained even until the days of David (Acts 7:7).

Like Joseph, David found favor in God's sight (compare v. 9; 13:22;

---

kiyyûn, sourced in the similarity of appearance of certain letters in the Aramaic alphabet of the Elephantine colony of the fifth century B.C., is helpful (Archer and Chirichigno 1983:151). It shows that a mistranslation of meaning is not necessarily present.

The NIV stops the quotation just before the word "Babylon," probably because the editors saw the discrepancy with Amos, which reads "Damascus," as an indication that Stephen is no longer directly quoting and has applied the concept of exile to the final deporting of Judah. Reasons have been offered for Stephen's introduction of this change—accommodation to a postexilic audience located in Judah, Luke's stage-managing to balance exile into Mesopotamia (Babylon) with the call out of Mesopotamia (7:4; Richard 1982:42)—the problem still awaits a resolution that shows Stephen's and Luke's use respects the original Old Testament context.

1 Sam 13:14). He asked that he might find a *dwelling place (skēnōma)* for *the house of Jacob* (NIV mg). *Skēnōma* is an ambiguous term, so it is difficult to know whether Stephen intends David to speak of the tabernacle or of the temple (Marshall 1980:146). From the Old Testament accounts, however, we know that David desired to prepare a more permanent structure (2 Sam 7:2-16; 1 Chron 17:1-14).

If God had granted David's request, God's covenant dynamic would have been violated, for this transcendent, sovereign God always takes the initiative and makes all the provisions for worship. God denied David's request but promised him that his son Solomon would build a house for him (2 Sam 7:11-16) and that God would establish Solomon's house.

Stephen qualifies and completes this thought with a slight break as he announces, *But it was Solomon who built the house for him* (Acts 7:47). He then immediately introduces a strongly contrasting thesis: *However, the Most High does not live in houses made by men.* This assertion that the transcendent God (compare Lk 2:14; 19:38) is not confined to things "made with human hands" would have jolted his hearers. The Jews commonly used "made with human hands" to refer to idol worship (*Sibylline Oracles* 14:62; Is 31:7; Wisdom of Solomon 14:8). To apply this phrase to the temple could well enrage them.

But Stephen's thinking is biblical, as the subsequent Old Testament quote shows (Is 66:1-2/Acts 7:49-50; compare 1 Kings 8:27). God's transcendence and role as Creator of all demonstrate his self-sufficiency. He can never be finally dependent on humans, not even if they build him a temple (Acts 17:24-25).

If this is Stephen's point, we need not conclude that in the process he rejects the temple itself as apostasy (Haenchen 1971:285) or as inappropriate for the pilgrim people of God (Bruce 1990:206). And he does not balance his negative statement with a positive one, so that we know what replaces the temple. God's transcendence, his reign in heaven above, as Stephen will shortly see and testify to, must be the controlling perspective for any proper use of a house of worship (7:55-56; Sylva

---

7:46 The NIV margin says "Some early manuscripts *the house of Jacob.*" Internal evidence—the flow of thought (Kistemaker 1990:270)—favors *God* to such an extent that the other reading seems not simply more difficult but, in the minds of some, nonsensical and therefore probably a primitive corruption (Longenecker 1981:347). Still, external evi-

1987; 1 Kings 8:17-20, 27-53).

Stephen has effectively answered the second charge, that he speaks blasphemy against "God" and "this holy place" (Acts 6:11, 13). In so doing he identifies the real blasphemers: anyone who so venerates the temple that it ceases to be a place where the transcendent God is glorified and becomes a place where self-glorying men take pride in what they have done for God.

Today too the church may face the temptation of an "edifice complex," assuming that unless a visible structure for the worship of God is raised and maintained, we haven't truly worshiped or borne an effective witness. Stephen gives us perspective. Remember, it is the transcendent God we are worshiping. He does not need our buildings to receive our praise. *We* may need them to facilitate worship and witness. But we must make sure we need them and use them for the right reason.

Indictment: Present Rebellion and Lawlessness (7:51-53) Stephen's indictment works from the inside out. The Jews are *stiff-necked,* unwilling to bow to authority (compare Ex 33:3, 5; 34:9, in the context of the idolatrous worship of the golden calf; Acts 7:39-41). Their resistance is not to human beings but to God *the Holy Spirit* (Is 63:9-10). They have never truly come into a saving covenant relationship with God, for though outwardly circumcised and proud of their ethnic-religious heritage, they are *uncircumcised* in their *hearts* (Lev 26:41; Jer 9:26). In their disposition toward God they do not differ from pagans, who refuse the sign of the covenant. They have *ears* that spiritually do not hear. It is as though they were covered with uncircumcised foreskin (Jer 6:10). This unrepentant, unregenerate condition is the same as that of their *fathers* (compare Acts 7:39).

Their ancestors' rebellion issued in persecution of God's messengers, the prophets (2 Chron 36:16; Lk 6:23; 11:49; 13:34). They even killed those who proclaimed *the coming of the Righteous One,* the Messiah (see Acts 3:14). And this generation has proceeded further. They have betrayed and murdered the Messiah himself (Lk 9:44; 18:32; 22:4, 6; 24:7;

---

dence—major Alexandrian and Western witnesses, together with a similar thought in the Qumran literature (1QS 9:3-6)—persuades me that the more difficult marginal reading *house of Jacob* should be adopted as the original (see Metzger 1971:351-53). The potential influence of Psalm 132(131):5 on the other reading should not be overlooked.

Acts 3:14). Thus they stood condemned of the very charges they level against Stephen. By doing away with the Lord's anointed, God's one provision of salvation, they have shown themselves to be truly against him and his presence. They are also against Moses' *law,* altering its authority through selective obedience (Ex 20:13, 16). In fact, they leave their man-made traditions, "customs handed over by Moses," intact, even if it means violating the plain command of the law (Mt 15:3-6). Yes, they received the law at the direction of *angels* (probably a circumlocution for God; see Acts 7:38), yet they have not kept this divinely given standard.

Religious performance fueled by fear or pride is an obstacle to the true knowledge of God's provision of salvation. But more, it sets itself in competition with worship of the one true God by raising up idols. In the end it will wage war on true worship. What dangers do the religious find themselves in, far from God's covenant provisions for a saving relationship through the only mediator, Messiah Jesus! And by and large they are blind to it.

Stephen's Martyrdom (7:54—8:3)

Justin Martyr, beheaded for the faith in A.D. 165 said, "The more we are persecuted, the more do others in ever increasing numbers embrace the faith and become worshippers of God through the name of Jesus" (*Dialogue with Trypho* 110). Contrast the impact of modern-day martyrs for other causes. Who remembers what Che Guevara stood for? Luke's account of Stephen's death helps us understand the effect dying for the gospel has, and in so doing challenges us to accept its truth claims.

Stephen's stoning climaxes his witness and introduces an important turning point in the witness of the Hellenistic Jewish Christians of Jerusalem. The intensity and scope of persecution and the extent of witness both take quantum leaps.

Stephen's Accusers Respond with Rage (7:54) Stephen's indict-

---

7:56 The significance of *standing* versus "sitting" at God's right hand (compare Ps 110:1) should not be sought in the posture. It is not a sign that Jesus stands to worship as the angels do or to welcome the martyr Stephen. He is not coming to Stephen in a personal parousia, or serving as his advocate, confessing his name before the Father (many commentators prefer this—for example, Schneider 1980-1982:1:475; Bruce 1990:210; Marshall 1980:149;

ment (7:51-53) so penetrates "uncircumcised hearts" that the Sanhedrin is *furious* (literally "sawn through in their hearts"; compare 5:33). They are "torn up" not with repentant sorrow for their sins but with seething anger against the preacher of repentance. They grind their teeth with such a hissing sound, such a hateful screwing of the mouth, that Stephen knows they have but one aim: to do away with him (compare Ps 34:16 LXX; 36:12 LXX). As we have seen before, when faced with the truth those in error will either accept the message or seek to silence the messenger, even permanently (Acts 4:18; 5:28, 40).

Stephen's Execution (7:55-58) One man *full of the Holy Spirit* faces a gallery of men full of hate. Luke is not describing a special momentary gifting in Stephen (as Haenchen 1971:292; Bruce 1990:240), but the fitting climax of a life in the Spirit (6:5, 8, 15; Williams 1985:132). The gallery concentrates on him; Stephen gazes into heaven (*atenizō* is stronger than the NIV *looked up to;* compare 1:10; 3:4, 12; 6:15). God grants that Stephen may peer into heaven itself with his mind's eye and see *the glory of God* (either a circumlocution for God the Father or the shekinah glory that both conceals and reveals the divine presence and nature; compare 7:2; 22:11).

This vision positively culminates the climactic thesis of Stephen's sermon: God dwells in heaven, not in temples made with hands (7:48-50). *The Son of Man standing at the right hand of God* is at the center of Stephen's attention and the heart of his confession. *Son of Man,* a phrase otherwise present primarily on the lips of Jesus during his earthly ministry, points at once to Jesus' incarnation, saving death and resurrection, and heavenly exaltation, universal dominion, and glorious future reign (Mt 8:20; Lk 9:22, 44; 18:31; 19:10; 21:27, 36; 22:69/Dan 7:13; Ps 110:1). When we think of the title against its background (Dan 7), the divine nature of this figure comes to the fore.

By this confession Stephen and Luke invite us to see Jesus for who he really is, and in that vision to recognize him as worthy of worship, of

---

Lk 12:8). He is not acting as judge, or overseeing an interim in salvation history before the church age, with its Gentile mission, truly dawns (Longenecker 1981:350). Rather, it is a matter not of posture but of position (compare Acts 7:33; Richard 1978:295). Stephen is emphatically confessing Jesus' transcendent place in heaven.

complete devotion and obedience even to death.

The Sanhedrin will have none of this "Jesus worship." To them it is a blasphemy (Mk 14:61-64) that their loud yells must drown out and their hands must prevent from entering their ears (Strack and Billerbeck [1978:2:684] relate the rabbinic teaching on such a pious duty). And what a perfect picture of their spiritual deafness, these who are "uncircumcised in ear" and refuse to take that essential first step to salvation—having ears to hear God's message (7:51; Lk 4:21; 8:8; 9:44; 14:35; Acts 28:27/Is 6:10).

Like a herd of stampeding animals (compare Lk 8:33), yet intent on one purpose (NIV *all*), they rush together against Stephen, drag him out of the city and begin to stone him. Throwing him down from a high place, they gather and heave paving stones on top of him until death comes. These are the appropriate punishment, place and executioners (the witnesses) for the sin of blasphemy (Lev 24:14; Deut 17:7; *m. Sanhedrin* 6:1, 4; 7:4).

In an extraneous note indicating the custodian of the witness-executioners' cloaks Luke introduces us to *a young man named Saul.* He will figure prominently in the advance of the church in the near and long term (Acts 8:3; chaps. 9, 13—28).

When we reflect on how quickly a dignified high court was transformed into a lynch mob, we see how thin can be the veneer of civility and judicial order in society. This is especially true when those opposing God's truth see themselves as guardians of his message. There is nothing to stop their violence, as Stephen and many martyrs in his train have learned.

Stephen Dies Peacefully (7:59—8:1) Jewish custom prescribed that the condemned be given opportunity to confess his sins on his way to execution so that he might have "a share in the world to come" (*m. Sanhedrin* 6:2). Stephen's declarations reveal his innocence and his

---

7:58 Stephen's death is a true execution after a Jewish trial. As a rule, the death penalty could be carried out only with the approval of the Roman governor, but here it is not necessarily the case either that the incident occurred in an interregnum between governors (E. F. Harrison 1986:137) or that Pilate was lax in administration at the end of his tenure (Williams 1985:134). Rather, the Jews had a special dispensation when it came to violations concerning the temple. They could execute a death sentence without prior Roman permission (Josephus *Jewish Wars* 6.126; Bruce 1988:159).

Meanwhile masks the fact that the witnesses were the first executioners in the stoning

Christian grace to those who have wronged him. In prayer he calls on Jesus to take him into his presence at death (compare Acts 2:21). He echoes his Lord's words of confident trust on the cross and again confesses Jesus' divinity (compare Lk 23:46/Ps 31:5). Having used *Lord* very sparingly in his sermon (Acts 7:31, 33, 49), now without hesitation he addresses *Lord Jesus* with the most important petition any human can bring to God. He is answered, and so can we be, for the Lord Jesus stands at God's right hand, ever ready to receive us to be with him in glory at the time his sovereign will has ordained (Lk 23:43).

Whether falling under the weight of a paving stone hurled from above or deliberately kneeling in prayer, Stephen cries out with a loud voice (contrast Acts 7:57), asking that Jesus not "establish the sins" of his executioners (Rom 10:3; compare Lk 23:34). How will this happen? If they will hear and receive the good news (24:47; Acts 2:38; 3:19; 5:31; 10:43), then their sins will be forgiven, and they will not have to face the final punishment for a sin standing against them.

Is Stephen's prayer answered? Augustine said, "The Church owes Paul to the prayer of Stephen" (quoted in Barclay 1976:62). In fact, Saul is the one adversary named in the incident. Luke is laying the groundwork for the great victory God will win through Saul's conversion and subsequent missionary service.

Like his Lord, Stephen dies at peace with God, himself and the world—even his enemies. *He fell asleep.* By showing us how to die, he also shows us how to live and models the secret of staying power of Christian witness even to death. If he can die for his Lord like that, confidently, forgiving his enemies, there must be something to this Jesus who he says reigns at God's right hand.

Persecution and the Church's Advance (8:1-3) In what may be a reverse parallelism, Luke concludes Stephen's martyrdom with the twin

---

procedure (*m. Sanhedrin* 6:4).

The *young man named Saul* could have been anywhere from twenty-four to forty years old (Josephus *Jewish Antiquities* 18.197; Longenecker 1981:352). This age range is suitable for both presence at the stoning and involvement in the subsequent persecution. Galatians 1:22 does not contradict Acts 8:3, for when the Galatians text is considered in the light of the verse that follows, one can see that the ignorance of the Christians was not of Paul the persecutor but of Paul the Christian (Krodel 1986:154).

themes of persecution and the church's further advance. The hinge phrase on which they turn is *except the apostles*. Whether because Hellenistic, not Hebraic, Jewish Christians are targeted in the persecution or because the apostles feel a duty to hold things together at Jerusalem, they stay there. Their continued presence in Jerusalem certainly does provide stability and continuity for the young church's life and mission. There is no hint from Luke that their lack of initiative at this point is disobedience to Acts 1:8.

From this apostolic center the centrifugal forces of persecution and ever-expanding witness push out. The main impetus is a great persecution against *the church at Jerusalem*. It is closely connected with Stephen's death, for it happens *on that day*. Persecution—"harassing somebody in order to persuade or force him to give up his religion, or simply to attack somebody for religious reasons"—encompassed a wide range of activities from ridicule to social ostracism to occasional beatings to confiscation of property to imprisonment to execution (Marshall 1980:151; Krodel 1986:158). Saul "tried" (attempted, not incipient, action as NIV; E. F. Harrison 1986:140; Gal 1:13, 23) *to destroy the church*, as a wild animal mangles its prey (Lake and Cadbury 1979:88; compare Acts 20:28; Is 65:25). He goes *from house to house* and drags both *men and women* off to prison. This imagery and these actions give us a sense of the severity of the persecution.

But the dispersion through persecution creates a band of missionaries, not refugees. All are scattered, as seed is sown, and go about evangelizing (Acts 8:4; compare Lk 8:5, 11). Judea and Samaria, the second two theaters for the Great Commission's fulfillment, have now been entered. A Christian witness is raised in Jerusalem even after Stephen's death. Devout men, whether non-Christian Jews (E. F. Harrison 1986:139; compare 2:7) or Hebraic Christian (Williams 1985:136), bury Stephen and publicly mourn him (NIV does not point out the public aspect with its wording *mourned deeply*). This is a courageous witness to Stephen's innocence, for Jewish custom forbade public mourning of one executed for blasphemy (*m. Sanhedrin* 6:5-6).

Indeed, "the blood of martyrs is the seed of the church." And today the same dynamic is at work, whether in China since the coming of communism or in Uganda and East Africa with their political turmoil or

in the previously predominant religious hostility of Latin America. The fruit of witness under persecution, even martyrdom, is now being harvested. The gospel born by Spirit-filled Christians is life. Death cannot stop it!

Samaria Responds to the Gospel (8:4-25)

The tarot cards of psychic readers, the crystals of New Age devotees and the amulets of a witch doctor are common in many societies today. Many are following magic to find the power to cope with life.

As the church advances across another cultural threshold, from Hellenistic Jew to half-breed Samaritan (compare Acts 1:8—"in all Judea and Samaria"), it encounters a society steeped in occult magic and syncretistic religious practice. It learns through its missionaries, who must also be theologians, that the power of the gospel is not magic and cannot be bought. In the process it discovers again the true power of the gospel.

The Gospel's Power Is Superior to Magic (8:5-13) Philip, another member of the seven (6:5), undertakes a mission to Samaria. Was the Samaritan city he evangelized Gitta—Simon Magus's home according to Justin Martyr, who himself hailed from the region *(Apology* 1.26)—or Samaria's religious center, Shechem—which was also the site of some of John the Baptist's and Jesus' ministry (Jn 3:23; 4:4-42; Bruce 1988:165; Lake and Cadbury 1979:89)? Luke does not tell us.

The syncretism and the mixed race of the post-Assyrian-exile Samaritans (2 Kings 17:24-41), together with the reciprocal reprisals against both Mt. Gerizim and Jerusalem worship centers in intertestamental times (Josephus *Jewish Antiquities* 13.255-58; 18.29), so heightened prejudice and animosity between Jew and Samaritan that the best that could be said for their relations in the first century was "Jews do not associate with Samaritans" (Jn 4:9).

Instead of the Davidic Messiah, the Samaritans looked forward to the coming of the *tāhēḇ*, "the restorer" (Deut 18:18), a herald of the last day—a day of final judgment, of vengeance and reward, when the temple of Gerizim would be restored, the sacrifices reinstated and the heathen converted (R. T. Anderson 1988:307). What Theophilus and we know about Samaritans from Luke's writings is a mixed picture that on balance is positive (Lk 9:52-56; 10:29-37; 17:11-19).

Philip "preaches" (4:18-19/Is 61:1-2; Lk 24:47) the Christ in whose

person the kingdom of God has come and by whose name it spreads. God accompanies this announcement with *signs* of healing (compare Acts 4:16, 22, 30; 5:12; 6:8; interestingly, *signs* are mentioned only two more times in Acts at 14:3; 15:12). In enemy territory, where false worship is practiced, it is not surprising that one encounters the spiritual powers behind such worship: *evil spirits* (NIV puts the literal rendering, *unclean,* in the margin; they are ritually unclean and make those whom they possess ritually unclean).

God in his mercy does signs of his kingdom's advance in syncretistic Samaria, granting release through the herald of his liberating gospel. And tokens of the coming messianic age appear as well, when Philip heals the paralyzed and the lame (Is 35:3, 6; compare Lk 7:22; 5:24-25; Acts 9:33-34). No wonder the people *paid close attention* (*prosechō* may even have the sense "to attend to, i.e., to believe and act on"—compare 16:14—Lake and Cadbury 1979:89; but Haenchen 1971:302 doubts it).

And there is much joy (8:8; compare 8:39; 13:48, 52). They have been looking for a *tābēb,* "restorer," who will herald the day; now they meet a herald who preaches that the restorer has already come and signs of that restoration can be experienced even now.

The nature of this first-time advance of the gospel across the cultural threshold to Samaria may primarily account for the signs' presence. But the fact that Philip faces a situation of spiritual encounter not unlike what pioneer church planters among unreached peoples face today should encourage us to expect the powerful working of the gospel in these situations as well.

Simon is described by Luke as practicing magical arts with the effect that the whole population of Samaria, regardless of social standing, has been for a long time held in his sway, completely astonished at his power (8:9, 11; compare 2:7, 12; Philo *De Specialibus Legibus* 3.100-103;

8:9 Simon the sorcerer is probably identical with the alleged founder of a Gnostic heresy (Justin Martyr *Apology* 1.26, 56; Irenaeus *Against the Heresies* 1.23; Hippolytus *Refutation of all Heresies* 6.2, 4-15; R. T. Anderson 1988:304; Meeks 1977; R. M. Wilson 1979). The scholarly consensus (Meeks 1977) says Luke describes Simon as a magician, a Gnostic only in the wider and vaguer sense of *gnōsis.* The assertion that he taught the Gnostic doctrines of the Simonian sect is probably traceable to his later followers or to heresiologists (R. M. Wilson 1979:491). Lüdemann (1987) seeks in the confession (Acts 8:10) and the use of *epinoia* (8:22) evidence of incipient Gnostic thought.

Plato *Laws* 909A-B; Josephus *Jewish Antiquities* 20.142; Delling 1967:356-59). Simon capitalized on their attention and presented himself as the embodiment of the occult power. He received praise as if he were an angelic or divine supernatural being: "This is the power of God, [the power] that is called 'Great' " (NIV has smoothed over the syntax but in the process has altered the second title).

The Samaritans believe the gospel of the reign of God in the powerful name of Jesus and are baptized. Simon believes, is baptized and devotes himself to Philip. The one who amazed the Samaritans (8:9, 11) is now himself continually amazed at Philip's signs and great miracles (compare the title in 8:10).

And today when God chooses to do signs and wonders through his servants as his church advances, the immediate "quantitative" effect, amazement, may be expressed in outward profession of belief and even baptism. But if the signs and wonders, when combined with the Spirit-empowered preaching of the word of salvation, do not have a "qualitative" effect, regeneration, then the convert will adopt a syncretized Christianity. Jesus will be no more than a magical name, though the most powerful one. What makes the difference is repentance from a magical mindset through an affirmation of the sovereign power of God, who grants salvation blessings when and where he will. We must affirm that it is not the power of miracle, so easily seen in our unregenerate mindset as magic, that saves us, but the power of the Word of God which by the Spirit we receive, believe and follow and so are liberated (Krodel 1986:165; Lk 16:29-31; Jn 2:23-25).

The Gospel's Power Includes All and Cannot Be Bought (8:14-25) News reaches the apostles in Jerusalem that Samaria has *accepted the word of God* (compare Lk 8:13; Acts 11:1; 17:11). The apostles send two of their number, Peter and John, to Samaria. When they arrive, they

---

8:10 *This man is the divine power known as the Great Power* (literally, "this is the power of God, the power that is called 'Great' ") may be read either as an explicit claim to deity— *chilah rabbah* is a favorite divine designation in the Samaritan Targum traditions (Coggins 1982:430)—or a claim to be a subordinate heavenly being, "Grand Vizier of God Almighty" (De Zwaan 1979:58). Both could be having their effect on a half-breed Samaritan audience.

Though it is commonplace to take "of God" as Luke's insertion for clarification (Marshall 1980:155; compare Lk 22:69), it makes good sense as part of the original confession if one sees that the Samaritans make this confession within a monotheistic framework.

discover that the gift of the Holy Spirit has not been given. They immediately pray to the Lord (compare Lk 11:13) that the Spirit may fall on the Samaritan believers. As they lay hands on them, the Samaritan believers receive the Holy Spirit.

The clear teaching of the apostles and their customary practice is that the giving of the Spirit is a birthright of every Christian, received at conversion (Acts 2:38; 1 Cor 12:3, 13). Acts gives no consistent pattern for a second-stage giving of the Spirit by apostolic laying on of hands, as Roman and Anglo Catholic teaching on confirmation would assert, or with extraordinary manifestations such as prophesying and speaking in tongues, as Pentecostal and charismatic teaching on baptism with the Spirit would contend (Acts 8:14-17; 10:44-48; 16:31-34; 19:1-6). Therefore the Samaria experience must be viewed as extraordinary, not normative.

But why does God sovereignly delay the coming of the Spirit in this case? In order to preserve the unity of the church and the integrity of the church's crosscultural mission to all nations in the face of the inbred animosity between Jew and Samaritan. If God had not withheld his Spirit until the Jerusalem apostles came, converts on both sides of the cultural barrier might have found Christ without finding each other. Neither Samaritan nor Jewish Christians would have been assured that the Samaritans were truly regenerate and the spiritual equals of regenerate Jews (compare Acts 15:8-11). What Luke teaches us, then, is that the unity of the church and the unhindered advance of its mission into all cultures is so important to God that he will delay giving to a converted people what is their birthright, the salvation blessing of the Spirit, in order to ensure that these realities will be fully preserved. So the church today

8:14 Instead of assuming that Luke is representing the whole region as acting in a Christian manner, though represented by only one or two congregations (Longenecker 1981:358; compare Rom 15:26; 2 Cor 9:2), we should see his words as pointing to the qualitative fact that Samaritans have now received the gospel.

8:16 See John Stott's thorough discussion (1990:151-59) of the normativeness of the Samaria experience of the Spirit. Not only does he speak to Anglican and Roman Catholic, Pentecostal and charismatic concerns, he also critiques the explanations of some who hold to a one-stage giving of the Spirit: James D. G. Dunn's defective gospel-presentation approach (1970:63-68) and the Reformed understanding that what is given is not the regenerating Spirit but extraordinary graces of the Spirit, charismatic manifestations (Calvin 1965:236; compare Kistemaker 1990:301). Luke supports neither explanation, and the

should deal with the matter of the Spirit's coming from the same stand-point.

When Simon sees the technique and the office involved in the grant-ing of the Spirit, he makes a syncretizing request. He brings the apostles money and asks for "authority" (NIV is less exact with *ability)* to grant the Holy Spirit to whomever he lays hands on. What Simon is seeking to purchase is an office, a priesthood subordinate to that of the apostles. Purchasing a priesthood was not uncommon in the ancient world, even in Israel (Suppl. Epigr. Gr. IV 516B[35-36], cited in Derrett 1982:61; 2 Mac-cabees 4:7-10). It reflects the typically idolatrous and pagan understand-ing of the way to acquire supernatural power that one would then con-trol (Derrett 1982:61-63).

Peter's condemnatory reply tells Simon the truth about what God thinks of his request and what that request reveals about Simon's spir-itual condition. In a "curse formula," ironically similar to those found in pagan magical papyri (Haenchen 1971:304), Peter places both Simon and his money under a ban, consigning both to eternal destruction (compare Josh 6:17-18; 7:13-15). His rationale is Simon's presumption that he could obtain the gift of God through money (compare Acts 2:38; 10:45; 11:17). To pay money for God's power violates its essential nature as the gift of a sovereign God who always has the receiver in his control and is not controlled by any human (Derrett 1982:62). But worse, such an approach reveals one has not left the "authority of Satan" (see 26:18).

Peter declares Simon unregenerate. He has no *part or share.* For Luke this can refer to either salvation (26:18) or ministry (1:17). Peter's further references to a *heart . . . not right before God* (8:21) and being *full of bitterness and captive to sin* (8:23), as well as his call to repentance

---

answer must be found in the unique salvation-history position of the initial Samaritan mission and the historic enmity between Jew and Samaritan.

The NIV marginal note is misleading; *eis* is not necessarily the equivalent of *en* here but points to a commercial or cultic context in which the phrase would mean "The one who is baptized becomes the possession of and comes under the protection of the one whose name he bears; he is under the control of the effective power of the name and the One who bears the name, i.e., he is dedicated to them" (Bauer, Gingrich and Danker 1979: s.v. ὄνομα).

Bruce (1988:168) proposes that the baptism was into the name of the Lord Jesus rather than in the trinitarian formula.

(8:22), which the early church normally addresses to the unregenerate (Lk 24:47; Acts 2:38; 3:19; 17:30; 26:20), and the earlier mention of destruction (8:20), all support the view that Simon is not regenerate.

Peter's remedy is repentance from the wicked disposition and the evil stratagem it generated. Simon must pray to the Lord for release—forgiveness—of the sin that now holds him in bondage to unrighteousness (compare Is 58:6, 9). His continuing syncretizing thought, which is no different from continued participation in idolatrous false worship, can issue in no other result than the bitter fruit of final destruction (Deut 29:18).

The uncertainty in Peter's promise of forgiveness is based not on doubts about God's ability but on a recognition of Simon's current disposition of heart. Simon's request was so presumptuous that to promise certain forgiveness would allow him to continue in the mindset that God's free grace is indeed cheap grace. Simon's repentance must cast him totally on the mercy of God. He must not even presume to immediately appropriate God's promised forgiveness to himself. Peter may also be warning Simon of the seriousness of his lost condition. Humanly speaking, there is no way that he can, and therefore that he necessarily will, extricate himself from this captivity to sin.

It is uncertain whether Simon's request for the apostles' intercession is a sign of true repentance. Is he sensing the seriousness of the sin and asking the apostles to join in intercession? In humility does he feel so incapable of praying or so distrustful of his own prayers that he must ask for the intercession of others? Or do the content of his request—to be spared the consequences of his sin—and the very fact that he asks others to intercede indicate that here is remorse and not true repentance (Williams 1985:143)? What is clear is that the apostles conclude their mission to Samaria with the preaching of the gospel, including a warning about the consequences of not embracing the gospel wholeheartedly (compare Acts 2:40; 10:42).

In our day some nominal Christians have syncretized their faith with

---

8:21 NIV translates *logos* (matter) as *ministry*, which some opt for (Barrett 1979:294; Kistemaker 1990:305), while the majority see it as referring to salvation (Haenchen 1971:305; Marshall 1980:159; Krodel 1986:165). Bruce (1990:222) suggests we see the Jewish concept of "portion in the age to come" (*m. Sanhedrin* 10:1-4).

cultural religious ways. They may be Christopagans in Two-Thirds World traditional societies or practitioners of Western spirituality accommodating consciously or unconsciously to postmodern New Age thinking. Like Simon, they must realize the seriousness of their condition. Those who think they have "the best of both worlds" must repent, or in the age to come they will experience the worst of all possible worlds.

Philip and the Ethiopian Eunuch (8:26-40)

We are fascinated by missionary tales of "chance" encounters. Along a lonely road in the African bush, a man suddenly appears and asks a missionary traveler, "Can you tell me who Jesus is?" Luke's account of Philip's divinely guided encounter with the Ethiopian would have been just as fascinating to first-century Romans or Greeks, for in their view Ethiopians lived literally at the southern edge of the earth (Homer *Odyssey* 1.23—*eschatoi andrōn;* see Acts 1:8).

God is actively fulfilling his purposes for the scope of the church's mission (Lk 24:47; Acts 1:8). If it reaches an Ethiopian so soon after its beginning, Theophilus can know for sure that the gospel that is to be preached among all the nations is true. It *is* for him, and for us too.

This scene is a fitting climax to the Grecian Jewish Christians' mission thrust, for here they complete the geographical aspects of the Acts 1:8 commission: Jerusalem (6:8-8:3), Judea and Samaria (8:4-25) and the ends of the earth (8:26-40). Further, it is a harbinger of the full-fledged Gentile mission to come (Acts 13—28).

An Evangelist Guided by God (8:26-31) Through his angel, God takes the initiative and directs Philip to take the road *from Jerusalem to Gaza.* The phrase translated *south (kata mesēmbrian)* may also be taken temporally, "at noon" (so regularly in the LXX). This would make the command all the more unusual, for few travelers would be on the road in the harsh midday sun. *Desert road* might be better translated "wilderness road." This fits the topography of the northern route from Jerusalem to Gaza, which was paved (suitable for a carriage), was more direct and

---

8:23 The phrase *full of bitterness* does not point to Simon's evil effect in the church (as Williams 1985:143) or a bitter attitude that he imparts to others (as Kistemaker 1990:306). Rather, the phrase taken as a whole as a Hebraic genitive, "bitter gall," points to the consequences in punishment for such a life.

had abundant water at Ein Yael (Rapuano 1990:47; contrast Williams 1985:146).

In immediate obedience, with little information but complete trust in the God who guides, Philip sets out. For God to summon Philip from a thriving ministry in Samaria to the wilderness of the Judean hills is not an irrational move. God's goal is not only "quantity" but also "quality," in the sense of an ethnically diverse body of Christ (Rev 5:9). In a day when four of six billion have yet to hear the gospel within their own language and culture, we should not be surprised to see God calling our most effective evangelists to go to remote places. And like Philip, they should obey immediately and unquestioningly.

Philip encounters an Ethiopian eunuch and his retinue. He is at once exotic, powerful and pious. Greeks and Romans were particularly fascinated with dark-skinned Africans (Martin 1989:111; Diodorus Siculus *Library of History* 3.8.2-3; Strabo *Geography* 17.2.1-3). Although *Ethiopian* was used generally for anyone with these physical characteristics, here it refers to an inhabitant of the ancient kingdom of Meroe, which covered what is now northern Sudan south of Aswan to Khartoum (see NIV marginal note; compare Youngblood 1982:193; Crocker 1986). This man is powerful, the chief treasurer of a kingdom wealthy from its iron smelting, gold mining and trading position. It was a conduit for goods from the rest of the continent. *Candace, queen of the Ethiopians* (better "Queen Mother, ruling monarch of the Ethiopians," since *candace* is a title, not a proper name), cared for the duties of state. The king was regarded as a god, "child of the sun," too sacred to engage in administration. The candace in this instance was Amanitare (A.D. 25-41; Wead

8:26 To say that the *angel* is identical with "the Spirit" (8:29, 39) and is only a vivid way of depicting divine guidance through inner prompting (Bruce 1988:174; Williams 1985:146) fails to reckon with the variety of ways God may choose to guide his witnesses.

Grammatically, *the desert* may be taken with either *road* or *Gaza;* NIV opts for the former. This is preferred because it points out both which road and the unusual nature of the command, thus highlighting God's guidance. If it refers to the latter, it appropriately describes Old Gaza, destroyed by Alexander Jannaeus in 96 B.C. Strabo the geographer describes the site as "remaining desert" (Strabo *Geography* 16.2.30).

8:27 *Eunuch* in ancient times could mean a castrated male (Lev 21:20; Deut 23:1); a castrated male who served in high government office, particularly under a woman ruler or in duties involving women (such as oversight of a harem) or in a treasury (Plutarch *Vitae Parallelae: Demetrius* 25.5); or any male high government official (Jer 34:19). It is difficult

1982:197; Crocker 1986:67).

Luke does not identify the eunuch as either a proselyte, a Gentile convert to Judaism, or a God-fearer, a Gentile adherent to the Jewish monotheism, ethic and piety (compare Acts 2:11; 6:5; 10:2; 13:26, 43; Levinskaya 1990). He presents him only as pious according to the Jewish faith. The eunuch is returning to Meroe after a pilgrimage to Jerusalem for one of the feasts, and he is *sitting in his chariot* reading Scripture. The chariot is probably a four-wheeled covered vehicle, like an oxcart, large enough to accommodate the eunuch, his driver, Philip and possibly another servant (who would be reading the manuscript aloud if the official is not doing so himself). The carriage is moving slowly enough to allow for reading and for Philip to approach it on foot. Reading aloud was the common practice in ancient times, and was especially necessary when words were strung together on a manuscript without spacing or punctuation (Bruce 1990:226).

Under the guidance of the Spirit (compare 10:19; 11:12; 13:2, 4; 16:6-7), Philip obediently overcomes any social reticence, approaches the wagon, walks briskly alongside and engages the eunuch in conversation about his reading. Luke consistently tells us that reading and understanding Scripture are not the same thing, especially for those who do not have the hermeneutical key (13:27; compare Lk 6:3; 10:26). Correct spiritual understanding is a gift (8:10; 10:22). The eunuch admits his need. His humble, teachable stance is the essential first step to achieving knowledge of salvation (compare Acts 17:11).

God in his mercy has provided not only the text but also the interpreter, a Spirit-filled teacher. The eunuch urgently, but politely, asks

---

to determine which use Luke is making here. Marshall (1980:162) says that the piling on of phrases, *dynastēs* immediately following *eunouchos,* renders the former redundant if it does not point to a physical condition, but this could be read the other way: *dynastēs* explains *eunouchos,* so that the latter does not indicate the physical condition (compare Haenchen 1971:310). In what sense the Ethiopian was a eunuch has a great bearing on his religious status in Israel, for physical eunuchs could not become proselytes (Deut 23:1). Luke's clarifying description seems to point to eunuch as high official, not castrated, and therefore allowably a proselyte. His possession of a scroll of the Scriptures, very difficult for a Gentile to come by, may also support this.

See Levinskaya's (1990) sober assessment of the evidence for regarding *hoi phoboumenoi ton theon* as an identifiable group of Gentiles who worshiped the one true God and identified with the Jewish synagogue yet stopped short of becoming full proselytes.

guidance (13:42; 16:9; contrast Lk 6:39). And today these two gifts are still present. Where are those of teachable spirit?

Jesus Is Preached from the Scriptures (8:32-35) Luke reports that the eunuch was reading the Septuagint of Isaiah 53:7-8 (Acts 8:32-33). Though the wording reflects "a gravely deviant translation" (Archer and Chirichigno 1983:123) at this point, the basic intention of Isaiah is not completely lost (Williams 1985:147). Luke is very interested in the content of this quote, introducing it with a phrase meaning the "content or wording of the passage" (compare v. 35; not *passage of Scripture* as the NIV). In it we have a description of the innocent, righteous sufferer, the objective basis for vicarious atonement. Luke has already portrayed Jesus in his passion in these terms: silent before authorities (Lk 23:9), deprived of justice, an innocent man condemned (Lk 23:4, 15, 22; 23:47; compare Acts 2:22-23; 3:14), his life taken (Lk 23:18; 22:2; 23:32; compare Acts 2:23; 10:39; 13:28).

The eunuch wants to know whether the prophet is talking about himself or someone else. For the Jew in the first century "someone else" was either the humiliated but vindicated "righteous sufferer" of the apocalyptic and wisdom traditions (Is 53:11; *1 Enoch* 46, 62, 63; Wisdom of Solomon 2:12-5:23; Sirach 11:13/Is 52:15; Decock 1981:114). Or, as the targum has it, wicked Gentile nations suffer at the hands of the victorious Messiah, who vindicates his people (*Targum of Isaiah* 53:7-8; note Israel suffers in *Targum of Isaiah* 52:14; 53:2, 4, 10, and the wicked Gentile nations in 53:3, 7-9, 11). The messianic interpretation is original with Jesus (Lk 22:37/Is 53:12; Longenecker 1981:364; Bruce 1988:176).

Philip "opened his mouth" (NIV omits this phrase; compare 10:34)

8:32-33 See Archer and Chirichigno (1983:123) for details on deviations between the Hebrew and LXX texts. Also note that the NIV takes some further liberties in its translation of the Acts passage. Archer asserts that inerrancy is not violated by the presence of the LXX text form, since Luke is accurately reporting what the eunuch was reading and no apostolic approval is given or doctrine built on it. Some claim that Luke avoids a vicarious-atonement soteriology (with no quote of the immediate context, Is 53:6 and end of 53:8) and instead offers a "humiliation/exaltation of the righteous sufferer" soteriology, based on the LXX wording (Decock 1981; Krodel 1986:169). But a slaughtered sheep is referred to (compare Jn 1:29), and the quoted verses could be intended to serve as context pointers to other verses that do mention vicarious atonement (Bruce 1988:176). Further, Luke does present a vicarious-atonement soteriology (Lk 22:19-20; Acts 20:28). The presentation of a righteous sufferer can serve as the objective basis for such a soteriology (Larkin 1977).

and beginning from this passage (compare Lk 24:27) tells the eunuch the good news about Jesus. Christ is the salvific key to the Old Testament. Does Philip simply expound Isaiah 53 and then show the fulfillment in Jesus' life, vicarious death and victorious resurrection/exaltation (see E. F. Harrison 1986:152)? Does he continue a connected exposition through succeeding chapters of Isaiah, dealing with baptism at Isaiah 54:9-10 (compare 1 Pet 3:21) and the new day of salvation at 55:1, to 56:4-8, where a eunuch participates without hindrance in the people of God (Porter 1988)? Does he proceed from Isaiah 53 via early Christian testimonia on the suffering servant and righteous sufferer to show the Ethiopian how Christ and his salvation are preached in all the Scriptures (Is 42:1-44:5; 49:1-13; 50:4-11; Ps 22, 34, 69, 118; Longenecker 1981:365)?

Whatever the method, Philip both answers the eunuch's question and points to Jesus' saving significance. Just as a messenger fresh from the field of battle would "evangelize" the citizens with news of their army's triumph (2 Sam 18:19-20, 26, 31), Philip evangelizes the Ethiopian that Jesus, the righteous sufferer, crucified and risen again, has won the victory over sin and death, and now repentance and forgiveness of sins are available in his name (compare Lk 4:18/Is 61:1; Acts 13:38-39).

Do you want to understand the Old Testament? Stand in the empty tomb, under the shadow of an empty cross, within earshot of the teaching of Jesus and the preaching of the apostles, and *read!*

Convert and Evangelist Sent on their Way (8:36-40) When the carriage arrives at some water, the eunuch exclaims, "Behold water! What is hindering me from being baptized?" (NIV *Why shouldn't I be bap-*

8:36 Rapuano (1990:48) lists the various options for the water's location: Wadi el-Hasi, north of Gaza on the coastal plain; Ein ed Dirweh, near Beth Zur in the Judean hills on the southern route; Ein Yael, five miles south of the old city of Jerusalem on the northern route; and Ein Hanniya, one mile west of Ein Yael. Although there cannot be final certainty (Lake and Cadbury 1979:98), Rapuano argues persuasively for Ein Yael.

The NIV marginal note correctly states that there is only late manuscript evidence—the earliest E (sixth century)—to support the inclusion of the eunuch's confession (Metzger 1971:359), though it should be noted that most minuscules, not just a few manuscripts, contain it (see the second-century reference to the confession in Irenaeus *Against Heresies* 3.12.8). Since the style of the verse is not Luke's, the quality of the manuscript testimony is poor, and there is sufficient motive for a copyist to insert a confession that was mandatory in his own church's practice, it makes sense to see this verse as not originally part of Acts.

tized?). One of Luke's great concerns is that obstacles of age (Lk 18:16), religious tradition, old or new (Lk 9:49-50; 11:52), race or ethnic origin (Acts 10:47; 11:17), or physical condition (8:36, if the eunuch were one physically) must not keep people from hearing and applying to themselves the gospel of salvation. His ideal is found in the closing phrase, indeed the closing word, of Acts: "Boldly and *without hindrance* he preached the kingdom of God and taught about the Lord Jesus Christ" (28:31).

The eunuch is baptized as Philip stands with him in the water. Is it by immersion (Williams 1985:148) or pouring (Stott 1990:162)? The account will accommodate both understandings. The act's theological significance is cleansing for sin and incorporation into the fellowship of those who have experienced Christ's salvation blessings (Lk 24:47/Acts 2:38-39; 10:47-48; 16:31-33).

Though Philip is taken away *suddenly,* the eunuch goes on his way *rejoicing.* For Luke and us, joy is a manifestation of a person's salvation (8:8; Lk 6:23; 10:20), particularly of reception of the Holy Spirit (Acts 13:52).

The episode ends as it began, with divinely guided and empowered outreach. Miraculously transported over thirty miles to the seacoast town of Azotus (Old Testament Ashdod), Philip continues his witness on non-Jewish soil until he comes to Caesarea (compare 21:8).

The conversion of the Ethiopian eunuch graphically demonstrates the inclusiveness of the gospel. No apparent obstacle—whether physical defect, race or geographical remoteness—can place a person beyond the saving call of the good news. Athanasius, in his comments on Psalm 68:31, marvels that "by 'Kushites' God indicates the end of the earth. . . . For how Kush ran to the preaching is possible to see from the believing Ethiopian. God shows that all the other nations also believe in Christ with their kings" (quoted in Martin 1989:116). For persons of black African lineage, the eunuch's conversion means the "inclusion of black Africans among the charter members of the faith . . . all of which sym-

---

8:39-40 A number of scholars consider it unnecessary to interpret Philip's removal as a "supersonic ride of miraculous velocity" (Stott 1990:162; Williams 1985:149; Kistemaker 1990:321; contrast Krodel 1986:171). Yet the fact that suddenly the eunuch does not see Philip anymore, though he had arrived on foot, and that the verb *harpazō* is used (compare

bolizes from the beginning the African involvement in the new faith that spread throughout the world" (C. E. Lincoln 1984:24).

□ Paul's Conversion and Early Ministry (9:1-31)

The church's mission is indeed unstoppable if the risen Lord can reach down to save the movement's chief enemy, Paul. We know Paul's conversion is important to Luke because he relates it three times (see 22:6-16; 26:9-18). After its first telling Luke gives us two episodes from Paul's early ministry and a summary statement of the church's stability, vitality and growth in Judea, Galilee and Samaria. This concludes Luke's account of the advance of the Jerusalem church through the first two steps of Acts 1:8. And with this demonstration of the genuineness of Paul's conversion and call to Jew and Gentile, recognized by the Jerusalem apostles, everything is now in place for the church's next great advance: taking the gospel to the Gentiles, to the ends of the earth.

Paul's Conversion (9:1-19)

The most important event in human history apart from the life, death and resurrection of Jesus of Nazareth is the conversion to Christianity of Saul of Tarsus. If Saul had remained a Jewish rabbi, we would be missing thirteen of twenty-seven books of the New Testament and Christianity's early major expansion to the Gentiles. Humanly speaking, without Paul Christianity would probably be of only antiquarian or arcane interest, like the Dead Sea Scrolls community or the Samaritans.

Saul the Enemy (9:1-2) With Old Testament imagery for anger—snorting through distended nostrils (Ps 18:8, 15)—Luke builds up the picture of Saul as a rampaging wild beast in his hateful opposition to the disciples of the Lord (compare Acts 8:3; Gal 1:13, 23). When the NIV renders "threats and murder" as *murderous threats,* something is lost of the reference to the two-part Jewish judicial process (Longenecker 1981:368) and the highlighting of Saul's violence (Lake and Cadbury 1979:99). Saul does not just make threats (compare Acts 4:17, 29); he

---

2 Cor 12:2; 1 Thess 4:17; also compare 1 Kings 18:12; 2 Kings 2:16; Ezek 3:14; 8:3, though the LXX does not use *harpazō* at those places) indicates that we are dealing with a miraculous translation.

helps bring about actual executions (8:1; 26:10). Aside from this initial note, Luke gives us no indication of Saul's inner thoughts and motives before, during or after his conversion (but see 7:54-8:1; 26:9-11; Rom 7:7-12; Gal 1:13, 14; Phil 3:4-11).

Saul takes action. He goes to Caiaphas (4:6) and receives letters of introduction to the synagogues in Damascus, some 140 miles northeast. He seeks to enlist their aid, or at least permission, to arrest any fugitive Hellenistic Jewish Christians and return them to Jerusalem for trial (22:5).

The hostility to Christianity of pre-Christian Saul presents both challenge and hope to any non-Christian. The hope is that if God can turn the fiercest opponent of the Lord into his most willing servant, he has the ability to save anyone. The challenge is not to be deceived by self-satisfaction. Saul was quite content with his life spiritually. But God's sovereign grace arrested him.

Saul's Encounter with Christ (9:3-9) As Saul travels to Damascus at midday, he experiences the divine presence: *a light from heaven* flashing around him and a *voice* addressing him (compare 7:31/Ex 3:4-10). The descent from Mt. Hermon to Damascus in the plain goes through a region known for violent electrical storms. Though this flashing light may have had the effects of lightning, however, it was a supernatural midday phenomenon.

Saul and his traveling companions see the light, but Saul sees more: the risen Lord Jesus in all his resplendent glory (9:17, 27; 22:14; 26:16; 1 Cor 9:1; 15:8). So overwhelming is the sight that Saul falls to the ground (compare Ezek 1:28; Dan 8:17). The sound or voice probably reminds him of the *baṭ-qôl* ("daughter of the voice"), the way pious Jews

---

9:2 Though Saul's credentialing by the Sanhedrin to extradite Jews in Damascus lacks immediate first-century parallels (Hultgren 1976:107; Haenchen 1971:320), there is precedent (1 Maccabees 15:15-21; Josephus *Jewish Antiquities* 14.190-95; *Jewish Wars* 1.474). The Romans did allow Jews freedom in governing their religious affairs (Sherwin-White 1963:100). Through moral suasion the Sanhedrin did exercise authority over the Jews in the Diaspora (Schürer 1979:218; Safrai 1974:204). This is sufficient historical basis for Saul's action. Mann (1988) proposed that Saul was targeting recent converts among those deputized to check the ritual purity of pilgrims.

If he found: the uncertainty has to do not with whether there were Christians in Damascus or how many (as Kistemaker 1990:331), but with whether Paul would be able to find them (Williams 1985:153). Damascus had a very ancient Jewish settlement which was large and

believed God had directly communicated with human beings since the gift of prophecy had ceased with Malachi (Longenecker 1981:370). But the divine presence creates confusion for Saul, for if God is speaking with him, who is this heavenly figure addressing him?

The voice gives the divine perspective on Paul's activity. With a repeated address (compare Gen 22:11; Ex 3:4; 1 Sam 3:10; Lk 10:41; 22:31) the voice asks, *Saul, Saul, why do you persecute me?* Jesus identifies with his disciples, his body (see Lk 10:16; Acts 1:1; 9:1; 1 Cor 12:27; Eph 4:12). In doing so he reveals that Saul's teacher Gamaliel's worst fears have materialized (Acts 5:39).

Saul grapples with his dawning realization that his life, though lived in zeal for the one true God even to the point of persecuting the church, has in reality been one of "ignorance in unbelief" (1 Tim 1:13). Through the question "why?" he begins to see that in proving his commitment to God by persecuting the church, he has actually been proving himself an enemy of God. As Saul deeply considers that "why?" and accepts the divine perspective on his actions, his whole spiritual world will be turned upside down. What was gain will become loss (Phil 3:6-9). What was a badge of honor will become a lifelong shameful blot on his character (1 Cor 15:9; 1 Tim 1:13, 15).

Out of his confusion, Saul calls, *Who are you, Lord?* Is he simply addressing the heavenly being with respect (Marshall 1980:169), or is he for the first time confessing Jesus as his Lord (compare Rom 10:9-10; 1 Cor 12:3; Kistemaker 1990:332)? His inquiry about the person's identity may indicate the former. He receives a divine disclosure in the clear reply, "I am Jesus, whom you are persecuting." Jesus of Nazareth is risen from the dead! Stephen was telling the truth when he bore witness to

---

influential in the first century. During the Jewish war of the late sixties 10,800 Jews were rounded up in the gymnasium and killed (Josephus *Jewish Wars* 2.559-61; he says 18,000 in 7.368).

9:3 Meinardus (1981:58) surveys the possible sites of Saul's conversion: two miles from Damascus (sixth-century tradition, according to Antonius of Placentia); one mile from Damascus (fourteenth-century tradition of Antony of Cremona); half a mile south of the Roman city walls, in a Christian cemetery between the tomb of St. George and the place of the apostles' refuge (scholars have pointed out that this is not even near, let alone on, the Roman road connecting Jerusalem with Damascus); at Kaukab, fifteen kilometers southwest of Damascus on the road to Jerusalem (a local tradition and a rotunda church site provide attestation). Meinardus prefers the last possibility.

the Son of Man standing at God's right hand (Acts 7:56). Jesus is the Christ, the Son of God, the Savior, the Lord (9:20, 28).

Immediately Jesus issues a divine demand that requires Saul's trust and obedience. In the city he will learn what he *must do* to fulfill God's purposes (compare 9:16; 14:22).

Saul's companions probably include a number of wayfarers banded together in a caravan for protection against the hazards of the journey, as well as temple police to aid Saul in his work (Lake and Cadbury 1979:101; Bruce 1988:185). At this encounter they stand speechless, hearing a voice or the sound of a voice but not understanding the words (9:7/22:9). They do not see Jesus, though they see the light (22:9).

Thus Saul's conversion experience is an objective event with third-party witnesses. It is also a very personal event. The witnesses do not participate in the theophany the way Saul does (compare Jn 12:29-30; Acts 7:56).

For Saul the physical effects are devastating. Getting up from the ground, he opens his eyes and discovers he is blind! Led by the hand (Judg 16:26; Tobit 11:16) into the city, he neither eats nor drinks *for three days.*

But the spiritual effects on Saul will last a lifetime. The spiritual significance of a Jewish rabbi's being physically blinded by the light of the glory of God in the face of Jesus Christ is not lost on Saul or Luke (2 Cor 4:4-6). Major themes in Luke-Acts are God's final salvation as a recovery of sight to the blind and as a light to the nations (Is 40:5/Lk 3:6; Is 61:1-2/Lk 4:18-19; Is 42:6/Lk 2:30-32; Is 49:6/Acts 13:47; compare 26:23; Lk 7:21-22; 18:35-43—last miracle before the cross; 14:21; Acts 26:18-23; Hamm 1990:68). The Jews, especially the rabbis, used the image "guide to the blind" to describe their God-given role among the

9:8, 18 The details of the blinding and healing have to do with scientific fact more than popular tradition (contra Haenchen 1971:328; his evidence is Tobit 3:17; 11:13). In 1977 John D. Bullock read a paper to the annual convention of the American Academy of Ophthalmology and Otolaryngology in which he cited treatment of patients with similar symptoms (*The Columbia Record* 80 [October 4, 1977]: 7A). They had been struck by lightning. What Ananias probably wiped away from Paul's eyes was scar tissue.

9:10-19 There was probably a mutually confirming relationship between the direct revelation on the Damascus Road (Acts 26 and Gal 1) and the word of the Lord through Ananias in Judas's house (Acts 9 and 22; Bruce 1988:188); if so, there is no final contradiction between Paul's insistence that he received his gospel and apostleship directly from Christ

Gentiles and the 'am hā'āreṣ (*1 Enoch* 105:1; *Sibylline Oracles* 3:194; Josephus *Against Apion* 2.41; Rom 2:19). As Saul meditates on the light during those three days of darkness, then, the greatness of the divinely promised final salvation available only in the last person he saw must become more and more clear and precious (Acts 26:18). And the role he is to play in becoming a light to the Gentiles must become increasingly evident (26:17).

What is Saul to make of his blindness? It is not a punishment (as Hamm 1990:70) nor an indication of divine disfavor (as Hedrick 1981:419) nor simply a concrete proof of the vision (as Haenchen 1971:323). An acted parable, it shows Saul the spiritual bankruptcy of his pre-Christian condition.

Saul's fast may be caused by the shock. Eye doctor John Bullock notes that the electrical shock from being struck by lightning causes violent muscular contractions; the throat can be so affected that it is hard to swallow (see notes for 9:8, 18). Or the fast may be a conscious act of penance for past sins (Haenchen 1971:323). The former seems more likely, since in 9:19, after his healing, Saul takes nourishment and is strengthened.

All conversion experiences are unique to the individual. What of Saul's experience does Luke intend us to take as normative? We should focus on the dynamic pattern of conversion, which includes a personal encounter with Jesus Christ via a witness to the gospel, a response of surrender in penitence and faith, and the reception of salvation blessings and incorporation into the church.

Saul the Chosen Vessel (9:10-19) In a *vision* the Lord speaks to Ananias, sending him on a mission to restore the new convert. The mission serves to preserve Paul's apostleship as by "revelation from Jesus

---

and Luke's portrayal of Ananias's role (Gal 1:1, 11-12; Acts 9:10-18; 22:12-16; Lake 1979b:191). Ananias functions as a prophet speaking a direct revelation of Christ (Williams 1985:158).

Paul and Luke do not differ on the basic facts about Paul's apostleship. Paul has seen the risen Lord and received his gospel and apostleship from him (9:17; 22:14; 26:15-18; 1 Cor 9:1; 15:8; Gal 1:1, 11-12, 15-16). Yet there is an irregularity: Paul does not meet the qualifications of "the Twelve" (Acts 1:21-22; 1 Cor 15:9). Luke deals with the irregularity by reserving the term *apostle* almost exclusively for "the Twelve" and only occasionally calling Paul an apostle, and then in company with Barnabas (Acts 14:4, 14).

Christ" (Gal 1:12), to bring him into the church, despite his notorious reputation, and to ensure that the Gentile mission will take place with the approval of the church (Acts 13:1-4; compare other visions that guide the church's advance: 10:3, 17; 16:9-10: 18:9-10).

Ananias, a resident of Damascus and a devout disciple (22:12), is part of a "double vision" divine encounter (9:12) in which both he and Paul are made aware of the next step. Ananias should proceed to the main east-west thoroughfare of Damascus, *Straight Street.* With great porches and gates at each end and colonnades for commerce running along each side, this fashionable address would be as well known in its day as Regent Street in London or Fifth Avenue in New York is today. He is to look for Saul of Tarsus in Judas's house. Tradition locates Saul's abode at the west end (Lake and Cadbury 1979:102). Saul *is praying,* probably in preparation for his restoration (compare 1:14).

To be converted means to move from self-centered independence to dependence on the Lord and interdependence with fellow disciples. Saul the convert needs the support and encouragement of the church. Today too the gospel witness should emphasize by word and deed that being born again is being born into the family of God, the church.

Ananias protests. He has misgivings grounded in the convert's past reputation. All the Lord has told him is that this Saul is blind and praying. When Ananias puts that together with the *harm* Saul has perpetrated against the saints (9:21; 26:10) in Jerusalem, he is not sure he wants the assignment. Besides, Saul's mission in Damascus, with the authority of the high priests (either Annas and Caiaphas [Kistemaker 1990:329] or the high-priestly families [Bruce 1990:238]), is *to arrest all who call on [the Lord's] name.* By negative example, at this point, Ananias teaches us that reluctant gospel messengers must not only love their enemies but also trust that the gospel has such redemptive power that a praying converted persecutor is a persecutor no more.

The Lord does not directly answer Ananias's misgivings; he simply repeats his command: "Go!" The sovereign Lord has spoken. That is all the rationale Ananias or we need. Yet in his mercy the Lord also tells Ananias Saul's new status as *my chosen instrument* (Jer 18:1-11; 2 Cor 4:7; 2 Tim 2:20-21), his new mission, *to carry my name before the Gentiles and their kings and before the people of Israel,* and new rela-

tionship to persecution, to *suffer* for Jesus' name. These new realities mean Ananias has nothing to fear from Saul.

Though Paul later seems to practice a "to the Jews first" strategy (Rom 1:16; for example, Acts 13:5, 14, 46; 14:1; 16:13; 17:1, 10; 18:4; 19:8; 28:23-28), he will remain aware of his definite calling to the Gentiles (18:6; 22:21; 26:17, 20; also 13:46-47/Is 49:6). Suffering for the Lord Jesus' name will indeed be his portion (Acts 20:23-24; 21:11; 26:17; 2 Cor 11:23-27; Phil 1:12-14; 3:10; Col 1:24).

Every convert then and now needs to know "it has been granted to you on behalf of Christ not only to believe on him, but also to suffer for him" (Phil 1:29). This verse was used to charge inquirers in Russian churches in the days of active persecution under atheistic communism. New Christians must know that discipleship is purposeful and costly.

Ananias obeys and performs his ministry to Paul. Laying hands on Saul, he declares that he has been sent by the Lord Jesus so that Saul may see again and *be filled with the Spirit* (Acts 9:17). Saul's vision (v. 12) linked only the healing and the laying on of hands, consistent with other passages in Luke-Acts (Lk 4:40; 13:13; Acts 28:8). Ananias also seems to link it with Paul's being filled with the Spirit (Williams [1985:157] and Marshall [1980:172] say no). Saul's filling with the Spirit is not a delayed reception of the baptism of the Spirit as a salvation blessing, but is the first of many empowerments for apostolic witness (compare 13:9; also see 2:4; 4:8, 31). This is Paul's "Pentecost," further validating his apostleship.

Ananias ministers to Saul as a convert. He heals him—sight is regained as *something like scales* (film or scar tissue) falls from Saul's eyes. He instructs Saul, confirming that the Jesus whom Saul saw on the road is indeed the Lord. He comforts Saul, addressing him as a Christian brother. He baptizes Saul, formally incorporating him into the body of Christ. Finally Saul knows full physical restoration as he takes nourishment. In all, Ananias's ministry models for us the supportive, restorative role the church is to play in the lives of newly converted Christians.

Paul's Witness in Damascus and Jerusalem (9:19-31)

Reports of "foxhole religion" and deathbed conversions leave us uneasy. And having just read about Saul's conversion, we might be wondering

about him. How do we know his and others' experiences are genuine?

Witness in Damascus (9:19-25) For several days Saul is "in the company of" Damascus disciples, probably both refugees from Jerusalem and Damascus Christians. His reception by the community and his desire to share in fellowship with them are certainly signs of a genuine conversion. "True conversion always issues in church membership" (Stott 1990:178).

Yet Saul does not bask exclusively in the church's fellowship for long. Immediately he embarks on a mission of powerful Christ-centered preaching in the synagogues. Just as instantaneous as his healing is his fulfillment of his calling (vv. 15, 18). Filled with the Spirit, without training or a probationary period, he proclaims on numerous occasions (Haenchen 1971:331; not *began to* as NIV) that Jesus is the Son of God. The historical Jesus is central to his proclamation (v. 27; 17:7, 18; 19:13; 20:21; 28:23, 31). Saul consistently argues for Jesus' messiahship and boldly declares that he is the only source of salvation (17:3; 18:5; 19:4; 13:23; 16:31).

Only here and at Acts 13:33 (quoting Psalm 2:7) does Saul proclaim Jesus *the Son of God.* Within a messianic and monotheistic framework (2 Sam 7:14-16; Ps 2:7) this title is like "Son of Man" (compare Acts 7:56). For Jews, "Son of God" both conceals and reveals who Jesus is. For them it may be nothing more than a messianic title (compare 4QFlor 1:10-11; *1 Enoch* 105:2; 4 Ezra 7:28-29). Yet when understood literally it implies participation in the divine nature, having a unique relationship and fellowship with God the Father (Lk 22:69/Ps 110:1; Dan 7:13; Lk 22:70). Saul, who has just seen Jesus in all his glory as the risen and exalted Lord, makes this the theme of his first sermons (9:3-5; compare Rom 1:1-4; Gal 1:16).

All who hear Saul are beside themselves with "astonishment" (see comment at Acts 2:7). The radical conversion of one who *raised havoc* against Christians is clearly a miracle. Saul's activity had been as humanly

---

9:19, 23 The period described may include the three years spent in Damascus, including sojourn in Arabia (Gal 1:17-18). The time markers are general, and a break in sequence is hinted at in verse 23.

9:23-25 Compare 2 Corinthians 11:32-33. Although the precise political relationship between Nabatea and Damascus at this time is not certain (Longenecker 1981:376; Williams

devastating to God's people as the sacking of Jerusalem in 586 B.C. (Josephus *Jewish Antiquities* 10.135; compare Gal 1:13, 23; Menoud [1978a] sees it as only spiritual harm). What a turnabout that he should now be declaring that same Jesus to be the very Son of God!

As Saul grows *more and more powerful* spiritually (Williams 1985:160; Longenecker 1981:376 thinks this also includes his apologetic skills), his apologetic for Jesus as the Messiah produces bafflement among non-Christian Jews (Acts 6:10). His method is to set details of Jesus' life and the Old Testament messianic prophecies side by side in order to prove that Jesus is indeed the Christ (9:22; compare 17:3; 18:5; 26:23). What moral courage it takes for Saul to speak the gospel to the very persons who had been asked to help in his anti-Christian crusade! What more powerful evidence could be needed to persuade Theophilus—and us— that the conversion is genuine?

After time in Arabia (Gal 1:17; in New Testament times the region east of Palestine) Saul returns to Damascus, takes up his witness in the synagogues and faces a plot against his life. In collusion with forces of the governor under Nabatean King Aretas IV, the Jews seek to ambush Saul when he leaves the city (see 2 Cor 11:32-33). Saul escapes with the help of *his followers,* converts under his ministry *(mathētai;* all other uses are of "followers, disciples, of Christ"; see Metzger 1971:366). They locate a house built in the city wall, with a window facing out (2 Cor 11:33). At night they put Paul in a large hamper, possibly of rope ("a large woven or network bag or basket suitable for hay, straw . . . or for bales of wood," Lake and Cadbury 1979:106) and lower him through the window (compare Josh 2:15). He flees to Jerusalem, where he again takes up his witness for Christ in the Hellenistic Jewish synagogues.

George Bernard Shaw once said that the biggest compliment you can pay an author is to burn his books. Luke would add, the biggest compliment to a preacher is to conspire to silence him (compare Lk 22:2; Acts 2:23; 5:33, 36; 10:39; 13:28; 23:15, 21, 27; 25:3). Paul's persistent

---

[1985:160-61] is certain Aretas IV controlled the city through an ethnarch), a cooperative endeavor against Saul by both Nabateans (2 Cor) and Jews (Acts) is plausible, especially if Saul had evangelized while in Arabia and thereby annoyed the authorities (Marshall 1980:174; Krodel 1986:179).

stand in persecution was a strong proof of a genuine conversion and fruitful life and ministry.

Witness in Jerusalem (9:26-30) Saul arrives at Jerusalem a true outsider. His old compatriots, non-Christian Jews, are now his adversaries. His old enemies, the Christians, are not yet his "brothers." He may be staying with his sister while he tries to make contact and associate with *the disciples.* The church is *afraid.* So notorious are this persecutor's past deeds that even after several years they continue to place a cloud over the reports of his conversion.

What a contrast this fearful band of disciples is to that fearless group that only a few years earlier boldly defied its persecutors (4:19-20, 31; 5:12-14, 29)! Opposition can take its toll. Still, one of them, Barnabas, has courage (4:36). Being a "bridge person" (11:22, 25; 15:22, 25, 35), Barnabas takes Saul to the apostles (literally as NIV, not figuratively— "take an interest in"—as Kistemaker 1990:355) and tells them of Saul's conversion, call and subsequent ministry (grammatically it could be Saul who does the telling [Marshall 1980:175], but context indicates it is Barnabas, as in NIV; Haenchen 1971:332).

Increasingly in Acts *the apostles* fulfill the role of guarantors of the church's message and mission (8:14-15; 11:1-17; 15:1-29). Here they receive Saul and validate his call to preach the gospel of grace to the Gentiles. Barnabas summarizes the marks of Saul's call, which are congruent with the marks of the apostleship of the Twelve: Saul has seen the risen Lord, although he did not accompany him during his earthly ministry (22:14; 1 Cor 9:1; Gal 1:12; compare Acts 1:21-22). Saul has received a commission *(the Lord had spoken to him),* although it was not during preascension resurrection appearances (Lk 24:46-47; Acts 1:8). Like the apostles, Saul has been filled with the Spirit and has preached fearlessly in the name of Jesus (4:8, 13, 31, 33).

In a day when we often elevate individualistic, personal, subjective

9:26-27 Compare Galatians 1:18. That after three years the Jerusalem Christians would be fearful of Saul, unaware or unconvinced of his conversion and call (Acts 9:26-27/Gal 1:18), is plausible (contrast Haenchen 1971:336) when we consider that Saul has been away in Arabia a good portion of that time and that a persecuted community is naturally suspicious of any good news about its most violent adversary. A story of conversion can be a ruse for infiltration.
9:27-30 Compare Galatians 1:18-24. Via a generalizing plural Acts gives the general pic-

experience over communal, ecclesial, corporate judgments, Saul's example shines. His call is "for real" because it stands up to the test of the apostles, those charged with guaranteeing the message and mission of Christ's church. Any contemporary claims to God's call must similarly be tested by the deposit of the apostles and prophets: the Scriptures.

Saul moves about *freely*, . . . *speaking boldly in the name of the Lord* (v. 28; compare v. 27; see comment at 4:29). In Luke's understanding and Paul's, bold speaking is both characteristic of Christian witness and the result of a supernatural filling with the Spirit (4:8, 13, 31; 9:17, 27-28; 13:46; 14:3; 18:26; Eph 6:19-20; Phil 1:20; 1 Thess 2:2).

Saul's preaching again involves apologetic to Jews. A Hellenistic Jew himself, Paul picks up where Stephen left off, disputing in the Hellenistic synagogues (Acts 6:9). The church's mission has come full circle: its chief opponent has become its chief protagonist!

As with Stephen, the Grecian Jews try to do away with Paul. "Suffering . . . is the badge of true discipleship," said twentieth-century martyr Dietrich Bonhoeffer (1963:100). The church gets wind of the plot and spirits Saul out of Jerusalem, to the seaport Caesarea and off by ship to Tarsus in Cilicia, East Asia Minor (22:3). In a vision God lets Saul know that his departure is according to divine plan (22:17-21). The church is not personally rebuffing Saul, nor self-interestedly removing him as a flash point for potential persecution (22:17-20).

The persecution and divine preservation are further evidences of the genuineness of Saul's call. Through his experience we also learn that avoidance of known trouble is not necessarily a sign of cowardice (Krodel 1986:181). If undergoing a known danger, especially a life-threatening one, will prevent a Christian missionary from fulfilling the known plan of God, then he or she should avoid it by every legitimate means possible.

The State of the Church in Palestine (9:31) Looking both back-

---

ture, while Galatians gives the particulars. Saul sees Peter and James the Lord's brother. The details of his contact with the churches of Judea (Acts 9:28-29/Gal 1:22) are not easy to reconcile (Bruce 1988:194). Still, if we take into account the church's continuing fear or shunning of Paul and his public ministry focus—evangelization of Hellenistic Jews—then limited personal contact with the churches of Judea is plausible (Hemer 1977a:87). Williams (1985:163) points out that *moved about freely* could point to a series of private meetings with the apostles.

ward and forward, Luke summarizes the outward condition and the inner health of *the church throughout Judea, Galilee and Samaria*. In a reverse parallelism, Luke begins and ends with the qualitative and quantitative outward circumstances: *peace* and growth (Lk 1:79; 2:14; 19:42; Acts 2:41, 47; 4:4; 6:1, 7; 12:24). This is a foretaste of what heirs of the messianic kingdom will one day enjoy (Jer 3:16; 23:3; 33:6; Ezek 37:26). In between Luke notes the characteristics of inner health that make this possible: godliness and Spirit-empowered encouragement. Peace has come primarily through the conversion of the chief persecutor and through changing political realities in the Empire (Williams 1985:164), but Luke also points to the strengthening the church has experienced (compare Acts 20:32). The church's growth is due in no small part to the Christians' godliness, *living in the fear of the Lord*. The Holy Spirit also has a role, empowering the preaching that *encouraged* (*paraklēsis*, meaning "exhortation," Schneider 1980-1982:2:41; not comfort or protection after persecution, as Haenchen 1971:333) unbelievers to come to Christ.

Is the Christian church for real? When it fits the description of Acts 9:31, the watching world has evidence that the church is authentic and its message true.

THE JERUSALEM CHURCH: ITS MISSION TO THE GENTILES (9:32—12:25)

After two thousand years of the successful spread of Christianity among nearly every major ethnic group except the Jews, the natural question for us is, Will the Jews ever come to Christ in large numbers? In the church's earliest days the opposite question was the obvious one: Will the Gentiles ever be saved? Jewish Christians did believe that God had a saving purpose for the Gentiles, but it would be fulfilled at the very end of time (Is 2:1-4; 42:6; 49:6; Tobit 14:5-7). So deeply ingrained was the abhor-

9:31 *Ekklēsiai* ("churches"), a variant reading followed by the KJV and NKJV, is in line with Luke's normal practice (see 15:41; 16:5) but less well attested. Its origin through copyist adjustment is more understandable than the reading *ekklēsia* ("church"; Metzger 1971:367). Giles (1985) suggests that the variant *ekklēsia* with plural verbs (pointing to the Jerusalem church dispersed) be given serious consideration.

9:32-43 Peter's ministry to Aeneas and Dorcas parallels that of Elijah and Elisha (1 Kings 17:17-24; 2 Kings 4:18-37) as well as that of Jesus (Lk 5:17-26; 8:41-56) and Paul (Acts 14:8-

rence of any contact with the ritually unclean that if it had been up to Hebraic Jewish Christians to take the first step toward Gentiles with the gospel, that initiative might never have occurred.

After a preparatory account of Peter's healing ministry in an ethnically mixed area (Acts 9:32-43), Luke uses four episodes to describe how God took the initiative to bring Gentile seeker Cornelius and Jewish Christian apostle Peter together, thus inaugurating the Jerusalem church's mission to the Gentiles (10:1—11:18). The Jerusalem church's confirmation, through Barnabas, of Hellenistic Jewish Christians' successful evangelistic initiatives among Gentiles at Antioch manifest the continuity and extension of that mission (11:19-30). God's miraculous intervention to rescue Peter from death and the subsequent divinely ordained death of the persecutor Herod strongly emphasize how important and how unstoppable the mission to the Gentiles is (12:1-25).

□ The Mission Is Inaugurated Through Peter (9:32—11:18)

When does God "outflank" and when does he make a "frontal assault" to advance the gospel? It depends on whether those who stand in the way are essential to its success. The Jerusalem church, as the mother church and guarantor, is essential to the inauguration of a successful, sustainable Gentile mission that will preserve the church's unity and its continuity of mission. So after strategically placing Peter near Caesarea (9:32-43), God through a combination of visions and acts of human obedience brings Cornelius and Peter together so that the Gentile might hear the gospel and be saved (chapter 10). When challenged by the church at Jerusalem, Peter so defends the Gentile mission that all the church can do is break out in praise of God (11:18).

Peter's Healing Ministry at Lydda and Joppa (9:32-43)

When Jews use the all-purpose greeting/farewell "Shalom!" (peace),

---

12; 20:7-12). Clearly Peter acts in continuity with the prophets, the Old Testament "apostles" who spoke and acted for God. This shows also that what the risen Lord commands is in continuity with what the earthly Jesus did. And it implies that Paul's mission did not deviate from that of his Jewish Christian predecessors (Talbert 1986:43).

9:32 Luke consistently imitates Old Testament style with the phrase "and it came to pass" (Hebrew *wayᵉhî:* 9:32, 37, 42-43; not in NIV).

they are wishing that your life be more than hassle-free. They desire for you that sense of well-being born of full health. The church too "enjoyed peace" (9:31), the shalom of a formerly bedridden Aeneas walking about in the Lydda Christian assembly and a once deceased Dorcas again busily sewing garments for the needy.

These transitional episodes flesh out the summary statement of 9:31, demonstrating that the mission to the Jews in Jerusalem, Judea and Samaria (1:8) has been completed all the way to the coast. They are preparatory for the next great advance of the church: the Jerusalem church's Gentile mission (10:1—11:18). They place Peter in an advantageous geographical position to respond to the summons of Cornelius.

Peter and Aeneas (9:32-35) We last saw Peter evangelizing Samaritan villages (8:25). Now he appears itinerating about the countryside, probably the regions mentioned in 9:31 (Haenchen 1971:338) as opposed to the territory between Jerusalem and Lydda (Bruce 1990:246). We are not told whether he is providing edificatory oversight to believers (Haenchen 1971:338) or evangelizing the unreached (Bruce 1990:246 calls it missionary work) or both.

The apostle arrives at Lydda, twenty-five miles northwest of Jerusalem at the intersection of highways from Egypt to Syria and from Jerusalem to coastal Joppa. It was the capital of a toparchy, or administrative district, and had a predominantly Jewish population in an ethnically mixed region. It is the Old Testament city of Lod, near which modern Israel's international airport of the same name is located (1 Chron 8:12; Ezra 2:33; Neh 11:35). There Peter finds *saints* (compare 9:13) who were converted under the witness of pilgrims returning from Pentecost or of Hellenistic Jewish Christians dispersed by persecution or of Philip (Acts 8:1, 40; Longenecker 1981:381; E. F. Harrison 1986:171; Kistemaker 1990:358).

Among the saints there—not Lydda's population in general, and therefore a Christian, not a non-Christian, gathering—Peter meets the Hellenistic Jewish Christian Aeneas. For eight years he has had a chronic ailment that has left the lower part of his body paralyzed. One such type of paraplegia is tuberculosis spondylitis, a paralysis that results from compression of the spinal chord (R. K. Harrison 1979:958). Aeneas has been confined to his mat, which is his bed.

Peter declares, *Jesus Christ heals you* (compare 1:1; simple action present—"this moment Jesus Christ heals you," Longenecker 1981:381). Then follows the command *Get up and take care of your mat.* As a sign of instantaneous and full recovery Aeneas immediately gets up (compare 3:7-8; Is 35:6). Luke points to the great impact this miracle has for the advance of the church. All who see Aeneas in Lydda and the coastal plain of Sharon, stretching from Joppa to Mt. Carmel beyond Caesarea, *[turn] to the Lord.*

What is the relationship between miracleworking and evangelism (9:35, 42)? In Acts, miracles accompany about half of the occasions of effective preaching of the gospel (2:4/14-41; 2:43/47; 3:1-10/11-26; 4:29, 30/33; 5:12-16; 6:8, 10/7:1-53; 8:5/6; 9:34/35; 9:40-41/42; 13:10-11/12; 14:1/3; 14:10/15-17); on the other occasions they do not (8:35-38; 9:22; 9:28-29; 10:34-43; 11:20-21; 13:16-41; 16:14-15; 16:31-34; 17:1-4; 17:22-34; 18:4-5; 19:8-10; 20:18-21).

We need to avoid two extremes. Rather than despising the role of the miraculous in evoking saving faith, we should recognize its legitimate role in giving credence to the preached word. In the end, saving faith must rest not on the impression the miracle has made but on the truth of the message to which it points. Furthermore, there is nothing superior about preaching that is accompanied by the miraculous. Luke knows well that experience of the miraculous can bring misunderstanding and confusion and even throw up a hindrance to saving faith. Those who interpret it according to an unregenerate worldview will be blind to its true origin and significance (Lk 11:15; 16:27-31; Acts 14:8-18; 16:16-21). When miracles do occur as the gospel is being preached, the evangelist must fearlessly interpret God's acts by his Word to the audience, so that misunderstanding is put down and Jesus Christ is exalted.

Peter and Dorcas (9:36-43) Eleven miles farther northwest, in Joppa (the ancient seaport for Jerusalem, Josh 19:46; modern Jaffa), lives Tabitha, or Dorcas, a disciple famous for her kindness to the poor. She lives in the fear of the Lord (Acts 9:31) by adopting correct values concerning material things (compare Lk 12:33; Acts 10:2, 4; 20:35; 24:17). Dorcas becomes sick and dies. Funeral arrangements begin with the cleansing of the body with oil and rinsing it clean with water (*m. Šabbat* 23:5). Then she is placed in an upper room (compare *Semahot* 11:2).

Outside Jerusalem, burial was not necessarily carried out on the same day, especially if the shroud or the coffin needed to be prepared (Safrai 1976:776). Luke notes Lydda's nearness to Joppa and the sending for Peter.

Out of honor to such a saint, Peter does come. As he is conducted to the upper room, the noisy wailing of widows greets him. They are probably among the Christian poor Dorcas had helped (Acts 6:1; compare Jesus' special interest in widows in his teaching and ministry: Lk 4:25-26; 7:12; 18:1-8; 20:47; 21:1-4). In fact they are wearing some of her handiwork. Dorcas customarily made (*epoiei,* customary use of the imperfect [Williams 1985:167], not pluperfect as NIV) undergarments and outergarments—cloaks—for them (NIV *robes and other clothing* is less precise).

In Dorcas Luke gives us a model of Christian charity to the marginalized in society. Then orphans and widows were the most economically vulnerable (Lk 20:47). No government safety net was there to catch them. And today too, Christians must bring as much "shalom" as possible to those on the margins.

Peter's actions show his total dependence on God. Ordering everyone out of the room (Mk 5:40) and falling on his knees in prayer, he asks the risen Lord to apply his resurrection power to this corpse. Then turning toward the dead woman (literally, "to the body"), he issues the simple command *Tabitha, get up.* In a reversal of the first act of preparation for burial, closing the eyes of the deceased (*m. Šabbat* 23:5; *Semaḥot* 1:4), Dorcas opens her eyes and, seeing Peter, sits up.

What joy there must be as Peter, helping her to her feet, calls through the door to *the believers* (literally "the saints"), and especially *the widows,* to whom he presents her *alive* (compare Acts 1:3). News of the resurrection leads many to saving faith in the Lord, and Peter remains quite awhile in Joppa, in the house of Simon the tanner.

The way God resurrected Dorcas apart from any actions by Peter

---

9:37 Most commentators assume the burial has been delayed in the hope that Peter will raise Dorcas (Haenchen 1971:339; Marshall 1980:179; Longenecker 1981:382; Kistemaker 1990:360). Nothing in the account, however, explicitly states this. The absence of a reference to oil does not imply it. The supposed indications of unusual delay were not outside normal Jewish burial practice (compare *Leviticus Rabbah* 34:10).

9:43 Luke uses the detail that Simon was a tanner simply to distinguish him from his

which could be interpreted as magical manipulation shows us that prayer and the Word of God must be central to every healing God grants.

Cornelius's Vision (10:1-8)

Are genuine seekers after God saved, if they have responded to the light they have but have never heard the gospel? The experience of Cornelius begins to answer this question.

Fearing God and Helping the Needy (10:1-2) At Caesarea, a mainly Gentile city, residence of the Roman proconsul (from A.D. 6 onward), lived Cornelius, a Roman centurion. He was in command of sixty to one hundred men and was the equivalent of an army captain or company commander. His unit was part of the Italian Regiment (the *Cohores II Miliaria Italica Civium Romanorum*). A cohort had ten centuries and was the equivalent of a modern military battalion. This battalion was an auxiliary unit, not part of a regular Roman legion. Such a battalion of archers was first made up of Roman soldiers and then filled out in the provinces.

Cornelius would have been a winsome figure for Luke's Roman audience. Polybius said of centurions, the backbone of the Roman army, "They wish centurions not so much to be venturesome and daredevil as natural leaders, of a steady and sedate spirit. They do not desire them so much to be men who will initiate attacks and open the battle, but men who will hold their ground when worsted and hard pressed and be ready to die at their posts" (*Histories* 6.24.9).

This "solid citizen" along with *all his family* (literally "all his household," which would have included household servants and military orderlies and their families) was *devout and God-fearing*. Luke does not quite use "God-fearer" (*hos phoboumenos* or *hos seboumenos*) as a technical term (Acts 10:2, 22, 35; 13:16, 26, 43, 50; 16:14; 17:4, 17; 18:7). But it does point to that class of monotheistic Gentiles who worshiped the

---

guest, Simon Peter the fisherman. Tanning was a ritually unclean trade, since it dealt in the skins of dead animals; thus some have seen Peter's choice of accommodation and Luke's note of it as foreshadowing Peter's leadership role in taking the gospel to the Gentiles (Longenecker 1981:383; but Marshall 1980:180 doubts it; see *m. Ketubot* 7:10). Would the religious significance of this detail have registered with a Gentile audience?

God of the Old Testament, kept the Old Testament ethical code, attended synagogue, observed the sabbath and practiced the main requirements of Jewish piety (Levinskaya 1990). Because they refused to become proselytes, Jews still regarded them as ritually unclean Gentiles. Luke emphasizes Cornelius's piety: regular prayer (the Jewish practice was three times a day: *m. Berakot* 4:1; compare Dan 6:10) and many acts of charity among the needy of the Jewish people (Tobit 1:16; Sirach 7:10; 16:14; compare Mt 6:1-14).

God may do preparatory work in a culture before missionaries arrive. But note Cornelius's worship is directed to the one true God.

The Opportunity to Receive "More Light" (10:3-6) *At about three in the afternoon* (literally, "the ninth hour," the Jewish afternoon hour of prayer and sacrifice), in broad daylight, Cornelius, wide awake, sees clearly a vision in which an angel approaches him and addresses him by name. Staring *in fear* (compare 1:10; 3:4, 12; 6:15; 7:55), Cornelius responds, *What is it, Lord?* (compare 9:5). *Lord* can mean anything from a courteous "sir" (so here says Bruce [1990:254]) to a divine title (E. F. Harrison 1986:176 says it indicates that Cornelius knows he is in God's presence). Cornelius probably is indeed giving some worshipful acclaim, although he may not know the exact identity of the one to whom he is speaking (Longenecker 1981:386).

The angel says Cornelius's prayers and acts of charity have risen as the aroma of the meal offering rose as a memorial before God (Lev 2:2, 9, 16; Ps 141:2; Tobit 12:12; Longenecker 1981:386). It is too much to say that Cornelius has been praying that he might be fully incorporated into the fellowship of the people of God (as Pesch 1986:1:337; Kistemaker 1990:373).

What we see emerging to this point is the basic outline of the "more light" principle of God's redemptive mercy (compare Lk 8:18; 19:26). Cornelius has responded in faith and obedience to the "light" he has received, as evidenced by his piety. He fears the one true God, prays to him regularly and acts in love to the needy among God's people. Such obedience is not a "works righteousness" that earns salvation. This we

---

10:3 Visions—often double visions—occur in four episodes in Acts. Each time they function to give divine guidance for the advance of God's mission, especially in the face of human resistance or uncertainty (Ananias and Paul, 9:10, 12; Gentile Cornelius and Jewish

can see by God's response. He does not declare Cornelius saved. Rather, he grants him "more light" by which he and his household may be saved (Acts 11:14). God's response is embodied in a command to send for the messenger who carries the gospel, the essential "more light" (4:12). What have we done with the light we have received?

The angel tells Cornelius to send to Joppa, thirty miles south, and fetch *Simon who is called Peter* from the house of *Simon the tanner,* located by the sea (a good water supply was needed for the tanning trade). God deals with Cornelius this way to demonstrate that salvation comes to all people in the same divinely commanded and enabled way: through human messengers who proclaim the gospel (Lk 24:47).

We need to constantly remind ourselves of this, whether we are considering the claims of the gospel and are tempted to wait for some extraordinary experience, or whether having received it and become a witness to it we are tempted to become lax in evangelism, thinking that there may be other ways God will save people.

Cornelius Obeys (10:7-8) Cornelius calls two household servants (an *oiketēs* had a particularly intimate relationship with the master, since he served him in very personal matters; Philo *De Plantatione* 55) and a soldier who is an orderly (the NIV translation of both terms misses the intimate relation these men have to Cornelius). He tells them *everything that had happened* (Williams [1985:172] notes the emphatic position of *everything* in the Greek text). As members of his household, all three would be God-fearers (compare Acts 10:2), though Luke emphasizes the devoutness of the military orderly.

Cornelius sends them to Joppa to find and bring back Peter. Some have supposed that the thirty-mile distance requires that they ride (Marshall 1980:184). Others suggest that a determined march through the night with rest stops would permit them to arrive about noon the next day (Haenchen 1971:347; compare 10:9, 17). In any case, Cornelius's immediate obedience to limited information models for us the kind of faith that will truly receive salvation. It depends on God's word of promise alone.

apostle Peter, 10:3, 17, 19; 11:5; Paul and the European mission, 16:9-10; Paul and the evangelization of Corinth, 18:9; compare 5:19-20; 8:26).

Peter's Vision (10:9-23)

A Muslim doesn't consider it impolite to go into the kitchen of non-Muslim hosts to make sure milk and meat are not mixed in the meal preparations. So strong is our commitment to ethnic distinctives of diet, especially when they are grounded in religion. We do not readily leave the comfort zone of our religio-ethnic identity. But if Peter is to spearhead the Jerusalem church's Gentile mission, God must move him out of his Jewish comfort zone.

A Culinary Vision (10:9-16) Luke dovetails the actions of Cornelius's messengers with those of Peter. *About noon* (literally, the sixth hour, with daylight hours reckoned from six a.m.) on the following day, as they are *approaching the city,* Peter climbs, probably via an outside stairway, to the flat rooftop of Simon the tanner's house. His purpose is prayer, according to the pattern of pious Jews who prayed three times a day, though this was not necessarily one of the officially prescribed times (*m. Berakot* 4:1; Ps 55:17). The rooftop provides solitude, possibly an awning for shade, and the refreshment of breezes off the Mediterranean.

During his prayers Peter becomes very hungry. As the meal is being prepared (the normal Jewish pattern was a light meal in the forenoon and the main meal about sunset, so this was not a regular meal), *a trance* comes on him. It is not a dream (contra Williams 1985:173), nor does Peter lose control of his senses. Rather, the presence of the Lord so comes upon him that he is in a profound state of concentration. He is partially or completely oblivious to external sensations but fully alert to subjective influences as God communicates with him visually and audibly (Kistemaker 1990:377; compare 22:17). Commentators have suggest-

---

10:9 Lake and Cadbury (1979:114) suggest that in the light of Acts 10:30 *the following day* should be understood as calculated from the time of the journey's start. If Cornelius receives the vision on Monday and the men begin their journey on Tuesday, verse 9 points to Wednesday noon.

10:12-13 Derrett (1988:206) makes a case for the primary reference being to the animals at and after the flood. The order of categories is closest to that of Genesis 7:14 and 8:19, and the lack of mention of fish makes sense not only because fish were absent from the ark but because they do not have "the breath of life" in them and were given as food (Gen 6:19-20; 7:2-3, 8, 14-15).

Derrett believes that this command (Acts 10:13) is a auditory substitute for Deuteronomy 12:15, 21 and has the effect of repealing the food laws of Leviticus 11 and Deuteronomy 14 (1988:211). If the allusions to Genesis 6—9 are accepted, the heavenly vision appears to be reestablishing the eating practices permitted to Noah (Gen 9:3). As long as blood is

ed that Peter's hunger, his thoughts of conflict between Jews and Gentiles in the churches of the coastal plain, and the flapping of the awning or the sight of ships in full sail on the Mediterranean are psychological influences on the vision's details (Longenecker 1981:387; Marshall 1980:185). Luke, however, speaks only of Peter's hunger. What we do learn from this narrative's setting is that God is again taking the initiative to bring Peter and the Gentiles together.

Peter sees heaven opened and a "vessel" or "container" (NIV's *something* is too general) like a "linen sheet" (in *Martyrdom of Polycarp* 15.2 the word refers to a ship's sails) being *let down . . . by its four corners*. The four corners probably refer to the worldwide dimensions of the vision's significance ("four corners of the earth," Rev 7:1; less certain is an allusion to Noah's ark, as Derrett 1988:206).

The categories of animals it contains do correspond to a comprehensive Old Testament cataloging of the animal kingdom on land and in the air (Gen 1:24; 7:14; 8:19; Lev 11). Whether *all kinds* indicates that the assemblage includes both clean and unclean animals (E. F. Harrison 1986:178; Longenecker 1981:387) or just the unclean (Haenchen 1971:348; Marshall 1980:185) is not clear. Peter's protest at the command to *kill and eat* indicates that at least some unclean animals are present. The vision's purpose—proving a new freedom in association of Jew and Gentile—is best accomplished if a mixture is present.

Peter is commanded to slaughter these animals according to the proper method and eat (Deut 12:15-16; *m. Ḥullin*). Luke lets us know this mandated behavior change is from God by showing a rare free intercourse between heaven and earth (compare 1:10-11; 2:2; 7:55-56) and

not eaten, both Jew and Gentile can eat clean and unclean food.

10:14 *Unclean* in the Old Testament is "anything associated with a foreign cult, or hostile to Yahweh." It defiles, making those who come in contact with it ceremonially unclean (Hauck and Meyer 1965:416). In Leviticus 11 and Deuteronomy 14 the clean-unclean distinction marks what the holy people of God are and are not permitted to eat. Gordon Wenham (1981) closely critiques and finds inadequate all the suggested rationales for the distinction: hygiene, association with idolatry, carnivores as unclean, and ethical symbolism. He proposes an overarching symbolism of purity understood as integrity and wholeness. Animals that do not seem to fit their class are unclean (for example, those having many more legs and wings than normal—Lev 11:20-23). Wenham applies this to Israel's relation to God. The diet was limited to certain meats in imitation of God, who had restricted his choice among nations to Israel. It reminded them of their calling to be a holy nation.

a direct voice from heaven (Lk 3:22; 9:35; Acts 9:4, 7; compare 7:31). Divine revelation is required if Old Testament revelation and the layers of ethnic prejudices built upon it are to be set aside.

In the strongest possible terms and appealing to Ezekiel 4:14, Peter faces what he may view as a temptation or test of loyalty. He refuses, announcing his firm resolve to live in ritual purity (compare Mt 16:22; Lk 22:33): *I have never eaten anything impure or unclean* (Lev 10:10; 11:1-47; Deut 14:3-21). That is, I have never eaten anything that is accessible to every human being (NIV *impure,* literally "common") but by divine mandate is forbidden to me as part of God's holy people. Such food is *unclean,* not only because God declares it to be such but also because if I eat it I will become ritually defiled, unfit to come into God's presence in worship.

The voice comes again, this time providing the rationale: God has declared all foods clean. Peter is not to go on declaring some foods profane or "common." Jesus' teaching and behavior had certainly prepared the way for such a declaration (Mk 7:14-23; Lk 11:39-41), and the cross was the salvific basis for it (Eph 2:14-15; Col 2:14). The sheet from heaven and the voice both bear witness that all God's creatures are now to be viewed as clean and good, not to be refused (Gen 1:31; 1 Tim 4:3).

This whole transaction occurs three times. What is the basic truth here? It is divine mandate, not something inherent in the creature, that establishes the dividing line between clean and unclean.

Divinely Sent Gentile Guests (10:17-23) Peter is thoroughly perplexed (NIV's *wondering about* is too weak; compare 2:12; 5:24; Lk 9:7). Is he confused by an evident divine contradiction, a heavenly voice commanding him to disregard food laws that God had given Moses for Israel? Or is he wondering what significance this boundary abolition will have for his identity and behavior as a Jewish Christian?

10:19 B (Vaticanus), an important fourth-century witness, is the *one early manuscript* referring to "two" men to which the NIV marginal note points. A group of Western and Byzantine manuscripts do not have any number. If the "two" reading, which would count the soldier only as a guard, is original, then the readings that have "three" or that omit the number are corrections in the light of Acts 10:7 and 11:11. But because the soldier seems to be more important than a mere guard and the diversified manuscript witness to the reading "three" gives it the strongest support among the options, it seems best to follow that reading (Metzger 1971:373).

By providential coincidence, Cornelius's men appear at the gate and call out for Peter just as he is puzzling over the vision. God the Holy Spirit speaks to Peter, telling him that three men are seeking him (compare v. 21). In describing their pursuit of Peter who will tell them how to be saved (11:14), is Luke presenting a model of the spiritual stance every Gentile should take (17:27; compare Rom 2:7)?

Peter is to go with them without making a distinction for himself (NIV *do not hesitate;* Greek *diakrinō*). In the middle or passive voice this verb can mean either "to take issue with" or "to be at odds with oneself, to doubt, to waver, to have misgivings" and is so understood here by many (NIV; Bruce 1990:257; Kistemaker 1990:382; compare v. 29). But since Peter's objections are really based on continuing prejudicial distinctions between Jew and Gentile, and the vision as he comes to properly interpret it has to do with removing such distinctions (v. 28), it seems best to take the verb here in an intensified form of its active meaning, "to make a distinction, to differentiate" (compare 11:12; 15:9; Marshall 1980:187; Stott 1990:187; Krodel [1986:191] takes it as meaning both). So taken, the Spirit's instruction is Peter's focal point of illumination concerning the vision. If he will act out "not making distinctions" with these Gentiles even to the extent of table fellowship in their household, he will understand the vision and its implications. And today if we would understand God's Word, especially where it challenges our prejudices, we too must wrestle with its meaning and its implications. We may expect to understand it more and more fully as we obey it more and more readily.

Peter meets the men with a declaration that he is the one they are "looking for." He asks why they have come. Placing Cornelius in the most favorable light possible, the messengers describe their master's character, his reputation among *all the Jewish people* (compare Lk 7:5)

One must be careful neither to reduce the Spirit's communication in "some direct un-mistakable way" to "growth of inward conviction" (Marshall 1980:187) nor to lump the angel (10:3), the heavenly voice and the Spirit into one divine reality that "it is both exegetically and experientially difficult, if not impossible, to draw any sharp lines between" (Longenecker 1981:389). While there is certainly a unity of purpose and action from the Triune God, the distinct methods of communication must not be ignored (compare 8:26, 29; 13:2; 16:6, 7).

and the angel's instruction.

Peter invites the men in to be his guests. In this he does not go beyond what a law-abiding Jew might do (Marshall 1980:187). Still, because of their visit's purpose, Peter's hospitality is a sign that he agrees to their request, which was not permitted for a Jew. Peter in this brief encounter grows in his discipleship. Obedience to the Spirit will lead to understanding. Understanding demands further obedience.

God by his word was breaking down prejudicial barriers as his witnesses obeyed. What breakthroughs does God want to bring about through us as we obey?

Peter's Witness to Cornelius (10:23-48)

"The ground is level at the foot of the cross." There is no platform of religious or ethnic heritage or practice that one must climb to qualify for God's saving favor. First-century Jews, even Jewish Christians, would have disagreed. Today, some nominal Christians look to bloodlines or certain religious rites to erect their platform. But the startling good news of Peter's message is that no religio-ethnic or cultural conditions must be met to qualify for God's salvation blessings.

Peter and Cornelius Meet (10:23-33) Because of the precedent-setting nature of Peter's visit to Cornelius (compare 15:7) or possible trouble the visit would cause Jewish Christians back in Jerusalem, Peter sets out with a delegation of six *brothers* who can serve as witnesses (10:45; 11:12). The journey to Caesarea takes somewhat longer than it had taken Cornelius's envoys, maybe because of the larger group and their lack of mounts (Williams 1985:175).

Cornelius's expectancy in many ways models the stance of the people of God toward the final salvation (Lk 3:15; 7:19-20; 12:46; compare Ps 119:166). Obediently and magnanimously he too gathers a delegation including *relatives and close friends* (Josephus *Jewish Antiquities* 7:350; compare Acts 11:14).

There is some understandable awkwardness when Peter and Cornelius meet. It is not because of Peter's reluctance. Luke chronicles his determined progress (10:24-25, 27). Rather, it's due to Cornelius's enthusiastic greeting in which he falls at Peter's feet in homage (NIV *in reverence;* literally, "he worshiped"). Is this indeed "worship" from a God-fearer?

Everett F. Harrison (1986:180) says no. But if Cornelius is showing only respectful gratitude, Peter probably would not correct him so forcefully. (All other uses of the term refer to true or false worship—Lk 4:8; 24:52; Acts 8:27; 24:11; Lk 4:7; Acts 7:43). Filled with joy at the sight of the one whose message will bring salvation and filled with awe at seeing the one whom an angelic vision said to summon, Cornelius naturally falls down in worship.

Peter will have none of this. Grabbing him by the arm, he tells him to get up, letting him know that he himself is only a human being. Peter is living out his commitment to a strict monotheism that will brook no worship of any but God (Lk 4:8; compare Ex 20:3-5; Deut 5:7-9; Rev 19:10; 22:8-9; contrast Haenchen [1971:350], who says he is just modeling humility). At the same time he places Cornelius and himself on the same footing. Peter avoids two extremes when he treats humans as neither "gods" nor "dogs" (Acts 10:26, 28; Stott 1990:189; compare Acts 3:11-12; 14:15). With a simple act and firm words, Peter removes from Cornelius's mind and heart the difference between Jew and Gentile. This is the starting point for any who would take the gospel to those who have never heard. There must at the least be acknowledgment of the level ground of creation: "I too am a human being."

Conversing, they enter the house and encounter a *large gathering.* Luke consistently uses this phrase to describe the effect of miracles and response to the gospel at each stage of the fulfillment of Acts 1:8 (2:6; 4:4; 5:16; 8:7). The response of the Gentiles potentially will be as enthusiastic as that of the Jews.

When Peter says that *it is against our law* to associate or visit with a Gentile (literally, "a person of another race"), he is not pointing to explicit Old Testament teaching as much as to Jewish custom. Nehemiah did take the mandate excluding Ammonites and Edomites from the assembly (Deut 23:3-4) and extended it to all Gentiles (Neh 13:3). Rabbinic law extended the separation, however, by proscribing Jewish social contact with Gentiles, particularly accepting hospitality in their homes (*m. 'Aboda Zara* 5:5; *m. Toharot* 7:6; compare *m. Demai* 3:4). In the end, in Jewish eyes, Gentiles themselves became a source of ritual impurity (*t. Demai* 3:14; *t. 'Aboda Zara* 4:11).

Despite this deep-seated taboo, Peter announces he has learned

the lesson of the heavenly vision, which providentially converged with the arrival of Gentile messengers and the Spirit's instruction "Go with them, not making any distinctions" (10:9-19). Peter puts it tersely: *God has shown me that I should not call any man impure [common] or unclean* (v. 28; compare vv. 14-15). Just as the external cultural barrier between holy and profane (the common), clean and unclean, has come down, so the prejudicial barrier between races and ethnic groups is forever removed. No human being is to be treated as profane, somehow beyond the reach of a sacred God's saving and sanctifying work. No human being is to be viewed as unclean, a hindrance to my pursuit of spiritual purity before God (compare Jesus' example in Lk 5:30; 7:34; 15:1).

Peter has acted on his new insight by coming without objection (compare Acts 10:20). Now he wants to know why he has been called. Cornelius's response indicates that God has orchestrated this historic meeting, the inauguration of the Gentile mission.

Cornelius's vision and his subsequent obedience are the most repeated features of his conversion narrative (10:3-7, 22, 30-33; 11:13-14). Thus Luke continues to emphasize that the Gentile mission is God's will and would not have happened without divine intervention. In Cornelius's retelling here Luke emphasizes that it was while at prayer, and possibly in answer to a particular prayer for further knowledge of the way of salvation, that the angelic vision was given (compare 10:4; Lk 1:13). Cornelius's comments conclude with an expression of polite gratitude— *it was good of you to come* (compare 3 Jn 6)—and a statement of the receptivity of all present. Cornelius also stresses the message's divine origin and universal applicability, along with his audience's accountability. Is Luke holding up Cornelius as a model for hearing the gospel?

Peter's Speech (10:34-43) Luke introduces Peter's speech with solemnity: "having opened his mouth" (compare Acts 8:35; 15:7). Peter's speech proceeds in three stages: an introduction with the theme (the impartial God sends the message that Jesus, through whom peace comes, is Lord of all people—10:34-36), a statement of the kerygma,

---

10:30 NIV translates *idou* ("behold") as *suddenly* and may miss some of its importance as a demonstrative marker. It serves to point out divine intervention and providential con-

which proves the theme (vv. 37-41) and a conclusion (the witness of apostle and prophet, which applies Christ's judicial and saving lordship to the hearers—vv. 42-43).

Peter begins by declaring, *God does not show favoritism.* He uses an idiom reflecting ancient Near Eastern practice. Literally the concept is "to receive the face" (Hebrew *nāsā' pānîm*/Greek *lambanō prosōpon*). To greet a social superior, one lowered the face or sank to the earth. If the one thus greeted raised the face of the greeter, it was a sign of recognition and esteem. Such favoritism may have been welcome to those who experienced it, but it was not to be found in a judge (compare the Old Testament picture of God as impartial judge: Deut 10:17; 2 Chron 19:7).

Peter applies this character quality to God's dealing with persons *from every nation (ethnos).* This term refers not simply to nation-states but also to any racial, ethnic or cultural grouping by which humans distinguish themselves. Peter says that persons in every *ethnos* who fear God and do right are acceptable *(dektos),* welcome, to him.

Does this statement teach a "larger biblical hope" that the vast majority but not absolutely all will be saved? Does it teach that God will judge the heathen by light they have, not according to "the light that did not reach them" (Pinnock 1990:367; compare Anderson 1970:102; Marshall 1980:190)? It is true that *dektos* means "pertaining to that which is pleasing in view of its being acceptable" (Louw and Nida 1988:1:299). It is used in the Old Testament of acceptable sacrifices and prayers and of moral acts (Lev 1:3; 19:5; Prov 15:8). In each case, however, God declares the conditions for acceptability. Is the acceptability or welcome spoken of in Acts 10:35 right standing with God, salvation? Only if the verse is divorced from its immediate and larger contexts. If Cornelius is already a saved believer, why does the angel tell him to send for Peter, who would bring "a message through which you and all your household *will* be saved" (Acts 11:14; Fernando 1987:133)? That Cornelius or anyone else can be acceptable to God for salvation without hearing the gospel or confessing the name of Christ contradicts the angel's message

vergence of events throughout the narrative (vv. 17, 19, 21; 11:11).

and Luke's understanding of the way one comes to salvation through the gospel message (11:14; compare 11:1; Lk 8:11-15; Acts 16:30-31).

In Acts 10:35 Peter and Luke are seeking to avoid two extremes: the Jews' ethnic pride and prejudice, which saw no Gentile as a fit object of God's saving call, and the view that the religions of all cultures are equally valid bases for being acceptable to God.

What Peter is saying is the same thing that the writer to the Hebrews points out: "anyone who comes to [God] must believe that he exists and that he rewards those who earnestly seek him" (Heb 11:6). In turning away from idols to the one true God, Cornelius demonstrated belief in God's existence; in turning away from pagan immorality to doing *what is right* according to the Old Testament ethic, he showed his earnestness in seeking God. He had made the first steps of repentance, which did not save him but made him a proper candidate to hear the good news, according to a "more light" principle (compare Acts 11:18).

In a day of religious pluralism, when compassionate Christians seek to guard against prejudicial bias and see the good in all religions, Peter's speech clearly teaches us that though God does not play favorites with nations, he does make distinctions in matters of religion. Only those who worship him, the one true God, and Jesus Christ whom he has sent can know eternal life (Jn 17:3).

Peter now states the theme of his message (Acts 10:36). Within the framework of God's dealings with a particular nation, *the people of Israel,* God sent a message (see references at 10:44), *telling the good news* (see comment on "evangelize" at 8:35) *of peace [accomplished] through Jesus Christ* (compare 10:43). Peter next highlights the universal scope of salvation blessings. This Jesus Christ is Lord of all people. The peace

10:35 Bassler (1985) contends that Luke's view of God's impartiality differs from Paul's radical eschatological approach (Rom 2:10). She says Luke seems to incorporate the distinction in Greco-Roman universalism between those who use reason to live virtuously and those who do not. She contends that Luke employs the Jewish Christian ideal as the standard of behavior for the virtuous life. In this way God's impartiality "acknowledges the ability of Gentiles to conform to Jewish-Christian standards of merit" (1985:551). But such a view does not take into account the fact that Cornelius still needs to hear a message in order to be saved (Acts 11:14).

10:36 Due to the lack of a connecting particle, the precise relation of verse 36 to its immediate context should not be determined by linking it to what precedes, thus making impartiality the context of the gospel (contrast Marshall 1980:191). Then the reception of

Christ achieved is not just for the Jews but for all people. The peace Christ wrought is the basis for tearing down the platforms of ethnic pride and the barriers of ethnic religious prejudice so that Jew and Gentile, indeed all persons, can be at peace with each other.

Peter's bold declaration draws out clearly God's intention announced from the very beginning of his Son's saving mission (Lk 2:10, 14). Now we know that "all the people" (Lk 2:10) includes the Gentiles. When the shattering good news "Jesus Christ is Lord of all people" is heard and heeded, the church is liberated from its cultural parochialism, set free to witness "across the tracks" and across the world.

Peter now offers proof, through the kerygma, for Christ's universal lordship (Acts 10:37-41). Twin themes run throughout his account of Jesus' life, death and resurrection: historical verifiability and divine accomplishment. He marks the events in terms of time and place (vv. 37, 39-40). He identifies the apostles as eyewitnesses to the events (vv. 39-41). Peter realizes that Jesus was not seen generally after his resurrection, and he explains this. God chose those who would see the risen Lord, thus indicating that their witness not only has his approval but has its origin in divine initiative, not human motivation (compare Lk 6:13-16; Acts 1:2). Peter further testifies to the resurrection's historical authenticity by saying that during the postresurrection period the apostles *ate and drank with him* (Christ). To be a witness of one who eats and drinks with you is to experience him with all your senses (Lk 24:30, 39-43; Acts 1:3-4; compare Jn 20:19-23, 27; 21:12; Tobit 12:19). In all these ways Peter proves that Jesus' life, death and resurrection, which demonstrated that he is *Lord of all,* happened in space and time. This was of utmost importance to Luke's readers, for his narrative was intended to help them

---

forgiveness by all those who believe (v. 43) becomes unnecessary. Nor should we link the verse to what follows, making *the message* the object of *you know* (see v. 37; compare RSV). Then verse 37 following cannot properly function as proof of the sermon's theme contained in this verse (Burchard 1985:293; compare Lk 2:15, 17). Rather, verse 36 should be allowed to maintain its independent status with a minimum of emendation. It contains the gospel message on the pattern of its first announcement to the shepherds (Lk 2:10-14). The NIV permits such a reading, though it does deemphasize the verse's climax by making it a dependent clause. The verse should read, "As to the word [accusative of respect] that God sent to the children of Israel, bringing good news of peace through Jesus Christ: This [Jesus Christ] is Lord of all [people]."

"know the certainty" of "the things that have been fulfilled among us" (Lk 1:4, 1).

What God accomplished in Jesus' ministry, death and resurrection is the proof of his universal lordship. Peter says God anointed Jesus with the Holy Spirit and power for his ministry (compare Lk 4:18/Is 61:1; Lk 3:22; 4:1, 14; 10:21). It is interesting that Isaiah presents the servant of the Lord as having a ministry that extends to all nations (Is 42:6; 49:6; compare 11:1-5). Peter focuses on the power of Jesus' ministry. He exercised his lordship by *doing good* (*euergetōn;* Hellenistic kings held a related royal title, *euergetēs,* Lake and Cadbury 1979:121; compare Lk 22:25) and by releasing those oppressed by the devil's power (Lk 13:16; compare 11:14-23; this should not be limited to physical healings, as Marshall 1980:192; it should extend to exorcisms—E. F. Harrison 1986:183). This ministry showed God was with him (compare Mt 1:23/ Is 7:14).

It is his resurrection-exaltation that decisively demonstrates his lordship (Acts 2:36). Peter simply states that God raised him and caused him to be seen (1:2-3; 3:15; 4:10; 13:30, 37). In the Great Commission delivered by the risen Lord we begin to see the essential link between resurrection and universal lordship. The apostles were commissioned to carry the message *He is the one whom God appointed as judge of the living and the dead.* Only the One who has conquered the power of death is qualified to judge all humankind, living or dead, and render and execute verdicts of eternal life or death.

Peter mentions only briefly Jesus' death, the jarring antithesis to his universal lordship (10:39). What was a cursed death to the Jews (note the allusion to Deut 21:22 in Peter's phrase *hanging him on a tree)* was equally despicable to Romans. Crucifixion was fit only for non-Roman citizens, slaves and provincials. Only if a Roman citizen was convicted of treason would he be crucified. How could One whose followers claimed was "Lord of all people" have been crucified? Peter does not answer that question here, though the allusion to a cursed death, under-

---

10:42 Though some see *the people* as referring to both Jew and Gentile because of verse 34 (Williams 1985:181; Kistemaker [1990:399] says it refers to Gentiles), this understanding fits neither the usage in the immediate context (v. 41) nor Peter's and the Jerusalem church's practice to this point in carrying out a Jewish mission (Longenecker 1981:393). Though it

stood in both a promise-and-fulfillment and a vicarious-atonement framework, would certainly go a long way to legitimize it (compare Lk 22:35-37/Is 53:12).

Peter's conclusion applies Christ's universal lordship to his audience (Acts 10:42-43). In Jesus they face both a final accounting and a unique opportunity. Part of the message the risen Lord commanded the apostles to proclaim (Lk 24:47) and testify or warn *(diamartyromai,* Acts 2:40; 8:25) the people is that God has appointed Jesus the judge of all human-kind in the last day. The theme of final judgment occurs consistently in speeches to Gentiles (17:31; 24:25). It seems to be a way to talk about repentance in terms relevant and motivating to them. Indeed, Peter moves easily in this one sentence from a particularist view, *he com-manded us to preach to the people* (the Jews), to a universal view, *he is the one whom God appointed as judge of the living and the dead* (all humankind). To this universal Judge all must answer.

Peter immediately turns to the good news that through the name of this universal Lord (2:38; 4:12) all are presented with the unique oppor-tunity to receive the forgiveness of sins. He grounds this expression of salvation blessings, *forgiveness of sins* (Lk 24:47; Acts 2:38; 5:31; 13:38; 26:18; compare Lk 1:77; 4:18), in the witness of all the Old Testament prophets (Is 33:24; 53:4-6, 11-12/Lk 22:37; Jer 31:34; Dan 9:24; compare Lk 24:25-27, 44-47). And he moves again from the particular, the Jewish prophets' witness, to the universal, the promise that *everyone who be-lieves in him* receives forgiveness.

Peter's preaching on the impartial God and the universal Lord and Savior now shows how Christ's Great Commission lies at the heart of a "go" theology (Lk 24:47; Acts 1:8). Such a centrifugal momentum must drive the church today.

God's Confirmation (10:44-48) Salvation blessings come to those who hear, receive, believe and hold fast to the Word, the gospel message (Lk 8:15; Acts 2:22; 3:22-23; 4:4; 15:7; 13:44; 19:5; 26:29; 28:26-28). So here the Spirit falls on them, just as Peter speaks *these words* of the

---

may explain the delay in the direct Gentile mission (E. F. Harrison 1986:184), Peter's articulation should probably be understood as saying that the gospel reaches the Gentiles through the Jews (Krodel 1986:198; compare 3:25-26).

welcome promise of forgiveness to all who believe and the audience hears *the message* (probably referring to the gospel, not just Peter's sermon—Lake and Cadbury 1979:122; compare Lk 8:15; Acts 4:4; 8:4; 10:36; 11:19; 15:7; 17:11).

In our day Western society is increasingly turning its back on its rational, cognitive heritage in favor of high-impact, "high-touch" experience. Some Christians engaged in crosscultural mission hail this mindlessness as a liberation that permits us to frame a truly contextual gospel free of Western rationalism. Yet at the very beginning of crosscultural mission, Peter neither depended on power encounter nor denigrated the cognitive. In fact, the Word and the Spirit were interdependent. And so must it ever be.

Luke's description of the Spirit's coming lets us know that the Gentiles' salvation is divinely worked, complete and authentic. It is all of God, for Peter has not even finished his speech. He has not given an invitation. God, the knower of all hearts, has chosen to cleanse their hearts by faith (15:8-9). He demonstrates that these Gentiles have indeed been given "repentance unto life" (11:18) by pouring out the gift of his Spirit on them, as he did on Jewish believers at Pentecost (2:4, 17, 33; compare 2:38; 8:20; 11:17). That the Spirit *came* on them (literally, "falling on," 8:16; 11:15) points not only to arrival but also to suddenness and intensity (Turner 1981:49). By combining this description with the imagery of "pouring out on," inundating with as with an overwhelming tidal wave (10:45), Luke highlights the completeness of the salvation experienced. Its authenticity is manifested by the Gentiles' *speaking in tongues.*

As the NIV marginal note indicates, there is some uncertainty about what the word *tongues* refers to and hence how it is to be translated. The literal translation *tongues* here would refer to Spirit-inspired ecstatic utterances of "heavenly languages" that require an equally inspired interpreter (1 Cor 14; compare Acts 19:6; Longenecker 1981:394: Haenchen 1971:354). The marginal reading *other languages* (note that *other* is not present in the Greek text) points to human languages (2:4-8). If we

---

10:45 *Circumcised believers* probably refers to a certain party within Jewish Christianity that believed circumcision was necessary for incorporation into the church, as Kistemaker

opt for the "ecstatic utterances" interpretation, we have to explain the claims that the experience paralleled that of Acts 2 (10:47; 11:15, 17). Williams says they need to be similar though not identical to satisfy the claims of the text (1985:184). If we opt for the "foreign languages" explanation, we must account for the lack of the term *other* and how such an outburst of foreign languages could have been convincing to the Jewish believers. It would have been convincing if these Gentiles spoke in languages including Hebrew and Aramaic, which the Joppa believers could follow.

Though it is difficult to be certain about the nature of the "tongues" (Kistemaker 1990:400), what the early believers conclude from this manifestation is certain: salvation blessings have been poured out on uncircumcised Gentiles. This challenges the Jews' basic assumption that a holy and pure God would not pour out his Holy Spirit on profane, common and unclean Gentiles, unless they became holy and ritually pure through becoming Jews. No wonder that Jewish Christians with a commitment to circumcision showed the same "astonishment" at this phenomenon as the Pentecost crowd did (2:7, 12; compare 8:13; 9:21).

The experience of salvation always evokes praise to the Giver of salvation. So here, as at Pentecost (2:11) and in Ephesus, the last evangelized area of Paul's missionary journeys (19:17), the newly converted or newly filled-with-the-Spirit magnify God.

Expecting a negative answer, Peter asks, in essence, "Who is going to stand in the way of God's work?" Only at the risk of resisting God would someone dare to hinder the full incorporation into the church via baptism of Gentiles who have the Spirit's baptism (compare Lk 18:16; Acts 5:39; 8:36; 28:31). So Peter orders their baptism and enjoys their hospitality for *a few days.*

The ground is indeed level at the foot of the cross. What a comfort to all the racially and culturally despised in our day, who thirst for the dignity that comes from spiritual equality in the "Christ identity." What a challenge to the church to live out, through acceptance across racial,

(1990:403) contends, not simply to Jewish Christian believers in general (Lake and Cadbury 1979:122).

class, ethnic and gender lines, our profession that we serve an impartial God who has sent us a universal Lord and Savior.

Peter's Defense of His Gentile Mission (11:1-18)

What would convince a charismatic that the cerebral theological discourses that pass for sermons in emotionless orthodoxy can call people to genuine faith? What would convince those in a formal tradition that the faith of those who have responded to emotionally charged charismatic preaching is authentic?

How Peter convinced Jerusalem church members who had been prejudiced against uncircumcised Gentiles becomes a model for us as we seek to sort through claims to God's working which challenge our biases.

Peter Encounters Criticism (11:1-3) The conversion of Cornelius's household was a truly momentous event: *the Gentiles also had received the word of God* (10:44-45; compare 8:14; 17:11). The gospel had decisively crossed its last cultural threshold. The scope and level of the reporting also shows the import of this milestone. The church *throughout Judea,* even *the apostles,* heard about it.

Peter is not summoned, yet he may anticipate some trouble, so he goes up to Jerusalem, taking along corroborating witnesses (see v. 12). There he immediately encounters criticism from *circumcised believers.* The reference to *circumcised believers* does not seem to refer here to the whole church, which was completely Jewish at this time (contrast Longenecker 1981:397). Rather, it points to certain believers who were particularly zealous for the law and insisted on no social intercourse between circumcised and uncircumcised (Bruce 1988:220; Gal 2:12). They charged Peter with making himself ritually unclean by entering a Gentile's house and eating with him (see comment and background information at Acts 10:28).

Commentators may speculate about the motivation behind these charges—perhaps fear of persecution from unbelieving Jews (Bruce 1988:219) or Jewish-Roman tensions under Caligula (Kistemaker

---

11:3 The table-fellowship issue, the heart of the charge against Peter, is not mentioned explicitly in Acts 10. But it is a concern that arises naturally from the conversion of Gentiles (compare Gal 2:11-14; Acts 10:14, 28) and would be much on the minds of Jewish

1990:408). But what is clear is that prejudice led to a myopic view of the situation (compare the Pharisees' treatment of Jesus: Lk 5:30; 15:1). How sad it is when man-made rules designed to protect our holiness and bring us close to God prevent us from seeing and rejoicing when God grants salvation to those who had not known his grace.

Peter Defends His Actions (11:4-15) Early reports of Cornelius's conversion may have been fragmented and garbled. To set the record straight, Peter explains (18:26; 28:23) the situation in an orderly fashion (compare Lk 1:3; NIV's *everything . . . precisely as it had happened* communicates more the intent than the method itself). Peter's report is an orderly, reliable, factual account of the divine initiatives in word and deed that brought Cornelius and him together.

Luke shows the reliability of his account by using it as a second witness to the events of Acts 10 (compare Deut 19:15). He presents it as a first-person eyewitness report. All the events are relayed either as Peter experienced them (his vision, Acts 11:5-10; the arrival of Cornelius's men and the Spirit's command, vv. 11-12; the Spirit's coming, vv. 15) or as they were reported directly to him (Cornelius's vision, vv. 13-14). The *six brothers* are brought in as witnesses as well (vv. 12-15). Their number may be significant for commending the truthfulness of the account to Luke's Roman audience, since it was the custom in Rome to authenticate a really important document by attaching seven seals to it (Barclay 1976:87). Finally, Peter calls on his audience as witnesses when he likens what happened at Caesarea to what they themselves experienced at Pentecost (v. 15).

This is above all a factual report of the divine initiative via interpreted acts to bring salvation to the Gentiles. Peter makes no comment on his personal circumstances, his perplexity about the vision or his own interpretation of the events' significance (10:9-10, 17, 19, 28-29, 34-35). He lets the facts speak for themselves. Any interpretation of their significance is objective and revealed, for it comes from heaven, the Spirit and the angel (11:7, 9, 12, 14).

In this way Peter teaches the main lessons of his experience. God

Christians, given that if it were practiced the result could well be persecution (Marshall 1980:195).

has cleansed all foods (v. 9). The dietary laws that marked the distinction between Jew and non-Jew are abolished. The Spirit commands that Peter live out this new freedom by accompanying uncircumcised men to their master's house, "not making any distinctions" (v. 12). He is not to treat them as he would have when the food laws, which made distinctions, were still in force (*diakrinanta* should be taken as a true active [Marshall 1980:196], not with its middle meaning, "hesitation," as in NIV, probably under the influence of 10:29; compare 10:20). The angel tells Cornelius that the purpose of Peter's visit is to proclaim a message by which uncircumcised Gentiles may enter into salvation (11:14).

Indications of Peter's understanding of the events' significance are not entirely lacking. He emphasizes the divine origin of his vision (11:5/ 10:11). He stresses the providential ordering of events by his immediate juxtaposition of them: his vision and Cornelius's men's arrival (11:11/ 10:17-18), the beginning of Peter's preaching and the coming of the Spirit (11:15/10:44). Finally, he hints at the divine rejection of the Jewish taboo against entering a Gentile's house when he notes that the angel appears *in his [Cornelius's] house* (11:13).

From the content of Peter's report we learn again that the real hero of the Cornelius conversion narrative is God, "the gracious prodding One who makes bold promises and keeps them, who finds a way even in the midst of human distinctions and partiality between persons" (Willimon 1988:99). Where distinctions born of racial, ethnic, class or gender prejudice stand as obstacles to the advance of the gospel, we can be sure that God will prod us to eliminate them.

Peter's method shows that "the proof of Christianity always lies in facts" (Barclay 1976:87). God speaks a word and then fulfills it. God acts

11:11 The more difficult textual reading of Acts 11:11 (*ēmen*, "we were"; NIV follows the *ēmēn*, "I was," reading) implies that the six men are already in the house; this is no contradiction to Acts 10:17-23, which is silent on the matter.

11:12-13 Cornelius is not named when first introduced, and the angel is also introduced without explanation. But this does not indicate that Luke composed the account assuming his readers' knowledge. These details could have been part of the report that reached the ears of the church at Jerusalem (v. 1).

11:14 The angel's disclosure of Peter's purpose in preaching—Cornelius and his household's salvation—does not originate with Luke. Acts 10:33 could imply that Cornelius had been informed originally of the saving purpose of Peter's message.

to fulfill his saving purposes and then interprets that act so that we may understand and appropriate it to ourselves. Whether for the Christian or the non-Christian, the method and the expected response are always the same: report the facts through reliable witnesses; receive, believe and act on the report.

An Interpretive Case for God at Work (11:16-17) Peter now seizes on the similarity of the coming of the Spirit to Cornelius's household and the Spirit's coming to the disciples at Pentecost. He points to the divine origin and the salvation-history significance of the Pentecost experience by remembering Jesus' words of promise (Acts 1:5; compare Lk 3:16). John's baptism of repentance, in preparation for the coming of the Messiah at the last day, would be superseded by the Spirit's baptism, inaugurating the presence of the salvation blessings of that last day. At Pentecost, Peter says, we experienced this same gift, the Holy Spirit himself (Acts 10:45-47; 15:7-11; compare 2:38; 8:20), by meeting only one condition: belief in the Lord Jesus Christ (15:7, 11; compare 2:44; 4:4, 32; 8:12; 10:43). If Cornelius's household has received this gift without being circumcised, then Gentiles too must be acceptable to God on the same condition.

To refuse to incorporate the Gentile believers into the church via baptism and full table fellowship would be to thwart God's purposes. Peter cannot, indeed he would not be able to, stand in the way of God (NIV's *Who was I to think that I could oppose God?* makes explicit the element of judgment; see comment at 10:47). It was incumbent upon Peter, if he was to follow God's lead, to treat these Gentiles as full brothers and sisters in Christ by accepting their hospitality and eating with them.

As with the Samaritans (8:14-17), the external manifestation of the

---

11:15 The Spirit's falling as Peter *began to speak* does not necessarily contradict Acts 10, where Peter had preached for some time before the Spirit fell (vv. 43-44). *Began* may not be a strict time marker here (Kilgallen 1990). Both passages affirm that Peter was interrupted (10:44; 11:15). Could it be that Peter had only begun in the sense that he introduced his gospel in summary form and intended to develop it further in discussions with his audience in the days ahead (compare Kistemaker 1990:413)?

11:16 The marginal note "or *in*" provides a locative as opposed to an instrumental way of rendering the dative *hydati.* Either is possible, but the parallelism with *en pneumati hagiō* (Lake and Cadbury [1979:126] say the variation in construction is stylistic, without significance for interpretation) probably requires that *hydati* also be taken instrumentally.

Spirit's coming and presence serves a limited though vital purpose in salvation history. It should not be taken as a normative pattern for all Christians in all times and places. This time the Spirit comes before any profession of faith or water baptism, demonstrating that God the knower of all hearts has indeed cleansed these Gentiles' hearts by faith, making them fit to receive the Holy Spirit. Not only does this sequence of events convince Jewish Christians of the soundness of Gentile conversions, it also links the Spirit's coming to conversion so as to call into question any view of baptism of the Spirit as an experience subsequent to conversion/regeneration (see note at 1:5).

The Church Responds in Praise (11:18) The facts, the divinely given interpretation and the apostle's application prove convincing. The critics *had no further objections* (literally, "became or were quiet"; see Lk 14:4; Acts 21:14) and glorified God with a confession that the Gentiles' faith is genuine. Such praise usually occurs in Luke-Acts in response to a miracle or to news of the Gentile mission (Lk 5:25-26; 13:13; 18:43; compare 2:20; Acts 13:48; 21:20; compare Lk 23:47). *So then, God has even granted the Gentiles repentance unto life.* The phrasing indicates that the Jewish believers understand the "revolution in principle" that has occurred. It is not just an isolated God-fearer's household but *the Gentiles,* all non-Jews, to whom the door of salvation is wide open. Further, this *repentance* is not a precondition produced by human effort. It is a gift from God to the Gentiles, just as it was to the Jews (Acts 3:26; 5:31).

What then should convince us that God is at work even in ways that cut across the grain of our prejudices? A plain hearing of the facts and their interpretation, judged by the promises of God's Word, is where we start. And when we keep in mind that salvation begins with the gift of repentance, our prejudices, which will always demand that the outsider meet certain performance standards, will melt away. In their place will come wonder and praise to God that his salvation has touched people whom we, left to ourselves, would not.

□ **The Mission Continues and Faces Opposition (11:19—12:25)**
Two vignettes of life in the Antioch and Jerusalem church provide a transition from the mission to Jews to the mission to Gentiles; from

Peter, the apostles and the Jerusalem evangelists to Paul and his missionary band; and from Jerusalem as the sending base to Antioch.

The Gentile Mission at Antioch (11:19-30)

Ancient Antioch was famous for its humor, especially the coining of
jesting nicknames. When an organized brigade of chanting devotees of
Nero led crowds in adulation, this band of imperial cheerleaders with
their ludicrous homage was quickly dubbed *Augustiani.* And earlier,
when the devotees of the one called Christ came to public attention, they
were named *Christianoi,* partisans of Christ (11:26). What may have been
first coined by outsiders as a term of derision (see Acts 26:28 and 1 Pet
4:16, the only two other New Testament occurrences of the term—both
on the lips of hostile unbelievers), the followers of the Way embraced
it as a fitting label.

Theophilus and his peers had heard the name, though not always
distinctly. It was confused by many with *Chrēstianos,* possibly deriving
from *Chrēstos,* "useful," a common name for a slave (compare Suetonius
Claudius 25.4). What does it mean to be a *Christianos,* a Christian
(Tacitus *Annals* 15.44; Suetonius *Nero* 16.2)? Luke clears this up for
Theophilus and us by pointing to Antioch.

Inclusive Evangelism (11:19-21) To show the origin of the direct
mission to the Gentiles, Luke picks up the thread of the story from Acts
8:4 and notes the geographical progress of Hellenistic Jewish Christians
who spread the life-giving seed of the word (Lk 8:11) even as they were
scattered by "affliction" (NIV *persecution;* compare Acts 14:22; 20:23)
brought on by Stephen's martyrdom. They evangelized the Jews of
Phoenicia—modern Lebanon, the coastal strip seven and a half miles
wide and about seventy-five miles long from Cape Carmel north to the
river Eleutheros. Congregations in Tyre, Sidon and Ptolemais were the
fruit (21:4, 7; 27:3). They extended their mission to Cyprus, the location
of a very early and now very large Jewish colony (Philo *Legatio ad Gaium*
282; compare Acts 4:36) and then on to "Antioch on the Orontes" in
Syria. Three hundred miles from Jerusalem and fifteen to twenty miles
east of the Mediterranean, it stood at a point where the Orontes River
breaks through at the convergence of the Lebanon and Tauros mountain
ranges.

Of the sixteen cities built by the Seleucid general Seleucus I Nicator and named for his father Antiochus, Syrian Antioch was the largest and most prosperous. With a population of over 500,000, including a Jewish colony of 70,000, and a thriving economy because of its strategic position at the crossroads of trade routes south to Palestine and Egypt, east to Persia and west to the Asia Minor peninsula, Antioch was justly called "Antioch the Great, Queen of the East." Josephus ranked it as the third greatest city of the Roman Empire, behind Rome and Alexandria (Josephus *Jewish Wars* 3.29).

This free city, capital of the Roman province of Syria, was "a melting pot of Western and Eastern cultures, where Greek and Roman traditions mingled with Semitic, Arab, and Persian influences" (Longenecker 1981:399). Cicero (*Pro Archia* 3) praised its art and literature. Juvenal referred to its reputation for immorality, writing of "the Orontes pouring pollution into the Tiber" (*Satires* 3.62)—the invasion of Rome by eastern superstition and profligacy (compare Barclay's [1976:89] description of the cult prostitution associated with the worship of Daphne and Apollo; the temple was near Antioch).

To such a city came Hellenistic Jewish Christians from Cyprus and Cyrene (a city on the Mediterranean coast of modern Tunisia) and directly evangelized Gentiles, while continuing the outreach to Jews (note *also* in v. 20). Luke gives us neither the motive nor the date of this bold new mission thrust. Because Luke sees Peter as the inaugurator of the witness to the Gentiles (15:7, referring to 10:1—11:18), and the church sends Barnabas and not the apostles to investigate the Gentile mission at Antioch, it appears that this witness follows Peter's preaching to Cornelius. Indeed, it may be consciously following Peter's precedent.

Preaching of *the good news* of *the Lord Jesus* to Gentiles points them to Christ's sovereignty and deity. "Many were trying to find in various mystery cults a divine lord who could guarantee salvation and immortality to his devotees" (Bruce 1988:225). The good news is that "this can be found in *the Lord Jesus*" (compare 10:36; 16:31;

11:20 *Greeks* (Hellēnistas) should be understood in the broad sense of "Greek-speaking persons who practice Greek ways"—that is, the mixed non-Jewish population of Antioch.

20:21; 28:31).

The Lord's hand, an Old Testament metaphor for God's power and favor (Ezra 9:7; Is 66:14; compare Lk 1:66), is with this witness—not in signs and wonders (Acts 4:30; so Krodel 1986:207), for they are not explicitly mentioned here, but in the convicting and convincing work of the Spirit such that significant numbers *believed* and *turned to the Lord* (4:4; 6:7; 9:24; 10:27; 14:15; 15:19; compare 9:35; 26:18, 20).

Though Luke uses *Lord* interchangeably for the Father and the Son, if all the uses in 11:19-26 speak of Jesus, we learn the comprehensive role he plays in bringing salvation to the Gentiles. He is the gospel's content, power and goal. He is the sustainer and the identity of those who receive it.

In a day when a misapplication of church-growth theory's "homogeneous unit principle" can produce monocultural churches, God's blessing on inclusive evangelism across ethnic lines at Antioch is a necessary reminder of where God's heart is. While he may indeed give growth within homogeneous ethnic units, such units are not his ideal, and neither should they be ours.

Authentic Growth (11:22-24) Though Luke does not tell us the Jerusalem church's motive for dispatching Barnabas, the circumstances and the church's disposition are probably not unlike what we find in Acts 11:1-3. The church as a whole is sympathetic, which their choice of Barnabas indicates, but a segment, "those of the circumcision," are not so sure and need to be placated (Marshall 1980:202).

The Jerusalem church's action reflects a concern for continuity and accountability in the advance of the church's mission. Sometimes missionaries today hesitate to tell all that is happening in their work, believing that unorthodox strategies or methods required by crosscultural witness will not be understood by "the folks back home." The early church never manifested such lack of trust, and the resulting churches were the stronger for their willing accountability.

Barnabas authenticates this church growth both in his initial reaction, joy, and in his encouragement to perseverance. Unlike "those of the

(Contrast Longenecker [1981:401], who says it refers to Gentiles who had some relationship to the synagogue.)

circumcision" in verse 2, but very much like the hosts of heaven (Lk 15:7, 10), Barnabas rejoices at seeing *the evidence of the grace of God* (Acts 11:23; NIV introduces the phrase *the evidence of*). The grace that Barnabas sees is not so much the change in lifestyle or the more manifest spiritual gifts (as Williams 1985:193), though these are undoubtedly present; rather, it is the great numbers of newly and soundly converted Gentiles. "In Acts grace is that power which flows from God or the exalted Christ and accompanies the activity of the apostles giving success to their mission" (Esser 1976:119; Acts 4:33; 15:11; 18:27; 20:24). Do we, with Barnabas, rejoice "at the spectacle of God's free favor, unlimited by racial or religious frontiers, embraced and enjoyed by all without distinction" (Bruce 1990:273)?

Barnabas, true to his name ("Son of Encouragement," 4:36), encourages (note continuous action imperfect *parekalei*) the Antioch believers to steadfast loyalty to the Lord (compare Josephus *Jewish Antiquities* 14.20; Wisdom 3:9; Lk 8:15). Note that the "glue" of their perseverance in salvation is a personal relationship with Christ embraced from the inside out, not the external mark of circumcision and Jewish practice. And such must be the case for new converts to Christianity from any culture. If the heart is first abiding in Christ as Lord and Savior, the new ways of living will necessarily follow as the person learns to walk according to God's will as revealed in his Word.

Luke now authenticates Barnabas, showing approval of this "bridge person's" authentication of the Gentile witness at Antioch. He attests his character as *a good man* (Lk 8:8, 15; compare 6:45). He presents that character's source: *full of the Holy Spirit and faith* (see comment at Acts 6:3; compare 6:5; 7:55). Instead of operating by sight, insisting that Gentiles show outwardly, through circumcision and ritual observance, what they claim to have happened inwardly, Barnabas chooses by faith to apply God's promise of a universal offer of salvation to the Antioch situation (Lk 24:47; Acts 2:21, 39). Finally, Luke tells us of the fruit of such character: numerical growth of the church (compare 2:41, 47; 5:14; 6:7; 8:6). In any age those full of the Spirit and good character, "faith"

11:28 The frequent famines of Claudius's reign (A.D. 41-54; Suetonius *Claudius* 18; Tacitus *Annals* 12.43) and the great famine of Palestine (A.D. 46-48; Josephus *Jewish Antiquities* 20.51,

vision and fruitfulness will be on the cutting edge of the church's advance.

Doctrinally Sound Nurture (11:25-26) Though Luke does not give the motive, the explosion in numbers and the need to conserve the harvest through careful grounding in the faith may have moved Barnabas to recruit Paul, still called Saul (E. F. Harrison 1986:194). He travels northwest to Tarsus in Cilicia, east Asia Minor, to *look for Saul* in his hometown (the term implies a thorough search; compare Lk 2:44-45; Acts 9:30; 21:39; 22:3). For a whole year Barnabas and Saul work together in the church, teaching *great numbers of people*. As Luke uses the concept and as Paul articulates his calling (2 Tim 1:11), teaching (Christian nurture) and evangelism are not necessarily mutually exclusive activities (compare 4:2; 5:42). When the gospel and the Christian way of life are correctly understood, teaching and evangelism are distinct but must be seen as inseparable.

The believers are first *called* Christians at Antioch. Literally the verb means "to transact business." Hence to transact business under a particular name is to be known by that name (Bruce 1988:228).

Holistic Liberality (11:27-30) For Antioch to model fully what it means to be *Christians,* it must demonstrate orthopraxy by meeting physical needs (compare 2:42-47).

Antioch learns of a need through the word of prophets, Agabus in particular. Itinerant prophets ministered in the first-century church. They were evidence that the last days, the time of salvation, has dawned (2:17-18; Longenecker 1981:403). They "spoke revelation from the Spirit (1 Cor 14:29-30), usually in terms of edification and encouragement (1 Cor 14:3, 31) and even fundamental doctrine (Eph 3:4-5). But occasionally their ministry included prediction" (E. F. Harrison 1986:197). Prompted by the Spirit, Agabus "makes a prediction" (in extrabiblical usage this action points to enigmatic speech [Lake and Cadbury 1979:131], but not here, according to Haenchen [1971:374]): a great famine will spread over *the entire Roman world.* Luke tells us this prediction was fulfilled during Claudius's reign (see note). *The entire Ro-*

---

101) adequately fulfilled the prophecy (Marshall 1980:204).

The expanded Western reading *synestrammenōn de hēmōn* ("and when we were gath-

man world, literally, is the inhabited world politically, not geographically. At this time it was often viewed as coterminous with the Roman Empire (Lake and Cadbury 1979:131; Marshall 1980:204). This prediction was probably made before Claudius's reign (A.D. 41-54; Bruce 1990:277).

Since we too live in the last days, should we in the church expect to find prophets foretelling the future? Christians are divided on this issue, based on beliefs regarding how the closing of the canon of Scripture relates to the presence of revelation today. That factor must certainly be taken into account. Any claims to divinely inspired prophecy must be tested and must meet the criteria in Scripture for true prophecy (Deut 18:20-22). Alleged divinely inspired prophecy must be completely fulfilled. Anything less is not biblical.

The church responds in holistic liberality. Each member as he or she is financially able—that is, from discretionary income (compare Lev 25:49; Acts 19:25)—decides what to give and contributes it to a fund for famine relief. Their liberality is holistic in two ways. First, it extends beyond spiritual concern—"we will pray that God provides for you in your affliction"—to practical physical aid. Hence the collection is labeled a "service" (*diakonia;* Acts 6:1; 12:25; Rom 15:31; 2 Cor 8:4). Second, this interchurch relief involves the receiving church serving the sending church—a mixed Jewish and Gentile congregation serving a Jewish assembly. Such unity is based on the conviction that the church is a body greater than any single congregation within any culture. This unity carries with it a responsibility for the well-being of all disciples, wherever they are (note the use of the terms *disciples* and *brothers*). Barnabas and Saul take this collection to the *elders* (see comment at Acts

---

ered together") introducing Agabus's prediction would constitute the first "we passage" in Acts. Although Bruce views it as possibly original (1988:230), Longenecker (1981:405) is quite certain it is secondary, arising from an appropriation of Acts 13:1 (Lucius of Cyrene) or the tradition that Luke hailed from Antioch.

11:30 This visit is the same as the one reported in Galatians 2:1-10. If we date both the first and second visits from Paul's conversion, so that the three and fourteen years run concurrently (Gal 1:18; 2:1; the phrasing of Galatians permits this) and allow for some flexibility in rounding off years (Longenecker 1981:405), then an A.D. 33 date for Paul's conversion puts a second visit fourteen years later (Gal 2:1-10), within the time frame of the Palestine famine of Claudius's reign (A.D. 44-48; compare Acts 11:28). The trip's purposes—for Paul to lay before the apostles the gospel preached among the Gentiles (Gal

15:2), who have emerged as the administrators of physical aid in the Jerusalem church after the evident dispersal of the "Seven" at Stephen's martyrdom.

In our time, in the Western world and increasingly elsewhere, decades of social legislation have made the state responsible for meeting the physical needs of our neighbors, including fellow Christians. Antioch's example, then, raises the hard question: How much personal responsibility do I feel for the physical needs of others, especially the church in the Two-Thirds World? Though we cannot meet every need that global news brings to our attention, we can still do something to live out the holistic liberality that is an essential mark of being *Christians.*

Herod's Opposition at Jerusalem (12:1-25)

Citizens of today's nation-states often succumb to an "almost religious reverence for the power of the state" (Willimon 1988:112). Theophilus and his peers lived under regimes where homage to the emperor was not only a civic duty but a welcome way of expressing appreciation for the "safety net" the emperor had provided. But the demand for total loyalty will turn into total opposition when the state faces Christians who confess, "Jesus is Lord!"

The narrative of Herod's opposition and demise can help Christians face political opposition with discerning confidence and lets the inquiring unbeliever know that the state cannot stop the church in its mission.

A King Attacks (12:1-4) Herod Agrippa I (10 B.C.-A.D. 44), grandson of Herod the Great (Lk 1:5) and nephew of Herod the Tetrarch (Lk 3:19; 13:31; 23:7-12), spent his childhood and some of his adult life in the highest imperial circles in Rome. He had recently returned to Palestine

2:2) and for Paul and Barnabas to deliver the famine-relief collection (Acts 11:30)—though distinct, are not mutually exclusive. Paul hints at the famine-relief purpose in Galatians 2:10. The characterizations of the meetings ("official" in Gal 2, "unofficial" in Acts 11) are not contradictory.

Positively, both were prompted by revelation (Acts 11:27-28; Gal 2:2) and involved the same personnel (Acts 11:30; Gal 2:1). Peter's backsliding (Gal 2:11-14) is better explained at the point of an interim solution (distinct spheres for Jewish and Gentile mission) after the second visit and before the Jerusalem Council (Acts 15).

12:3-4 For Luke's interchangeable use of "Days of Unleavened Bread" and "Passover" compare Luke 22:1. Technically, Passover is 14 Nisan and the Days of Unleavened Bread are 15-21 Nisan.

to rule over territory that by A.D. 41 extended as far as his grandfather's kingdom (see Schürer 1973:442-54 for a complete description). Committed to maintaining the Pax Romana by supporting the Jewish majority in Palestine, he was both a pious observer of Jewish practices and a ruthless suppressor of minorities when they became disruptive (Longenecker 1981:407-8).

Whether influenced by Pharisees or by Sadducees among the Jewish leadership, Herod decides to arrest (literally, "lay hands on"; compare 4:3; 5:18; 21:27) some of *the church,* presumably the apostolic leaders (Bruce 1988:233). We are not told explicitly why Herod intends to *persecute* (literally, "harm, mistreat"; 18:10; compare Ex 7:6, 17) them. He may be responding to a stir caused by the apostles' "apostate" fraternizing with the Gentiles (compare 21:27-32). Or, like his grandfather (Mt 2:16), he sees the movement's messianic claims posing a political threat. All Luke tells us is that the beheading of James (a fulfillment of Mk 10:39) pleases the people (contrast 5:26). In Jewish law death by the sword was the penalty for murder or apostasy (*m. Sanhedrin* 9:1; compare Deut 13:6-18).

The martyrdom of James, the son of Zebedee and the brother of John (Lk 5:10; 8:51; 9:28), is an especially heavy blow to the church. Only some ten years after Jesus' resurrection/exaltation, one of the twelve apostles has been removed from the scene. To make matters worse, Herod seems bent on a systematic dismemberment of the movement, for next he arrests Peter. He places him under a secure guard of *four squads of four soldiers each,* rotating in three-hour shifts at night (Vegetius *De Re Militari* 3.8). Ever scrupulous in his Jewish observance, and possibly wishing to avoid an uproar at festival time (compare Mk 14:2), Herod leaves Peter in prison during the seven-day Feast of Unleavened Bread, which immediately followed Passover.

Luke teaches us that Satan's sphere of control is directly related to political governance (Lk 4:6; 22:53). Jesus warned that its power would be used against his followers (Lk 12:11-12; 21:12-19). Will we stand for Jesus as our Lord, realizing that sooner or later we will pay the price for doing so? Those who have lived in religious freedom for generations have much to learn from brothers and sisters in Christ just now emerging from the oppression of totalitarianism.

The Lord Delivers (12:5-11) Luke skillfully juxtaposes the power of the state—*so Peter was kept in prison*—and the power of the church, prayer—*but the church was earnestly praying to God for him*. In continuous (the verb construction indicates duration), fervent (Lk 22:44; 1 Pet 1:22; 4:8), united prayer, the church intercedes for Peter. Prayer is the only weapon it has, but it is more than enough. Luke presents prayer as "the natural atmosphere of God's people and the normal context for divine activity" (Longenecker 1981:409; Acts 1:14, 24; 2:42; 6:4; 13:2). If extended, fervent, united prayer is not a church's *first* resort in a time of crisis, the church reveals that it is ultimately depending on something or someone other than God.

As if to test the church's faith to the limit and emphasize his consummate power over his enemies, the Lord waits to act until the eve of Peter's show trial and probable summary execution. By his sleep Peter models a deep trust in God's sovereignty (Ps 3:5; Lk 8:23). Herod takes extra security measures, for normally one chain was enough (Seneca *Epistles* 5.7; compare Herod's own experience as recounted in Josephus *Jewish Antiquities* 18.195-96; Williams 1985:200 disagrees and sees the *two chains* as normal security precautions); thus he betrays his inherent insecurity in the face of this movement (Acts 5:19-26).

Suddenly (literally, "and behold," a phrase consistently used to introduce angelic appearances—1:10; 10:30) *an angel of the Lord appeared*. We should not take this simply as another way of referring to divine intervention (compare Longenecker 1981:409), for Peter himself clearly distinguishes between the Lord and the angel he sends (12:11). For Luke the angel of the Lord not only provides deliverance for God's witnesses (5:19) but also gives strength (Lk 22:43), brings judgment (Acts 12:23) and above all reveals God's will about the advance of his saving purposes (Lk 1:11; 2:9; Acts 8:26; 10:3). The angel comes to Peter with the same suddenness as the church's enemies do when arresting believers (same term here and at 4:1; 6:12; 17:5).

At the same time *a light shone in the cell*. We are not told its source— is it a case of chiaroscuro, with the light actually coming from the angel? And we are not told its effects—are the guards rendered unconscious by it? Peter's absence is a total mystery to them (12:18), and this leaves us even more in the dark. With either a kick in the ribs or a push in the

side, the angel rouses Peter and orders him to get up quickly and prepare to leave. Freed from sleep by the angel's action and command, and freed from his jailers by the miraculous falling away of the manacles from his hands, Peter can obey the further orders to put his belt around his tunic (Bruce 1990:283; not *Put on your clothes,* as in NIV), tie on his sandals, throw his cloak around himself and follow the angel. These step-by-step commands, like those given to a child, show that Peter is drowsy and disoriented. They certainly underline the fact that this escape is all the Lord's doing.

Luke relates Peter's evaluation of his experience. Though awake enough to obey the orders, he does not think what he is experiencing is real. He thinks he is seeing a vision. Quite naturally his prior experience of a vision in which he was commanded to act may be coloring his judgment here (10:10-16). Verses 11 and 12 chronicle his progressive realization of what is happening. Luke describes the escape in the most matter-of-fact terms. Peter and the angel pass two guards (possibly each one is standing at an entryway [Marshall 1980:209], or maybe the two are patrolling one corridor [Haenchen 1971:384]), then come to the final barrier, an iron gate leading to the city.

A street away from the prison and alone, the angel having withdrawn, Peter comes to himself—that is, to a correct interpretation of what has just happened. He affirms the reality, the source, the result and, by inference, the purpose of the rescue (12:11). Christianity is indeed a space-time faith that confesses that its Lord can and will act in history on behalf of his saints. Peter knows that the escape has happened "in truth" (NIV *without a doubt;* compare 26:25; 12:9). The Lord has the same power to rescue now as he did when he delivered Israel from Egypt (7:10, 34/Ex 3:8).

The reason that Peter is rescued while James was executed may be found in the term *rescued.* Acts 26:17 uses the word to describe God's protecting hand on his witnesses to make sure they fulfill their respon-

---

12:10 The Western reading speaks of Peter and the angel "descending seven steps" upon exiting. Though this has a "verisimilitude reflecting local knowledge" (Metzger 1971:394), it is right to be cautious, even negative, about the authenticity of the detail (Longenecker 1981:412). Further, the precise identity of the prison is unknown, though many suggest the Antonia fortress adjacent to the temple.

12:15 Kistemaker (1990:442) gives a sober, balanced assessment of Scripture's teaching

sibilities. As long as it is necessary that a particular servant of the Lord be actively deployed in accomplishing Christ's mission, he or she will be rescued. Any martyrdom is still a mark of God's sovereignty, not a sign of his weakness; his gracious purposes, not his sadistic pleasure, may be traced in it. Any rescue is a sign of the triumphant advance of God's mission and a mark that nothing can thwart the accomplishment of his purposes.

The Church Is Astonished (12:12-17) Peter proceeds to the home of Mary, the mother of John Mark (12:25; 13:5, 13; 15:37; Col 4:10; 2 Tim 4:11; Philem 24; 1 Pet 5:13). From the description of the home's entryway, "door of the gate, gateway, or vestibule," we learn that the house was spacious. Its layout included at least a main building separated from a gatehouse or vestibule by an open court. Whether it was the site of the upper room (1:13) is disputed (E. F. Harrison [1986:203] says perhaps; Marshall [1980:210] says there is no positive evidence). It was probably the gathering place of the house church to which Peter belonged (compare 12:17). At the moment it was serving as the venue for extended fervent prayer for Peter, which evidently included all-night sessions.

In a playful touch of comic irony, which lends realism to the account, Luke relates how a maidservant named Rhoda ("rosebud"), charged with answering the door, is so overcome with joy (Lk 24:41) at the sound of Peter's voice that she leaves him standing there while she rushes in to announce (NIV *exclaimed;* compare Acts 5:22, 25; 12:17) his arrival. While the church members argue over the truthfulness of her report (Lk 24:22), Peter is left knocking and calling at the door. The very answer to their prayers is knocking, and they do not believe it! They declare Rhoda crazy. When she sticks to her story, they conclude that Peter's guardian angel—who according to their Jewish tradition would take on his attributes—has arrived either to bring good news or to announce Peter's death. Going to investigate, they are "beside themselves in astonishment" when they open the door and see Peter standing there (com-

concerning guardian angels (Gen 48:16; Ps 91:11; Mt 18:10; Lk 16:22). "The Bible teaches that God has commissioned his angels—to be precise a particular class of angels—to protect the believers on earth. Scripture nowhere indicates that every believer throughout his earthly life is protected by one particular angel. Angels are God's servants who take care of believers." For the Jewish speculation see Tobit 5:21; Strack and Billerbeck 1978:2:707.

pare Lk 8:56; 24:22; Acts 2:7, 12; 10:45).

How does God answer prayer? He can do it while we are still praying. We should not receive God's surprises with disbelief but with joy born of expectation, that "blend of confident trust and sanctified imagination" (Ogilvie 1983:204).

Motioning with his hand for silence (13:16; 19:33; 21:40), Peter briefly recounts his rescue in terms of its ultimate source, *the Lord,* and instructs that *James and the brothers* be informed of his escape. James the half-brother of Jesus had some form of administrative leadership with the apostles by the mid-thirties (Gal 1:19; 2:9), presided at the Jerusalem Council in A.D. 49 (Acts 15:13) and by the late fifties was head of the Jerusalem church (21:18; Longenecker 1981:410-11; Bruce [1988:239] sees him in a position of undisputed leadership at this point). This is the first reference to him in Acts and may be another indicator of Luke's interest in presenting orderly transitions in the life of the Jerusalem church, showing its continuity even in the face of persecution (8:1; 9:31). Even though Peter must pass off the scene to *another place,* the church leadership is still in the capable hands of *James and the brothers.* Though Haenchen (1971:385) thinks *brothers* simply means "fellow Christians," it is better understood as a reference to church leaders or elders (compare E. F. Harrison 1986:205).

The Lord's deliverance is complete. With this rescue from the king's attack, the church remains unscathed. So today, even when there are changes in personnel, God will superintend the healthy advance of his church.

The Persecutors Are Defeated (12:18-23) In the morning there is not a little "consternation" among the guards over Peter's whereabouts (the term can refer to mental agitation as well as the *commotion* that flows from it). Herod interrogates the guards and according to Roman custom has them led away to suffer the same penalty, in this case execution that the escapee would have faced (*Code of Justinian* 9.4.4).

12:17 There have been various suggestions for the identity of *another place:* an unknown hiding place (Stott 1990:211), the coastal plain cities of the 9:32-43 mission (but this is still within Herod's territory), Syrian Antioch (Gal 2:11-14; Marshall 1980:211), north central Asia Minor (1 Pet 1:1; Williams 1985:203) or Rome (J. W. Wenham 1972; the Roman Catholic tradition). Wenham's case for Rome and his proposed chronology need to be given due consideration.

Though Herod had chosen Jerusalem as his place of residence, Caesarea on the coast was still the administrative capital. For whatever reason he now leaves the environs of Jerusalem (*Judea* should be understood here in this narrower sense) and goes to Caesarea.

Herod had power of life and death not only over individuals but also over regions, as the inhabitants of Tyre and Sidon knew well. These coastal cities of northwest Palestine depended on the breadbasket of Judea for grain (compare Ezek 27:17). We are not told the cause of Herod's exasperation, even "fury" (NIV *quarreling*), with the cities. Haenchen (1971:386) suggests a trade war sparked by competition between Caesarea and these Phoenician ports. We do not know the precise action Herod took; it may have been an economic boycott. It was effective, for now the cities send a joint delegation with the aid of Blastus, the king's trusted personal servant, to ask peace for themselves (note the middle voice, *ētounto*).

Herod was at the very zenith of his power. Not only had Rome granted him rule over as great a territory as his grandfather Herod the Great ruled, but he could force self-governing cities adjacent to his domain into submission. On the appointed day to conclude the peace, which was during games in honor of Caesar, as Josephus reports it, "clad in a garment woven completely of silver so that its texture was indeed wondrous, he entered the theatre at daybreak. There the silver, illumined by the touch of the first rays of the sun, was wondrously radiant and by its glitter inspired fear and awe in those who gazed intently upon it" (*Jewish Antiquities* 19.343-44 [whole account 343-59]; note that the theater seats faced west). No wonder that as Herod addressed the assembly, which included the populace of Caesarea as well as the delegation from Tyre and Sidon (Bruce 1990:288 says the populace of Caesarea), they cried out, *This is the voice of a god, and not of a man.*

Herod does not refuse their homage. Immediately an angel of the Lord strikes him down and he is *eaten by worms.* He experiences pain in the

12:20 The roots of the conflict may lie in some events from earlier in Herod's life (see Josephus *Jewish Antiquities* 18.147-50).

12:21 It is uncertain whether these games were those of the March 5 festival, held every five years in honor of the founding of Caesarea and its namesake Augustus, inaugurated by Herod the Great (Josephus *Jewish Wars* 1.415), or whether they were instituted by Herod himself to celebrate Claudius's August 1 birthday.

heart and stomach—peritonitis from a perforated appendix, combined with intestinal roundworms, ten to sixteen inches long. (Bunches of these can obstruct the intestines, causing severe pain, copious vomiting and finally death.) This excruciating condition continues for five days until he dies.

Luke tells us why Herod experiences the Lord's immediate judgment: because he does not give "glory" *(praise)* to God (Lk 2:14; 19:38). In receiving the worship of people who are economically dependent on him (12:20; contrast 14:17), Herod made himself the object of false worship, violated the first two commandments and justly earned God's immediate judgment. All political leaders and followers in whatever day, Theophilus's or ours, and under whatever political system, must be duly warned by Herod's defeat. The Lord is "Lord of all" (Acts 10:36), and he will not share his glory with any other (Is 42:8; 48:11).

The Word of God Triumphs (12:24-25) With poignant contrast Luke summarizes the Lord's victory over political powers. Worms spread and devour Herod's body, but the word of God, the Christian message, also spreads and multiplies (see comment at 6:7; compare Acts 19:20; Lk 8:11). This should work confidence in our hearts. We need not cower before threatening political power. We will boldly continue to spread the message of life. Though those in power may stop us, even by death, they cannot stop the gospel!

12:23 The death of Herod Agrippa I as reported by Josephus *(Jewish Antiquities* 19.343-59) and Luke (Acts 12:20-23) is witnessed to, as the similarities and differences of the accounts indicate, by two independent but mutually confirming records (Longenecker 1981:413; Talbert 1984:53 disagrees).

Eaten by worms (skōlēkobrōtos) was used as a metaphor for the unpleasant end of evil persons (for example, 2 Macc 9:5-12; Josephus *Jewish Antiquities* 17.168-70; Lucian *Alexander* 59; Eusebius *Ecclesiastical History* 8.16.3-5). Hence some commentators say that we cannot precisely identify the natural causes for Herod's death (Bruce 1988:242). Of the medical options—arsenic, ruptured hydatid cyst, roundworms, peritonitis, a perforated appendix, or a combination of peritonitis and roundworms—the last seems to fit best the descriptions given by Josephus and Luke. Because Luke combines reference to the angel with a description of a natural disease, Marshall (1980:212) says Luke is not thinking of an angelic appearance but merely pointing to the divine origin of the disease. But because Josephus's account mentions Herod's awareness of heavenly judgment and Luke elsewhere speaks of such judgment without reference to angels (see Acts 5:5, 10; 13:11), it is best to conclude that since we have an explicit reference to angels here, we are indeed dealing with an angelic appearance.

12:25 Luke does not present a famine-relief visit (11:30; 12:25) to meet the Jerusalem church's needs in the drought of A.D. 46 and Herod's attack and his death (A.D. 44; 12:1-23)

Herod was cut off just four years into his reign, but the church's work knows no such incompleteness in any aspect. Barnabas and Saul, having finished their *mission* (literally, "service") at Jerusalem, return to Antioch, taking John Mark with them.

THE CHURCH IN ALL NATIONS: PAUL'S MISSIONARY JOURNEYS (13:1—21:16)

The Jerusalem church has faithfully carried the gospel across many cultural thresholds as witnesses in Jerusalem and in all Judea and Samaria (Acts 1:8). Through Paul it will embark on fulfilling the "to the ends of the earth" phase of the Great Commission (9:15-16; 13:2).

What the non-Christian seeker and the believer find in Luke's account of this next phase is an effectively contextualized message for increasingly diverse audiences (13:16-41; 14:15-17; 17:22-31); a mission progressing triumphantly, even over the forces of darkness (13:8-12; 14:8-20; 16:16-18; 19:11-20; 13:45-52; 14:19-20; 16:16-40; 19:21-40); a church spiritually united though ethnically diverse (15:1-35); and a movement innocent before the state (16:35-40; 18:12-17; 19:37-40).

☐ The First Missionary Journey (13:1—14:28)

The first missionary journey presents in microcosm all the main features

---

in incorrect chronological order. The general time marker that introduces the Herod episodes ("it was about this time," 12:1) need not imply a strict sequencing of events. Luke may have opted to order according to subject matter, dealing fully with Antioch's story first, then Jerusalem's (Longenecker 1981:407).

The marginal reading "Some manuscripts *to*" *(eis)* gives the harder reading, which is attested by the earliest and best manuscripts (Metzger 1971:398). The easier reading, *from (ek* or *apo),* which the NIV places in the text, is not as well attested. It is evidently a secondary solution. Acts 11:30 has already recorded Barnabas and Saul's arrival at Jerusalem. This passage clearly speaks of their departure. While some see the more difficult reading as primary but an instance of a primitive error (Longenecker 1981:417), others (Metzger 1971:399; Bruce 1988:243) understand *eis* as the Hellenistic equivalent of *en* and read it with *had finished their mission.* This yields the satisfactory rendering "Barnabas and Saul returned, after they had finished mission at Jerusalem, taking with them John also called Mark."

13:1—14:28 Though Paul's direct mission to the Gentiles is an identifiable advance in the church's mission, Luke should not be seen as reserving the Gentile mission for Paul (contrast Longenecker 1981:415). There is continuity between Paul, Peter and the Hellenistic Jewish Christians in their witness to Gentiles (10:34-48; 11:19-20; 15:7). The main difference is that Paul's direct Gentile witness is at the heart of a conscious proactive strategy.

of Paul's missionary call (9:15-16). Paul does indeed carry Christ's name "before the Gentiles and their kings" (14:27; 13:7-12, 46-48; 14:8-18) and "before the people of Israel" (13:14-41). He does suffer for that name (14:5, 19).

The Commissioning (13:1-3)

Large numbers of North American and European missionaries who were deployed after World War II are now retiring. The need for replacements raises the key question, Who sends the missionary? Clarity is needed in a time when some missionary candidates "lay hands" on themselves, without involving the church. On the other hand, some churches insist that unless candidates defer totally to their guidance, they should not go. The work of the Spirit in the lives of Saul and Barnabas and the church at Antioch gives us God's perspective on who sends the missionary.

Church Leaders as Missionary Candidates (13:1) Luke sets the scene by listing the Antioch church's leaders, at once spiritually gifted *(prophets and teachers)* and multiculturally and socioeconomically diverse. *Barnabas,* a Levite from Cyprus (4:36), labors alongside *Simeon,* a black man (with the nickname *Niger*), and *Lucius,* a Roman from Cyrene in North Africa (compare 11:20). *Manaen,* who in his youth was chosen as a companion to a prince, Herod Antipas, ministers with *Saul,* a Pharisee from Cilicia in southeast Asia Minor (22:3; Phil 3:5).

This leadership roll is actually a list of potential candidates for missionary service, for those who head and complete it are called by the Spirit to such work (13:2). And today, the "apostolic" function—cross-cultural pioneer church planting among unreached peoples—is still the highest calling (Rom 15:20; 1 Cor 12:28; 2 Tim 1:11). Will the church give its "best and brightest" to this calling?

The Spirit Directs Missionary Deployment (13:2) Is worship and fasting a part of this church's routine practice, or is it a special seeking of guidance? The purpose of fasting can be to withdraw as far as possible from the influence of the world and make oneself receptive to commands from heaven (Ex 34:28; compare Lk 2:37); this combined the

---

13:1 Some would identify *Simeon called Niger* as "Simon of Cyrene" (Mk 15:21; Lk 23:26;

emphatic Greek *dē* in the Spirit's directive, which may indicate an evaluation of a proposal (Williams 1985:210), probably indicates a quest for
particular guidance. Are the participants just the leaders (Bruce
1988:245) or the whole church (Marshall 1980:215)? In view of the
mutually interactive decision-making process of Acts 6:1-7 (see comment
there) and the fact that Paul and Barnabas report back to the entire
church (14:27), it is best to say the leaders in the presence of the entire
church take this action.

Whether by internal prompting in the entire church (Stott 1990:217)
or external directive through one of the believers (Longenecker
1981:417) or more particularly one of the prophets (Haenchen
1971:396), the Spirit communicates that now is the time for deployment.
The church is to *set apart* Barnabas and Saul for the evangelization of
Jew and Gentile (compare Rom 1:1; Gal 1:15). God had previously
personally called Saul and Barnabas, a call that was still in effect (so the
perfect tense; compare 9:15-16; 26:16-18).

In this simple command we meet God's basic answer to the question,
Who sends the missionary? God sends the missionary through two essential and complementary means: the personal, inward call to the individual and the outward confirmation through the church.

The Church Releases the Missionary (13:3) It is interesting that
Luke describes only the end of the process of confirmation. The church
is the key to timing in deployment. There is no mention of testing Saul
and Barnabas's ministry gifting as part of confirmation, probably because
they have been ministering in the Antioch congregation for over a year
(11:26). The need for testing must be deduced from other Scriptures
(such as 1 Tim 3:10).

The "release" (NIV *sent off*) of the missionaries from their duties so
that they may undertake this other work is marked by prayer, fasting and
the laying on of hands. Fasting and prayer constitute earnest intercession
for full equipping in the grace of God and the Spirit's full and successful
working through Barnabas and Saul in the mission (compare 14:26 and
the answer to the prayers in 13:9-12, 43, 48; 14:3, 10; compare also 4:29,

Rom 16:13; Longenecker 1981:416), but the difference in spelling indicates two different
names and hence different persons.

31, 33). The laying on of hands is probably not ordination for lifelong ministry (14:26 declares the work complete; contrast Kistemaker 1990:456) nor authorization to the apostolate. Rather, the church in an act of solidarity with the missionaries both commissions them as its representatives in this evangelistic mission (note the use of "apostle" to describe both Barnabas and Paul in Acts 14:4, 14) and commends them to God's grace and blessing (14:26). Luke is silent regarding the church's responsibility for financial support of these missionaries.

Antioch, then, becomes a model for the missionary vision and missionary deployment of every church. A church that embodies cultural diversity and has spiritually gifted, sensitive and obedient leaders will release into Christ's service those so called, earnestly interceding for them and standing in solidarity with them. With more than half the world's population yet to hear the gospel for the first time, our Lord needs many more Antiochs.

Witness on Cypress (13:4-12)

Nero had his court astrologers, who predicted his rule of the east, including sovereignty over Jerusalem. Sergius Paulus had his court prognosticator, Elymas (13:7). And today it is not unheard-of that world leaders consult astrologers as they schedule key events. But what happens when the power of the gospel confronts the power of the occult? The contest on Cyprus and its outcome show us.

The Missionary Thrust: Proclaiming the Word (13:4-5) Highlighting the divine initiative in the church's proactive Gentile mission, Luke describes the church's "release" of Paul and Barnabas (13:3) as *sent on their way by the Holy Spirit* (compare Lk 4:1, 14). Traveling to Seleucia, a Mediterranean port of Syrian Antioch, sixteen miles west and five miles north of the mouth of the Orontes, the missionary band embarks for Cyprus.

13:4-12 That the proconsul came to saving faith, even though his baptism is not mentioned, can be maintained (contrast Lake and Cadbury 1979:147; Haenchen 1971:403) when we take into account the condensed nature of the narrative (E. F. Harrison 1986:219), the role it plays as a satisfying conclusion to the account, and Luke's assumption that his readers understand faith, conversion and baptism as a unity—thus he does not need to mention each element every time someone comes to faith (Krodel 1986:230; Longenecker 1981:420; compare 14:1; 17:34).

13:5 *Hypēretēs* is a general term for "attendant" or "assistant" and is used for such a role

They land at an eastern port and administrative center, Salamis, some 130 miles west of the Syrian coast. Cyprus, 132 miles northeast to southwest, is traversed by two mountain ranges that enclose a fruitful central plain. The island itself is situated on shipping lanes between Syria, Greece and Asia Minor. From Ptolemaic times a large Jewish colony has been present (Josephus *Jewish Antiquities* 13:284, 287; 1 Macc 15:23; Philo *Legatio ad Gaium* 282), and a Christian witness appears to have been born there early (Barnabas is a Cypriot—Acts 4:36; compare 11:19-20).

There in the Jewish synagogues Saul and Barnabas "began to solemnly proclaim" (compare 4:2; 13:38; 15:36; imperfect ingressive action—Kistemaker 1990:460) *the word of God,* that is, the gospel, God's message of grace and salvation (13:7, 44, 46, 48; compare 13:12, 26, 49; 14:3, 25). *John*—that is, John Mark (12:12, 25; 13:5, 13; 15:37; Col 4:10; 2 Tim 4:11; Philem 24; 1 Pet 5:13) is there as "an assistant."

Frequent references to *the word of God* throughout the account of this first missionary journey show us that communicating the message of salvation must be the main activity of missions. In a day when specialist short-term work, humanitarian relief and support services are all being called missions, and rightly so, the church needs to make sure it does not shift its primary focus away from the central purpose of missions—the communication of the gospel.

Repelling a Sorcerer, Attracting a Governor (13:6-8) Traveling west across the island, Saul and Barnabas arrive at Paphos, ninety miles away. This was the senatorial province's official capital. In the governor's court a Jew, Bar-Jesus (transliteration of the Aramaic "Son of Salvation"), operates as a *sorcerer* and *false prophet. Sorcerer (magos)* was a venerable term for students of the metaphysical, including members of the Median priest class (Mt 2:1), possessors and users of supernatural knowl-

---

in a variety of contexts, including medical, military, political and religious. John Mark's function is not further specified. Is it practical, physical help (Acts 20:34; 24:23, Williams 1985:213)? Is it aid in spiritual ministry—providing eyewitness accounts of Jesus' life and ministry, especially his passion (Lk 1:2, Bruce [1988:247] reports this option approvingly), or keeping the scrolls of Old Testament Scriptures (Lk 4:20), or being a catechist of new converts (Longenecker 1981:419)? Probably we should take it in a broad general sense that could encompass both physical and spiritual ministry (Marshall 1980:218).

edge and ability (Josephus *Jewish Antiquities* 10.195, 216), magicians who used demonic magic (Acts 8:9-10), and charlatans and deceivers (compare 19:13-16; Delling 1967:356). Bar-Jesus is probably a court astrologer with demonic powers (Haenchen 1971:397; contrast Krodel [1986:229], who calls him part of the world of "religious con-artists who practiced quackery and interpreted dreams"). As a *false prophet*, Bar-Jesus—also called Elymas—claims wrongly to be a medium of divine revelation (Bruce 1988:249). As a *sorcerer* he claims to know magic formulas by which he can break the bonds of fate and give the governor control over the future. When faced with the truth of the gospel, Bar-Jesus actively opposes the missionaries (compare Lk 21:15; Acts 6:10). He makes every effort to "completely turn aside" the governor from the faith (compare 13:10; 20:30).

In sharp contrast, Sergius Paulus, the *proconsul* (the correct title for the governor of a senatorial province, which Cyprus became in 22 B.C.), *wanted to hear the word of God*. Luke calls him *intelligent*, probably complimenting him for his inquiring mind. His desire *to hear the word of God* is not simply a matter of administrative prudence (as Longenecker 1981:419). Rather, Luke holds up this Roman official from the highest levels of society as a positive model of the proper response to hearsay about Christianity. The proconsul's interest would surely impress

---

13:7 Inscriptional evidence points to a Lucius Sergius Paullus, one of the "curators of the Tiber" under Claudius, who could possibly have served as proconsul on Cyprus, and Quintus Sergius Paullus, who did (van Elderen 1970:151-56). Longenecker (1981:419) supports the former and Marshall (1980:219) the latter. Because the dating on the L. Sergius Paullus inscription places him on Cyprus later than the period of the first missionary journey, I prefer the other.

13:8 The explanation of the meaning of *Elymas* has proceeded along two lines. Theodore Zahn (cited in Lake and Cadbury 1979:144) adopts the Western reading *Hetoimas*, "ready" (compare the account of the sorcerer Atomos on Cyprus in Josephus *Jewish Antiquities* 20.142). He then relates it to a variant spelling of *Bar-Jesus* (*Bar-Iēsouan* [Hebrew *br-šwh*], *from the piel of šwh*, which might mean "make ready"). The need to use a less well attested reading and emendations and above all the need to see *Elymas* as the translation of *Bar-Jesus* when the grammar indicates that *Elymas* is translated *sorcerer* make this explanation unsatisfactory. It is better to see *Elymas* as the preferred reading and derived either from a Semitic word akin to the Arabic *'alīm* (wise) or an Aramaic form of *ḥālōmā* (magician; see Marshall 1980:219; Krodel 1986:229; Metzger 1971:403).

The faith is the content of the gospel (Lake and Cadbury 1979:144; note the definite article, though that could be understood possessively) and not the governor's "act of believing" (as Bruce 1990:297; compare Williams's [1985:214] middle position).

Theophilus and his fellow inquirers, just as a political, entertainment or sports celebrity who declares openly his or her spiritual hunger for the gospel would draw attention today.

Blinding the False Guide (13:9-11) Filled with the Holy Spirit (compare 4:8), Saul (here first called Paul) *[looks] straight at* Elymas (compare 3:4; 14:9) and delivers a verdict that reveals the sorcerer's true character, stance and activity. All that fills Elymas is deceit and the trickery of wrongdoing (contrast 1 Thess 2:3). He is a *child of the devil* in his stance as *an enemy of everything that is right,* literally "of all righteousness" (compare Lk 8:12). He perverts the *right ways of the Lord* in that he twists the path that would lead to salvation (taking *tou kyriou* as an objective genitive; Hos 14:9; compare Ps 119:1; Is 40:3, 5; Lk 1:79; Acts 8:21).

The divine sentence is that the sovereign *hand of the Lord,* which directs his saving purposes in history (Acts 4:28) and otherwise acts in healing and salvation blessing (4:30; 11:21), will be against Elymas, placing temporary physical blindness on him. Is the blindness to picture his own spiritual blindness (compare 9:8; 26:18)? Since it is temporary, is it intended to bring the sorcerer to repentance?

By juxtaposing the judgment to Sergius Paulus's faith response, Luke clearly shows how the gospel's power is greater than the power of the occult. *Immediately,* though not instantaneously, the sentence is carried

---

13:9 A Roman citizen had three official names: a praenomen (like our Christian or first name), a nomen (denoting the clan of the city of Rome to which he belonged) and a cognomen (a family or last name). Compare Lucius Sergius Paullus. Sometimes a signum or supernomen, a nickname, was added. In the case of the apostle, *Saul* was probably his signum, a Hebrew name used among his own people. *Paul* was his cognomen. His praenomen and nomen we do not know (Bruce 1988:249). Scholars propose three reasons why Luke puts the apostle through a name change at this point in the narrative: personal (Paul through a miracle proves himself to be filled with the Spirit and the real head of the Christian group [Haenchen 1971:399]), environmental (Paul from now on is operating in a Gentile environment [Marshall 1980:220]) or ministry (the conversion of Sergius Paulus, a Gentile with no prior links with the synagogue, was a major turning point and inaugurated a new policy, direct approach to and full acceptance of Gentiles [Longenecker 1981:420]). Paul has already been engaged in Spirit-filled ministry (9:17, 22, 28; 11:26). His Gentile mission, while distinctive, is not unique (compare 10:1—11:20). It is better to see the change as environmental.

13:10 The NIV reverses the order of the verdict pronounced on Elymas. Literally it reads, "O full of all kinds of deceit and trickery, child of the devil; enemy of everything that is right, will you never stop perverting the right ways of the Lord?"

out. The blindness comes on gradually as a gathering *mist* and in the end becomes total. Elymas finds himself groping about, *seeking someone to lead him by the hand.*

In Luke's account, the church's evangelists consistently meet overt demonic opposition through practitioners of occult arts when they first thrust into new ethnic or geographical territory: Samaria (8:9-24); Cyprus, first missionary journey (13:4-12); Philippi, thrust into Europe (16:16-18); Ephesus, third missionary journey (19:11-20). There is no culture today where, to one degree or another, such a spiritual battle is not joined. Not presumptuously, but confidently—by prayer, filled with the Spirit—we must boldly proclaim the gospel and, as the Lord directs, confront hostile spiritual powers.

The Magnificent Result: Winning the Governor (13:12) The power encounter yields saving results: the governor comes to faith (2:44; 4:4, 32; 11:21; 13:39). But Luke is careful to let us know the necessary interdependence of gospel word and mighty act. He says Sergius Paulus *believed, for he was amazed* (literally, "struck out of his senses"), not at the miracle but *at the teaching about the Lord.* With this last little phrase Luke informs us about the proper role of miracle in evangelistic witness (see comment at 9:35). Sergius Paulus, the first totally pagan Gentile convert and a representative of the upper echelons of Roman society, stands as a model inquirer and convert for Theophilus, his fellow seekers and all since their time.

Witness at Pisidian Antioch (13:13-52)

The human spirit can come under bondage because of external political and economic oppression and because of self-imposed religious legalism. First-century Jews needed relief from both. Paul came preaching a dying and rising Messiah who would free people from inner bondage so they could cope with external oppression. His message of hope should resonate with all those who long to be able to say, "Free at last!

13:13 Why did John Mark leave? At the least we may conclude from Acts 15:38 that decision was viewed as a serious desertion that rendered him, in Paul's eyes, unfit to go along on the second journey. Richard Longenecker strongly argues that John Mark disagreed with Paul over the validity of a direct Gentile mission (1981:421; see E. F. Harrison 1986:221 for a list of explanations).

Free at last! Thank God Almighty, I'm free at last!"

The Sermon's Setting (13:13-15) Setting sail from Paphos, *Paul and his companions* (literally, "those around Paul," a Hellenistic phrase that indicates the change in leadership; contrast 13:2, 7) travel 160 miles to the bay of Attalia on the south central Asia Minor coast. They evidently bypass the port city of Attalia (14:25), proceeding eight miles up the Cestrus River and on to Perga, five miles from the river. John Mark leaves the group at this point and returns to Jerusalem.

The missionary band does not evangelize Perga but takes a six-day journey some eighty miles up the river valleys to Pisidian Antioch. They must pass through rugged, hostile terrain infested with robber bands and onto the central Anatolian plateau, elevation over thirty-six hundred feet.

Pisidian Antioch was also founded by Seleucus I Nicator (see comment at 11:19). The Romans made it a Roman colony in 25 B.C., settling army veterans and their families there. It served as the main garrison city for a number of Roman outposts to the south. Pisidian Antioch sat astride the Via Sebaste, the Roman road from Ephesus to the Euphrates. Such a location and history meant that the population was a diverse mixture of Phrygian, Greek, Jewish and Roman.

Luke gives us a fascinating glimpse of a diaspora synagogue service. He notes in passing the Scripture readings. These came from the Pentateuch, possibly on a triennial lectionary cycle, and often but not always from the Prophets. For the latter, the reader was free to choose a passage from anywhere in the Former and Latter Prophets. A translation into the local language would follow.

Luke notes that at this point the *synagogue rulers* invite one of Paul's group to preach. These officials supervised and officiated at the service, maintaining order, choosing participants and making sure all went smoothly (Lk 8:41; 13:14; *m. Yoma* 7:1; *m. Soṭa* 7:7). The sermon, *a message of encouragement,* would both exhort and comfort Jews as they lived in faithful obedience to the law and waited for the final salvation

Why did the missionary band bypass Perga and travel inland to Pisidian Antioch? William M. Ramsay's proposal, based on Galatians 4:13, that Paul contracted malarial fever in the swampy coastland and fled to the highlands for relief has had continuing popular support (Barclay 1976:102; Ogilvie 1983:213; Stott 1990:221). Bruce correctly concludes, however, that it is "an interesting speculation, but nothing more" (1990:300).

of Israel (Lk 2:25; 1 Macc 12:9). It would be based on a text of the preacher's own choosing but would also weave in texts from the Scripture readings of the day (see Bowker 1967:101-10; Dumais 1979; compare Philo *De Specialibus Legibus* 2.62).

Paul's Word of Consolation: Old Testament Promise (13:16-25) Paul stands and, with a wave of the hand to gain attention, addresses both Jews and Gentile God-fearers (see comment and note at 8:27). He begins with what could be called the Old Testament kerygma: a rehearsal of four key events of God's gracious promise and liberating fulfillment, together with a declaration of the messianic promise to David (Deut 26:5-10; Josh 24:2-13, 17-18; Ps 68-72; 89:3-4, 19-37).

Paul commences with the confession that God is *the God of the people of Israel* (literally, "this people Israel"). With Gentile God-fearers in the audience, Paul articulates the particularity of God's dealings with Israel but within an international context. Second, he announces God's choice of the patriarchs for himself. Third, he proclaims the redemption of Israel from Egypt and the leading through the wilderness. This liberation is recounted in language reminiscent of the Pentateuch (Ex 6:6; Deut 1:31; 26:5, 8). Israel knew great blessing during its sojourn in Egypt, for God literally "exalted" them by greatly increasing their numbers (Ex 1:7), yet the people sinned, and God had to "bear with" them forty years in the wilderness (Num 14:34).

Fourth, God caused them to inherit their land after he had overthrown seven nations in the land of Canaan (Deut 7:1; Josh 3:10; 24:11). God's

---

13:16 Paul's position, *standing* rather than sitting, probably reflects Diaspora as opposed to Palestinian practice (Philo *De Specialibus Legibus* 2.62; Bruce 1988:253), not an exhortation versus an exposition as Longenecker contends (1981:424). Paul's body language is typically Jewish and not, as Ernst Haenchen (1971:408) proposes, part of Luke's presentation of Paul as an Hellenistic orator (Longenecker 1981:425).

13:18 The marginal note "Some manuscripts *and cared for them*" points to a variant reading that differs by one letter (text: *etropophorēsen*, "endure . . . conduct"; margin: *etrophophorēsen*, "care for"). The Hebrew *nāśā'* has the basic meaning "to bear, carry" and has within its range of meaning both nuances, "bear with" and "bear up." Two complicating factors in deciding which reading to prefer are the interchangeable use of the forms by copyists at Deuteronomy 1:31 (*etrophophorēsen* with the reading *etropophorēsen*, in a few manuscripts) and the fact that in Hellenistic spelling *trophophoreō* could be represented as *tropophoreō*. Though I. H. Marshall (1980:223) sees the positive meaning "care for" as making better sense, actually the negative meaning "endure, bear with" is very congruent with the growing indictment of Israel throughout the sermon. Since the positive meaning can be explained by Septuagint influence and is on the whole the easier reading, it is best

initiatives in mighty fulfillment of his gracious promises to the fathers *took about 450 years.* This involved four hundred years of sojourn in Egypt (Gen 15:13), forty years of wilderness wandering (Num 14:34) and ten years to possess the land of Canaan (Josh 14:10).

God raised up David and gave him a promise. Paul sets this within the context of God's orderly superintendence of Israel's national life through judges, up to the last judge and first prophet Samuel (compare Acts 3:24; 1 Sam 3:20). Paul highlights, though subtly, the sin that both led to and terminated Saul's forty-year reign (compare Josephus *Jewish Antiquities* 6.378). The monarchy was instituted because the people took matters into their own hands by asking for a king (note the middle voice— literally, "they asked for themselves"; compare 1 Sam 8:4-9). Saul's reign and the continuance of his line effectively ended when after disobedience God "removed"—deposed—him (compare 3 Kingdoms 15:13). David, by contrast, was a "man after God's own heart, who will do all God's will" (1 Sam 13:14). He is the model for all those who would receive God's covenant blessings of salvation.

David received a promise (2 Sam 7:12-16; compare 22:51; Ps 89: 29, 36; 132:11, 17), which Paul declares was fulfilled when God *brought to Israel the Savior Jesus.* Paul both tempers and heightens the Jewish hope. He avoids the use of *Messiah,* with its connotations of a purely political deliverer. He indicates that the liberation is much greater, for God is its source, bringing the final salvation according to the Old Testament (Is 49:6, 8; 45:21-22; compare Ps 27:1; 89:26; Lk 1:69; 2:11; Acts 5:31; 13:26).

to concur with the NIV's choice (Metzger 1971:405; compare R. P. Gordon 1974:286-89 for supplementary targumic evidence).

13:20 The Western reading that reverses the reference to 450 years and the phrase "after this" probably arose to avoid the misunderstanding of taking the large number for only the period of settling the land (Metzger 1971:407). The shift creates the further problem of making the time of the judges 450 years long and contradicting 1 Kings 6:1. Although the textus receptus follows this reading and Eugene Merrill (1981) has developed an ingenious method for showing how the number can square with what is reported about the times of the judges, it is best to follow Vaticanus, as the NIV does, and see the statement as an affirmation of God's faithfulness from the nation's entry into Egypt until it entered its inheritance.

13:22 *I have found David* alludes to Psalm 89:20 (LXX 88:21), and *a man after my own heart* to 1 Samuel 13:14. *He will do everything I want him to do* is probably not an allusion to Isaiah 44:28, which refers to Cyrus, not David, Gleason Archer and G. C. Chirichigno's explanation notwithstanding (1983:51). Rather, compare the targum of Jonathan's paraphrase of "after my own heart" at 1 Samuel 13:14 (Bruce 1990:305).

This focus on the spiritual or vertical dimension of salvation continues in Paul's mention of the last prophet, John the Baptist, the messenger who would prepare the way for the coming of the Messiah (Lk 1:76-77). *John preached repentance and baptism* (literally, "a baptism of repentance"), a ritual washing as a visible sign of repentance in preparation for the Messiah's coming holy kingdom. He made very clear both that he was not the Messiah and that this coming Savior was much greater than he. He said he did not even qualify to perform the most menial of tasks, untying the Messiah's sandals as he prepared for daily washing. John issued this denial repeatedly (*elegen*, imperfect pointing to repeated, customary action) as he was "finishing his course" (NIV *work;* compare Acts 20:24; 2 Tim 4:7).

Through John's steadfast denial of very natural Jewish expectations, Paul puts his audience and us on notice. We must be careful lest we misunderstand what God is doing to provide salvation.

The Word of Salvation: Christological Fulfillment (13:26-31) With greater intimacy *(brothers)* Paul readdresses his audience, proclaiming the promise's fulfillment. *To us,* as opposed to the patriarchs, *this message of salvation* (literally, "the message of this salvation") *has been sent* by God (not simply from Jerusalem, an option Williams [1985:223] notes; compare Lk 24:49; Gal 4:4, 6).

The central events of the kerygma, Jesus' death and resurrection, now come into view. Paul emphasizes three features of Jesus' death: its cause, its character and its reality.

1. Cause. Inhabitants of Jerusalem, ignorant of Jesus' messiahship and of the Scriptures (NIV does not represent this parallelism), fulfilled those very Scriptures by condemning him to death and making sure Pilate carried out the sentence. Though they were immediately culpable, ultimately God ordained it. He had planned it long ago and declared it through the prophets (Acts 2:23; 4:28; 3:17-18). It came to a complete fulfillment (Lk 12:50; 18:31; 22:37; 24:44). The people's ignorance was not simply a lack of knowledge but "a false understanding, a false path

---

13:26 The contrast to *us* is the people of the Old Testament who received the promises (Haenchen 1971:410), not the Palestinian Jews who rejected the Messiah (as Marshall 1980:225).

13:27-28 It is true, as Gerhard Krodel (1986:237) points out, that Luke's passion narrative

in knowing and thinking" that led them to turn away from a relationship to God in Jesus Christ (Schütz [1976:407] citing Otto Michel; compare Rom 10:3; 2 Cor 3:14-4:6).

One of the great ironies of our sinful human existence is that religion can make us blind to the true way of salvation. Even years of studying the Bible can leave us without understanding of the liberation Christ desires to bring. The experience of the people of Jerusalem in Jesus' day must ever stand as a warning to the religious.

2. Character. Luke is often faulted for not presenting Jesus' death as a substitutionary atonement (so Willimon 1988:124 here). Yet critics fail to take into account that when Luke notes Jesus' death as an innocent sufferer, he is presenting the objective conditions of vicarious atonement. For unless his death was a waste, a perverse miscarriage of justice, Jesus had to be suffering the penalty for someone's sins. So here Paul maintains Jesus' innocence: *no proper ground for a death sentence.* Pilate declared as much three times during the proceedings (the charges—Lk 23:2, 5; the governor's judgment—23:4, 14-15, 22; compare Acts 3:13-14). Jesus even received a proper burial (compare Lk 23:53, 55). At the same time Paul portrays Jesus' suffering as that of a criminal— he was condemned by the Jews, who requested a Roman execution for him, and he was crucified (hanging on *the tree* was a cursed death; compare Gal 3:13/Deut 21:23; Acts 5:30; 10:39).

3. Reality. To mention Jesus' burial is to affirm the reality of his physical death, a truth on which many ancient and modern heresies stumble. Note how later Paul recalls it as an essential of the gospel (1 Cor 15:4).

As Paul proclaims Jesus' resurrection he emphasizes its divine origin: *God raised him from the dead* (compare 3:15; 10:40; 13:37; Rom 10:9; Gal 1:1; Eph 1:20; Col 2:12; 1 Thess 1:10). He highlights its supernatural character when he says that Jesus "appeared" to those who had accompanied him from Galilee (compare Gen 12:7; Judg 6:12; Luke 1:11; 24:34; Acts 2:3; 7:2; 9:17; 26:16). He stresses the resurrection's historical reality. Eyewitnesses had opportunities to see Jesus over a period of

---

does not record a condemnation verdict from the Sanhedrin (compare Lk 22:71 with Mk 14:64). Still, it is certainly implied by the rhetorical question and the Sanhedrin's subsequent actions and demands.

many days (compare Acts 1:3). They were in a good position to identify him, since they had been part of his ministry band and had *traveled with him from Galilee to Jerusalem* (compare 1:21-22; 10:40-41). Theophilus and inquirers into Christianity's credibility in any time or place are given assurance once again that the central events of its saving message can stand, indeed invite, the test of public scrutiny.

The Testimonia of Proof: Scriptural Demonstration (13:32-37) Paul approaches the climax of his sermon by bringing together the word of promise and its fulfillment. On the one hand he tells *the good news* (5:42; 8:4, 12, 25, 40; 10:36; 11:20) that in *raising up Jesus*—bringing him into the arena of human history—God *has fulfilled* what he *promised* to the fathers. On the other hand Paul quotes Old Testament texts that articulate the promises and their means of fulfillment.

Paul begins with the divine declaration to the Lord's anointed: *You are my Son; today I have become your Father* (Acts 13:33/Ps 2:7; compare 2 Sam 7:12-16). The Jews and early church did take this psalm messianically (*Psalms of Solomon* 17:21-23; Strack and Billerbeck 1978:3:675-77; Heb 1:5; 5:5/Ps 2:7; Acts 4:25-26/Ps 2:1-2). Jesus is God's Son in the fullest sense of the word, for he shares his very nature (see comment at Acts 9:20). For this reason he can be the means by which God completely fulfills the promises made to the fathers.

The crowning good news is that *God raised him [Jesus] from the dead, never to decay.* Isaiah 55:3 undergirds this assertion by setting Jesus'

13:32-33 The answers to three interlocking interpretational matters determine whether we take these verses as referring to Jesus' resurrection or to his whole messianic mission. In what event was the "promise" fulfilled? What is Paul referring to when he says God was *raising up Jesus?* In what event was Psalm 2:7 fulfilled? *Raising up Jesus* occurred not at the resurrection, as many argue (Haenchen 1971:411; Marshall 1980:226; Krodel 1986:239; O'Toole 1979:366; Williams 1985:231). *Anastēsas* (raising up) unqualified by *ek nekrōn* (from the dead) can refer to God's bringing a person onto the stage of human history (3:22, 26; 7:37). It seems best, then, to take the phrase as referring to the entire messianic mission, and the fulfillment of the promise as entailing everything God accomplished in Jesus through his incarnation, earthly ministry, suffering, death, resurrection and exaltation. Psalm 2:7, then, would point to the incarnation, the beginning (Lk 1:35; Bruce 1988:260 argues strongly for the baptism, 3:22), not the resurrection, the climax of Jesus' messianic mission (contrast commentators listed above).

Paul's appropriation of Isaiah 55 and Psalm 16 does not violate the original context of either, especially of Isaiah 55:3 (contrast Haenchen 1971:412). Paul is not simply following a rudimentary rabbinic interpretational approach based on the Greek text. The *g^ezerâh šāwâh* word-link method *(ta hosia . . . ton hosion)* is not the only connection between these

resurrection within the larger context of the covenant blessings that flow to God's people because of God's "pledged mercies" to David (Kaiser 1980:227-28; Bruce 1988:260). They are "the unassailable proofs of grace which Yahweh will give in faithfulness to His promises" (Hauck 1967:491; 2 Sam 7:8-16; 2 Chron 6:42). If the "pledged mercies to David" centered on the promise that he would reign forever, they are given to God's people in the form of the blessings of life under that "forever reign."

The link between the "pledged mercies" and Messiah's resurrection involves this interpretational reasoning. If the Messiah has to undergo an atoning death for the sins of the people but is to reign forever, a resurrection must decisively intervene. If that "forever reign" is to happen at all, the king must experience a resurrection that will so transform him that "his flesh will never return to decay," the normal destiny of humans (Ps 16:10/Acts 13:35). In fact, Paul's hermeneutic for identifying the risen Jesus, not the dead David, as the reference of this assertion depends on this distinction. Using the same interpretational tools as Peter—the question of identity and a literal understanding of *You will not let your Holy One see decay*—Paul establishes that the Messiah rises (compare 13:30; see comment at 2:25-31).

If we would receive the divinely intended spiritual good from the Old Testament, we must fix our eyes firmly on the fulfillment, Jesus Christ, and ask of each passage of promise, What does it teach us of Christ? What

---

two passages. Joachim Pillai deals with this negative evaluation of Paul's hermeneutics (1979:101-3).

13:33 The best manuscripts read "to our children." Because *for us, their children* (NIV) makes better sense in the immediate context and has good evidence to support it, we should treat it as more probably original (Metzger 1971:410) and possibly, as Marshall (1980:226) suggests, treat the former reading as a primitive corruption.

Gegennēka, translated by the NIV *I have become your Father* with the marginal reading "Or *have begotten you*" renders the Hebrew verb *yālad* in the qal. While the hiphil normally means actual paternity, the qal points to general relationship of love (Harris, Archer and Waltke 1980:1:379; compare the same sentiment in 2 Samuel 7:14). While the NIV appears to represent the general or metaphorical use in the text and the literal use in the margin, if this verse does refer to the incarnation the term should be understood literally, yet in such a way that both the reality of the virgin birth and the full deity of the Son, including his eternity, are preserved. The Nicene Creed's phrase "begotten, not made" captures this truth.

13:36 The syntax permits the alternate translation "David after he served his own generation died in the will of God" (Haenchen 1971:412). This way more decisively eliminates David as the referent of the Psalm 16 quote.

can we learn about the salvation that is appointed for the last day?

The Offer of Liberation and Warning of Judgment (13:38-41)
The sermon reaches its climax as Paul solemnly proclaims salvation blessings, *the forgiveness of sins* and a release "from all for which the law was unable to provide justification." Here is the promised liberation—a spiritual salvation. The law could never "justify from"—that is, acquit of sin—since it could not produce perfect obedience in the one who observed it (compare 7:53; Jer 31:32-34; Lk 18:14; Acts 15:7-11; Gal 2:16; 3:11). Do we know this liberation? And these salvation blessings are for *everyone who believes,* again implying that Gentiles as well as Jews are within the scope of God's offer of salvation (Lk 24:47; Acts 2:38-39; 10:43).

Parallel to the offer of liberation is the warning of judgment for those who fail to recognize that God is truly effecting salvation through Jesus (supported by Hab 1:5/Acts 13:41; compare 1QpHab 2:7-16). Understood typologically, the spiritual pattern seen in God's surprise move of raising up the evil Chaldeans to punish Judah, even to the point of exile, could well be repeated in Paul's day and ours. The difference is that then God's work was judgment, whereas now it is salvation. But the warning is the same: Take heed lest you miss what God is doing. And the remedy is still the same: repentance. The warning was necessary, and is necessary today for those of a legalistic mindset to whom the "good news" of Jesus' offer of salvation by faith alone is unbelievable.

The Aftermath: Division, Rejection, Withdrawal, Progress (13:42-52) From what transpired immediately, a week later and in the subsequent weeks or possibly months we can trace out a divinely ordained spiritual dynamic in Jewish and Gentile response to the gospel and the Christian missionary's reaction.

As Luke reports division, he highlights for us the positive response. The *people invited* (compare 13:15) Paul and Barnabas to speak further about these things on the next sabbath. *Many of the Jews and devout converts to Judaism* (proselytes), however, made a definite positive de-

---

13:41 Two variations in text form between the Hebrew Masoretic Text and the LXX, which Luke picks up following the LXX, require comment. *Hoi kataphronētai* ("scoffers") may point to a Hebrew *Vorlage* that has *bōgdîm* ("treacherous ones") instead of *baggôyim* ("nations"; see Archer and Chirichigno 1983:159). There is no separate Hebrew word underlying *aphanizō*

cision, for they *followed Paul and Barnabas* (used only here in Acts to indicate Christian commitment; compare Lk 5:27; 9:23, 59; 18:22). By encouraging them to *continue in the grace of God,* Paul is not urging them to pursue Christ as they had trusted in God's grace given in the Old Testament (contrast Marshall 1980:229). Rather, in light of his exhortation (Acts 13:38-39) and the parallel thought at Acts 11:23, they are to remain in the salvation offered in the gospel (13:23, 26, 38-39) and not return to the performance way of obedience of the Old Testament law and Jewish tradition. This encouragement was well placed when we remember the attacks that these churches subsequently sustained from Judaizers (compare Gal 1:6-7; 3:1-6; 5:7-12; 6:11-13).

The next sabbath almost the whole city gathered to hear the word of the Lord. Evidently the word had spread and brought fruit through those who had heard the gospel. Again, the preaching of the Word, in particular a word about the Lord Jesus Christ, is central to the church's missionary enterprise and its advance. The negative response seems only to be hinted at.

The initial rejection comes when the Jews' jealousy is aroused by the crowds of Gentiles flooding into synagogue service. Though envy over the newcomers' success may be a factor (Marshall 1980:229), the main issue seems to be Paul's willingness to receive Gentiles directly into the people of God. He offers them an equal share in the spiritual blessings of the Messiah's kingdom simply based on faith, without requiring that they become Jews first (Longenecker 1981:429). The Jews speak out against Paul's message *abusively*—from the Christian perspective "blasphemously" (compare Acts 18:6; 26:11).

The final rejection occurs when the unbelieving Jews *[incite] the God-fearing women of high standing*—that is, Roman women who are attracted to Judaism but have not received Paul's message (13:50). These, in turn, probably influence their husbands, *the leading men* or magistrates of the city (compare 28:7). Thus the Jews *[stir] up persecution against Paul and Barnabas* (8:1; 2 Macc 12:23) and have exile imposed on the

(in passive, "I perish"), though we should note that it has been used to translate Hebrew *tāmâh* ("to be astonished") at Baruch 3:19.

13:45 The blasphemy was not directed primarily against Paul, as some contend (Marshall 1980:227-28), but against his message and its central content, Christ (Haenchen 1971:414).

missionaries. The magistrates banish them from the municipality. Since the magistrates' tenure was only for a year, the banishment is in effect temporary (Williams 1985:229; a violent expulsion is not necessarily indicated, despite Stott 1990:228).

Though the church's battle is for human hearts and minds and its weapons are spiritual, Christians must be prepared to face governmental attempts to restrict their evangelizing activities. Today, with the militant advance of Islam, the revival of traditional religions tied to resurgent nationalism, and secular humanism's systematic attack on religious faith expressions in public life, Christians have many opportunities to encounter the tactics employed against Paul and Barnabas at Pisidian Antioch.

In an initial but decisive withdrawal from the Jews, Paul and Barnabas set forth the divine priority of Christian mission: "to the Jew first." Although Paul consistently spoke of himself as "apostle to the Gentiles" (Rom 11:13; 15:16; Gal 1:16; 2:9), his mission was always to be carried out by going to "the Jew first" (Rom 1:16-17). This priority was a matter of theological necessity, and it applies to the conduct of Christian mission today. We must make sure Jews are not overlooked but are a priority in any evangelistic thrust into an unreached-peoples area.

The Jews' rejection of the gospel was a decision to judge themselves unfit for *eternal life,* the life of the age to come (compare 5:20; 11:18; 13:40-41, 48). Because of this and the Lord Jesus' mandate (Lk 24:47; Acts 1:8), Paul now turns to direct his preaching completely to the Gentiles. He finds his warrant in Isaiah 49:6, the Father's command to the Servant-Messiah. The Gentile mission is not "plan B." The declaration and quo-

13:47 If we take this quote as the content of the Lord Jesus' command, then we face the interpretational challenge of a change of referents. It is no longer the Lord God who appoints the Servant-Messiah to bring salvation to the Gentiles (Lk 2:30-32). It is the Servant-Messiah, now risen and exalted Lord, who commands his missionaries to preach salvation to the Gentiles. This problem is solved in one of four ways. (1) Most popular is an appeal to the "solidarity principle." For example, the mission of the servant is also the task of his followers (Marshall 1980:230; Krodel 1986:248; Stott 1990:227). (2) A variation on this is a "completion theory": the church as the body of Christ completes the mission of its risen and exalted Lord by proclaiming the good news to the ends of the earth (Longenecker 1981:430). (3) Some take the servant's identity with Israel and say it is now applied to the church (Williams 1985:227). (4) Some see the solution in the deity of Christ. "Luke discloses the identity of Jesus, . . . [portraying] the risen Lord Jesus acting and speaking with the authority that belongs uniquely to Yahweh himself" (D. E. Johnson 1990:353). A more

tation comfort Theophilus (and us as well) by asserting that the Gentile mission was part of God's original intent.

At their final, forced withdrawal, the missionaries *[shake] the dust from their feet in protest against them* (NIV adds *in protest,* v. 51). Some take the action as a sign of contempt, parallel to the Jews' practice of shaking off the dust of "unclean" foreign lands as they reentered the Holy Land (Lake and Cadbury 1979:160). Others, more correctly, see it, according to the Lord's instruction, as a sign of disassociation from a community doomed to destruction (Lk 9:5; 10:10-11; compare Acts 18:6). Such destruction will be so complete that if one is to avoid it, one must remove from oneself the very dust of the place. Because the disassociation is from the persecutors, Paul can later return to the city and work there.

Sometimes people reject the gospel so decisively that the only way to speak "the good news" is to inform the opponents of "the bad news" of the eternal judgment that they continue to face, in the hope that this "shock therapy" will lead to repentance (compare Rev 9:20-21; 16:9, 11, 21).

Jewish rejection never defeats the advance of the gospel (13:48-49, 52). There is always further progress. The Gentiles rejoice that the gospel is indeed for them (compare 15:31). They honor (literally, "glorify") *the word of the Lord.* And they believe and come to salvation (13:12; 14:1, 23; compare 13:39; contrast 13:41). Using predestination terminology, Luke is careful to point out here, as elsewhere, that this faith is above all God's work (2:41, 47; 5:14; 6:7; 11:21, 24; 21:19-20; compare Is 4:3; Dan 12:1; Lk 10:20; Phil 4:3; Rev 20:12-15; 21:27; *Jubilees* 30:20; *1 Enoch*

---

satisfactory approach is to see the Isaiah passage as directed to Jesus and serving as a warrant for Christ's commission to his disciples.

13:48 There have been a number of attempts to read the verse as other than an affirmation of predestination. Some appeal to the verb's basic meaning "to enroll" *(tassō)* and say either (1) the verse points to those who were already believing in accord with Old Testament revelation and were enrolled in God's people or (2) the enrollment does not have to do with a predetermined number but with a conferring of status (Delling 1972:28). Others take the verb as a middle and translate "as many as had set themselves [by their response to the Spirit's prompting] for eternal life became believers" (Williams 1985:228). Others view the statement at the level of salvation history and say the Gentiles believed by virtue of a plan that already included them. Marshall (1980:231) lists this option. Each of these understandings is less likely than a predestinarian one, which accords with Luke's affirmations of God's election and saving initiative elsewhere (Lk 10:20; Acts 2:47; 13:17; 16:14; 18:10).

104:1). We too must always keep before us the antinomy of faith as a personal human decision and as a divine gift according to God's election.

In conclusion, Luke notes that the gospel spreads to the whole region from this main garrison city with road links to five outposts (Acts 19:10). Qualitatively the gospel sustained itself in the disciples' joy though their church planter was forced to leave them (13:52; compare 8:8; 5:41; 11:23; 12:14; 15:3). Outward circumstances do not finally determine the well-being of the spiritually liberated.

Witness at Iconium (14:1-7)

How often have we heard, "What happens in a politician's private life is his own affair; it only concerns the voters when it affects performance in office"? Yet often sexual or financial indiscretion means the ruin of political ambitions, no matter how cogent the political message. A message's truth is judged by the messenger's integrity.

Luke's narrative about the gospel's advance at Iconium sets side by side the Jewish persecutors and the Christian witnesses. By focusing on the courageous Christian witnesses, he helps us decide between the Jewish attacks on the gospel and that gospel's truth claims.

Believing Hearts Versus Poisoned Souls (14:1-2) Expelled from Pisidian Antioch, Paul and his band travel eighty miles southeast on the Via Sebaste. They move across rolling country to Phrygian Iconium, also in the Roman province of Galatia. Iconium, which maintained its Hellenistic culture as a Greek city-state, was a prosperous commercial and agricultural center with five roads radiating from it.

The apostles go to the synagogue first (13:5, 14). In response to their speaking, *a great number of Jews and Gentiles [believe].* Luke delights

---

14:1 While *kata to auto* would normally be taken as a variant of *epi to auto*, meaning "together," most commentators and the NIV take it as "in the same way" (compare Gen 45:23 LXX; 1 Macc 8:27; *kata ta auta,* Lk 6:23, 26; 17:30). Haenchen (1971:419) finds inadequate attestation for this meaning.

14:2-3 The narrative tension between persecution and immediate continuation of ministry, though causing difficulties for the Western text copyists (Metzger 1971:419-21), may be readily resolved if we understand the aorists of verse 2 as ingressive and the *men oun* not as inferential *so* (NIV) but as a resumptive "now." Luke picks up the story line from

in portraying the effectiveness of preaching in quantitative terms (13:43, 44; 14:21) and the church in a growth mode (2:47; 4:4; 5:14; 6:7; 9:31; 11:21). This is certainly a challenge to church leaders in status quo or declining situations.

Unbelieving Jews, however, engage in counterevangelism. They *stirred up* the Gentiles and *poisoned their minds against the brothers.* Literally they "made their souls evil against," pointing to an assault on the feelings not intellect. (The "soul" is that inward place of feeling that may be influenced by others.) The Gentiles, in turn, become hostile toward the missionaries (not all the Christian converts). As in physics every action spawns an equal and opposite reaction, so in the spiritual realm the proclamation of the truth will always encounter opposition (Lk 8:12).

Persevering Boldness (14:3) Resuming the story line of the missionary journey's itinerary (13:51; see notes for 14:2-3), Luke highlights the persevering boldness of Paul and Barnabas's witness. Like Peter, John and "the Twelve" in the face of the Sanhedrin's threats (4:31), Paul and Barnabas speak openly the plain truth *for*—better "because of, relying on"—*the Lord*—that is, the Lord Jesus Christ (*epi;* Bauer, Gingrich and Danker 1979:287; Krodel 1986:252). Bold perseverance in the face of hostility is as much an evidence of the power of God as the great numbers who come to Christ (compare 4:8, 13).

The Lord, for his part, *confirmed* (literally "bearing witness to") "the word about his grace" through *signs and wonders* by the evangelists. Luke labels the gospel *the message of his grace* in order to show that the signs and wonders confirm the reality of the salvation blessings claimed by that word (see comment at 11:23; compare 4:33; 13:43).

Luke's presentation of signs and wonders here gives us criteria for judging claims today. Their true source must be God alone. They must

---

Acts 13:51 after a conclusion and some introductory remarks (13:52—14:2; compare 13:4; Longenecker 1981:432).

14:2 The term the NIV translates *refused to believe (apeisthēsantes)* in general Greek usage means "to disobey." In biblical thought the supreme disobedience is not to believe God's word, in this case the gospel. It is a key term in the Pauline description of the Jewish rejection of the gospel (Rom 11:30-32; 10:21/Is 65:2; compare Lk 1:17; Acts 19:9; Rom 2:8).

14:3 Haenchen (1971:420) says we cannot tell whether God the Father or God the Son is referred to by *the Lord.* Krodel (1986:252) says it points to Jesus as God and shows the inseparability of Jesus Christ from the God of Israel.

occur at his initiative. Their fruit will not necessarily be an irresistible compulsion, so that all who witness and hear of them will believe. Rather, their true purpose and effect is "establishing the Gospel in its full and genuine authority" (Calvin 1966:3). Far from denigrating the verbal, cognitive appeal of the gospel in favor of the visual, experiential impact of miracle, Luke sees signs and wonders as confirming support to the gospel. These miracles at Iconium place the work of Paul and Barnabas in continuity with the mission of Jesus and "the Twelve" and bear witness to unbelieving Jews that the salvation blessings Israel experienced in the past and hoped for at the end of the age are now not only theirs but also the Gentiles' (2:22; 5:12; 15:12; Ex 7:3; Ps 135:9; Acts 2:19/Joel 2:30; Gal 3:4-5).

Final Rejection: Plotters Versus Apostles (14:4-7) The city is divided. Taking advantage of the situation, Jews and Gentiles, together with their leaders, plot to mistreat and stone the missionaries. Their "plotting" manifests itself as uncontrolled irrational violence (*hormē;* Lk 8:33; Acts 7:57; 19:29; compare Bertram 1967:470). The persecution is so fierce (Lk 18:32) that a mob intends to stone the missionaries (compare Diodorus Siculus *Library of History* 17.41.8).

Paul and Barnabas flee some eighteen and then sixty miles to the southeast, finding refuge in the Lycaonian Roman outposts of Lystra and Derbe. They act from prudence, not cowardice, for there *they continued to preach the good news.*

The gospel's opponents stirred up and poisoned souls against messengers of the truth, creating division and spawning a bloodthirsty plot of mob violence. The gospel messengers manifested evangelistic effec-

---

14:4 This is one of two times in Acts when *apostles* does not refer to the Twelve (14:14; compare Lk 11:49). At other points Luke distinguishes Paul and Barnabas from "apostles" (9:27; 15:2, 4, 6; 16:4), but here he applies the term to them. What does he mean here? Does Luke differ from Paul in his understanding of Paul's apostolic status? Luke, like Paul, appears to use *apostles* both in a restricted sense for "the Twelve," chosen by Christ during his earthly ministry and witnesses of his resurrection, and in a broad sense for "missionaries," commissioned messengers of the gospel (compare 2 Cor 8:23; Gal 1:19; Phil 2:25). The latter meaning is intended here (compare 13:1-3).

Both Paul and Luke were aware of Paul's apostleship and its extraordinary nature (Acts 26:16; 1 Cor 15:8). They simply chose different ways to present Paul's similarity to and distinctiveness from the Twelve. Paul freely used the term *apostle,* while Luke in the main reserved it for the Twelve, though he employed cognates to describe Paul's calling (22:21;

tiveness, persevering boldness, miraculous divine confirmation, tactical prudence and persistence in witness. Whose message should Theophilus and we believe?

Witness at Lystra (14:8-20)

It is increasingly obvious that we live in a religiously pluralistic society. Star athletes in Western nations have Islamic names; a Hindu worship center may be across the road from our church. The challenge is not that our neighbors are not Christians but that they are often adherents of a non-Christian cult or religion. How can we begin to witness to them? Luke gives us one strategy in his narrative of Paul's first proclamation to a completely pagan Gentile audience.

God's Power Displayed (14:8-10) At Lystra, a fortified Roman frontier outpost eighteen miles south-southwest of Iconium, Paul is preaching the gospel to people of the local ethnic groups. Luke tells us that a man crippled from birth is sitting (possibly as a beggar), hears Paul's message and has faith to be made whole. To describe the man's aspirations Luke uses a term that is part of a word group he also uses to describe salvation; thus he links the healing that is about to take place with the salvation Paul has been proclaiming (13:26). The miracle will picture the completeness of restoration brought by God's salvation in Christ.

Paul fixes his attention on the man and sees that faith is present. So he calls out a command that is a creative word. The crippled man, showing faith by his obedience, leaps up and begins to walk. The healing is instantaneous and complete (compare 3:7-8).

26:17). Paul said he was "untimely born," while Luke described that untimely birth in the context of the ministry of the Twelve and highlighted its distinctiveness by consistently avoiding references to Paul as an apostle.

If *to plēthos tēs poleōs* is employed here as a technical term for an assembly of citizens of a city-state, the division may reflect an official response (Longenecker 1981:433).

14:9 Luke mainly links this kind of fixing of attention to viewing the supernatural or miraculous (1:10; 3:4, 12; 6:15; 7:55; 10:4; 11:6; 13:9; compare 23:1).

14:10 Standard dispensational and Reformed theology limits the working of signs and wonders to the apostolic age (Edgar 1988; Gaffin 1979:89-116).

Jacob Jervell and Robert L. Hamblin provide helpful characterizations of Luke's view of miraculous deeds and their relation to the church's witness (Jervell 1984:87; Hamblin 1974:34).

Should miraculous deeds be an essential part of a contemporary strategy for approaching adherents to non-Christian religions? John Wimber's initial articulation of "power evangelism" would answer with an emphatic yes. His analysis of the Acts account of the early church's mission concludes, "Rarely was church growth attributed to preaching alone. . . . [Signs and wonders] were the catalyst to evangelism" (1986:118). Others would limit the working of signs and wonders to the apostolic age.

Luke takes a middle position that gives exclusive support to neither of these options. While Luke gives no evidence that miraculous gifts will necessarily cease with the close of the apostolic age, he does not present them as essential to the church's advance. When miraculous deeds and gospel proclamation occur together, proclamation is primary. During the first missionary journey, proclamation accomplishes God's saving purposes apart from miraculous deeds at Pisidian Antioch and Derbe. Jesus teaches that miraculous deeds, even his resurrection, in and of themselves cannot produce faith (Lk 16:27-31; 24:25-27). Indeed, they may be misinterpreted. Proclamation—the proper interpretation—is needed to declare the source and purpose of miraculous deeds. What miraculous deeds do accomplish is to manifest the divine power of God's Word and to authorize the preacher. Just as Paul, through spiritual discernment and Spirit-impelled command, was the means for the crippled man's restoration, so today God can choose to accompany the faithful preaching of his Word with miraculous deeds, especially in cultural contexts in which Satan's control is most evident.

God's Power Misinterpreted (14:11-13) The crowd's response to the miracle shows both total excitement and total lack of comprehension. They cry out in Lycaonian, their heart language, that the gods Zeus and Hermes have come in human form. They repeatedly address Paul and Barnabas with divine homage. This is not surprising, for Ovid the Roman poet relates a legend of a previous visitation by Zeus and Hermes to the Phrygian region. They came in human form and inquired at one

14:11-12 Ovid *Metamorphosis* 8.611-724 contains the legend about the gods visiting the vicinity of Lystra. There is archaeological evidence of worship of Zeus and Hermes in this region as late as the third century A.D. (Lake and Cadbury 1979:164).

14:12, 19 There is corroborating evidence for the historicity of the account from Paul's own writings, especially references to his reception and persecution at Lystra (2 Tim 3:10-11; compare 2 Cor 11:25; Gal 4:14; 6:17).

thousand homes, but none showed them hospitality. Only a poor elderly couple, Baucis and Philemon, took them in. The pair were rewarded by being spared when the gods flooded the valley and destroyed its inhabitants. The couple's shack was transformed into a marble-pillared, gold-roofed temple, and they became its priests.

The crowd's reaction to Paul and Barnabas, then, is understandable. They want to avoid punishment and garner any blessings that the gods may desire to dispense. They see Zeus, the weather god, and Hermes his messenger as the providers of fruitful harvests.

The crowd's response clearly illustrates the problem of communication to people with a non-Christian background. Unless the Holy Spirit opens their hearts and minds to receive and understand the gospel message as true, they will continue to interpret it and any miraculous manifestations in the only way they know how, in terms of their non-Christian religious beliefs and values. From one angle, this reinterpretation process simply is a communication problem. But from another angle, if the reinterpretation persists, it becomes syncretistic, permitting other worldviews to maintain themselves over against Christian truth claims.

God's Power Proclaimed (14:14-18) Paul and Barnabas react with intense disgust. In Jewish fashion they show their revulsion at this blasphemous false worship by tearing their clothes. They rush out into the crowd, insisting that the worship stop.

Paul's speech begins with an attack on idolatry. His initial question, *Men, why are you doing this?* assumes that there is common ground between his audience and himself—that they can join him in his negative evaluation of idolatrous practices. He points out the miracleworker is not worthy of worship, since he is a human being like they. He identifies idols as *worthless things* that his preaching has called them to turn from. Idols are worthless, empty, indeed deceitful, because they do not produce the effect they promise (compare Jer 2:5).

14:13 The NIV rightly interprets the priest's and the crowd's movement as toward the city gates (E. F. Harrison 1986:233) and not the temple gates (as Williams 1985:239) or house gates (as Bruce 1990:322).

14:14 Other examples of this Jewish reaction are 2 Kings 18:37 and 19:1 and Matthew 26:65.

Paul next proclaims the one true *living God,* the Creator of all that is. He is the true source of the miraculously benevolent. Later Paul says the supply of rain that makes the ground fruitful, providing human beings with abundance of food and gladness of heart, is the ongoing witness that the living God, not Zeus and Hermes, exists. Such arguments occur throughout the Scriptures (Ps 147:8; 104:13-15; Jer 14:22; Mt 5:45). Paul also implies the moral consequences of not recognizing the living Creator as God. Paul's call to conversion and his explanation of God's permissive will in allowing all nations to *go their own way* assume human accountability. He is explaining why in every past generation God did not act in judgment as he did in Noah's generation.

Paul's speech models elements that must be included in any strategy of effective witness to adherents of a non-Christian religion. We must assume common ground with the person, our humanity. We are both made in the image of God with an ability to reason and evaluate experience. We must have a flexibility of approach in presenting the gospel. We must be familiar enough with the person's religious beliefs to know what they are substituting for the one true God and his ways. We must correct them, but just as important, we must figure out how the gospel is "good news" so we may tell them how to truly fulfill their religious aspirations. Finally, we must witness with urgency, making the person aware of the consequences. Since we are all accountable before God, our dialogue with non-Christians is not a simple exchange of religious opinions but a discussion of life-and-death issues.

The Mission Advances Through Suffering (14:19-20) Disgruntled by Paul and Barnabas's rejection of their worship, a crowd, incited to riot by Jews from Antioch and Iconium, stones Paul. They drag him out of the city, discarding what they think is a corpse.

Paul's suffering issues in a quiet victory. Lystran believers gather

---

14:16 Almost all recent commentators state or imply that Paul's statement implies the nations are not culpable for past idolatry (Lake and Cadbury 1979:166; Haenchen 1971:428; Marshall 1980:239; Williams 1985:239). Such an understanding sets Acts 14 over against the teaching of Romans (Rom 1:18-23; 3:21-26). God's letting the nations *go their own way* simply explains why humankind sins by responding to general revelation with false worship.

14:17 Paul's assertion about God's witness to his existence does not affirm a natural theology that sees the knowledge of God in the various religions of humankind (contra Pickard 1970:49). It is a claim for objective revelation through creation for which all humans

around him. He gets up, reenters the city and the next day proceeds to Derbe to preach there. Victory is manifest in his recovery, as instantaneous as the cripple's healing, and in his freedom of movement.

This last scene teaches us that being an instrument of God's saving blessing to others, even of miraculous workings, is no guarantee that we will be immune from persecution, including physical suffering.

Witness at Derbe and the Return Trip (14:21-28)

The ruins of ancient religious temples, whether in the Peruvian highlands or the Cambodian jungle, are mute testimony to the assertion "A religious faith is always one generation from extinction." What can guard Christianity from extinction? Paul's example, at the end of the first missionary journey, of strengthening the just-planted churches through confirmation, consolidation and communication shows us the way.

Confirmation (14:21-22) In the eastern provincial border town of Derbe (Lycaonian for "juniper tree"), sixty miles east of Lystra, Paul and Barnabas *preached the good news*. They make many disciples and evidently face no opposition (compare 2 Tim 3:11).

Afterward, instead of moving straight east to Tarsus, a straight shot of 150 miles, Paul and Barnabas decide to retrace their steps. As will become Paul's practice (see comment at Acts 15:36), the apostle will maintain contact with the churches he has planted, providing ongoing counsel and encouragement. Though Paul focused on church planting (1 Cor 3:6), the goal of his labors was to "present everyone perfect in Christ" to the Lord at his coming (Col 1:28; Rom 15:16; 1 Thess 2:17-20). So today, an evangelist or church planter who does not make provision for discipleship is like a farmer who harvests well only to see the crop spoil because it is not properly stored.

Paul's purpose is "to strengthen the souls of the disciples." He wants

---

are responsible. Yet because of willful ignorance no one subjectively comprehends it apart from the Spirit-illumined reception of special revelation.

14:19 If the few Jews at Lystra were under the official or unofficial jurisdiction of the synagogues at Pisidian Antioch and Iconium, then the Jews' pursuit of Paul and Barnabas as far as Lystra is understandable historically.

14:20 Did the disciples surround Paul to mourn over him (E. F. Harrison 1986:236) or to pray for him (Ogilvie 1983:224)? Luke gives us no indication. At the very least Luke is showing us the young believers' courageous solidarity with the apostle.

the new Christians to become "more firm and unchanging in attitude or belief" (Louw and Nida 1988:1:678). They have known persecution and will know the pressure of Judaizers' attempts to turn them from the "faith way" (Gal 1:6-7; 3:1-3; 6:12-13). Paul commands them to *remain true to the faith* (literally, "remain in"; compare Acts 11:23; 13:43). As it was Christ's divinely appointed destiny *(dei)* "to suffer these things and then enter his glory" (Lk 24:26), so his followers *must [dei] go through many hardships to enter the kingdom of God* (Acts 14:22; compare Rom 8:17; Phil 3:10-11; Col 1:24). *Many hardships* are to be expected as a normal, indeed necessary, part of the Christian life. For Luke, they mainly come in the form of persecution (Acts 5:41; 11:19; 20:23). We must endure through them if we would hope to *enter the kingdom of God,* experience the full enjoyment of salvation blessings either at death (2 Tim 4:18) or at Christ's return. And today, if authentic Christianity is to be propagated and survive, it will be because we have said no to any "gospel" that promises glory without the suffering, and yes to the way of the cross, which leads to a crown.

Consolidation (14:23-25) Paul and Barnabas combine encouragement with provision of a leadership structure. They appoint elders for each church.

We need to be careful not to use this passage alone to build a whole theology of leadership selection, complete with policies and procedures. When Luke is more expansive on these matters, he shows the congregation as having a role in leadership selection, as the postapostolic church did (*Didache* 15:1; compare Ignatius *Letter to Polycarp* 7.2). Acts 14:23 does teach us that there may be circumstances, especially in the life of a newly planted church under threat of persecution and false teaching, where missionary appointment of leaders is the wisest course.

14:23 The NIV marginal reading "Or *Barnabas ordained elders; or Barnabas had elders elected*" probably says more about the views of church government represented on the translation team than about the range of possible translations of *cheirotoneō* in this context. While the word did become a technical term for ordination in later church history (Eusebius *Ecclesiastical History* 6.43.10), the syntax of verse 23 places the verb's action before the ordination procedure of fasting and praying and commitment to the Lord. To turn the verb into a causative passive with the congregation evidently as the assumed agent of election— "had elders elected (by the congregation)"—is not supported by the verb's form or meaning, nor demanded by the immediate context. The plain fact is that Luke portrays Paul and Barnabas as selecting and appointing the elders. Some commentators argue from the larger

The swiftness of these appointments has bothered some church-planting strategists (compare 1 Tim 5:22). But if the core of the membership came from the synagogue, they had sufficient biblical and theological background to permit rapid spiritual maturation. Further, "perhaps Paul and Barnabas were more conscious of the presence and power of the Holy Spirit in the believing communities" than we are today (Bruce 1988:280).

Paul and Barnabas, *with prayer and fasting, committed them to the Lord.* This shows us that eldership was a spiritual ministry of the most vital kind (compare Acts 13:1-3; 20:28; 1 Tim 4:14; 5:17). Their teaching, spiritual governance and exercise of discipline could be undertaken only with the same total dependence on the Lord that characterized their abiding belief in him for salvation (compare Acts 20:28-32). Indeed, Paul and Barnabas place these elders "on deposit with the Lord" (*paratithēmi;* 20:32; compare 2 Tim 1:12, 14). Such leadership will take the church into the next spiritual generation.

Paul and Barnabas make their way southward through wild, mountainous Pisidia to the fruitful alluvial plain of Pamphylia to preach at Perga, a major Greek city near the coast (compare 13:13). Departing from the port city Attalia, eight miles southwest, they sailed for Syrian Antioch and their sending church.

Communication (14:26-28) As will become his custom (18:22), Paul reports fully to the church at his home base, Antioch. As Luke makes clear, God is truly the hero of the first missionary journey. Only because the Antioch church *had . . . committed* Paul and Barnabas *to the grace of God* (compare 13:3) have they been able to complete the journey. As Everett F. Harrison observes, the missionaries have carried out their task to the "full limits of possibility" (1986:238; compare Rom 15:19; Col

context of Acts that the congregation had a role, whether of concurrence (Longenecker 1981:439) or actual selection (Kistemaker 1990:525; Acts 1:23; 6:1-6; 13:1-3), and Luke's brief note may leave room for such understandings; still, the basic sense of the verb points to the missionaries as making the choice.

Luke's use of *elders* is not an anachronism (contra Bruce 1990:326 and Marshall 1980:240, among others), though none of the uncontested Pauline letters use it to designate church leaders (only in 1 Tim 5:17, 19; Tit 1:5). We may harmonize Paul's and Luke's usage if we realize that Paul often describes leadership in terms of function (Rom 12:8; 1 Thess 5:12; compare 1 Tim 5:17). He seems to reserve *elder* for times when the position itself is in focus (compare Luke's similar approach in Acts 20:17, 28).

4:17). What they report to the gathered church is *all that God had done through them*—better, "for them" (see comment at Acts 15:4). The phrasing emphasizes their awareness of God's presence and his saving work throughout the mission (11:21; 15:4; compare 1 Cor 3:9). Finally, it was God who *opened the door of faith to the Gentiles.* This image captures what the first missionary journey was all about (Acts 9:15-16; 13:1-3). God did swing wide open *to the Gentiles* the *door of faith,* giving access to salvation by faith (Lk 13:24-25; Acts 13:38-39; 13:12, 43, 46-48; 14:1, 23). The church will survive to the next generation when it maintains this kind of fruitful communication between the just-planted church and the sending church.

□ The Jerusalem Council (15:1-35)

In a day when the cultural diversity of world-class cities is more "stew pot" than "melting pot," the church needs to relearn lessons from the Jerusalem council. These lessons will help the body of Christ seize the moment for further evangelistic advance, for we will be able to model a harmonious cultural diversity that the world with all its ethnic strife can only hope for. Here is great good news for Theophilus and us: a gospel that recognizes diversity yet enables harmonious living based on a higher unity, our identity in Christ.

The Problem Surfaces (15:1-5)

The grand reunion at Antioch continues for some time (14:28). And in due course some from Judea come and begin to teach (*edidaskon* imperfect is ingressive) "another gospel." They baldly claim, *Unless you are circumcised, according to the custom taught by Moses, you cannot be saved.* This incident may have been the same as the one described in

15:1-35 When Acts 15 and Galatians 2:1-10 are viewed as reporting the same event, a number of discrepancies call into question the historical plausibility of Acts 15. Although there have been a number of attempts to harmonize Acts 15 and Galatians 2 and at the same time preserve the historical reliability of both (Williams 1985:248; Kistemaker 1990:536), they prove unsatisfactory. They have to rely on arguments that make Peter act out of character or make Paul choose to keep silent about certain aspects of the apostolic decree. It is much simpler to conclude that Acts 15 and Galatians 2 refer to two different events (Bruce 1988:231, 284; Marshall 1980:244-45; Longenecker 1981:405, 440). See note at Acts 11:30, which argues for Galatians 2:1-10 and Acts 11:29-30 reporting the same event.

Paul's other letters are silent on the decree. Their handling of food issues (Rom 14; 1 Cor

Galatians 2:11-14, although from what we learn at the council the visitors should not be organically linked to Peter or James. Though they claim the latter's name, they are probably more rigorous concerning the law than he. It is likely that they come from among *the believers who belonged to the party of the Pharisees,* since their doctrine is the same (15:5).

These teachers are adding a performance condition to salvation: circumcision and, as their Jerusalem compatriots articulate it, obedience to the law of Moses. Such a "proselyte model" of Gentile conversion was natural to Jews steeped in the Old Testament, which promises that in the last days Gentiles, through the witness of a restored Israel, will flow to Jerusalem and be incorporated into the one people of God (Is 2:2-3; 25:6-8; 56:6-7; 60:2-22; Zech 8:23).

Paul and Barnabas disagree so strongly with this group that a *sharp dispute,* turbulent quarreling, arises as they debate the issue (compare 23:7, 10). When the church (including its leaders—Longenecker 1981:443) sees that discussion is not producing a resolution, it orders that a delegation be sent to the apostles and elders at Jerusalem to address the problem. Such an appeal is most appropriate, for the Judean visitors came from the Jerusalem church, and naturally it is the next highest court of appeal. Not only do Jesus' apostles lead this original post-Pentecost church, but it is also the mother church of Antioch (11:19-21) and has expressed some proprietary interest (11:22-23).

The behavior of Paul and Barnabas teaches us that it is right to contend for the truth of the gospel in spite of the debate that may ensue. No local church or denomination should settle for politically expedient peace at the expense of doctrinal purity. At the same time, Antioch's decision to appeal to Jerusalem shows us that doctrinal purity maintained in an atmosphere of contentiousness—at the expense of peace—is an equally

8—10) seems out of step with Acts 15. At Corinth Paul is dealing with Gentile Christians still influenced by their pagan background and operating in an intensely pagan environment. His instructions to them pursue another tack and, understandably, don't refer to the decree. The "weaker brother" vegetable eaters of Romans 14 represent a more analogous situation, though the issue may have been simple lifestyle. Paul's reasoning in Romans is quite similar to that which undergirds the decree. The decree deals in the main with practical matters of accommodation for unity, not adherence to a universally normative moral imperative. It accords well with Paul's attitude in 1 Corinthians 9:19-23. Nothing in Paul's letters, then, prevents us from seeing him as assenting to, even disseminating, the apostolic decree of Acts 15.

wrong situation.

Sent . . . on their way, escorted some distance by the church, the delegation travels by land, visiting fellow believers in Phoenicia and Samaria. These rejoice at the report of the conversion of the Gentiles (14:27; 15:12). What a contrast to the suspicious reaction of the teachers from Judea! Luke's note shows not only that the Judaizers are in the minority but, positively, that joy is the appropriate response to news that persons of any cultural group have come to salvation (Lk 1:14; 15:7, 10, 32; Acts 11:23). One of the best litmus tests for the presence of the saving grace of God in our hearts is whether they overflow in joy at the news that another has found the Savior.

The church and its leaders welcome the delegation and receive a report of *everything God had done through* (preferably "for"; Bauer, Gingrich and Danker 1979:509; compare 14:27) *them* (15:4). A Judaizing response comes from the Pharisaic *party* (*hairesis*—not heresy or sect, but "wing," like evangelicals and Anglo-Catholics in the Anglican Church). To them, to allow Gentiles to be converted and incorporated into the church by faith and baptism is a truncated approach: *The Gentiles must be circumcised and required to obey the law of Moses.* Before we are too hard on these zealous Jewish Christians, let's ask ourselves, What cultural dos and don'ts have we appended to the gospel as conditions for church membership?

The Witness of the Spirit and the Word (15:6-21)

Church leaders and members must learn to debate with each other so that the truth may be embraced by all. The Jerusalem Council shows us the right ammunition for debate and a church leader's responsibilities in it.

Peter's Speech (15:6-11) At an official gathering of the Jerusalem church leaders, *apostles and elders,* there is much debate (compare 15:2). Finally Peter rises to speak. He begins by stressing the divine initiative in the inauguration of the Gentile mission. He reminds the church, alluding to the Cornelius incident, that *some time ago* (ten to

---

15:10 Nolland (1980) makes a strong case for the inability to bear the yoke of the law being the futility of achieving salvation by responsible obedience.

15:11 The NIV and many translators and commentators take *pisteuomen sōthēnai* as "we believe that we will be or have been saved," an expression of opinion or conviction about

twelve years) God chose him to be the mouthpiece by which Gentiles would hear the gospel and come to saving faith (10:33, 36, 43; 11:13-14). Next he points to the divine acceptance of the Gentiles: *God, who knows the heart* (1:24), a person's true spiritual state, gave the Holy Spirit to them as he had to Jewish believers at Pentecost (10:44-48; 11:15, 17). Here Peter strongly challenges the Jewish view that the only acceptable outward evidence of the conversion of Gentiles is their willingness to be circumcised and live as Jews. If God has taken initiative toward the Gentiles and accepted them for salvation, God's lack of prejudice against the Gentiles is obvious.

Peter draws a negative and positive conclusion from his experience with Cornelius and his household. Negatively, to insist on circumcision and living under the Jewish law is actually to put God to the test. Though secondarily this would be to call "into question [God's] power to cleanse the hearts of the uncircumcised by His Spirit" (Williams 1985:253), primarily it means tempting God to inflict punishment, even eternal condemnation, by placing the Gentile convert back in the "law performance" way of trying to relate to God. Taking on the yoke of the law and carrying it was a positive image in Judaism (*m. Berakot* 2:2; *m. 'Abot* 3:5). Peter here claims that with respect to obtaining salvation, the responsible keeping of the law is futile (Acts 13:38-39; Gal 3:10-12). Positively, using the Gentiles as the standard, Peter declares that it is *through the grace of our Lord Jesus Christ* that "we believe so as to be saved," *just as they [the Gentiles] are* (compare 2:21; 4:12; 14:3; 16:30-31).

We must let this simple truth sink deep into our hearts, for as Lloyd Ogilvie observes, "The struggle for faith alone never ends. It's a part of our own inability to accept a gift. And deeper than that: we want to be loved because of what we do for God" (1983:227).

The Testimony of Barnabas and Paul (15:12) In the face of Peter's cogent theological reasoning *the whole assembly became silent.* The groundwork for settling the issue in favor of Paul and Barnabas has

---

one's salvation. Given the importance of faith for salvation in the whole argument, it is better to take the phrase as referring to one's conversion: "we believe so as to be saved" (Nolland 1980:112-13).

been laid, and basic unity has been restored. Now Barnabas and Paul speak, *telling about* (providing "detailed information in a systematic manner"—Louw and Nida 1988:1:411), all (literally, "so many"—not in NIV) *the miraculous signs and wonders God had done among the Gentiles through them.* As at Cornelius's conversion, God's miracleworking has accompanied this Gentile mission (14:3, 9-10). Therefore Paul's mission and message—the law-free gospel of grace—has the same divine legitimacy as Peter's. Here we again encounter a focused function for signs and wonders: confirmation to Jews of God's approval of the Gentile mission (see comment at 14:3).

James's Assessment (15:13-21) James, the half-brother of Jesus, who as the chief elder may well be chairing the meeting, *spoke up*—literally, "answered." He will now give his assessment of the evidence presented and offer a solution to the controversy. He interprets Peter's experience with Cornelius as a major event in God's salvation history. *At first*—that is, long ago (compare v. 7)—God *showed his concern* (v. 4; literally, "visited"). James's wording places the salvation of the Gentiles on a par with God's saving acts toward Israel, past and future (Ex 3:16; 4:31; Jer 39:41 LXX; Lk 1:68, 78; 7:16; *Testament of Levi* 16:5; *1 Enoch* 25:3). His purpose is to take a people for his name from among the Gentiles. By using phrasing that closely echoes God's choosing of Israel, James heightens the radical nature of the new thing God has done (Ex 19:5; Deut 7:6). Now *a people [laos] for himself* (literally, "for his

---

15:12 The NIV subordinates the second member of a parallel construction *(esigēsen . . . kai ēkouon)*, leaving the impression that the silence is more closely related to a polite listening to Barnabas and Paul than to the effect of Peter's speech.

Though commentators sometimes see indications of the Jerusalem church's esteem for Barnabas in the reversal of order to *Barnabas and Paul* (for example, Williams 1985:253), Haenchen (1971:447) rightly says it is only a matter of stylistic variation that occurs throughout the narrative.

15:13 James's (see comment at 12:17) piety and asceticism earned him the nickname "Old Camel's Knees," for he was so frequently in the temple kneeling in prayer for the forgiveness of the people that his knees developed callouses as camels' do (Eusebius *Ecclesiastical History* 2.23.4-8). He was in the perfect position to assess the debate, for the Judaizers would have heard him sympathetically.

15:14 The NIV margin points out that the Greek text contains *Simeon* at this point, which it calls "a variant of *Simon;* that is, Peter." Actually *Simeon (Symeōn)* is an indeclinable transliteration of the Aramaic *Šim'ôn* and hence what Peter would have been called in his native tongue. *Simon* is a similar-sounding but genuine Greek name that is often substituted for Simeon in references to Peter (compare Lk 4:38; 6:14; 22:31; 24:34).

name"; compare Acts 15:17) will be taken from among the Gentiles.

Though the Jews expected God's salvation to reach to the Gentiles, they thought that Gentile participation would occur through incorporation into the already existing people of God, Israel. They never thought that the people of God would comprise both Jew and Gentile but not be Jewish. Note that Luke uses *laos* consistently in Acts to refer to the Jews as the people of God (4:10; 10:42; 13:17; 26:17, 23; 28:17; contrast 18:10).

Though this may be a radically new thought to the first-century Jew, it is not new to God. *The words of the prophets are in agreement with this* (15:15, referring to either the book of the twelve minor prophets—Acts 7:42; 13:40; compare Zech 2:11—or the fact that many prophets so agree). Here we have a reversal of roles for the promise and fulfillment. Usually it is the alleged fulfillment that must agree with the promise. Here the fulfillment becomes the hermeneutical key for understanding how the prophet Amos could prophesy that in the last days the "people of God" would include Gentiles who had not first become Jews.

The wording of the Amos 9:11-12 quotation (Acts 15:16-17) is a comprehensive statement of what God has done through Peter. The rebuilding of *David's fallen tent* may point ultimately to the whole saving program of God in his Messiah (Kaiser 1977:108; compare the Qumran use of the passage—CD 7:16; 4QFlor 1:12) and hence to Jesus' saving death and resurrection (Bruce 1988:293-94), but it does not do so in a

---

15:16-17 The wording of the quotation varies significantly from the Hebrew text of Amos 9:11-12. The differences between Acts 15:16 and Amos 9:11 involve stylistic adjustments but no change in meaning. At Acts 15:17/Amos 9:12 the MT reads "that they may possess the remnant of Edom" and Acts and the LXX read *that the remnant of men may seek* (Acts has the object *the Lord*). This is not Luke's appropriation of a LXX spiritualization, which has transformed a messianic recovery of territory into the conversion of the Gentiles (contra Bruce 1988:293-94). Rather, the MT is likely a corruption of the Hebrew text that stands behind the LXX and Acts (compare CD 7:16; 4QFlor 1:12; Archer and Chirichigno 1983:155; Braun 1977:117). Hebrew *ydršw* ("they shall seek") could easily have been copied as *yyršw* ("they shall possess"), the *d* and *y* often being confused in transmission. The object may have been either "him" or "me," both referring to God (*'ōtô* or *'ōtî*). The consonants *'dm* can be pointed to spell either *'ādām* ("men") or *'edōm* ("Edom"). Other scholars argue that the MT as it stands can still support James's interpretation (Kaiser 1977; King 1989).

15:16 The dispensational interpretation that takes *after this* to refer to the gospel dispensation and the Amos quote to refer to the future restoration of the Davidic messianic kingdom has been effectively critiqued by both E. F. Harrison (1986:248-49) and Walter Kaiser Jr. (1977:106).

spiritualizing way that violates the original context. To say that James equates the "house of David" with the church and the prophecy as a whole with "the church gathering to itself all the nations" does violate Amos's original intent (contra Williams 1985:254). Rightly interpreted, the rebuilt Davidic tent refers to a restored Israel, which in the person of Jewish Christians God chooses to inaugurate the Gentile mission (15:7, 14; compare Longenecker 1981:446). That was, after all, the purpose of Israel's restoration: *that the remnant of men may seek the Lord.*

James has grasped the very heart of Amos's eschatological message concerning the nature of the salvation that Messiah brings to the Gentiles. In so doing, James has replaced a proselyte model of Gentile salvation with an eschatological/christocentric one. The Lord has chosen to place his name on Gentiles as Gentiles, without requiring that they surrender their ethnic identity. That name, "the Lord Jesus Christ," is the basis on which they have repented and believed (Lk 24:47; Acts 4:12; 10:43), the identity they have adopted in baptism (2:38; 10:48; compare 11:26) and the reason they will suffer (compare 5:41; 14:22).

This Old Testament text teaches that Christians' new identity in Christ both supersedes and allows room for their cultural identity. Christians are saved from the error of prejudicial ethnocentrism. What a liberation, to respect and appreciate differences, not using them as weapons of prejudice but at the same time not being imprisoned by them!

James concludes the quote by affirming that this plan for Gentile salvation is not of human origin and is not new. It has been known by God for ages (compare Is 45:21). To oppose it with human cultural traditions, even those that appeal to Scripture, is to oppose God's eternal revelation.

What solution to the controversy does this freshly articulated understanding yield? James makes an "official" proposal of one negative and one positive action with respect to Gentile converts. *We should not make it difficult* for them: that is, Jewish Christians should not pressure Gentile

---

15:18 The NIV marginal reading is secondary. It is an example of an attempt by copyists to recast the elliptical expression of verse 18 as an independent sentence (Metzger 1971:429).

15:20, 29 In textual critical matters, the Alexandrian and most manuscripts have the four prohibitions; the Western text omits *meat of strangled animals* and inserts a negative form

converts (compare Judg 14:17; 16:16 LXX) into adopting circumcision and the yoke of the law as a necessary condition and sign of their salvation (contrast Acts 15:1, 5). Positively, the council asks Gentile converts *to abstain from food polluted by idols* (compare 15:29, "food sacrificed to idols"; Ex 34:15-16; compare Lev 17:7-8), *sexual immorality* (possibly meaning marriage within levitical degrees—Lev 18:6-18), *meat of strangled animals* (meat that has not been ritually slaughtered so as to drain the blood properly—Lev 17:13) and *blood* (eating blood—Lev 17:10).

Interestingly, each of these prohibitions was originally addressed not only to Jew but also to Gentile aliens living alongside them in the land. The rules' specifics and their rationale (Acts 15:21) show they are given to promote table fellowship between uncircumcised Gentile converts and Jewish Christians who observe the dietary laws. There is no surrender here of the gospel freedom alluded to in verse 19. Rather, that freedom is to be used in love to serve Jewish Christian brothers and sisters, but not beyond the bounds of Scripture (Gal 5:13). *Sexual immorality,* as an ethical matter, not having to do with ritual purity, may seem out of place. But given that one of the Jews' ongoing concerns was "low ethical and moral standards among Gentiles" (Scott 1992:14), it is appropriate in this list to represent the category of moral standards.

James's proposal, then, teaches us three things about life together in a culturally diverse church. We must say no to any form of cultural imperialism that demands others' conformity to our cultural standards before we will accept them and their spiritual experience. We must say yes to mutual respect for our differences. And we must live out that respect even to the extent of using our freedom to forgo what is permissible in other circumstances.

In a day when transportation and urbanization make it easier to stay apart than face the challenge of living together as a multicultural body of believers, the church has yet to model consistently what James calls

---

of the Golden Rule; the Caesarean text omits *sexual immorality.* Through omission, insertion and treating blood as a reference to murder, the Western text makes all the prohibitions moral. The Caesarean text treats the list as strictly ceremonial. Since both the Western and Caesarean readings can be accounted for as attempts to ease the difficulties of the Alexandrian, the latter should be taken as original (Metzger 1971:429-34).

for. But even our separate culturally homogeneous fellowships may face challenges of gender, music and generation gaps. We need to take Acts 15 to heart.

The Council's Letter (15:22-29)

James's assessment and proposal carry the day not only with the leaders but with the whole church. The Judaizers lose the argument, though their influence may continue (compare 21:20-25). The council decides to send a letter and personal envoys to Antioch with Paul and Barnabas. *Judas (called Barsabbas)* is possibly the brother of Joseph Barsabbas (1:23), though the patronymic Barsabbas (= son of Sabba, Seba or sabbath) was common. *Silas,* the diminutive of Saul (little wolf), later becomes a traveling companion of Paul (Lake and Cadbury 1979:179; compare 15:40). Both are leaders, prophets (v. 32) and possibly representatives of the Hebraic Jewish and Hellenistic Jewish wings of the church, respectively. They will carry the letter (not write it; contrast Campbell 1988:509) and verify the council's decision in person.

The letter's very address shows a balance between unity in Christ and respect for diverse cultural identities. *The apostles and elders, your brothers,* address Christian brothers and sisters, recognizing their ethnic identity: *To the Gentile believers,* literally, "to the brothers from among the Gentiles."

The body of the letter communicates in essence the decisions on the two key issues: the spiritual status of uncircumcised Gentiles who have joined the church and regulations for their table fellowship with Jewish Christians (vv. 24-27, 28-29). The council does not address the first issue directly. It indicates its position through a disassociation from the Jud-

---

15:22 *Decided* is the technical term for "passing a measure in a political assembly" (compare vv. 25, 28; Lake and Cadbury 1979:178).

15:23 Reference to Cilicia may be because the Judaizers have extended their influence that far (compare 16:4), though politically the eastern portion of Cilicia was at this time administered from Antioch and thus naturally connected with it and Syria.

15:28 While Krodel (1986:290) believes *the Holy Spirit* refers to the Cornelius incident, Bruce (1988:298) rightly concludes, "So conscious were the church leaders of being possessed and controlled by the Spirit that he was given prior mention as chief author of their decision."

Krodel (1986:280) views the decree as the apostolic interpretation of Luke 16:17 with respect to the social function of the Torah in interracial communities and hence an ethical

aizers and an identification with and commendation of Paul and Barnabas. It describes in the strongest terms the disturbing effects of the Judaizers (compare Gal 1:7; 5:10). *Troubling your minds* is quite literally "a ravaging of your souls," as destructive as an army's devastation of enemy territory (Josephus *Jewish Antiquities* 14.406). In blunt terms the council disowns their mission and message, saying that these *went out from us without our authorization.*

By contrast, Paul and Barnabas are owned as *our* (esteemed) *dear friends* (literally, "beloved ones"; compare Rom 16:5; Jas 1:16; 1 Pet 2:11) and commended as those *who have risked their lives for the name of our Lord Jesus Christ.* This commendation does not refer to their total commitment to Christ (contra Bruce 1990:345). Rather, it points to the literal hazarding of their lives (contrast the Judaizers—Gal 6:11-13).

The council handles the second issue through a Spirit-inspired apostolic decree (Acts 15:29). The rationale in verse 21, the presence everywhere of Jews with scruples in these matters, indicates the circumstances in which this responsibility or *burden* must be met. It is normative practical wisdom, applicable as a matter of courtesy and Christian love whenever fellowship with Jewish Christians with scruples should warrant. Abstaining from sexual immorality as an ethical norm, however, is universally applied.

The decree's prohibitions still come into play today, either universally in the case of sexual practices or particularly in the case of dietary regulations—wherever Gentile Christians encounter Jewish Christians who are keeping a kosher table. By extension these rules guide all Christians to use their freedom to abstain from practices that would offend the cultural sensitivities of another. What interethnic and intergenerational

requirement for Gentiles as Gentiles, not proselytes. But he fails to take into account the removal of the distinction between clean and unclean food among the people of God in the last days. This effectively abolishes the moral status of the ceremonial requirements.

Mark A. Seifrid (1987:40) argues for the decree as an ethic on a different basis: the enthroned Messiah through the Spirit places new demands on humankind. This view does not reckon with the Old Testament roots of the decree's content. It is best to see the decree as universally normative, but in the main only for the specific situation of table fellowship with Jewish Christians with scruples. Longenecker (1981:448) sees it in the category of practical wisdom for showing courtesy to Jewish Christians. The prohibition of sexual immorality, in the light of other Scripture (Ex 20:14; 1 Thess 4:3), should be treated as a universally applicable moral norm.

harmony the church could know if all rushed to give up their "rights" to please the others!

Antioch's Reception (15:30-35)

The Antioch church is *glad for* the letter's *encouraging*, indeed comforting, *message* (compare 9:31). Where there had been terror (v. 24) there is now joy. And rightly so, for the Gentile converts know where they stand with reference to Judaism and to Jewish Christian believers. There is no circumcision requirement, but full acceptance. They have received guidance on respect for Jewish Christian scruples so full table fellowship can be enjoyed. When gospel truth and Christian love are promoted, there is every reason for joy among all those who would enter and live in such an attractive, wholesome fellowship.

Being prophets, Judas and Silas are supernaturally gifted, like their Old Testament counterparts, to apply the word of God to the personal and corporate circumstances of God's people (compare 1 Cor 14:3, 31). They enter into a lengthy ministry of pastoral exhortation, *to encourage and strengthen the brothers.* They repair the Judaizers' damage (Acts 15:24) and enable the saints, in matters of the gospel, to re-lay a firm foundation (Bauer, Gingrich and Danker 1979:768; compare 14:22).

Ceremoniously, the prophet-envoys later take their leave of the Antioch church *with the blessing of peace to return to those who had sent them.* And the church with renewed vigor engages in outreach. Paul, Barnabas and *many others* remain to teach and "evangelize the word of the Lord." As living organisms are able to rejuvenate themselves when damaged, so the Spirit of God can and will repair the wreckage of hurt feelings, strained relations and wrong thinking brought to the body of Christ by the infiltration of false teaching. What it takes is a church willing to take the time, expend the human resources and make the effort to do the repair work.

□ The Second Missionary Journey (15:36—18:22)

The mission to plant the church in all nations now takes several new

---

15:34 This verse, noted in the margin, is found in later manuscripts. It is probably a copyist's insertion to account for the presence of Silas at Antioch in verse 40 (Metzger 1971:439).

directions. Strategically, there is the Lord's direct guidance throughout the journey (16:1-10; 18:9-10). Geographically, the gospel invades Europe (16:10—18:22). Politically, Christianity faces its opponents' challenge concerning its status in the empire (16:20-21; 17:6-7; 18:13). At the same time earlier themes continue: contextualized witness, persecution, power encounter and divine protection.

This account increases the momentum and magnifies the greatness of the gospel's advance to the ends of the earth in a way calculated to have maximum impact on a Roman audience. For the advance moves the witnesses closer and closer to Rome. There is effective witness in Philippi, a Roman colony. Roman provincial justice is dispensed by Gallio, scion of a leading upper-class family. What is made of Christianity in these contexts will certainly affect how Theophilus and his fellow seekers will view it.

And for us this journey raises questions about divine guidance; what status the church has in the eyes of the state, and how we might frame our gospel message so that it speaks to those whose beliefs and values are not so very different from those of the inhabitants of first-century Philippi and Athens.

Mission to Asia Minor and the Macedonian Call (15:36—16:10)

Part of St. Patrick's benediction, "May the wind be always at your back," well suits the experience of the Pauline missionary band at the beginning of its second journey. The wind is, of course, the wind of the Spirit, and it blows in some surprising directions. Hearing how this push west into Europe began under God's good hand is certain to give the reader confidence that the gospel message is more than just another Eastern cult threatening to pollute Roman minds and hearts. We too can gain confidence as we think about God's direction of the nature, personnel and carrying out of the same mission.

The Right Purpose: Nurture of Believers (15:36, 41; 16:4-5) The plan of the second missionary journey is follow-up nurture, then further outreach. Paul is not one to "dip and drop" his converts (Talbert

---

15:36 The emphatic particle *dē*, untranslated in the NIV, should probably be represented by an introductory "come" (Lk 2:15; Acts 13:2).

1984:68). He suggests to Barnabas that they *visit* (denoting caring over-sight; compare Lk 1:68, 78; 7:16; Acts 15:14) the brothers and sisters in the churches they have planted (13:13—14:20; 15:41; 16:1, 4-6; Gal 1:2, 21; 3:1-5). This was always Paul's practice (Acts 14:21-23; 18:23; 19:21; 20:1-6).

So after disagreeing with Barnabas and choosing Silas, Paul *went through Syria and Cilicia, strengthening the churches.* As had been done at Antioch, the emissaries shore up the Gentile Christians' faith, which has almost been dismantled by the Judaizers (compare 15:32). They probably also deliver the Jerusalem Council's decrees (15:23). The sum-mary statement about ministry in the Galatian churches explicitly notes such activity (16:4-5).

The result is the same: wise and healthy *decisions* (used of imperial decrees at Lk 2:1; Acts 17:7) help to strengthen Christians *in the faith* (compare 3:7, 16; Col 2:5; 1 Pet 5:9). Qualitative growth is matched by quantitative growth. With reaffirmation of the Gentiles' full acceptance by faith alone and instructions on how to fellowship with scrupulous Jewish Christians, it is not surprising that the churches *grew daily in numbers* (compare 2:41, 47; 4:4; 5:14; 6:7; 9:31; 11:21; 12:24). So today God's hand of blessing, manifest in quantitative growth, will be seen where Christians proclaim a gospel of grace without additional cultural requirements and promote multicultural unity. And this fruit will remain when we choose the right purpose: nurture.

The Right People: Silas and Timothy (15:37-40; 16:1-3) Paul gathers his companions for the journey in some unexpected ways. His recruitment begins logically enough when he asks Barnabas to accom-pany him (v. 36). But Barnabas's intention to take John Mark leads to *such a sharp disagreement,* literally "a heated disagreement" (compare Deut 29:27 LXX; Jer 39:37 LXX), that Paul and Barnabas decide they can no longer work together. So they separate.

Luke does not explain why Barnabas wants to take John Mark along. Is it that this encourager's sympathy reaches out to restore the deserter (compare Acts 4:36; 9:27)? Is it Barnabas's sympathy with the viewpoint

16:4 Jerusalem does not appear to commission Paul to hand on the decrees, yet the plural verb in this verse indicates that he does so even to the churches of South Galatia, to which they are not addressed. Bruce (1988:305) therefore doubts that this verse was in the original

of the strict Jewish Christians, which he may share with Mark, and which may have occasioned Mark's earlier defection (Gal 2:13)? Is it simply the family tie between them (Col 4:10)? What we do know is that from Paul's perspective, John Mark's desertion in the midst of the first missionary journey rendered him unfit for the second (Acts 13:13; compare Lk 8:13; 1 Tim 4:1). Luke has not told us why John Mark deserted. Paul does say that Mark *had not continued with them in the work,* and earlier that work was defined as "the door of faith" being opened to the Gentiles (14:26-27). It may be that on a journey to communicate the Jerusalem church's affirmation of the Gentile mission, this defector would have proved more of a liability than an asset.

In any case, the separation doubles the church's mission, for Barnabas takes John Mark and goes to his home area, Cyprus (4:36), and Paul chooses a new partner, Silas. Silas is well suited to the task. He is spir-itually gifted, a prophet (15:32). He embodies the church's commitment to a Gentile mission with the law-free gospel, for he was one of the envoys bearing the council's letter (15:22, 27). As a Roman citizen, he can move about easily within the Empire (16:37).

Given Luke's emphasis on unity as the mark of the Holy Spirit within the church, he can hardly approve of the divisiveness that led to the separation (2:44-46; 4:32; 5:12). Yet he does approve of Paul's team and notes that it is *commended [having been handed over to] by the brothers to the grace of the Lord* (compare 14:26).

This incident shows us that past performance reveals character and properly serves as a basis for judging suitability for future service. Fur-ther, even though differences in judgment may produce schism, God can so rule and overrule that there is no permanent barrier to the advance of his mission.

The other "right person" for Paul's mission is Timothy (16:1-3). Though he obviously fills the gap created by Paul's refusal to take John Mark, there is also an element of providential surprise in his selection (compare the introductory *kai idou,* "and behold," untranslated in the NIV). Timothy will be very useful for the mission. He is a disciple, a man

text. There is no manuscript evidence to support this view (Kistemaker 1990:580). Besides, Paul is mentioned in the letter as well (15:25).

of good character (Phil 2:20-22; compare Acts 6:3; 1 Tim 3:7) whose reputation has extended even to Iconium, a day's journey away. He is a person of mixed parentage.

Timothy's one defect is a lack of circumcision. If the Jews at this time traced Jewish descent of mixed marriages matrilineally *(m. Qiddušin* 3:12; *m. Yebamot* 7:5; Cohen [1986:267] questions whether the principle was applied this early), uncircumcised Timothy is a Jew by birth but apostate. The small Jewish community at Lystra was either too weak or too lax to enforce circumcision in a culture that determined ethnic and religious heritage patrilineally. Still, Timothy has a good spiritual heritage from his mother (2 Tim 1:5; 3:15). With his father now possibly deceased (the verb tense seems to indicate this), there is no impediment to circumcision. And there is every reason. If Paul condones Timothy's uncircumcised, apostate status, he will not have access to synagogues, his strategic point of contact in most cities. Further, the decree's underlying principle of respect for cultural identity will be compromised by the presence of a Jewish Christian who has "gentilized." So by circumcising Timothy, Paul clarifies his status for Jewish believer and unbeliever alike.

This is not inconsistent with the circumcision-free gospel to Jew and Gentile so recently affirmed at the council. Rather, it reflects Paul's higher consistency. For Paul never denied his religious heritage or its practices as an appropriate way to live out his Christian commitment (Acts 21:21-24), yet he could treat circumcision as a matter of indifference and use it as a means of cultural adaptation to further the gospel (1 Cor 9:19-23; Gal 5:6).

The "right people," then, to promote the advance of the church's mission are spiritually fruitful, morally faithful and culturally flexible. Today such men and women are God's gift to the church for the cutting edge of mission advance.

16:6 *The region of Phrygia and Galatia* has been understood in two basic ways: (1) denoting two distinct ethnic territories, Phrygia (Pisidian Antioch, Iconium) and Galatia to the north (Polhill 1992:345), or (2) denoting one territory, the Phrygian portion of the Roman province of Galatia (Longenecker 1981:457). Colin J. Hemer (1976; 1977c) has removed objections to the latter view with regard to the adjectival use of "Phrygia." The former view creates a major detour to the north. The latter view points to another stage in the journey (contrast Polhill 1992:345) and is consistent with Luke's use of territorial names. This latter view should be followed. Paul's route, then, is through Iconium and Pisidian

The Right Place: Divinely Chosen Macedonia (16:6-10) From
Pisidian Antioch in *the region of Phrygia and Galatia* Paul evidently
intends to make his way straight west into the Roman province of Asia
on the Via Sebaste, 150 miles to Colosse and then 150 more to Ephesus.
We are not told how, but the Holy Spirit clearly prevents them from
taking that route so that they could preach the word in Asia. This occurs
probably before they set off or early in their passage, for they evidently
turn northward almost immediately.

They come to Dorylaeum, or more probably Cotiaeum, at *the border
of Mysia* (the latitude of Mysia), the northern portion of the province of
Asia, and sought to head northeast into the province of Bithynia, *but the
Spirit of Jesus would not allow them to.* Again there is no indication of
the means he uses. Paul evidently takes this negative guidance to mean
that he must push the mission farther west, across the Aegean to Greece.
He heads for Troas, the port of embarkation for Macedonia, even though
there is no direct route to it from where he begins (compare Bowers
1979; Haenchen 1971:487 disagrees).

Troas, more properly Alexandria Troas, was an important seaport for
travel from the northwestern part of the Roman province of Asia to
Macedonia and the west. Ten miles south of the ancient site of Troy, the
now deserted site has ruins of an aqueduct, a theater and city walls six
miles in circumference, giving mute testimony to its prosperity and mag-
nitude. There *during the night* Paul receives positive guidance. In a
vision (compare 9:12; 18:9; 22:17; 26:16) he sees and hears *a man of
Macedonia . . . begging him, "Come over to Macedonia and help us."*
This "begging" is a strong appeal (compare 13:42).

Now that Paul has received extraordinary and circumstantial guidance,
his team corporately reasons, putting together *(symbibazō)* the positive
and negative guidance, to the conclusion that God has called them to

Antioch and to the northwest after the Spirit's hindrance.

16:8 Only if you take *passed by* in the sense of "bypassed, did not evangelize" can the
movements described fit with the geography. One has to physically pass through Mysia in
order to arrive at Troas, which is within its bounds. There are other examples of *parerchomai*
to mean "pass through and over" (1 Macc 5:48), and that is what it may well mean here
(Haenchen 1971:484).

16:10 The "we passages" (see introduction) are indicators of Luke's own participation
in the events recorded.

evangelize the Macedonians (compare 13:2). And they act immediately, getting ready (literally "seeking") to leave for Macedonia.

How does God guide his church to the right place for mission? There will be "closed" as well as "open doors." There will be guidance addressed to individuals as well as to the entire team. There will be guidance via circumstances, sometimes extraordinary, as well as through the use of reason in evaluating circumstances in the light of God's Word. And specific guidance will come only to those who are already on the road, living out their general obedience to the Great Commission. Being able to say, "God sent me; I come with the wind at my back," is a strong witness to one's hearers that one's message is from God and true.

Witness at Philippi (16:11-40)

"What must I do to be saved?" was the most pressing religious question of Luke's day. People believed they were in the grip of fate. All were looking for a savior, whether through traditional animistic worship, the mystery religions or the imperial cult.

Today life's basic question is "What must I do to put it all together? How can I gain control of my life and cope with seemingly uncontrollable forces around and within me?" The questions may be different, but the ultimate need is the same. Luke shows God's answer in three lives that were transformed by his power at Philippi, a Roman colony.

A Divinely Opened Heart (16:11-15) Paul and his team set sail northwest from Troas, making a straight line for Samothrace, a mountainous island navigational marker with its 5,577-foot Mount Fengari. About halfway on their voyage they anchor for the night on the north side of the island. They complete their 156-mile journey the next day, landing

---

16:12 The NIV wording *the leading city of that district of Macedonia* follows the oldest form of the text, witnessed to by A, ℵ, C and p⁷⁴, which includes a definite article before the word *district* and reads literally, "a first city of the district of Macedonia" (Metzger 1971:444). Commentators have found it difficult to decide in what sense Philippi was "a first city." This was not true politically. Philippi did not qualify to use *prōtos* as an honorific title. Was it a matter of local pride or prowess in economics (mines of precious metals) or education (a world-renowned medical school)?

Some have argued for a conjectural emendation based on some Latin versions and the historical realities of the times. If an *s* were added to *prōtē*, making it a modifier of *meridos,* the phrase would be "a city of the *first district* of Macedonia." In 168 B.C., upon conquest by the Romans, Macedonia was divided into four administrative districts. This emendation

at Neapolis. Favorable winds have given them "Godspeed," for another time the voyage in the opposite direction will require five days (20:6).

The team now takes the Via Egnatia, the Roman road that stretched from Dyrrhachium and its port city Egnatia on the Adriatic to Neapolis on the Aegean. They proceed nine miles inland over some hills to Philippi, on the central Macedonia plateau.

Philippi's reputation was well deserved from the time the father of Alexander the Great, Philip II of Macedon, renamed it after himself and established it as a commercial center. It dealt in agricultural produce of the rich plain and gold and silver mined from the surrounding mountains. Philippi had been made a Roman colony so it could serve as a home for retired army veterans after the decisive battle of the second civil war (42 B.C.) and the battle of Actium (31 B.C.). Bearing witness in Philippi was the closest thing to preaching in Rome without actually being there. Theophilus and his peers would understand well the Philippians' reactions.

Following his normal "to the Jew first" strategy, Paul seeks out the synagogue on the sabbath (13:14, 46; 14:1). Local reports or his awareness of the Jewish custom of locating synagogues outside the precincts of idolatrous pagan cities but near water (for ritual purification) may lead Paul to suppose the synagogue is outside the city gate by the river (the Gangites, one and one-half miles west of the city; Josephus *Jewish Antiquities* 14.258; compare *Mekilta Pisha* 1:64-65; Finegan [1981:103-4] proposes a site outside the east gate marked by a Christian basilica dating from the first half of the fourth century).

What Paul finds, however, is a group of women gathered to worship the God of Israel, probably in the open air. Evidently the Jewish com-

has been strongly argued for (Bruce 1988:308; Wikgren 1981), but since there is no basis for it in manuscript evidence, it is best to follow the NIV reading (Kistemaker 1990:588; Metzger 1971:446).

A *Roman colony* was a territory whose inhabitants, the core being Roman citizen colonists, enjoyed (1) *libertas*, the right of autonomous government, whether on Italian or provincial soil, using a Roman form of local administration and Roman law in local as well as external matters, (2) *immunitas*, freedom from tribute or taxation, though in the provinces land, even that owned by Roman citizens, was subject to taxes, and (3) *Ius Italicum*—the whole legal system in respect of ownership, transfer of land, payment of taxes, local administration and law became the same as that on Italian soil (Lake and Cadbury 1979:190).

munity in Philippi was so small that it did not have the requisite ten men to form a synagogue (*m. Sanhedrin* 1:6; *Pirqē 'Abot* 3:8). As Paul and his team sits down with them, they use the opportunity to speak of the Lord Jesus as the fulfillment of the divine promise of messianic salvation.

Lydia, a God-fearer and wealthy businesswoman—a dealer in expensive *purple cloth*—from Thyatira, a city in the Lycus Valley in the province of Asia, listens to what Paul is saying (compare Acts 13:50; 17:4, 17; 18:7). *The Lord opened her heart to respond* (*prosechō*, better "to pay attention to, give heed to, follow"; compare 8:6; Bauer, Gingrich and Danker 1979:714; Haenchen 1971:495) *to Paul's message*. Before salvation the heart—the inner life, the center of personality, the seat of spiritual and intellectual life (Sorg 1976:182-83)—is so controlled by sin that it is either slow to believe or actually antagonistic to the gospel (Lk 24:25; Acts 28:27; 7:51, 54). Only if God prepares the heart by opening it— enlightening it to understand the gospel, moving it to desire the salvation blessings (compare 24:32)—and strengthening its will to decide for and endure in the Lord (11:23) will it become the "noble and good heart" that receives salvation (Lk 8:15). What must I do to be saved? Listen to God's Word in such a way that you find him opening your heart to follow it.

Next come Lydia's public profession of her faith in baptism, together with her household (compare Acts 16:33; 18:8), and her exercise of hospitality. In ancient Greco-Roman society the household was the basic social, economic and religious unit. The typical household was large, including nuclear and extended family, slaves and economic retainers. "Roman households were united in a common religious cult (the *Lares*)

16:13 *A place of prayer* was used by both Jew and Gentile to refer to a synagogue in the sense of "meeting house" (Schürer 1979:439; Juvenal *Satires* 3.296). Many scholars think that given Luke's normal use of *synagōgē* for "meeting house" (Acts 17:1, 10, 17), here he is denoting just a gathering place for worship, possibly even in the open air (compare E. F. Harrison 1986:267; Longenecker 1981:461).

16:14 Thyatira was famous for making purple dye and dyeing *purple cloth*. The dye was very expensive, being extracted from the root of the Eurasian herb madder, or from shellfish (molluscs). Eight thousand molluscs were required to produce one gram of pure purple dye (Kistemaker 1990:590).

16:15 The usefulness of this verse to support the practice of infant baptism has been variously assessed. While Polhill's rejection is probably too strong (1992:350), it is a moot point whether children were included in the baptism (Stott 1990:263). Stott's further ob-

irrespective of age or personal beliefs" (Green 1970:210). The conversion of this female head of a household, who was either single or a widow, has necessary religious and spiritual implications for the other members. And today we must be ever mindful of the strategic importance of social networks for the rapid spread of the gospel, for multi-individual household conversions can snowball into people movements (see Hulbert 1978; 1979).

Luke's picture of Lydia's practice of hospitality demonstrates once again that those who experience the saving grace of God become gracious (2:42-47; 10:48; compare Rom 12:13; 1 Tim 3:2; 1 Pet 4:9). Though Paul normally does not accept hospitality and financial support of converts as he is planting a church in their midst (2 Cor 11:7-9; 1 Thess 2:9), he makes an exception here. He permits Lydia to live out the principle of sharing material goods with those who teach the Word (1 Cor 9:11, 14; Gal 6:6). Apparently his normal hesitation is overcome when she will not take no for an answer (*persuaded,* actually "prevailed"; compare Phil 1:5).

The Slave Girl with a Demonic Spirit (16:16-24) As Paul continues his outreach to Jews and God-fearers, he is accosted by *a slave girl who had a spirit by which she predicted the future* (literally, "a spirit, Python"; see note). She is twice bound, spiritually and economically, for her masters are making quite a profit by exploiting her occult powers. Yet what engages Paul with her is her spiritual opposition to his mission. Day after day she follows Paul and his team, *shouting* (literally, "crying out repeatedly"), *"These men are servants of the Most High God, who are telling you the way to be saved"* (literally, "a way of salvation"). This

---

servation is worthy of consideration: "it is worth mentioning that *oikos* [household] is certainly used sometimes for a family with children" (1 Tim 3:4-5, 12; 5:4).

16:16 "Python" referred originally to the serpent or dragon that guarded the abode of the Delphic Oracle, who predicted the future. Apollo slew the dragon and took to himself the power of prophecy, so that he became known as the Pythian Apollo, and all who claimed to prophesy while being indwelt by him were called "pythons." Plutarch compares and contrasts the phenomenon with "ventriloquism" (*Moralia* 414e). The LXX uses the latter term to translate Hebrew '*ôḇ,* "a medium or familiar spirit" (Lev 20:27; 1 Kingdoms 28:8), whereas rabbinic literature mentions *python* directly when dealing with the demonic (*m. Sanhedrin* 7:7; Strack and Billerbeck 1978:2:743). By using the term in apposition to *spirit* Luke gives the demon's name, later describing its function, fortune telling (*manteuomai;* compare LXX references: Deut 18:10; 1 Kingdoms 28:8; Ezek 13:6; 21:29; Mic 3:11).

announcement both helps and hinders the mission. To Jewish ears it rings of truth, using terminology ("Most High God," 'ēl-'elyôn) that they considered the Gentile way of referring to the one true God (Gen 14:18-20; Num 24:16; Dan 3:26; 4:32; 5:18, 21). But to polytheistic pagans, who were henotheists as opposed to monotheists, there were many "highest gods"; the title had been attached to Zeus, Isis the mother-goddess of the kingdom of Lydia in Asia, and Baal. A pagan hearer would understand the term to refer to whatever deity he or she considered supreme (Trebilco 1989:60; contrast Levinskaya 1993:125-28). And "a way of salvation"? For the pagan it was release from the powers governing the fate. of humankind and the material world (Longenecker 1981:462). So though initially this declaration may seem a help to Paul as it attracts crowds and provides a good starting point for discussing the gospel with pagans, it has to be corrected each time and thus soon becomes an annoyance (compare Acts 4:2). That a demon-possessed girl is the source of this true but potentially ambiguous statement is another difficulty (compare Lk 4:34, 41; 8:28). Such Satanic tactics have not changed in two thousand years. To counter them the message of salvation must always be proclaimed in clarity and fullness, with its divine source unambiguously credited.

The exorcism occurs via direct confrontation. *He turned around and said to the spirit* (authoritative command), *"In the name of Jesus Christ I command you to come out of her!"* The results are immediate: *at that moment the spirit left* (literally, "came out," compare the command). As at Jerusalem and Judea (Acts 5:16) and in Samaria (8:7), so now in a move across the sea toward the end of the earth, the advance of the gospel means the extension of the kingdom of God through a liberation of those under Satan's authority (26:18). What must I do to be saved? Experience the liberating power of the Lord Jesus Christ, who not only opens but also cleanses hearts (15:9).

This exorcism is both similar to and different from Jesus' ministry of

---

16:20-21 Daniel R. Schwartz's (1984) view—that the accusers are unbelieving Jews who are attacking Christianity and the reference to being Roman is concessive—is less likely than the normal interpretation that the accusers are Gentiles and the participle should be understood causally. The Jewish community in Philippi was small, and anti-Semitic feeling was strong in the Empire (Cicero *Pro Flacco* 67-69; Juvenal *Satires* 14.96-106).

exorcism. Christians confronting the forces of evil today can find guidance here. Persons who were certifiably demon-possessed, as indicated by their talk and action, attacked Jesus and Paul in order to hinder the preaching of the kingdom of God. Both Jesus and Paul dealt authoritatively with the demon-possessed using the simple command "Come out!" and the results were immediate (Lk 4:35; 8:29; 9:42; 11:14). There the similarities end. Jesus' authority is personal and direct. The demons fear Jesus and what he can do to them, though they still seem to taunt (Lk 8:28 and parallels). He rebukes them. Paul's authority and ours is christocentric and derived. *In the name of Jesus Christ . . . come out of her* (Acts 16:18; compare 19:13, 17). Exorcism must be approached today, then, with much care, humility and prayer. But there must also be bold confidence that Jesus is still bringing release to the captives (Lk 4:18).

Whenever the gospel threatens vested interests, especially economic interests, it is bound to meet opposition (compare 19:25-27). So the slave girl's handlers, far from being pleased with her liberation, can think only of their loss of revenue. *They seized Paul and Silas and dragged them into the marketplace to face the authorities* (compare 21:30). The four large stone steps that led up to the *bēma,* "speaker's platform or judgment seat" where the authorities held court, at the midpoint on the north side of the marketplace forum, are still there today (Finegan 1981:102). Roman local administration of civil and criminal cases was the responsibility of the *duoviri.* Luke terms them *stratēgoi* (16:20), the equivalent of the honorable title *praetor* by which they often preferred to be called. Each was assigned two *lictors,* police escorts who carried the *fasces et secures,* the symbol of their authority, a bundle of rods bound together with thongs and often accompanied by an ax.

Paul and Silas are brought before these magistrates and charged with disturbing the peace and introducing *customs unlawful* for Roman citizens *to accept.* The handlers appeal to law-and-order nationalism, anti-Semitic prejudice and ethnic traditionalism. At the same time there is

Rome was lax in enforcing its prohibition of proselytization of Roman citizens for a foreign cult that did not have state sanction (Sherwin-White 1963:79-82; see Cicero *Laws* 2.8.19 for the prohibition).

By converting the second charge (v. 21) into the means by which the first charge occurred, the NIV fails to represent the fact that two charges, not one, were brought to the magistrates.

actually a kernel of truth in their words. In the Roman Republic a cult of Apollo centered on healing and prophecy, and under Augustus a magnificent temple to Apollo was erected on the Palatine. "Apollo Palatinus was in some sort the equal of Jupiter Optimus Maximus" (Rose and Robertson 1970:82). Preaching the way of salvation in the Lord Jesus, in whose name the "spirit Python," inspired by Apollo, was cast out, might certainly be viewed as *advocating customs unlawful for us Romans to accept or practice.*

The crowd rises up against the missionaries, and the magistrates seem to apply rough summary justice by having the lictors use their rods to beat them (compare 2 Cor 11:25; 1 Thess 2:2). Such punishment was certainly within the magistrates' rightful power, though it was not to be used on a Roman citizen (see below, vv. 35-40). Since prisons functioned in ancient times more as places of detention for those awaiting trial than as places of punishment, the praetors' consignment of Paul and Silas to the jailer for safekeeping is not part of the summary justice (contrast Marshall 1980:271) but precedes handing them over for trial before the proconsul (Sherwin-White 1963:82). Security seems to have been of the utmost concern, for these pagan minds must have wondered, If they can cast out a soothsaying spirit, what will prevent them from using their magical powers to escape incarceration?

So delivered into the keeping of a jailer (probably a retired military man), placed in the innermost part of the prison (archaeology has identified a probable site adjacent to the forum; Finegan 1981:105) and with feet fastened in wooden *stocks* (there is no indication that it was for torture, as Bruce [1988:315] contends; compare Polhill 1992:353), the missionaries are left for the night. As Christians have found throughout history, the state is often an instrument of persecution.

16:25-34 Ernst Haenchen (1971:501) finds a "nest of improbabilities" in this portion, including the selective effects of the earthquake (the foundations shake but the roof does not fall in—v. 26), the jailer's seemingly irrational actions (he prepares to commit suicide without checking on the prisoners or taking into account that he probably will not be punished for escapes occasioned by an "act of God") and Paul's "omniscient" shout of comfort (he seems to know both the jailer's intentions and the location of all the prisoners). An earthquake fulfilling God's purposes could be designed by him to have selective results. Also, certain factors mentioned only very briefly in Luke's condensed narrative support the historical probability of both the jailer's and Paul's actions (Marshall 1980:272; Bruce 1990:364; see comments at 16:27-31).

A Jailer with a Hungry Soul (16:25-34) At midnight the missionaries follow their Lord's example, now embodied in the church and
especially its leadership (Lk 6:12; 9:18; Acts 2:42; 3:1; 6:4; 9:11; compare
Lk 18:1). They lift *hymns* of praise as they pray. This joy in the midst of
undeserved suffering manifests again the power of true salvation, which
is victorious whatever the circumstances (compare Acts 5:41; Phil 4:4).
As a result their fellow prisoners—most if not all with a polytheistic
mindset—are *listening* to a praise service exalting the excellencies of the
one true God, whose word alone can show the way of salvation (compare Acts 16:17, 32).

The Lord "made his praise glorious" when *suddenly* (compare 2:2)
"the rocks cried out" as *the foundations of the prison were shaken* by
a powerful earthquake, a phenomenon common in that region. The
prison doors *flew open* (12:10) and the chains *came loose,* literally
"came unfastened."

Though not responsible for escapes resulting from "acts of God"
(Haenchen 1971:497), the suddenly aroused jailer takes drastic personal
measures. Either to expiate for the disgrace of having failed in his duty
or to administer to himself, before his superiors did, the penalty for
having let any escape (*Code of Justinian* 9.4.4), the jailer draws his short
sword, a dagger, and is about to plunge it into his neck or heart when
Paul calls out, *Don't harm yourself! We are all here!* It is interesting that
other than physical healings and exorcisms, this is the first time in Acts
that a temporal need of a non-Christian is met. From it we learn that the
gospel must be preached within the context of concern for the whole
person.

The urgency, shakenness and respect, if not worship, shown in the
jailer's demeanor are matched by his question: *Sirs, what must I do to*

16:25 NIV and E. F. Harrison 1986:271 distinguish between the prayers and the praise,
leaving the implication that the prayers may have been entreaty for deliverance, to which
the earthquake was an answer. The Greek text subordinates "praying" as a participle to the
main verb "singing hymns," and thus points to the whole as an act of worship directed to
God (Haenchen 1971:497).
16:26 To explain the earthquake as shaking loose the chains' staples from the wall, so
that the prisoners were free though still attached to their chains (compare Marshall
1980:272), does not do full justice to Luke's wording (Haenchen 1971:497). The prisoners
were free of their chains.

be saved? The earthquake and the prisoners' willingness to remain have vindicated the message and the messengers (16:17). Temporal salvation is not the issue, since the prisoners are reported present; clearly, then, this seismic event has shaken loose from the jailer's heart the key religious question of his age (Harnack 1961:104-19). Today, too, often our personal world has to be shaken up by the onset of a life-threatening disease, a divorce, a vocational or financial reversal, before we consider the really important questions in life.

Paul's answer is the gospel in one simple command: *Believe in the Lord Jesus, and you will be saved—you and your household.* In almost every city evangelized on this second missionary journey the positive response to the gospel is described as saving faith (16:34; 17:12, 34; 18:8; compare 17:4). But it is belief *in the Lord Jesus* that brings salvation. Paul knows no separation between receiving Jesus as Savior and following him as Lord, as some contemporary theologians may argue (Hodges 1981; Ryrie 1989).

As with Lydia (16:15), personal salvation for the head of the household has spiritual implications for the rest of the members. It does not mean automatic salvation for all household members, for true salvation is grounded in a proper understanding of the gospel. So Paul takes time with the jailer and his household to explain to them the way of salvation. Each individual is responsible for what he or she will do with the gospel.

The care the jailer and the missionaries have for each other is captured beautifully in Chrysostom's words, "He washed and was washed, he washed them from their stripes, and was himself washed from his sins" (*Homilies on Acts* 36). Through baptism the missionaries confirm the jailer and his household in their faith. The jailer manifests the grace of Christ by gracious hospitality (compare 2:42, 46; 16:15; 17:5; 18:7). Those soundly converted (note the perfect participle "having believed," denoting complete action with continuing results) rejoice around the table (16:34). *Filled with joy* means "a state of great joy and gladness, often involving verbal expression and bodily movement, e.g., jumping,

---

16:34 *Brought . . . into* is literally "led up." The residence is above the prison.

16:35 Those who see the incarceration as punishment assume that the magistrates planned all along to release Paul and Silas, so that their release was unrelated to the earthquake (Lake and Cadbury 1979:200; Marshall 1980:274). Haenchen (1971:498) sees the

leaping, dancing" (Louw and Nida 1988:1:303; compare 2:46).

The jailer and his household are the quintessential converts. They come to faith through hearing the Word, confess that faith in baptism, experience the eschatological joy of their new vertical relationship, and live out their new life of grace through physical help and hospitality in their horizontal relationships (Krodel 1986:313). *What must I do to be saved? . . . Believe in the Lord Jesus, and you will be saved—you and your household.*

The Magistrates' Response (16:35-40) The missionaries are still in the jailer's custody. In the morning, however, in proper administrative fashion the magistrates send word by their lictors for the jailer to release Paul and Silas. Luke gives us no motive. Joyfully, the jailer brings the news and blesses them with the farewell *Go in peace.*

But Paul refuses the release. Providing a peaceful environment for the fledgling church is more important to him than pursuing personal peace (compare 9:31).

Paul announces his Roman citizenship and declares that two of his fundamental rights have been violated by the previous day's proceedings (16:22-23). The Lex Valeria (509 B.C.) and the Lex Porcia (248 B.C.), reaffirmed in the Lex Julia (23 B.C.), shielded Roman citizens from humiliating punishments in public, such as beating with rods (Cicero *On Behalf of Rabirius Charged with High Treason* 12; Bruce 1990:366). Further, a Roman citizen was always entitled to a trial before punishment was administered. Paul demands that the magistrates come and publicly escort them from prison. This will be a public admission that the magistrates were wrong and that Christians pose no threat to Roman law.

On hearing of the Roman citizenship of these traveling Jewish preachers, the magistrates are *alarmed.* A Roman citizen had a status in the Empire not unlike that of a British citizen in India in the days of the British Empire. "In theory he could travel anywhere without problems, being everywhere protected by the Roman law. He was not subjected to the local law unless he consented (though such consent would be usual

---

release as an expulsion, but the verbs in verses 36 and 39 do not bear this out. If the detention was actually a binding over for trial, the release might well have been motivated by the earthquake and the fear of further unfortuitous events.

16:37 *Quietly* is literally "secretly" and shows the strength of Paul's concern.

in business), and he could take matters into his own courts when these were sitting. He owed allegiance to Rome and Rome would protect him" (Lyall 1976:10). Further, a magistrate risked losing his office or worse, being disqualified from ever serving in governmental administration again, if he mistreated a Roman citizen (Lake and Cadbury 1979:201; compare Acts 22:22-29).

The magistrates do as Paul demands. They came and "appealed to" (not *appeased*) them. Escorting them out, they request that Paul and Silas leave the city. Are they uncertain that they can provide for the missionaries' safety in a situation made even more volatile by their release?

Paul and Silas accede to their request, but only after they have met with the church and encouraged it (compare Acts 15:32). Persecution will not end with Paul and Silas's departure, for that is the Christian's lot (Acts 14:22; Phil 1:27-30). Since the "we" sections of Acts stop after the Philippi episode and do not pick up again until Acts 20:5, again at Philippi, many have conjectured that Paul leaves Luke here to strengthen the church.

This concluding scene yields some valuable principles for guiding Christians in their relations with the state (Talbert 1984:70). Paul's insistence that justice be done encourages Christians to appeal to their legal rights as protection against unjust treatment by non-Christians. The fact that Paul's request was granted gives us confidence that the state can be reasonable and correct its mistakes. Paul's innocence of the charges establishes the pattern that Christians are not to be troublemakers; when we do suffer at the hands of state power, it should be as innocent victims of those with questionable motives (compare 1 Pet 4:15-16). Only by such exemplary lives can we witness with integrity and, by the Spirit's power, answer the haunting question of that age or any age: What must I do to be saved?

Witness at Thessalonica (17:1-9)
Though absolute monarchies hold sway over very few peoples today,

17:1-9 The impression here of a short stay (three weeks) and the implied longer stay presented in Paul's letters (Phil 4:16; 1 Thess 2:9) are not finally contradictory (contra Haenchen 1971:510). Luke's report deals mainly with the mission's initial phase to the Jews. Paul's letters fill in the gaps in our knowledge about the rest of the mission (Williams

many still live under totalitarian rule. When the Christian gospel invades such an environment, an authority struggle automatically arises. For the Thessalonians, Theophilus and his fellow seekers, the call to bow to King Jesus in repentance directly challenged Caesar's absolute rule. Luke's account helps us all learn how to count the cost of citizenship in the kingdom of God.

Christ the King Died and Rose Again (17:1-4) Proceeding south and west along the Via Egnatia, Paul and Silas travel thirty miles to Amphipolis, the capital of the first district of Macedonia; a further twenty-seven miles to Apollonia; and finally thirty-five miles to Thessalonica, the capital of both the second district and the whole province. Though he may want to distance himself from Philippi in Macedonia's first district, Paul is also making a strategic choice by targeting Thessalonica. This city was uniquely situated to serve as a center for the spread of the gospel to the whole Balkan peninsula (see Rom 15:19; 1 Thess 1:7-8). A seaport on the Thermaic Gulf, Thessalonica linked sea and land routes to the rich agricultural plain of the interior of Macedonia. So today, missions strategists rightly target world-class cities and key cultural groups so that the gospel, once taking root there, may naturally spread to whole peoples and whole nations.

Instead of recounting a speech, Luke describes Paul's pattern of verbal witness through a series of clauses (Acts 17:3). They form a rhetorical syllogism, a pattern of persuasion familiar to any first-century schoolboy (Kurz 1980). By deductive logic, Paul propounds major and minor premises, using irrefutable proofs (*tekmērioi:* evidence from authoritative texts and witnesses; compare Acts 1:3). Taken together, these premises lead by necessary logic to the conclusion, the speaker's goal in persuasion. The witness pattern is

Major Premise: The characteristics of the Christ (Messiah) are that he must suffer and rise from the dead (17:3a).

Minor Premise: Jesus modeled these characteristics in his death and resurrection (Kurz [1980:179] believes this premise is referred to in

---

1985:285).

17:2 *Reasoned (dialegomai)* is well defined by D. W. Kemmler as "reasoned, or discoursed argumentatively, either in the way of dialogue . . . or in that of formal and continuous discourse" (1975:35).

the clause *I am proclaiming to you*, 17:3b).

Conclusion: *This Jesus . . . is the Christ* (17:3b).

What stands out here is the role of the Old Testament and the interconnected nature of argumentation and proclamation in the process of persuasion. It was a matter of *explaining* (*dianoigō;* Lk 24:32, 45-46) *and proving [from the Scriptures]* the major premise (the Greek word order permits us to take this phrase with these verbs instead of with *reasoned,* as the NIV). *Proving (paratithēmi)* was "demonstrating by setting evidence side by side"—God's authoritative Word (such as Ps 2; 16; 110; Is 53) next to the premise that it was the divine plan that the Christ must suffer and rise from the dead (compare Lk 9:22, 44; 17:25; 18:31-33; 24:26, 46; Acts 2:31; 3:18; 13:27-29). Paul's argumentation aimed to overcome Jewish preconceptions about the Messiah as a victorious king with an eternal reign who neither suffers nor rises from the dead.

The proof for the minor premise comes in the form of proclamation (*katangellō,* the solemn declaration of a completed happening; 16:21; 17:13, 23; Schniewind 1964:71). With boldness Paul bears witness to the historical events of Jesus' life, death and resurrection.

Witness must always be pursued in this way. There is a time for dialogue, a time to deal carefully with the questions and doubts of those who hear our witness. But there must also be proclamation. The gospel is, after all, good news from God about what he has done in Christ, not the distillation of the best of human religious reflection.

A few *Jews,* possibly Jason (17:7) and Aristarchus (20:4) among them, *a large number of God-fearing Greeks* (there is not a redundancy here separating the men into two groups, pagans and God-fearers; contrast Stott 1990:272; compare Acts 13:43) and *not a few prominent women* (compare 13:50; 17:12) *were persuaded.* By the power of the Spirit Paul's reasoning has helped them understand the situation for themselves. As

---

17:5 Luke's description of the persecution accords well with 1 Thessalonians 2:13-16, for there Paul describes the Thessalonians' mistreatment at the hands of their fellow countrymen, probably both Jew and Gentile (contrast Krodel 1986:320-21).

Jealous (*zēloō;* compare 5:17; 13:45; 22:3) is better translated "zealous"—that is, as a jealousy for God's glory and the law which will take direct action on behalf of God, including persecuting Christian missionaries (Stumpff 1964:884, 887). Though commentators often infer jealousy born of loss of influence over the Gentile God-fearers or of contemplation of the now-diminished numbers of prospects for conversion to Judaism (Krodel 1986:318;

a result, they are able to make a free decision, in this case to embrace Jesus as their suffering and risen Messiah (Kemmler 1975:133; compare 26:28). And they immediately changed identities and *joined* (literally, "their lot was cast with," implying divine saving choice; compare 13:48) Paul and Silas as brothers and sisters in the kingdom of King Jesus the Christ.

King Jesus Is Mightier than Caesar (17:5-9) The Jews who did not believe, in their misdirected zeal for the glory of God and the law (compare Rom 10:2), take measures to thwart the gospel's advance. They "set the city in an uproar" (*ethoryboun;* compare cognate *thorybos,* Acts 20:1; 21:34; 24:18; Josephus *Jewish Antiquities* 18.65; it is more extensive than NIV's *started a riot*). They gather the rabble lounging in the marketplace and form them into a mob (compare Plutarch *Parallel Lives: Aemilius Paulus* 38.4, who represents the *agoraioi* as agitators).

The mob moves to Jason's house, looking for Paul and Silas with the intention of bringing them to trial before the free city's citizens' assembly. Not finding the traveling preachers, they drag some of their own citizens, Jason and some of the *brothers,* before the local city officials (*politarchai,* a term found only in inscriptions; Thessalonica had five or six). Possibly they feel it more appropriate to arraign their own citizens there. Maybe they suppose that the citizens' assembly would be more lenient with their own than the officials charged with public order. The charges are threefold: public disturbance—causing *trouble all over the world;* harboring disturbers of the peace; and *defying Caesar's decrees, saying that there is another king, one called Jesus.*

The forties had been a turbulent decade for Rome in dealing with the Jews. In A.D. 41 Emperor Claudius wrote a threatening letter to the Alexandrians, saying he would take measures against Jews who were "stirring up a universal plague throughout the world" (Sherwin-White 1963:51).

Bruce 1990:370), it is better to see it as a zeal, now misguided, in the tradition of Phinehas (Num 25:11, 13 LXX), Elijah (3 Kingdoms 19:10, 14) and Mattathias (1 Macc 2:24, 26, 50).

Dēmos (NIV *the crowd*) is also a technical term for a public assembly of citizens responsible for legislative-and judicial matters, hence the NIV marginal reading "Or *the assembly of the people.*" Though most take the term's uses here as ambiguous or as the less technical option (NIV and Polhill 1992:362; compare 19:30, 33), Marshall (1980:278) reconstructs a plausible sequence of events based on the technical meaning.

In A.D. 44 there were public disturbances in Palestine in the wake of Herod Agrippa I's death. In A.D. 49 Claudius expelled Jews from Rome because of public disturbances in the Jewish community at the instigation of *"Chrēstus"* (Suetonius *Claudius* 25.4; see comment at Acts 18:3). Though the Jews themselves had caused the uproar at Thessalonica, their trumped-up charges of public disturbance made sense within the Empire's current political climate.

The charge of defying Caesar's decrees is best understood against this background. "Augustus and Tiberius had been very sensitive about the activities of astrologers and other prognosticators and had issued decrees forbidding predictions and inquiries affecting the affairs of state or the emperor's personal well being" (Bruce 1988:325; Dio Cassius *Roman History* 56.25.5-6; 57.15.8; Tacitus *Annals* 6.20; 12.52; compare 14.9). Paul's eschatology could be easily twisted into declarations about a coming monarch who will displace Caesar (1 Thess 1:9-10; 2 Thess 2:5-8). Since Thessalonica would want to maintain its status as a free city through loyalty to the emperor, and since the local officials are charged with preserving order and making sure the imperial decrees are respected, the charges understandably throw the crowd and the city officials into turmoil *(tarassō,* 17:13; compare 12:18; 19:23).

From Acts 17:10 we can surmise the officials took bond from Jason and the others to ensure two things: there would be no more public disturbances, and Paul and Silas and their preaching would be gone from the city (Longenecker 1981:470). If either condition is not met, the bond will be forfeited (contrast Lake and Cadbury [1979:206], who see the bond involving Jason's denial of involvement with Paul and Silas; the forfeiture would occur if that were found not to be true). The practical result is Paul and Silas's forced departure from Thessalonica.

Although the persecutors had been the real disturbers of public order, the gospel always has an unsettling, even revolutionary effect on those who hear it. It calls for a repentance that means bowing to King Jesus in total allegiance. Totalitarian rulers, whether Caesar or modern-day

17:10-15 When comparing Timothy's movements according to Paul—Athens to Thessalonica (1 Thess 3:2)—with Acts—remaining at Berea, rejoining Paul at Corinth (Acts 17:14; 18:5)—some conclude either tentatively (Haenchen 1971:513) or with certainty (Krodel 1986:323) that only Paul is correct. Timothy and Silas, then, must have accompanied Paul

overlords, cannot peacefully coexist with King Jesus or his kingdom subjects.

Witness at Berea (17:10-15)

In these postmodern times people have learned to live without absolutes so long that they find it difficult to exercise simple faith or make long-term commitments. When they hear the Christian gospel's call to faith, they do not quite know how to respond. Luke helps through an example from a most unexpected place: the "off-the-beaten-path" city of Berea.

A People of Noble Character (17:10-12) The believers at Thessalonica comply with the terms of the bond (17:9) by sending Paul and Silas, and presumably also Timothy, away during the night. They travel west-southwest along the Via Egnatia some twenty miles and then leave it and head south thirty more miles to Berea. This strategic withdrawal into the third district of Macedonia and to a city that Cicero labeled "off the beaten track" (*Against Piso* 36.89) is not a retreat but a means of further advance. A populous city in another district of Macedonia will hear the gospel through Paul's synagogue witness (compare Acts 17:1).

The Berean Jews and God-fearers are of *more noble character (euge-nesteroi)*, with open minds willing to learn and evaluate this new message fairly (Louw and Nida 1988:1:332). In Greek and biblical understanding, to be *eugenos* primarily was to be "of noble birth" (compare Lk 19:12; 1 Cor 1:26) and, derivatively, to have qualities that go with "good breeding": "being open, tolerant, generous" (Polhill 1992:363; compare Lk 8:15; Acts 16:14).

This *noble character* manifests itself in two ways. There is *great eagerness* (literally, "all eagerness") to receive the message. Yet the people's enthusiasm is not gullibility, for they subject Paul's message, the word of God, to thorough scrutiny. Daily they meet to examine the Old Testament Scriptures to see if the gospel declarations square with them (compare 17:2-3). Their examination parallels the best in human jurisprudence, unbiased investigation to get at the truth (*anakrinō;* Lk 23:14;

---

on his trip to Athens. But both Paul and Luke are correct if Silas and Timothy joined Paul in Athens later, Paul sent them to Thessalonica and Philippi, respectively, and finally they rejoined Paul at Corinth.

Acts 24:8). The result is that a large number of Jews and Greeks, prominent women as well as men, probably both God-fearers and pagans, believe the message and are saved (compare 20:4; Rom 16:21).

To be believers, then, we must eagerly embrace the gospel message with all openness, hearing it on its own terms and letting it master us. Many postmoderns seem ready to take such a step. They call it adopting a "second naiveté."

To be a believer also means to engage our critical faculties in testing the gospel's truth claims. For postmoderns who will bow to no authority but what they have tested and approved, this is an essential step if faith is to have integrity. Yet since in the Christian order of things "faith precedes understanding," this scrutiny will be fruitful only after an initial positive embracing of the good news.

Protecting the Messenger (17:13-15) When the Jews in Thessalonica hear of Paul's evangelistic activity in Berea, they come and employ the same public-disturbance tactics used earlier, with similar results (17:5). They shake up (*saleuō,* used literally of earthquakes at Acts 4:31; 16:26) and stir up the crowds (15:24; 17:8). Possibly because the Berean Christians realize that the Thessalonian Jews have the ear of provincial authorities, they decide that in their situation "discretion is the better part of valor." Before any arrest and judicial action can be taken they courageously spirit Paul away toward the coast.

This second consecutive withdrawal will prove to be another advance: not only does Paul leave behind a newly planted church to be nurtured by Silas and Timothy, but his escape will take him to Athens, the center of Greco-Roman culture and Greek religion. Paul's progress is like wildfire: try to stamp it out in one place and it crops up in another. David Livingstone's words could well have been his: "I am prepared to go anywhere, *so long as it is forward"* (Barclay 1976:129).

If Paul and the Bereans engage in a ruse, heading to the coast but then turning south to approach Athens by land, then the Bereans' "accompanying" involves providing protection and care (compare Josh 6:23 LXX;

17:14 *To the coast* (literally, "in the direction of the sea," *heōs epi tēn thalassan*), in the manuscripts the Western text drops *heōs* and with its other additions definitely points to a sea voyage. The Byzantine reading substitutes *hōs* ("as") for *heōs* ("as far as," "to"), indicating a ruse on Paul's part. He made "as" to travel by sea but actually traveled by land. The neutral reading

2 Chron 28:15 LXX).

To be a believer means having not only *noble character* that commits itself to the message but also a courageous soul that commits itself to the messenger—and to all who are part of the body of Christ (Acts 16:15, 33-34; 17:4, 7). Postmoderns have a hard time with long-term commitment in relationships, as they do with bowing to the authority of a divine message. In both cases Luke's presentation of the Bereans' example gives them hope. By the power of the Spirit anyone can have what it takes to believe (2:42-47; 16:14).

Witness at Athens (17:16-34)

The prevailing philosophies of the West's post-Christian era—secular humanism's scientific empiricism and the New Age pantheistic type of postmodernism—are remarkably similar to the Epicureanism and Stoicism Paul encountered at Athens. Paul's speech becomes a model for how to witness to the educated post-Christian mind, even as it spoke to Theophilus and his fellow seekers with their first-century pre-Christian minds.

Proclaiming the Gospel with Integrity (17:16-21) When Paul arrived at Athens in the province of Achaia, he came to an anomaly. Though its population was no more than ten thousand and it had been reduced to poverty and submission by its war with Rome (146 B.C.), it was granted the status of a free city in view of its illustrious past. "Accordingly, although the time of her greatest glory was gone forever, Athens could still boast of her right to be called a great center of philosophy, architecture, and art"—and, we might add, religion (Madvig 1979b:352). In fact, what assaulted Paul's spirit was the ubiquitous idolatry (Livy *History of Rome* 45.27.11). Guarding the entrance to houses and shrines was a square pillar with the head of Hermes, the god of roads, gateways and the marketplace. What Paul met in Athens was "a forest of idols" (Wycherley 1968:619).

Paul is more than *greatly distressed,* for he experiences a paroxysm in

adopted by the NIV is ambiguous and could support either understanding. Though both land and sea voyages have their supporters (sea—Williams 1985:292; Finegan 1981:125; land—E. F. Harrison 1986:281; Longenecker 1981:472), the lack of reference to a port of embarkation, contrary to Luke's normal practice, weighs in favor of the land route interpretation.

his spirit, a provocation of anger or grief or both, because the glory due to God alone is being given to idols. The Lord reacted the same way to idolatry in Israel (Deut 9:7, 18, 22; Ps 106:28-29; Is 65:2-3; compare Is 42:8), and so should we. Any paraphernalia of false worship should provoke in us such grieving anger that we, jealous for the glory of God and his Christ, reach out and share the good news, which includes a call to repentance (Stott 1990:279).

Paul reaches out in witness not only in the synagogue (17:2, 10; 18:4) but also *in the marketplace day by day with those who happened to be there.* "The Athenian Agora [marketplace] was the center of the public and business life of the city, and people met there every day to learn the latest news and to discuss all manner of subjects. . . . Temples and government buildings, shops and offices, and altars and statuary filled the Agora, and stoas and colonnades gave protection against the summer sun and the winter rain and cold" (Finegan 1981:128). John Stott observes that the equivalent today is "a park, city square or street corner, a shopping mall or marketplace, a 'pub,' neighborhood bar, café, discothèque or student cafeteria, wherever people meet when they are at leisure" (1990:281). We, like Paul, must go to where the people are, and to those settings where serious discussion of ideas, even religious ideas, is natural and expected.

Paul's evangelism again follows the pattern of "reasoning" about *Jesus and the resurrection* (compare 17:2-3). Epicurean and Stoic philosophers, representatives of two of the three major philosophical schools of thought in Paul's day, react to his message. The Epicureans mock, *What is this babbler trying to say?* The Stoics are curious: *He seems to*

17:18 *Babbler (spermologos)* was a term of derision originally pointing to a seed-picking or scavenger bird and then applied to men who picked up odds and ends in the marketplace. In philosophical matters a "babbler" parroted a grab bag of ideas which did not originate with him and which he did not necessarily understand (Lake and Cadbury 1979:211).

17:19 The NIV translation *a meeting of the Areopagus (Areion Pagon)* correctly identifies the referent as the supreme legislative and judicial council of Athens, the body of former city administrators, rather than their traditional meeting place, the 370-foot outcropping northwest of the Acropolis. The introductory prepositional phrase "in the midst of" pretty much demands this understanding. *Areopagus* is a transliteration of a phrase meaning, literally, either "hill of Ares" (the Greek god of war; the Roman equivalent is Mars, hence the KJV "Mars Hill") or "hill of the Arai," the Furies who avenged homicides and whose

be advocating foreign gods.

Epicureans, atomic materialists, viewed reality as an endless chance combining and dispersion of atoms. They would find the concept of bodily resurrection laughable (Epicurus *Epistle to Menoeceus* 123-32). The Stoics, materialist pantheists, identified the divine as the principle of reason pervading all and, in the form of fate, governing all. Because of either their cyclic eschatology (belief that there were periodic conflagrations of the universe after which history simply repeated itself) or their later adoption of the Platonic concept of the soul's immortality, they could not conceive of resurrection (Chrysippus *Fragment* 625; Bahnsen 1980:11). Luke seems to indicate that they thought Paul was pointing to a female goddess, Anastasis, consort of the male god Jesus (McKay [1994] disagrees, finding no extrabiblical evidence for "Anastasis" as a female deity).

These reactions show us that Paul had proclaimed the simple gospel with integrity to the intellectual sophisticates of Athens. And we must reintroduce post-Christians to Jesus with freshness, without resorting to the traditional formulations they will call the "old, old story." But we must do so with faithfulness, telling it the way it was and is.

Paul's message has created such a stir among the Epicureans and Stoics that they bring him before the Areopagus, Athens's chief legislative and judicial council. This body licensed traveling lecturers, and Paul's hearers want to see whether he should be given freedom to continue to teach. They want to understand *this new teaching,* for *some strange* (rather, "surprising, astounding") *ideas* are coming *to their ears.*

The Athenians had an ambivalent relation to "foreign gods." On the

---

shrine was at its base (Madvig 1979a). The council also used to meet in the Stoa Basileios at the northwest corner of the Agora, adjacent to the Stoa Poikila, "the painted Stoa," where the Stoics used to assemble. This may be where the council met in this case (Hemer 1989c:240).

The council is probably holding a preliminary hearing to examine Paul for licensure as a public lecturer, whether before a commission of the council or before the whole body (Longenecker 1981:474; contrast Bruce 1988:331-32). The lack of a verdict and other judicial details makes it less likely that this is a formal trial (see Lake and Cadbury 1979:213; contrast Plato's account of the proceedings against Socrates in *Apology* 24B-C). Paul may have departed from Athens rather soon after the council meeting because the lack of a definitive verdict effectively suspended his mission (17:32-34; 18:1).

one hand, they were famous for incorporating alien deities into their pantheon (Strabo *Geography* 10.3.18). On the other hand, they believed they must stay vigilant lest "new gods" undermine the morals of the state (Stählin 1967:7). So the issue here is understanding followed by evaluation: is this something good or not?

The fearless and relevant witness that follows models an approach that some Christians in every society must take. They must engage the opinion-makers and shapers of thought and "do battle with contemporary non-Christian philosophies and ideologies and philosophies in a way which resonates with thoughtful, modern men and women, and so at least gain a hearing for the gospel by the reasonableness of its presentation" (Stott 1990:281).

Luke seems to prepare us for the relative lack of positive response to Paul's sermon by portraying Athenians as intellectual dilettantes more than genuine seekers after truth. With skepticism making major inroads in the first century, Athens's intellectual life was characterized by uncertainty, turmoil and lack of progress, so that hunger for and fascination with the new was very strong (Bahnsen 1980:12). The postmodernist phase of the post-Christian era manifests the same tendencies. W. D. Davies, veteran New Testament scholar, wonders, "Is ours one of those situations in which 'Things fall apart; the center cannot hold' because there is no one center and often no centers? . . . The new pluralism can often become banal, trivial and pretentious, like a fish in that ocean [of the transcendent] always keeping its mouth wide open, afraid to shut it, and therefore never taking a bite" (1986:58).

Introduction to the Areopagus Speech (17:22-23) With irony Paul gives his assessment of the Athenians. He "sees" *(theōreō,* in the sense of perceives or understands; 17:16; 21:20; 27:10) that they are *very*

17:22-31 Some claim the speech is a literary composition of the author of Acts because it appears to lack congruence with Paul's theology in the following ways: (1) it seems to excuse pagans (17:23, 30; contrast Rom 1—3); (2) its gospel presentation lacks the cross and justification by faith (compare 17:30-31); (3) it uses Hellenistic philosophical, not biblical, terminology (17:24-29; Haenchen 1971:528-29 and Krodel 1986:327, both following Dibelius 1956a and 1956b). But when we take into account the difference in audience and purpose of Acts 17 and Paul's letters, along with the contextualizing aim of Paul's speech— to clothe essentially Old Testament and Jewish beliefs in Hellenistic form—we can readily see both as coming from the same mind (Marshall 1980:282-83; Bruce 1988:334).

religious (hōs deisidaimonesterous). The Athenians' reputation for religious piety is well attested (Pausanias *Description of Greece* 1.17.1; 1.24.3;
Strabo *Geography* 9.1.16). *Hōs desidaimonesterous* may be understood
either negatively as superstitious fear of the gods (Plutarch *Moralia* 164E-
71F) or in a neutral, even positive sense, as the NIV (Aristotle *Politics*
5:9:15, p. 1315a). Paul puts the ambiguity to good use. In light of verses
of 23 and 30, he probably wants to say "they have a religion . . . but it
is wrongheaded" (Bock 1991:119). Here we have a respectful recognition of religious endeavors but not an acknowledgment that they lead
to true, saving faith. Paul is telling a simple but limited truth and creating
a basis for further comment.

Paul now uncovers the Athenians' admitted need: the knowledge of
the one true God. As he *walked around and observed* (literally, "looked
at again and again, examined carefully") their *objects of worship,* he
found an altar with the inscription TO AN UNKNOWN GOD. Though there are
a number of reports of such altars (Pausanias *Description of Greece* 1.1.4;
5.14.8; Philostratus *Life of Apollonius of Tyana* 6.3), only Diogenes
Laertes (*Lives of the Philosophers* 1.110) gives a reason for their origin.
Once when Athens was plagued by pestilence in the sixth century B.C.
and the city rulers had exhausted all their strategies to abate it, they sent
to Crete, asking the prophet Epimenides to come and help. His remedy
was to drive a herd of black and white sheep away from the Areopagus
and, wherever they lay down, to sacrifice them to the god of that place.
The plague was stayed, and Diogenes Laertes says that memorial altars
with no god's name inscribed on them may consequently be found
throughout Attica. Wycherley proposes, with some archaeological justification, that such altars may also have been raised to appease the dead
wherever ancient burial sites were disturbed by the building projects of

See Prior 1975 and Bahnsen 1980 for extended treatments of the evangelistic and apologetic value for today of the witness at Athens.

17:23 Don Richardson, missionary author, misreads the Diogenes Laertes account of
Epimenides' animistic polytheism as evidence that Epimenides was a prophet of the one
true God and taught vicarious atonement (Richardson 1984:13).

There is no literary or inscriptional evidence for an altar dedication to an unknown deity
in the singular. The ancient historical evidence for altar dedications in the plural "are merely
generalizing, and do not justify the literalistic and hypercritical objection that each altar must
have been dedicated to a plurality of such gods" (Hemer 1989c:241).

later generations (1968:621).

Paul now makes his point of contact, saying that *what [they] worship as something unknown* (literally, "what they worship being ignorant") he will *proclaim* to them. Those who take these words as expressing both a positive and a negative relation between the religious pagan and the one true God see the positive relation as an ignorant worship of God (Haenchen 1971:521; Talbert 1984:74; Stott 1990:285). No new god is being introduced; it is simply that God's identity is being unveiled to those who admit, if only unconsciously, their ignorance.

And what about those in cultures who have never heard the gospel? Does the "positive" relationship Paul points to mean these ignorant worshipers are saved? Clark Pinnock is agnostic and says Acts 17:23 does not speak directly or decisively to this question (1991:110).

Yet the phrasing of the statement and the immediate context point to the conclusion that there is no such positive relation with the one true God. Paul is stressing the ignorance with which they worship, and this is again a limited point of contact; it is just a way to raise the basic question, Who is God? (Williams 1985:297). If Paul's audience has been worshiping the one true God all along, why is their ignorance culpable, something they must repent of (v. 30; compare vv. 27, 29)? Paul carefully uses the neuter "what" *(ho . . . touto)* in reference to his starting point: their objects of worship. He is probably making a transition to the subject of the divine nature (*to theion,* neuter). In so doing Paul stands clear of a direct equation of the unknown god and the one true God (Dupont 1979b:541).

Today we must note where post-Christians admit ignorance and study how the light of God's good news dispels that darkness.

The One True God as Creator, Ruler and Sustainer of All (17:24-29) Paul challenges Stoic pantheism and Epicurean materialistic deism by testifying that *the God who made the world and everything in it is the Lord of heaven and earth* (Ps 146:6; Is 42:5). The implication

17:26 Though some see *every nation of men* as simply referring to humankind as a whole (Marshall 1980:287), the references to time periods and boundaries point to nations as the main referent. *The times* are not the yearly fruitful seasons (Bruce 1988:338), the life span of individuals or periods of human history (compare Lk 3:1-2; 16:16; 19:44; 21:24; Acts 1:7; compare Krodel 1986:334). They are the divinely appointed times for a given nation's flourishing. *The exact places where they should live* (literally, "boundaries of their habita-

for worship is that God *does not live in temples built by hands* (1 Kings 8:27; Acts 7:48-50). Interestingly, this was a tenet of Zeno, the founder of Stoicism; Plutarch takes subsequent generations to task for abandoning it in practice (Plutarch *Moralia* 1034B). In chiastic fashion Paul moves immediately to another implication: God is *not served by human hands, as if he needed anything.* Service *(therapeuō)* is "cultic ministry [and] consists in the bringing of sacrificial fruits and any cultic action which might give the impression that the deity is referred to some human performance" (Beyer 1965:129). God's self-sufficiency is affirmed in the Old Testament (Ps 50:7-15) and developed in Jewish prayer (2 Macc 14:35; 3 Macc 2:9). It was also a tenet of Epicureanism (Lucretius *On the Nature of Things* 2.650; Philodemus *Pros eusebeias* fr. 38). Paul brushes aside the necessity, let alone appropriateness, of idolatrous worship servicing the divine nature by affirming that, conversely, it is God who *gives all men* (NIV has supplied *men;* the reference could be much more comprehensive—all living creatures) *life and breath and everything else* (Gen 1:29; 2:7; 9:3; Is 42:5; Acts 14:17).

What good news Paul had for the Epicureans and Stoics living as they did under impersonal chance or inexorable fate! Behind or within reality stands neither of these but rather a gracious, personal Creator, Ruler and Sustainer of all. For modern scientific humanity, living as it does within an impersonal universe that has evolved quite by "chance" from the big bang to the last whimper of a dark and frigid night without starfire, Paul's message is also very good news. And for postmodern humanity this gracious, personal God breaks the bonds of pantheistic "karma."

Paul now concentrates on humankind. He affirms the creation of human beings by a direct act and declares that God's design was for various cultures ("every nation," *pan ethnos*) to cover the face of the earth in a harmonious patchwork of diversity (Gen 1:28; 9:1, 7; 10:5, 20, 31-32). That harmony is born of God's governance of the time period and the

---

tion") are not the natural boundaries between earth and sea (Job 38:8-11; Ps 74:17; 104:5-9) but national boundaries.

Nation (ethnos) "is the most general and therefore the weakest of [biblical] terms [for "a people"] having simply an ethnographical sense and denoting the natural cohesion of a people in general" (Bertram and Schmidt 1964:369).

space each culture would inhabit (Deut 32:8; Ps 102:13; Dan 2:36-45; compare Stoics on divine providence—Seneca the Younger *De Providentia;* see Winter 1993:133-36). While Stoicism looked at humankind in its diversity and urged it to consider itself one community, "even as a herd that feeds together and shares the pasturage of a common field" (Plutarch *Moralia* 329B), Paul affirms both our unity and our diversity.

God's second design (not necessarily growing out of the first, as the NIV states, but parallel to it) was that *men would seek him.* In the biblical understanding this is "the thankful and reverent longing of the whole man for God whose goodness he has experienced" (Marshall 1980:288; Ps 14:2; Prov 8:17; Is 55:6; Jer 29:13; Amos 9:12 LXX; Heb 11:6).

Yet sin has interjected itself into the human experience, so that our "seeking" has become "groping" with no certainty of success, even though God is still very much present with us (compare Rom 1:18-32). The NIV's presentation of parallel purposes *that men would seek him [God] and perhaps reach out* (better "grope") *for him and find him* turns the qualifier clause about groping into a positive part of God's design. This lessens a main theme of the passage: ignorance of God (groping after him) is morally culpable and must be repented of.

Paul goes on to reinforce human responsibility for failing to seek and find God. He asserts God's presence in terms of our dependence on him. *For in him we live and move and have our being.* This is the converse of the Stoic pantheistic assertion that the divine spark of Reason, God, is in us (compare Dio Chrysostom *Discourses* 12.27; Posidonius as quoted in Barrett 1961:65). Paul appeals to the fourth- and third-century Stoic philosopher Aratus for confirmation: *We are his offspring* (Aratus *Phenomena* 5). His introductory remark (not a quote as NIV) cleanses the Aratus quotation of both its reference to Zeus and its pantheistic metaphysic (compare Renehan 1979:347; Edwards 1992). What is left is some recognition of the true nature of God, especially what humankind's being made in his image says about the divine nature (Bruce 1988:339). Being his offspring refers only to creation, not salvation, as the subsequent call to repentance clearly shows (Bock 1991:119).

17:27 The groping is not because of the amount of revelation received (Bruce 1988:338; E. F. Harrison 1986:286) or finite humankind's limited capacity to find God (Polhill 1992:375). Rather, it is because of the Fall. Ignorance of the one true God is culpable

For first-century Epicureans and twentieth-century moderns, the fact that God is the Father of humankind is challenging good news. No longer need we settle for the reductionistic explanation of humankind and its activity. We are not simply a complex interplay of electrical impulses, chemical processes, subatomic DNA and environment. And for Stoics and postmoderns, this good news makes us both less and more than they understand us to be. Pantheism or the "God within" is revealed as false, but in its place is the person made in God's image, living in conscious dependence on God.

As twice before (vv. 24-25) Paul draws implications for worship from these truths about God. His basic line of argument, found often in the Old Testament and Jewish literature, is that if like begets like, it is illogical to suppose that the divine nature that created living human beings is like an image made of an inanimate substance, no matter how valuable (Deut 4:28; Is 40:18-20; 44:9-20; Wisdom of Solomon 13:10; 15:7-17). Since such images are the product of human *design and skill,* they cannot be analogous to the divine being who made humankind.

This posed a direct challenge to some Stoic thought, which claimed that by following traditional myths of the poets and prophets along with innate reason, the divine spark within, idol-makers could appropriately represent the gods (Dio Chrysostom *Discourses* 12.44-46, 60). Postmodern thinking influenced by the New Age would find itself similarly challenged.

Conclusion: A Call for Radical Personal Change (17:30-31) In "the times of ignorance"—all those past generations from the first human beings until Christ (except Noah's generation, Gen 6:5-8; 9:11-17)—God overlooked humankind's sin, especially false worship. He "overlooked" it not by excusing it or failing to notice it, but rather by not punishing it as it deserved (Rom 3:25; Acts 14:16). *Now,* however, God commands *all people everywhere to repent.* Each generation's problem is that their ignorant worship is culpable, rebellious, false worship. God's solution is not to receive more information but to make a radical turn from idolatry to the one true God (Acts 14:15; 26:20). Formerly

throughout the passage, and the immediate context places emphasis on human responsibility.

humankind lived in a sinful ignorance that God in his mercy passed over. Now, after sin has been judged in Jesus' death and resurrection, comes the "day of salvation" in a gospel proclaimed in his name, calling for repentance and promising forgiveness. Today there is no room in God's economy, as Paul preaches it, for so-called B.C. Christians—persons saved without knowledge of Christ and his saving work (contrast Kraft 1979:231).

The call to repentance is urgent because the consequences for not repenting—a final judgment and eternal condemnation—are inescapable. The judgment is definite (*he has set a day;* Lk 17:24, 30; 21:34-36), universal (*he will judge the world,* or "whole inhabited world"; Acts 11:28; 17:6), fair (*with justice;* Ps 96:13) and personal (*by the man he has appointed,* Jesus; Jn 5:27; Acts 10:42). Though the Greek philosophers might envision a judgment on souls in the hereafter as part of a reincarnation scheme, they find a final judgment, as Paul declares it, incredible (Büchsel and Herntrich 1965:933-34).

The *proof* Paul offers to establish his argument is Jesus' resurrection. That event, itself established by many "undeniable proofs" (1:3), guarantees the reality of this future event and thus authenticates the urgency of the call to repentance. The resurrection is, then, the linchpin for both potential ways of applying the death and resurrection of the Christ to one's eternal destiny. It establishes both the warning of judgment and the promise of salvation blessings (2:32-33; 5:30-32; 10:40-42).

Results: Mockery, Curiosity, Faith (17:32-34) For the Greeks, and especially the Epicureans, resurrections simply didn't happen. Interestingly, Aeschylus said that at the inauguration of the court of the Areopagus, Apollo stated, "Once he [man] is slain; there is no resurrection" (*Eumenides* 648). No wonder some Areopagus members, especially Epicureans who saw death as merely a dispersal of atoms, respond to Paul with mockery. And modern empiricists respond to such incredible claims in the same way. Greg Bahnsen's point is well taken (1980:9, 17-22): we will be following Paul's example and spend our energies wisely

──

17:34 Though commentators uniformly reject the view that Paul viewed his mission at Athens as a failure because he abandoned the simple gospel for an intellectual approach (1 Cor 2:2 is often appealed to), some still see the mission as basically unsuccessful because of the Greeks' attitudes and the lack of spiritually prepared hearts (Longenecker 1981:478;

if we try to help moderns wrestle with the presuppositions that prevent them from even entertaining the possibility of a resurrection, rather than trying to prove its historicity within a modern scientific framework.

The Stoics seem to respond to Paul with jaded curiosity: *We want to hear you again on this subject.* Though at other times during his missionary witness Paul was able to capitalize on people's genuine curiosity (13:42, 44; 17:2, 11), Luke does not tell us whether Paul ever had opportunity to take the Areopagites up on their request. At the very least, their response delays Paul's licensing and effectively curtails his activity. Paul will encounter such exercises in procrastination again (24:25; 26:28). Procrastination leaves people in their unrepentant state, facing only certain judgment. They must embrace the Savior now if they are to be rescued from wrath later, when he comes as Judge. Postmoderns who delay commitment must watch out lest they procrastinate all the way to the judgment seat of Christ.

But some (*tines;* NIV's *few* may be too negative) of Paul's hearers do decide to become followers of ("associate intimately with"; 5:13; 9:26; 10:28) Paul and express saving faith (16:31, 34; 17:12). Luke names Dionysius, a member of the Areopagus council, and Damaris, probably part of the crowd and a foreign-born courtesan, since no Greek women of polite society would have had an opportunity to hear Paul in public (Metzger 1971:459-60, following Ramsay; Polhill 1992:378-79 thinks this is a general summary statement about fruit from witness in synagogue, marketplace and Areopagus, and therefore does not necessarily say anything about Damaris' social status). Luke desires the same believing response from his readers—Theophilus, his fellow seekers and us.

Witness at Corinth and Return to Antioch (18:1-22)

First-century Roman jurisprudence at its best models for us what every state should be for the Christian: the protector of religious freedom and the promoter of religious toleration. At Corinth, the arena for the final stage of Paul's second missionary journey, Proconsul Gallio's decision

Dupont 1979b:536). For others the mention of Dionysius the Areopagite and the report of the speech itself point to a more positive view of the results (Lake and Cadbury 1979:219; E. F. Harrison 1986:290).

sets a precedent of shielding the church from pagan and Jewish attacks and opens a decade-and-a-half-long period of opportunity for the gospel's progress.

The Saints' Practical Protection (18:1-8) Paul, leaving Athens, travels fifty-three miles south-southwest to Corinth. Corinth was politically and economically the main city of Achaia, for it was ideally situated on the three-and-a-half-mile-wide isthmus between the Peloponnesian peninsula and the Greek mainland. Cenchrea was its eastern port city on the Saronic Gulf leading to the Aegean, while Lechaeum was its western port city on the Gulf of Corinth leading to the Adriatic. Thus Corinth (population 200,000) was a key commercial center at the juncture of north-south land and east-west sea routes. Having risen from ruins a little more than a century earlier, when Julius Caesar constituted it a Roman colony (44 B.C.), the city was now dubbed "wealthy Corinth" and had served since 27 B.C. as the capital of the senatorial province of Achaia. The cosmopolitan mix of "local Greeks, freedmen from Italy, Roman army veterans, businessmen and government officials, Orientals, . . . including a large number of Jews," lived in a "rip-roaring town" where, as Horace put it, "none but the tough could survive" *(Epistles* 1.17.36; Longenecker 1981:480).

To such a city, with all its peril and promise, Paul comes alone (1 Cor 2:3). Given that by the year 2000, we are told, there will be five hundred "world-class" cities (one million-plus population) and twenty-three "megacities" (ten million-plus population), we must have the same strategic eyes Paul had in choosing to evangelize Corinth.

Paul experiences Christian companionship in a common trade when he finds (NIV *met)* Aquila ("eagle") and Priscilla ("ancient or venerated woman"; this form is a diminutive of Prisca; compare Acts 18:26; Rom 16:3; 1 Cor 16:19; 2 Tim 4:19). Luke introduces Aquila as a *native of Pontus,* an area of north-central Asia Minor, bordering on the Black Sea, which formed an administrative unit with Bithynia. Aquila and his wife

---

18:2 *All the Jews* is not Luke's exaggeration of the decree (contra Krodel 1986:342). The decree's content may well have differed from the extent of its implementation. "The edict does not seem to have been totally or permanently effective, for the Jews were too numerous and too essential to the life of the capital to be banished for long" (E. F. Harrison 1986:292).

18:3 Bauer, Gingrich and Danker (1979:755) believe the extrabiblical evidence is incon-

have recently arrived from Rome, having been expelled with *all the Jews* by Claudius (A.D. 49). Suetonius tells why—"since the Jews constantly made disturbances at the instigation of *Chrēstus*" (*Claudius* 25.4). Writing seventy years after the event, Suetonius may have assumed *"Chrēstus"* was simply a local troublemaker; however, the dispute in the Jewish community over Jesus *Christus* (the names would have been pronounced similarly) was the real issue. Through the Roman Jews' resistance to the gospel and an emperor's edict, God's sovereign care worked to bring Paul and this couple together.

Their common trade is "tentmaking," or better "leatherworking." Most tents in that day were constructed of leather, but the meaning of *skēnopoios* was extended (as was the case with the English "saddler") to refer to an artisan who produced a variety of leather articles. While Jewish rabbis were bivocational so that they would not have to charge for their teaching (*m. 'Abot* 2:2), other traveling teachers in the Hellenistic world received remuneration for their lectures. In Greco-Roman culture the manual labor of the artisan class was despised.

Paul engaged in leatherworking to offer his gospel without charge and model a good work ethic (Acts 20:34-35; 1 Cor 4:12; 9:15, 18; 1 Thess 2:9; 2 Thess 3:8). He probably used his workshop as a place of witness, as some Greek philosophers used theirs as a teaching venue (Hock 1979). His departure from the workshop and exclusive devotion to preaching after Timothy and Silas's arrival from Macedonia probably shows that he did not view his leatherworking as essential to his evangelism strategy (18:5).

Today "tentmaker" missionaries enter "creative access" countries through secular employment when there is no way to enter as a full-time missionary. If they keep Paul's motives in mind, they will be able to see their bivocationalism as beneficial to the spiritual health of churches they plant. Not only will they model a work ethic that is essential to sanctification, but they will avoid creating wrongful dependency, for they will

clusive concerning the precise trade denoted by *skēnopoios,* and F. F. Bruce (1988:346) basically stays with "tentmaker"; however, Wilhelm Michaelis (1971:393-94) makes a strong case for "leatherworker" based on patristic understandings of the passage. To continue to take *cilicium*—the goat's hair of Paul's home region, Cilicia, which was woven into material for tents—as decisive for the issue imports an extraneous cultural detail into the discussion.

18:5 For an explanation of Paul's coworkers' movements see comment at 17:15.

be offering the gospel of grace "free of charge."

When Timothy and Silas arrive from Macedonia, they likely bring Paul a monetary gift (2 Cor 11:9; Phil 4:15). Paul can now be exclusively *devoted to* ("engrossed or absorbed in") *preaching* (literally, "the word"; compare Acts 6:4). Bivocationalism may be a good pattern for evangelistic church planting, but for Luke it is not the best. To be free to be fully engrossed in evangelism is best. Paul's work now is to engage in an apologetic *(reasoned . . . trying to persuade)* and proclamation *(testifying)* that "the Messiah is Jesus" (so the word order in 18:4-5; compare 17:2-3).

The saints' practical protection now takes the form of a co-opted meeting place. The familiar pattern of the gospel's confrontation with Judaism—proclamation, division, rejection, separation, further advance—occurs here in rapid succession (see comment at 13:42). Jews "oppose and blaspheme" the gospel and the Lord Jesus Christ, who is at its center. In an acted parable, "shaking out his robes," Paul disassociates himself from the Jews for several reasons. He wants to be clear of the judgment that their blasphemy will incur. He wants them to know that their rejection of the message places them in the same position as Gentiles: facing judgment. He wants to declare his freedom from any further responsibility for their eternal destiny (Neh 5:13; Lk 9:5; 10:10-11; Acts 13:46, 51). Using Old Testament phraseology (2 Sam 1:16; compare Mt 27:24-25), Paul's declaration says as much. Their guilt and coming punishment are their own responsibility.

Through with his mission to the Jews here, though he will continue it elsewhere (see Acts 18:19), Paul will now focus on the Gentiles. His base of operations will be the house of God-fearer Titius Justus, next door. Again God has providentially protected his mission by giving it an ideal venue for harvesting Gentile God-fearers. That harvest is not long in coming: first *Crispus, the synagogue ruler,* holding that highly visible position of supervising sabbath services and maintaining order, and *his entire household believed in the Lord* (compare 16:15, 33). Then *many*

18:6-8 Though a case can be made for Crispus's conversion as the catalyst for the break with the synagogue, there is no indication in the text that Luke is presenting the material other than chronologically. The present ordering of events is equally plausible (Marshall 1980:295).

18:7 Many commentators have given *Titius Justus* the praenomen "Gaius" and identified

of the Corinthians who heard him believed and were baptized.

The Lord's Promise of Protection (18:9-11) Earlier Paul has received guidance and encouragement in visions from the Lord (9:12; 16:9-10). Now the Lord appears to him at night again, with a threefold command attached to a threefold promise, all expressed in biblical language (Deut 31:6; Josh 1:5; Is 41:10; 43:5; Jer 1:7-9):

Do not be afraid (literally, "Stop being afraid")/*I am with you*

Keep on speaking/No one is going to attack and harm you

Do not be (literally, "become") *silent/Because I have many people in this city*

For Paul—or for us—to be afraid is to doubt the last promise of the risen Lord (Mt 28:20). Though Paul has territorially moved beyond the Macedonian call (16:9-10), the Lord is here to guide, telling him to *keep on speaking.* He promises that no one will *attack* Paul to *harm* him (see fulfillment of this in 18:12-17; NIV turns the purpose or result expression into a parallel promise: *to attack and harm).* Persecution would aim to stop the freely proclaimed, life-changing gospel message (compare 4:18-20; 5:18-20, 28-29; 16:21; 17:7, 13). Therefore Paul is not to become *silent.* The Lord has already chosen *many people* (see comment at 15:14) for his own in this city. The Lord's predestination (13:48) not only guarantees a fruitful ministry but demands that Paul responsibly fulfill his obligation to witness. And that he does, *teaching . . . the word of God* in Corinth *for a year and a half.*

In light of the vision of Revelation 5:9-10 and 7:9-10—"a great multitude that no one could count, from every nation, tribe, people and language, standing before the throne and in front of the Lamb"—it is right for us today to claim the promises and obey the commands of Acts 18:9-10 for the eleven thousand people groups that have yet to hear the gospel.

The State's Precedent-Setting Protection (18:12-17) The Jews mount a *united attack on Paul* (4:1; 6:12; 17:5), bringing him *into court* (literally, "to the judgment seat"). Lucius Junius Gallio, the proconsul

---

him with the Gaius of Romans 16:23 and 1 Corinthians 1:14.

18:9 Though some commentators see the presence of present and aorist prohibitions *(mē phobou . . . mē siōpēsēs)* as just a matter of stylistic variation (Haenchen 1971:535), A. T. Robertson (1934:890) rightly points out the significance of the contrast: "He had been afraid, he was to go on speaking, he was not to become silent."

who hears the case, was the son of Spanish orator and financier Marcus Annaeus Novatus, who, after the relocation of his family to Rome, participated in the highest and most influential circles of society. Gallio's brother Marcus Annaeus Seneca, a Stoic philosopher, politician and dramatist, was tutor to the young Nero. Gallio pursued a career in government and between his praetorship and admission to the consulate served as the governor of the senatorial province of Achaia. A series of inscriptions help us date his tenure fairly precisely and give us good extrabiblical evidence for placing Paul in Corinth between A.D. 49 and 51 (Barrett 1961:48-49). Seneca described his brother's affable personality thus: "No other human being is so charming to just one person as he is to all people" (*Naturales Quaestiones* 4A, preface 11). Paul probably appeared before Gallio at the beginning of the governor's tenure and near the end of the apostle's stay in Corinth (A.D. 51).

The Jews bring an ambiguous charge. Who are *the people* Paul *is persuading* (better, "inciting")? Are they Jews or Gentiles? More to the point, are they Roman citizens? Against what *law* are they being incited *to worship God?* Is it the Roman law against proselytizing citizens for "foreign cults" (see note at 16:20-21; compare 17:7)? Is it the Jewish law as Gallio understands it (18:15)? Or is it an application of the edicts of Claudius that the Jewish people are to be treated as a *collegium lictum*— a legal, social and in this case religio-ethnic entity whose customs and practices are to be respected and whose lives are to be left undisturbed (Josephus *Jewish Antiquities* 19.278-91)? Possibly the Jews mean for Gallio to extend Claudius's edicts into their internal affairs. In their view Paul's teaching of *the word of God* is contrary to the Jewish law and creates an internal disturbance. In this sense he is violating the edict.

Before Paul can utter a word in his defense, Gallio decides not to render a verdict in the matter. God is fulfilling his promise of protection. Gallio evaluates how the charges relate to the spheres of necessary and discretionary jurisdiction. Using technical legal language (*kata logon*

18:12 The actual "judgment seat"—*bēma*—of Corinth, the ruins of which can still be seen, was a high, broad platform raised on two steps with raised benches at the back and partway along the sides. An impressive blue and while marble structure, it stood in the forum and was used for formal occasions (Finegan 1981:151). Paul was probably tried not before it but in the northern basilica beside the Lechaeum road (Williams 1985:311).
18:17 Though the Western text, Bruce (1988:353) and Longenecker (1981:486) all see

aneschomēn hymōn, "I would have been justified in accepting your complaint"), he says that *some misdemeanor,* open or violent wrongdoing, or *serious crime,* an offense involving fraud, deception, unscrupulousness (13:10), would be a legitimate matter for his jurisdiction. But the Jews have brought him controversial *questions* (15:2; 26:3) about *words* (literally, "a word"—the gospel message, 18:11) and not deeds, about *names* (messianic titles and Jesus' identity as the Christ, v. 5) and about *[their] own law* (a law-free gospel for the Gentiles, vv. 6-8). *I will not be a judge of such things.*

Here Gallio articulates two principles of church-state relations that, when lived out in any political structure, will pave the way for the gospel's unhindered progress. First, by saying that Paul is not accused of a *misdemeanor* or *serious crime,* Gallio declares Christianity's innocence before the state. Missionary activity is not illegal (contrast the Jewish leaders' assessment: 4:18, 21; 5:28). Second, by refusing to adjudicate an intramural religious dispute, Gallio declares that religious questions do not fall within the competence of secular state powers (Lk 20:25). For the fifties of the first century this was truly a precedent-setting decision. The decision of so eminent a proconsul would carry weight wherever such issues arose throughout the Empire (Longenecker 1981:486).

Yet there is a dark side to Gallio's lack of involvement. Not only does he *eject* the defendant and plaintiffs—possibly by physical force through the lictors—from the court, but he takes no action when the Jews begin to beat one of their own, Sosthenes. If Sosthenes is a Christian sympathizer (compare 1 Cor 1:1), then this breakdown of law and order within the *collegium lictum* is a warning that a state's hands-off policy in religious matters may simply make room for persecutors to continue opposing the gospel. Paul's instructions concerning prayer for state rulers should always be on our hearts (1 Tim 2:1-4).

Completion of the Mission (18:18-22) Shielded by the state, Paul remains in Corinth *for some time.* Eventually, in full fellowship he *left*

the Gentile bystanders beating Sosthenes, the NIV renders it as much more likely a beating by the Jews, probably because of the circumstances.

18:18 *M. Nazir* 3:6 and 5:4 and Josephus *Jewish Wars* 2.313-14 give evidence that a Nazirite vow could be undertaken outside Palestine. Bruce (1988:355) disagrees and sees the vow as a private one. What is new in Luke's account is the commencement of the vow's completion, the cutting of the hair, outside Palestine.

(better "said farewell to") *the brothers* and, accompanied by Priscilla and Aquila, sails for Syria. This refers either to his final destination or to eastern territory that included Judea.

At Corinth's eastern port city, Cenchrea, seven miles southeast, Paul cuts his hair, signaling the beginning of the end of a Nazirite vow (Num 6; *m. Nazir*). Evidently he had begun this vow after either the Macedonian or Corinthian vision, as a sign of earnest beseeching of the Lord for success in the mission to which Paul had been called (Acts 16:9-10; 18:9-10). Now in thanksgiving Paul ends the vow and thus recognizes that the Lord made good on his promises. In our life of faith we too may be confident that what God calls us to do he will enable us to complete (Phil 1:6).

The first leg of Paul's journey involves a flying visit to Ephesus, politically and economically the leading city in the province of Asia—in fact the third largest city in the Roman Empire (population 250,000 plus; see comment at 11:19 on Syrian Antioch, the second largest city in the Empire). Jews had been resident there since early Hellenistic times. Quite a number had Roman citizenship, and the Romans upheld the Jews' rights consistently from Augustus onward (Josephus *Antiquities* 14.228-30, 234, 236-40; 16.162-66, 171-73; see Stern 1974:152). Though Paul receives a positive response to his synagogue preaching (*dialegomai*, 17:2, 17; 18:4; see note at 17:2)—he is asked to stay longer—he makes a hasty departure. Though the time is short, perhaps he is still intent on getting to Jerusalem by Passover. The sea lanes opened on March 10, and in A.D. 52 Passover was in early April (Bruce 1988:356). Or he is hurrying there to complete his vow. In any case, he expresses his intention to return *if it is God's will* (18:21; Rom 1:10; 15:32; 1 Cor 4:19; 16:7).

Here Paul and we learn that personal desires and divine guidance so interact that all our planning will be implemented only if it is part of God's sovereign design. This makes us at once more flexible and more confident as we face our future, and more thankful as we reflect on our past.

In a very abbreviated fashion Luke describes Paul's arrival at Caesarea,

---

18:22 Gerhard Schneider (1982:2:255) doubts the historicity of a Jerusalem visit because Acts 21 does not mention it and Romans, Galatians and the Corinthian correspondence seem to exclude it. But given evidence for the Jewish custom that a vow begun in the Diaspora would be completed in Jerusalem (see note at 18:18), as well as Paul's desire to maintain

his "going up" and "coming down" from Jerusalem (8:15; 11:2; 25:1, 6-7) after greeting the church there, and his return to Antioch (compare 14:26-27). Paul models considerate communication, promoting the unity of the body and the continuity of the mission. Today too, the stability of the gospel's advance will be only as strong as the lines of communication with praying and supporting sending churches.

□ The Third Missionary Journey (18:23—21:16)

The third missionary journey displays Paul at the height of his apostolic powers, fulfilling his calling as a guarantor of the church's gospel and its mission. Through Paul God proclaims a powerful gospel and performs extraordinary miracles, the signs of an apostle. Paul embraces an equally significant apostolic mark: suffering. How shall we apply to ourselves the encouragement and challenge of the example of the divinely empowered, yet obediently suffering, apostle?

Witness at Ephesus: Planting the Church (18:23—19:22)

In the business world competition is the name of the game: "Lead, follow, or get out of the way!" The religious/spiritual environment of first-century Ephesus was not much different. Nominal Christians clinging to "the baptism of John," Jews steeped in their tradition, pagans and even Christians practicing magic all seemed to be saying in their own ways, "Can you match this?"

Filling Out an Incomplete Gospel (18:23—19:7) Paul's fifteen-hundred-mile journey begins with an orderly revisiting of churches in *the region of Galatia and Phrygia* (literally, "the Galatian region and Phrygia"). Luke is probably pointing here to the portion of Lycaonia in the province of Galatia and the ethnic region of Phrygia, also located within the province. Here Paul had planted churches during the first missionary journey (Acts 13—14; see note at 16:6). With exhortation Paul "shores up" all the disciples, making them firm to face persecution from without and false teaching from within (14:22; 15:32, 41; compare Ex

---

contact and promote unity among all the churches, there are appropriate motives to provide a rationale for the itinerary as a whole, including the visit to Jerusalem (Williams 1985:314). Sufficient time can be found for it in the Pauline chronology.

17:12 and Judg 16:26, 29 LXX). Paul's continuous practice should be ours: to continue to affirm and confirm converts in their faith so that they may become lifelong disciples.

Luke now catches us up on Apollos's ministry at Ephesus and Corinth in the interval between Paul's visits (18:24-28). Apollos (short form of Apollonius), an Alexandrian Jew, had evidently taken advantage of the education of that city and especially its Jewish community. Alexandria, known for its museum, library and ancillary learning facilities, boasted a Jewish population containing scholars who had produced the Septuagint and later counted Philo the philosopher among their ranks. Luke characterizes Apollos as *learned* and proceeds to specify his area of competence: *a thorough knowledge of the Scriptures* (literally, "being mighty in the Scriptures"). Luke further defines his expertise: Apollos has *been instructed in the way of the Lord* and is able to teach *about Jesus accurately.*

If Luke had not added the qualification *he knew only the baptism of John,* we would be inclined to think Apollos was a Christian, for he knew the gospel, *the way of the Lord,* which is to be identified with "things *about Jesus*" (compare Bruce 1988:358-59). When we understand *with great fervor (zeōn tō pneumati)* in the same way as Romans 12:11, "aglow with the Spirit," the picture of a regenerate Apollos lacking only Christian baptism seems complete. Luke normally presents Christian baptism as the outward sign that the inward reception of the Spirit at conversion has taken place (Acts 2:38-39; 9:17-18; 10:44-48). To present Apollos as having the Spirit without having obtained Christian baptism would be an anomaly. Of course some see the lack of reference to Christian baptism as an indicator that Apollos is considered to have the Spirit and therefore not to need the rite (Krodel 1986:355).

We encounter less difficulty, though, if we take Apollos to be a knowledgeable, fervent but unregenerate disciple of John the Baptist who believes Jesus is the Messiah but does not understand the present saving significance of his death and resurrection. Further, he is unaware of what Pentecost means for all who are baptized in the name of Jesus. *The way*

18:27 Though in word order *through grace* most naturally goes with *believed* (as in NIV),

of the Lord that he knows, then, is not the gospel, but God's way of salvation set forth in the promises of the Old Testament (Is 40:3-5/Lk 3:4-6; compare 1QS 8:13-14). The "boiling over of spirit" with which he speaks is the *fervor* of his own spirit (NIV) and not the Holy Spirit's glow. Apollos preaches *boldly* from the perspective of promise and preparation, an "underrealized eschatology" if you will, as if Ezekiel 36:25 had occurred but not verses 26-27.

The best analogy to Apollos today is a nominal, cultural Christian raised in the liberal theological tradition of the West. Such a person may display the same fervor and the same knowledge about the earthly Jesus' life and teachings. Whether in the "social gospel" of a prior generation or current calls to work for peace, justice, human rights and a safe, clean environment, there are echoes of the preparatory repentance preaching of John (Lk 3:10-14). These concerns rightly answer the venerable question "What would Jesus do?" But since they focus only on human effort, they trap the adherents in, at best, a life of humanly induced goodness and, at worst, the emptiness of dull religious practice. Salvation by grace and the blessing of the indwelling Holy Spirit are completely missed.

Priscilla and Aquila, having heard Apollos's preaching, *invited him to their home* (also possible: "took him aside") *and explained to him the way of God more adequately.* This couple's grace in considerately instructing Apollos out of the limelight and his grace in receiving their words mean that another person has entered the kingdom of the Messiah. Apollos needed and received "what all religious people desperately need—an experience of the substitutionary sacrifice of Calvary as the only basis of righteousness with the Lord, and an infusion of His Spirit as the only source of power to live life as He meant it to be lived" (Ogilvie 1983:271).

Complete in gospel and truly incorporated into the faith, Apollos desires to go to Achaia. The church encourages him and writes letters of commendation (compare 2 Cor 3;1). There Apollos proves a *great help . . . by grace* to the believers (1 Cor 3:6; 16:12; compare Acts 6:8; 14:26; 15:40; 20:32). Through a very effective apologetic ministry, completely

---

it may be placed last in the sentence for emphasis and actually modify the *great help* Apollos was (Bruce 1990:404).

refuting the Jews in public debate (compare 6:10), Apollos clearly demonstrates *from the Scriptures* (literally, "through the Scriptures") *that Jesus was the Christ* (literally, "that the Messiah is Jesus"—the word order shows the direction of the argument; compare 18:5).

Apollos now bears the unmistakable marks of a Christian: recognition and encouragement within the body of Christ, divine grace suffusing his natural abilities so that the effect is powerfully of God, and a clear witness to the person and work of the Lord Jesus Christ. Here is the standard for any knowledgeable professing Christians who with ability and enthusiasm are trying to follow the teachings of Jesus in their own strength. If such persons are teachable like Apollos, they will learn the whole gospel and come to the Spirit and eternal life.

Luke picks up Paul's itinerary with the note that the apostle takes a hilly, higher-elevation route west to Ephesus. This was more direct than the regular trade route down the Lycus and Maenander valleys. Ephesus, "the principal trading center of Asia" (Strabo *Geography* 12.8.15), with its harbor and network of roads reaching into the interior, has caught Paul's strategic eye. It will serve well his purposes for penetrating a whole province evangelistically (19:10, 26).

From Paul's diagnostic questions and the response of the Ephesian *disciples* we quickly learn what Paul evidently suspects: these persons are not truly regenerate. Luke labels them *disciples* probably because at first their outward identification with the Christian believers led Paul to take them for true Christians. Does Paul's first question about receiving the Holy Spirit indicate that he sees none of the Spirit's fruit or giftings in their lives? The combination of questions certainly tells us that Paul assumes that saving faith, the reception of the Spirit and Christian baptism converge at conversion (see references at the discussion of Apollos, above, for Luke's accord with this view).

The disciples' response about the Spirit, which the NIV translates lit-

19:1 *Interior:* the underlying phrase suggests a region of higher elevation and in context explains why Paul was a stranger to the churches of the Lycus Valley (Bruce 1988:362). John B. Polhill disagrees, saying Paul traveled the valley but simply did not stop to witness (1992:398).

19:2 While the NIV marginal reading *after* is possible from the syntax, it is not probable, for both "receive" and "believe" are in the past tense and more likely point to coincident time (Marshall 1980:306). The grammar of the passage therefore does not support the

erally, should probably be taken to mean that they have not heard of the Holy Spirit's contemporary presence (compare Jn 7:39). If they do not know the Old Testament's witness to the Spirit's existence (Num 11:16-17, 24-29; Is 63:10-11; Joel 2:28-32), they certainly would know such a witness from the preaching of John the Baptist, whose baptism they had received (Lk 3:16). In fact, John's preaching of the imminent arrival of a Messiah in eschatological judgment tied closely together the baptism "with the Holy Spirit and with fire." His followers, even if they had heard about Pentecost, probably would not have seen it as the fulfillment of John's prophecy, for the purifying fire of final judgment had not immediately followed Pentecost. As Paul's corrective steps show (Acts 19:4-6), these disciples, like Apollos, are at best nominal Christians, and at worst simply disciples of John. In either case they are living without either the truth or the power of the Christian gospel.

How many professing Christians today could make the statement these twelve made: *we have not even heard that there is a Holy Spirit?* Perhaps they heard the good news of the Spirit's presence but did not really hear it, because they were resistant or not ready. Maybe they have not been taught a whole gospel, so that they do not expect to find the Spirit active today.

Paul's corrective is to preach the gospel to the twelve by pointing out the preparatory and therefore partial nature of the baptism of repentance and of John's message pointing to the Messiah who was to come. Though the Gospels never explicitly state that John called for faith in Christ, the status and role he gave to Jesus certainly imply it (Lk 3:16-17; Jn 1:27; 3:23-30). Paul makes the point that Jesus is this "coming one."

To receive the gospel qualifies one to be baptized in the name of the Lord Jesus, and this is what the twelve do (Acts 2:38-39). This is no "rebaptism," for after the triumph of Easter and the provision of full salvation blessings at Pentecost, a preparatory baptism of repentance is

necessity of a second, separate experience of the Spirit after regeneration, as Pentecostal and some branches of charismatic thought contend.

19:5 Richard Longenecker's explanation (1981:494) of the different treatments of Apollos and the twelve "disciples"—the former was not baptized because he viewed his baptism as pointing to Jesus the Messiah, but the latter were because they viewed their baptism as rivaling commitment to Jesus—has only slight support in the text.

more than incomplete—it is obsolete (Lk 16:16; Eph 4:5).

Not as part of baptism but in order to communicate to these twelve that they are now incorporated into the church and the Spirit has indeed come, Paul lays hands on them (compare Acts 8:17). The Lord in his mercy gives outward manifestations, "other languages" (the NIV margin should be followed if the parallel to Pentecost [2:4] is to be fully shown) and prophecy, confirming to them that full salvation blessings are indeed theirs now.

As we reflect on conversion experiences at Pentecost, in Samaria and at Caesarea with Gentile God-fearers, what is unique to the various first-century situations and what is normative for all time? Unique items, given to demonstrate to various groups and to Jewish Christian observers the direct incorporation of various groups of non-Jews into the body of Christ, are the apostolic laying on of hands and the extraordinary manifestations of the Spirit's presence, speaking in other languages and prophecy. Necessary precedents having been set, there is no need in God's economy for their normative repetition in every Christian's experience (Acts 15:7-11). But "repentance, faith in Jesus, water baptism and the gift of the Spirit . . . belong together and are universal in Christian initiation" (Stott 1990:305; Lk 24:46-47; Acts 2:38-39).

Separating from Unbelieving Tradition (19:8-10) Following the strategy perfected on his previous journeys, and in fulfillment of his promise (18:21), Paul engages in synagogue preaching. For three months he speaks boldly, holding nothing back (20:20, 27). *Arguing persuasively* (literally, "reasoning and persuading"), he pursued his customary method of rhetoric in formal address and the give-and-take of dialogue (see comment and notes at 17:2-4). Marshaling arguments from the evidence—Old Testament promises and New Testament eyewitness reports of fulfillment—he removed all obstacles to his hearers' being convinced (18:4). Luke sums up his message's content as *the kingdom of God.* Later, reporting Paul's farewell discourse to the Ephesian elders, Luke is more expansive: Paul's message was "repentance" toward God and "faith in our Lord Jesus" Christ, "the gospel of God's grace" (20:21,

---

19:15 Though the two words for *know* are different *(ginōskō . . . epistamai),* they are

24). These themes in cosmic, ethical, sanctification and soteriological dimensions all speak of the reign of God in the lives of those for whom Jesus is Lord.

The Jews' reaction—becoming *obstinate* (literally, "being hardened" or "hardening themselves"; compare Ex 8:15; 9:35; Ps 95:8; Acts 7:51) and refusing to believe (literally, "disobeying"; see comment at 14:2)—shows the negative effects of rejecting the gospel over a period of time. We cannot remain neutral; we are either softened toward or hardened against an oft-repeated message. Their rejection was expressed in a public maligning of Christianity *(the Way)*. This may mean a formal rejection, since *publicly* translates a phrase that literally means "before the assembly." Paul's withdrawal is also described in semiformal terms. *He took the disciples* may present a type of self-excommunication (*aphorizō;* Lk 6:22).

As always, Paul's withdrawal leads to further advance, for he now reasons *daily in the lecture hall of Tyrannus* (either the teacher or the proprietor). The Western text has an interesting time reference, "from the fifth to the tenth hour" (Acts 19:9). The Mediterranean "siesta" occurred from the fifth hour (11:00 a.m.) onward, and we know from Acts 20:34 that Paul worked at his trade while in Ephesus. This gives us a picture of a tireless apostle and an eager audience. Each is willing to give up the normal time of rest in order to speak and hear of the kingdom.

Only where there is such commitment to teach and such hunger to receive the word of the Lord will there be advances like that portrayed in the next verse. For two years, during a mission lasting as Bruce estimates from fall 52 to summer 55 (1988:366), Paul keeps up this pace, and as a result—probably via his converts—an entire province hears the gospel (Col 1:7; 2:1; 4:13). The churches of the prison epistles, the letters to Timothy and the book of Revelation are proof of the mission's effect (1 Cor 16:19; Rev 2—3).

Mastering Magic (19:11-20) The private side of paganism in the ancient world was the attempt to manipulate spiritual forces via magical incantations, ritual acts and paraphernalia in order to ward off evil and bring well-being. Ephesus was a city most hospitable to magicians, sor-

---

probably used for stylistic variation (Haenchen 1971:564) and do not indicate different types of knowledge (contrast NIV; Williams 1985:328).

cerers and charlatans of all sorts. Attached to the statue of Artemis, the city's chief goddess, were certain symbols, *ta Ephesia grammata,* which had been turned into a magical formula (Plutarch *Moralia* 706E; 85B; Arnold 1989:15-16).

In a divine initiative, God weds *extraordinary miracles* with the spread of the Word of the Lord throughout Asia, a territory that Satan had firmly and manifestly in his grasp. We have met such strategic "power advances" before in Acts: in Jerusalem and its Judean environs, Samaria, and Macedonia (5:16; 8:7; 16:16-18). Now, at the climax of Paul's efforts as a missionary free to move about as he will, Luke presents another. These evidences of the presence of the reign of God (19:8) in liberating wholeness occur through a unique means. The application of *handkerchiefs* (*soudaria,* sweatbands for the head; compare Jn 11:44; 20:7) and *aprons* (better "belts"—*simikinthia,* a loanword from the Latin *semicinctium;* Martial *Works* 14.153; Petronius *Works* 94.8; Leary 1990), carried away from contact with Paul's skin during his leatherworking, bring healing and release from evil spirits (compare Lk 8:43-48; Acts 5:15).

The skeptic and the mimic will immediately draw the wrong conclusions about these happenings: either they did not occur, or they should be copied. Neither response is the intention of Luke or the rest of biblical teaching (Stott 1990:306). Paul, by his own testimony, was a miracleworker; this was part of his credentials as an apostle (Rom 15:19; 2 Cor 12:12; Gal 3:5). These healings did occur, but to imitate them—as some media evangelists have been wont to do with "prayer cloths" or other "prayed-over" trinkets sent through the mail—is to reduce miracle to magic, or impersonal manipulation (contrast Lk 8:43-48). Following James's instructions is still the best way to call on the Lord for healing (Jas 5:14-15).

Power encounters can sometimes lead to syncretistic responses (Acts 8:19). Though the Old Testament expressly forbade dabbling in the occult, Jews in ancient times played an important role in mediating the magical wisdom of the East to the Greco-Roman world (Lev 20:6, 27; Deut 18:10-11; Josephus *Jewish Antiquities* 8.45-49; Lk 11:19). In fact, some Jews were apparently familiar with the magic formula "the Ephe-

---

19:16 *Bleeding* translates *tetraumatismenous,* which means battered or wounded, but not necessarily with a flow of blood (Bruce 1988:369).

sian letters" (*Testament of Solomon* 7:1-8; 8:11). So it is not surprising to find *seven sons of Sceva, a Jewish chief priest,* acting as exorcists. Since the high priest was the only one permitted to utter the "unpronounceable name of God" and enter his presence in the Holy of Holies on the Day of Atonement, it makes sense that these brothers would use that title as part of their "hype" (*m. Yoma* 3:8; 5:1; 6:2; compare Mastin 1976).

The sons' syncretistic appropriation follows the time-honored practice of piling name upon powerful name so as to create incantations strong enough to require spirits to do one's bidding. One such conjuration goes "I conjure you by the god of the Hebrews/Jesus, IABA IAĒ ABRAŌTH AIA THŌTH ELE ELŌ . . ." (Betz 1986:96). *The name of Jesus, whom Paul preaches* is these men's newest and most potent "power name" (compare Eph 1:21).

As the evil spirit responds to their attempted exorcism, the power encounter is transformed into demonic manhandling. Neither the exalted Lord Jesus nor Paul is directly involved. Yet the results reveal the unquestioned superiority of *Jesus, whom Paul preaches.* The demon displays spiritual insight: he knows both Jesus and Paul (compare Lk 4:34, 41; 8:28), but he does not recognize the magicians.

From the mouth of a demon we learn the valuable lesson that Jesus will not allow his name to be reduced to a magical formula (Ex 20:7). Only those with a personal relationship with Christ and who invoke his name in humble faith are in the correct position to see God act to drive out demons.

The evil spirit's mastery of the sorcerers now turns physical. Galvanized by superhuman strength, the demon-possessed man pounces on them and overpowers them (*ephallomai,* often indicating overpowering by superior spiritual beings; 1 Kingdoms 10:6; 16:13; Moulton and Milligan 1974:269). They receive such a beating that they barely escape with their lives. The magicians, powerless to command the demon, are defenseless against his assault.

From "power advance" to syncretistic response to demonic manhandling to respect and repentance: such is the progress of power encounter

---

19:18-20 Simon J. Kistemaker (1990:693) helpfully notes that all the finite verbs in these verses except those translated *calculated* and *came to* are in the imperfect tense. This portrays a progression and repetition of action.

at Ephesus. *Fear* seizes (literally, "fell on") all who hear about the incident, and *the name of the Lord Jesus* is accorded respect. Here again, demonstrations of divine power do not automatically produce conversions (see comment at Acts 9:35, 42, where they do). They do, however, demonstrate the reality of the Lord's spiritual power and its superiority to, and difference from, magic. Realizing that Jesus' name is not to be manipulated, the populace is now in a better position to hear the good news of repentance and forgiveness of sins declared in that name (Lk 24:47). And for Christians who have *believed* for a while (perfect tense of *pisteuō* so indicates), it is now time for a final break with their past.

They make the break in word by coming and *openly* confessing (literally, "confessing and announcing") *their evil deeds,* their magic practices, possibly revealing the spells themselves. Then they collect books of magic spells and burn them. Their repentance is costly. *Fifty thousand drachmas,* the fees for all the formulas in the books, was thirty-five thousand dollars in today's U.S. currency. The repentance is complete: these believers have removed any temptation to go back to the old life.

Today the temptation is still present to syncretize a newfound faith with pre-Christian ways of using "power" to cope with life. Whether it be worship and manipulation of the new power levers of secularization—money, education, science, technology—or the traditional practices of occult magic in their time-honored or New Age form, those who live under Jesus' lordship must sooner or later come to terms with any compromise in these matters and follow the Ephesian Christians' example of making a clean break with their "power" past.

In a summary statement declaring the gospel's complete triumph over the competition, Luke stresses the life-giving nature of God's saving message by personifying it: *The word of the Lord spread* (literally,

---

19:19 Though the type of silver coin is not explicitly designated, a drachma is normally assumed. Rather than figuring the value on a customary or minimum wage for a day laborer (so the NIV margin), it may be better to calculate it based on the weight of the metal. An Attic drachma equals 67.5 grains of silver (14 percent of a troy ounce). Polhill's sum (1992:406)—thirty-five thousand dollars—is figured on silver selling at five dollars per ounce, a drachma being worth seventy cents.

19:21-22 Longenecker (1981:500) sees *after all this had happened* as a programmatic transition referring to the fulfillment of the Gentile mission of panels four and five (12:25—19:20; compare Krodel [1986:365], who compares it to the transition at Lk 9:51). Given the lack of parallel usage of the phrasing elsewhere in Acts, it is probably better to take the

"grew") *widely and grew in power* (Acts 6:7; 12:24). Luke highlights the power of the message through adverbial phrase and verb (*kata kratos,* NIV *widely; ischyen,* NIV *grew in power,* possibly "prevailed"; compare Lk 1:51; Eph 1:19; 6:10). Luke's theology places proclamation of the gospel message at the center of any "power advance" in the church's mission, and so should ours.

Preparing for Future Advance (19:21-22) To set in bold relief the final episode at Ephesus, Luke, as he has done before (18:21; compare 15:36), breaks in with an overview of Paul's future movements expressed though his desires. Though there is a description of the intervening stops on the itinerary—Macedonia, Achaia, Jerusalem—the emphasis is on the final destination, Rome (23:11; Rom 1:13-15; 15:30-32). The NIV presents these plans as simply Paul's human desires and purposes: *Paul decided.* This translates the admittedly ambiguous phrase "he purposed in the spirit" (his spirit or the Holy Spirit?—compare the equally ambiguous Acts 20:22 and the definite 21:4). When this phrase is taken in combination with the *must* of the next sentence (*dei,* a term often used by Luke to indicate divine necessity—for example Lk 4:43; 9:22; 17:25; 22:37; Acts 1:21-22; 3:21; 9:16; 23:11; 27:24), Luke seems to be declaring Paul's conviction by the power of the Spirit that it is God's will for him to continue pursuing his calling by preaching the gospel in Rome. Once the northeastern portion of the Mediterranean basin is evangelized, there will be no more room for the apostle to the Gentiles to work (Rom 15:23). What better way to fulfill a calling to all the nations, to "kings" and the small and the great, than to proclaim the message of the kingdom at the very center of it all, the capital of the Empire? Through his converts, in centrifugal fashion, he can then reach to the ends of the earth, even the regions of the west, including Spain, which he also hoped to evangelize

phrase as simply referring to the events at Ephesus (Lake and Cadbury 1979:244).

19:22 Paul's deployment of Timothy here, versus Timothy's and Titus's activities as presented in the Corinthian letters (1 Cor 4:17; 16:10; 2 Cor 2:13), is not a problem for Luke's historical reliability (contra Haenchen 1971:569-70). A harmony of evidence is achievable if we take the Acts deployment as occurring after Timothy returned from the assignments mentioned in 1 Corinthians (Marshall 1980:313). Luke's silence on Titus is part of his selectivity—limiting the number of characters so that Paul stays in the spotlight.

Erastus is a fellow worker mentioned in 2 Timothy 4:20 but probably not the city official referred to in Romans 16:23.

personally (Acts 9:15; 26:22; Rom 15:24). Ever the strategic thinker, ever under the Spirit's guidance, Paul plans for this divinely ordained "new Macedonia." And he works his plan by sending Timothy and Erastus to get a collection for him to take to Jerusalem (Rom 15:26).

Today the church desperately needs to listen to visionary strategists whose "mission advance and church growth" eyes help them define and articulate the task in doable terms. They call the church to finish the task: "It can be done; it ought to be done; it must be done—a church for every people and the gospel for every person."

Witness at Ephesus: Facing Opposition (19:23-41)

An anthropologist studying the effects of Christianity on an Amazonian tribe may ask, "Does Christianity kill culture?" Demetrius, the Ephesian craftsman in silver, his colleagues and the Ephesian populace would say "Yes!" But just what effects does Christianity have when introduced into a culture? Luke wants Theophilus, his contemporaries and us to find answers in the account of the riot at Ephesus.

A Craftsman's Complaint (19:23-27) With an indefinite time marker (compare 12:1) and by way of general statement, Luke introduces the last recorded episode of the Christian Gentile mission in the book of Acts. The incident is probably near the end of Paul's ministry at Ephesus (see 20:1). *A great disturbance* arises concerning *the Way* (12:18; 17:6-8, 13). The gospel's continued spread throughout Asia, not just Paul's witness, is at issue here (19:10, 20). Christianity is a way of life, a new belief system with a new Lord at the center, and a new set of mores and behavior patterns—in short, a new culture. Because every culture survives through the dynamic of coercive conformity, the presence of a new way, which claims to be "the Way," will by definition create a disturbance.

The catalyst for the disturbance is Demetrius, a manufacturer of *silver shrines of Artemis*. These were plaques, silver reliefs of the goddess within her temple. The New York Metropolitan Museum of Art has a second/first-century B.C. bronze matrix of Artemis in her temple (Reeder 1987). It is the form into which a sheet of silver or bronze was pressed

---

19:24 Longenecker (1981:503) views the *silver shrines of Artemis* as miniature statuettes of the goddess, but the phrasing *naous argyrous Artemidos,* "silver temples of Artemis," does not substantiate this interpretation. David John Williams (1985:332-33) sees them as replicas

to make such a plaque. Once dedicated in the Great Temple of Artemis, these would serve local worshipers and pilgrims as votive offerings, family worship centers, amulets or just souvenirs.

The Anatolian "Great Mother" was identified by Greek settlers with the Greek Artemis—virgin huntress, goddess of wild animals, wild nature, chastity and childbirth. It is difficult to discern which of her three roles—mother goddess, fertility goddess or nature goddess—was primary in the minds of first-century devotees (LaSor 1979b:306; Arnold 1989:26). Details of her statue, however, do reveal the powers attributed to her. The multiple bulbous objects on her chest have been variously interpreted: are they "breasts, bee eggs, ostrich eggs, steer testicles, grapes, nuts, acorns"? They point to her role as a goddess of fertility (Arnold 1989:25). The dreadful animals on her skirt show she has the power over them and is able to deliver from fear, since she is the supreme "ghost goddess." The signs of the zodiac around her neck show she can mediate between her followers and the cruel fate that dogs them. Indeed, she possesses authority and power superior to astrological fate (Arnold 1989:25, 21). In sum, Artemis had unsurpassed cosmic power. She was called Savior, Lord, Queen of the Cosmos and heavenly goddess. Each year in March or April, Ephesus hosted the monthlong festival Artemisa, a time of carnival and religious celebration. Pilgrims flocked from all over the Empire to participate in the impressive ceremonies to Artemis, including offerings at her sacred grove, to enjoy athletics, plays and concerts, and to partake of great banquets and revelry.

Demetrius's product, an important item in the Artemis cult, *brought in no little business* (better, "profit") *for the craftsmen.* Possibly as president of the guild of silversmiths, Demetrius assembles his fellow craftsmen along with *workmen in related trades,* workers in lead, marble, and semiprecious stones (religious objects of the Artemis cult have been discovered made of those materials [Crocker 1987:77]).

Demetrius reviews two facts from their current situation: their *good income* from the "silver shrine" trade and the effect of Paul's polemic against polytheistic idolatry. As with the Jews (17:4; 18:4; 19:8), with the

of the temple, terra-cotta and marble examples of which have been found. See comments for Ellen Reeder's evidence.

Gentiles Paul has engaged in a rhetoric of persuasion. The result has been that the apostle has *led astray large numbers of people . . . in Ephesus and in practically the whole province of Asia* (19:26; compare 19:10). The basic meaning of *led astray (methistēmi)* is "mentally and spiritually *to bring to a different point of view, cause someone to change his position"* (Bauer, Gingrich and Danker 1979:499). Since the Christian message is about repentance and conversion, could there be a play on words here as Demetrius speaks disparagingly of the transformation called for by Paul's Christian witness (Col 1:13; compare Acts 26:18)? The message that has caused such defection is that *man-made* (literally, "those coming into being through hands") *gods are no gods at all* (17:29; Is 44:9-20; 46:1-7; compare 1 Cor 8:4-6; 10:20).

At the very center of each culture is a religion, whether sacred or secular, expressed in a set of myths of origin, power and destiny. These in turn spawn the culture's worldview, which generates social structures and behavior patterns. Paul's message here shakes Ephesian, indeed Greco-Roman, culture to its very core by showing one of its religious power centers, the Artemis cult, for what it is: nothing. In that sense it does mean the death of the culture, as it does for any culture today with its gods, whether they be a traditional pantheon of tribal deities or the media and educational icons of secular humanism.

Demetrius sees the gospel as a threat to economic prosperity, national pride and religious fervor. *Our trade* (literally, "this branch of the business") will come into disrepute among those who have shunned idolatry, so that orders and sales will dry up. *The temple of the great goddess Artemis,* the pride of Ephesus and Asia, will be reckoned as nothing. It may be hard for Demetrius's hearers to imagine that this structure could totally lose its value in the eyes of the world. After all, Antipater deemed it one of the seven wonders of the world. Its precincts covered an area 425 × 225 feet, four times the size of the Parthenon, with 127 sixty-foot columns. It was the foremost worship center of Asia and a world-renowned bank (Pausanias *Description of Greece* 7.5.4; Dio Chrysostom *Orations* 31.54). But if the image for which it was built were judged no

---

19:29 Since Gaius is a common name and does not necessarily refer to the Corinthian Christian (Rom 16:23; 1 Cor 1:14), it is better to take the plural *Macedonas* as the original reading (so the NIV) and see the text variant as the result of scribal haplography (Bruce

goddess by all, it would indeed be *discredited.*

If the Christian witness succeeds, the *divine majesty* of Artemis literally "will be torn down" (Lk 12:18). Demetrius's claims for the extent of the worship of Artemis are quite accurate. Thirty-three worship sites have been located across the Roman Empire from Spain to Syria (Strabo *Geography* 4.1.5). According to Pausanias this cult received the most extensive and highest worship in the ancient world (*Description of Greece* 4.31.8). In Rome the Aventine temple of Diana (Roman equivalent of Artemis) had a statue modeled on the Ephesian type, and on the occasion of the marriage of Emperor Claudius to Agrippina, commemorative coins were struck at Ephesus with the profiles of the newlyweds on one side and a figure of the statue with the legend "Diana Ephesia" on the other (Kreitzer 1987:61). To have such divine majesty torn down would be quite a feat. Yet from what Demetrius has seen of the mighty advance of a gospel of repentance from vain idols, it is "a clear and present danger."

Demetrius's appeal to economic, patriotic and religious motives for a defense of paganism against the gospel shows how interrelated are these cultural aspects. Any Christianity worth its salt will be a challenge to the pocketbook, the flag and the shrine.

A Crowd's Confusion (19:28-34) Demetrius's audience reacts in angry defiance, with a cultic chant of adoration: *Great is Artemis of the Ephesians!* (compare Bel and the Dragon 18, 41). This throws *the whole city* into confusion. The craftsmen and workers become the core of a mob that rushes violently into the theater, having laid hold of two of Paul's traveling companions, Gaius and Aristarchus (Gaius is otherwise unknown; Aristarchus is mentioned at Acts 20:4; 27:2; Col 4:10; Philem 24).

The theater (capacity twenty-four thousand) was the largest and most impressive of all structures in ancient Ephesus. Built into the steep western slope of Mount Pion with a view of the city and the broad street to the sea, it was used for large gatherings of inhabitants, as well as the citizens' assembly (Finegan 1981:162). This gathering is probably an unofficial meeting of the city assembly in which Demetrius hopes to put pressure on civic authorities to take action against the apostolic group

---

1988:375) rather than, with Longenecker (1981:505), taking the singular as original and viewing the plural form as secondary, the result of dittography.

(Sherwin-White 1963:83). The declaration of the truth has wounded religious and ethnic pride, which reacts with a destructive mixture of mindless zeal and fury (compare Lk 4:28; 8:33; Acts 5:17; 7:57; 13:45). Today the same reaction to the gospel from zealots of the world's great religions or of antireligious ideologies should be no surprise.

Whether to witness or to show solidarity with his arrested fellow workers, *Paul wanted to appear before the crowd* (literally, "purposed to go into the *dēmos*" [popular assembly]), probably emboldened by the way his Roman citizenship and the Empire's authorities have protected him (Acts 16:37-40; 18:12-16). But his fellow disciples shield him this time by not permitting him to go to the theater (9:24-25, 30; 14:5; 17:10, 14). Further, *some of the officials of the province,* "Asiarchs" by title, beg him not to go. An Asiarch was an aristocrat, a member of the provincial council. Made up of representatives from the major cities, this council had particular responsibility for the work of the temples devoted to the imperial cult. For such men to be Paul's friends and take such an interest in him shows not only the high levels of society to which the gospel had penetrated but also that Christianity evidently was not yet viewed as a threat to the imperial cult. In fact, the educated classes seemed to treat it with greater tolerance than did the masses.

Paul again balances prudence and bravery, and so should all witnesses for Christ. When the church body functions with Spirit-endowed wisdom, there is a good source of guidance. There may be times when Spirit-directed personal conviction will override the church's counsel (Acts 21:13-14), but the church's word must always be received gratefully.

The assembly was confused, divided *(some were shouting one thing, some another)* and ignorant of its purpose *(most of the people did not even know why they were there).* Here is an apt picture of the disorient-

---

19:30 Luke uses three terms to describe the gathering: *ochlos,* "crowd" (vv. 33, 35); *dēmos,* "people, populace, crowd" gathered for any purpose, "popular assembly" for the transaction of public business (vv. 30, 33; NIV renders "crowd . . . the people"); and *ekklēsia,* "assembly," a regularly summoned political body (vv. 32, 29, 41). Since Luke intersperses these three terms, it is probably best to let each, especially *dēmos,* have its most distinctive force. Hence I understand *dēmos* as referring here to a "popular assembly," though a highly irregular one.

19:33 There is ambiguity about the subject and the meaning of the main verb *shouted instructions (synebibasan).* The verb can mean "instruct" (Is 40:13), "prove" (Acts 9:22), "conclude or infer" (16:10). There is also the text variant *katebibasan* ("take down"), which

ing nature of misguided religious fervor. We find it today not only in the frenzied rituals of traditional religions but also in the verbal pounding that combatants in the postmodern "culture wars" inflict on each other.

In the end, the Artemis cult's opposition to the gospel proves futile. The Jews in the crowd push forward Alexander to determine the cause of the tumult. When some from the crowd tell him it is the Christian "Way," he seeks to speak to the assembly to make a defense for the Jewish community, presumably to distance it from "the Way," if not also to provide ammunition to the Gentiles in their persecution of this "self-excommunicated" group. But the crowd will have none of it. They draw no distinction between Jews and Christians, for both groups are monotheistic and oppose idolatry. Recognizing that Alexander is a Jew, they drown out his attempted defense with a two-hour chant: *Great is Artemis of the Ephesians!* (compare 19:28). And today we know that a culture's religious lies are asserting themselves against the truth when in response to the calm and clear proclamation of the gospel, all the culture's proponents can do is shout louder. Does Christianity kill culture? It exposes what is not true in order to cleanse and transform culture.

A Clerk's Clear Thinking (19:35-41) The city clerk quieted the crowd. He is the head of the city executive, the annually elected chief administrative assistant to the magistrates. He also serves as liaison to the Roman authorities. Three assertions by the clerk show that the assembly is unnecessary, a fourth that it is positively dangerous to this free city's well-being: (1) The Ephesians' reputation as guardians of the temple and image of Artemis is safe (vv. 35-36). (2) These Christians' reputations are unsullied (v. 37). (3) The crowd can have recourse before regular courts and legislature (vv. 38-39). (4) The crowd is in danger of coming under the charge of rioting without cause (vv. 40-41).

---

is favored by some (Bruce 1990:419). The subject could refer to "some of the Jews of the crowd" or "some of the Gentiles of the crowd." The options are "the Jews put Alexander forward" (1) "and the Gentiles conclude he is the cause of the disturbance" (one option for E. F. Harrison [1986:319]), (2) "and the Gentiles take him down" (Bruce 1990:419), (3) "and the Jews instruct Alexander to address the crowd" (Williams 1985:337); (4) "to find out what is happening and the Gentiles instruct him" (Haenchen 1971:575; NIV). Option 4 seems to make the best sequence of events: the Jews thrust Alexander forward to find out the cause of the tumult. Some in the crowd instruct him that it concerns Paul, a Jewish Christian. Alexander then attempts to make a defense of the Jewish community and so distance it from the Christians, but only triggers an anti-Semitic reaction.

The clerk declares as "undeniable facts" the universal reputation of Ephesus as *guardian* (*neōkoros,* a title later used of cities responsible for a temple devoted to the imperial cult [Sherwin-White 1963:88]) of the temple and the *image, which fell from heaven (diopetēs).* While a meteorite at Taurus was worshiped as an image of Artemis (Euripides *Iphigenia in Taurica* 87-88; 1384), no extrabiblical source reports such at Ephesus. The clerk may be speaking of the ancient age of the image, which was so old that it was viewed as fashioned in heaven (Longenecker [1981:502] takes the reference literally). Such an affirmation speaks to both Demetrius's anxiety and Paul's polemic about gods made with human hands (vv. 26-27). The clerk announces that Artemis's reputation is safe and she does not fall into the category of idols that Paul is critiquing.

A temple's roles as a bank and a worship center were interdependent. Fear of the god deterred robbers. The wealth of the bank enhanced the prestige of the god. Thus "to commit sacrilege" literally was "to rob temples" (noun *hierosylos*). This the Christians have not done. Further, their challenges to polytheism and idolatry have not involved the crime of public blasphemy. Either the clerk views the "heaven-fashioned" image as beyond Paul's charges. Or, if Paul's approach has been the same as at Athens, Paul's polemic involves reasoning on a generic level: the nature of deity and the worship appropriate to it from human beings, who are its offspring. No direct attack on Artemis, a concrete case, is necessary. Paul's tactics have much to teach us about effective "speaking the truth in love" to devotees of non-Christian religions.

The clerk suggests two legitimate means of redress: the court system and the legislature—the citizens' assembly meeting at its duly constituted times (one regular and two extra sessions per month, per Sherwin-White [1963:87], using the inscription of Salutaris and Chrysostom *Homilies* 42). The courts could handle private financial disputes, while the citizens' assembly could deal with any alleged attack on the city's prestige.

19:38 *The courts are open* could mean they were in session at that time or, because the proconsul or his representative moved on a circuit, they were open from time to time.

Proconsuls is a generalizing plural, since there was one proconsul per province. He or his representative performed judicial functions.

20:1 Luke tells us nothing of Paul's immediate plans, his changes of plan or the anxious

The real *danger* (contrast v. 27) is to be charged with rioting without cause; the city could lose status as a free city if it failed to maintain law and order through its own local authorities. With this caution the clerk exercises his authority by dismissing the assembly.

Luke teaches us through this clerk that so long as Christians do not strain the social fabric of a culture through "public blasphemy of the gods," fair-minded government officials should protect Christians from rash, illegal acts of persecutors. This is one of the means by which law-abiding witness to the gospel, which transforms culture, may advance unhindered.

To Jerusalem—Macedonia, Achaia, Troas (20:1-12)

One of the greatest gifts a parent, a teacher or a coach can give is encouragement. Luke describes Paul's ministry of encouragement as he summarizes his movements at the end of his third missionary journey and focuses on a local church gathering in Troas. From these we learn how salvation blessings come in the ministry of mutual encouragement within the church.

Encouragement amid Goodbys (20:1-6) When the highly charged situation in Ephesus has settled down, Paul decides it is a propitious time to depart. But he does not do so until after he has called the disciples together for some encouragement *(parakaleō)*. Growing out of the basic meaning "to call to one's side," this verb can mean "to appeal to or beseech," "to exhort" or "to comfort." For Paul and Luke, exhortation/encouragement is verbal ministry that by the Spirit's power seeks to strengthen Christians to persevere in the faith in the face of trials, especially persecution (Acts 11:23; 14:22; Rom 12:8). Paul consistently ministered encouragement in the churches, especially when he was about to leave them, when he visited them after an absence or when he could be with them only via letter (Acts 14:22; 15:32; 16:40; compare Eph 4:1). So in his leavetaking from Ephesus (Asia) and in his itineration through

---

frame of mind with which he moves to Troas and then into Macedonia, as he looks for Titus and the news he brings of how the Corinthian church has responded to his "sorrowful letter" of correction. For this we must turn to 1 Corinthians 16:5-8 and 2 Corinthians 1:15—2:1; 2:12-13.

Macedonia and Achaia on his way to Jerusalem, Paul speaks *many words of encouragement*. His three-month stay is probably due to winter, when sea travel was avoided (compare Acts 27:12; 28:11; Tit 3:12).

Paul's example in itself is an encouragement to us, for it challenges us to be encouragers ourselves. It comforts us as well to know that the physical presence of those who brought us to birth in Christ is not essential to our further progress in the Christian life.

As Paul is about to set out on the last leg of his journey to Jerusalem, sailing directly from Achaia to Syria, he encounters a plot of the Jews against him (Acts 20:3; compare 9:24; 23:30). With cunning prudence Paul changes his plans and moves overland back through Achaia and Macedonia. This way he avoids possible harm, even death, as a passenger aboard a vessel crowded with Jewish pilgrims heading to Jerusalem for Passover. He divides his party, sending some—the Asians Tychichus and Trophimus—or possibly all his companions ahead to Troas by ship. After celebrating Christian Easter in Philippi (Passover A.D. 57 was April 7-14) and a five-day sea journey against contrary winds (the normal voyage in this direction is three or four days; Lake and Cadbury 1979:254; contrast 16:11), Paul and Luke rejoin the party at Troas (the "we sections" that left off in Philippi [16:10-17] recommence here at 20:5). Courage and prudence so combined in Paul's life that divine purposes were not thwarted by threatening circumstances (19:21-22). And so it should be with us.

Encouragement in Local Focus (20:7-12) At the end of a week's stay in Troas, Paul continues his ministry of encouragement in the context of a worship service. In the earliest unambiguous reference to early

_____

20:2 Luke tells us nothing of Paul's probable activity during these travels: Titus's report and the writing of 2 Corinthians in Macedonia (2 Cor 7:5-16), the evangelistic mission along the Via Egnatia as far west as Illyricum (Rom 15:19; 2 Tim 4:10), the making of arrangements with the churches for a collection for the poor in the Jerusalem church (Rom 15:25-32; 1 Cor 16:1-4; 2 Cor 8—9) and the writing of Romans in Corinth (Rom 16:1, 21-23).

20:4 Though Luke mentions the party of traveling companions, evidently representatives of the contributing churches, he makes no explicit reference to the collection itself. John Polhill (1992:417) notes that Luke's silence has been explained as due to (1) a failure to deliver it because of robbery or confiscation by authorities, (2) the embarrassment it was to Jewish Christians in front of the Jews, or to Christians before Roman authorities, who closely regulated the analogous Jewish temple tax (Josephus *Jewish Antiquities* 16.162-65), (3) the Jerusalem Jewish Christians' negative reception of Paul (Acts 21:20-21). The potential

church practice concerning Sunday worship, Luke tells us that *on the first day of the week we came together to break bread* (compare 1 Cor 16:2; Rev 1:10; *Didache* 14:1; *Epistle of Barnabas* 15:9). In a letter to Trajan from Bithynia in the early second century, Pliny the Younger describes Christian practice. "They had met regularly before dawn on a fixed day to chant verse alternately among themselves in honor of Christ as if to a god. . . . After this ceremony it had been their custom to disperse and reassemble later to take food of an ordinary, harmless kind" (*Epistles* 10.96.7). Hence although the first day of the week was a workday, Christians hallowed it at its beginning and end, through corporate worship in celebration of Christ's resurrection (Lk 24:1). *To break bread* in Christian parlance probably points to a fellowship meal begun and completed by the sacrament of the Lord's Supper (Lk 22:19-20; Acts 2:42, 46; 20:11; 1 Cor 10:16; 11:24).

Paul's words to the Christians of Troas constitute a formal address, possibly with discussion and conversation (*dialegomai*, Acts 20:7, 9; compare 17:2, 17; 18:4, 19; 19:9; 24:25; *homileō*, 20:11; also Lk 24:14-15). Luke emphasizes the speech's length: it extends to midnight and, then, after the Lord's Supper-fellowship meal, until daybreak. Paul spares no effort in verbal exhortation as he prepares the disciples for what he thinks will be life permanently without his presence (Acts 20:25).

What principles for Christian worship is Luke teaching us through this narrative? The first day of the week, the Lord's Day, is when Christians should consistently gather for worship. The sermon, the exposition and application of the Word of God, is an integral part of worship. The Lord's Supper, the "visible Word," is just as important as a means of spiritually

misunderstanding of the collection by Roman authorities and citizens, Luke's target audience, seems the best explanation.

Sopater represents Berea and is the same person as the Sosipater of Romans 16:21. Of the Thessalonians we meet Aristarchus again in Acts 19:29 and 27:2, Colossians 4:10 and Philemon 24. Gaius of Derbe is one of several Gaiuses in the New Testament (Acts 19:29; Rom 16:23; 1 Cor 1:14; 3 Jn 1). Timothy does not represent Lystra but serves as Paul's junior colleague (Bruce 1988:382; Acts 16:1; 19:22). Tychichus and Trophimus we meet later in Acts and Paul's prison and pastoral epistles (Acts 21:29; Eph 6:21; Col 4:7; 2 Tim 4:12, 20). Luke, as indicated by *we,* may represent Philippi. For other explanations of representation for Corinth see Bruce 1988:382-83.

20:6 For Haenchen (1971:582) *after the Feast of Unleavened Bread* is only a time marker and does not indicate Paul's observance; for Krodel (1986:376) it points to Paul's keeping of the Jewish Passover; for Marshall (1980:325) it is Christian Easter.

strengthening the church gathered. The two certainly belong together, but the frequency for taking the sacrament varies (2:46, daily; 20:7, weekly). When because of abuses the church came to separate the sacrament from the fellowship meal (1 Cor 11:17-22), something of the "family atmosphere" present in the combination may well have been lost. In an increasingly rootless society, where individuals find themselves without meaningful personal relationships in an impersonal urbanscape, recapturing "family" around the Lord's Table could be a saving grace for many. Urban Rome may well have found this an inviting picture too.

Into the midst of such an encouraging scene comes tragedy. Eutychus (good fortune), probably a lad between seven and fourteen years old, falls into a deep sleep. The room's atmosphere must have been heavy, with many smoking small torches *(lampas)*, and the boy must have tried to catch the night air by sitting on a windowsill. But the lateness of the hour, the hypnotic effect of the flickering lights and Paul's lengthy discourse all probably contribute to his drowsiness. He loses his balance, falls out the window (probably no more than an open slit in the wall) and is *picked up dead*. With poignant simplicity Luke tells us what we all know: death is an unwelcome intruder that suddenly renders those who witness it speechless, immobilized.

Paul's action and words bring comfort. Not unlike Elisha of old, Paul *threw himself on* (better "fell on") *the young man and put his arms around him* (2 Kings 4:32-35; compare 1 Kings 17:19-24). The boy's life returns, for Paul calls out, *Don't be alarmed* (literally, "Stop being distressed"; compare Mk 5:39, where it describes the noise of mourning). *He's alive!* (literally, "his life [*psychē*, soul] is in him"). Then almost matter-of-factly Luke tells us that Paul returns to the upper room, partakes of the Lord's Supper and the fellowship meal, continues his exhortation-encouragement via personal conversation until daybreak, then departs.

When Luke caps the episode with the lad's being led away, probably home, *alive,* and the disciples' being *greatly comforted,* he certainly

20:9 The boy's age may be properly specified as between seven and fourteen because he is identified as a *pais* in verse 12 (Philo *De Opificio Mundi* 105, quoting Hippocrates).

Some claim it is impossible to be sure, given the phrasing in verses 9, 10 and 12, whether Eutychus was clinically dead or not (Bruce 1988:385). A plain reading of the text, however, does point toward actual death. He is not taken up "as dead" (*hōs nekros;* Mt 28:4; Mk 9:26; Rev 1:17) but simply "dead" *(nekros)*. His life is described not as "still in him," but as "in

focuses on this miracle of resurrection as a source of comfort to the Christians. It is the last recorded miracle of Paul as a missionary moving about in freedom. But there are other sources of comfort/encouragement: the preaching of the Word of God and the taking of the Lord's Supper together. Luke says to his audience and to us that though the apostles are gone, the Lord is not. He has left tokens of his grace for all who would be encouraged and encourage: the restored Eutychus and the Spirit-enabled means of grace, Word and sacrament.

To Jerusalem—Miletus (20:13-38)

What do you say when you say goodby? When an apostle says farewell and addresses leaders of the next spiritual generation for what he thinks is the last time, a "farewell discourse" is in order. As Paul reviews his past as a model for the Ephesian elders' future work and charges them as Spirit-appointed pastoral overseers, we quickly become aware that Luke intends this message for all church leaders in every spiritual generation.

Gathering the Elders (20:13-17) The party departs Troas by ship ahead of Paul, instructed to take him on board at Assos. Paul walks the twenty-mile distance overland. Assos, a port city with the only good harbor on the north shore of the Adramyttian Gulf, stands on a seven-hundred-foot volcanic hill and faces south to the island of Lesbos. The port would have been known to Romans as the birthplace of the Stoic philosopher Cleanthes and the venue for three years of Aristotle's teaching career (Strabo *Geography* 13.1.57-58). Paul may make his rendezvous by sighting the ship while on his way and being taken on board before Assos, for so the verb tense indicates (Williams 1985:344).

They proceed forty-four miles south to Mitylene, a chief city on the island of Lesbos, some sixty miles south of Troy. Its position near old trade routes between the Hellespont and ports south and east made it an important seaport. Mitylene, a free city, was a favorite resort for Roman

---

him" (v. 10). Taken with verse 9 this declaration implies that life has returned to the boy. The NIV's *He's alive!* may be slightly more ambiguous. Leading the lad *alive* at the narrative's conclusion, even after Paul's departure, suggests not so much a process of recovery, regaining of consciousness, as a climactic statement of the proof of the power of God (Acts 1:3; 9:41).

aristocrats.

Setting sail the next day, they arrive *off Kios.* Kios, an island shaped like a drawn bow facing Asia Minor, is twelve miles from ancient Smyrna and five miles from the mainland. The birthplace of Homer, it was struck with a violent earthquake in the time of Tiberius, who helped rebuild it.

The following day they cross *over to Samos.* One of the most famous of the Ionian islands, Samos lies at the mouth of the Bay of Ephesus, separated from the mainland by the milewide strait of Mycale. Samos was renowned not only for its works of art but also for its chief manufacture: pottery of a fine, smooth clay, deep red in color.

The next day they put in at Miletus. This most illustrious Ionian seaport on the west coast of Asia Minor was situated on the south promontory of a gulf into which the Meander River once emptied. It was economically prosperous, architecturally beautiful and religiously significant. The Milesian temple of Apollo at Didyma, famed for its oracles, was nearby.

These background comments show that this "name-dropping" itinerary would have been of interest to a Roman audience. Such an island-hopping method of travel was necessitated by the meteorological and topographical demands on first-century navigation. On the Aegean, summer winds customarily blew only during daylight hours, so sailing vessels could make no headway at night. Further, the narrow channels along the west coast of Asia Minor were so dotted with small islands that night navigation was dangerous.

Paul consciously bypasses Ephesus, and Luke tells us why: he does not want to be slowed down on his way to Jerusalem, for he desires to arrive there, *if possible, by the day of Pentecost.* Though Jewish piety may

---

20:15 *Parebalomen,* which NIV translates *crossed over,* can also be rendered "pass by" or "stop at" (Polhill 1992:421). Given the geography and the progress of the voyage, the NIV is preferred.

20:18-35 The farewell discourse is a genre present throughout Scripture (Gen 47:29—49:33; Deut 31:14—33:29; Josh 23:1—24:30; 1 Sam 12:1-25; 2 Kings 2:1-14; Mt 28:18-20; Jn 13—17; 2 Tim; 2 Pet; see also *Jubilees* 7:20-39; 2 Baruch 44:1—46:7; *Testaments of the Twelve Patriarchs;* Kurz 1990; Lövestam 1987:2). The departing leader's life is reviewed as an example for imitation and an apologetic for his conduct. There are warnings concerning future dangers to the faith, exhortations to faithfulness and God's benediction in an affec-

motivate him (see Deut 16:16), a celebration of the Spirit's outpouring on the first Christian Pentecost is certainly reason enough (Acts 2:1-13). Still, Paul's pastor's heart overcomes his personal schedule. He cannot do without one last contact with the church in Asia. With earnestness and authority he summons the elders from Ephesus, thirty-odd miles away.

An Apostle's Model Work (20:18-27) In a reverse parallelism structure Paul reviews his past and anticipates his future (vv. 18-21, 22-24), and then in particular relation to the Ephesians he describes his future and makes an apologetic for his past conduct (v. 25, 26-27). He appeals to their personal experience—*you know*—as he points to his consistency during *the whole time* he was with them.

Paul reminds them of the model life he has lived as he *served the Lord.* The term Paul uses *(douleuō)* points to the slave-master relationship (Judg 10:16; 1 Sam 12:20; Lk 16:13). Paul's allegiance to his Lord determined the conduct of his ministry. His leadership was servant leadership, the *humility* of a lowly mind (22:25-27; Eph 4:2). His involvement was intensely personal, for he shed the *tears* of a tender heart, sorrowing over rejections of the gospel without the church and resistance to its full work within the church (Acts 20:31; 2 Cor 2:4). His was the steadfast endurance of a tough skin in the face of trials (NIV *severely tested* [*peirasmos:* "trial," "test," "temptation"], Lk 22:28) from *plots of the Jews* (Acts 9:24; 20:3; compare 19:33-34).

For Luke, orthopraxy—in this case the messenger's character and manner of ministry—is just as important as orthodoxy, the message. One effectively says goodby by reminding those left behind of a model life lived before them.

Paul's past ministry also includes a "model word" characterized by comprehensiveness in presentation and in the looked-for response. In

---

tionate, sorrowful, prayerful farewell. Paul's address falls into this category and parallels Jesus' farewell discourse at the Last Supper table (Lk 22:15-38, uniquely in Luke of the Synoptic Gospels). According to Kurz, the primary function of the biblical version of the farewell genre is to describe and promote the transition from original religious leaders to their successors in such a way that community tradition and the authority to preserve the tradition for later generations is maintained (1990:50).

20:19 The NIV introduces a concessive clause beginning with *although.* This breaks up Luke's straightforward presentation of the three qualities of Paul's service to the Lord: humility, intense personal involvement and endurance.

audience, *both Jews and Greeks* (19:8-10; Eph 2:11-22), in venue, *publicly and from house to house* (Acts 19:9; compare 5:42), in content, *anything that would be helpful,* Paul did not hesitate (*hypostellō,* "shrink back in fear," opposite *parrēsiazomai,* "speak boldly") to preach (*anangellō,* " 'to announce, to inform, to tell,' provide information with the possible implication of considerable detail" [Louw and Nida 1988:1:411]) and to teach them. This reminder of his approach arms the elders for the future, when false teachers will claim that their "other gospel" is an essential supplement to Paul's (20:21, 27).

The looked-for response from both Jews and Gentiles is *that they must turn to God in repentance* (literally, "repentance toward God") *and have faith in our Lord Jesus.* The brief phrase "repentance toward God" captures the whole process of conversion, which Luke elsewhere describes as "repent and turn to God and prove . . . repentance . . . by deeds" (26:20). What is in the forefront is turning to God with all one's being, an absolutely serious reckoning with him as one's God in all one's decisions, as the Old Testament prophets called for (Jer 34:15; 26:3-5; Hos 6:1-3; Behm and Würthwein 1967:985). For the Jew it is a returning, for the Gentile a turning to the one true God for the very first time (Acts 14:15; 1 Thess 1:9).

As repentance is paired with the salvation blessing "forgiveness of sins" in Luke's seminal statement of the gospel (Lk 24:47), so here the repentance response is coupled with *faith in our Lord Jesus.* Only unconditional trust in the Lord, in whose name—that is, on whose authority and by whose saving work—forgiveness can be proclaimed, secures this salvation provision (Acts 16:31; see these themes at 19:4-5, 10, 18, 20; Eph 1:13, 15, 19; 2:8; 3:17; 4:5, 13; 6:16, 23). In such brief compass Theophilus and we could not be told better what is required to become a Christian. Repentance, total surrender to God, complete trust in his Son: with these the journey on the path of grace into and in the kingdom must be begun, continued and completed (Acts 20:24-25).

Saying, "And now behold," Paul turns abruptly to sketch his future as far as he knows it. In the process he models some further character traits

———————————————————————————

20:25 Paul's statement does not necessarily refer to his death, as many who see Luke addressing the church in his own day contend (for example, Haenchen 1971:592). It can

that, because they reveal faithfulness to the ministerial calling, these elders also need for the future. Paul's next steps are in obedience to the Spirit's compulsion. He says he goes to Jerusalem "having been bound by the Spirit." There may be a play on words here, for the same verb is used for the divine necessity that compels and guides Paul and the binding of being handcuffed and incarcerated (*deō,* Lk 9:22; Acts 1:16; 19:21; 21:11, 13, 33; 22:29; 23:11; 24:27; 27:24; compare 20:23, *desma*).

Paul's obedience includes an ability to live with uncertainty even when what he does know about the future is not encouraging. Whether by prophet or direct revelation, the Holy Spirit testifies to him in every city that *prison and hardships* (better "afflictions" born of persecution, *thlipsis*) await him in Jerusalem. Though all Christians may not be called to endure imprisonment for the faith, if they would enter the kingdom they must so live under Jesus' lordship that, like their Lord, they will find themselves walking the path of suffering leading to glory (Lk 24:26; Acts 14:22; compare 11:19).

There is, then, no final contradiction between the Spirit's compulsion and the Spirit's warning. God mercifully prepares his servant to count the cost of his daily cross-bearing in a fallen world that hates his Christ and those who own his name (Lk 9:23; 12:4-12; 21:12-19).

Paul expressly counts the cost and does it in terms of his *life* (*psychē,* "soul, life"). In biblical understanding the *psychē* can mean "life on earth in its external physical aspects; seat and center of the inner life of man in its many and varied aspects; and seat and center of life which transcends the earthly" (Bauer, Gingrich and Danker 1979:893). With this range of meaning human beings can face in one word the choice of which dimension to invest themselves in (Lk 9:24; 12:23). Paul states the choice and his decision in the form of relative worth. In the face of impending *prison and hardships,* he makes his *psychē* (his physical existence) of no value in the sense that he does not choose to preserve it at all costs. Rather, he chooses to pursue the purpose *the Lord Jesus* has for him: *the task of testifying to the gospel of God's grace* (Acts 9:15-16). Paul calls this pursuit "finishing a race" (compare 13:25; 2 Tim 4:7)

just as well point to Paul's intentional departure from the Aegean world, which he now views as comprehensively evangelized (Acts 19:21; Rom 15:23-29).

and "completing a task" (*diakonia*, a ministry or service). Paul sees his presence in Jerusalem as an integral part of his apostolic gospel ministry. Certainly the good news is all about grace, God's unmerited saving favor bestowed on Jew and Gentile without distinction (Eph 2:5, 7-8; 3:2). And what better, more needy place to testify to it than Jerusalem, that bastion of works righteousness.

Paul's future and his past are all of a piece, and so should ours be. No matter the outward circumstances, even if they include impending threats, our conduct should consistently fulfill our one calling as servants of the Lord Jesus who testify to his one message: the gospel of God's grace.

Paul now relates his future prospects to the Ephesians: *None of you . . . will ever see me [literally, "my face"] again.* Again his ministry is in the forefront of his thought. These Ephesians are those *among whom [he has] gone about preaching [kēryssō] the kingdom.* Of the terms for preaching and evangelizing, this one

> characterizes the concrete proclamation of the message in a particular instance, with special reference to the claim that is being made, and its authority to set up a new order. It includes information, but is always more than mere instruction or a bare offer, and is equally distinct from the communication of philosophical teaching or general wisdom. *Kēryssō* sets a standard which to ignore is not simply indifference but refusal. (Coenen 1978:57)

Preaching the kingdom not only ushers persons into a personal relationship with the King, Jesus, but creates a personal bond between evangelist and evangelized, now both subjects of the kingdom. Paul's statement also shows that the pioneer church planter, though he is a church's first pastor, must have an itinerant ministry. He must know when to let go: when the planting is done and the pastoral team, leaders in the next spiritual generation, must water so that the harvest may bear fruit to

---

20:28 The NIV translation of *episkopoi* as *overseers* with the marginal alternate *bishops* correctly emphasizes function over office. The New Testament uses "elder" and "bishop" without distinction, even interchangeably (Acts 20:17, 28; Tit 1:5, 7; 1 Pet 5:1-2 [the verb]). Stott's apt phrase "presbyter-bishop" seems to comprehensively capture the role and office (1990:323).

The phrase *church of God* followed by *with his own blood* could and probably did lead to an anthropomorphic misunderstanding: how can God who is spirit have blood? Some

maturity (1 Cor 3:6). To stay too long is to allow dependency to stifle growth.

Paul now turns to his past and its significance for the Ephesians' eternal destiny. Like the watchman of Ezekiel 33:9, Paul has no blood on his hands. He is *innocent* (literally, "clean"; 18:6) *of the blood of all men.* Why? *I have not hesitated to proclaim to you the whole will of God* (compare v. 20 for the same verbs: hesitate, preach/proclaim). *Will of God (hē boulē tou theou)* combines the ideas of purpose and plan and often refers to the divine plan of salvation accomplished through the Messiah's suffering (2:23; 4:28; compare 13:36). Here Paul affirms that he held nothing back of the gospel revelation, especially those parts dealing with judgment. Do we preach the whole gospel, so when God calls us to another field we too can say with good conscience that we have told the people everything they need to know about the plan of salvation?

Gearing Up for Future Challenges (20:28-35) Paul prepares the elders for their future with charges to spiritual watchfulness over the flock (vv. 28-31) and physical aid to the weak (vv. 33-35), with a blessing in between, the word committing them *to God and to the word of his grace* (v. 32). Since Luke gives few specifics about church government, Episcopalians, Presbyterians and Congregationalists can all feel at home in this passage. But these charges do set forth values that should guide the exercise of leadership in the church. The intervening committal shows the true source of strength for doing the work.

Leadership exercised in spiritual watchfulness over a flock is first of all collegial. Christian elders are always referred to in the plural by Luke (11:30; 14:23; 15:2, 23; 20:17). In a day when individualism, monarchial authoritarianism or simple economic necessity turns the pastoral role into a "one-man show," we would do well to consider, no matter our polity, how we may promote teamwork in the pastoring of the local

copyists substituted the phrase "of the Lord." The misunderstanding may have actually arisen because copyists no longer recognized *his own* as a term of endearment referring to Christ (compare "my beloved": Gen 22:16; Rom 8:32). A better solution is to take the latter phrase to refer to Christ and retain the phrase "of God." Paul is charging the leaders to shepherd "the church of God which he bought with the blood of his own [Son]" (Metzger 1971:480-82).

flock.

Second, leadership must be spiritual: *the Holy Spirit has made you overseers*. The Holy Spirit, either through gifting that the church then recognized or by prophecy at the point of selection, appointed these persons as overseers (Polhill 1992:426-27; Barrett 1977:114; Acts 13:2-4; 1 Cor 12:7-11; 1 Tim 4:14). Their function is to be careful, pastoral and corrective (20:28, 31). They are to live out their "watchcare" of themselves and the congregation through shepherding and admonishing. As a shepherd protects, cares for and feeds the sheep, so through teaching and exhortation these presbyter-bishops are to nurture those in their charge (Eph 4:11-12; 1 Pet 5:1-3). Sometimes that teaching will be admonition *(noutheteō)*, the correction of the will that presupposes opposition (Rom 15:14; Col 1:28; 3:16).

Finally, in manner, this leadership will be serious, conscientious and intensely personal. This Paul communicates by describing the church's infinite worth and his own demeanor. The congregation is not the elders' church but *the church of God, which he bought with* "the blood of his own"—Jesus (Ps 74:2; Is 43:21). Paul constantly and *with tears* continued his ministry of admonition among them.

In our day there is a great emphasis on specialties in ministry—administrator, educator, counselor, church-growth strategist, social worker— roles not unlike the helping professions found in society at large. This passage can especially help us to recapture a coherent focus for leadership in local church ministry. As John Stott says, it will help us "rehabilitate the noble word 'pastors,' who are shepherds of Christ's sheep, called to tend, feed, and protect them" (Stott 1990:323).

Paul's charge has a sense of urgency because of future dangers. Syncretizing pagans and persecutors from outside will spiritually ravage the flock with the destructive force of wolves (Ezek 22:27; Mt 7:15; Lk 10:3). Within the church, heresy leading to schism will be the order of the day (note 1 Tim 4:1-3; 2 Tim 1:15; in Rev 2:1-7 there are reports of its

---

20:35 Many scholars have been impressed with alleged parallels to this saying in Greek literature (Plutarch *Moralia* 173D; 778C; Thucydides *History* 2.97.4). They have suggested that Jesus (Marshall 1980:336) or the Christian church (Krodel 1986:392) or Luke himself (Haenchen 1971:595) has taken and Christianized a Greek proverb. Thucydides has the form closest to this saying, but interestingly enough it describes the custom of Persian kings. Plutarch is quoting the Persian king Artaxerxes in *Moralia* 173D, Epicurus in *Moralia* 778C.

occurrence at Ephesus).

In the face of such threats, the elders and we might be tempted to ask, with Paul, "Who is equal to such a task?" (2 Cor 2:16). There is hope in Paul's blessing, which comes in the form of a committal (Acts 20:32). He commits *(paratithēmi)* the elders, puts them on deposit with *God and . . . the word of his grace* (14:23; compare Lk 23:46; 2 Tim 2:2). In the safekeeping of God and the gospel, they will not be destroyed but will grow spiritually (*which can build you up;* Acts 9:31). In fact, they will be empowered for perseverance all the way to heaven: *give you an inheritance with all those who are sanctified* (Lk 12:32; Acts 26:18; Eph 1:14, 5:5, 26; Deut 33:3-4).

More important than the leaders' commitment to their charge is God's faithfulness to his. For by it the leaders receive the ability to keep theirs.

Paul completes his exhortations to the elders with the charge to physically aid the weak. Using his own example and an otherwise unknown beatitude of the Lord, in a reverse parallelism he addresses both attitude and conduct concerning material things. The attitude is to say no to covetousness, as Paul among them did not desire *anyone's silver or gold or clothing* (precious metals, clothing and foodstuffs were the standard forms of wealth in ancient times; Josh 7:21; Mt 6:19; Jas 5:2). We must replace covetousness with liberality, knowing the truth of the Lord Jesus' declaration that the one whose disposition is "giving not receiving" (Mt 10:8) is blessed. Such an attitude will issue in a lifestyle of labor (*kopiaō,* "toil which wears you out"), not for personal gain but in order to have something to *help the weak,* those who are incapable of work (Eph 4:28). In Luke-Acts "the weak" are normally the chronically, physically ill who come to Jesus or the apostles for healing (Lk 4:40; 9:2; Acts 9:37; 19:12). Paul modeled such a lifestyle of giving when he supported himself and his party by practicing his leatherworking trade while with them (18:3; 19:9—Western text implies his labor).

Is Luke mandating a precise imitation of Paul in the matter of the

So where the form is close, the source is even more remote. We are not dealing here with an exclusively Greek proverb but a sentiment found in various contexts in the ancient world. It is better, then, to take the reverential way it is introduced as an indication that it indeed originated with the one to whom it is attributed, Jesus (Hemer 1989b:82-83; compare Lk 6:38).

source of financial support for full-time Christian workers? Does he view self-support as the duty of all Christian leaders (so Haenchen 1971:594)? If so, then all will need to be bivocational. But Scripture also teaches that it is legitimate for spiritual ministry to be supported financially (Lk 10:7; 1 Cor 9:11, 18; Gal 6:6; 1 Tim 5:17-18). This should qualify the extent of the application of Paul's practice to any spiritual leader's duty. Whether "tentmaker" or paid Christian worker, the one who is in line with Paul's charges and exercises leadership graciously, eagerly and humbly will manifest a kind of leadership that the world—with its concern with money, prestige and power—does not know but desperately needs to know (Lk 22:25-27; 1 Pet 5:1-3).

An Affectionate, Sorrowful Farewell (20:36-38) Paul now seals his farewell with prayer (compare Acts 1:24; 6:6; 13:3; 14:23). Falling on his knees, he acts out his total submission to the Lord (1 Chron 29:20; 2 Chron 6:13; Acts 21:5; Eph 3:14). The elders, in their affectionate devotion to Paul, join him in much weeping, just like the sound of mourning (Lk 7:13; 8:52; 23:28; compare Lk 6:21; Acts 21:13). They fall on Paul's neck and repeatedly kiss him. In ancient culture a parting kiss on cheek, forehead, shoulder or hand was a sign of grateful respect and love; erotic inclination was secondary (Lk 15:20; compare Gen 50:1; 1 Kings 19:20; 3 Macc 5:49). The emotion of the parting is especially heightened by the anguish of knowing they will not see Paul again. So they accompany him to the ship, possibly also supplying provisions for the journey (*propempō;* Rom 15:24).

Prayer for us too must be the natural way to seal the spiritual transaction of passing the torch to the leadership of the next generation. And when such business necessitates the departure of the previous leadership, prayer will bring out such filial emotion that it will be hard to tear ourselves away (Acts 21:1).

To Jerusalem—By Sea to Palestine (21:1-16)

Patrick Henry's rallying cry in the American Revolution, "Give me liberty or death!" captures the essence of the determination needed to pursue a goal no matter the cost. This Paul displays on his way to Jerusalem. Following in the steps of the Lord Jesus, Paul by his life sets the seal of authenticity on the gospel (Lk 9:22, 44, 51/Acts 20:22-24; 21:4,

10-11; compare Lk 18:31-34; Mt 16:23/Acts 21:4, 12; compare Lk 9:45). So far the only reason Luke has given us for Paul's willingness to embrace danger is his determination to complete "the task of testifying to the gospel of God's grace" (Acts 20:24).

Miletus to Tyre (21:1-6) Paul completes the Aegean/Asia Minor leg of his journey to Jerusalem by sailing south and east on successive days to the islands of Cos and Rhodes, probably stopping at the ports of the same name, then on to Patara. Patara was a major port of Lycia and a favorite haven for large vessels traveling from the eastern Mediterranean to the Aegean. Headquarters of the Roman governor of Lycia, it was celebrated for its oracle of Apollo. Romans would have been familiar with Cos as a health resort with a salubrious climate, hot ferrous and sulfurous springs, medical school, and sanctuary of Asclepius. Emperor Claudius, influenced by his own physician, Xenophon of Cos, had recently made the port a free city and conferred immunity from taxation (A.D. 53). Its own Cassius had plundered Rhodes (43 B.C.), which was now "little more than a beautiful city with a glorious past" (Couch 1988:183).

Paul and his party change ships at this point because (1) their sailors know only the Aegean, (2) the ship is a small coastal vessel unsuited for the four-hundred-mile trans-Mediterranean route to Phoenicia or (3) it is committed to taking the slower coastal route east (Lake and Cadbury 1979:265). Two-thirds of the way into their journey, Cyprus, the site of Paul's first missionary campaign (13:4-12), comes into view. They pass it and leave it behind, literally "on the port side." After a journey of five days (so Chrysostom *Homilies* 45) they arrive at Phoenicia, the seacoast of central Syria between Mount Carmel on the south and the Eleutherus River on the north. They put in at Tyre, a city built on an island with its port on the south side. An earthen mole constructed by Alexander the Great connected the city to the mainland, and subsequent action of the harbor waters had left a sandy beach.

Paul's party uncovers (compare Lk 2:16) the whereabouts of a church, probably founded by Hellenistic Jewish Christians scattered in the aftermath of Stephen's martyrdom (Acts 11:19; see the positive disposition of Tyrians to Jesus' ministry, Lk 6:17; 10:13-14). Paul may have previously visited this church at least twice (12:25; 15:3). Here the party stays a week, either during the unloading and loading of their vessel (Bruce

1990:440) or until they can find another ship (Haenchen 1971:600).

The fellowship Paul enjoys at many stops on his journey illustrates Barclay's maxim "The man who is in the family of the Church has friends all over the world" (1976:154). For Paul "the church has become a countercultural, global network of communities caring for their own subversive missionaries who are now traveling to and fro throughout the Empire" (Willimon 1988:159).

As Paul said happened in every city, the Holy Spirit predicts his coming suffering. This time the disciples conclude that the prediction is not just a warning but actually a prohibition. So Luke expresses it: *through the Spirit they urged* (literally, "were repeatedly saying") *Paul not to go on to Jerusalem* (compare 20:23). Since the same Spirit has compelled Paul to go to Jerusalem (19:21; 20:22), we would be confronted with a contradiction if the prediction were actually a prohibition, but such need not be the case (see note). Paul, then, is not disobedient to the Spirit by disregarding the prohibition. As with all the Spirit's predictive warnings, it is intended simply to stiffen his determination as he once again realistically counts the cost (20:22-24).

Sometimes the counsel of friends, filtered through the grid of their fears and concerns for our safety, can be misguidance. Like Paul, we must determine to "do the right thing" even when outward circumstances and projected outcome do not appear to be stamped with the blessing of God.

As the whole church, including women and children, escorts the party to the port via the beach, they kneel in a solemn prayer of committal reminiscent of the leavetaking at Miletus (20:36-38). The bonds of Christian fellowship forged in this short week are strong, and they cannot but help give strength to the apostle as he continues down the road to certain suffering. We too should never miss an opportunity, by fellowship and prayer, to strengthen the determination of fellow Christians as they face hard tests.

21:4 *Mē epibainein* is either a present prohibition, "cease going on" (Bruce 1990:439), or a negative purpose statement, "not to go" (Kistemaker 1990:747). Acts 20:18 supports the latter option.

That Acts 21:4 combines the Holy Spirit's prediction with the church's conclusion is allowed for by a use of *through (dia)*, which points to the occasion for the statement, not its efficient cause (Longenecker 1981:516); it is paralleled by Acts 20:22-23 (Stott 1990:333).

Tyre to Caesarea (21:7-14) The party makes a voyage of twenty-seven miles to Ptolemais, situated on a small promontory on the north side of a broad bay between it and the modern city of Haifa. The site of ancient Acco (Judg 1:31) and modern Acre, Ptolemais, a prosperous metropolis and Roman colony, had the best anchorage on that part of the central Syrian coast. Here during a one-day stopover Paul and his party *greeted the brothers* in a church probably planted at the same time as Tyre's (Acts 11:19).

Though they could proceed by road to Caesarea, skirting Mount Carmel (forty miles), probably they go the thirty-two miles by sea. Caesarea, with its magnificent harbor and city built by Herod the Great to serve as the port of Jerusalem, was also the Roman provincial capital of Judea. This is the third time Paul has passed through Caesarea (9:30; 18:22). *Philip the evangelist* and his *four unmarried* (literally, virgin) *daughters* host his group. Philip is identified according to function, if not office, not only to distinguish him from the apostle of the same name but probably also to bring to mind his chief work, the early evangelization of Samaria to the coast (8:4-40). This is one of the three occurrences in the New Testament of the title *evangelist* (Eph 4:11; 2 Tim 4:5). Our modern appropriation of the term may be too specialized, applied only to those gifted to proclaim the gospel to the unconverted. Pastors who like Timothy preach the Word must remember that they too do the work of an evangelist (2 Tim 4:2, 5). And evangelists must aim for pioneer crosscultural church planting, the missionary work of apostles. Philip's daughters with *the gift of prophecy* are a reminder that in fulfillment of Joel 2:28/Acts 2:17, without regard to gender, God is pouring out his Spirit in each spiritual generation of the time period called "the last days."

It is not Philip's daughters but Agabus (compare 11:27-28), come down from Judea—that is, Jewish territory—who in an acted prophecy offers another opportunity for Paul to renew his determination to go to

---

21:7 Though the main meaning of *dianyō* is "to complete" (so Bruce [1990:440] takes it here), another possible meaning is "to continue" (Bauer, Gingrich and Danker 1979:187), which the NIV chooses.

21:9 *Prophesied* (had the gift of prophecy) translates a participle *prophēteuousai,* "prophesying," which could point to the activity as well as the gift, though without its specific content.

Jerusalem. The action and word together communicate the effective and self-fulfilling word of God (Is 55:11; Bruce 1988:401; see Old Testament examples: 1 Kings 11:29-40; Jer 13:1-11). Agabus takes *Paul's belt*, probably a long strip of cloth which he would wrap around himself several times and in which he would fold money (Mt 10:9; *m. Šabbat* 10:3; *m. Berakot* 9:5). He binds himself hand and foot and says, *The Holy Spirit says, "In this way the Jews of Jerusalem will bind the owner of this belt and will hand him over to the Gentiles."*

Though neither of these actions is recorded, both are assumed in what Luke tells us of the Jews' treatment and the Romans' handling of Paul (21:30-33; 24:1-9; compare 28:17). We do not need to conclude, as many do, that based on Luke's report of the arrest, Agabus is mistaken. The prophecy's wording, especially *hand him over to the Gentiles,* parallels Jesus' predictions of his suffering (Lk 9:44; 18:32; 24:7). The theological significance is similar. It is neither the desire nor the just deserts of a righteous person to be given over to the power of enemies (Ps 26[27]:12; 40[41]:3; 73[74]:19; 117[118]:18; 139[140]:9). That is what God has determined as the fate for Israel in punishment for its sins (3 Kingdoms 8:46; 14:16; 2 Chron 25:20). So for this to be prophesied of Paul points to his innocence. As Peter will point out later, Christians are called upon to suffer for the right reason (1 Pet 4:15-16).

If anything divides Christians today, it is this question: Is the miraculous—signs and wonders, the gift of healing or prophecy—intended to continue beyond the apostolic age or the closing of the canon of Scripture? Some who answer in the affirmative with regard to prophecy use this passage to argue that New Testament prophecy is qualitatively different from the prophetic revelation reported in the Old Testament. They define it as simply "telling something that God has spontaneously brought to mind" and claim for it an authority less than Scripture's and even less than recognized Bible teaching (Grudem 1988:29-30). They reason that Paul disobeyed the prophecy of Acts 21:4; Agabus was wrong when his prophecy is compared with Acts 21:30-33; and the daughters of Philip may have prophesied, but as women they would not have been permitted to teach authoritatively (1 Tim 2:12).

We have already seen that these assessments of Acts 21:4 and Agabus's prophecy are not the preferred ones. The distinction between prophecy

and teaching and the implications for 1 Timothy 2:12 for Philip's daughters' ministry activity are well taken. Still, for Luke a New Testament prophet

is the Lord's instrument, one among several means by which Jesus leads his church. As one who makes known *(gnōstos)* the meaning of Scripture, exhorts and strengthens the congregation, and instructs the community by revelations of the future, the Christian prophet manifests in the power of the Spirit the character of his Lord, who is the Prophet of the end-time. (Ellis 1970:67)

This is the standard for defining and testing all alleged prophetic utterances in our day.

The prophecy triggers an interaction between Paul and his fellow believers, including members of his traveling band. With tender affection the believers *pleaded* (better, "were pleading," imperfect) *with Paul not to go up* (better as a present prohibition, "cease going up"; Bruce 1990:442) *to Jerusalem* (compare 20:37-38; 21:4). They want to preserve the beloved apostle from physical harm, possibly death, and so keep him for themselves and the church's mission.

Paul responds with unwavering determination as he seeks to help them sort out the will of God in this matter. In such a process he recognizes the effects of their emotions on him. They are *weeping* for him as the women did for Jesus on the way to the cross (Lk 23:28). They are *breaking [his] heart,* his resolve, as stone is pulverized. He reaches back for the rationale that guides his whole life: *for the name of the Lord Jesus.* The One under whom he serves (Acts 20:19, 24) and in whose name he preaches, heals and baptizes (9:27-28; 16:18; 18:15; 19:5) is the One for whose name he is willing to suffer, even die (9:16; compare Lk 21:12; Acts 5:41). He reaffirms his resolve: he is *ready . . . to be bound* (21:33) and, like the prophets and Jesus before him, *to die in Jerusalem* (Lk 13:33-34).

In devout resignation, unable to persuade him otherwise, they *gave up* (literally, "became quiet"; Lk 14:4; Acts 11:18), saying the only thing a Christian can say in such perplexing circumstances: *The Lord's will be done* (Lk 22:42).

We learn from Paul that suffering for the right reason, for the Lord's sake, is the key to a determination that correctly sorts out God's will.

From the Christians we are instructed positively and negatively. Negatively, we must ask ourselves, "Has our own fear of radical obedience ever prompted us to crush someone else's determination to do the Lord's will? Has tender affection ever been substituted for courageous love in wanting God's best for someone else?" (Ogilvie 1983:298). Positively, do we know when to cease striving with one another and in humility, recognizing our lack of definitive knowledge of God's plan for the other, start asking God to carry out his desire for their lives?

Caesarea to Jerusalem (21:15-16) Having prepared for the sixty-four-mile journey overland, and comforted by the presence of some from the Caesarean church, Paul *went up to Jerusalem* (compare Lk 18:31; 19:28). He is received by Mnason (an authentic Greek name, but possibly a Hellenization of Manasseh). Luke identifies him as a Cypriot Christian and *one of the early disciples*. He may have been among the original 120 or, at least, part of the converted Pentecost throng (Acts 1:15; 11:19-20). His Hellenistic Jewish Christian background makes him the ideal host for Paul's party of Jewish and Gentile Christians.

THE CHURCH IN ALL NATIONS: PAUL'S PALESTINIAN MINISTRY (21:17—26:32)

From the moment the military tribune handcuffs Paul in the court of the Gentiles, the apostle conducts his ministry as a prisoner awaiting final trial and verdict. This last quarter of Acts, parallel to the passion narrative of Luke's Gospel, provides a realistic and necessary balance to Luke's report, to this point, of the church's triumphant advance (Lk 24:26; Acts 14:22).

In this section Jewish opposition contrasts with Roman protection as Paul continues to witness with urgency and integrity. As a Roman tribune, two governors and a friendly local monarch inquire into Paul's case, Luke draws us in to ask the same questions and face the same answers about the truth of the gospel.

□ Paul at Jerusalem (21:17—23:35)

In the midst of some Jews' death-dealing intentions counterbalanced by Roman protective justice stands the Christian witness Paul. He shows that rare combination of loyalty to his ethnic traditions (that's what gets him

into trouble in the first place) and boldness to seize every opportunity to proclaim the universal gospel.

Promoting Harmony (21:17-26)

When a person becomes a Christian, what becomes of his or her religious past? Must all previous pious practice be left behind? Or may some be made fit patterns for the new life in Christ? A patient thinking through of Luke's teaching on the Christian, the Old Testament law and religious tradition, as modeled in Paul's conduct, will give us guidelines by which we can make judgments about our own religious past.

Joy over the Successful Gentile Mission (21:17-20) At the home of Mnason, Paul receives a "warm welcome" from fellow Christians. Since Luke does not specify that only like-minded Hellenistic Jewish Christians so greet Paul and his party, we should probably think of a delegation representative of the whole Jerusalem church. From them news of his coming would filter back to all segments of the church (v. 22). The next day there is a respectful reunion, an official reception by the chief elder, James, half-brother of Jesus, and the church's ruling elder board (see note at 15:13). James receives a solemn greeting from Paul, perhaps an embrace, a kiss and a verbal greeting such as "Hail!" "Peace be with you!" or "Grace and peace to you!" (Windisch 1964:500).

Then Paul offers a praiseworthy report. As at the Jerusalem Council, he *reported in detail* (idiomatically, "one item after another") *what God had done among the Gentiles through his ministry* (Acts 15:12, 14; also see 14:27; 20:24). Luke's phrasing reminds us that anything accomplished through a ministry from the Lord, for the Lord and in his name is, in the final analysis, accomplished by the Lord alone. This is a necessary reminder, for often we are so busy doing *our* demographics, planning *our* outreach strategies, preparing *our* people and materials for *our* next big advance for God that we forget that he must do the work. True ministry *for* him will always be ministry *by* him.

When the elders heard this, *they praised God* (*edoxazon,* "were glorifying"). Not unlike Jesus' "triumphal entry" into Jerusalem (Lk 19:37-38), Paul's arrival is surrounded by praise. Interestingly, after reporting the glorifying of God at Jesus' birth, for his teaching and especially his healing ministry, and at the way he died, Luke makes the salvation of the

Gentiles his crowning reason for praise (Acts 11:18; 13:48).

Indeed, if we bear the mark of grace we will respond in praise when we hear of saving grace coming to others. That grace will be especially evident when they are persons against whom we were formerly prejudiced because of race, class or culture. Praise for their salvation is the only proper starting point for building a framework of harmony within which all can deal properly with their religious past.

False Reports About Paul's Teaching (21:20-22) In full spiritual unity, the elders point out to Paul that massive numbers of *Jews, . . . all of them . . . zealous for the law,* have become believers. These may be the converted Pharisees of Acts 15:5. Literally "zealots for the law," they lived out their loyalty to God by combining ardent nationalism with strict observance of the whole Mosaic code. Phinehas, Elijah and the Maccabees were their worthy predecessors (Num 25:10-13; 1 Kings 19:10, 14; Josephus *Jewish Antiquities* 12.271).

These converts have been particularly troubled by reports that Paul has been teaching Diaspora Jews *to turn away from Moses.* This phrase translates *apostasia,* which refers to either political or spiritual rebellion (2 Chron 29:19; 1 Macc 2:15; Acts 5:31, 39; 2 Thess 2:3). Specifically, Paul is alleged to have instructed these Jewish believers to stop having their children circumcised and "to stop walking according to the customs" (so the prohibitions should be understood).

While it is easy to see how such implications might be drawn from Paul's teaching of a law-free gospel, there is no evidence that Paul ever instructed Jewish Christians this way (Rom 2:25-30; Gal 5:6; 6:15). In fact, Paul was most scrupulous not to offend the conscience of the "weaker brother," the Jewish Christian who maintained ancestral customs, and even went so far as to have Timothy circumcised (Acts 16:3; Rom 14:1—15:13).

21:20 *Many thousands of Jews have believed:* although the most commonly accepted estimate of Jerusalem's resident population is twenty-five to fifty-five thousand, there need be no hyperbole here if we conclude that *thousands* includes many visiting Christians who are in Jerusalem for the festival (Williams 1985:361; Bruce [1990:445] disagrees with including visitors in the number).

21:24, 26 *Join in their purification rites. . . . Paul . . . purified himself along with them:* we can clear up potential confusion concerning the nature of the purification Paul pursued if we understand that Paul, having contracted ritual uncleanness from his time abroad in

Our religious past can make distortions of the truth attractive to us, especially those that reinforce our pride in loyalty to our traditions. What can be done to overcome such falsehood, which always threatens to bring disunity to the church?

Conciliatory Respect of Ritual Observance (21:23-26) The church leaders counsel Paul to combat words with action. Four pious but indigent men in the congregation have taken on themselves a Nazirite vow of limited duration (Num 6). By abstaining from products of the vine, not cutting their hair and avoiding ritual impurity, they have been showing thankfulness for past blessings, earnestness in petition or strong devotion to God. The multianimal sacrifice and cleansing ceremony at the end of the vow period, when the hair is cut and offered to God, is financially prohibitive (6:13-20). Paul is asked to bear the expenses of the four. This was a commonly recognized act of piety (Josephus *Jewish Antiquities* 19.294). To do so he must go through a seven-day ritual cleansing himself, because he has recently returned from Gentile lands (*m. Oholot* 2:3; 17:5; 18:6; Num 19:12). The intended result is that the rumors about Paul will be shown to be baseless and he will be seen *living in obedience to the law*. Lest Paul's action be misunderstood in another direction, as making Jewish custom normative for Gentile Christians, the elders hasten to add that the Jerusalem Council decree is still in place (see discussion above at Acts 15:20, 29). It is repeated here in essential detail.

The next day Paul begins his own ritual purification and declares to temple authorities the date that the Nazirite vow, here called *the days of purification* (Num 6:5 LXX), would be completed through a sacrificial ceremony (*m. Nazir* 6:7).

What does the elders' counsel to Paul say about Luke's view of Christians and their religious past? Before we can draw general principles, we

---

Gentile lands (*m. Oholot* 2:3; 17:5; 18:6), must make himself ritually pure through a seven-day ceremony (Num 19:12) so that he will be in a position to accompany the four and pay the expenses for the sacrifices by which they will complete their Nazirite vow (Num 6:13-20; *m. Nazir* 6:7). Such an explanation is possible because the LXX (and subsequently Luke) uses purification terminology (*hagnizō, hagnismos*) to refer both to the process of removing ritual impurity (Num 19:12) and to undergoing a Nazirite vow (Num 6:3, 5). Luke's telescoped account, especially the phrases *hagnistheti syn autois* (Acts 21:24) and *syn autois*

must deal with unique and theologically significant factors concerning the Jewish law. At its core was divine revelation in three aspects: moral, civil and ceremonial. Surrounding that were oral tradition and rabbinic exposition. Luke's use of terminology often prevents us from easily distinguishing which aspects of the law he is referring to. Still, Luke's use of the term *customs* does seem to show he is aware of the difference between divine revelation and human tradition (15:1; 21:21; 26:3; 28:17). And there may be a distinction in Luke's thinking between the moral, ceremonial and civil aspects which will enable us to make decisions about normativeness based on content (Lk 10:25-28).

If we focus on the divine revelation component of a Jewish Christian's religious past, the Old Testament law, we can see Luke says it has no relevance for salvation (Acts 13:38-39; 15:10-11). While the moral aspect is universally normative (Lk 10:25-28; 18:18-23), Luke also sees a positive use for the ceremonial laws, to aid Jewish Christians in the expression of their piety. He does not make these laws binding on Gentiles, however. Only when Gentiles are in the company of Jewish Christians with scruples should they keep ceremonial ritual purity, and then not beyond what God mandated in the Old Testament for aliens living in Israel.

What guidelines does this incident yield for today? There is a large measure of freedom, but that freedom is to be used to promote (1) the advance of the gospel and (2) the unity of an ethnically diverse church. So long as our conscience is not bound by non-Christian traditions and practices and the Christian gospel is not syncretized with the thought behind non-Christian practice, our pre-Christian religious past, properly cleansed, may move into a transformed spiritual future.

---

hagnistheis (21:26), in which Paul's activity is closely associated with the four, has created the potential confusion.

21:24 There are at least three options for understanding the status of the ceremonial law in Luke's thinking. Jacob Jervell claims that Luke has a most conservative outlook: "by insisting on Jewish Christian universal adherence to the law, he succeeds in showing that they are the restored and true Israel entitled to God's promises and to salvation" (1972b:147). Stephen G. Wilson argues against Jervell and ends at a mediating position, saying that living according to the law has no bearing on achieving salvation for Jew or Gentile, but Luke views it in a wholly positive light as a means of expressing piety (1983:102; compare Downing 1986). Craig Blomberg claims that Luke understands the law only in a promise-and-fulfillment framework and that this passage does not speak to the issue of

Arrested in the Temple (21:27-36)

"Will we survive?" is the pressing question for Jews in every generation. Twentieth-century Jews in the shadow of Hitler's holocaust vow "Never again!" First-century Jews saw Paul's Gentile mission as equally a threat to their survival, for it effectively erased the line between Jew and Gentile within the people of God. The eternally decisive issue, however, is, Which "people of God" does God intend to survive?

Accusations That Stir Up a Crowd (21:27-29) Toward the end of the seven-day purification process (Num 19:12)—probably the seventh day, when he will receive the "water of atonement"—Paul is in the temple. Jews from Asia see him there—to them this is an unusual sight (*theaomai;* compare Acts 1:11; 22:9). From the time of his witness in the Ephesian synagogue, Paul has faced constant opposition from Asian Jews, and now, under cover of a Pentecost pilgrimage, they have dogged his steps to Jerusalem (19:9; 20:19; compare 6:9; 20:29). *They stirred up the whole crowd,* so that a mob scene ensues (19:32). Paul is *seized* by his persecutors as they broadcast the charges against him (compare Lk 21:12; Acts 4:3; 5:18; 12:1).

Agitation, confusion and physical violence are the hallmarks of persecution. For the disciple of Christ they are neither a surprise nor beyond God's providential control and saving purposes (Lk 21:15, 18).

Whereas the Gentiles of Macedonia asked for help in hearing the message of salvation, the Jews of Jerusalem request help for destroying the messenger (Acts 16:9). The Asian Jews raise a general charge against Paul's teaching: it opposes *our people [laos] and our law and this place,* that is, the temple (compare 6:11, 13-14; 24:5-6; contrast Paul's understanding of his stance toward Judaism, 24:14-16). Acts does not record

---

lawkeeping at all (1984:67-68; compare Bruce [1990:447], who says that from Paul's perspective ceremonial regulations are *adiaphora*). When we view Luke's work as a whole, Wilson's position is probably the most accurate rendering of Luke's approach, though freedom in matters of ethnic practice may be more of a factor for Luke.

21:26 Would the Paul of the epistles compromise his stand for a law-free gospel by following James's counsel in verse 24? This question of authenticity may be answered by pointing to another of Paul's qualities: cultural flexibility (1 Cor 9:19-23; Marshall 1980:346). There is no final inconsistency here.

The Greek phrasing here does not indicate, as Marshall (1980:347) contends, that the date of the Nazirite vow's completion and Paul's ritual cleansing coincided (Bruce 1990:448).

Paul's views on the temple (but compare 7:48-50 and 17:24). He does say the law is unable to free from sin or bring forgiveness (13:39). Paul does not teach against *the people*. Rather, the Jews who oppose Paul and his gospel—the good news of the fulfillment of the promises made to their forebears—reveal by their opposition that they are not part of the true people of God. So it is with any opposition to the gospel. It is a revelation of the persecutor's error, not a valid judgment against the message.

The specific charge is that Paul has brought Greeks into the temple and thus defiled it. The Asian Jews have seen the Asian Trophimus in Paul's company (Trophimus is part of the delegation bringing the collection—20:4; 2 Tim 4:20). They *assumed,* wrongly (compare 14:19; 17:29), that this apostle whose preaching so effectively has torn down barriers between Jews and Gentiles would not hesitate to take a Gentile beyond the court of the Gentiles into the court of women, even the court of Israel.

Though Gentiles were welcome to worship in the outermost court, they were forbidden on penalty of death to enter beyond the balustrade into the two inner courts (*m. Kelim* 1:8). Josephus informs us, and archaeological evidence confirms, that at intervals there were signs posted in Greek and Latin saying "No foreigner is to enter within the forecourt and the balustrade around the Sanctuary. Whoever is caught will have himself to blame for his subsequent death" (Segal 1989:79; Polhill [1992:452] has information on the present location of such an inscription; Josephus *Jewish Wars* 5.193). This prohibition enforced Numbers 3:38.

It is ironic indeed that Paul is arrested while doing the very opposite of what he is accused of. In the process of seeking to show his respect for Jewish ethnic identity within the church by practicing ritual purification, he is arrested for allegedly defiling the temple. All this occurs because Paul is committed at one and the same time to the unity of all through their identity in Christ, no matter racial and ethnic background, and to the respect of cultural diversity in the body of Christ. Any Christian

---

21:30, 32 Those who view the crowd's reaction as the irregular action of a lynch mob

who insists on standing in such a tension will probably be similarly misunderstood as both too free in associations and too strict in ethnic loyalties.

Apprehension That Shakes a City (21:30) Luke graphically takes us from the panoramic view of a whole city *aroused* (*kineō;* literally, "moved, shaken"), to the people *(laos)* becoming a mob (*syndromē tou laou;* compare v. 36), to the man at the vortex: Paul *seized* (18:17) and *dragged* (16:19) out of the temple's sacred courts to the court of the Gentiles. *And immediately the gates were shut.*

In these few brief details of the Jerusalem Jews' final rejection of the Christian gospel, we see the last major spiritual and geographical turning point in Acts. Never again will Paul return to Jerusalem for worship or witness. By shutting out the messenger and the message of salvation, Paul's opponents have sealed the city's doom (Lk 13:34-35; 21:6, 20). Israel's ethnic pride, which constantly fueled its determination to survive, prevented it from fulfilling its divinely intended mission as "a light for the Gentiles" (Is 49:6). It robbed the temple of the universal glory God planned for it as "a house of prayer for all nations" (Is 56:7; compare Lk 19:46). May every "people of God" (church) in every nation and culture heed Jerusalem's negative example, lest it too find itself under God's judgment for failing to reach out with the gospel to those beyond its own kind.

When we understand the Jewish view of Paul's alleged crime, we will know the mortal danger he was in as the temple police proceeded to beat him. As implied by the wording of the last phrase of the inscription—"whoever is caught will have himself to blame for his subsequent death"—the penalty for defiling the temple sanctuary was summary execution, "death at the hands of heaven." This applied as much to a Jew who brought a defiling person into the sanctuary as to the unclean person himself (*b. 'Erubin* 104b). No trial was required. The charge alone was sufficient to warrant being delivered into the hands of the temple police, dragged into the outer court, the court of the Gentiles, and beaten to death (for example, having one's brain split open with

---

(Bruce 1990:451; E. F. Harrison 1986:351) do not take the Jewish background sufficiently into account.

clubs—*m. Sanhedrin* 9:6; Philo *Legatio ad Gaium* 212). The Romans normally did not interfere with such executions (Josephus *Jewish Wars* 6.124-26). Such summary justice was demanded not only by the nature of the crime but by its consequences. The Jews believed the temple remained profaned until the trespasser had been executed by the priestly authorities on behalf of God. This background not only explains the bloodthirsty reaction of the crowd now and as they interrupt Paul's speech but also supplies an understandable motive for the curse vow of those who subsequently conspire to murder him (21:36; 22:22-23; 23:12). If the commander of the Roman garrison had not arrived, Paul would have been beaten to death.

An Arrest That Saves the Apostle (21:31-36) Adjacent to the temple area, at the juncture of the western and northern porticoes that formed the outer boundary of the court of the Gentiles, was the Antonia fortress. It was headquarters of the Roman garrison stationed at Jerusalem. Herod the Great reinforced it for the safety and protection of the temple and named it for Antony. This spacious sixty-foot-high building had the general appearance of a tower; turrets stood at its four corners, the one on the southeast being 105 feet high. From it Roman soldiers commanded a view of the whole temple area. Stairways into the northern and western porticoes gave direct access to the court of the Gentiles (see Josephus *Jewish Wars* 5.192, 238-247; *Jewish Antiquities* 15.409). A cohort stationed in Jerusalem had, at least on paper, 760 infantry with 240 cavalry (Lake and Cadbury 1979:275). During festival times they would be on guard at the porticoes of the outer court, alert to any signs of insurrection (Josephus *Jewish Wars* 5.244). The decade and a half before the outbreak of the Jewish war against Rome was marked by constant disturbances against the Roman political order (Josephus *Jewish Antiquities* 20.160-72; *Jewish Wars* 2.254-65).

It is not surprising, then, that when the commander of the garrison heard *that the whole city of Jerusalem was in an uproar,* he himself, with some centurions and soldiers, *ran down* the steps of the fortress into the court of the Gentiles to restore order. The commander's arrest

---

21:33 To be *bound with two chains* meant to be handcuffed to two soldiers. This was

(which was a rescue), his interrogation of the crowd (though unsuccessful) and his removal of Paul to the barracks, away from the crowd's murderous intent, all model what Luke sees as the state's proper role toward the Christian. The state's order must protect Christians against anarchic persecution. State justice must be exercised based on getting at the truth based on the facts (22:24, 30). By affirming these values through his positive portrayal of Roman military officials, Luke certainly gained a hearing among his Roman audience, whom he would encourage to follow the same example by getting at the facts of the gospel (Lk 1:4).

By contrast, the Jews are thoroughly discredited, for all they want is to do away with the gospel messenger (Lk 23:18; Acts 21:36; 22:22). When ethnic survival in this life is the highest priority, one is bound to miss salvation for eternity (9:23-26).

Defense Before the Mob (Acts 21:37—22:21)

What's a Jewish Christian to do? He feels very comfortable in his new faith with its Old Testament roots. At the same time this faith has radically transformed him into a "world Christian." He is now at home in the ethnically diverse body of Christ. Misunderstandings, even opposition, are bound to arise. How do you explain that following a universal gospel does not mean surrendering one's Jewishness, especially one's piety? In Paul's defense he declares that the risen Christ is the key.

Correcting Wrong Thinking (21:37-40) At the top of the stairs, just as the Roman soldiers are about to take Paul into the Antonia fortress barracks, away from the tumult of the pursuing mob, the apostle asks permission to speak with the commander. Paul's polite and polished Greek catches the tribune off guard; he replies, *Do you speak Greek?* He had expected the cause of such a disturbance to be a Jew of rough character and no education. Now he tries to place him among foreigners who were potential troublemakers. Is he that *Egyptian* false prophet who, some four to five years earlier (A.D. 54), had raised up a large following, *four thousand terrorists,* taken them *into the desert* and re-

---

not proper for a Roman citizen (see comment at 22:29) and seemed to be something of a badge of suffering for Paul (26:29; 28:20).

turned to the Mount of Olives? From there, he had promised his band, he would command the walls of Jerusalem to fall flat. The Roman garrison would then be an easy conquest, and the Egyptian could be installed as ruler (Josephus *Jewish Wars* 2.261-63; *Jewish Antiquities* 20.169-72). Governor Felix's troops, however, took preemptive action, slaying four hundred, taking two hundred prisoner and scattering the rest, including the Egyptian. Has he now returned to Jerusalem, and is the populace venting its anger on him for the failed revolt and its aftermath?

Paul answers that he is *a Jew,* not a foreign false prophet. This also explains why he is in the temple. He is *citizen* of *Tarsus in Cilicia,* not an Egyptian; a person with civic status, not a disenfranchised revolutionary. Tarsus of Cilicia, southeastern Asia Minor, was ten miles from the Mediterranean Sea on the Cydnus River, population 500,000 at the height of its prominence. It was of strategic importance, for it commanded the Cilician Gates, a pass through the Taurus Mountains which led to the central Asia Minor plateau and trade routes to the west. It was not an idle boast to call it *no ordinary city.* From the early days of the Empire, the life of Tarsus had been closely intertwined with that of the highest levels of Rome. Julius Caesar visited the city in 47 B.C., and Antony granted it the status of a free city in 42 B.C. Augustus sent Athendorus, his former tutor, a Stoic philosopher, back to his native Tarsus to reestablish just administration. Nestor, tutor to Marcellus, Augustus's intended heir, continued the Rome-decreed line of "philosopher-governors." The people of this university town had a zeal for learning and philosophy beyond that of Athens and Alexandria, though it did not attract as many students as the latter centers. Tarsians were known for finishing their schooling abroad and finally settling in Rome or elsewhere (Hemer 1988).

What Theophilus and we should learn from this interchange is not to

---

21:40; 22:2 William LaSor (1979a:233) argues convincingly that though Aramaic was more commonly understood than Hebrew, the Dead Sea Scrolls demonstrate that Hebrew was more widely known among the masses in the first century than scholars usually assume. These references to the "Hebrew language" may indicate an exception to Paul's normal practice of speaking in Greek or Aramaic. Using Hebrew attracted attention and demonstrated his loyalty to his Jewish roots.

22:1-22 Haenchen (1971:628-29) contends that Paul does not address the issue of temple defilement or the other general charges, and that he climaxes his speech with a reference

confuse the gospel's liberation with political revolution. The Lord Jesus and his kingdom present a more radical challenge than that.

Paul asks and receives permission to speak to the crowd. His courage and determination are at once remarkable and readily understandable. What would cause him to want to address a crowd that had slandered him, given him an executioner's beating and, only minutes before, so violently rushed on him and called for his death that Roman soldiers had to physically pick him up so they could make a hasty exit? It is a total commitment to his Lord and his calling (20:23-24; compare Lk 21:13). This perspective gives the gospel its integrity. It's a stance we must all adopt.

With the stairs as his platform and the crowd below as his ready-made congregation, *Paul stood . . . and motioned to the crowd* with his hand (Acts 12:17; 13:16; 19:33). Miraculously, they become silent. Here is not simply the force of personality or even of a courageous character. Here the power of God is at work to gain a hearing for the battered, arrested, faithful apostle. Paul addresses the people *in Aramaic* (better, as the NIV margin states, *in Hebrew—tē Hebraídi dialektō,* literally, "in the Hebrew language"; see notes).

Exordium and Narratio: Declaring Paul's Jewish Piety (22:1-3)

Paul's address, *Brothers and fathers,* together with his use of Hebrew, is a proper and effective exordium or opening. He shows respect to the dignitaries, priests and Sanhedrin, the older members in the crowd. He identifies with his audience in the use of their sacred language. They quiet down and listen.

Paul's brief narratio, a statement of the facts adapted to persuade his listeners that the charges are groundless, follows the common ancient pattern for describing one's formative years: birth, rearing, education. He is *a Jew, born in Tarsus of Cilicia.* Hence he is not against the Jewish people. He was *brought up in* Jerusalem. One can hardly expect the son

---

to the Gentile mission. He sees this as evidence that the speech's true setting is Luke's own community's struggle with the relation of Christianity to Judaism, especially the Gentile mission. Using the tools of rhetorical analysis, however, we can see that the heart of Paul's answer is verse 3, the narratio, his statement of the facts (Long 1983:104). These do directly speak to the charges (21:28). In fact, the reference to a divinely ordained Gentile mission is not irrelevant either, for it is really the underlying occasion and cause for the assumption that Paul had defiled the temple by bringing in a Gentile.

of Diaspora Jews, returned to Jerusalem for his formative years, to be against the temple. *Under* (literally, "at the feet of") *Gamaliel* Paul was *trained* "according to the strictness of the law of the fathers." How could one who had allowed himself to "be dusted by the dust" of such an eminent scholar's feet now teach against the law (*Pirqe 'Abot* 1:4; see comment at Acts 5:34)? Would one who is *as zealous for God* (see comment at 21:21) as any in the crowd bring a Gentile into the temple's sacred courts and defile them? Paul prizes his Jewish heritage, and so should every Jewish Christian. Such loyalty will get Theophilus's attention.

Probatio—Proof One (22:4-5) Paul's probatio (body of proof section) offers four scenes from his conversion and its aftermath. They provide evidence, substantiated by witnesses, that his life of Jewish piety and his calling to preach the universal gospel are compatible.

Scene one portrays Paul as the persecutor of the followers of the way. The extent of his persecution (*women* as well as *men*) and the outcome (sometimes *death*—7:58; 8:1; 26:10) proved Paul's zeal for the Jewish God (Phil 3:6). They were also a silent witness to his sin and rebellion against God. Luke consistently portrays sinful ethnic Israel as the persecutors and murderers of God's true apostles and prophets (Lk 11:49; Acts 7:52; compare Lk 21:12). Paul never recovered from the shame of what had been for him a badge of honor (1 Cor 15:9; 1 Tim 1:13-15).

In the larger context of Acts this is the second of three times that Paul's conversion experience is related (9:1-19; 26:12-18). Though other events like Cornelius's conversion are repeated to stress their importance, Paul's conversion has supreme significance, for it has the "longest run on stage," bracketing Paul's ministry and his suffering witness. For Luke, Paul's personal history as testimony becomes a model for the conversion of Jew and Gentile alike. Here it challenges and gives hope that other Jews can turn from their ethnocentric blindness to the light of a liberating universal gospel. Any defense speech by Paul, then, must always be viewed as an example of Paul going on the offensive with a witness to the gospel's saving message.

Drawing on rhetorical handbooks' instructions on the forensic defense speech (the apology), Jerome Neyrey (1984) and William Long (1983) explain the flow of this speech. It must move from an exordium, in which the speaker presents himself in such a way that the audience becomes docile and attentive, to a narratio, where the basic facts of the case are so stated that the audience will be persuaded to the speaker's view. Next comes the body of the apology, the probatio (the proof), where evidence is marshaled to prove arguments presented on behalf of the speaker's view. The refutatio and peroratio elements do not seem to appear in Paul's speeches.

Fred Veltman (1978:252) presents a more general structure for a defense speech, taken

At this point Paul simply wants his audience to know his zeal, and he appeals to the records or the memory of high priest and Sanhedrin as testimony to the fact. One of the most exasperating things about self-righteous rebellion against God is that it can appear in the guise of zeal for God.

Probatio—Proof Two (Acts 22:6-11) Scene two, the risen Lord's encounter with Paul on the Damascus Road, places under judgment his life of persecuting believers out of zeal for God. Luke highlights the overpowering nature of the divine encounter by noting that in the brightness of the midday sun a divine light *flashed* around Paul. Blinding at noontime and being cast to the ground picture the spiritual judgment under which Paul found himself (Is 25:12; 26:5; 29:4). Jesus' haunting question *Saul! Saul! Why do you persecute me?* reveals that *Jesus of Nazareth,* in his resurrection power, is the key for distinguishing between proper and misguided zeal for God. And it is the same today for Jew and Gentile alike. Jesus is the litmus test. Any zeal for God that turns a person against the followers of Jesus is misguided.

Paul makes sure that this supernatural event can serve as a sign and undeniable proof in his probatio by describing the experience of corroborating witnesses, his companions. Paul's encounter with Christ was objective yet personal. His companions saw the *light* surrounding Paul but not the risen Lord who appeared to him (Acts 22:9, 14; 9:7). They

---

from his study of the form in ancient histories. It is useful for understanding the speech in its context.

22:3 The NIV makes two interpretational choices that, while individually permissible, when taken together do not account for all the elements of the Greek syntax. If *kata akribeian* is taken as an adverbial modifier of *pepaideumenos,* yielding the phrase *thoroughly trained* (NIV), then the genitive phrase "of the law of our fathers" must be related to the subsequent verb "to be zealous." If not, the genitives are left dangling in the Greek syntax. It is better to translate the whole as a prepositional phrase with genitival modifiers modifying "train"—that is, "having been trained according to strictness of the law of our fathers."

22:9 What the companions did or did not hear of the voice from heaven is not at odds with the account in Acts 9 (v. 7). A. T. Robertson (1934:506) explains how aspects of the range of meaning of *akouō*—"hear, understand"—can be indicated by objects in the genitive and accusative. This leads to the proper harmonization of 9:7, "they heard a voice" (genitive), and 22:9, "they did not understand the voice" (accusative).

22:11 Is the cause of blindness natural or supernatural (compare 9:18)? There is no necessary contradiction of the two presentations of Paul's blinding, for God can use secondary means to accomplish his ends.

heard a *voice* addressing Paul but were not privy to its message (9:7; 22:9).

Paul's enlightenment concerning his guilt led to enlistment in Christ's cause. Neither as a good Jew responding to divine revelation (contra Longenecker 1981:525) nor as one simply stupefied, realizing he must change (contra Marshall 1980:355), but like the Pentecost crowd, realizing it was under judgment, Paul asked, *What shall I do, Lord?* (2:37). The Lord did not answer directly but called for trust and allegiance as he directed Paul to the city. Paul's blindness was another sign that something supernatural had indeed happened to him on the Damascus Road. Luke's phrasing, *brilliance of the light* (*doxa tou phōtos,* "glory of the light") leaves little doubt in the reader's mind that this is the splendor of the exalted Lord Jesus appearing from heaven (Lk 24:26; 21:27; also see 9:26, 31-32; 2:9; Acts 7:2, 55).

Probatio—Proof Three (22:12-16) Scene three, in Damascus, expounds, possibly by reverse parallelism, the meaning of Paul's conversion in terms of divine and human initiative (vv. 13, 16) and relates his calling to preach the universal gospel (vv. 14-15). Paul's witness to all this was Ananias, whose piety according to the law was attested by all the Jews of Damascus. He embodies the continuity and discontinuity of Jewish Christianity, for the man of such renowned piety was also the Lord's instrument and mouthpiece for equipping Paul in the first steps of his newfound faith and mission.

The acted parable of the Lord's saving work, moving from blindness to sight, was completed as Ananias *stood beside* Paul *and said, "Brother Saul, receive your sight!"* (*anablepō,* "to see again" or "to look up"; when Luke describes the restoration he uses the same verb with Ananias as the object, so that possibly both meanings are meant here—Paul saw again as he looked up at Ananias). The key role Ananias played in Paul's conversion demonstrates to the audience that being a pious Jew and being a Christian convert are not necessarily mutually exclusive.

As Ananias interpreted to Paul his calling on the Damascus Road, the

_____

22:15 The NIV does not translate the *boti* that begins this verse and may point to a causal connection with what precedes or introduce a substantival clause giving us the content of the voice in verse 14 (Lake and Cadbury 1979:281).

22:16 *Be baptized (baptisai)* is an aorist causative middle that means, literally, "have

continuity was emphasized. It was *the God of our fathers* who had appointed him (3:13; 5:30; 7:32; Ex 3:13). God had chosen Paul to *know his will.* From the Damascus Road encounter Paul had the haunting realization that his persecution had been actually directed at Jesus of Nazareth, the risen and exalted Messiah. From this he knew that God's will must have something to do with his saving purposes and their implementation through the gathering of a body of believers called followers of the Way. But God had chosen Paul for more. He was privileged like the other apostles, though "as one abnormally born" (1 Cor 15:7-8), to see the risen Lord (Acts 1:22; 2:32; 3:15; 4:33).

Ananias used the messianic title *the Righteous One* (Jer 23:5-6; 33:15; Zech 9:9; Acts 3:14; 7:52). This points to the heart of the gospel: the risen, exalted Jesus of Nazareth, whom Paul sees, is the vindicated victim of an innocent death. And Paul was destined to hear from the voice of *his mouth* the gospel message, to which he was called to bear lifelong witness. This full-orbed revelation of the gospel would both fulfill and supersede the document of promise, the law.

Paul's responsibility was to be Christ's *witness to all men of what [he had] seen and heard* (Lk 24:46-48; Acts 1:8; 9:15). The universal scope of the gospel's offer of salvation is stated in general terms here. In the end it will prove to be the stumbling block to those who hear this speech (22:21-22). Note how much of the gospel message (Lk 24:46-48) is stated or implied in Acts 22:7-10, 14. Ananias rightly contended that Paul's gospel was revealed to him from heaven (compare 26:14-18; Rom 10:9-10; 1 Cor 15:1-4; Gal 1:12, 15-16).

Either as a mild rebuke (so the NIV) or possibly as a simple question (Marshall 1980:357), Ananias completed his mission by encouraging Paul in the next step: fulfilling his responsibility in response to his conversion. He was to "get himself baptized," picturing in that outward purification the inward cleansing from his sins that had resulted from his calling on the name of the Lord for salvation (Acts 2:38, 21; 9:14, 21).

Paul is a model for all those who become disciples in answer to the

yourself baptized." Since regeneration, though accomplished in the individual, is not exclusively an individual matter (1 Cor 12:13), Acts never presents baptism as self-administered (Acts 2:38, 41; 8:36, 38; 9:18; 16:15, 33). The NIV preserves this truth here by rendering the command in the passive.

call of those who are fulfilling their Lord's commission (Mt 28:18-20). For identification with the church through public profession of faith and baptism is not only a matter of obedience, it is a matter of spiritual health, now and in eternity (Lk 12:8). We need the outward sign of our salvation applied to us like a stake in the ground.

Probatio—Proof Four (22:17-21) In the last scene Paul himself models the tension of continuity and discontinuity in a Jewish Christian's life. He remained loyal to the Lord's holy place, exercising piety in worship in the temple upon his return to Jerusalem. Even after conversion, then, he practiced a piety that gave the lie to the recent charges that he taught against the temple and cavalierly defiled it by bringing Gentiles into its sacred precincts.

During worship, in a trance, Paul saw Jesus, the Lord of the temple (Lk 19:45-48; compare 2:46-49). The Lord directed him, *Leave Jerusalem immediately, because they will not accept your testimony about me.* This heavenly command and rationale declared the scandalous proposition that the risen and exalted Messiah would direct his messengers of salvation tidings away from Israel. Its rationale was an indictment of Israel's unwillingness to receive the gospel.

Paul showed his zeal for the people by remonstrating with the Lord. Surely his life as a persecutor and his service as an accomplice to Stephen's death would be enough evidence of his Jewish loyalty and would gain him a hearing (7:58; 8:1, 3; 9:2; 22:4). The Lord did not argue with Paul. He had already given his rationale: Israel did not oppose the messenger but the message, *your testimony about me.* All that remained was for the Lord to repeat the command and for Paul to obey. *Go; I will send you far away to the Gentiles* (2:39; 13:46; Eph 2:13, 17). The Gentile mission was the focus of Paul's ministry, yet always within a "to the Jew

---

22:17 Paul's presence in the temple does not contradict his claims that he was not personally known to the Judean churches (Gal 1:22). Both can be true.

22:18 The speech gives a supernatural reason for Paul's departure from Jerusalem, while earlier Luke tells only us of a human one (Acts 9:29-30). These are not mutually exclusive causal factors. Bruce observes that this is not the only place in the narrative where divine direction and human action coincide (1988:419).

22:20 The NIV margin *witness* gives the literal meaning of *martys.* The text *martyr* gives a transliteration of the term, which has come into the English language with the meaning "a Christian who under persecution gives his or her life for the faith." Stephen was the first recorded example, and the use of the term in the phrase *tou martyros sou* (your witness)

first" strategy (Acts 9:15; 13:46; 14:27; 15:3, 12; 21:19).

In the divinely commanded mission to the Gentiles and the Jewish people's refusal to accept the gospel we have the explanation of the Jews' opposition to Paul. The charges are false, but the opposition is real. Should our Lord's directive to Paul become a paradigm for church-growth strategy today—for example, "hold resistant fields lightly; concentrate harvesters where the response is greatest"? The Jewish people's unique position in relation to the Gentiles in salvation history (Rom 11:25-26) prevents us from extrapolating principles about responsiveness and concentration of forces. The momentum, however, always seems to be toward the frontiers, toward those who have never heard the gospel.

Conversation with a Roman Tribune; Defense Before the Sanhedrin (22:22—23:11)

When people react to gospel preaching, they are either glad or mad. Luke wants Theophilus, his contemporaries and us to see this again as he presents the various reactions to Paul and his witness. In the process we will learn the two aspects of Paul's gospel that excite Jewish opposition: the offer of salvation to Gentiles, on the same basis as Jews, and the resurrection of the body.

Ethnic Combativeness (22:22-23) That a supposed heavenly vision in the temple would send Paul *to the Gentiles* was an unthinkable, blasphemous notion. The crowd reacted to this "red flag" vocally, even turbulently. Raising their voices to drown Paul out, they took up again their cry "Away with him!" (21:36; Lk 23:18). Their reason: the proclaimer of such apostasy is *not fit to live!* Screaming excitedly, *throwing off* (better shaking out) *their cloaks and flinging dust into the air,* the crowd

---

may be an instance in Greek of this new meaning.

22:23 Throwing or waving cloaks and throwing dust in the air may express (1) excitement, especially anger (2 Sam 16:13; Cadbury 1979a:275), (2) severe displeasure as one tears one's clothes and adopts the position of one under the curse that will come to a blasphemer (Job 2:12; Acts 14:14; the difficulty with this interpretation is that *hriptō* does not mean "to tear"), (3) preparation for stoning, with dust as a symbolic substitute (7:58), or (4) separation from Paul, treating him as one would an unclean Gentile, as indeed the pious Jew shook out his clothes when he returned from Gentile lands (compare Acts 13:51; 18:6). This last option seems to most fully convey the kind of revulsion the mob would want to express against Paul's Gentile mission.

shows that they want to have nothing to do with Paul. To them he is as repulsive as an unclean Gentile.

The Jews show themselves to be unfit evaluators of Christianity. Their ethnic pride and prejudice are a warning to us all. We have our own "red flags" that cause the same paralysis of mind and hearing. They put an immediate stop to reason and substitute a blind, violent mob spirit or a granitelike imperviousness to gospel truth (Ogilvie 1983:311).

Governmental Curiosity (22:24-29) The tribune has to determine why the people were shouting against Paul (21:34). He decides to interrogate the apostle, using torture to bring out the truth. The NIV rendering *flogged and questioned* leaves the impression that the flogging is a separate punishment, not an instrument of interrogation (the literal phrase is "interrogate with lashes"). Though Paul had been beaten five times by the Jews and felt the Roman lictors' rods three times, this flogging would eclipse all these in its severity and potential for permanent physical damage, even immediate death (Acts 16:22-23; 2 Cor 11:24-25). In flogging, a whip of thongs studded with pieces of bone or metal, attached to a wooden handle, was applied repeatedly to the back of a person positioned on the floor, at a pillar or suspended from the ceiling. He was stretched out with bound arms secured so he could not deflect the blows.

As the soldiers are stretching their prisoner out with thongs about his wrists to secure him for the scourging, he asks a question that transforms him from victim to master of the situation. *Is it legal for you to flog a Roman citizen who hasn't even been found guilty?* Though from the Augustan age the Lex Julia contained an absolute prohibition on binding or beating a Roman citizen, Paul's qualified statement accords with later practice (Sherwin-White 1963:72-73; compare Acts 16:37). The centurion is dismayed and immediately reports Paul's Roman citizenship to the tribune. The tribune verifies it by a simple question to Paul, which the apostle answers in the affirmative. To wrongly claim Roman citizenship was a serious, even capital offense (Suetonius *Claudius* 25.3; Epictetus

---

22:28 Though Adrian Sherwin-White (1963:151) rightly cautions about the fruitlessness of speculating about where, when and how Paul's family acquired citizenship, the best guess is that they received it for valued services rendered to a Roman administrator or general (perhaps Pompey) either in the Gischala region of northern Palestine or at Tarsus (Longe-

Discourses 3.24.41). Because most citizens did not travel far from their hometown, they did not normally carry with them proof of citizenship. But a traveler such as Paul may have carried with him a copy of his birth registration (Sherwin-White 1963:148-49). Paul's bearing and his previous cultivated interaction with the commander, in which he had revealed his Tarsian citizenship (21:39), may be enough to assure the commander that he is telling the truth.

The tribune responds, possibly sarcastically, *I had to pay a big price for my citizenship*. He is referring to the bribes he paid to intermediaries in the imperial secretariat or provincial administration to ensure that his name would appear on the list of candidates for enfranchisement. Given his name, Claudius Lycias, he had probably received his citizenship recently, during the reign of Emperor Claudius, his benefactor, whose name he took as his *nomen*. He may have worked his way up through the ranks and moved from centurion to tribune rank.

Paul responds simply, *But I was born a citizen*. Paul is at least the tribune's social equal, if not his slight superior by longevity of Roman citizenship in his family.

The declaration of citizenship has its desired effect: the military interrogators *withdrew immediately*. Paul, though still a prisoner, will be viewed differently from now on. In fact, alarm or fear grips the tribune as he realizes that he violated one of the basic rights of a Roman citizen when he *put Paul . . . in chains* (21:33). As the Roman orator Cicero exclaimed, "To bind a Roman is a crime, to flog him is an abomination, to slay him is almost an act of murder" (*Against Verres* 2.5.66).

Paul's use of his Roman citizenship teaches us that as an expression of God's moral order, and when the laws governing its exercise of power are just, the state may be appealed to for protection of the physical well-being of law-abiding citizens. The Christian's appeal must always be in the interest of the advance of the gospel.

Though at this point the tribune is no closer to knowing why Paul

---

necker 1981:528).

22:29 There is no contradiction between the commander's alarm at having chained Paul and his supposed waiting until the next day to release him from them. *Released* may refer to bringing Paul out of prison for the hearing (Bruce 1988:422).

caused the city to be in a tumult, his integrity in subordinating his methods of interrogation to the laws of Rome is an admirable quality which at least will allow the investigation to continue. He also becomes a silent witness to Paul's innocence.

Sophisticated Cynicism (22:30—23:5) The commander faces a dilemma. To preserve the life of this Roman citizen, he should probably keep him in custody. And in order to keep him in custody, he should at least have charges. Yet these he has not yet uncovered. His desire is *to find out exactly why Paul was being accused by the Jews.* He decides to assemble the chief priests and the Sanhedrin and listen to Paul's defense before them.

Though the tribune is just doing his job in a case of public disorder, he becomes a model for Luke's readers and for us. Just as he persists in his pursuit to know the certain facts of the case (*gnōnai to asphales;* compare 21:34), Luke's readers should study his works to know the certain truth of the gospel (*epignōs . . . tēn asphaleian;* Lk 1:4).

With the same spiritual intensity that accompanied God's miraculous work through him, Paul *looked straight at the Sanhedrin* (Acts 14:9; 13:9). He confesses that he has lived a blameless life. *Fulfilled my duty to God* means, literally, "lived as a citizen before God" (Phil 1:27; 3:20). As the Jews appropriated this term for describing a life of piety, they expanded its scope of reference to the whole conduct of life (3 Macc 3:4; 4 Macc 5:16). Probably the Old Testament concept "to walk before the Lord" is the best equivalent (Gen 17:1). When Paul says that he has all his life, *to this day,* "walked before God" *in all good conscience,* he means that he is conscious of no wrongdoing (1 Cor 4:4; Phil 3:6; 2 Tim 1:3). Though he is very much aware of his sinful pre-Christian actions, these he did in ignorance and unbelief, while at the same time being blameless before the law as far as he knew (Rom 7:9-12; Phil 3:6; 1 Tim 1:13). He has lived as a Christian through a renewed mind and cleansed conscience (Rom 12:1-2; 2 Tim 1:3; compare Heb 9:14).

What triggers the high priest's physical response? Is it (1) Paul's manner of speaking (his simple form of address [Lake and Cadbury

---

22:30 The commander's exercise of authority to summon the Sanhedrin, a right normally reserved for the governor; this ritually unclean Roman's meeting with the Sanhedrin; and that body's usefulness to him in this case are not historical difficulties if we remember that

1979:287] or impolite speaking out of turn [Haenchen 1971:637]), (2) the content of Paul's confession (the arrogant, even blasphemous, assertion that he can be a good Jew though now he is a Christian [Stott 1990:351]) or (3) the high priest's frustration with Paul's holy boldness as he bears witness to the truth, leaving the Jewish cleric at a loss for words? Ordering Paul to be slapped is very much in character for high priest Ananias, son of Nedebaeus (or Nebedaeus), who served A.D. 47-59. He was both greedy and ruthlessly violent, using beatings to extort tithes from common priests' allotment and leaving them destitute (Josephus *Jewish Antiquities* 20.205-7).

With his cheek still burning from the slap's sting, Paul fires back, *God will strike you, you whitewashed wall!* Paul's predictive curse follows proper Old Testament form (Deut 28:22; *m. Šebuʿot* 4:13). He uses an image for hypocrisy that Ezekiel invoked against false prophets who prophesied peace but could no more stand against the onrushing judgment of God than a stone wall held together only by whitewash can withstand an oncoming flood (Ezek 13:10-16). Paul's rationale is that in a judicial system where one is innocent until proven guilty, to punish before the verdict has been rendered is not to judge fairly (Lev 19:15). Paul's prediction came true: Ananias met a violent death at the hand of brigands in A.D. 66 (Josephus *Jewish Wars* 2.441). But despite all that seems right about Paul's response, it is, as Paul will quickly admit, still wrong. It is blessing, not cursing, that is to be on our lips. The Lord Jesus calls us to turn the other cheek (Lk 6:28-29).

The servant's remonstrance, either as a question (so the NIV) or as a complaint, reveals the high tension of the moment. Here is *God's high priest,* Israel's chief leader since it has no king, and Paul has declared God's judgment on him!

Paul pleads ignorance, declares the Old Testament law's requirement and in so doing subordinates himself to the authority of the Word of God. He does not speak ironically: "I didn't know he was the high priest, because he was certainly not acting like one" (contra Marshall 1980:364). Nor was his curse a simple sin of ignorance because Paul did not know

he was the chief representative of Roman authority in Jerusalem, a coping strategy had probably been developed for such official contacts, and the Sanhedrin was the most competent body to counsel in a religious matter (Marshall 1980:361-62; Bruce 1988:422).

from whom the command came or did not understand that he was the high priest (contra E. F. Harrison 1986:367). Rather, it was a sin of omission. Paul did not take into consideration the man's position when he made the declaration (Polhill 1992:469). Paul's prophetic curse, given in hasty anger, had violated a basic biblical precept lived out by David in his dealings with Saul. Though an officeholder dishonors the office through his conduct, one does not have liberty to dishonor him (1 Sam 24:6; 26:9-11). *Do not speak evil about the ruler of your people* (Ex 22:27 LXX).

How do we cope when a sophisticated cynic's punishing rejection of our integrity drives us to lash out in anger? Like Paul, we must respond in humility, quickly admitting our fault and subordinating ourselves again to the authority of God's Word. "It is not our mistakes that do us in; it's our pride that keeps us from admitting them" (Ogilvie 1983:316).

Theological Controversy (23:6-10) Paul now *called out in the Sanhedrin, "My brothers, I am a Pharisee, the son of a Pharisee. I stand on trial because of my hope in the resurrection of the dead."* Is this only a clever diversionary ploy? Is Paul simply trying to divide the assembly, so that they cannot agree to request and be given this prisoner for trial and certain execution? No, Paul's confession focuses on that aspect of the gospel that will be central to his apologetic throughout his trial witness (24:15; 26:6-8; compare 28:20). It tells the truth about the ultimate reason for his arrest by the Jews. For Paul and Luke, resurrection, especially the resurrection of Messiah Jesus, is the key issue that determines the nature of the continuity and discontinuity between Jews and Christians as part of the true people of God. *Hope in the resurrection of the dead* (literally, "hope and resurrection of the dead") as a hendiadys is better rendered "hope, even the resurrection of the dead." Paul specifies Israel's future hope of messianic salvation by the event that inaugurates it. This was indeed Israel's understanding, and as Christians affirmed it they stood in direct continuity with the Old Testament people of God (Dan 12:2; 2 Macc 7:14; *1 Enoch* 51:1-5; *Psalms of Solomon* 3:11-12). But the belief that the foundational fulfillment of that hope had

_____

23:6 There is no contradiction to Philippians 3:7-8 in Paul's identification of himself as

occurred in the raising of Jesus created the discontinuity. The Jews, on the whole, did not embrace this truth.

Paul finds himself on trial because of the Messiah's resurrection and the new realities it introduced. For if Jesus had not risen from the dead, he could not have appeared to Paul on the Damascus Road, or in the temple, and commissioned him to take the gospel to the Gentiles (Acts 22:15, 21). Paul would, then, not have promulgated a message or lived a lifestyle that his fellow Jews would have opposed.

And today, when many have contented themselves with pinning their hope on social or material progress in this life, we need to declare the good news of a true hope at the end of history, a resurrection to eternal life.

The Sanhedrin was composed of the priestly and lay nobility of the Sadducean theological persuasion together with scribes of the Pharisee faction. An uneasy peace existed between them, for though the Sadducees were the council's majority, the Pharisees had the good will of the people and were able to get their way regarding regulations for Israel's religious life (Josephus *Jewish Antiquities* 18.16-17).

As Luke points out and Josephus and other ancient Jewish literature document, the Sadducees and Pharisees differed on what happens to human beings after death. The Pharisees affirmed both an intermediate state as "angels and spirits" and a final resurrection (Josephus *Jewish Wars* 2.163; *Jewish Antiquities* 18.14; see 2 Baruch 51:5, 10 for evidence of Jewish belief in an intermediate state as angels; *1 Enoch* 22:3, 7; 103:3-4 for postdeath existence as spirits; Daube 1990). The Sadducees affirmed neither (Josephus *Jewish Wars* 2.165; *Jewish Antiquities* 18.16; compare Lk 20:36).

These social, political and theological factors more than account for the *dispute* that breaks out, the *great uproar* that follows and the violence that might well leave Paul *torn to pieces* (Acts 23:7, 9-10). The debating point leads to a division—a number of the Pharisees argue vigorously that Paul is innocent. Their worldview enables them to admit the possibility that an angel or spirit had spoken to him on the Damascus

---

presently a Pharisee, if we focus on his continuing personal piety according to the law and his belief in the resurrection (Longenecker 1981:532).

Road or in the temple. They are not confessing Jesus as risen Messiah, let alone exalted Lord, but they are on the way.

The gospel's worldview assumptions will always challenge the givens in any of today's myriad cultural, religious, philosophical and ideological outlooks. Like Paul, we need to so know our audience's worldview so that we may communicate the truth in love, where possible identifying common ground yet knowing there is always bound to be disagreement.

Things are getting out of hand. The commander sends word for more troops to come down from the Antonia fortress and "snatch" Paul out of the midst of the Sanhedrin. With this second rescue by the Romans, Agabus's prediction has come to its complete fulfillment (21:34, 11): Paul is now fully in the Romans' custody.

Divine Confirmation (23:11) Paul believed that it was God's will—at least he purposed "in the Spirit"—to bear witness in Jerusalem and Rome (19:21). He admitted that he did not know whether he would succeed, for the divine guidance he received also included warnings that affliction and imprisonment awaited him in Jerusalem (20:23; 21:4, 11). On more than one occasion he stated his readiness to face death, even in Jerusalem, if that was what faithful witness demanded (20:24; 21:13).

As he is violently opposed by the Jews, an enigma to his Roman protectors, what must be racing through his mind? What's next for him? Though we do not know Paul's mind and heart at this point, the Lord does. *The following night the Lord stood near Paul and said, "Take courage! As you have testified about me in Jerusalem, so you must also testify in Rome."* This word of comfort, assuring Paul that it is God's will (*dei*, "must"; 19:21; 27:24) that he bear witness in Rome, is also a word of guidance. Directed by this knowledge, Paul will avoid death by ambush on the way to or in Jerusalem (23:12-35; 25:1-12).

From this vision and subsequent events we learn that because martyrdom is never suicide, the gospel witness can be assured of divine guidance and protection, in the midst of life-threatening circumstances, so that his mission is not cut short.

Plot Uncovered; Paul Taken to Caesarea (23:12-35)

The Romans, like late-twentieth-century Americans or Koreans or Germans, were a "can-do" people. They would expect any gospel that prom-

ised its spread to all nations to show results (Lk 24:47; Acts 1:8). But in this episode Luke seems to paint himself into a corner. On the heels of a divine vision assuring Paul that he will witness in Rome comes a report of plotters determined to take the apostle's life. Is God able to fulfill his purposes to bring the gospel to all nations, especially to Romans? Like the book of Esther, without ever mentioning God, Luke reveals the divine hand, frustrating the schemes of human beings and ordering all things so that his purposes for the gospel's advance will come a step closer to fulfillment.

Deadly Plot (23:12-15) Twice the Romans have rescued Paul from the Jews' deadly intent (21:32-36; 23:10; see also 22:22-24). But his removal into the safekeeping of the Roman authorities only seems to intensify the Jews' determination to do away with him. From Acts 22:30 forward Luke consistently highlights Israel's rejection of the gospel by using the general term *the Jews* to refer to those who oppose Paul.

More than forty men take a "curse oath" *(anathematizō)*. They " 'accursed themselves' or 'wished for themselves the curse of God' or 'declared their lives forfeit' if they did not bend every effort to fulfill their voluntarily accepted obligation to kill Paul" (Behm 1964:355). They declare their fanatical devotion in a complete fast from food or drink until Paul is dead. Such a vow means death either way, for any ambush of a Roman military contingent would lead to the immediate death of most of the attackers.

Is this vow an extension of a commitment to remove the curse of God from a defiled temple by seeing to it that the perpetrator will experience death "at the hands of heaven" (see comment at 21:28-32)? In Jewish thinking, zealous ones should take on themselves that curse if God's offended holiness is not avenged.

Although the plotters are unsuccessful, we do not need to conclude that they die. Jewish casuistry provided for the breaking of a vow "[that cannot be fulfilled by reason] of constraint" (circumstances that kept the conditions of the vow from being met; *m. Nedarim* 3:1, 3).

The enemies of the gospel, in the end, have only the self-destructive power of self-imposed curses to try to realize their plans. What a feeble hope in comparison to the providential, saving power of God! And how ironic! Those who place themselves under a curse in order to remove

a curse assume that they are in the will of God but are really picturing what is already true of them. These enemies of the cross are persons under God's condemnation and only increase their punishment by taking such action against a messenger of the gospel.

These devoted plotters are also deceptive plotters. In order to maneuver Paul into a situation where they can get at him, they ask the Sadducean segment of the Sanhedrin, *the chief priests and elders,* to persuade the council to officially *petition the commander* to "bring Paul down" (NIV *to bring before*) from the Antonia fortress to them. The pretext will be to secure *more accurate information about his case;* the purpose will be *to kill him* (*anaireō;* Acts 23:15, 21; 25:3; compare Lk 22:2; Acts 21:36; 22:22).

Persecutors of the gospel have no interest in the truth about the gospel messenger. Not only must we continually show ourselves interested in the truth (21:34; 22:24), but we must be wise as serpents and innocent as doves when confronting such schemes (Mt 10:16).

Divine Providence (23:16-22) Paul's nephew, a young man probably in his early twenties, *heard of this plot* (literally "ambush"; Josh 8:7, 9 LXX). He reports it to Paul, who then sends him with his message up the chain of command through a centurion to the commander.

Since Paul's imprisonment, like most incarceration in ancient times, is not a punishment but a custody until his case can be determined (in Paul's case it is also protective custody), his nephew's access to him is not unusual. That Paul can call for a centurion to take the young man to the tribune, and that the "command" would be obeyed, reflects not only his status as a Roman citizen but also the urgency of his message.

As the centurion reports to the commander, he gives Paul a title that will become for the apostle a mark of persecution and a badge of honor.

23:17-18, 22 The nephew is described as *neanias* and *neaniskos* (diminutive of the former). Though commentators reflecting on the commander's treatment of him often conclude that he is a teenager (for example, Williams 1985:387), Hippocrates' definition of *neaniskos* as reported by Philo would place him between twenty-two and twenty-eight (*De Opificio Mundi* 105). The commander's taking him by the hand would point to the lower end of that range.

23:23 Sending 470 troops would not unduly deplete the garrison if its normal strength was one thousand (Bruce 1988:433; contra Haenchen 1971:650; Krodel 1986:432).

The exact translation of *dexiolaboi* (NIV *spearmen;* etymologically, "holding in the right

From now on Paul is consistently "Paul, the prisoner" (23:18; 25:14, 27). For freedom-loving ancients to identify with someone in prison, deprived of liberty because of alleged or proven wrongdoing, could be a matter of shame (2 Tim 1:8). But for Paul that shame turns to honor when he lengthens the title to say "Paul, the prisoner of Christ Jesus" or "prisoner for the Lord" (Eph 3:1; 4:1; Philem 1, 9). So may all Christians who suffer shameful circumstances in persecution realize the honor that rests on them because of the One for whom they suffer.

In a kindly *(by the hand)* and discreet *(drew him aside)* way, the commander interrogates the nephew. Evidently the Sanhedrin has already lodged its request, for the young man urges the tribune, *Don't give in to (peisthēs;* better "yield to, be persuaded by") them. The commander takes the plot seriously, asking the young man to depart and not tell anyone that he has reported this.

This unmasking of the plot is a silent witness to God's providential ruling and overruling in the affairs of humankind to fulfill his saving purposes (Prov 21:30; Is 8:10). Human beings play an essential role. The courageous nephew, the determined apostle, the compliant centurion and the discerning tribune all are essential to seeing that the cunning plot is foiled. Here is the first time the promise of the night vision, "so you must also testify in Rome" (Acts 23:11), guides Paul as he responds to unfolding events. Strong courage must be matched by canny wisdom if the persecuted witness is to avoid a premature death.

Roman Precautions (23:23-30) The commander calls two of his centurions and orders them to prepare for Paul's transfer to Caesarea. *A detachment of two hundred soldiers, seventy horsemen and two hundred spearmen* indicates the Roman assessment of the seriousness of the threat and the importance of the prisoner. The *mounts* provided for Paul

---

hand") cannot be recovered because of lack of other occurrences in ancient literature. Some have viewed it as pointing to additional mounts (leading horses). The poorly attested *dexiobolous*, "throwing with the right hand," is adopted by the Syriac Peshitta as "slingers or javelin throwers." The Vulgate has *lancearios*, "spearmen" (so the NIV). George Kilpatrick (1963) proposed that "local police spearmen" are spoken of.

The time marker is literally "from the third hour of the night." According to Roman reckoning, figuring from sundown at 6:00 p.m., this would normally be 9:00 p.m. (so the NIV). But with more daylight hours at this time of year—late spring or early summer—we should probably think of 9:30 p.m.

will be for relays, baggage, the soldiers to whom he is chained or his friends (Williams 1985:390). They are to leave under the cover of darkness—at 9:30 p.m.—for Caesarea on the coast, the provincial capital for Judea. The might of Rome's legions willingly deployed to protect one witness to the Lord Jesus is silent but powerful testimony to who is really Lord in that world and in ours.

Since the tribune lacks the necessary authority to deal judicially with prisoners of provincial status once he has restored public order, he may have already decided to transfer Paul to the governor's direct jurisdiction before he heard of the plot (Sherwin-White 1963:54; Marshall 1980:369). That news only accelerated the process.

The governor in question is Felix. He had served under Cumanus administering Samaria (A.D. 48-52) and succeeded him as governor until his recall in A.D. 59. Originally a slave, he was emancipated either by Antonia Minor, daughter of Mark Antony and mother of Emperor Claudius, or by Claudius himself, depending on whether Antonius (Tacitus *Histories* 5.9) or Claudius (Josephus *Jewish Antiquities* 20.137) is his correct nomen. Felix's tenure was marked by ongoing disturbances among the people, whether from the old-style terrorist-hoodlums *(lēstēs)*, messianic impostors and false prophets, or the new threat, *sicarii*, assassins with their "short dagger" terror (Josephus *Jewish Antiquities* 20.160-61; *Jewish Wars* 2.252-53). The brutal measures he took to deal with these only turned the Jews more against him and stirred up more unrest. Tacitus said that he "practiced every kind of cruelty and lust, wielding the power of king with all the instincts of a slave" (*Histories* 5.9).

In standard epistolary form the tribune's letter identifies the sender, Claudius Lycias (see comment at 22:28), and the receiver, Governor Felix, who is addressed with the honorific title "His Excellency" (this was appropriate to his office though he was not a member of the equestrian class). The body of the letter rehearses the tribune's conduct with reference to the prisoner and his assessment of the charges against Paul.

23:24 F. F. Bruce's (1978:33) argument for Claudius as Felix's nomen, based on an incomplete inscription, has been effectively critiqued by Colin Hemer (1987:45-49), who favors Antonius. He concludes, however, "But all is still in the realm of circumstantial probabilities, and we yet await unambiguous epigraphic testimony."

His recounting of Paul's rescue deals loosely with the truth in order to place himself in the best professional light. In fact, he learned Paul was a Roman citizen only after the rescue-arrest and at the point of scourging as a part of interrogation (22:25-29). His assessment, however, is accurate. The tribune concurs with Gallio before him that charges brought against Christians by Jews are theological, stemming from an intramural religious debate (18:15; compare 25:19). Paul is innocent of all crimes before Roman law.

By example and testimony the commander reminds us of three things about the interrelationship of the Christian and the state: (1) The state's proper role is to protect the rights of its citizens (Rom 13:4; 1 Tim 2:2-4). This the Christian may insist on. (2) The state is incompetent to make judgments on theological/religious matters. Whenever it does so it transgresses the boundary articulated by Jesus (Lk 20:25). (3) Christians must follow their Lord's example in guarding their innocence before the laws of the state (23:14-15, 22, 41, 47; compare Acts 25:8, 10-11, 18-19; 26:31-32).

Roman Protection (23:31-35) The thirty-five-mile nighttime leg of Paul's transfer proceeds without incident. Traversing the Judean hill country, either through Bethel or via the more southerly route to Lydda and then ten miles north, the military contingent comes to Antipatris, identified by most with modern Kulat Ras el Ain. A military station at a trade-route crossroads on the border of Samaria and Judea, just at the foot of the Judean hill country, it signals safety to the troops, both geographically and ethnically. The topography and populace most amenable to Jewish ambush lie behind them now. Ahead lies a flat coastal plain inhabited predominantly by Gentiles. The infantry and spearmen can return home while the cavalry takes Paul the remaining twenty-five miles to Caesarea. There the officers *delivered the letter to the governor and handed Paul over to him.* This transfer models God's ability to use even the military might of an empire to protect his gospel messengers.

Paul's movement toward Rome is at the same time a final movement

---

23:25-30 The letter is not Luke's invention (contra Haenchen 1971:650; Krodel 1986:432), for it is introduced by the phrase *echousan ton typon touton* (literally, "having this form"; NIV "as follows"), which in the papyri indicates a verbatim account (Bruce 1988:434, reporting E. A. Judge).

away from Jerusalem. Though he will continue to witness "to the Jew first" (28:17-27), Jerusalem's refusal to receive the gospel message (22:18, 22) and constant intent to destroy its messengers (Lk 13:34; Acts 25:3) seals its judgment from God (Lk 13:35; 21:20, 24).

Felix asks Paul his province of origin, either because he wonders about the need to show courtesy to a monarch of a client kingdom or he seeks a way to be rid of a troublesome case involving a Roman citizen in an imbroglio with the Jews. Paul's reply, however, gives Festus no relief. Eastern Cilicia at that time was part of the united province of Syria-Cilicia. The governor may not have wanted to trouble legate Ummidius Quadratus with the case. Or he is aware that Tarsus is a "free city" whose citizens are exempt from normal provincial jurisdiction. Or he may be wishing not to further antagonize Jerusalem Jews, who would have to take their case to Syria if it is remanded there. In any case, Felix decides to hear the case himself, after the accusers arrive. Herod the Great had built in Caesarea a very costly palace (Josephus *Jewish Antiquities* 15.331), which now served as the headquarters of the Roman procurator of Judea. Here, literally "in the praetorium of Herod," Paul was kept under guard.

Even in this initial, seemingly tangential interrogation we find God's purposes fulfilled through the thwarting of the governor's desires. Pilate was unable to transfer jurisdiction over Jesus to Herod Antipas. As a result, Jesus' prophetic declaration that he would suffer in Jerusalem was fulfilled. Similarly, Felix does not succeed in sending Paul to Cilicia or Tarsus. As a result, the road to Rome lies more directly before Paul (Acts 23:34-35/19:21; 23:11; compare Lk 23:6-7/9:51; 13:33). God's "finger-prints" are certainly all over what happens to Paul in these last days and hours. These turns of events authenticate his message and mission.

□ Paul at Caesarea (24:1—26:32)

During the Caesarean phase of Paul's Palestinian "ministry in chains,"

23:31-32 David John Williams (1985:390) notes that either aurally or by sight Luke could have access to the letter's contents.

While Bruce (1988:435; contra Haenchen 1971:648; Krodel 1986:433) believes the over-night forced march was doable, Marshall (1980:372) suggests that the infantry did not go the whole way to Antipatris while the cavalry did. Longenecker (1981:535-37), who takes the *dexiolaboi* (23:23) as extra mounts ("led horses"), sees the infantry alternately jogging

Luke highlights a persistent Jewish opposition that hopes to capitalize on the moral weaknesses of Roman governors. Still, humanly speaking, Roman law continues to be Paul's final line of protection. The innocence of Paul and his gospel before the state and the Jewish religion neutralizes the objections of Christianity's enemies. Theophilus and his peers may in all good conscience embrace a gospel that neither despises its roots nor threatens public order. Paul again uses his defenses as an occasion for powerful witness. The Spirit's work is evident, though no positive decisions are made.

Before Felix (24:1-27)

"Don't call me, I'll call you" is not only a way to dismiss telemarketers and door-to-door solicitors. Modern-day Felixes treat the gospel with the same indifference. Paul's trial witness before Felix at Caesarea helps us understand the reasons for and the hazards of putting off saying yes to Jesus.

Jewish Accusations (24:1-9) Shortly after Paul's removal to Caesarea, the Sadducean contingent of the Sanhedrin, *the high priest Ananias . . . with some of the elders,* arrives to bring charges before the governor. After Paul is *called in* by the crier at the beginning of the court session, Tertullus presents the Jews' case. He was probably a Hellenistic Jew who served as the Sanhedrin's expert legal counsel in Roman affairs.

Tertullus's exordium with its extensive *captatio benevolentiae* (it takes up half the speech as Luke reports it, vv. 2-4) curries the judge's favor with conventional flowery rhetoric. First is an appreciative assessment of Felix's tenure in office. In fact, the governor's rule brought anything but *a long period of peace,* and there is no record of many improvements, *reforms.* Felix did maintain a tense peace through an ongoing series of search-and-destroy missions against hoodlum terrorists (Josephus *Jewish Wars* 2.253, 264-65; *Jewish Antiquities* 20.160-61). Yet this fanned the fires of Jewish political rebellion into fiercer and fiercer flame. Second,

---

and riding.

24:4 Though the NIV takes *enkoptō* as "to weary" (compare Job 19:2 LXX; Is 43:23 LXX), it is better to take it according to its basic meaning, "to hinder," and understand it here as "to detain" (see the rhetorical introduction in Lucian *Two Indictments* 26—"But not to prolong my introduction when the water [in the water clock] has been running freely this long time, I will begin my complaint").

Tertullus curries favor by declaring his intent to move to the charges directly and deal with them briefly, depending on Felix's kindness to hear him.

Moving from general to specific, Tertullus carefully clothes the charges in mainly political terms so that they may be viewed as violations of Roman law. He begins with empirewide insurrection. The lawyer labels Paul a *troublemaker* (literally, "plague-spot") and accuses him of *stirring up riots among the Jews all over the world.* Whether the implication is general insurrection (Latin *seditio*) or simply disrupting Jewish communities, this charge is serious (compare Lk 23:2; Acts 17:6-7). Emperor Claudius's letter to the Alexandrines (November 10, A.D. 41) uses similar language. He warns the Jews that if they persist in suspicious activities, he "will by all means take vengeance on them as fomenters of what is a general plague *[nosos]* infecting the whole world" (*Greek Papyri in the British Museum [P. Lond.]* 1912, line 99).

Tertullus next charges disruptive heresy, which may carry with it the implication of fomenting theologically motivated civil unrest. He uses a contemptuous nickname for Christians, *Nazarene* (compare Jn 1:46; *nosrim* in the Talmud [for example, *Ta'anit* 27b]; Williams 1985:397), and labels them a *sect*—no more than an unauthorized minority movement within Judaism—and Paul their *ringleader.* Felix had to constantly deal with civil uprisings from such movements (Josephus *Jewish Wars* 2.253-65).

The temple defilement charge is cautiously stated as an attempted desecration. Does this show that the Jewish leaders know they have a weak case? They have witnessed no defilement, and the Asian Jews are not present to give testimony (Acts 24:19). Such testimony in any case would have been perjured. Has Tertullus also turned this into a political charge, since the Romans had given the Jews permission to impose the death penalty on any who defiled the temple (Josephus *Jewish Wars* 6.124-26)? Tertullus is at least justifying the Jews' initiative in Paul's arrest. He

---

24:7 The NIV rightly relegates to the margin a longer Western reading that came into the KJV via the Textus Receptus. Its use of *snatched* appears to mix in a word from a less-attested longer reading (Metzger 1971:490). Evidently the abrupt ending of the shorter reading at *ekratēsamen* seems to require a sequel that the longer reading supplies.

24:11 *Twelve days ago* is not merely a literary addition of seven (21:27) and five (24:1;

is confident that the judge's cross-examination of the defendant will verify the accusations. As the enemies of the righteous one surround him to attack (Ps 3:6 [7 LXX]), so the Jews *joined in the accusation* against Paul.

This full formulation of charges reveals several characteristics of persecutors' words. They will be broad, exaggerated, unsubstantiated, untruthful allegations. Double entendre and a trimming of charges will be used to fit what can barely be proved. Should we expect any less from those in the kingdom of the "father of lies" (Jn 8:44; Acts 26:18)?

Paul's Christian Affirmations (24:10-21) With a nod, a gesture befitting his rank (NIV translates it more generally, *motioned*), Felix indicates that Paul may take up his defense. His exordium with its *captatio benevolentiae* is respectful, affirming, within the bounds of truth, and brief. Paul *gladly* makes his defense because Felix's long tenure in Palestine has provided experience, knowledge and insight on Jewish affairs. Felix may well have spent a decade already in Palestine, first as administrator of Samaria under Cumanus (A.D. 48-52) and then as governor from A.D. 52 to the time of Paul's trial, A.D. 58 (Tacitus *Annals* 12.54; Josephus *Jewish Wars* 2.247; *Jewish Antiquities* 20.137). Paul's introduction models the bold, yet respectful, demeanor that Peter counsels us all to adopt when we stand before civil authorities and are required to "give the reason for the hope" that is within us (1 Pet 3:15-16).

Paul's answer to the insurrection charge (Acts 24:11-13) is framed in terms of his recent activity in Jerusalem, since this only is within the governor's jurisdiction. Motive, method, opportunity and proof of the alleged crime do not exist. As to motive, whether to celebrate Pentecost (20:16), render account of his stewardship thus far or rededicate himself to the next phase of ministry, Paul went up to Jerusalem to complete a spiritual pilgrimage, *to worship* (compare 8:27), not to start a "holy war." While on an earlier visit he had engaged in debate and witness to non-Christian Jews, this time he evidently confined himself to the Christian community (9:28-30/22:18; 21:17-26). His method of operation did not

---

contra Lake and Cadbury 1979:300). Rather, it encompasses the time of Paul's reported activity in Jerusalem: day 1—arrival (21:17); day 2—negotiations with James (21:18); days 3-9—purification (21:27); day 10—before council (22:30); day 11—discovery of plot (23:16-21); day 12—transfer to Caesarea (23:32; after 6:00 p.m. Jewish reckoning [Haenchen 1971:654]).

include *arguing . . . at the temple, or stirring up a crowd* for insurrection (*epistasis;* 2 Macc 6:3). In fact, if anyone could be accused of stirring up a crowd and inciting the city to riot, it was Paul's initial accusers (Acts 21:27-28, 30, 34-35). He lacked opportunity to orchestrate a revolt, since he had arrived in Jerusalem only twelve days before he was arrested. Besides, no proof of the charges can be now offered.

Paul's solid defense teaches us that though proclaiming a controversial message may spark an uproar, messengers themselves must always be peace-loving, circumspect and law-abiding.

As Paul answers the heresy charge, he reveals the uniqueness of Christianity vis-à-vis first-century Judaism. All Paul did in his life as a service of worship to God, he did as a follower of "the Way." Both the Dead Sea Scroll community and the New Testament church via John the Baptist's ministry used as their mandate Isaiah 40:3, "prepare the way for the LORD" (Lk 3:3-6; 1QS 8:13-16). Christianity, or the lifestyle it commended, became known as "the Way" (Acts 9:2; 19:9, 23; 22:4, 22; compare 1QS 9:16-21). The Dead Sea Scroll community prepared "the way for the LORD" through the study of the law, but Jesus' teaching set his followers on a more eschatologically imminent, ethically radical, profoundly personal and dynamically evangelistic "way" (Lk 14:25-33; Jn 14:6; Acts 1:8; Pathrapankal 1979:537-38).

Paul also emphasizes the Christian's continuity with Old Testament Jewish faith. He worships the same God, *the God of our fathers* (3:13; 5:30; 7:32/Ex 3:6). He does so with the same belief. He believes all that is written according to *the Law* and *in the Prophets* (Lk 24:25-27, 44; Acts 26:22). His worship involves *the same hope, . . . that there will be a resurrection of both the righteous and the wicked* (Is 26:19; Dan 12:2; *1 Enoch* 51:1-2). And his worship has the same aim: to live with *conscience clear before God and man,* no conscious record of misdeeds, in light of the coming judgment at the final resurrection (Acts 23:1).

For Jewish seekers and believers in any age, Paul's confession gives an encouragement that Christianity is, in the end, not a betrayal but the fulfillment of the Old Testament faith. The challenge is that this fulfill-

---

24:17 *An absence of several years* (literally, "many years") is conventional speech. He had been away six (18:22).

24:20 *In me* is found in the manuscripts of the Textus Receptus. Since it is a natural

ment will radically transform the Jewishness of those who step onto the "Way" inaugurated by Messiah Jesus.

Paul answers the temple defilement charge by emphasizing the purpose and propriety of his visit and pointing out that the eyewitness accusers of this alleged violation are not present (24:17-19). Paul's purpose was that of any pious pilgrim: *to bring my people gifts for the poor and to present offerings.* A person with such a purpose would hardly have temple defilement in his plans. In fact, his propriety—he was *ceremonially clean,* at least concluding his purification on his return from Gentile lands (21:26-27), and orderly, for he assembled *no crowd* or *any disturbance*—demonstrates this. The lack of eyewitness accusers to this most specific and immediately life-threatening of charges (see comment at 21:30) is an essential point in Paul's defense. He is relying on the time-honored Roman judicial principle that before any verdict, accusers must face the accused in person and there must be opportunity for a defense (25:16; Appian *Roman History: Civil Wars* 3.54). Converts from Judaism and nominal Christianity do well to emulate Paul's pursuit of the true worship of God through respect for and constructive engagement with his religious past.

One "crime" Paul will own up to: his shout before the Sanhedrin, *It is concerning the resurrection of the dead that I am on trial before you today* (23:6). The witnesses are present, but for two reasons this is no "crime." To the Romans Paul's statement is a matter of theology, irrelevant to their jurisprudence. To first-century normative Judaism, it is not heresy to confess hope in messianic salvation inaugurated through the resurrection of the dead (24:14-15). To see these hopes finding their initial and crucial fulfillment in the resurrection of Jesus of Nazareth is, of course, another matter.

Paul's introduction of the resurrection issue is not only good legal-defense strategy but also good evangelism. To speak of the final accounting before God and the eternal destiny that flows from it is to point out one of the certainties of human existence. Many may run from it, following alternate paths of personal eschatology—reincarnation or immediate annihilation. But all will have to face judgment. The resurrection of

addition rounding out the phrase, it is unclear whether the NIV introduced it because of its translation practice or by textual critical choice. It is best to delete it (Longenecker 1981:543).

Jesus—proof of coming judgment, promise of eternal salvation—must be at the heart of all "good news" preaching (17:30-31; 26:23; Lk 24:46-47).

Judicial Procrastination (24:22-27) Luke gives two reasons that Felix delays his verdict: his thorough acquaintance with Christianity and his desire to hear the testimony of Claudius Lycias, the only independent witness to any civil disturbances. Whether from Drusilla or from his decadelong tenure in Palestine, Felix knew "the Way," the opposition to it from the Jewish leaders-and increasingly from the people—and the potential for civil unrest that its very presence seemed to create.

Since Felix already has all the facts, are truth and justice compromised by his delay (Krodel 1986:442)? There may still be confusion over discrepancies among the testimonies of Tertullus, Paul and Claudius Lysias. Felix may want to interrogate the tribune in order to get to the bottom of the matter (Bruce 1988:446; Sherwin-White 1963:53). At the very least Felix protects himself from further civil unrest sparked by Paul's being at large and does the Sanhedrin a favor. And providentially, in protective custody Paul is kept from the hands of Jews intent on his death.

Paul's circumstances in custody include some measure of *freedom* and access to *his friends* (at least his traveling companions [Krodel 1986:442]; possibly also Christians of Caesarea [Haenchen 1971:656]). They take care of him, communicating with him, maybe even bringing food. These details serve as silent witness to Paul's innocence, for he is being treated as a Roman citizen simply detained for trial.

The judicial delay leads to gospel declaration (vv. 22-25). After several days, Felix and his Jewish wife Drusilla come to the section of the palace where the prisoners are kept and send for Paul.

Drusilla, one of the three daughters of Agrippa I (12:1-23), was born A.D. 38 and promised at a young age to Epiphanes, the son of Antiochus king of Commagene, if he would become a Jewish proselyte (Josephus *Jewish Antiquities* 19.354-55; 20.139-40). He refused to do so. So after the death of Agrippa I (A.D. 44), Drusilla's brother Agrippa II (Acts 25:13—26:32) gave her in marriage to Azizus, King of Emesa, a small domain

---

24:24 *Righteousness* should be taken not in the forensic but in the ethical sense, in line with both Felix's reaction and Luke's normal usage. Stott (1990:364) disagrees, saying that

on the Orontes. Azizus did consent to be circumcised. Enter Felix, whom Tacitus said indulged in "every kind of barbarity and lust" (*Histories* 5.9). Captivated by Drusilla's beauty, he wooed her away from Azizus with the aid of a Cyprian Jew named Atomus, who pretended to be a magician. Drusilla married Felix as much to escape the enmity of her sister Bernice, who abused her because of her beauty, as in response to his amorous spell (Josephus *Jewish Antiquities* 20.139-44). Felix was thrice married (Suetonius *Claudius* 28). This Drusilla replaced another Drusilla, granddaughter of Antony and Cleopatra. The couple would have been known to some in Luke's Roman audience, since they repaired to Rome after Felix was removed from his procuratorship in A.D. 59.

To such a dissolute couple Paul preaches *faith in Christ [Messiah] Jesus* (Acts 3:20; 5:42; 17:3; 18:5; 20:21). Given Felix's and Drusilla's past, it is not surprising that Paul focuses on matters that are foundational to a call to repentance: *righteousness, self-control and the judgment to come* (Jn 16:8-11). The couple, indeed, need to understand God's standard, their accountability and the reality of a final reckoning. In brief, they must face the bad news of their lost spiritual condition before they can grasp and embrace the good news.

Neither has pursued *righteousness,* "right conduct before God which follows the will of God and is pleasing to him" (Schrenk 1964:198; Lk 1:75; compare Acts 13:10). *Self-control,* whether in regard to sex, money or power, is foreign to them. While Drusilla would know of *the judgment to come* from her Jewish upbringing (see 24:15), Felix, a Roman freedman, knows of it only in a different form, probably being "vaguely persuaded that souls went down from the tomb to some deep places where they received rewards and punishments" (Cumont 1959:86).

In an age when the majority view all moral values as relative, the Christian witness needs to find a way to speak of God's righteousness again in such a way that it raises a standard for all. In a time when sin is viewed as alternative lifestyles, psychosocial dysfunctions, addictions or even disease, the gospel witness needs to find a way to speak mean-

"righteousness, self-control, and coming judgment" presents salvation in past, present and future perspective.

ingfully of responsible moral self-control. In an age of anxiety when humans know "something is wrong," though they have rejected the moral categories—absolutes, sin and guilt—that would enable them to know "some*one* is wrong," the Christian witness must learn how to declare a judgment to come in terms that make sense. Unless this happens, repentance will be impossible and the salvation rescue will appear unnecessary and hence irrelevant.

Paul always preached for a decision, and under the conviction of the Holy Spirit Felix knows this message is for him. It fills him with fear. He is startled, terrified, at the prospect of the last day (Lk 24:5, 37; Acts 10:4). But this does not lead to humble faith. Felix uses procrastination to stay in control of his own destiny. He will determine when and to what extent these matters are considered in the future.

How often does fear hide behind a busy schedule? How many have fooled themselves into thinking that by not deciding they have truly "kept all the options open" and at a *convenient* time in the future they will give the claims of Christ the serious attention they deserve? Actually indecision is a decision—a choice to remain where we are, outside God's saving grace, with the condemnation of the judgment to come our only prospect (Jn 3:18, 36).

But Felix's procrastination is more than a coping strategy. It also expresses his greed. Following common provincial administrative practice, he demands gold—seeks a bribe—from Paul in exchange for his release (Josephus *Jewish Antiquities* 20.215; *Jewish Wars* 2.273). He is evidently willing to trade hope of life eternal later for hope of money now (24:15, 26). Jesus warned of the unevenness of such a trade (Lk 9:25; compare 8:14).

Felix's desire for glory led him to trade the approval of fellow human beings for justice. He left office under a cloud. A Jewish delegation's complaint to the emperor about his ruthless suppression of a dispute between Jews and Gentiles in Caesarea led to his removal (Josephus *Jewish Antiquities* 20.182; *Jewish Wars* 2.266-70).

24:27 Though Eusebius placed the change of governors from Felix to Festus at A.D. 55-56, Bruce (1990:484) correctly argues—from the impression Josephus gives of a brief tenure and the change of coinage in Palestine—that Festus probably commenced his tenure in A.D. 59 (Josephus *Jewish Antiquities* 20.182-97; *Jewish Wars* 2.271).

As he leaves, he curries the Jews' favor by leaving Paul in prison. Paul's plight, clearly a miscarriage of justice and unworthy of a Roman citizen, nevertheless continues to provide the protection that is needed if Paul is ever to experience the divine promise—witness in Rome.

Felix's profligate life warns us all not to let sex, money or power put us into a "don't call me, I'll call you" stance toward the gospel.

Before Festus (25:1-12)

"I am sending you out like sheep among wolves. Therefore be as shrewd as snakes and as innocent as doves'" (Mt 10:16). The Jews' persistent, pernicious opposition had corrupted the exercise of Roman justice in Palestine, and only a shrewd and timely appeal to Caesar would extricate innocent Paul from the process. Paul's loyalty to and reliance on the rule of law would certainly endear him to Luke's audience. How they and we should once more marvel at our sovereign Lord's providential working, this time through the shrewd yet innocent Paul. It brings the apostle's witness one step closer to his divinely ordained goal: to bear witness to his Lord in Rome (Acts 19:21; 23:11).

The Venue Question (25:1-6) The brief but firm and honorable rule of Porcius Festus began with efficiency and wisdom (A.D. 59-61; Josephus *Jewish Antiquities* 20.182-97; *Jewish Wars* 2.271). Only three days after setting foot in the province he proceeded to his territory's true capital, Jerusalem, to meet the Jewish leaders.

Luke describes the leaders in general terms as *chief priests and Jewish leaders,* probably indicating that more than the Sanhedrin was involved. *They urgently requested* (better "persistently implored") the governor for a favor (the imperfect and present tenses point to importunate repetition): a change of venue for Paul's trial. Such a request was not out of the ordinary (Pliny *Epistles* 10.81.3-4). Yet it masked a deadly purpose: *an ambush to kill him along the way* (compare Acts 23:21, 16). They would use treachery to be rid of Paul, as they had with his Lord (Lk 22:2-6; Acts 2:23).

25:2 Longenecker (1981:544) provides a good explanation of how the frequent changes of high priest during this era and the continuing influence of those out of office would fit this general description. Bruce (1990:486) sees this as referring to the Sanhedrin; Williams (1985:409) sees the wording as possibly more inclusive.

Persistence and deceit are the trademarks of the church's persecutors. Therefore Christians must be "wise as snakes"—realistic, not naive or cynical. Nothing should take them by surprise, and they must try to anticipate all eventualities.

Festus's reply is a reasoned denial. The accused is incarcerated in Caesarea and the judge, the governor, is about to go there shortly; it makes sense for the accusers to go there as well. Festus issues a friendly invitation for the leaders to accompany him to Caesarea.

The soldiers' attempt to restore order in the temple area, the prisoner's transfer after the uncovered plot, and his continued incarceration as Felix's favor to the Jews when he left office were all occasions when military officers and governors acted on purely temporal or self-serving motives (21:32-36; 23:23-35; 24:27). Here too Festus makes a decision simply for his own convenience. But again, God is providentially directing human affairs so that the might of Rome will continue to protect his messenger. All who obey God's call and commit themselves to fulfill his purposes can have the confidence that the same providence protects them until their mission is done.

The Trial: Accusations and Affirmations (25:6-8) With customary efficiency Festus _convened the court_—literally, "sat down on the judgment seat" _(bēma)_. "This formality was necessary for his verdict to have legal validity" (Bruce 1988:451). Like predators after their quarry _the Jews . . . stood around him, bringing many serious charges against him_. But they are unprovable charges (compare 24:13, 19).

Before the bar of blind justice persecution will never prove a case built on lies. Here again the opponents of the gospel will be frustrated (6:10; 19:9-10). But Christians must always be sure they suffer for the right reason—because they are Christians—and that there is no case against them (1 Pet 4:14-16).

Though Festus's subsequent comments reveal that Paul is charged with much more (Acts 25:19), Luke presents Paul's defense as a brief

---

25:9 The nature of Festus's offer and his motives and intentions are variously assessed by commentators. He may be making a well-intentioned offer of a change of venue out of his genuine perplexity, as well as political motivation—to gain the Jews' good will (Bruce 1988:452). But why does Paul speak of being handed over to the Jews (v. 11)? If a change of immediate jurisdiction is being proposed (Williams 1985:408), is Festus being deliberately deceitful? Does he intend Paul to think change of venue while he means change of

affirmation: *I have done nothing wrong against the law of the Jews or against the temple or against Caesar.* The Jews have indeed consistently charged Paul with teaching and acting against the law (21:28; compare 24:5), the temple (21:28; 24:6) and Caesar (24:5). Paul has stoutly defended himself in each of these areas (law—22:3; 24:14-16; temple—22:17; 24:17-18; Caesar—24:11-13).

In this affirmation Luke capsulizes his conviction about first-century Christianity's two defining relationships. As to Judaism, it has not betrayed its religious roots. It stands in direct continuity with the Old Testament faith in its ethics and worship. The Jews can find no apostasy here. As to the state, Christianity is no revolutionary disrupter of the civil order, though in its own way it will produce a radical transformation of society, one heart at a time.

The Disposition and Paul's Appeal to Caesar (25:9-12) The next step in a trial featuring unsubstantiated charges and a solid defense should be acquittal. But Luke lets us know that a miscarriage of justice is in the making when he notes that Festus's next question is motivated by a desire *to do the Jews a favor,* what they have asked for (25:3; compare 24:27). Favoritism takes the blindfold off justice (Lev 19:15; Prov 17:15). Instead of declaring Paul innocent, Festus asks whether he is willing for the trial to be continued but with a change of venue to Jerusalem.

Paul's response and the way Festus later recounts the offer in conversation with Agrippa indicates that Festus's apparently innocent question about change of venue may cloak an inference of change of jurisdiction (25:11, 19-20). He could be implying that the Sanhedrin would be given immediate jurisdiction over this "religious" case and he would ratify whatever decision they take. In that way he promises that Paul will *stand trial before me.*

In a reverse parallelism construction, which climaxes with his appeal to Caesar, Paul evaluates his present and future judicial dealings with the

---

jurisdiction (Krodel 1986:446)? Or is Festus, knowing that Paul is aware of the dangers of ambush along the way, seeking to make the prisoner responsible for any consequences of a transfer to Jerusalem and at the same time to clear himself of any accountability (E. F. Harrison 1986:391)? Given Paul's response, Krodel's understanding seems to best account for all the facts.

Roman court and the Jews. He makes his statements turn on a profession of his integrity.

A. *I am now standing before Caesar's court, where I ought to be tried.*

B. *I have not done any wrong to the Jews, as you yourself know very well.*

C. *If, however, I am guilty of doing anything deserving death, I do not refuse to die.*

B. *But if the charges brought against me by these Jews are not true, no one has the right to hand me over to them.*

A. *I appeal to Caesar!*

Not only does Paul reveal his own integrity, stating that if guilty he will not refuse to undergo the law's full penalty, but he also unmasks the governor's failings. The governor knows Paul's innocence but won't declare an acquittal. The governor has proposed a change of venue which will in some way involve an illegal change of jurisdiction. To "hand Paul over" *(charizomai)* to the Jewish leaders is indeed to grant the Jews *a favor (charis,* 25:9). The only way to overcome these failings is for Paul to take the proceedings out of the hands of this lower court. By appealing directly for a trial before the imperial court, which was the right of every Roman citizen, Paul stops the judicial proceedings (Ulpian *Digest* 48.6.7, cited in Sherwin-White 1963:58).

Paul's shrewdness allows him to overcome the governor's moral failings and the fatal results that they would likely produce. It also enables Paul to retain the initiative of the divine "must" that has ultimate control of his personal destiny (23:11). Again God has providentially so ordered the decisions of individuals and nations that embedded in Roman law is an appeal mechanism that can now be employed by his witness, who was born a Roman citizen. But it requires Paul to exercise faith, courage,

---

25:11 The wisdom of Paul's appeal to Caesar, given that the Caesar in question is Nero, is vindicated if we remember that in the early part of Nero's reign (A.D. 54-59) the imperial administration was carried out "under the influence of his tutor Seneca, the Stoic philosopher, and Afranius Burrus, prefect of the praetorian guard" and was looked upon as "a miniature golden age" (Bruce 1988:454).

25:13-22; 26:31-32 Because Acts 25:13-22 is a private conversation and its purpose seems to be to rehabilitate Festus so he may join Luke's parade of upstanding Roman officials who testify to Christianity's innocence, some have taken the scene as Luke's composition (Haenchen 1971:673; Lake and Cadbury 1979:311). For some evangelical scholars the private character of this scene constitutes a real obstacle to its acceptance as a report based on

integrity and shrewdness.

Festus *conferred with his council.* It was customary for the governor, even the emperor, to have a body of assessors—higher-ranking military officers, younger civil servants in training and dignitaries from the local population—to help him evaluate court cases. Festus wants to make sure the appeal is in order based on the type of charges that have been brought. So assured, he makes the terse declaration *You have appealed to Caesar. To Caesar you will go!* The might of Rome protects; the might of Rome provides the transport. Paul will bear witness in Rome, possibly before the emperor himself (9:15; 23:11).

Before Agrippa and Bernice (25:13—26:32)

There are certain "defining moments" that forever change the identity and destiny of an individual, a movement, a nation. The moment may be as commonplace as the birth of a child or as unique as the extraordinary British defeat of the Spanish Armada. The defining moment for all of human history and for every individual is the resurrection of Jesus Christ. Prisoner Paul boldly proclaims this before Festus, Agrippa and Bernice in the final missionary preaching in Acts. To embrace this proclamation is to permit the purpose of Luke-Acts to be fulfilled in one's life (Lk 1:1-4).

A King's Curiosity (25:13-22) The King Agrippa who comes *to pay his respects to Festus* was Marcus Julius Agrippa II (A.D. 27-100), son of Agrippa I (Acts 12:1-25) and great-grandson of Herod the Great (Mt 2:1-23). Brought up in Rome in the court of Claudius, he was a favorite of the emperor, though too young to immediately succeed his father at his death in A.D. 44. In A.D. 50, following the death of his uncle (Herod of Chalcis, A.D. 48) he was granted the petty kingdom of Chalcis, northeast

---

eyewitness testimony. They assert, however, that the content is reliable, being reconstructed from subsequent public interaction and not constructed simply to forward Luke's theological purposes (Longenecker 1981:547). Marshall (1980:400) concludes that the private conversation of Acts 26:31-32 is Luke's dramatic composition. I join Williams (1985:411) in the suggestion that it is hard but not impossible for Luke to have had access to informants for both private scenes.

25:13 Either following a textual variant (future participle) or treating the aorist participle as indicating purpose, the NIV renders it *to pay their respects*. This is the sense called for by the verb's meaning and the immediate context, and thus should be preferred to seeing the relationship to the main verb as prior action (contra Williams 1985:411).

of Judea. He later exchanged it for the tetrarchy of Philip, Abilene (or Abila), Trachonitis and Acra (the tetrarchy of Varus) in A.D. 53. In A.D. 56 Nero added to his kingdom the Galilean cities of Tarichea and Tiberias with their surrounding lands and the Perean city of Julias (or Betharamphta) with fourteen villages belonging to it (compare Josephus *Jewish Wars* 2.220-23, 247, 252; *Jewish Antiquities* 20.104, 138, 159; Longenecker 1981:547). He had supreme power in Jewish religious life, for the Romans gave him the right to appoint the high priest and custodianship of the temple treasure and the high priest's vestments (Josephus *Jewish Antiquities* 20.213, 222). He was the last of the Herodian line.

Accompanying him now is his sister Bernice, a year younger than he. She had been engaged to Marcus, a nephew of the philosopher Philo of Alexandria. Then she married her uncle Herod, king of Chalcis. At his death she returned to live with her brother Agrippa II and engaged in an incestuous relationship with him. This gained her notoriety both in Palestine and in Rome (Josephus *Jewish Antiquities* 20.145-46; Juvenal *Satires* 6.156-60).

Festus discusses Paul's case with Agrippa, laying it before him so he could get his opinion on it. In the process Paul is described in four ways.

1. He has been *left as a prisoner* (Acts 25:14). Luke's verb form (the perfect periphrastic) stresses the continuing results of Felix's past decision. Paul as prisoner lives out a paradox that persecution brings. Though he is innocent (23:29; compare Lk 23:4, 15, 22), he is treated as a criminal—in bonds, without freedom, knowing all the shame brought by incarceration and implied guilt (Acts 23:18; 26:29; 28:16; compare Lk 22:37; 23:32). Yet Paul's status has resulted from fulfillment of prophecy and obedience to the path of suffering that all faithful witnesses to the truth must tread (Lk 21:12; Acts 20:23; 21:11, 13; also see Lk 22:37, 42).

2. Paul was opposed yet protected (Acts 25:15-16). Now it becomes clear: it was not just a change of venue that the Jerusalem Jews sought (vv. 2-3); they wanted a change of jurisdiction, as Paul had asserted (v. 11). They wanted Festus to agree that Paul was guilty of a capital offense

---

25:18-20 The descriptive imperfects throughout this section, "bringing," "suspecting,"

against their law and that he should be handed over to them for summary execution. Had they taken the time to explain to Festus about crimes that merited "death at the hands of heaven" and how the Romans had accommodated the Jews' concern about "temple defilement" offenses (see comment at 21:30)? Festus's reliance on a basic principle of Roman justice was Paul's protection. "Our law, Senators, requires that the accused shall himself hear the charge preferred against him and shall be judged after he has made his own defense" (Appian *Roman History: Civil Wars* 3.54; compare Ulpian *Digest* 48.17.1, cited in Haenchen 1971:672). So it was not only a desire for convenience but also a commitment to justice that preserved Paul's life. That justice is also the biblical way (Deut 19:15-21).

3. Paul was tried, but no punishable charges resulted (Acts 25:17-19). Festus with customary efficiency *convened the court* (compare 25:6). Taking a hostile stance, the accusers surprised the governor by making religious charges: *some points of dispute . . . about their own religion* (compare 25:7). This was the consistent understanding of Roman officials about the nature of Jewish opposition to Christianity (18:15; 23:29). Evidently Festus has concluded there is nothing to the sedition charges; Paul has indeed *done nothing wrong . . . against Caesar* (25:8). Paul is not guilty of violating Caesar's decrees against creating disturbances in the Jewish community. Festus has not decided about Paul's culpability in the temple defilement matter, an issue of dual jurisdiction.

The main point of dispute is *a dead man named Jesus who Paul claimed was alive* (v. 19). The phrasing reveals Festus's attitude toward Christ's resurrection and innocently communicates the prominent role it played in Paul's defense. Though more general references to "resurrection of the dead" have peppered Paul's defense (23:6; 24:15, 21), we now know that Jesus' resurrection is the central point of contention. Paul certainly made that clear in his speech before the temple mob (22:7-10, 14-15, 17-21).

Paul began with the objective historical fact of the resurrection, and so must we. It is the essential foundation for any supernatural working

---

"claiming," "asking," are missed by the NIV, and with them some of the vividness of the progressive action of the scene (Kistemaker 1990:876).

whereby we come to our "defining moment" of meeting our risen Savior and entering into a personal relationship with him.

4. Paul was offered a change of venue but instead appealed to Caesar (25:20-21). Festus *was at a loss*—perplexed—about this testimony to supernatural events (compare Lk 24:4; Acts 2:12; 5:24; 10:17). Not only the nature of the evidence but also the limits of his sphere of authority rendered Festus incompetent to judge these matters (Lk 20:25). This trial was about "God's" sphere, not "Caesar's." But Festus's perplexity did not keep him from trying, as his offer of a change of venue shows.

Festus and all governmental officials following him do well to learn the limits provided by a biblically grounded distinction between the proper spheres of authority of church and state. The state's judicial wisdom is never competent to decide matters of theology. Its power is never a valid enforcer of church/temple decisions.

The way Luke describes Paul's request as an *appeal to be held over for the Emperor's* (literally, "His Majesty's") *decision* shows that he was asking not only for removal from a Roman provincial tribunal to the imperial court but also for protection during the process. Festus' order was, literally, "to send him up to Caesar" (*anapempō*, a technical term for transfer to a superior tribunal; Josephus *Jewish Wars* 2.571).

With some curiosity, possibly disdain, Agrippa says he *would like to hear* "the person." The imperfect *eboulomēn* is either a true past indicating a wish he had entertained for some time (compare Lk 9:9; 23:8) or a desiderative intended to soften the remark and make it more polite, diffident or vague (Williams 1985:414). Festus accedes to his desire: *Tomorrow you will hear him.*

To hear a messenger with the word of God is the first step on the path to saving faith (Lk 8:8, 15, 18; Acts 4:4; 10:22, 33; 13:44; 18:8). Agrippa and Festus at this point unwittingly appear to model two essential prerequisites for receiving the gospel: a teachable spirit and a desire to hear the message.

25:24 The NIV fails to translate *andres* (males) in the form of address: *pantes hoi symparontes hēmin andres*. Bruce (1988:458) notes that the address is formal, and in that cultural setting Bernice would not have felt herself expressly ignored.

25:26 NIV's *His Majesty* translates *tō kyriō*, "my sovereign Lord," which was given a divine connotation when addressed to Roman emperors by subjects in the eastern provinces. There

A Governor's Dilemma (25:23-27) As Luke sets the scene, a majestic court in full regalia assembles. In come *Agrippa, Bernice, . . . high ranking officers* (Festus's tribunes, who commanded the cohorts stationed at Caesarea; compare Josephus *Jewish Antiquities* 19.365) *and leading men of the city,* a group mainly, if not entirely, Gentile. What a contrast when prisoner Paul is led in chained! Does Luke want us to look beyond the trappings of earthly, temporal power and see where the real power lay, in the manacled hands of a Spirit-filled witness to an eternal gospel, "the power of God for salvation"?

Festus articulates his dilemma by setting side by side the Jewish and Roman assessments of Paul, including the prisoner's appeal, and then presenting his need (vv. 24-27). Either by command or by exclamation Festus invites all present to consider Paul. As someone observes an unusual sight, whether the supernatural/miraculous (3:16; 4:13; 7:56; 8:13; 10:11; 28:6) or the innocent suffering (Lk 23:35, 48), so the assembled dignitaries should look at this man. This one whom Festus will shortly declare innocent has aroused the hostility of *the whole Jewish community.* What was previously presented as a request for a change of venue or a statement of charges and request for a death penalty we now learn was a petition delivered with bloodthirsty *shouting* (*boaō,* "to cry or shout with unusually large volume"; Louw and Nida 1988:1:398) *that he ought not to live any longer* (compare 22:22). The same zeal for the purity of the temple and the sanctity of Jewish religious identity that fired the arresting mob and the plotters continued unabated throughout Felix's tenure and greeted Festus (21:27-36; 22:22; 23:12-22). Little did Paul's opponents realize that their "ought not" (*mē dein*) stood in direct opposition to the divine "ought" (*dei*) of Paul's mission to Rome (23:11; 27:24).

All persecution in the final analysis is born of religious, ideological or ethnic pride or fear. It is a blind, irrational hostility against the truth of the gospel, which seeks to frustrate the purposes of God but in the end

---

was a remarkable rise in the frequency of such usage under Nero and his successors (Deissmann 1978:353).

Stott's (1990:369) understanding that Festus was seeking evidence to substantiate charges does not fit with verse 27.

only finds itself "kicking against the goads" (26:14).

Festus now gives us for the first time his assessment of Paul's status before Roman law: *I found he had done nothing deserving of death*. Like his Lord, Paul has been declared innocent three times, a full exoneration in a judicial system where the accused was given three opportunities to defend himself (Lk 23:4, 15, 22; Acts 23:29; 25:25; 26:31). Festus fails to mention the political pressure and perplexity that led to his offer of a change of venue and in turn to Paul's appeal to Caesar (25:9-11, 20-21). Rather, he proceeds directly to the matter of Paul's appeal, leaving the impression, which is made explicit at the end of the hearing, that Paul is to blame for his continuing incarceration (26:32). Neither the governor nor the king explicitly takes into account that the decision to send an innocent man to Caesar, once he has appealed, is as much a political as a judicial decision. In Paul's case, not only would Caesar be insulted but the Jews would be infuriated if this prisoner were set free.

When persecutors use the state to further their ends and the result is a failure in the administration of justice, Christians must live in such integrity that even then their innocence before the laws of the state will be apparent to all.

Festus needs to find charges that may accompany the prisoner (Ulpian *Digest* 49.5-6, cited in Bruce 1990:494). With his search for things *definite [asphales] to write,* Festus joins Claudius Lycias in the desire to get at the truth about the Jewish opposition to Christianity (21:34; 22:30). He also models the stance that Luke desires all his readers to take toward the Christian gospel (Lk 1:4).

An informal hearing before Agrippa should help. He is well acquainted with Judaism. In a face-saving expression, Festus again affirms Paul's innocence and states his dilemma: it is *unreasonable* (*alogon;* Josephus *Jewish Antiquities* 1.24)—in the sense of "illogical, absurd," not "unfair"—that a prisoner be sent on to Caesar without prosecutable charges. Doing the right thing, even after a failure of judicial administration, will put Festus in a position to hear and respond to the truth of the gospel.

26:4 In the light of Acts 22:3 *in my own country (ethnei)* should be rendered "among

The Prisoner's Defense, Part 1 (26:1-8) Agrippa, in the chair, directs Paul to speak. The apostle "stretches out" his hand in the stance of an orator commencing his speech. The *captatio benevolentiae* of Paul's exordium places Agrippa in the right frame of mind for hearing him by declaring the "good fortune" he reckons he has in making his defense before one so *well acquainted with all the Jewish customs and controversies* (see 21:21; 23:29; 25:19 to see how such relate to Paul's case). Further, with polite address (*deomai;* 21:39) Paul "begs" the king's "patience" in listening to him (compare 24:4). By this introductory appeal in Paul's exordium Luke emphasizes not only the apostle's respectful demeanor, worthy of emulation by all who are judged for their faith, but also that what is at issue is a theological matter.

As Paul moves in his exordium from introductory appeal (26:2-3) to the presentation of his ethos, himself (vv. 4-5), he affirms that his background as a strict Pharisee places him in continuity with his Jewish religious roots. Within his nation, particularly in Jerusalem, he has consistently lived out the Old Testament and Jewish ideal of piety *ever since I was a child* (1 Kings 18:12; Ps 70[71]:5, 17 LXX; Lk 18:21; Sirach 6:18). He has done this publicly; the Jews, who have known it *for a long time* (*anōthen;* Lk 1:3), can so testify *if they are willing* (compare Acts 23:1; 24:16, 19). He has practiced piety strictly, according to the Pharisee *sect of our religion.* Josephus says of them, "There was a group of Jews priding itself on its adherence to ancestral custom and claiming to observe the laws of which the Deity approves" (*Jewish Antiquities* 17.41). Luke uses *thrēskeia,* which means "*religion,* esp. as it expresses itself in *religious service* or *cult*"(Bauer, Gingrich and Danker 1978:363). He may have particularly in mind the Pharisees' laws of ritual purity and their regulations for the performance of temple worship. This life of piety has continued up until this day (*ezēsa,* culminative aorist, "I have lived"). Paul places himself squarely within Jewish orthopraxy. The accusers' charges are baseless (21:28; 24:5-6).

In a reverse parallelism construction that begins and ends with a

my own nation," referring not to Cilicia but to the Jewish nation, with Jerusalem further specifying the reference geographically (Williams 1985:416).

statement of the charge Paul believes is the reason for his trial, the apostle commences his narration, the statement of the facts of the case (26:6-8). The point at issue is the hope for messianic end-time salvation (23:6; 24:15; 28:20). In the middle of this articulation Paul states that the *twelve tribes* also *are hoping* to arrive at that same goal. Thus he affirms a continuity of his gospel message with Jewish orthodoxy.

Paul is certainly on solid ground when he claims that "the hope" for the Old Testament saint and the Intertestamental Jew was messianic end-time deliverance (Is 25:6-12 [see v. 9 LXX, *ēlpizomen*]; 51:5 LXX; 2 Macc 2:18; *1 Enoch* 40:9; *Testament of Benjamin* 10:11; 2 Baruch 30:1). Indeed, the Jews looked forward to the fulfillment of the promises made to the fathers in the end time (2 Baruch 51:3). They did see the end-time salvation as commencing with a resurrection of the righteous, though admittedly the Sadducees did not (2 Macc 7:11, 14, 23; compare Acts 23:6; 24:21). Luke does not hesitate to populate his narrative with pious Jews living expectantly for that deliverance (Lk 2:25, 38; 7:19; 23:51). Paul emphasizes the way they live out their expectation: in fervent (*en ekteneia,* often descriptive of prayer; Lk 22:44; Acts 12:5), consistent (*day and night,* at morning and evening sacrifice; Lk 2:37) corporate worship of God (*latreuō;* Acts 24:14; 27:23). It is certainly a "living hope," a goal which they were expecting to attain (compare Phil 3:11-14, where Paul shows the same stance toward the full manifestation of the hope).

If Paul has such strong continuity with pious Jews, why is there such opposition to him and his message of *hope?* Paul declared that in the risen and exalted Lord Jesus the promises have been fulfilled and the hope is now a present reality (Acts 13:32/2 Sam 7:11-17; Acts 13:23). This Paul will explicitly proclaim at the climax of the proof section of his

---

26:7 The NIV translates *katantēsai* as *to see fulfilled,* but the term has the basic meaning "to reach a goal." The momentum toward the goal embodied in a hope that demands total commitment needs to be maintained by a rendering such as "are hoping to attain" (Michel 1965:623-24).

26:9-23 Jerome Neyrey (1984:216, 221) details the types of proofs Paul employs in his probatio. He defends the concept of resurrection by presenting "authorized testimony of a valid witness" (v. 16), the "first among proofs"; tokens (*tekmēria,* "irrefutable proofs") in the form of an eyewitness narrative of the appearance of the resurrected Jesus (compare 1:3); signs (the light, 26:13); corroborating witnesses (vv. 5, 12-13); and probabilities based

speech (26:22-23).

This is the main question for every individual, whatever his or her religious, ideological or cultural heritage: Is Jesus your hope? The Christian message asks, Will you repent of your false hopes—the American dream for the next generation, the Hindu's Nirvana, the Muslim's paradise—and let Jesus be your true hope?

Paul concludes his narratio by stating the point for the judge's decision: *Why should any of you consider it incredible that God raises the dead?* Though Paul thinks of Jesus' resurrection in particular, he puts the point as a general question. In so doing he reveals what a challenge the resurrection of Christ is to any human worldview. To Agrippa, if he is under the influence of aristocratic Sadducean thought, God's raising the dead is unbelievable (23:8). Festus has already declared himself on this subject (25:19). If, in general, resurrections do not happen, then what is claimed about Jesus did not occur. But if it did happen to Jesus, then a central feature of one's worldview, belief about what happens after death, must be radically reoriented. Here there is certainly a radical discontinuity between Paul's claims about Jesus' resurrection and the assumptions of Jew and Gentile alike. Yet there is continuity with the Old Testament faith and Israel's living hope (26:6-7, 22-23). And for all humankind, because of this resurrection's saving significance, it is our defining moment.

The Prisoner's Defense, Part 2 (26:9-23) Paul begins his probatio (proof) by removing any suspicion that he was positively disposed to belief in Jesus as the crucified and risen Messiah. He details the scope, extent and intensity of his opposition to Christians as Christ's persecutor (26:9-11). Pharisee though he was, Paul did not believe that a resurrec-

---

on cultural expectations—epiphanies (vv. 14-16) and prophetic commissionings (vv. 16-18).

26:10 How can verse 10 be accurate if we take it literally to mean that Paul voted with the Sanhedrin for the death penalty for a number of Christians? Wasn't he too young to be a member? Anyway, under Roman rule the Sanhedrin could not exact the death penalty. Further, only Stephen is reported as martyred. Though the reference to Paul's voting may point figuratively to his agreement with them (Marshall 1980:393), the reference to multiple Christian deaths may be taken literally and viewed as historically plausible when we remember that the circumstances in Judea at Stephen's death were ripe for others to suffer the same fate (Williams 1985:417).

tion had occurred in the case of Jesus. It seemed to him that it was his moral duty *(dei) to do all that was possible to oppose the name of Jesus of Nazareth*—that is, Christ's presence and power among his people (Polhill 1992:500) or the message about Jesus, especially his resurrection (O'Toole 1978:49). The scope of his persecution target was large: he pursued *many of the saints, . . . many a time,* going *from one synagogue to another.* His persecution of Christians extended from synagogue punishment intended to get them to recant (this Paul relates from a Christian perspective in his reference to "blaspheming"; compare Pliny *Letters* 10.96.5) to imprisonment to consenting to their deaths. So intense was Paul's opposition that he pursued Christians to cities outside Palestine. An "exceedingly furious rage" drove him to do it (NIV *obsession against* may not be strong enough). Yet even such strong persecution was not outside the sovereign plan of God; and Jesus has promised such for all true disciples (Lk 12:4, 8-12; 21:12-19).

Paul's conversion and commissioning transformed him from Christ's persecutor into Christ's apostolic convert (26:12-18). Here we meet not only the most telling evidence that Jesus is risen but also the clearest exposition of that resurrection's significance.

In this third recounting of his conversion (compare 9:1-9; 22:5-11) Paul, traveling with the high priest's *authority and commission* to arrest Christians, is himself arrested by Christ on the Damascus Road. In this account of the light that drove him to his knees, Luke, following Paul, emphasizes its power and its concrete or objective nature. Its brilliance is *brighter than the sun,* and that at noontime. It "shines around" not only Paul but his companions (*perilamptō;* NIV's *blazing around* renders *periastraptō* present in 9:3; 22:6). As in the other two accounts, we are reminded that although part of the experience—seeing the risen Lord and receiving the message—occurred personally to Paul and no one else, it was an objective experience in space and time, for the companions heard a voice, though not the message. They saw a light, though not Jesus (9:7; 22:9).

26:14 See note at 21:40; 22:2 for discussion of whether *Hebraïdi dialektō* should be understood as Hebrew or Aramaic. Because *Saoul* is a Hebrew transliteration, "Hebrew" is the preferred translation here as well.

The proverb of Acts 26:14 is absent from the other accounts (9:4; 22:7) but a commonplace in Greek literature (see Bruce 1990:501 for examples). It has not been placed on Jesus' lips by either Luke (contra Lohfink 1976:78) or Paul (contra Longenecker 1981:552). Though

Light is appropriate to the theophany of the heavenly risen Lord in his divine mode of being (Ex 20:18; Deut 4:12; Is 60:1-3; O'Toole 1978:63). It is a fitting metaphor for the revelation and salvation he brings (Is 42:6; 49:6; Lk 2:32; Acts 26:18, 23; Krodel 1986:461). Our Lord's dealing with Paul here teaches us that to get the attention of those who are self-confident enough in their religion to persecute others, God may take extraordinary steps to literally bring them to their knees.

Saul, Saul, why do you persecute me? This question at the same time declares Paul's guilt and opens the way for him to be free of it. To this point in his life Jesus was just the name of a dead messianic pretender, which Paul did everything in his power to make his followers renounce (26:9-11). Now he is overpowered by Jesus' living presence; indeed, he had been in a losing battle with Christ all along. *It is hard for you to kick against the goads.* Did Ecclesiastes 12:11, "The words of the wise are like goads," come to his mind? To change the metaphor, the word of the Lord had kept growing and spreading like wildfire, especially in the time of persecution (Acts 8:3-4). Those who tried to stamp it out simply sent more sparks into the wind to ignite hearts in many more places. Paul learned, as does anyone who consistently says no to the faith, that it takes work to resist the truth of the gospel and the life of the Spirit.

Paul's response of humble submission, *Who are you, Lord?* places him in the only position that can turn the condemnatory accusation into an answer full of hope. *I am Jesus, whom you are persecuting.* In these simple statements from heaven Jesus declares that he is risen from the dead and exalted to the Father's right hand. He proclaims his supremely triumphant salvation victory. Paul cannot successfully oppose Christ and his mission—and why would he want to anyway? Jesus further announces that Christians are peculiarly the Messiah's people. To persecute them is to persecute him.

These truths are the light Paul needs to be converted. And any conversion involves that defining moment when we enter into a personal

---

such a saying could crop up in any "ox-cart society," which Palestine certainly was, there is rabbinic evidence of the use of Ecclesiastes 12:11 with its figure "goads," which may be a more direct background (*Psalms of Solomon* 16:4; Philo *De Decalogo* 87; compare rabbinic use of the Eccles 12:11 figure—Strack and Billerbeck 1978:2:770). It is not historically improbable for the risen Lord to so address the Pharisee Saul.

relationship with the risen Jesus Christ by embracing the good news that this suffering and risen Messiah is mighty to save those who repent of their rebellion against him (Lk 24:46-47).

Paul's conversion is at the same time a commissioning to a lifework of gospel witness (Acts 26:16-18). In words reminiscent of the call of the Old Testament prophets, Jesus commands him, *Get up and stand on his feet*, for he is to bear a divine message that will place him in danger. Hence a promise of divine protection must be added (Jer 1:7-8, 17-19; Ezek 2:1-2).

What is distinctive in the appointment, though not necessarily unique, is the nature of the mission and the nature of the audience. The Lord appoints Paul a servant *(hypēretēs)*. With this term for "assistant" Jesus stresses that Paul is to do exactly his master's bidding (Lk 1:2; 4:20; Acts 13:5). And he further specifies the service as *witness of what you have seen of me and what I will show you* (compare 22:17-21). He will proclaim a message that he is convinced of and that is based on "direct personal knowledge" (Strathmann 1967b:476; Acts 23:11; 26:22). His audience is both Jews (Luke refers to them by that spiritually significant term, *laos,* "the people"; the NIV rendering obscures this; see 13:15, 31; 28:26-27) and Gentiles. The direct Gentile mission, so offensive to his fellow Jews, is so necessary in God's saving plan that it is even part of the gospel message (Lk 24:46-47). It must ever determine the target audience of Paul's mission and ever be the flash point of opposition to it (9:15; 13:46-50; 22:15, 21-22). All who will answer Christ's call to be witnesses will face the challenge of responding with courage and confidence.

26:16-18 These verses are unparalleled in chapters 9 and 22; but Luke is not telescoping commissions given by Ananias and the risen Lord in the temple and placing them on the lips of Jesus during the Damascus Road appearance (contra Marshall 1980:396; compare Bruce [1990:501], who says there is a telescoping of commissionings by Ananias and in the temple with one given on the Damascus Road). Stott's (1990:381) protestations to the contrary, such a literary explanation does not square with historical accuracy. A better explanation is that Luke, for maximum dramatic effect, has delayed relaying this fact of Paul's conversion until his last recounting (Hedrick 1981:427). A close look at Ananias's role reveals that he never gives Paul his commission; his role is confirmation through healing and baptizing (9:17-18; 22:16). In fact, Ananias's own words contain an allusion to the risen Lord's commission on the Damascus Road (22:14-15). Paul did receive his commission from Jesus on the Damascus Road.

Never missing an opportunity to fulfill his ministry, Paul climaxes his report of Jesus' commissioning by proclaiming its purpose in terms of outcomes (26:18; compare Col 1:12-14). He winsomely lays before his audience the salvation blessings that can be theirs if they too will but trust in this risen Savior. With a healing metaphor Jesus tells Paul he is *to open their eyes*. This stands for "the spiritual health of those who find salvation in Christ and receive his revelation" (O'Toole 1978:74). Luke will use the metaphor of "closed eyes" for a sinful condition (Acts 28:27/ Is 6:10; compare Lk 19:42) and "seeing eyes" for those blessed to witness of God's saving purposes (Lk 2:30; 10:23; compare Is 42:7).

Paul further enlarges on the transformation that this salvation brings: those who receive Paul's witness will *turn . . . from darkness to light, and from the power of Satan to God.* They can abandon the gloom, ignorance and evil of an environment without the messianic Savior (Lk 1:79; 11:33-36; 22:53; Acts 13:11) for the light of hope, revelation and goodness found in the living presence of the Risen One (Lk 2:32; Acts 13:47/Is 49:6). The bondage of Satan's *power* ("authority"; Lk 4:6; 22:53) can be exchanged for the gracious sovereignty of God, who is greater (Lk 4:36; 5:24; Acts 8:19).

The positive blessings that flow from this transformation encompass one's past, present and future. There is *forgiveness of sins,* one of Luke's favorite ways of describing what salvation provides for us (Lk 4:18/Is 61:1; Lk 24:47; Acts 2:38; 5:31; 10:43; 13:38). And there is a new eternal destiny grounded in a new identity. We have *a place* (*klēros,* a lot or portion of an inheritance, Ps 77[78]:55 LXX; compare Acts 1:17; 8:21) *among those who are sanctified by faith* in Jesus (16:31; 20:32; 20:21;

26:16 What the NIV renders literally as two parallel thoughts, *as a servant and as a witness,* may be a hendiadys with the latter term specifying the former: "a servant, i.e., a witness."

26:18 The NIV renders the three parallel purpose statements by linking the second more closely to the first and by making the third a result clause issuing from the first two. The NIV renders *epistrephō* as a transitive whereas Bauer, Gingrich and Danker (1978:301) see it as intransitive. Used elsewhere in Acts and the lack of an expressed object here make the latter rendering more likely (Acts 3:19; 9:35; 11:21; 14:15; 15:19; but see Lk 1:16).

26:19 Wilhelm Michaelis (1967:372) points out that Luke consistently uses *horama* to refer to "visions" (9:10-11; 10:3, 17, 19; 11:5; 12:9; 16:9-10; 18:9). It is better, then, to translate the phrase *tē ouraniō optasia* as "heavenly appearance" or "appearance from heaven."

24:24). Trust in Christ is our defining moment.

As further proof of the reality of this encounter and in order to bring its significance to bear on his present circumstances, Paul now portrays himself as Christ's obedient witness (26:19-23). As a faithful witness, he follows the risen Lord's command by preaching in *Damascus* (9:19-22), *in Jerusalem* (9:26-28; 22:17-21), *in all Judea* (9:28-30) and *to the Gentiles also* (11:25-26; 13:46; 14:27; 22:21). Paul stresses the radical about-face involved in embracing the good news. "To convert is not just to give one's life a new direction but in practice to reorientate oneself continually to the goal by the radical setting aside of evil" (Behm and Würthwein 1967:1004). With conversion, repentance and the new life that proves the genuineness of that repentance, there is no room to drive a wedge between Jesus as Savior and Jesus as Lord. If one is not truly committed to him as Lord, one cannot rightly claim he is one's Savior.

Paul's faithful witness has also been a contested witness. Paul preached the same gospel to Jew and Gentile alike, inviting both to receive salvation blessings in the same way: by repentance and faith in Messiah Jesus. This obliterated the religious distinction between Jew and Gentile that ethnic pride had so carefully preserved. On account of this mission and message the Jews seized him in the temple and tried to kill him (21:30-31). And so today, the universal offer of salvation based on grace received by repentance will still be resisted.

Paul gives one final proof that his mission is from God. He was arrested and beaten by a bloodthirsty mob, and while he was in Roman custody the Jews hatched ambush plots, even involving newly arrived Festus. But with *God's help* he is still alive and bearing witness *to small and great alike.*

Now he wants to engage Festus, Agrippa and the rest in a consideration of the truth of the message, especially its fulfillment of Old Testament prophecy (Lk 24:46; Acts 3:18). With an introductory *ei,* with its

---

26:20 The reference to Paul's evangelizing *in all Judea* at first sight is awkward grammatically (in the accusative not dative) and does not agree with Galatians 1:22-23. It is not necessary to resort to the expedient of an early corruption of the text, for which there is no manuscript evidence (contra E. F. Harrison 1986:406), or Luke's literary method of modeling the phrase on Luke 4:44 or Acts 10:39 to suggest a Jesus-Paul parallel (contra Krodel 1986:464), or an understanding that Luke is pointing to the effect of the fact that Paul the former persecutor is now a gospel preacher, not his actual presence (Kistemaker

implication "that the proposition which follows is denied and must be argued out" (Lake and Cadbury 1979:321; compare Acts 17:3), Paul lays out two central propositions of the gospel: the Messiah's suffering and, since the resurrection, his provision of salvation blessings to Jew and Gentile alike. Both stand in continuity with the Old Testament but move beyond the current Jewish understanding of it. A Messiah who suffers is possible only if he is the same person as the Suffering Servant (Lk 22:37/ Is 53:12). Only a Messiah who rises *first* from the dead can be the source of salvation blessings: *light* now proclaimed through his disciples to all (Acts 2:25-36/Ps 16:8-11; 110:1; Acts 13:46-47/Is 49:6). The point is clear. Without the resurrection of Christ, the defining moment in human history, there is no future hope for anyone. But when we let Christ's resurrection be our defining moment, the lights come on for our past, present and future.

The Rulers Respond (26:24-29) The Roman governor's "commonsense" outburst shows that he sees neither Jesus' resurrection nor the salvation blessings that flow from it as fit topics for rational discussion (compare 25:19). Such notions can come only from one who is out of his mind, whose *great learning* and exploration of such mysteries are driving him insane.

Paul is preaching for a decision with convincing conviction, and the only way Festus can rationalize his rejection is to declare the messenger mad and his message gibberish. Festus's reaction is instructive for Luke's audience. Their initial response might well be the same. And how many today, with their "commonsense" approach to life, would react as Festus did? It is obviously not the response Paul or Luke is looking for.

Paul answers Festus calmly but firmly. He denies the governor's estimate of his mental condition. He declares that what he is saying (*rhēmata apophthengomai* implies Spirit-filled speech; 2:4, 14; 10:44; 13:42) is *true and reasonable*. Its veracity (1 Kings 17:24; Lk 20:21) and

---

1990:901). Rather, if the accusative is taken as an accusative of extent and seen to refer to all Paul's subsequent witness activity in Judea, the phrase makes both harmonious grammatical and historical sense (Williams 1985:423).

26:23 The NIV renders the *ei* as *that* and turns propositions for debate into affirmations.

26:24 *Mainomai, mania* can refer to a madness inspired of the gods, as well as insanity. But given the cause Festus identifies, it is better to see his interruption as derogatory, not complimentary (O'Toole 1978:125-28; contrast Bruce 1990:505; E. F. Harrison 1986:407).

rational soundness commend it as reliable (note "reasonable" *[sōphrosynē]* contrasted with "mania" in Greek literature: Xenophon *Memorabilia* 1.1.16; Plato *Phaedrus* 244D; *Protagoras* 323B). In fact, Paul can make such an assertion because his message is about an objective historical fact, a public event of which even King Agrippa is aware.

In the post-Enlightenment secularized West, where religion has for some generations been removed from the arena of public discourse and confined to private feelings and opinion, Paul's ringing defense of the gospel as *true and reasonable* utterances of things *not done in a corner* should give us courage to bring gospel truth back into the public arena. Christianity does make sense. It will stand up to public scrutiny. In response to "commonsense" dismissals of the faith as insanity, we must call for patience and a judicious assessment of the facts. Christians have nothing to fear from such scrutiny. Indeed, we believe because of, not in spite of, the facts.

Paul turns to Agrippa, seeking common ground in acceptance of the Old Testament prophets' authority. But Agrippa will not be drawn into a discussion of spiritual matters. His sophisticated avoidance of the slightly embarrassing prospect of discussing matters of religion in public is expressed in the dismissive: "Do you want to convince me that in such a short time you have made me a Christian?"

But Paul won't let him off the hook. Time is not the issue. Paul doesn't care how long it takes. So important is this salvation for Agrippa and all who hear Paul that he prays God they may receive it, "become what he is." Then, with a touch of humor or nobility, he adds, *Except for these chains.*

How tragic is Agrippa's sophisticated avoidance of a confrontation with the risen Christ! At least Festus looked at it directly and called it madness. Agrippa sets conditions that the evangelist cannot meet. To all those who say, "It will take more than this to make me a Christian," Paul warns, "Your conditions are irrelevant in the light of the supreme importance

---

26:28 Agrippa's reply is ambiguous. Does *en oligō* mean "in a short time" (O'Toole 1978:141-45) or "with little effort" or "with few arguments"? Following the more difficult reading, *poiēsai*, should it be rendered "to make" or as a theatrical technical term, "to play"? Should its subject be "Paul" (O'Toole 1978:144) or, as in the NIV, "Agrippa"? What is the tone of the remark? Is it "a trivial jest, a bitter sarcasm, a grave irony, a burst of anger" or

of the salvation this gospel offers. Don't let your requirements prevent you from receiving God's provision."

The Consensus: The Prisoner Is Innocent (26:30-32) The hearing is over. The dignitaries exit and in private discussion agree on Paul's innocence: *This man is not doing anything that deserves death or imprisonment* (compare 23:29; 25:18). And as if to explain the anomaly of an innocent Roman citizen in chains, Agrippa adds, *This man could have been set free, if he had not appealed to Caesar.* This is not a matter of Roman jurisprudence but of Roman politics. Even though a person could be acquitted and released after an appeal to Caesar (Sherwin-White 1963:65), not to honor such an appeal would be to slight the emperor's prestige. These declarations of innocence make it clear that Paul and Christianity cannot be charged with sedition against the state. Nothing in the conduct of the messenger calls into question the truthfulness of the message. Luke's Roman audience and we must come to terms with the gospel and the defining moment it offers by dealing directly with its truth claims.

THE CHURCH IN ALL NATIONS: PAUL'S JOURNEY TO ROME (27:1—28:31)

"To a Roman the city of Rome was the centre of the world; from the golden milestone in the Forum at Rome roads went out in all directions to all parts of the Empire. So when The Acts ends with Paul in Rome preaching the gospel, Luke must mean that now from the centre of the world the gospel is beginning to go out in all directions to all parts of the Empire" (Filson 1970:76). The "salvation applied" portion of the gospel—good news preached to all the nations—indeed finds its fulfillment in Paul's bold and unhindered proclamation at Rome of "the kingdom of God" and the king, the Lord Jesus Christ (28:31; compare Lk 24:46-47).

This phase of Paul's "ministry in chains" has parallels and contrasts

---

"an expression of sincere conviction" (Stott 1990:376; compare Williams 1985:426)? Paul's response seems to require the following rendering: "Do you want to convince me that in such a short time you have made me a Christian?" The tone is sophisticated avoidance by a slightly embarrassed king.

with Christ's death and resurrection. Paul, not unlike Jonah, faces the prospect of a watery grave, but he comes through triumphantly (compare Jonah 1; Lk 11:29-32). Human wisdom (Acts 27:10, 31), encouragement of fellow travelers (27:21-26, 33-38), divine personal protection (28:3-6) and gracious mercy ministry (28:8-9) are all involved. But God's providential working to fulfill his saving purposes through Paul—the gospel's proclamation in Rome—will not be thwarted. This is Luke's final challenge to his Roman audience and to us. If the advance of the gospel is so unstoppable, what is stopping us from embracing it?

□ By Sea to Malta (27:1-44)

When we hear of sudden storms on lake or ocean wreaking havoc on recreational sailors, we are reminded that "even today the sea represents a place of peril, of human vulnerability, the place where would-be sailors are at the mercy of the elements" (Willimon 1988:183). This first-century account of a sea voyage pits the death-dealing opposition of the storm (27:14-20, 27-32, 39-44) against God's gracious providence surrounding and working through wise, courageous, encouraging, nurturing Paul (27:21-26, 33-38). As that gracious providence prevails for Paul and all 275 with him, we who are Christians may ask, "Am I the same source of preservation for those around me?"

Caesarea to Crete; the Storm (27:1-26)

During the apostle Paul's "ministry in chains" he has successfully maneuvered around mob attack, scourging, plot and ambush (21:32-33; 22:22-25; 23:10, 12-34; 25:3-12). Just when he appears to be "home free," granted safe passage to Rome, Paul faces his greatest challenge: a storm at sea. Will natural forces do what human opponents have been unable to do—thwart God's gracious purposes for Paul to preach the gospel in Rome (19:21; 23:11)?

Prologue—Journey to Fair Haven (27:1-8) As Paul embarks on his journey to Rome, Luke reminds us of his prisoner status. Paul is

---

27:1 The ancestor of Julius, as his nomen suggests, probably acquired Roman citizenship under Julius Caesar or Augustus (Bruce 1988:477).

Imperial Regiment (speirēs Sebastēs) probably does not refer to an auxiliary cohort (six hundred men, tenth part of a legion) from *Sebastē* ("Samaria") or to the *speculatores,* "a

handed over along with other prisoners into centurion Julius's custody (compare Lk 23:25). Julius chooses a homeward-bound coasting vessel that is about to call at ports on the western *coast of the province of Asia* until it came to its home port, Adramyttium, located south of Troas, east of Assos and facing the island of Lesbos. Paul's traveling companions include at least Luke and the Macedonian Christian Aristarchus (Acts 19:29; 20:4; Col 4:10, 14; Philem 24).

Borne along by the Syrian coastal current—the Nile water that runs north—the ship, moving at a speed of three knots, covers the sixty-nine nautical miles to Sidon in twenty-three hours. Sidon, mother city of the Phoenicians, with its double harbor, figures prominently in Luke's Gospel as a model of repentant Gentile receptivity to the teaching of Jesus (Lk 6:17; 10:13-14; compare 4:26). It was probably evangelized during the Hellenistic Jewish Christian dispersion after Stephen's death. There were a number of times during Paul's earlier ministry when he may have visited the church there (Acts 11:19, 30; 12:25; 15:3). Through the *kindness* of the centurion Paul is freed, probably under guard, to visit *friends* in the city. They *provide for his needs,* which, as I. Howard Marshall (1980:404) conjectures, may have included conversation, a meal and some gifts to help on the journey.

In contrast to Jesus' suffering, Paul knows relief both from a centurion who shows kindness and from the companionship of friends on board and along the way. The importance of the support of Christian friends should not be underestimated.

On the next leg of the journey, as they strike out to the west, the travelers encounter adverse weather. Contrary winds from the west block their progress. Since their square-rigged vessel does not readily tack into the wind and make headway in a zigzag fashion, the crew chooses to use the island of Cyprus as a shield, sailing on its *lee,* its northern side which faced away from the wind. They may also want to take advantage of the westward two-mile-per-hour current along the southern coast of Asia Minor, as well as the land breezes that at night flow down the valleys

---

special body of imperial guards" (contra Longenecker 1981:558), but to an auxiliary cohort stationed in Palestine that had received the honorary title *Sebastē,* "Augustus, Imperial" (Haenchen 1971:697).

perpendicular to the sea (see Heliodorus *Aethiopica* 4.16.10). So as Luke narrates, *We . . . sailed across the open sea off the coast of Cilicia and Pamphylia, [and] landed at Myra in Lycia.* Myra, on the western third of Asia Minor's south coast, was a chief port of the imperial grain service, a regular port of call for grain vessels taking the northerly route from Alexandria to Rome. Archaeological remains of the grain storage facilities attest to its importance.

The *Alexandrian ship sailing for Italy,* on which the centurion books passage for himself and his prisoners, is probably a vessel in the imperial grain fleet. Since the main time for the Alexandria-to-Rome run was in late spring and early summer, the ship's presence at Myra in early fall probably indicates it is on a second run that the owners are trying to squeeze in before winter (Casson 1971:298).

On this portion of the trip—Myra to Fair Havens, Crete—the same contrary winds from the west accost them. After *many days* they only succeed in making Cnidus, a port at the western end of a long promontory of southwest Asia Minor which stretches out into the Adriatic. As they leave Cnidus and enter the open sea, the northerly winds of the Adriatic blow against them, preventing them from maintaining their westward course. So they drop under *the lee of Crete,* sailing along its southern coast, again using an island as a shield. Even so, keeping close to the coast and making westward progress is difficult. The ship barely makes Fair Havens, a harbor at the midpoint of Crete's south coast, twelve miles east of Cape Matala and five miles from Lasea.

Rejecting an Apostolic Warning (27:9-12) The ancients divided the navigational year on the Mediterranean into four periods (Hesiod *Works and Days* 663-68; Vegetius *Military Institutions of the Romans* 4.39; compare *Genesis Rabbah* 6:5b, "The crossing of the Great Sea too: Thus saith the Lord, who giveth a way in the sea [Is 43:16]—from Pentecost until the Festival [Tabernacles]"—mid-May to mid-October). Op-

---

27:6 It is difficult to obtain a clear picture of the dimensions of such a vessel, for none has been archaeologically recovered (Hirschfeld 1990:28). This one was large enough to accommodate passengers and crew numbering 276 (v. 37). Josephus reports one such ship carrying six hundred persons (*Life* 15). Lucian describes a ship 180 feet long, well over a quarter as wide and 44 feet deep. Since he does not give us the shape of the hull, we still don't know its precise capacity (*The Ship or the Wishes* 5).

27:10 *Can see [theōreō]* may indicate that supernatural insight is involved (Lk 10:18; Acts

timum sea travel could be expected during the summer months, May 15 to September 15. Dangerous times for sailing were September 16 to November 10 and March 11 to May 14. Sea travel on the Mediterranean ceased between November 11 and March 10.

As the ship lies in port at Fair Havens, it is already the *dangerous* period—*after the Fast,* the Jewish Day of Atonement, which occurred in the fall, the tenth day of Tishri. In A.D. 59 this would have been October 5 (Marshall 1980:406).

Paul's warning is well founded (v. 10). Vegetius described the dangers of "winter sailing" as scant daylight, long nights, dense cloud cover, poor visibility and the double raging of winds, showers and snows (*Military Institutions of the Romans* 4.39). The dangerous period saw the beginning of such conditions.

As the centurion, the ship's captain (NIV *pilot*) and the ship's owner or his representative confer, *the majority,* possibly including most of the rest of the crew, reject Paul's counsel and decide to risk a forty mile-journey out in open sea around Cape Matala to Phoenix. Fair Havens's harbor was open to the east, leaving ships unprotected against winter winds (Earle 1982). Phoenix, at the west of the promontory Cape Mouros, was better suited for a wintering ship. The present Phoinika Bay fits the description, for it has an inlet that faces southwest, and there are traces of a inlet, now marred by silting and an earthquake, that faced northwest (Finegan 1981:196). Paul's cautionary word is the first of a number of initiatives in which the apostle demonstrates that he is indeed his "brother's keeper."

The Storm's Fury (27:13-20) A *gentle south wind* comes up, like those common during the summer sailing season, and the officers and crew judge, though wrongly (12:9; 17:18; 26:9), that they have gained their purpose. They *weighed anchor and sailed along the shore of Crete* some three or four miles to Cape Matala. It is probably as they round

7:56; 10:11), though most take it as the common sense of Paul the experienced traveler (Williams 1985:431; Bruce 1988:482). Krodel (1986:474) takes it as a combination of the two.

27:11 *Pilot* is a literal rendering of *kybernētēs* (better "captain"). In Paul's day, "particularly on large ships the captain was a hired professional who had full authority over the running of the vessel and full command of its crew" (Casson 1971:316; compare Plutarch *Moralia* 807B).

the cape that they meet a *wind of hurricane force, called the "Northeaster,"* blowing down from 8,056-foot Mount Ida. The strong cold wind that blows across the Mediterranean in the winter from a general northeasterly direction is caused by a depression ("low") over Libya which induces a strong flow of air from Greece (Finegan 1981:197).

The storm so seizes the ship that the crew is unable to head the vessel into the wind and position it so that the waves will not strike it broadside and break it apart. Though in the main they had to give way to the wind, lower the sails and allow themselves to be driven, they did not do so totally. A small sail on the mast was used to tack and make headway into the wind. Otherwise the ship would have been broken apart by the waves (Haenchen 1971:701).

When people reject the wisdom gained from observing God's natural order, foolish decisions are likely to follow. As one mountaineer said as he turned back from the challenge of climbing an Alaskan peak because his equipment was inadequate for the icy conditions, "There are old mountaineers, bold mountaineers, but no old, bold mountaineers" (Robinson 1993).

The crew takes at least four steps to cope with the storm (Acts 27:16-19). First, under the protection of *the lee,* the south coast, *of a small island called Cauda* some twenty-three miles west of Cape Matala, they hoist and secure on deck the dinghy (NIV's *lifeboat* limits its uses) they are towing. They do this not only to rescue a waterlogged boat from the battering of the waves but also to prevent the rough seas from smashing it against the stern of the ship (Lake and Cadbury 1979:332). Second, they "frap" the ship, undergirding it with cables running vertically under its center hull, four or five turns. This strengthens the hull against the continual pounding of the waves.

27:14, 16 The differences between the NIV and KJV in spelling the storm's name—*Eurakylōn (northeaster)* versus *Euraklydon,* "rough water"—and the island's name, *Cauda* versus *Clauda,* can be accounted for by different manuscript traditions. The KJV follows a later manuscript tradition that manifests copyists' adjustments to explain difficult spelling. *Eurakylōn* is a hybrid compound of Greek *Euros* (east wind) and Latin *Aquilo* (north wind). Metzger (1971:497) says it does not occur elsewhere in ancient texts, though Hemer (1975:103) has found it in a Latin inscription, a twelve-point wind-rose incised in a pavement at Thugga in proconsular Africa. *Kauda,* the true form of the island's name, was frequently spelled with an *l* (Metzger 1971:498).

Third, *they lowered the sea anchor*. This was a broad piece of wood held vertical by a weight below and an empty barrel on top. It would slow the ship's movement from crest to crest and help keep it on course (Haenchen 1971:703). The lowering of the mainyard with its sail and the setting of a storm sail may also be included in this lowering (compare Lucian *Toxaris: Or, Friendship* 19). If some sort of course westward could be maintained, they could avoid the *sandbars of Syrtis*. One hundred miles off the Libyan coast and three hundred miles in circumference, this area has deep waters with shallows; "the result is, at the ebb and the flow of the tides, that sailors sometimes fall into the shallows and stick there, and that the safe escape of a boat is rare" (Strabo *Geography* 17.3.20). So ancient sailors sailing along the North African coast kept a safe distance and took precautions not to be "driven by winds into these gulfs" (Strabo *Geography* 17.3.20).

Fourth, if we may understand verses 18 and 18 as dealing with the same gear, it is probably the mainyard spar, as long as the deck, and the accompanying gear and tackle that, after a failed first attempt, they succeed in throwing overboard on the third day (Clark 1975:145; NIV's *cargo* in v. 18 must then be differently understood). Thus lightening the ship by removing movable gear and tackle from the deck, the crew hopes to avoid further storm-induced damage to the ship's structure.

These herculean efforts to secure the ship, its course and their safety still left these sea voyagers at the mercy of the elements. The cloud cover and darkness of the storm meant they didn't know where they were *for many days*. The sun and the stars—in ancient times the only means of navigation on the open sea—were out of sight. Besides all this, *the storm continued raging. Finally all hope* was being abandoned (imperfect passive) that they would be saved (compare Lk 23:35, 37, 39).

27:17 Haenchen (1971:703) notes four methods of frapping: vertically in the hold or underneath the hull, horizontally on deck or around the hull (he opts for the last method). Casson (1971:91) says that vertical frapping was customary for merchant ships and horizontal for warships. The NIV follows this understanding.

Since Luke uses a general term, *skeuos* or "gear" (NIV *sea anchor*) to refer to what was lowered, a variety of interpretations have surfaced: mainyard carrying the main sail (Williams 1985:435; E. F. Harrison 1986:417), sails (Krodel 1986:475), all equipment on which the ship's course and speed depended—rudder, tackle, anchor—or sea anchor (Marshall 1980:409; Bruce 1988:486; NIV). The latter seems to best suit the action's purpose.

When do we abandon hope? When we do not know where we are but do have the terrible knowledge that we may not get out alive. And such is the condition of many people today, disoriented in emotional, relational, social or physical storms.

The Apostle's Encouragement (27:21-26) *The men had gone a long time without food.* Asitia indicates this is voluntary. Is it anxiety, seasickness or the inedibility of the foodstuffs (because the storm spoiled them or made cooking impossible)?

Paul stands up in their midst (not as NIV, *before them*) and says, in essence, "Cheer up! The outcome will be positive." He reviews the counsel he gave at Fair Havens (27:10), not so much to say "I told you so" (contrast Longenecker 1981:561) as to partly establish why he should be believed now. Indeed, he frames what they *should* have done using his favorite verb for divine necessity (*edei;* compare Lk 24:44; Acts 23:11; 27:26). This may point to the revelatory quality of his prior warning (see note at v. 10). Paul, then, "urges" (same word translated "warned" in v. 9) them, *Keep up your courage, because not one of you will be lost; only the ship will be destroyed.*

Paul immediately proceeds to give his source of information. His allegiance and his piety are devoted to the one true God (compare Lk 1:74; 2:37; Acts 24:14). That God has sent his angel "this very night" (NIV *last night*). He "approached me" (NIV *stood beside me;* compare 9:39) and gave this message of encouragement, which reaffirms a divine promise and announces a gracious gift. As at Corinth, the angel urged Paul to "stop being afraid" (18:9). He reiterated the divine necessity *(dei)* of standing *trial before Caesar* (23:11). He announced the good news: *God has graciously given you the lives of all who sail with you* (the perfect tense, *has . . . given,* communicates certainty). Luke does not explicitly say that this is in answer to Paul's intercession (contrast Marshall [1980:410], who cites Gen 18:23-33 as a parallel). All we can be sure of is that God is determined that Paul not perish at sea, and has further

27:23 The *angel* is not really a christophany presented according to an angel christology to communicate to Luke's audience and also accommodate the pagan understanding of Paul's fellow travelers (contra Krodel 1986:476). As Bruce (1990:521) puts it, Paul knows the difference between the appearance of an angel and the appearance of Christ to him (Acts 18:9; 23:11; 22:8, 14). Interestingly, this is the only appearance of an angel to Paul recorded in Acts. Luke may have included it to complete a parallelism with Peter and Jesus (Lk 22:43).

decided to preserve all those with him.

Paul's application of the angel's message to his fellow travelers is a call to keep up their courage. He also states that they will *run aground on some island*. He bases his call on his own faith that God's deed will match this prophetic word.

Paul models for us the stance of one who is convinced that God's gracious purposes cannot be thwarted, even when outward circumstances call that conviction into question. It is not that he is simply a practical man in a critical emergency—"keeping his head when all about him are losing theirs" (contrast Bruce 1988:475). Rather, it is precisely because he is an "impractical" holy man, a Christian apostle who receives messages from angels, that he can be an encouragement in the fury of the storm. His strength comes from beyond the storm: he "believes God," that he can accomplish what he has promised. Such faith is the foundation for a life of encouragement.

The Shipwreck (27:27-44)

Eric Liddell, "the Flying Scotsman," won the four-hundred-meter race at the 1924 Paris Olympics in world-record time. But his real heroics occurred twenty years later, in the Weihsien concentration camp in China. This missionary's faith and energy encouraged many of the eighteen hundred trapped in the camp's squalid conditions. "Uncle Eric" to children separated from their parents, he "organized activities, served as a teacher and a guardian for youth, and fulfilled the role of pastor until a brain tumor claimed his life in February 1945" (Williamson 1991:127).

Many centuries and many miles away on the dark, storm-tossed Mediterranean, Paul too determined to make a difference to those around him. His example helps us understand what it is to proclaim by one's life the salvation blessings found in Christ alone.

Warning: Conserve Skilled Human Resources (27:27-32) Two weeks, or 324 hours, have passed since Cauda. If the ship has been *driven*

The angel's role in Peter's and Paul's experiences is basically the same: to promote the extension of the apostles' witness through powerful release or guidance (Acts 5:19; 10:3, 7, 22; 11:13; 12:7-11; compare 8:26).

27:26 This is not necessarily a matter of divine revelation (contrast Haenchen 1971:705). It could be the deduction of an experienced traveler based on faith in the promise (Williams 1985:437). Malta is the only island in the stretch of open water between Tunisia and Sicily.

across the Adriatic Sea at a rate of one and one-half knots, it has covered 482 nautical miles. On a course of a very shallow curve, the ship would find itself at Malta, 474 nautical miles from Crete (Haenchen 1971:705; Smith 1978:124-28). *About midnight,* whether from the waves' change of motion into a running swell or the sound of surf crashing against Point Koura, a quarter of a mile away, *the sailors sensed they were approaching land.* Luke actually speaks from the point of view of the seafarers, who see the boat as stationary, and says, "The land was approaching."

The sailors test their sense that land is near by casting a leadline overboard to take depth soundings. The "lead had a hollow on the underside which, filled with tallow or grease, brought up samples of the bottom" (Casson 1971:246; Herodotus *History* 2.5). Their unit of measure is "fathom," the distance between fingertips when the arms are extended— approximately six feet (E. F. Harrison 1986:420). Probably no more than thirty minutes later (Smith 1978:130-31), a second sounding finds that the sea floor is thirty feet closer.

The sailors take immediate action to halt the ship's drift toward a coast that they cannot make out in the dark. They hurl four anchors from the ship's stern, probably by casting a cable with two anchors attached from each side of the stern. This would not only halt the ship's progress but also position its bow facing the shore to prevent the waves from making damaging broadside blows.

The vessel is now poised for its approach at daybreak. The sailors have done all they know to do. Now all that is left is to keep on wishing for daylight (NIV *prayed for daylight*). Though God is sovereign, human beings still have responsibility. These sailors met theirs, and we must meet ours, especially in adverse circumstances that can tempt us to despairing passivity.

So important is the crew to the survival of all that when some seek to escape, under the pretext of using the dinghy to position anchors from

---

27:27 *Being driven (diapherō)* may refer to the zigzag movement of a vessel tossed about in heavy seas (Philo *De Migratione Abrahami* 148; Lucian *Hermotimus* 28; Plutarch *Moralia* 552C; so some map renderings of this journey). Given Luke's use of *dia* in compounds as an intensifier, his other use of this term (Acts 13:49), and the time and distance involved, it is better to take the term as the NIV does.

In New Testament times *the Adriatic Sea* designated a portion of the Mediterranean

the bow, Paul draws this to the attention of the centurion and his men: *Unless these men stay with the ship, you cannot be saved.* Luke may be playing on his leitmotif of salvation here, speaking of physical rescue but intending to point beyond it (compare Acts 4:9, 12; 16:30-31). The word of promise is "God has graciously given you the lives of all who sail with you" (27:24). If the sailors jump ship, this promise cannot be fulfilled for them or for the passengers.

The assurance of physical salvation through belief in the divine message to Paul and the commitment to remain with him is an acted parable of the essentials of spiritual salvation: believing the gospel message and solidarity with the gospel messenger (14:3-4; 16:14-15, 32-34; 17:2-4, 34; 18:8). Impulsively or wisely, the soldiers cut the ropes so that the dinghy falls away. The passengers' and crew's fate will now be the same.

Encouragement to Gather Strength (27:33-38) Each successive appearance of Paul in the voyage narrative moves him more to the center. As the key to the physical survival of all on board, he encourages these who because of *constant suspense* (anxious expectation; compare Lk 21:26) have not gone to the galley to prepare a meal for a fortnight (they may have nibbled, however, on their own supplies—Williams 1985:438). He urges them to gather strength for the final push to shore by taking a meal. Again he uses salvation terminology: *You need it to survive* (literally, "This is for your salvation"). His reassurance comes in the form of a proverbial saying present in the Old Testament and Jesus' teaching: *Not one of you will lose a single hair from his head* (1 Sam 14:45; 2 Sam 14:11; 1 Kings 1:52; Lk 21:18). So certain is physical rescue under divine providence that not even a hair—the most easily detachable part of the human body—will be lost in the process.

Paul matches words with actions: *he took some bread and gave thanks to God. . . . Then he broke it and began to eat.* We should not doubt that Luke wants us to understand that Paul eats here with eucharistic intent

including the stretch between Crete and Malta (Pausanias *Description of Greece* 5.25.3; Ptolemy *Geography* 3.4.1, 15).

27:35 Many have concluded that given the occasion, the presence of unbelieving soldiers, crew and passengers, and the absence of references to the cup and of explicit references to the Lord's Supper, Paul ate no more then an ordinary meal (Lake and Cadbury 1979:336; Haenchen 1971:707; Marshall 1980:414; Stott 1990:392; Kistemaker 1990:936). But the clustering of a number of terms distinctive to the "words of institution" (Barrett 1987:60)

(Lk 22:15-20; 24:30-31, 35; Acts 2:42, 46; 20:7, 11). Originally the words of institution probably bracketed everyday meals of the believers, so the sanctifying giving of thanks and inaugural breaking of bread took on a kerygmatic significance in combination with Jesus' words, "This is my body given for you." Paul could have done this here, but to what effect? This is the climax of this acted parable, in which physical salvation by divine providence, mediated by the wisdom and guidance of God's apostle, points to the spiritual salvation of which this apostle is also a messenger. To those who "just don't get it," Paul is simply being prudent—eating food in thankfulness and confidence. But to those who hear the Lord's death proclaimed until he comes, Paul's eucharistic example leads to the open secret of the apostle's life: faith in Christ's saving work.

The ship's company are *encouraged.* They turn away from their anxious, despairing vigil (27:20) and regain sufficient heart to take food. Indeed, all 276 on board eat their fill (Lk 9:17) and then set about final preparations for approaching the shore. The precious cargo of grain, which has served as ballast in the storm, would now prevent them from running aground as high on the shore as possible. So they begin to jettison it. The effect of Paul's encouragement and eucharistic example demonstrates the power of one who has determined to be "salt and light," as well as a witness, to those around him.

A Saving Presence—the Prophecy Fulfilled (27:39-44) At daybreak the crew makes a decision based on their observations. They "tried to recognize" the land (conative imperfect; Williams 1985:441). All they can make out is *a bay with a sandy beach,* but they hope that here they can "beach the ship." That is their plan, if they "might be able" to pull

---

suggests either that Luke is portraying an ordinary meal in such a way as to remind the reader of the Eucharist (Krodel 1986:478) or that he is offering a more nuanced understanding of what Paul was actually doing. Bruce suggests, "To the majority it was an ordinary meal, while for those who ate with eucharistic intention (Paul and his fellow-Christians) it was a valid eucharist" (Bruce 1988:492).

27:39 Malta was part of the northerly run from Alexandria to Rome (Casson 1971:297). Therefore they probably could not identify the island from the landscape, not because Malta was not a part of normal shipping routes (contra Haenchen 1971:707) but because this part of Malta, which came to be known as St. Paul's Bay, was remote from the main habor and therefore not familiar to them (Bruce 1990:526; Williams 1985:441).

27:41 *Sandbar* correctly translates *topon dithalasson* (literally, "place of two seas"). James Smith (1978:142), followed by Bruce (1988:494), identifies it with a channel that runs

it off (*dynainto:* the optative mood of personal wish shows the level of uncertainty under which they continue to labor; compare 27:12-13).

They "cut loose the anchors," or simply let the anchor ropes fall into the sea (Haenchen 1971:707). They untie *the ropes that held the rudders.* These two large paddles, secured during the storm, are now lowered into place on each side of the ship at the stern to provide steerage (Casson 1971:228). They hoist *the foresail to the wind;* this sail sloped forward almost like a bowsprit and also provided steerage (Lake and Cadbury 1979:338). Then the crew "began to head" for the beach (inceptive imperfect; Kistemaker 1990:941).

At the entrance to the bay they unexpectedly *struck a sandbar;* today the shoal is thirty-nine feet below the surface, but then it probably stood in only thirteen feet of water. The ship effectively *ran aground,* for *the bow stuck fast and would not move.* The rocks of Malta disintegrate into extremely minute particles of sand and clay when acted upon by currents or by surface agitation. They form a tenacious deposit of clay (Smith 1978:144). The combination of the bay floor's composition and the direction of the wind made this sandbar the ship's final resting place. But the sea was not through with the ship. The *pounding of the surf* gradually broke up *the stern* (continuous imperfect). Paul's prophecy was coming true: *only the ship will be destroyed* (27:22).

The soldiers knew that they could pay with their lives for any prisoners who escaped when all abandoned ship for land. So they *planned to kill the prisoners.* But the centurion had other plans (compare previous Roman protection: 21:33-36; 23:10, 23; 25:1-12). *To spare [diasōsai] Paul,* he thwarted their plan and *ordered those who could swim to jump over-*

---

between an island and the bay's shore. This identification does not take into account the consciously analogical nature of Strabo's description of the Bosporus (*Geography* 2.5.22) as a *dithalasson.* The term consistently describes the geographical feature of land that creates "two seas"—a sandbar, promontory or isthmus (Dio Chrysostom *Discourses* 5.9; Strabo *Geography* 1.1.8).

Of the surf represents an expansion of the curt expression *by the pounding* (literally, "by the force"). The latter phrase is found in many ancient manuscripts but not all. Because Alexandrian scribes who produced the manuscripts that lack the phrase were known for their penchant for brevity, the UBS text editors gave it a "C" rating and chose to include it in square brackets (Metzger 1971:500). Haenchen (1971:708) suggests that the phrase may better refer to the force of the impact that threw the bow high.

board first and get to land. In a very real sense Paul was a "saving presence," for saving him automatically meant saving the other prisoners. Thus as a mediator of physical preservation, Paul again becomes a living parable of spiritual salvation, which is just as certain when persons take refuge in the name Paul preaches (16:31). Whether swimming, floating on planks (which may have been used to hold the grain cargo in place) or riding on the backs of swimmers, *everyone reached land in safety.*

The comforting prophetic word had been fulfilled to the last letter (27:22, 34). The strongest of natural forces threatening Paul's existence had been unable to thwart God's providential purposes for him. Solidarity with Paul meant physical life. For those considering the claims of Christ, the question is, If God's messenger can be so salubrious to old salts, what can his message do for me?

☐ Ministry at Malta and Rome (28:1-31)

Among the watchwords of the 1989 evangelical world congress on evangelism, Lausanne II in Manila, was for the "whole church" to bring the "whole gospel" to the "whole world." For many at the conference, "the whole gospel" meant, as it did for Paul, proclaiming Christ in "word, deed and sign."

At Rome Paul engages in personal evangelism (28:23-31). On Malta he is involved in a mercy ministry (28:3, 8-9). And the apostle himself, unaffected by a poisonous snake grasping his hand, is proclamation "in sign" (28:3-6). Taken together and in proper relation to each other, these scenes help us understand what it is to proclaim "the whole gospel."

Malta: Mercy Ministry (28:1-10)

"At least I have my health!" How many times have we heard this dec-

---

27:44 *On pieces of the ship (epi tinōn tōn apo tou ploiou)* could be translated "on some of the ship's people." The form *tinōn,* an indefinite pronoun, may be either masculine or neuter (Lake and Cadbury 1979:339). The picture, then, would be of swimmers helping nonswimmers.

28:1 *Malta* refers to an island 58 miles south of Sicily and 180 miles north of Cape Bon in Tunisia. Angus Acworth's (1973) and Otto Meinardus's (1976) proposal of Mljet, off Dubrovnik in the Adriatic, is effectively answered by Hemer (1975; see commentary and notes at 27:14, 27). Heinz Warnecke's (1987) more recent suggestion of the western Greek island of Kephallenia, five hundred kilometers south of Mljet, though defended as a possibility by Alfred Suhl (1991), has been thoroughly critiqued by Jürgen Wehnert (1990).

laration of the high, if not supreme, value placed on physical well-being? What is God's perspective on physical health? How is it related to the saving "wholeness" the gospel announces?

Health Preserved by the Power of God (28:1-6) Though the crew and passengers were *safely on shore* (*diasōthentes;* compare 27:43-44), they still faced the possibility of slavery or death if they met unfriendly islanders. The inhabitants of Malta could well have been such. Luke labels them "barbarians" (note NIV's softening to *islanders*). Their language was a Punic (Carthaginian) dialect. The island, strategically located at the narrows of the Mediterranean, had been settled from Phoenician Carthage in the sixth century B.C. Though Rome had captured it from Carthage in 216 B.C. and Augustus had settled veterans and their families on it, those who met Paul at this remote bay were of the original settlers' stock.

God in his providence made the rescue complete, for these uncouth, uncivilized *islanders* showed *unusual kindness* and *welcomed* the shipwreck survivors with a *fire*. Though the temperature may have been about 50 degrees Fahrenheit, the rigors of the journey and the swim to shore had soaked the travelers to the bone. A fire was necessary relief from the rain and cold. Paul's promise, *Not one of you will lose a single hair from his head* (27:34), continued to be true.

Jesus and Paul modeled the "character of authority as service" (Lk 22:25-27; L. T. Johnson 1992:461). Thus Paul *gathered a pile of brushwood and . . . put it on the fire.* No act of service for the health and well-being of others was too menial for him or his Master, nor should it be for us. But in that act danger struck: *a viper, driven out by the heat, fastened itself on his hand.* Lawrence of Arabia relates a similar experience: "When the fire grew hot a long black snake wound slowly out into

---

28:2 Many interpret *barbaroi* ("barbarians") not culturally but linguistically (Hemer 1985:101; Bruce 1990:531) as "non-Greek speakers," whose language sounded to Greeks like "bar-bar-bar-bar." But the islanders' unusual kindness in hospitality indicates that Luke wants us to think in terms of both language and culture—that is, non-Greek speakers and uncivilized (Miles and Trompf 1979:266; E. F. Harrison 1986:424; contrast Stott [1990:394], who thinks the hospitality shows that they were civilized).

It was raining: Bruce 1990:531 and NIV correctly render *ephestōta* (perfect tense) as a past event with continuing results, rather than as an impending event (as Kistemaker 1990:950).

our group; we must have gathered it, torpid, with the twigs" (Lawrence 1927:107, quoted in Bruce 1988:497).

The islanders, steeped in an animistic worldview, thought of the gods as using the forces of nature, especially storm and sea, for retributive justice. They interpreted Paul's snakebite as the work of the goddess "Justice" against Paul, who must be a murderer. In a Greek epigram Statyllius Flaccus tells of a mariner who escaped the whirlwind and fury of the deadly sea, only to be slain by a viper on the Libyan sand (*Greek Anthology* 7.290).

The islanders were following the conventional wisdom: "bad things happen to bad people." Yet Paul's innocence (23:29; 26:31) encourages Luke's readers and us to take a second look at the significance of this snakebite. At the very least, it calls into question the adequacy of any worldview that solves the problem of evil in such a mechanistic fashion.

In a very matter-of-fact way Paul *shook the snake off* and *suffered no ill effects.* Thus he proved true Jesus' promise to his messengers (Lk 10:19; compare Ps 91:13). Still, suffering no harm is the exception, not the rule, for Christian disciples in general and for Paul in particular (Acts 14:22; 9:16).

The islanders kept on expecting Paul to either *swell up* (compare Num 5:21, 27) or burn with fever (*pimprasthai* can mean either; Bauer, Gingrich and Danker 1979:658) and *suddenly fall dead* as the poison acted to destroy blood corpuscles and vessels. But their expectations went unfulfilled. How were they to explain Paul's preservation in health? They began to say, or repeatedly said, "He is a god!"

28:3-5 No poisonous snakes are currently found on Malta. Because poisonous snakes generally strike and release, rather than biting and holding on, some conclude that this is not an eyewitness account (Conzelmann 1987:223; Haenchen 1971:713, 716). But conditions on the island may reasonably be thought to have changed over the centuries, so the absence of poisonous snakes now does not necessarily call into question a report of their presence in Paul's day (Krodel 1986:479). That the snake was indeed poisonous, although it did not behave as expected, should be our conclusion based on the islanders' eyewitness reaction. We should expect them to know their snakes.

28:4 The Greeks viewed Justice as a virgin daughter of Zeus who kept watch for any injustice done on earth and reported it to her father, who then dispensed retributive justice to make it right, including destroying ships at sea (Hesiod *Works and Days* 239, 256; Plutarch *Moralia* 161F). The Phoenicians also had a god (or at least demigod) called Justice. Philo of Byblos's *Phoenician History,* as reported in Eusebius's *Preparation for the Gospel* 1.10, speaks of the generation from the gods—mortals responsible for the development of

The islanders' about-face shows the power of a worldview for interpreting experience—and how a non-Christian worldview often won't "get it right." Those who have a non-Christian worldview and observe a "witness in sign" are likely to misconstrue what is happening unless an interpretation, a "witness in word," is provided. Even then, unless the Lord opens the heart to understand the gospel witness, the miraculous sign will not serve to point unambiguously to the power of Jesus the Savior. The Maltese are not alone in misinterpreting a "witness in sign" (Acts 2:12-13; 3:12; 8:18-21; 14:11-18; 19:13-16). And today Luke calls the "signs and wonders" movement to reckon with this ambiguity and aim to make the Spirit-empowered, Spirit-illuminating proclamation of the gospel message central to any "power encounter."

Paul Ministers Divine Healing (28:7-10) In parallel with the islanders' initial welcome is the official welcome by Publius, *the chief official* on the island. Luke's report of the survivors' *three days* of hospitality at Publius's *estate* would certainly enhance Paul's status in the eyes of Luke's readers, especially if *us* referred only to Paul and his Christian companions.

Paul's host has an older relative who needs physical healing (compare Jesus' and Peter's ministry: Lk 4:38; Acts 9:33-34). Publius's father *was sick in bed, suffering from* bouts of *fever and dysentery* (*pyretois*, plural). It is probably the "Malta fever" (*Micrococcus melitensis*), which in the nineteenth century was traced to the milk of Malta goats and for which a vaccine was developed in 1887. Untreated, it lasted an average of four months, but in some cases up to two to three years (Longenecker 1981:565).

---

various aspects of culture—among whom was Sydyk, Justice.

28:6 The lack of rebuke to the islanders' exclamation is not because Luke contradicts himself and presents Paul as a "divine man" (contra Conzelmann 1987:223). Rather, Luke lets the confused fickleness of the Maltese be its own rebuke. Longenecker (1981:564) says that because the rebuke is not reported, there was probably no worship (contrast Acts 14:11-18).

28:7 *Chief official of the island:* Hemer's (1985:100) analysis of Maltese inscriptions shows that *ho prōtos tēs nēsou* refers not to the Roman procurator, who was over both Gozo and Malta, but to the chief local magistrate of Malta (the principal island of the two). Publius, the official's first name, was used either because of local custom or because of the relationship he developed with the survivors (Longenecker 1981:564). Though some say that *us* may refer only to Paul and his Christian companions (Polhill 1992:533), the size of the estate, its servant staff and the limited time involved may indicate that the entire group was accommodated (Williams 1985:445).

Paul parallels Jesus' and Peter's practice in some ways: he goes to the bedside and lays hands on the man (Lk 4:39-40; Acts 9:34; compare Paul's experience in 9:17). But he makes a significant addition: he prefaces the laying on of hands with prayer, thus showing as explicitly as possible the true source of the healing power (compare Jn 11:41-42).

The islanders' misunderstanding of Paul's survival after the snakebite—"He is a god!"—explains his methods here. Publius's father and the Maltese must learn for the first time—and we must never forget—that any restoration of physical health comes from God, whether it be directly or through the practice of medicine. We, like Paul, show that we are convinced of this truth if we ask for healing in prayer.

The sick on the island respond to the news of the healing by "approaching" Paul, one after another, and "being healed" by him (imperfect continuous action; compare Lk 4:40-41; Acts 5:15-16). Though Christians may differ on what aspects of Paul's miraculous ministry were unique to him as an apostle and which are possible today, all should agree that the proclamation of the "whole gospel" will involve prayer-saturated witness to and concern for the "whole person" (compare Jas 5:13-18).

Paul experiences what he had instructed the Corinthians about—the dynamic of sowing spiritual things and reaping physical things (1 Cor 9:11; also see Rom 15:27). The islanders *honored* Paul's party *in many ways* and *furnished* them *with the supplies . . . needed.* A mercy ministry embraced in truth will not simply amaze or bring physical restoration—it will make one merciful.

To Rome: Imprisonment and Witness (28:11-31)

Today the operative word in computers is "interactive." Books in soft-

---

28:10 *Honored us in many ways,* taken together with verse 9 (with *therapeuō*), does not necessarily indicate that Luke added his medical skills to Paul's miraculous healing ministry. Bruce (1988:500) raises this as a possibility (but compare Lk 6:18, where *therapeuō* and *iaomai* are used interchangeably to speak of miraculous healing; Polhill 1992:534). The first-person plural simply signifies that Luke and the other Christian companions were indirect beneficiaries of the honors given (Williams 1985:446).

Though *timē* can refer to a fee for professional services rendered, particularly a physician's (Sirach 38:1; 1 Tim 5:17), the NIV has a better rendering for the phrase, which literally is "honored with honors," given the nature of the ministry.

ware permit us to interact with the text by writing our own endings. By the way Luke concludes Acts, he shows us that he wants us to interact fully with its message—not that we control it, but that it controls us.

Arrival at Rome (28:11-16) The shipwreck survivors were probably on Malta from mid-November to mid-February or the beginning of March. Then Paul and the rest of the passengers and crew *put out to sea* again. At one of Malta's large harbors they had found *an Alexandrian ship with the figurehead of the twin gods Castor and Pollux.* Twin sons of Tyndareus, king of Sparta, the *Dioscouroi* had been immortalized as gods from the union of Leda, queen of Sparta, and Zeus. Seeing their constellation, the Gemini, while on the high seas was thought to be a sign of good fortune. They were the patron deities of sailors and protectors of innocent seafarers, and their cult had devotees in Egypt as well as Italy (Epictetus *Discourses* 2.18.29). Euripides presents them as guardians of truth and punishers of perjurers (*Electra* 1342-55).

It is probably with an intended ironic twist that Luke notes Paul's embarkation on "The Castor and Pollux." For though the unbelieving ancients would have attributed Paul's rescue to "the Twins" and taken it as a token of his innocence, Paul has made clear he belongs to, serves and believes in the one true God, who was his protector and deliverer (27:23-25). So today, though others tout the gods of non-Christian religion or secular technopolitical ideology as protectors and saviors, the Christian knows who is really in gracious control.

After a sixty-mile voyage north, the ship *put in at Syracuse,* on the southeast coast of Sicily, the triangular island at the tip of the boot of the Italian peninsula. They stayed for *three days* at this provincial capital city, famed for fishing, shipbuilding and bronze work.

The seventy-mile passage to Rhegium was uneventful. This Italian port

28:11 Pliny (*Natural History* 2.47) says that sea travel resumed after February 7; Vegetius (*Military Institutions of the Romans* 4.39) says after March 10 (compare Josephus *Jewish War* 2.203).

28:13 The NIV's *set sail* follows the better attested but more difficult reading (*perielontes,* a nautical term of uncertain meaning; Metzger 1971:501). The other reading, *perielthontes* ("sailing around or along," possibly pointing to tacking), could be original and the other due to the scribal error of skipping the theta. More likely *perielthontes* is a scribal attempt to make *perielontes* intelligible (Metzger 1971:501). A number of commentators and modern translations prefer *perielthontes,* "sailing around" (Stott 1990:396; Polhill 1992:536). If Acts 27:40 may guide us, in this context *perielontes* probably means "weigh anchor, cast loose."

is six or seven miles from Messina, across the strait that separates Sicily from Italy. On the strength of a *south wind* the ship moved northward and in two days covered the 175 nautical miles (overall speed five knots) to Puteoli.

Puteoli, because of its location in the Bay of Naples and its man-made jetties, was at this time, in Strabo's words, "a very great emporium," Rome's main port of entry from the east (Strabo *Geography* 5.4.6; Seneca *Epistles* 77.1). Since Josephus mentions a Jewish colony at Puteoli (*Jewish Wars* 2.104), it is not surprising that Paul and his Christian companions *found some [Christian] brothers.* Their invitation to *spend a week with them* of course presupposed a request to the centurion and his consent (compare 27:3).

What an attractive picture of the worldwide network of support and encouragement that Christians know! To the cosmopolitan Roman then, and the sophisticated but unconnected urbanite now, Paul's experience of instant but genuine intimacy and full-orbed mutual commitment in the company of *brothers* at Puteoli is a refreshing picture of what they long for and can have in the gospel (compare 16:15, 33-34; 21:7; 27:3).

And so we came to Rome. The word *so* brings out two themes in Acts. It looks back and climactically marks the precise fulfillment of God's promise to Paul (23:11; 27:24). But it also points forward, telling the reader to note the way Paul and his party came to Rome: in the company of Roman Christians who came to give them the kind of welcome reserved for dignitaries (*apantēsis;* Cicero *Letters to Atticus* 16.11).

Paul made his way twenty miles up the Via Compana to its intersection with the Via Appia, the Appian Way. Statius called this Roman road "the worn and well-known track of Appia, queen of the long roads" (*Silvae* 2.2.12). The 130-mile trek to Rome probably took five days. Moving

---

28:14 The double reference to arrival at Rome (28:14, 16) may be explained either by Luke's desire to set in bold relief Paul's encouraging encounter with the Roman Christians or by his frame of mind—his eagerness to bring the account to a climax (Longenecker 1981:567). Harmonizing the double reference by seeing the first as pointing to a larger geographical area, the "administrative district of Rome" (Ramsay 1896:347), has been consistently rejected (for example, Lake and Cadbury 1979:345; Polhill 1992:536). Simon Kistemaker's "so we started for Rome" (1990:955), while it permits the phrase to function as a title framing the next sequence of events, reduces its effectiveness as a climactic statement of fulfillment.

through hill country and returning to the coast only three times, this road passed through the Pontine Marshes, in which a canal had been constructed in an attempt at draining them. At the northern end of the marsh, forty-three miles from Rome, was *the Forum of Appius,* "crammed with boatmen and stingy tavern-keepers" (Horace *Satires* 1.5.3-6). Ten miles farther was *Three Taverns* (Cicero *Letters to Atticus* 2.10). At both these "halting stations" Christian *brothers* from Rome, who *had heard that* Paul and the others *were coming,* greeted him and provided a reception and escort to Rome fit for an emperor.

What an irony: Paul the imperial prisoner makes a triumphal procession to the capital of the Empire! Thus proceeds the advance of the gospel in fulfillment of Acts 1:8, a demonstration of the truth of its declaration that it would be proclaimed in all nations.

At the sight of these men Paul thanked God and was encouraged (literally, "took courage"). Why? From his letter to the Romans and from Acts we know that one of Paul's long-standing desires was to bear witness in Rome (19:21; Rom 1:10-12; 15:22-24, 30-32). Along the way to that goal, he had anticipated and met some significant obstacles. When, with God's help, we achieve divinely appointed goals, the only proper response is thankfulness.

And as for the future? Paul "took courage" especially at the sight of the Roman Christians. Because the Judaizing opposition either followed Paul to Rome or greeted him there (Phil 1:15-19), this show of support was surely most significant to him. As Christians today face the future, they too need support from one another, especially in prayer, if they are to "take courage."

As Paul and his companions *got to* (better "entered") *Rome,* they were no doubt struck with, as Horace says, "the smoke, the riches and the din

28:16 Scholars have differed over the precise identification of the officer, *stratopedarchēs,* to whom Paul was handed over according to the longer Western reading. Was it the *princeps peregrinorum,* commandant of the *castra peregrinorum* on the Caelian hill, the headquarters of legionary liaison officers on furlough in Rome (Ramsay 1896:348)? Was it the *praefectus praetorii,* the prefect of the Praetorian Guard, to whom prisoners of the provinces were entrusted (Haenchen 1971:718; Pliny *Letters* 10.57.2)? Or—more likely, in view of a prefect's exalted position—was it the commandant of the Praetorian barracks near the Viminal Gate who actually processed Paul? (See Sherwin-White 1963:108-10 and Bruce 1990:537; Pliny's wording allows for such an understanding.)

of wealthy Rome," the ancient world's largest city, capital and hub of the Empire (*Odes* 3.29.12). Here Paul experienced a more lenient form of custody, his own rented quarters, where he remained chained at the wrist to one soldier of the Praetorian guard, who served a four-hour shift (Phil 1:13; Josephus *Antiquities* 18.169).

Encounter with Jewish Leaders (28:17-22) *Three days* after Paul's arrival, in accordance with his "to the Jew first" strategy, he *called together the leaders of the Jews* (13:5, 14; 14:1; 16:13; 17:2, 10, 17; 18:4; 19:8). The Jewish community at Rome in mid-first century is estimated to have numbered forty to fifty thousand, most being slaves and freedmen. They inhabited "the great section of Rome on the other side of the Tiber" (Philo *Legatio ad Gaium* 155). The names of ten to thirteen synagogues have been recovered from inscriptions in the catacombs (Dunn 1988:xlvi).

As Paul began to speak (NIV *said;* the Greek is inchoative imperfect—Robertson 1934:885), he addressed his hearers as *brothers.* The apostle never finally turned his back on his compatriots. He saw each new audience of Jews as potentially containing some of the elect remnant who would hear and respond to the gospel (Rom 10:9-15; 11:5). And today Paul's initiative teaches us that centuries of Jewish rejection and Gentile anti-Semitism or neglect cannot erase the responsibility that all witnesses have to make sure the gospel goes "to the Jew first."

This brief address is in a chiastic structure highlighting four affirmations. First, Paul is innocent before the Jews (28:17b, 19c). They can bring no sustainable charges against him, and he has none to bring against them. The Jews may charge that Paul is working against "the people" and *the customs of our ancestors,* as they did when they tried to lynch him and when they accused him at the hearings (21:28; 24:6; 25:7). But the charges won't stick, because Paul always acted for and not against his people (26:17, 23) and always respected Jewish customs (21:23-24, 26). Further, Paul does not view his nation as at odds with himself (compare 24:17; 26:4).

28:21 This verse, Acts 9 and Justin Martyr *Dialogue* 17 are the only evidence that central

Second, Paul is a prisoner, and there are reasons for this (28:17c, 19b). Paul *was handed over (paradidōmi)* as a prisoner from Jerusalem *to the Romans* (compare Lk 22:21; 23:25; Acts 21:11). With the implication of treachery and injustice that often accompanies the biblical use of the term *paradidōmi,* and by juxtaposing Paul's prisoner status to an affirmation of his innocence (28:17b), Luke leads us to understand that Paul does not deserve to be a prisoner. The mystery of why he remains a prisoner after the Romans declared him innocent will be explained in the chiastic parallel: *I was compelled to appeal to Caesar* (v. 19; also see 25:11).

Third, Roman and Jew had opposite dispositions toward Paul (28:18a, 19a). The Romans *wanted* ("were purposing, planning"—imperfect, possibly tendential) *to release* him. It was their plan, maybe when Festus first considered the case as he entered the governorship of Judea. By bringing charges and insisting on a trial in Jerusalem, a ploy for their deadly ambush, the Jews *objected* to Paul's release (25:3, 7).

Fourth, the one affirmation on which the chiasm turns is *because I was not guilty of any crime deserving death* (28:18). Paul is innocent before the Roman state (23:28-29; 25:25; 26:31-32).

It is hard to avoid the conclusion that this speech is as much for Roman middle-class ears as for the Jewish hearers. To be actually innocent by Jewish standards seriously undercut the Jewish arguments against Paul's gospel. This is important for Theophilus's and his fellow seekers' receptivity to the gospel. Innocence before the state would strongly commend the faith to the law-abiding Roman.

Paul's speech climaxes by answering the question: "Why do the Jews oppose the Christian message and me?" *It is because of the hope of Israel that I am bound with this chain* (see comment at 23:6; compare 24:15; 26:6-8).

The leaders respond to Paul's witness to his innocence in a very politic manner. They have heard nothing bad about Paul, whether by letter or by word of mouth, officially or unofficially. They have heard nothing good about *this sect* but would like to hear Paul's *views* on it. The scope

supervision from Jerusalem via envoys extended into the Diaspora during the first century A.D. (Safrai 1974:206).

and effect of the gospel witness—it is spreading everywhere—has been matched by opposition to it *everywhere* (17:30; compare Lk 2:34; Acts 13:45).

Explaining the Gospel to Jews (28:23-28) On a set day the Jews *came in even larger numbers* (compare 13:44) to Paul's rented lodgings (vv. 16, 30). So intent was he to win them that he discoursed *from morning till evening* (compare Western reading of 19:9; 20:7, 11; Ex 18:13). Time should never be a factor in witnessing to the truth that leads to eternal life. As long as the audience has the time, the Christian witness should have the inclination (compare Jn 4:31-35).

As the Jewish leaders requested, Paul *explained* the Christian faith to them. But it was not his *views* about a *sect* that he expounded. Rather, he *declared,* even "warned," *(diamartyromenos)* about *the kingdom of God* (Acts 10:42; 23:11). More that just a shorthand way of referring to the gospel message (1:3; 8:12; 19:8; 20:25; 28:31), *the kingdom of God* was the eschatological highway into the heart of the pious Jew (Lk 13:28, 29; 14:15; 19:11; 23:42, 51; Acts 1:6). And the good news was that God's reign was in their midst in the victorious life, death and resurrection-exaltation of Messiah Jesus and his salvation blessings.

Today utopias of the left and the right are in shambles. People are uncertain, even apprehensive, whether the kingdoms of this world can manage the present, let alone the future. They are ready for the good news about *the kingdom of God.*

The Jewish leaders' acceptance of this good news hinged on the answer to several important questions: Had the Messiah already come? If so, who was he? So Paul in his exposition also entered into reasoned discourse, "persuading" (NIV *tried to convince,* not necessarily a cona-

---

28:23 *Where he was staying (xenia)* has as its primary meaning "hospitality," which a number prefer here (Lake and Cadbury 1979:346; Marshall 1980:423). The secondary meaning, "lodging," better fits the context (Haenchen 1971:723; Kistemaker 1990:965).

The NIV placement of the main verb, *explained,* and the subordinate participles of manner, "declaring, persuading," parallel with one another miscommunicates the nature of Paul's witness (see the way Stott [1990:398] builds on the NIV's rendering). Paul's main activity was exposition of his views, as the leaders had requested. He did it through proclamation as well as reasoned argumentation.

28:24 Were the *some* who *were convinced* truly converted? Polhill (1992:542) and Krodel (1986:499) say yes, pointing to the pattern of mixed results elsewhere in Acts and the evidence that the verb can unambiguously point to true conversion (13:43; 14:1-2; 17:4;

tive imperfect) them from the Scriptures, *from the Law of Moses and from the Prophets,* about Jesus (see comment at 17:4; compare 13:23-29; 17:3-4; 26:22, 27-28; Lk 24:25-27, 44-48). He is indeed the Messiah whose earthly mission and resurrection-exaltation had brought in *the kingdom of God* and made it visible to the eyes of faith. Any witness for Christ will involve not only bold declaration but also clear reasoning, lucid give-and-take.

The response to the message was mixed: *some were convinced, . . . but others would not believe* (13:44-45; 14:1-2; 17:4-5). This division among the Jews could leave the impression that Paul's teaching was just that of a Jewish *sect,* attracting some Jews but not others. It certainly could not be the good news of *the kingdom of God;* otherwise all Jews would embrace it. So to interpret this mixed response in a true biblical light, Paul quotes from the Old Testament (28:26-27/Is 6:9-10).

As Luke sets up the quote, he tells the Jews' reaction to it. They *began to leave,* "disagreeing among themselves" (NIV's *they disagreed among themselves and began to leave* creates finite verbs in sequence out of a main verb, "to leave," and a present participle that gives the manner in which they left). They could not come to consensus on whether their ancestors' resistance to God's message was paralleled by the present Jewish rejection of the Christian gospel. Nor could they agree that *God's salvation has been sent to the Gentiles, and they will listen!* Paul's *final statement (rhēma hen)* was a dynamic utterance that bound together Old Testament promise and New Testament fulfillment (2:14; 5:20; 13:42; 26:25; Bovon 1984:229-30).

The quotation's introductory formula stresses the divine origin of Scripture as well as the immediacy of its address to its original audience,

---

19:8-9). Haenchen (1971:723) and Marshall (1980:424) say no, noting the negative Isaiah quote Paul appears to apply to all and the fact that none return to hear more (28:26-27). Yet nothing in the immediate context prevents us from seeing the usage as similar to that in the larger context: being *convinced* means being converted.

28:26-27 The text form follows the LXX except for pushing forward *to this people* to follow the first verb. The shift from imperatives to finite causative verbs in the description of the dullness of heart, hardness of hearing and closed eyes probably reflects the Sopherim's theological preference for emphasizing Judah's willful disobedience over against God's judicial blinding through the prophet's message (Archer and Chirichigno 1983:93). A pointing of the text as hiphil verbs shows that this is an allowable interpretation.

your forefathers, and by necessary implication to Paul's present audience, the "sons" (7:51). Here we have a "typology of judgment" in which the pattern among the ancestors in the time of promise is repeated and brought to a climax in the time of fulfillment.

The prophet speaks of what happens when people perceive saving truth without appropriating it: *You will be ever hearing but never understanding* (compare Lk 8:10/Is 6:9). Then in chiastic order, dealing with heart, ear and eyes, the prophet lays bare the cause of this mysterious condition and shows the proper pattern of receptivity to the gospel. There is nothing defective in the message. The defect is in the audience's sinfulness. If they would but *see with their eyes, hear with their ears, understand with their hearts and turn,* God *would heal them* (note the Targum and Mk 4:12 speak of God's forgiveness). For Jew and Gentile alike, unless outward perception is matched by inner spiritual insight, hearing and seeing will be in vain (Sand 1991:250; Lk 2:50; 8:8, 12, 15; 18:34; 24:25, 45; Acts 2:37; 7:54; 15:7-9; 16:14).

With *therefore* Paul draws an inference from the quote, showing that God will not be thwarted—his gospel will still bring salvation (Dupont 1979a:403). Although this is the third and final time Paul speaks of Jewish

_____

28:28 Does Paul's quote and statement indicate that Luke believes the rejection of the Jews is final and therefore there is no continuing mission to the Jews? Some answer the question yes on both counts. Either they see a failure of the Jewish mission and a "replacement" of it by the Gentile mission (Tyson 1988:137; compare Haenchen 1971:128-129), or they declare the mission a success according to God's purposes and view the church of Jewish remnant and Gentile according to a "restoration-exclusion" model (Jervell 1972a). Others respond with a qualified yes to these questions. They distinguish between an official or corporate Jewish rejection, which is final, and individual Jews who as part of the believing remnant do accept the gospel (Polhill 1992:544-45; Krodel 1986:503-4). They conclude that the Jewish mission may be over, but not the obligation to witness to individual Jews. David Moessner (1988:101-3) cites the Old Testament pattern concerning God's interaction with a rebellious Israel: the people's sinfulness; God's messengers' plea for repentance; Israel's rejection of the messengers; God's judgment (see Deut 31—32). He says that now is still the time of proclamation and warning. Luke holds in tension the witness to all nations, including the Jews, and the fact that the "the 'days of retribution' upon an unrepentant people are straining to fulfilment" (Moessner 1988:103). Though the rejection is "final," the mission is not.

28:29 The sentence in the NIV margin reflects a Western reading that came over into the KJV via Byzantine manuscripts. It is probably a copyist's addition to ease the somewhat abrupt transition from verse 28 to verse 30 (Metzger 1971:502).

28:30 The reference to *two whole years* and Luke's silence about the trial's outcome and the rest of Paul's life has puzzled commentators. Earlier attempts (Cadbury 1979b:330) to

rejection and Gentile reception (13:46; 18:6), it is carefully nuanced. We must not jump to the conclusion that Luke is saying that the Jews' rejection is final or that the mission to the Jews is over. Notice that of the three statements, this is the only one in which Paul does not explicitly say he is turning from the Jews to the Gentiles. Further, his statement about salvation being sent to the Gentiles is in the past tense, a parallel activity of God. What is contrasted is not the missions but the different audiences' responses to the one mission.

Indeed Paul *welcomed all who came to see him,* presumably both Jew and Gentile, as the Western text makes explicit. *God's salvation has been sent to the Gentiles.* And it is part of the momentum of salvation history for them to embrace it. *They will listen!* It's as if Luke were saying to his audience, "What's stopping you from making these salvation blessings your own?"

The Proclamation Continues (28:30-31) This final summary statement captures what Acts has set out to prove: that through the fulfillment of the design of Acts 1:8, "repentance and forgiveness of sins will be preached in [Jesus'] name to all nations" (Lk 24:47). It does so with a simple picture of Paul that stresses the "how" more than the "what" of

see the time marker as pointing to a statute of limitation by referring to Philo *In Flaccum* 128 have not worn well under scrutiny (see Sherwin-White 1963:119; note David Mealand's evidence [1990:589] that two years was often the term of a lease). At the very least we can say that Luke and his readers may well have been aware of a change that took place after the two years (Krodel 1986:507).

What happened to Paul? Was he tried? Longenecker (1981:572) says this is the proper inference from 27:24. Sherwin-White says it is a possible but not necessary conclusion that the case was simply dropped because of Nero's practice of leniency and his desire to clear court dockets in his early years (1963:119; Tacitus *Annals* 13.11). But this flies in the face of Acts 27:24. That Paul was tried, convicted and martyred is against the evidence of the Pastoral Epistles and early church writers, though many have challenged the credibility of the evidence and such a reconstruction of Paul's further movements (2 Tim 4:16; *1 Clement* 5.5-7; Eusebius *Ecclesiastical History* 2.22).

Why is Luke silent about subsequent events in Paul's life? The most satisfying answer draws together Luke's historical circumstances and his purpose in writing Acts. If Acts 20:25 is any guide, Luke probably did not know the outcome of the trial before Caesar. Even if he did, he probably completed the work shortly after Paul's release (Kistemaker 1990:966).

If Luke's purpose in writing Acts was primarily evangelistic and secondarily to encourage the church in its mission, then Acts ends at a very appropriate point in Paul's life and in a very appropriate way (Trompf 1984:233; Williams 1985:451, 455). The design set forth in Acts 1:8 is fulfilled, and the advance of the gospel message rather than the fate of one messenger is suitably highlighted (Krodel 1986:508).

his witness. *For two whole years Paul stayed there in his own rented house and welcomed* (literally, "was welcoming"—iterative or continuous imperfect) *all who came* (literally, "were coming"—present participle of continuous action) *to see him.* The gospel continues to be for all. The Christian witness must always welcome seekers, as Paul did.

Luke's literary artistry carries us to an open-ended conclusion. Paul's witness is a combination of continuous preaching and instruction. The distinction is important: preaching appeals to the will, calling for a decision, while teaching informs the mind, requiring growth in knowledge and understanding. But it should not be overemphasized, for as Stott notes, "all Paul's preaching had a doctrinal content, while all his teaching had an evangelistic purpose" (1990:400; Acts 5:42; 15:35; 20:20).

Proclaiming *the kingdom of God* must always be accompanied by teaching about its Sovereign, the Lord Jesus Christ, and his saving work in his death and resurrection. In this way the whole gospel is covered (Lk 24:46-47).

How did Paul bear witness? With complete freedom. Inwardly, he knew no pressure of fear to conceal or obscure or hesitate about the truth. Rather, *boldly* (literally, "with all boldness") by the power of the Spirit—candidly, clearly, and confidently—he was preaching and teaching (Acts 2:29; 4:13, 29-31; 9:27; 13:46; 14:3; 19:8; 26:26). Paul's prison epistles from this period mention serious adversaries and ask for prayer that he might be bold (Eph 6:19-20; Phil 1:15-20). If even Paul had to ask for prayer for boldness, there is hope for the rest of us.

The outward freedom Paul knew is framed by the very last word of Acts: *akōlytōs,* "unhindered." This shows the Roman government's attitude toward Christianity: it did not pose such a threat to either the civil order or the Roman way of life that one of its advocates would have to be muzzled during house arrest. This should strongly commend the faith to Roman inquirers.

But more than government tolerance, this term points to a sovereign God whose saving plan—that the gospel will be preached in Jesus' name

---

In his own rented house uses a secondary meaning of *misthōma*, which Mealand has confirmed (1990:585) in his computer-assisted studies. He found the word used positively for "rent." This meaning is better suited to the immediate context than the primary meaning, "his own earnings" or "at his own expense" (contra Bruce 1988:509).

to all nations—will not be thwarted. Though there may be incarceration, the Word of God is not bound. Luke has fully demonstrated that the implementation/application portion of the salvation message is indeed true (Lk 1:4; 24:47). And if his readers in any day embrace that message, they will soon find themselves embodying it, proclaiming repentance to the forgiveness of sins in his name to all the nations "with all boldness, unhindered." So may it be till Jesus comes.

Bibliography

Acworth, Angus
    1992   "Where Was St. Paul Shipwrecked? A Re-examination of the Evidence." *Journal of Theological Studies* 24:190-93.

Allen, David L.
    1990   "Acts Studies in the 1990's: Unity and Diversity." *Criswell Theological Review* 5:3-13.

Anderson, J. N. D.
    1970   *Christianity and Comparative Religion.* London: Tyndale Press/Downers Grove, Ill.: InterVarsity Press.

Anderson,
  Robert T.
    1988   "Samaritans." In *International Standard Bible Encyclopedia,* 4:303-8. Rev. ed. Edited by Geoffrey W. Bromiley. 4 vols. Grand Rapids, Mich.: Eerdmans.

Archer, Gleason L.
    1964   *A Survey of Old Testament Introduction.* Chicago: Moody Press.

    1982   *Encyclopedia of Bible Difficulties.* Grand Rapids, Mich.: Zondervan.

Archer, Gleason L.,
  and G. C.
  Chirichigno
    1983   *Old Testament Quotations in the New.* Chicago: Moody Press.

Arnold, Clinton E.
    1989   *Ephesians—Power and Magic: The Concept of Power in Ephesians in the Light of Its Historical Setting.* Cambridge: Cambridge University Press.

Aune, David
    1987   *The New Testament in Its Literary Environment.* Philadelphia: Westminster Press.

Bahnsen, Greg L.
    1980   "The Encounter of Jerusalem with Athens." *Ashland Theological Bulletin* 13:4-40.

Baird, William
1980   "Ascension and Resurrection: An Intersection of Luke and Paul." In *Texts and Testaments: Critical Essays on the Bible and the Early Church Fathers,* pp. 3-18. Edited by W. Eugene March. San Antonio, Tex.: Trinity University Press.

Barclay, William
1976   *The Acts of the Apostles.* Rev. ed. Daily Study Bible Series. Philadelphia: Westminster Press.

Barrett, C. K.
1961   *The New Testament Background: Selected Documents.* New York: Harper & Row.

1977   "Paul's Address to the Ephesian Elders in Acts 20." In *God's Christ and His People: Studies in Honour of Nils Alstrup Dahl,* pp. 107-21. Edited by Jacob Jervell and Wayne A. Meeks. New York: Columbia University Press.

1978   "Shaliach and Apostle." In *Donum Gentilicum: New Testament Studies in Honour of David Daube,* pp. 88-102. Edited by Ernst Bammel, C. K. Barrett and W. D. Davies. Oxford: Clarendon.

1979   "Light on the Holy Spirit from Simon Magus (Acts 8, 4-25)." In *Les Actes des Apôtres: Traditions, rédaction, théologie,* pp. 281-95. Edited by J. Kremer. Louvain, Belgium: Leuven University Press.

1982   "Salvation Proclaimed, Part 12: Acts 4[8-12]." *Expository Times* 94:68-70.

1987   "Paul Shipwrecked." In *Scripture—Meaning and Method: Essays Presented to Anthony Tyrell Hanson for His Seventieth Birthday,* pp. 51-64. Edited by Barry P. Thompson. Hull, U.K.: Hull University Press.

Bassler, Jouette M.
1985   "Luke and Paul on Impartiality." *Biblica* 66:546-52.

Bauer, Walter,
  F. Wilbur Gingrich
  and Frederick W.
  Danker
1979   *A Greek-English Lexicon of the New Testament and Other Early Christian Literature.* 2nd rev. and aug. ed. Chicago:

University of Chicago Press.

Baugh, Steven M.
1990   "Phraseology and the Reliability of Acts." *New Testament Studies* 36:290-94.

Behm, Johannes
1964   "ἀνατίθημι κτλ." In *Theological Dictionary of the New Testament,* 1:353-56. Edited by Gerhard Kittel and Gerhard Friedrich. 10 vols. Grand Rapids, Mich.: Eerdmans.

Behm, Johannes,
and E. Würthwein
1967   "νοέω κτλ." In *Theological Dictionary of the New Testament,* 4:948-1022. Edited by Gerhard Kittel and Gerhard Friedrich. 10 vols. Grand Rapids, Mich.: Eerdmans.

Bengel, John A.
1860   *Gnomon of the New Testament.* 2 vols. Philadelphia: Perkinpine & Higgins.

Bennett, Dennis,
and Rita Bennett
1971   *The Holy Spirit and You: A Study Guide to the Spirit-Filled Life.* Plainfield, N.J.: Logos International.

Bertram, Georg
1968   "ὁρμή κτλ." In *Theological Dictionary of the New Testament,* 5:467-74. Edited by Gerhard Kittel and Gerhard Friedrich. 10 vols. Grand Rapids, Mich.: Eerdmans.

Bertram, Georg,
and Karl Ludwig
Schmidt
1964   "ἔθνος κτλ." In *Theological Dictionary of the New Testament,* 2:364-72. Edited by Gerhard Kittel and Gerhard Friedrich. 10 vols. Grand Rapids, Mich.: Eerdmans.

Betz, Hans Dieter
1986   *The Greek Magical Papyri in Translation, including the Demotic Spells.* Chicago: University of Chicago Press.

Beyer, Hermann W.
1965   "θεραπεία κτλ." In *Theological Dictionary of the New Testament,* 3:128-32. Edited by Gerhard Kittel and Gerhard Friedrich. 10 vols. Grand Rapids, Mich.: Eerdmans.

Blomberg, Craig L.
1984   "The Law in Luke-Acts." *Journal for the Study of the New Testament* 22:53-80.

Bock, Darrell L.
1991   "Athenians Who Have Never Heard." In *Through No Fault*

of Their Own: The Fate of Those Who Have Never Heard,
pp. 117-24. Edited by William V. Crockett and James G.
Sigountis. Grand Rapids, Mich.: Baker Book House.

Bonhoeffer,
Dietrich
1963   *The Cost of Discipleship.* Rev. ed. New York: Macmillan.

Borger, Rylke
1988   "Amos 5, 26, Apostelgeschichte 7, 43 und Šurpu II, 180."
Zeitschrift für die alttestamentliche Wissenschaft 100:70-81.

Bovon, François
1984   " 'Schön hat der heilige Geist durch den Propheten Jesaja
zu euren Vätern gesprochen' (Apg 28, 25)." *Zeitschrift für
die neutestamentliche Wissenschaft* 75:226-32.

Bowers, W. Paul
1979   "Paul's Route Through Mysia: A Note on Acts xvi.8." *Journal
of Theological Studies* 30:507-11.

Bowker, John W.
1967   "Speeches in Acts: A Study in Proem and Yelammedenu
Form." *New Testament Studies* 14:96-111.

Braun, Michael A.
1977   "James' Use of Amos at the Jerusalem Council: Steps Toward
a Possible Solution of the Textual and Theological
Problems." *Journal of the Evangelical Theological Society*
20:113-21.

Brock, Sebastian P.
1974   "Barnabas: *HUIOS PARAKLĒSEŌS.*" *Journal of Theological
Studies* 25:93-98.

Brown, Schuyler
1978   "The Role of Prologues in Determining the Purpose of
Luke-Acts." In *Perspectives on Luke-Acts,* pp. 99-111. Edited
by Charles H. Talbert. Edinburgh: T & T Clark.

Bruce, F. F.
1951   *The Acts of the Apostles: The Greek Text with Introduction
and Commentary.* Grand Rapids, Mich.: Eerdmans.

1954   *The Book of Acts.* Grand Rapids, Mich.: Eerdmans.

1974   "The Speeches in Acts—Thirty Years After." In *Reconciliation and Hope,* pp. 53-68. Edited by Robert Banks. Grand
Rapids, Mich.: Eerdmans.

1976   "Is the Paul of Acts the Real Paul?" *Bulletin of the John*

Rylands Library 58:282-305.

1978   "The Full Name of Procurator Felix." *Journal for the Study of the New Testament* 1:33-36.

1988   *The Book of Acts.* Rev. ed. Grand Rapids, Mich.: Eerdmans.

1990   *The Acts of the Apostles: The Greek Text with Introduction and Commentary.* 3rd rev. and enl. ed. Grand Rapids, Mich.: Eerdmans.

Büchsel, Friedrich, and Volkmar Herntrich

1965   "κρίνω κτλ." In *Theological Dictionary of the New Testament,* 3:921-53. Edited by Gerhard Kittel and Gerhard Friedrich. 10 vols. Grand Rapids, Mich.: Eerdmans.

Burchard, Christoph

1985   "A Note on *Rhēma* in Jos As 17:1f.; Luke 2:15, 17; Acts 10:37." *Novum Testamentum* 27:281-95.

Cadbury, Henry J.

1979a   "Note XXIV: Dust and Garments." In *Additional Notes to the Commentary,* pp. 269-77. The Beginnings of Christianity. Edited by F. J. Foakes Jackson and Kirsopp Lake. Grand Rapids, Mich.: Baker Book House.

1979b   "Note XXVI: Roman Law and the Trial of Paul." In *Additional Notes to the Commentary,* pp. 297-337. The Beginnings of Christianity. Edited by F. J. Foakes Jackson and Kirsopp Lake. Grand Rapids, Mich.: Baker Book House.

Calvin, John

1965   *The Acts of the Apostles 1—13.* Calvin's Commentaries. Edited by David W. Torrance and Thomas F. Torrance. Grand Rapids, Mich.: Eerdmans.

1966   *The Acts of the Apostles 14—28.* Calvin's Commentaries. Edited by David W. Torrance and Thomas F. Torrance. Grand Rapids, Mich.: Eerdmans.

Campbell, Robert C.

1988   "Silas; Silvanus." In *International Standard Bible Encyclopedia,* 4:509. Rev. ed. Edited by Geoffrey W. Bromiley. 4 vols.

Grand Rapids, Mich.: Eerdmans.

Carson, D. A.,
  Douglas J. Moo
  and Leon Morris
  1992   *An Introduction to the New Testament.* Grand Rapids, Mich.:
                  Zondervan.

Casson, Lionel
  1971   *Ships and Seamanship in the Ancient World.* Princeton, N.J.:
                  Princeton University Press.

Clark, David J.
  1975   "What Went Overboard First?" *Bible Translator* 26:144-46.

Coenen, Lothar
  1978   "κηρύσσω." In *New International Dictionary of New
                  Testament Theology,* 3:48-57. Edited by Colin Brown. 3 vols.
                  Grand Rapids, Mich.: Zondervan.

Coggins, Richard J.
  1982   "The Samaritans and Acts." *New Testament Studies* 28:423-
                  34.

Cohen, Shaye J. D.
  1986   "Was Timothy Jewish (Acts 16:1-2)? Patristic Exegesis,
                  Rabbinic Law and Matrilineal Descent." *Journal of Biblical
                  Literature* 105:251-68.

Conzelmann, Hans
  1987   *Acts of the Apostles: A Commentary.* Philadelphia: Fortress.

Coppens, Joseph
  1979   "L'imposition des mains dans les Actes des Apôtres." In *Les
                  Actes des Apôtres: Traditions, rédaction, théologie,* pp. 405-
                  438. Edited by J. Kremer. Louvain, Belgium: Leuven Univer-
                  sity Press.

Couch, Aaron J.
  1988   "Rhodes." In *International Standard Bible Encyclopedia,*
                  4:182-83. Rev. ed. Edited by Geoffrey W. Bromiley. 4 vols.
                  Grand Rapids, Mich.: Eerdmans.

Crocker, Piers T.
  1986   "The City of Meroe and the Ethiopian Eunuch." *Buried
                  History* 22:53-72.

  1987   "Ephesus: Its Silversmiths, Its Tradesmen and Its Riots."
                  Buried History 23:76-78.

Cumont,
Franz V. M.
1959   *Afterlife in Roman Paganism.* New York: Dover.

Daube, David
1976   "A Reform in Acts and Its Models." In *Jews, Greeks and*
               Christians—Religious Cultures in Late Antiquity: Essays in
               Honor of William David Davies, pp. 151-63. Edited by
               Robert Hamerton-Kelly and Robin Scroggs. Leiden: Brill.

1990   "On Acts 23: Sadducees and Angels." *Journal of Biblical Lit-*
               erature 109:493-97.

Davies, W. D.
1986   "Reflections on Thirty Years of Biblical Studies." *Scottish*
               Journal of Theology 39:43-64.

Decock, Paul B.
1981   "The Understanding of Isaiah 53:7-8 in Acts 8:32-33."
               Neotestamentica 14:111-33.

Deissmann, Adolf
1978   *Light from the Ancient East: The New Testament Illustrated*
               by Recently Discovered Texts of the Graeco-Roman World.
               Grand Rapids, Mich.: Baker Book House.

Delebecque,
Édouard
1980   "Trois simples mots, chargés d'une lumiere neuve (Acts des
               Apôtres II, 47b)." *Revue thomiste* 80:75-85.

Delling, Gerhard
1967   *"μάγος κτλ."* In *Theological Dictionary of the New*
               Testament, 4:356-59. Edited by Gerhard Kittel and Gerhard
               Friedrich. 10 vols. Grand Rapids, Mich.: Eerdmans.

1972   *"τάσσω κτλ."* In *Theological Dictionary of the New*
               Testament, 8:27-48. Edited by Gerhard Kittel and Gerhard
               Friedrich. 10 vols. Grand Rapids, Mich.: Eerdmans.

Derrett,
J. Duncan M.
1977   "Ananias, Sapphira and the Right of Property." In *Studies in*
               the New Testament, vol. 1, *Glimpses of the Legal and Social*
               Presuppositions of the Authors. pp. 193-200. Leiden: Brill.

1982   "Simon Magus (Acts 8:9-24)." *Zeitschrift für die*
               neutestamentliche Wissenschaft 73:52-68.

1988   "Clean and Unclean Animals (Acts 10:15; 11:9): Peter's Pronouncing Power Observed." *Heythrop Journal* 29:205-21.

de Waard, Jan
1971   "The Quotation from Deuteronomy in Acts 3, 22.23 and the Palestinian Text: Additional Arguments." *Biblica* 52:537-40.

De Zwaan, J.
1979   "The Use of the Greek Language in Acts." In *Prolegomena II: Criticism,* pp. 30-65. The Beginnings of Christianity. Edited by F. J. Foakes-Jackson and Kirsopp Lake. Grand Rapids, Mich.: Baker Book House.

Dibelius, Martin
1956a   "Paul in Athens." In *Studies in the Acts of the Apostles,* pp. 78-83. London: SCM Press.

1956b   "Paul on the Areopagus." In *Studies in the Acts of the Apostles,* pp. 26-77. London: SCM Press.

Dillon, Richard J.
1981   "Previewing Luke's Project from His Prologue (Luke 1:1-4)." *Catholic Biblical Quarterly* 43:205-27.

Dodd, C. H.
1964   *The Apostolic Preaching and Its Developments.* New York: Harper & Row.

Downing,
 F. Gerald
1986   "Freedom from the Law in Luke-Acts." *Journal for the Study of the New Testament* 26:49-52.

Dumais, Marcel
1979   "Le langage des discours d'évangélisation des Actes: Une forme de langage symbolique?" In *Les Actes des Apôtres: Traditions, rédaction, théologie,* pp. 467-74. Edited by J. Kremer. Louvain, Belgium: Leuven University Press.

Dunn, J. D. G.
1970   *Baptism in the Holy Spirit.* London: SCM Press.

1988   *Romans 1—8.* Word Biblical Commentary 38A. Dallas: Word.

Dupont, Jacques
1964   *The Sources of Acts: The Present Position.* London: Darton, Longman & Todd.

1979a   "La conclusion des Acts et son rapport à l'ensemble de l'ouvrage de Luc." In *Les Actes des Apôtres: Traditions, rédaction, théologie,* pp. 359-404. Edited by J. Kremer.

Louvain, Belgium: Leuven University Press.

1979b   "Le discours à l'Aréopage (Ac 17, 22-31) lieu de rencontre
               entre christianisme et hellénisme." *Biblica* 60:530-46.

1979c   "The First Christian Pentecost." In *The Salvation of the
               Gentiles: Essays on the Acts of the Apostles,* pp. 35-60. New
               York: Paulist.

Earle, Ralph
1982   "Fair Havens." In *International Standard Bible Encyclope-
               dia,* 2:270. Rev. ed. Edited by Geoffrey W. Bromiley. 4 vols.
               Grand Rapids, Mich.: Eerdmans.

Edgar, Thomas R.
1988   "The Cessation of the Sign Gifts." *Bibliotheca Sacra* 145:371-
               86.

Edwards, M. J.
1992   "Quoting Aratus: Acts 17:28." *Zeitschrift für die
               neutestamentliche Wissenschaft* 83:266-69.

Ellis, E. Earle
1970   "The Role of the Christian Prophet in Acts." In *Apostolic
               History and the Gospel: Biblical and Historical Essays
               Presented to F. F. Bruce on His Sixtieth Birthday,* pp. 55-67.
               Edited by W. Ward Gasque and Ralph P. Martin. Grand
               Rapids, Mich.: Eerdmans.

Esser, Hans-Helmut
1976   "Grace, Spiritual Gifts." In *New International Dictionary of
               New Testament Theology,* 2:115-23. Edited by Colin Brown.
               3 vols. Grand Rapids, Mich.: Zondervan.

Fernando, Ajith
1987   *The Christian's Attitude Toward World Religions.* Wheaton,
               Ill.: Tyndale House.

Filson, Floyd V.
1970   "The Journey Motif in Luke-Acts." In *Apostolic History and
               the Gospel: Biblical and Historical Essays Presented to F. F.
               Bruce on His Sixtieth Birthday,* pp. 68-77. Edited by W. Ward
               Gasque and Ralph P. Martin. Grand Rapids, Mich.:
               Eerdmans.

Finegan, Jack
1981   *The Archaeology of the New Testament: The Mediterranean
               World of the Early Christian Apostles.* Boulder, Colo.:
               Westview.

Foulkes, Irene W.
1978   "Two Semantic Problems in the Translation of Acts 4:5-20."

Bible Translator 29:121-25.

Gaffin,
 Richard B., Jr.
  1979   *Perspectives on Pentecost: Studies in New Testament
                Teaching on the Gifts of the Holy Spirit.* Phillipsburg, N.J.:
                Presbyterian and Reformed.

Gasque, W. Ward
  1978   "The Book of Acts and History." In *Unity and Diversity in
                New Testament Theology,* pp. 54-72. Edited by Robert A.
                Guelich. Grand Rapids, Mich.: Eerdmans.

  1988a   "A Fruitful Field: Recent Study of the Acts of the Apostles."
                Interpretation 42:117-31.

  1988b   "Recent Commentaries on the Acts of the Apostles."
                Themelios 14:21-23.

Giles, Kevin N.
  1985   "Luke's Use of the Term *Ekklēsia* with Special Reference to
                Acts 20.28 and 9.31." *New Testament Studies* 31:135-42.

Gordon,
 Alasdair B.
  1971   "The Fate of Judas According to Acts 1:18." *Evangelical
                Quarterly* 43:97-100.

Gordon, Robert P.
  1974   "Targumic Parallels to Acts xiii.18 and Didache xiv.3."
                Novum Testamentum 16:285-89.

Grässer, Erich
  1979   "Die Parusieerwartung in der Apostelgeschichte." In *Les
                Actes des Apôtres: Traditions, rédaction, théologie,* pp. 99-
                127. Edited by J. Kremer. Louvain, Belgium: Leuven Univer-
                sity Press.

Green, Michael
  1970   *Evangelism in the Early Church.* Grand Rapids, Mich.:
                Eerdmans.

  1975   *I Believe in the Holy Spirit.* London: Hodder & Stoughton.

Grudem, Wayne
  1988   "Why Christians Can Still Prophesy." *Christianity Today* 32
                (September 16): 29-35.

Guthrie, Donald
  1990   *New Testament Introduction.* Rev. ed. Downers Grove, Ill.:
                InterVarsity Press.

Haenchen, Ernst
1971   *The Acts of the Apostles: A Commentary.* Philadelphia:
                       Westminster Press.
Hamblin, Robert L.
1974   "Miracles in the Book of Acts." *Southwestern Journal of
                       Theology* 17:19-34.
Hamm, Dennis
1984   "Acts 3:12-26: Peter's Speech and the Healing of the Man
                       Born Lame." *Perspectives in Religious Studies* 11:199-217.

1990   "Paul's Blindness and Its Healing: Clues to Symbolic Intent
                       (Acts 9, 22, and 26)." *Biblica* 71:63-72.
Harnack, Adolf
1961   *The Mission and Expansion of Christianity in the First Three
                       Centuries.* New York: Harper & Brothers.
Harris, R. Laird,
  Gleason L.
  Archer Jr. and
  Bruce K. Waltke
1980   *Theological Wordbook of the Old Testament.* 2 vols.
                       Chicago: Moody Press.
Harrison, Everett F.
1986   *Interpreting Acts: The Expanding Church.* Grand Rapids,
                       Mich.: Zondervan.
Harrison, Roland K.
1979   "Disease." In *International Standard Bible Encyclopedia,*
                       1:953-60. Rev. ed. Edited by Geoffrey W. Bromiley. 4 vols.
                       Grand Rapids, Mich.: Eerdmans.
Hauck, Friedrich
1967   "ὅσιος κτλ." In *Theological Dictionary of the New
                       Testament,* 5:489-93. Edited by Gerhard Kittel and Gerhard
                       Friedrich. 10 vols. Grand Rapids, Mich.: Eerdmans.
Hauck, Friedrich,
  and Rudolf Meyer
1965   "καθαρός κτλ." In *Theological Dictionary of the New
                       Testament,* 3:413-31. Edited by Gerhard Kittel and Gerhard
                       Friedrich. 10 vols. Grand Rapids, Mich.: Eerdmans.
Hedrick, Charles W.
1981   "Paul's Conversion Call: A Comparative Analysis of the
                       Three Reports in Acts." *Journal of Biblical Literature*
                       100:415-32.
Hemer, Colin J.
1975   "Euraquilo and Melita." *Journal of Theological Studies*
                       26:100-111.

1976   "The Adjective 'Phrygia.' " *Journal of Theological Studies*
                27:122-25.

1977a   "Acts and Galatians Reconsidered." *Themelios* 2:81-88.

1977b   "Luke the Historian." *Bulletin of the John Rylands Library*
                60:28-51.

1977c   "Phrygia: A Further Note." *Journal of Theological Studies*
                28:99-100.

1985   "First Person Narrative in Acts 27-28." *Tyndale Bulletin*
                36:79-109.

1987   "The Name of Felix Again." *Journal for the Study of the
                New Testament* 31:45-49.

1988   "Tarsus." In *International Standard Bible Encyclopedia,*
                4:734-36. Rev. ed. Edited by Geoffrey W. Bromiley. 4 vols.
                Grand Rapids, Mich.: Eerdmans.

1989a   *The Book of Acts in the Setting of Hellenistic History.*
                Tübingen: J. C. B. Mohr.

1989b   "The Speeches of Acts, Part 1: The Ephesian Elders at
                Miletus." *Tyndale Bulletin* 40:77-85.

1989c   "The Speeches of Acts, Part 2: The Areopagus Speech."
                Tyndale Bulletin 40:239-59.

Hick, John, and
Paul F. Knitter,
eds.
1987   *The Myth of Christian Uniqueness: Toward a Pluralistic
                Theology of Religions.* Maryknoll, N.Y.: Orbis.

Hirschfeld, Nicolle
1990   "The Ship of Saint Paul, Part 1: Historical Background."
                Biblical Archaeologist 53:25-30.
Hock, Robert F.
1979   "The Workshop as a Social Setting for Paul's Missionary
                Preaching." *Catholic Biblical Quarterly* 41:438-50.

Hodges, Zane C.
1981   *The Gospel Under Siege: A Study on Faith and Works.*
                   Dallas: Redención Viva.

Hoekema,
   Anthony A.
1972   *Holy Spirit Baptism.* Grand Rapids, Mich.: Eerdmans.

Holdcroft, L.
   Thomas
1962   *The Holy Spirit: A Pentecostal Interpretation.* Springfield,
                   Mo.: Gospel Publishing House.

Hubbard,
   Benjamin J.
1977   "Commissioning Stories in Luke-Acts: A Study in Their
                   Antecedents, Form and Content." *Semeia* 8:103-26.

Hubbard,
   Robert L., Jr.
1988   "Red Sea." In *International Standard Bible Encyclopedia,*
                   4:58-61. Rev. ed. Edited by Geoffrey W. Bromiley. 4 vols.
                   Grand Rapids, Mich.: Eerdmans.

Hulbert, Terry C.
1978   "Families Are Both the Means and Goal of Evangelism."
                   Evangelical Missions Quarterly 14:171-77.

1979   "Household Discipling Means Strong Families and Growing
                   Churches." *Evangelical Missions Quarterly* 15:4-16.

Hultgren, Arland J.
1976   "Paul's Pre-Christian Persecutions of the Church: Their
                   Purpose, Locale and Nature." *Journal of Biblical Literature*
                   95:97-111.

Jacobs, Henry E.
1979   "Barnabas." In *International Standard Bible Encyclopedia,*
                   1:432. Rev. ed. Edited by Geoffrey W. Bromiley. 4 vols.
                   Grand Rapids, Mich.: Eerdmans.

Jeremias, Joachim
1969   *Jerusalem in the Time of Jesus.* Philadelphia: Fortress.

Jervell, Jacob
1972a   "The Divided People of God: The Restoration of Israel and
                   Salvation for the Gentiles." In *Luke and the People of God: A*
                   New Look at Luke-Acts, pp. 41-74. Minneapolis: Augsburg.

1972b   "The Law in Luke-Acts." In *Luke and the People of God: A New Look at Luke-Acts,* pp. 133-52. Minneapolis: Augsburg.

1972c   "The Twelve on Israel's Thrones: Luke's Understanding of the Apostolate." In *Luke and the People of God: A New Look at Luke-Acts,* pp. 75-112. Minneapolis: Augsburg.

1984   "The Signs of an Apostle: Paul's Miracles." In *The Unknown Paul: Essays on Luke-Acts and Early Christian History,* pp. 77-95. Minneapolis: Augsburg.

Johnson, Dennis E.
1990   "Jesus Against the Idols: The Use of the Isaianic Servant Songs in the Missiology of Acts." *Westminster Theological Journal* 52:343-53.

Johnson, Luke T.
1981   *Sharing Possessions: Mandate and Symbol of Faith.* Overtures in Biblical Theology 9. Philadelphia: Fortress.

1992   *The Acts of the Apostles.* Sacra Pagina. Collegeville, Minn.: Liturgical Press.

Johnston, George
1981   "Christ as *Archēgos.*" *New Testament Studies* 27:381-84.

Kaiser, Walter C., Jr.
1977   "The Davidic Promise and the Inclusion of the Gentiles (Amos 9:9-15 and Acts 15:13-18): A Test Passage for Theological Systems." *Journal of the Evangelical Theological Society* 20:97-111.

1980   "The Promise to David in Psalm 16 and Its Application in Acts 2:25-33 and 13:32-37." *Journal of the Evangelical Theological Society* 23:219-30.

Kemmler, Dieter Werner
1975   *Faith and Human Reason: A Study in Paul's Method of Preaching As Illustrated by 1-2 Thessalonians and Acts 17, 24.* Leiden: Brill.

Kilgallen, John J.
1990   "Did Peter Actually Fail to Get a Word In? (Acts 11, 15)." *Biblica* 71:405-10.

Kilpatrick, George D.
1963   "Acts 23, 23: *dexiolaboi* [='spearmen from the local

police']." *Journal of Theological Studies* 14:393-94.

King, David M.
1989 "The Use of Amos 9:11-12 in Acts 15:16-18." *Ashland Theological Journal* 21:8-13.

Kingsmore, Brian
1990 "Track 650: Nominalism Today." In *Proclaim Christ Until He Comes: Calling the Whole Church to Take the Whole Gospel to the Whole World,* pp. 446-48. Ed. J. D. Douglas. Minneapolis: Worldwide Publications.

Kistemaker, Simon J.
1990 *New Testament Commentary: Exposition of the Acts of the Apostles.* Grand Rapids, Mich.: Baker Book House.

Kodell, Jerome
1974 " 'The Word of God Grew': The Ecclesial Tendency of *Logos* in Acts 6, 7; 12, 24; 19, 20." *Biblica* 55:505-19.

Koester, Helmut
1982 *Introduction to the New Testament.* 2 vols. Philadelphia: Fortress.

Kraft, Charles H.
1979 *Christianity and Culture: A Study in Dynamic Biblical Theologizing in Cross-Cultural Perspective.* Maryknoll, N.Y.: Orbis.

Kraybill, Donald B., and Dennis M. Sweetland
1983 "Possessions in Luke-Acts: A Sociological Perspective." *Perspectives in Religious Studies* 10:215-39.

Kreitzer, Larry J.
1987 "A Numismatic Clue to Acts 19:23-41: The Ephesian Cistophori of Claudius and Agrippina." *Journal for the Study of the New Testament* 30:59-70.

Krodel, Gerhard
1986 *Acts.* Augsburg Commentary on the New Testament. Minneapolis: Augsburg.

Kurz, William S.
1980 "Hellenistic Rhetoric in the Christological Proof of Luke-Acts." *Catholic Biblical Quarterly* 42:171-95.

1990 *Farewell Addresses in the New Testament.* Collegeville, Minn.: Liturgical Press.

Lake, Kirsopp
1979a "Note XII: The Communism of Acts ii. and iv.-vi. and the Appointment of the Seven." In *Additional Notes to the*

	Commentary, pp. 140-50. The Beginnings of Christianity. Edited by F. J. Foakes Jackson and Kirsopp Lake. Grand Rapids, Mich.: Baker Book House.
1979b	"Note XV: The Conversion of Paul and the Events Immediately Following It." In *Additional Notes to the Commentary,* pp. 188-95. The Beginnings of Christianity. Edited by F. J. Foakes Jackson and Kirsopp Lake. Grand Rapids, Mich.: Baker Book House.

Lake, Kirsopp, and
Henry J. Cadbury

1979	*English Translation and Commentary.* Vol. 4 of *The Acts of the Apostles.* The Beginnings of Christianity, Part I. Edited by F. J. Foakes Jackson and Kirsopp Lake. Grand Rapids, Mich.: Baker Book House.

Larkin,
William J., Jr.

1977	"Luke's Use of the Old Testament as a Key to His Soteriology." *Journal of the Evangelical Theological Society* 20:325-35.
1993	*Culture and Biblical Hermeneutics: Interpreting and Applying the Authoritative Word in a Relativistic Age.* Lanham, Md.: University Press of America.

LaSor, William S.

1979a	"Aramaic." In *International Standard Bible Encyclopedia,* 1:229-33. Rev. ed. Edited by Geoffrey W. Bromiley. 4 vols. Grand Rapids, Mich.: Eerdmans.
1979b	"Artemis." In *International Standard Bible Encyclopedia,* 1:306-8. Rev. ed. Edited by Geoffrey W. Bromiley. 4 vols. Grand Rapids, Mich.: Eerdmans.

Laubach, Fritz

1975	"Conversion etc." In *New International Dictionary of New Testament Theology,* 1:353-55. Edited by Colin Brown. 3 vols. Grand Rapids, Mich.: Zondervan.

Lausanne
Committee

1989	*Lausanne II Manila Notebook.* Monrovia, Calif.: Lausanne Committee for World Evangelization.

Lawrence, T. E.

1927	*Revolt in the Desert.* New York: George H. Doran.

Leary, T. J.
1990   "The 'Aprons' of St. Paul—Acts 19:12." *Journal of Theological Studies* 41:527-29.

Levinskaya, Irina A.
1990   "The Inscription from Aphrodisias and the Problem of the God Fearers." *Tyndale Bulletin* 41:312-18.

1993   "Syncretism: The Term and Phenomenon." *Tyndale Bulletin* 44:117-28.

Lincoln, Andrew T.
1985   "Theology and History in the Interpretation of Luke's Pentecost." *Expository Times* 96:204-9.

Lincoln, C. Eric
1984   *Race, Religion and the Continuing American Dilemma.* New York: Hill and Wang.

Linton, Olof
1974   "The List of Nations in Acts 2." In *New Testament Christianity for Africa and the World,* pp. 44-53. Edited by Mark E. Glasswell and Edward W. Fasole-Luke. London: SPCK.

Lohfink, Gerhard
1976   *The Conversion of Saint Paul: Narrative and History in Acts.* Chicago: Franciscan Herald.

Long, William R.
1983   "The Paulusbild in the Trial of Paul in Acts." In *SBL 1983 Seminar Papers,* pp. 87-106. Edited by Keith H. Richards. Chico, Calif.: Scholars Press.

Longenecker, Richard
1981   *Acts.* In *John and Acts,* by Merrill C. Tenney and Richard Longenecker. Expositor's Bible Commentary 9. Grand Rapids, Mich.: Zondervan.

Louw, Johannes P., and Eugene A. Nida
1988   *Greek-English Lexicon of the New Testament Based on Semantic Domains.* 2 vols. New York: United Bible Societies.

Lövestam, Ewald
1987   "Paul's Address at Miletus." *Studia Theologia* 41:1-10.

Lüdemann, Gerd
1987   "The Acts of the Apostles and the Beginnings of Simonian Gnosis." *New Testament Studies* 33:420-26.

Lyall, Frances
1976 "Roman Law in the Writings of Paul: Aliens and Citizens." *Evangelical Quarterly* 48:3-14.

McKay, K. I.
1994 "Foreign Gods Identified in Acts 17:18?" *Tyndale Bulletin* 45:411-12.

Madvig, Donald H.
1979a "'Areopagus." In *International Standard Bible Encyclopedia*, 1:287-88. Rev. ed. Edited by Geoffrey W. Bromiley. 4 vols. Grand Rapids, Mich.: Eerdmans.

1979b "Athens." In *International Standard Bible Encyclopedia*, 1:351-52. Rev. ed. Edited by Geoffrey W. Bromiley. 4 vols. Grand Rapids, Mich.: Eerdmans.

Mann, C. S.
1988 "Saul and Damascus." *Expository Times* 99:331-34.

Marshall, I. Howard
1971 *Luke: Historian and Theologian.* Grand Rapids, Mich.: Zondervan.

1977 "The Sign of Pentecost." *Scottish Journal of Theology* 30:347-69.

1980 *The Acts of the Apostles: An Introduction and Commentary.* Tyndale New Testament Commentary. Grand Rapids, Mich.: Eerdmans.

1989 "The Present State of Lucan Studies." *Themelios* 14:52-57.

Martin, Clarice J.
1989 "A Chamberlain's Journey and the Challenge of Interpretation for Liberation." *Semeia* 47:105-35.

Marx, Werner G.
1980 "Luke, the Physician, Re-examined." *Expository Times* 91:168-71.

Mastin, Brian A.
1976 "Scaeva the Chief Priest." *Journal of Theological Studies* 27:405-12.

Mealand, David L.
1990 "The Close of Acts and Its Hellenistic Greek Vocabulary." *New Testament Studies* 36:583-97.

Meeks, Wayne A.
1977   "Simon Magus in Recent Research." *Religious Studies Review*
               3:130-42.
Meinardus,
   Otto F. A.
1976   "St. Paul Shipwrecked in Dalmatia." *Biblical Archaeologist*
               39:145-47.

1981   "The Site of the Apostle Paul's Conversion at Kaukab."
               Biblical Archaeologist 44:57-59.
Menoud,
   Philippe H.
1978a   "The Meaning of the Verb *Porthein.*" In *Jesus Christ and the*
               Faith: A Collection of Studies, pp. 47-60. Pittsburgh, Penn.:
               Pickwick.

1978b   "The Plan of the Acts of the Apostles." In *Jesus Christ and*
               the Faith: A Collection of Studies, pp. 121-32. Pittsburgh,
               Penn.: Pickwick.
Merrill, Eugene H.
1981   "Paul's Use of 'About 450 Years' in Acts 13:20." *Bibliotheca*
               Sacra 138:246-57.
Metzger, Bruce M.
1971   *A Textual Commentary on the Greek New Testament.*
               London: United Bible Societies.
Michaelis, Wilhelm
1967   "ὁράω κτλ." In *Theological Dictionary of the New*
               Testament, 5:315-82. Edited by Gerhard Kittel and Gerhard
               Friedrich. 10 vols. Grand Rapids, Mich.: Eerdmans.

1971   "σκηνή κτλ." In *Theological Dictionary of the New*
               Testament, 7:368-94. Edited by Gerhard Kittel and Gerhard
               Friedrich. 10 vols. Grand Rapids, Mich.: Eerdmans.
Michel, Otto
1965   "καταντάω κτλ." In *Theological Dictionary of the New*
               Testament, 3:623-26. Edited by Gerhard Kittel and Gerhard
               Friedrich. 10 vols. Grand Rapids, Mich.: Eerdmans.
Miles, Gary B., and
   Garry Trompf
1976   "Luke and Antiphon: The Theology of Acts 27—28 in the
               Light of Pagan Beliefs About Divine Retribution, Pollution
               and Shipwreck." *Harvard Theological Review* 69:259-68.

Minear, Paul S.
1973   "Dear Theo: The Kerygmatic Intention and Claim of the
            Book of Acts." *Interpretation* 27:131-50.

Moessner, David P.
1988   "Paul in Acts: Preacher of Eschatological Repentance to
            Israel." *New Testament Studies* 34:96-104.

Moscato, Mary A.
1976   "Current Theories Regarding the Audience of Luke-Acts."
            Currents in Theology and Mission 3:355-60.

Moule, C. F. D.
1982   "The Ascension According to Acts 1:9." In *Essays in New
            Testament Interpretation,* pp. 54-63. Cambridge: Cambridge
            University Press.

Moulton, James H.,
   and George
   Milligan
1974   *The Vocabulary of the Greek Testament Illustrated from the
            Papyri and Other Non-literary Sources.* Grand Rapids, Mich.:
            Eerdmans.

Mullins, Terence Y.
1976   "New Testament Commission Forms, Especially, Luke-Acts."
            Journal of Biblical Literature 95:603-14.

Neil, William
1973   *The Acts of the Apostles.* New Century Bible. London:
            Oliphants.

Neusner, Jacob
1971   *The Rabbinic Traditions About the Pharisees Before 70, Part
            I: The Masters.* Leiden: Brill.

Neyrey, Jerome H.
1984   "The Forensic Defense Speech and Paul's Trial Speeches in
            Acts 22—26: Form and Function." In *Luke-Acts: New Per-
            spectives from the Society of Biblical Literature Seminar,* pp.
            210-24. Edited by Charles H. Talbert. New York: Crossroad.

Nolland, John L.
1980   "A Fresh Look at Acts 15:10." *New Testament Studies* 27:105-
            14.

Oepke, Albrecht
1964   "ἀποκαθίστημι κτλ." In *Theological Dictionary of the New
            Testament,* 1:387-93. Edited by Gerhard Kittel and Gerhard
            Friedrich. 10 vols. Grand Rapids, Mich.: Eerdmans.

Ogilvie, Lloyd J.
1983   *Acts.* Communicator's Commentary. Waco, Tex.: Word.

Orr, J. Edwin
1937   *The Church Must First Repent: Chapters on Revival.* London: Marshall, Morgan and Scott.

1953   *Good News in Bad Times: Signs of Revival.* Grand Rapids, Mich.: Zondervan.

O'Toole, Robert F.
1978   *Acts 26: The Christological Climax of Paul's Defense (Ac 22:1—26:32).* Rome: Biblical Institute Press.

1979a   "Christ's Resurrection in Acts 13, 13-52." *Biblica* 60:361-72.

1979b   "Luke's Understanding of Jesus' Resurrection-Ascension-Exaltation." *Biblical Theology Bulletin* 9:106-14.

Packer, J. I.
1984   *Keep in Step with the Spirit.* Old Tappan, N.J.: Fleming H. Revell.

Palmer, Darryl W.
1987   "The Literary Background of Acts 1:1-14." *New Testament Studies* 33:427-38.

Parker, David C.
1992   *Codex Bezae: An Early Christian Manuscript and Its Text.* Cambridge: Cambridge University Press.

Parratt, John K.
1969   "The Laying On of Hands in the New Testament: A Re-examination in the Light of Hebrew Terminology." *Expository Times* 80:210-14.

Pathrapankal, Joseph
1979   "Christianity as a 'Way' According to the Acts of the Apostles." In *Les Actes des Apôtres: Traditions, rédaction, théologie,* pp. 533-39. Edited by J. Kremer. Louvain, Belgium: Leuven University Press.

Pesch, Rudolf
1986   *Die Apostelgeschichte.* Evangelisch-katholischer Kommentar zum Neuen Testament. 2 vols. Zürich: Benziger.

Pickard, William M., Jr.
1970   "Biblical Perspective for Dialogue." *Encounter* 31:42-55.

Pillai, C. A. Joachim
1979   *Early Missionary Preaching: A Study of Luke's Report in Acts 13.* Hicksville, N.Y.: Exposition.

Pinnock, Clark H.

1990   "Toward an Evangelical Theology of Religions." *Journal of the Evangelical Theological Society* 33:359-67.

1991   "Acts 4:12: No Other Name Under Heaven." In *Through No Fault of Their Own: The Fate of Those Who Have Never Heard,* pp. 107-16. Edited by William V. Crockett and James G. Sigountis. Grand Rapids, Mich.: Baker Book House.

Polhill, John B.

1992   *Acts.* New American Commentary. Nashville: Broadman.

Porter, R. J.

1988   "What Did Philip Say to the Eunuch?" *Expository Times* 100:54-55.

Powell, Mark A.

1991   *What Are They Saying About Acts?* New York: Paulist.

Praeder, Susan M.

1987   "The Problem of First Person Narration in Acts." *Novum Testamentum* 29:193-218.

Prior, Kenneth F. W.

1975   *The Gospel in a Pagan Society: A Book for Modern Evangelists.* Downers Grove, Ill.: InterVarsity Press.

Ramsay, Wiliam M.

1896   *St. Paul the Traveller and the Roman Citizen.* London: G. P. Putnam's Sons.

Rapuano, Yehudah

1990   "Did Philip Baptize the Eunuch at Ein Yael?" *Biblical Archaeology Review* 16 (November-December): 44-49.

Reeder, Ellen D.

1987   "The Mother of the Gods and a Hellenistic Bronze Matrix." *American Journal of Archeology* 91:423-40.

Renehan, Robert

1979   "Acts 17:28." *Greek, Roman and Byzantine Studies* 20:347-53.

Rengstorf, Karl H.

1964   "ἀπόστολος." In *Theological Dictionary of the New Testament,* 1:407-45. Edited by Gerhard Kittel and Gerhard Friedrich. 10 vols. Grand Rapids, Mich.: Eerdmans.

Richard, Earl

1978   *Acts 6:1—8:4: The Author's Method and Composition.* Missoula, Mont.: Scholars Press.

1979   "The Polemical Character of the Joseph Episode in Acts 7."
                Journal of Biblical Literature 98:255-67.

1982   "The Creative Use of Amos by the Author of Acts." *Novum
                Testamentum* 24:37-53.

Richardson, Don
1984   *Eternity in Their Hearts.* Rev. ed. Ventura, Calif.: Regal
                Books.

Robertson, A. T.
1934   *A Grammar of the Greek New Testament in the Light of
                Historical Research.* Nashville: Broadman.

Robinson, Chris
1993   "Untamable: Climbers Find St.-Elias Too Tough to Handle,
                Opt to Take Safer Path." *The State* 102 (June 26): C1, C7.

Rodgers, Peter R.
1987   "Acts 2:18: *Kai Prophēteusousin."* *Journal of Theological
                Studies* 38:95-97.

Rose, Herbert
Jennings, and
Charles Martin
Robertson
1970   "Apollo." In *The Oxford Classical Dictionary,* pp. 81-82. 2nd
                ed. Edited by N. G. L. Hammond and H. H. Scullard. Oxford:
                Clarendon.

Russell, Walt
1986   "The Anointing with the Holy Spirit in Luke-Acts." *Trinity
                Journal* 7, no. 1: 47-63.

Ryrie, Charles C.
1989   *So Great Salvation: What It Means to Believe in Jesus Christ.*
                Wheaton, Ill.: Victor Books.

Safrai, Samuel
1974   "Relations Between the Diaspora and the Land of Israel." In
                *The Jewish People in the First Century: Historical Geography,
                Political History, Social, Cultural and Religious Life and
                Institutions,* 1:184-215. Edited by Samuel Safrai and
                Menahem Stern. Philadelphia: Fortress.

1976   "Home and Family." In *The Jewish People in the First
                Century: Historical Geography, Political History, Social, Cul-
                tural and Religious Life and Institutions,* 2:728-92. Edited by
                Samuel Safrai and Menahem Stern. Philadelphia: Fortress.

Sand, Alexander
1991   *"kardia."* In *Exegetical Dictionary of the New Testament,*

2:249-51. Edited by H. Balz and G. Schneider. 3 vols. Grand
Rapids, Mich.: Eerdmans.

Sanders, John E.

1988   "Is Belief in Christ Necessary for Salvation?" *Evangelical
Quarterly* 60:241-59.

Schlier, Heinrich

1967   *"παρρησία κτλ."* In *Theological Dictionary of the New
Testament,* 5:871-86. Edited by Gerhard Kittel and Gerhard
Friedrich. 10 vols. Grand Rapids, Mich.: Eerdmans.

Schneider, Gerhard

1980-1982   *Die Apostelgeschichte.* 2 vols. Herders theologischer
Kommentar zum Neuen Testament 5. Freiburg im Breisgau,
Germany: Herder.

Schniewind, Julius

1964   *"ἀγγελία κτλ."* In *Theological Dictionary of the New
Testament,* 1:56-73. Edited by Gerhard Kittel and Gerhard
Friedrich. 10 vols. Grand Rapids, Mich.: Eerdmans.

Schrenk, Gottlob

1964   *"δίκη κτλ."* In *Theological Dictionary of the New Testament,*
2:174-224. Edited by Gerhard Kittel and Gerhard Friedrich.
10 vols. Grand Rapids, Mich.: Eerdmans.

Schürer, Emil

1973   *The History of the Jewish People in the Age of Jesus Christ
(175 B.C.-A.D. 135),* vol. 1. Revised and edited by Geza
Vermes, Fergus Millar and Matthew Black. Edinburgh: T & T
Clark.

1979   *The History of the Jewish People in the Age of Jesus Christ
(175 B.C.-A.D. 135),* vol. 2. Revised and edited by Geza
Vermes, Fergus Millar and Matthew Black. Edinburgh: T & T
Clark.

1986   *The History of the Jewish People in the Age of Jesus Christ
(175 B.C.-A.D. 135),* vol. 3/1. Revised and edited by Geza
Vermes, Fergus Millar and Matthew Black. Edinburgh: T & T
Clark.

1987   *The History of the Jewish People in the Age of Jesus Christ
(175 B.C.-A.D. 135),* vol. 3/2. Revised and edited by Geza
Vermes, Fergus Millar and Matthew Black. Edinburgh: T & T
Clark.

Schütz, E.

1976   *"ἀγνοέω (agnoeō)* etc." In *New International Dictionary of*

New Testament Theology, 2:406-9. Edited by Colin Brown. 3 vols. Grand Rapids, Mich.: Zondervan.

Schwartz, Daniel R.
1983 "Non-joining Sympathizers (Acts 5, 13-14)." *Biblica* 64:550-55.

1984 "The Accusation and Accusers at Philippi (Acts 16, 20-21)." *Biblica* 65:357-63.

1986 "The End of the *Gē* (Acts 1:8): Beginning or End of the Christian Vision?" *Journal of Biblical Literature* 105:669-76.

Scott, J. Julius, Jr.
1992 "The Jerusalem Council: The Cross-Cultural Challenge in the First Century." Paper presented to the National Meeting of the Evangelical Theological Society, November 20, 1992, San Francisco, Calif.

Segal, Peretz
1989 "The Penalty of the Warning Inscription from the Temple of Jerusalem." *Israel Exploration Journal* 39, nos. 1-2: 79-84.

Seifrid, Mark A.
1987 "Jesus and the Law in Acts." *Journal for the Study of the New Testament* 30:39-57.

Sherwin-White, Adrian Nicholas
1963 *Roman Society and Roman Law in the New Testament: The Sarum Lectures, 1960-61.* Oxford: Clarendon.

1986 "Pilate, Pontius." In *International Standard Bible Encyclopedia,* 3:867-69. Rev. ed. Edited by Geoffrey W. Bromiley. 4 vols. Grand Rapids, Mich.: Eerdmans.

Smith, James
1978 *The Voyage and Shipwreck of Saint Paul.* Minneapolis: James Family Christian Publishing.

Sorg, Theo
1976 "Heart." In *New International Dictionary of New Testament Theology,* 2:180-84. Edited by Colin Brown. 3 vols. Grand Rapids, Mich.: Zondervan.

Stählin, Gustav
1967 "ξένος κτλ." In *Theological Dictionary of the New Testament,* 5:1-36. Edited by Gerhard Kittel and Gerhard Friedrich. 10 vols. Grand Rapids, Mich.: Eerdmans.

Stern, Menahem
1974 "The Jewish Diaspora." In *The Jewish People in the First*

Century: Historical Geography, Political History, Social, Cultural and Religious Life and Institutions, 1:117-83. Edited by Samuel Safrai and Menahem Stern. Philadelphia: Fortress.

Stott, John R. W.
1974   "Imprint of the Early Church: Exposition of Acts 2:42-47." *His* 34 (May): 12-15.

1990   *The Spirit, the Church and the World: The Message of Acts.* Downers Grove, Ill.: InterVarsity Press.

Strack, Hermann L.,
and Paul Billerbeck
1978   *Kommentar zum Neuen Testament aus Talmud und Midrasch.* 4 vols. 7th ed. Munich: C. H. Beck'sche.

Strange, W. A.
1992   *The Problem of the Text of Acts.* Cambridge: Cambridge University Press.

Strathmann,
Hermann
1967a   "Λιβερτῖνοι." In *Theological Dictionary of the New Testament,* 4:265-66. Edited by Gerhard Kittel and Gerhard Friedrich. 10 vols. Grand Rapids, Mich.: Eerdmans.

1967b   "μάρτυς κτλ." In *Theological Dictionary of the New Testament,* 4:474-513. Edited by Gerhard Kittel and Gerhard Friedrich. 10 vols. Grand Rapids, Mich.: Eerdmans.

Stronstad, Roger
1984   *The Charismatic Theology of St. Luke.* Peabody, Mass.: Hendrickson.

Stumpff, Albrecht
1964   "ζῆλος κτλ." In *Theological Dictionary of the New Testament,* 2:877-88. Edited by Gerhard Kittel and Gerhard Friedrich. 10 vols. Grand Rapids, Mich.: Eerdmans.

Suhl, Alfred
1991   "Gestrandet! Bemerkungen zum Streit über die Romfahrt des Paulus." *Zeitschrift für Theologie und Kirche* 88:1-28.

Sylva, Dennis D.
1987   "The Meaning and Function of Acts 7:46-50." *Journal of Biblical Literature* 106:261-75.

Talbert, Charles H.
1984   *Acts.* Knox Preaching Guides. Atlanta: John Knox.

Thornton,
Timothy C. G.
1977   "To the End of the Earth: Acts 1:8." *Expository Times* 89:374-
                75.
Trebilco, Paul R.
1989   "Paul and Silas—'Servants of the Most High God' (Acts
                16.16-18)." *Journal for the Study of the New Testament*
                36:51-73.
Trompf, Garry W.
1984   "On Why Luke Declined to Recount the Death of Paul: Acts
                27—28 and Beyond." In *Luke-Acts: New Perspectives from
                the Society of Biblical Literature Seminar,* pp. 225-39. Edited
                by Charles H. Talbert. New York: Crossroad.
Turner, Max M. B.
1981   "Spirit Endowment in Luke/Acts: Some Linguistic
                Considerations." *Vox Evangelica* 12:45-63.
Tyson, Joseph B.
1983   "Acts 6:1-7 and Dietary Regulations in Early Christianity."
                Perspectives in Religious Studies 10:145-61.

1985   "Acts of the Apostles, The." In *Harper Bible Dictionary,* pp.
                10-11. Edited by Paul J. Achtemeier. San Francisco: Harper &
                Row.

1988   "The Problem of Jewish Rejection in Acts." In *Luke-Acts and
                the Jewish People: Eight Critical Perspectives,* pp. 124-37.
                Edited by Joseph B. Tyson. Minneapolis: Augsburg.
Unger, Merrill F.
1974   *The Baptism and Gifts of the Holy Spirit.* Chicago: Moody
                Press.
Van der Horst, P. W.
1977   "Peter's Shadow: The Religio-Historical Background of Acts
                5:15." *New Testament Studies* 23:204-12.
Van Elderen,
Bastiaan
1970   "Some Archeological Observations on Paul's First Missionary
                Journey." In *Apostolic History and the Gospel: Biblical and
                Historical Essays Presented to F. F. Bruce on His Sixtieth
                Birthday,* pp. 151-64. Edited by W. Ward Gasque and Ralph
                P. Martin. Grand Rapids, Mich.: Eerdmans.
Veltman, Fred
1978   "The Defense Speeches of Paul in Acts." In *Perspectives on
                Luke-Acts,* pp. 243-56. Edited by Charles H. Talbert.

Vielhauer, Phillip
Edinburgh: T & T Clark.

1966   "On the 'Paulinism' of Acts." In *Studies in Luke-Acts,* pp. 33-
            50. Edited by Leander E. Keck and J. Louis Martyn. Nashville:
            Abingdon.

Wagner, C. Peter
1988   *The Third Wave of the Holy Spirit.* Ann Arbor, Mich.: Servant.

Warnecke, Heinz
1987   *Die Tatsächliche Romfahrt des Apostels Paulus.* Stuttgart:
            Katholisches Bibelwerk.

Wead, David W.
1982   "Ethiopian Eunuch." In *International Standard Bible Ency-
            clopedia,* 2:197. Rev. ed. Edited by Geoffrey W. Bromiley. 4
            vols. Grand Rapids, Mich.: Eerdmans.

Wehnert, Jürgen
1990   "Gestrandet: Zu einer neuen These über den Schiffbruch
            des Apostels Paulus auf dem Wege nach Rom (Apg 27—
            28)." *Zeitschrift für Theologie und Kirche* 87:67-99.

Wenham, Gordon J.
1981   "The Theology of Unclean Food." *Evangelical Quarterly*
            53:6-15.

Wenham, John W.
1972   "Did Peter Go to Rome in A.D. 42?" *Tyndale Bulletin* 23:94-
            102.

Wikgren, Allen P.
1981   "The Problem in Acts 16:12." In *New Testament Textual
            Criticism—Its Significance for Exegesis: Essays in Honour of
            Bruce M. Metzger,* pp. 171-78. Edited by Eldon J. Epp and
            Gordon D. Fee. Oxford: Clarendon.

Wilcox, Max
1977   " 'Upon the Tree'—Deuteronomy 21:22-23 in the New
            Testament." *Journal of Biblical Literature* 96:85-99.

Williams, David
John
1985   *Acts: A Good News Commentary.* San Francisco: Harper &
            Row.

Williamson, Denise
1991   *Chariots to China: A Story of Eric Liddell.* Brentwood, Tenn.:
            Wolgemuth & Hyatt.

Willimon,
William H.
1988   *Acts.* Interpretation: A Biblical Commentary for Preaching
            and Teaching. Atlanta: John Knox.

Wilson,
Robert McL.
1979   "Simon and Gnostic Origins." In *Les Actes des Apôtres: Traditions, rédaction, théologie*, pp. 485-91. Edited by J. Kremer. Louvain, Belgium: Leuven University Press.

Wilson, Stephen G.
1983   *Luke and the Law.* Cambridge: Cambridge University Press.

Wimber, John
1986   *Power Evangelism.* San Francisco: Harper & Row.

Windisch, Hans
1964   *"ἀσπάζομαι κτλ."* In *Theological Dictionary of the New Testament*, 1:496-501. Edited by Gerhard Kittel and Gerhard Friedrich. 10 vols. Grand Rapids, Mich.: Eerdmans.

Winter, Bruce W.
1993   "In Public and in Private: Early Christians and Religious Pluralism." In *One God, One Lord: Christianity in a World of Religious Pluralism*, pp. 125-48. Edited by Bruce W. Winter and Andrew D. Clarke. 2nd ed. Grand Rapids, Mich.: Baker Book House.

Wirt, Sherwood E.,
and Kersten
Beckstrom, eds.
1974   *Living Quotations for Christians.* New York: Harper & Row.

Wycherley, R. E.
1968   "St. Paul at Athens." *Journal of Theological Studies* 19:619-21.

Youngblood,
Ronald F.
1982   "Ethiopia." In *International Standard Bible Encyclopedia*, 2:193-97. Rev. ed. Edited by Geoffrey W. Bromiley. 4 vols. Grand Rapids, Mich.: Eerdmans.